RULE OF LAW DYNAMICS

This volume explores the various strategies, mechanisms, and processes that influence rule of law dynamics across borders and the national–international divide, illuminating the diverse paths of influence. It shows to what extent, and how, rule of law dynamics have changed in recent years, especially at the transnational and international levels of government. To explore these interactive dynamics, the volume adopts an interdisciplinary approach, bringing together the normative perspective of law with the analytical perspective of social sciences. The volume contributes to several fields, including studies of rule of law, law and development, and good governance; democratization; globalization studies; neo-institutionalism and judicial studies; international law, transnational governance, and the emerging literature on judicial reforms in authoritarian regimes; and comparative law (Islamic, African, Asian, and Latin American legal systems).

Michael Zürn is director of the research unit Transnational Conflicts and International Institutions of the Social Science Research Center Berlin and professor of international relations at the Free University of Berlin. From 2004 to 2009, he was founding Dean of the Hertie School of Governance in Berlin. Zürn is a member of the Berlin-Brandenburg Academy of Sciences. He is (co-)editor or (co-)author of numerous books, most recently *Handbook on Multi-Level Governance* (2010), *Transformations of the State* (Cambridge University Press, 2005), and *Law and Governance in Post-National Europe* (Cambridge University Press, 2005).

André Nollkaemper is professor of public international law at the Faculty of Law of the University of Amsterdam, where he previously directed the Amsterdam Center for International Law. He is an external legal advisor of the Minister for Foreign Affairs of the Netherlands and member of the board of the European Society for International Law. He has practical experience in cases before several international courts and tribunals and courts of the Netherlands. He is co-editor-in-chief of the journal *International Law in Domestic Courts* and member of the editorial board of *The Hague Journal of Rule of Law*. His books include *National Courts and the International Rule of Law* (2011) and, as editor, *New Perspectives on the Divide between International and National Law* (2007).

Randall Peerenboom is a law professor at La Trobe University and an associate Fellow of the Oxford University Center for Socio-Legal Studies. He was a professor at UCLA Law School from 1998 to 2007 and director of the Oxford Foundation for Law, Justice and Society Rule of Law in China Programme. He has been a consultant to the Asian Development Bank, Ford Foundation, EU-China, United Nations Development Programme, and other international organizations on legal reforms and rule of law in China and Asia, and is the co-editor-in-chief of *The Hague Journal of Rule of Law*. He is the author or co-editor of *Judicial Independence in China* (Cambridge University Press, 2010), *Regulation in Asia* (2009), *China Modernizes: Threat to the West or Model for the Rest?* (2007), *Human Rights in Asia* (2006), *Asian Discourses of Rule of Law* (2004), and *China's Long March toward Rule of Law* (Cambridge University Press, 2002).

Rule of Law Dynamics

IN AN ERA OF INTERNATIONAL AND TRANSNATIONAL GOVERNANCE

Edited by

MICHAEL ZÜRN

Social Science Research Center Berlin

ANDRÉ NOLLKAEMPER

University of Amsterdam

RANDALL PEERENBOOM

La Trobe University, Melbourne

CAMBRIDGE
UNIVERSITY PRESS

CAMBRIDGE UNIVERSITY PRESS
Cambridge, New York, Melbourne, Madrid, Cape Town,
Singapore, São Paulo, Delhi, Mexico City

Cambridge University Press
32 Avenue of the Americas, New York, NY 10013-2473, USA

www.cambridge.org
Information on this title: www.cambridge.org/9781107024717

First published 2012

Printed in the United States of America

A catalog record for this publication is available from the British Library.

Library of Congress Cataloging in Publication data

Rule of law dynamics : in an era of international and transnational governance / Michael Zürn,
André Nollkaemper, Randall Peerenboom.
p. cm.
Includes bibliographical references and index.
ISBN 978-1-107-02471-7 (hardback)
1. Rule of law – Research. 2. Human rights advocacy. 3. Political indicators. I. Zürn, Michael.
II. Nollkaemper, André. III. Peerenboom, R. P. (Randall P.), 1958–
K3171.R8487 2012
340′.11–dc23 2011049752

ISBN 978-1-107-02471-7 Hardback

Contents

PART II. ACTORS: STRATEGIES AND RESPONSES

List of Tables

List of Figures

List of Contributors

Helmut Philipp Aust, Doctor of Laws (Dr. iur.), is a senior research Fellow at the Humboldt University, Berlin. He was previously a Fellow at the University of Munich as well as a visiting Fellow at the Lauterpacht Centre for International Law, University of Cambridge. He is the author of *Complicity and the Law of State Responsibility* (Cambridge University Press, 2011).

Tim Gemkow is a doctoral student in the Research Unit on Transnational Conflicts and Institutions at the Social Science Research Center Berlin and a member of the Berlin Graduate School for Transnational Studies. His research is supported by a PhD stipend from the German National Academic Foundation. He studied political science at the Free University in Berlin and the Institut d'Etudes Politiques in Grenoble and has published on the ambiguous consequences of increased legalization for the legitimacy of international organizations. His doctoral research investigates state decisions to adopt extraterritorial law and the different interactions between national extraterritorial law and international cooperation.

John Gillespie is professor of law and director of the Asia Pacific Business Regulation Group, Department of Business Law and Taxation, Monash University. He teaches and publishes widely about legal change in East Asia. He has worked as a consultant with many international development agencies in East Asia. His most recent book (with Albert Chen) is *Legal Reforms in China and Vietnam: A Comparison of Asian Communist Regimes* (Routledge, 2010).

Linn Hammergren is an independent consultant specializing in rule of law, anti-corruption, and general governance issues. Before 2008, she spent 10 years with the World Bank and 12 as an internal consultant for the U.S. Agency for International Development managing Administration of Justice projects. Her research and publications focus on judicial politics and reform, judicial corruption, citizen security, and the politics of foreign assistance. She is best known for her work on Latin America but is now also focusing on Africa, Asia, and the South Pacific.

Monika Heupel is a political scientist and a research Fellow at the Social Science Research Center Berlin in the research unit Transnational Conflicts and International Institutions. Her work focuses on international organizations, security studies, and global human rights policy. Her work has been published in *Security Dialogue*, *Cooperation and Conflict*, *International Affairs*, and the *Journal of International Relations and Development*, among others.

Paulette Lloyd is assistant professor of sociology and international studies at Indiana University, Bloomington. She is a faculty affiliate of the Center for Law, Society, and Culture at the Maurer School of Law and the Center for the Study of Global Change. Her current research interests include social network methods, the process of consensus formation on international norms and policies, United Nations voting analysis, human rights, international law compliance, transnational crime, and international organizations.

Wolfgang Merkel is director of the Democracy and Democratisation research program at the Social Science Research Center Berlin and professor of political science at the Humboldt University, Berlin. He is a member of a number of key bodies, including the Berlin-Brandenburg Academy of Sciences and Humanities and the International Council of Advisors to Spanish Prime Minister José Luis Rodríguez Zapatero. His most recent publications include the co-edited volume *The Future of Representative Democracy* (Cambridge University Press, 2011); *Systemtransformation* (2010); and contributions on democracy and democratization, dictatorships, political parties, comparative public policy, social democracy, welfare states, and social justice.

André Nollkaemper is professor of public international law at the Faculty of Law of the University of Amsterdam. He is an external legal advisor of the Minister for Foreign Affairs of the Netherlands and member of the board of the European Society for International Law. He has practical experience in cases before the European Court on Human Rights, the Special Court for Sierra Leone, the International Criminal Tribunal for the Former Yugoslavia, the Extraordinary Chamber for the Courts of Cambodia, and courts of the Netherlands. He is co-editor-in-chief of *International Law in Domestic Courts* (Oxford University Press), author of *National Courts and the International Rule of Law* (Oxford University Press, 2011), and editor of *New Perspectives on the Divide between International and National Law* (Oxford University Press, 2007).

Georg Nolte is professor of law at the Humboldt University, Berlin, and a member of the International Law Commission of the United Nations. He was previously professor of law at the Universities of Göttingen and Munich as well as visiting professor at All Souls College, Oxford, and Université Paris II. He has published widely on issues of public international law and comparative constitutional law.

Sarah M. H. Nouwen is Mayer Brown Research Fellow in Public International Law at the Lauterpacht Centre for International Law and Pembroke College, Cambridge. She holds a PhD (Cantab) and LLM (Utrecht/Cape Town/Western Cape) in international law and an MPhil in international relations (Cantab). She was a visiting professional at the International Criminal Court and worked as a consultant for foreign ministries, Ugandan and Senegalese nongovernmental organizations, and the African Union High-Level Implementation Panel for Sudan.

Randall Peerenboom is a law professor at La Trobe University and an associate Fellow of the Oxford University Center for Socio-Legal Studies. He was a professor at UCLA Law School from 1998 to 2007 and director of the Oxford Foundation for Law, Justice and Society Rule of Law in China Programme. He has been a consultant to the Asian Development Bank, Ford Foundation, EU-China, United Nations Development Programme, and other international organizations on legal reforms and rule of law in China and Asia, and is the co-editor-in-chief of *The Hague Journal of Rule of Law*. He is also a China International Economic and Trade Arbitration Commission arbitrator, and he frequently serves as an expert witness on People's Republic of China legal issues. His recent sole-authored and co-edited books include *Judicial Independence in China* (Cambridge University Press, 2010); *Regulation in Asia* (Routledge, 2009); *China Modernizes: Threat to the West or Model for the Rest?* (Oxford University Press, 2007); *Human Rights in Asia* (Routledge, 2006); *Asian Discourses of Rule of Law* (Routledge, 2004); and *China's Long March toward Rule of Law* (Cambridge University Press, 2002).

Tilmann J. Röder is a senior research Fellow at the Max Planck Institute for Comparative Public Law and International Law in Heidelberg and is responsible for rule of law projects in Islamic countries, including Afghanistan, Pakistan, Iraq, Egypt, Libya, and Tunisia. He has published in the areas of constitution building, legal pluralism, rule of law promotion in postconflict societies, and water conflicts in international law. Legal history also belongs to his fields of interest. His recent co-edited works include *Constitutionalism in Islamic Countries: Between Upheaval and Continuity* (Oxford University Press, 2011) and *From Industrial to Legal Standardisation, 1871–1914: Transnational Insurance Law and the Great San Francisco Earthquake* (Brill, 2011).

Frank Schimmelfennig is professor of European politics at ETH Zurich and a member of the Center for Comparative and International Studies. His main research interests are in the theory of international institutions and European integration and, more specifically, in the enlargement and democratization of European regional organizations as well as in international democracy promotion. More information can be obtained at http://www.eup.ethz.ch/people/schimmelfennig.

Gunnar Folke Schuppert is Professor Emeritus for Public Law and Administrative Science at the Humboldt University, Berlin. He currently holds a research professorship in New Forms of Governance at the Social Science Research Center Berlin, where he is also managing director of the institute's Rule of Law Center. In addition to these tasks, he heads a research project at the Collaborative Research Center (*Sonderforschungsbereich*) 700, Governance in Areas of Limited Statehood, and teaches as adjunct professor at the Hertie School of Governance in Berlin.

Beth A. Simmons is Clarence Dillon Professor of International Affairs and director of the Weatherhead Center for International Affairs at Harvard University. Her new book, *Mobilizing for Human Rights: International Law in Domestic Politics* (Cambridge University Press, 2009), won best book awards from the American Society for International Law, the American Political Science Association, and the International Social Science Council. Simmons was elected in April 2009 to the American Academy of Arts and Sciences. Current research interests include international law compliance, the globalization of criminal law, and international economic law.

Brandon M. Stewart is a doctoral student in the department of government at Harvard University. He received his BA from the College of William & Mary in Government and International Relations. His substantive interests include security, terrorism, and conflict–cooperation dynamics. Methodologically, he is interested in automated content analysis, statistical methods, and data visualization. His research has been published in *Conflict Management and Peace Science*, *Small Wars and Insurgencies*, and other peer-reviewed publications.

Richard Zajac Sannerholm has experience in rule of law reform in postconflict, crisis, and transition countries, working as a researcher and advisor for international organizations, national agencies, and nongovernmental organizations. Assignments include research and programming on legal education, public administration reform, rule of law training, customary law and issues of harmonization, and human rights. Zajac Sannerholm currently holds a position as a researcher and project leader at the Folke Bernadotte Academy, and he conducts research on measuring rule of law in public administration, monitoring administrative justice, rule of law and security sector reform, and an empirical project on mapping UN rule of law reform in postconflict settings.

Michael Zürn is director of the research unit Transnational Conflicts and International Institutions of the Social Science Research Center Berlin and professor of international relations at the Free University of Berlin. From 2004 to 2009, he was founding Dean of the Hertie School of Governance in Berlin. Zürn is a member of the Berlin-Brandenburg Academy of Sciences. Among his recent co-edited and co-authored book publications are *Handbook on Multi-Level Governance* (Edward Elgar, 2010); *Transformations of the State* (Cambridge University Press, 2005), and *Law and Governance in Post-National Europe* (Cambridge University Press, 2005).

Preface and Acknowledgments

This volume is part of a larger multiyear interdisciplinary project on the rule of law entitled "The Internationalisation of the Rule of Law: Changing Context and New Challenges." The project is sponsored by The Hague Institute for the Internationalisation of Law (HiiL), Social Science Research Center Berlin (WZB), the University of Amsterdam, and La Trobe University. The aim of the project is to contribute to a better understanding of the success or failure of rule of law promotion strategies by states, civil society, and international organizations such as the United Nations and the World Bank, in view of increasing international and transnational dimensions of governance in an era of international and transnational governance. The key research question has been identified in cooperation with the Hague Rule of Law Network.

The first phase of the project consisted of an authors' workshop in Berlin in November 2009, followed by a conference in Amsterdam in November 2009. The present volume is the culmination of these events and concludes the first phase of the project.

Based on the conclusions of this volume, the second phase consists of three research projects, each one to be led by the individual co-editors of this volume. Randall Peerenboom will focus on the special challenges that middle-income countries face in implementing the rule of law. Michael Zürn will focus on the normative dynamics triggered by the incorporation of principles of law on the international level. André Nollkaemper will investigate the principles and practices that shape the contestation between requirements from the international rule of law on the one hand and the national rule of law on the other. Each project will result in an edited volume as well as other research publications. In addition, the authors will provide concrete policy recommendations for policy makers and rule of law promotion officials on the basis of the outcomes of the three projects.

The editors collectively thank HiiL and their own institutions for their support. They also thank Morly Frishman and the HiiL staff for their highly professional support in organizing the workshops and conferences and their efficient handling of the myriad other logistical details that are vital to the success of a multiyear project such as this. The editors are also extremely grateful to Niki Frencken and Yael Tibco at the Amsterdam Center for International Law for their conscientious copyediting and hard work during the manuscript preparation process, and to John Berger and the team at Cambridge University Press for their support. Randall Peerenboom also thanks the Australian Research Council for ARC Discovery Grant DP0985927. As always, the editors are deeply grateful to their families for allowing them the time to complete this project and bearing their physical and mental absences with good humor.

List of Abbreviations

ABA – American Bar Association
ABA ROLI – American Bar Association Rule of Law Initiative
ACP – Africa, the Caribbean, and the Pacific
AJC – Advisory Judicial Commission
AJP-9 – Allied Joint Publication 9
BITs – bilateral investment treaties
BMZ – Germany's Federal Ministry for Economic Cooperation and Development
BTI – Bertelsmann Transformation Index
CAS – Court for Arbitration for Sport
CERP – Commander's Emergency Response Program
CIMIC – civil–military cooperation/coordination
CIS – Commonwealth of Independent States
COIN – counterinsurgency
CPA – Coalition Provisional Authority
CSDP – Common Security and Defence Policy
DfID – Department for International Development
DPP – Director of Public Prosecutions
DRC – Democratic Republic of Congo
EC – European Community
ECA – Europe and Central Asia
ECJ – European Court of Justice
ECOWAS – Economic Community of West African States
EIDHR – European Instrument for Democracy and Human Rights
EU – European Union
EUJUST LEX/Iraq – EU Integrated Rule of Law Mission for Iraq
EUJUST THEMIS – EU Rule of Law Mission to Georgia
EULEX – European Union Rule of Law Mission in Kosovo
EUPOL AFGHANISTAN – EU Police Mission in Afghanistan

EUPOL PROXIMA/FYROM – EU Police Mission in the former Yugoslav Republic of Macedonia
FCO – Foreign and Commonwealth Office
FPA – Final Peace Agreement
GAL – Global Administrative Law
GDP – gross domestic product
GIZ – *Gesellschaft für Internationale Zusammenarbeit*
GNI – gross national income
GTZ – *Deutsche Gesellschaft für Technische Zusammenarbeit*
GWOT – Global War on Terror
HIC – high-income countries
HiiL – Hague Institute for the Internationalisation of Law
HN – host nation
HPCC – Housing and Property Claims Commission
HPD – Housing and Property Directorate
IADB – Inter-American Development Bank
ICC – International Criminal Court
ICCPR – International Covenant on Civil and Political Rights
ICR – Implementation Completion Report
ICRC – International Committee of the Red Cross and Red Crescent
IEG – Independent Evaluation Group
IFOR – Implementation Force
IJPC – Independent Judicial and Prosecutorial Commission
IMF – International Monetary Fund
IO – international organization
ISAF – International Security Assistance Force
ISO – International Standards Organization
JLOS – Ugandan Justice Law and Order Sector
KFOR – Kosovo Force
LCR – Latin America and the Caribbean
L&D – Law and Development
LICs – lower-income countries
LRA – Lord's Resistance Army
MCA – Millennium Challenge Account
MCC – Millennium Challenge Corporation
MENA – Middle East and North Africa
MICs – middle-income countries
MIS – management information system
MMA – monitoring, mentoring, and advising
MONUC – UN Organization Mission in the DRC
NAFTA – North American Free Trade Agreement
NATO – North Atlantic Treaty Organization

NGO – nongovernmental organization
NIE – New Institutional Economics
OAS – Organization of American States
ODA – official development aid
OECD – Organization for Economic Cooperation and Development
OHCHR – Office of the High Commissioner for Human Rights
OSCE – Organization for Security and Cooperation in Europe
OTP – Office of the Prosecutor
PACE – Parliamentary Assembly of the Council of Europe
PISG – Provisional Institutions of Self-Government
PPP – purchasing power parity
PRTs – Provincial Reconstructions Teams
RoL – rule of law
SDHC – Special Division of the High Court
SRSG – Special Representative of the Secretary-General
SSR – Security Sector Reform
TNCs – transnational corporations
UN – United Nations
UNAMA – UN Assistance Mission to Afghanistan
UNCHR – UN Commission on Human Rights
UNCTOC – UN Convention against Transnational Organized Crime
UN DPKO – UN Department of Peacekeeping Operations
UNGA – UN General Assembly
UNHCR – UN High Commissioner for Refugees
United States – United States of America
UNMIBH – UN Mission in Bosnia-Herzegovina
UNMIK – UN Interim Administration Mission in Kosovo
UNSC – United Nations Security Council
UNTAC – UN Transitional Authority in Cambodia
UNTAES – UN Transitional Administration for Eastern Slavonia, Baranja, and Western Sirmium
UNTAET – UN Transitional Administration in East Timor
UPDF – Ugandan Peoples' Defence Forces
USAID – U.S. Agency for International Development
U.S. GAO – United States Government Accountability Office
WCC – War Crimes Court
WGI – Worldwide Governance Indicators
WJP – World Justice Project
WTO – World Trade Organization
WZB – Social Science Research Center Berlin

Introduction

Rule of Law Dynamics in an Era of International and Transnational Governance

Michael Zürn, André Nollkaemper, and Randall Peerenboom

1. INTRODUCTION

The nature, objectives, and effects of rule of law promotion are undergoing major transformations as a result of the increasing international and transnational dimensions of governance. Rule of law promotion by its very nature has always been an international and transnational activity, as states, international organizations (IOs), and nongovernmental organizations (NGOs) have aimed to influence rule of law practices in other states.[1] However, contemporary rule of law promotion has become internationalized in two additional senses. First, the incorporation of rule of law principles into international law binding on states has become an important aspiration of rule of law promotion, in the hope that doing so will provide a common standard for all states in a manner similar to international human rights law. Second, the

[1] Although rule of law is a contested concept, there is general agreement that rule of law requires at minimum that law imposes meaningful limits on the state and state actors, as reflected in the principles of legality and a government of laws, the supremacy of law, and equality of all before the law. The concept of "rule of law" is therefore distinguishable from "rule by law" in which law is primarily an instrument or tool for governing but is not intended to impose meaningful limits on the state or state actors. Rule of law theories are generally divided into two types: thin (procedural) or thick (substantive) theories (see Peerenboom 2002: 65–71 and the citations therein). Briefly put, a thin theory stresses the formal aspects of rule of law – those features that any legal system allegedly must possess to function effectively as a system of laws, regardless of whether the legal system is part of a democratic or nondemocratic society, capitalist or socialist, liberal or theocratic. Although proponents of thin interpretations of rule of law define it in slightly different ways, there is considerable common ground, with many building on or modifying Lon Fuller's influential account that laws be general, public, prospective, clear, consistent, capable of being followed, stable, and enforced (Fuller 1969; see also Raz 1979). In contrast to thin versions, thick or substantive conceptions begin with the basic elements of a thin conception, but then incorporate elements of political morality such as particular economic arrangements (free-market capitalism, central planning, etc.), forms of government (democratic, single-party socialism, etc.), or conceptions of human rights (liberal, communitarian, collectivist, etc.) (Summers 1999; Tamanaha 2004). There are therefore many competing thick conceptions of rule of law (Peerenboom 2002, 2004; Tamanaha 2004).

rule of law agenda has increasingly targeted IOs, transnational actors, and nonstate parties that now play a more significant role in rule making and governance.

The international and transnational nature of modern governance presents major challenges for the rule of law promotion agenda, at a time when the less-than-stellar results of traditional state-oriented rule of law promotion have led to increased doubts about the wisdom and feasibility of the enterprise (Carothers 2006a; Taylor 2009; Trebilcock and Daniels 2008; Trubek 2006). Have the major actors in the rule of law field, including the "great powers" and IOs, altered their strategies, programs, and practices to reflect the shift to new levels and new forms of governance? Do rule of law standards apply to new international and transnational forms of regulation? Should they be modified to fit the different context? Can the interactions between national and international levels be structured so that they do not become a new source of rule of law violation? Does international law provide a clear and acceptable set of standards that can form a common baseline for rule of law promotion applicable to both states and new forms of governance? Finally, how does rule of law promotion, whether or not it is based on standards of international law, cope with the wide variety of forms of resistance from the targets of rule of law promotion?

To contribute to our understanding of rule of law promotion, this volume seeks to address *the dynamics of rule of law in an era of international and transnational governance*. It uses the term "dynamics" to refer not only to the increasing international and transnational dimensions of rule of law promotion[2] but also to the interaction between the international and domestic levels of law. It conceptualizes these levels as a two-way relationship: International law influences rule of law development at the domestic and local levels; at the same time, precisely because of its potential effects, rule of law standards are being sought at the international level itself.

The dynamics of rule of law also encompass the interaction between rule of law promotion and rule of law conversion. The success of rule of law promotion depends not only on the attractiveness of the rule of law concept but also on the ways it is promoted and the ways it is received. To be effective, rule of law promoters need to take into account the response and feedback from recipients, and they must adapt their methods accordingly. This long-recognized truth remains relevant when rule

[2] We follow the established practice in international relations, using "international" to refer to activities taking place between states and "transnational" to refer to societal cross-border activities (see, e.g., the chapters in Carlsnaes, Risse, and Simmons 2002). International problems are accordingly the result of dynamics between states, whereas transnational problems are the consequence of cross-border societal activities. Consequently, international governance refers to regulations set up and carried out by states. This includes international law, as defined by the state-controlled sources of international law. Transnational governance, in contrast, refers to self-regulation among societal actors. Such regulation is not part of international law as traditionally understood. Many uses of "global governance" contain both components, transnational and international governance. In this volume we look at international efforts of rule of law diffusion (see chapter by Schimmelfennig, this volume) as well as transnational efforts (see Heupel, this volume). We also look at developments in international norms (see, e.g., Aust and Nolte, this volume) as well as transnational norms (see Schuppert, this volume).

of law promotion uses the tools of international law. It is critically relevant when rule of law promotion efforts are directed at international and transnational actors that have not previously been bound by rule of law principles.

To explore these interactive dynamics, this volume brings together the normative perspective of law with the analytical perspective of social sciences. It builds on existing literature that has studied, from both a legal perspective and a political science perspective, how modern governance includes the national, the transnational, and the international realm. That scholarship includes work on transnational law (Koh 1996; Zumbansen 2008); global administrative law (Kingsbury, Krisch, and Stewart 2005; Krisch and Kingsbury 2006); and governance beyond the state (Scott 2004; Zumbansen forthcoming). Of particular relevance for our focus on diffusion and conversion is the earlier work by Halliday and Carruthers on the relation between international and national lawmaking that addresses not only how global norms are conveyed to national settings and how such norms are implemented nationally but also recursive processes through which global and national lawmaking interact dynamically (Halliday and Carruthers 2007).

This book is organized in two parts. The first part explores the diffusion of rule of law standards across states and to new international and transnational levels of government. An analysis of quantitative indicators for the rule of law provides information on the global and regional patterns of diffusion, consolidation, and possible retreat. This analysis is complemented by more qualitative inquiries into the extent to which rule of law promotion has led to the normative expectation and legal obligation that states, IOs, and private actors performing roles traditionally reserved for government as part of new regulatory forms of transnational governance must abide by rule of law norms, principles, and rules embodied in international law.

The second half of the volume focuses on the evolving strategies and behavioral patterns underlying and responding to the diffusion processes analyzed in Part I. We focus on major players in the industry, especially the major Western powers, as well as IOs such as the World Bank, the European Union (EU), the International Criminal Court (ICC), and NGOs and new institutional nonstate players that act transnationally. Several chapters demonstrate a perhaps surprising continuity in the strategies and tools of rule of law promotion, leading to the question of whether these actors have sufficiently adjusted to lessons learned from traditional rule of law promotion efforts and to the challenges posed by new levels and forms of governance. The chapters also indicate various ways in which international law has become an important tool of rule of law promotion, for instance by the conclusion of treaties on suppression of crimes.

We then shift the focus from the supply side to the demand side, that is, from the policies and strategies of major powers and international donors to the recipient perspective. These chapters show that the outcome of rule of law promotion is to a large extent dependent on how it is received and implemented in the targeted societies. Although the major actors in rule of law promotion have begun to realize this, their strategic and behavioral adaptations so far have not adequately responded to this dynamic. Indeed, the parallel recognition of the need for further international law development of the rule of law setting forth generally applicable standards for all states, on the one hand, and the importance of local context, on the other, creates a theoretical and practical tension that has yet to be resolved.

All chapters in this volume emphasize different strategies, mechanisms, and processes that influence rule of law dynamics across borders, and across the national–international divide, seeking to illuminate possible paths of influence broadly so as to provide a comprehensive basis for further investigations. Taken together, the chapters show to what extent, and how, rule of law dynamics have changed in recent years, especially at the transnational and international levels of government, and to what extent the renewed academic attention to the topic reflects real-world developments rather than intellectual fashion. Moreover, the book provides an updated overview of what we do and do not understand about the reasons and mechanisms behind these dynamics. The volume as a whole also provides a basis for addressing more normative as well as policy-oriented questions in the further development of rule of law globally.

2. AN ANALYTICAL OVERVIEW OF RULE OF LAW DYNAMICS

Rule of law dynamics may be conceptualized as involving the distinct but interrelated processes of rule of law promotion (the promoter perspective), rule of law conversion (the recipient perspective), and the modalities, mechanisms, and processes that link the two (the diffusion perspective). It thus brings together three distinct academic literatures and discourses on rule of law. The *promotion perspective* looks at different strategies and programs of exporting states and organizations and asks about the effectiveness of these efforts. In this sense, it focuses on the starting point of the chain of events that may eventually lead to the establishment of the rule of law. It is dominated by rule of law practitioners. The *diffusion perspective* observes the dissemination of the rule of law concept as part of the more general diffusion of Western norms and asks about the causes and mechanisms that lead to this development. Its major interest is in normative structures and the ways they develop, not so much in actor strategies. This is often the approach adopted by sociologists, political scientists, and international relations scholars. The *conversion perspective* emphasizes the decisive role that the reception of concepts plays. It looks mainly at the receiving end of norm diffusion, including the proper transfer of a concept, the translation into the local context, but also in some cases the rejection of the norms. It asks mainly about the ways in which concepts are transformed in the process of translation and about the sources of this transformation or their rejection. This approach, adopted by sociologists, anthropologists, and area specialists, is common in regional studies emphasizing the role of culture and in postcolonial studies.

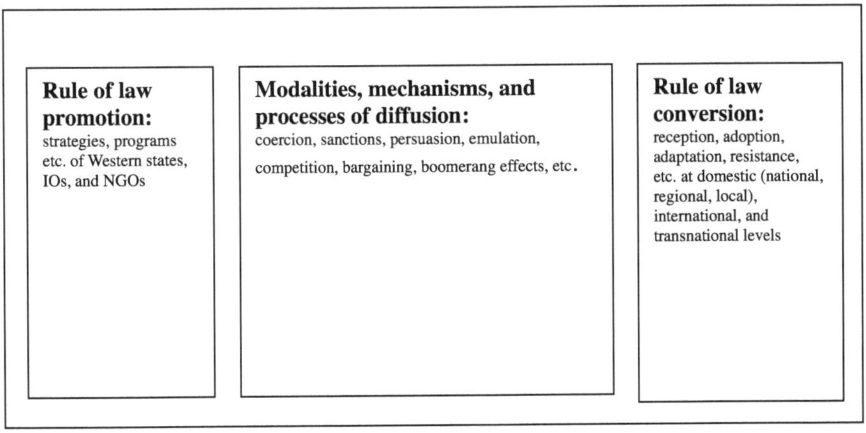

FIGURE I.1. Rule of law dynamics disaggregated.

Each of these perspectives thus analyzes similar processes from different angles. We use these three perspectives to disaggregate the notion of "rule of law dynamics" to better understand both the positive and negative developments in the rule of law field (see Figure I.1).

The rule of law promotion perspective focuses on the strategies, programs, and behavior of (predominantly Western) countries, IOs, and NGOs to strengthen and implement the rule of law. Rule of law promotion is itself a complicated dynamic process, in contrast to the simple ideal type that Twining (2004: 15) accurately characterizes as the naive model, namely "a *bipolar* relationship between *two countries* involving a *direct one-way* transfer of *legal rules or institutions* through the agency of *governments* involving *formal enactment or adoption* at a particular moment of time (*a reception date*) *without major change*."

Rule of law promotion generally involves multiple promoters, often advocating different and competing rules, concepts, and institutions. The process may be direct or indirect, with the result depending on numerous interactions between state and nonstate actors in multiple formal and informal settings. The subject matter may be traditional laws, legal rules, and institutions, but it may also be norms, "soft law," or nonstate regulatory mechanisms. Although the subject matter may be adopted by national governments and apply to the national level, it may also be international, regional, or local in character. The focus may be on the courts, or any other aspect of the legal complex (legislatures, police, prisons, notaries, arbitrators, mediators, law professors, and legal education) or the broader regulatory environment (administrative agencies, oversight committees, anti-corruption committees, security commissions, and private service providers). Rather than a particular moment of enactment, the norms and institutions may be established gradually and evolve and develop over time. Rarely is anything adopted without adaptation or implemented without resistance.

Although it is a useful starting point, rule of law promotion does not capture all significant aspects of rule of law dynamics. The rule of law promotion literature has not developed an understanding of the causal mechanisms through which promotion activities produce sometimes intentional and sometimes unintentional effects or results (the focus of the diffusion perspective). The rule of law promotion perspective also does not adequately attend to the recipient perspective and what happens to rule of law promotion efforts within the target country (the conversion process).

An equally important if less well studied aspect of rule of law dynamics is *rule of law conversion*. This refers to the dynamic process by which what is being promoted is received, adopted, adapted, and resisted. Rule of law promotion raises significant questions as to whether norms that have functioned well in one system can function similarly in other states with different legal systems, or if they have to be adjusted to fit the new context (compare Teubner 1998; Twining 2004: 19). Similar issues arise with respect to the application of rule of law standards to international law binding states and the activities of international institutions and transnational actors.

There are many metaphors that capture the complexity and interactive nature of the conversion process, such as legal translation (Langer 2004), legal transformation (Xu 2004), legal transposition (Orücü 2002), selective adaptation (Potter 2004), and legal irritant (Teubner 1998). Legal translation, legal transposition, legal transformation, and selective adaptation all call attention to the fact that institutions, rules, and practices may be changed in the process of adoption and implementation. However, selective adaptation places more emphasis on target-state agency. Rather than merely being passive recipients, legal actors in the target state (and now the international realm) actively choose certain elements and reject others, interpret terms consistent with local perceptions and understandings, and modify or rework institutions, rules, or practices in light of domestic circumstances. The term "legal irritant" captures the way a new rule or practice may disrupt the existing legal culture and current legal practices, sometimes in unexpected and far-reaching ways.

For present purposes, the conversion of concepts and ideas when arriving at the social targets may be conceived in terms of the *translation* paradigm utilized in a range of disciplines. In the debate about a "translational turn" (Bachmann-Medick 2009; Buden and Nowotny 2009), the category of translation is no longer understood solely or primarily as a linguistic and textual concept. History, sociology, and cultural studies not only use translation as an analytical category but also consider translation a transnational cultural practice, a category of action itself (for a sociology of translation, see Renn 2006). Hence, translation serves as a category to structure the analysis of the interactive processes of the transfer of meanings that are changed or transformed. The starting point of the translation concept is not the assumption of two separate, unconnected contexts but the interpenetration and entanglement of different contexts, discourses, and social fields (Fuchs 2009).

Translation as a social practice entails ruptures and is influenced by power asymmetries, fractures, and disparities. Because the introduction of new legal norms, rules, and institutions threatens entrenched interest groups and ways of life, they often meet resistance. Resistance marks the political awareness that cultural translation is not necessarily a harmonizing or bridge-building affair. The concept of "third space" (Bhabha 2004: 53–56) openly addresses the resistance perspective. Thus, the concept of resistance opens our analytical framework to include both the cultural and the interest dimension structuring the translation processes. Resistance and transformation of the original concept stem not only from political, economic, or coercive power attributed to the actors involved but also from the heterogeneous linguistic and cultural environments that frequently characterize the communication between predominantly Western actors and institutions and local representatives of the recipient state.

The existing rule of law literature has emphasized the rule of law promotion perspective and to a lesser extent the recipient perspective. The concept of diffusion, although not unknown in the literature, has been less well developed and underutilized.[3] However, rule of law dynamics also encompass the mechanisms, modalities, and processes through which rule of law is promoted and through which reception of and resistance to the concept of rule of law occur and feed back to the institutions involved in rule of law promotion. It includes the ways and means by which rule of law values and norms spread transnationally and across national and international levels and that may be employed by states that seek to make other states or international institutions accept rule of law standards, or by international institutions to make states accept rule of law standards (compare Barria and Roper 2008; Björkdahl 2005). It also includes the ways and means by which states and nonstate actors in target countries, or international institutions and transnational actors, resist and adapt rule of law values, as well as the ways they themselves seek to promote and project rule of law values and norms both internally and externally. These mechanisms, modalities, and processes include coercion, incentives, persuasion, emulation, and competition. There may also be more complicated interactive effects and processes, such as bargaining and negotiation, coalition building and alliances, and boomerang effects. In most cases, these modalities, mechanisms, and processes are not controlled by one actor or one set of actors but result from

[3] See Twining (2004) for a conceptualization of rule of law diffusion similar to our notion of rule of law dynamics. Whereas Twining uses "diffusion" to capture all three perspectives or components of rule of law dynamics, we have chosen to use "dynamics" as the more general concept because in our view "diffusion" as normally understood does not capture those processes of rule of law promotion that produce radically different outcomes than originally intended. It also does not include cases of successful resistance to rule of law diffusion. Both of these features seem to be particularly significant, however, when studying rule of law dynamics in an era of international and transnational governance. Moreover, although there is some overlap in the subject matter of promotion, diffusion, and conversion, they reflect different academic disciplines and have produced specialist literatures familiar to different actors. In an interdisciplinary volume, contributors and readers alike approach rule of law from particular perspectives. Keeping the three perspectives separate serves as a reminder that the reader may be entering unfamiliar territory.

the interplay of a multiplicity of social actors and forces, and in that sense they are themselves interactive and iterative processes with intended and unintended effects.

In using the concept of diffusion to capture this important aspect of rule of law dynamics, we are drawing on an extensive literature in other disciplines. In economics, diffusion research focused first on the spread of new technologies and its determinants, before turning to the diffusion of corporate practices (overview in Geroski 2000). Rogers (1983, first published in 1962) and Mansfield's (1961) fundamental work developed the rationales and models explaining the S-curve phenomena, in which the object (technology, practice, etc.) in the beginning slowly diffuses among an adopter population, gaining momentum, and in the end approaches the saturation level, reaching almost 100 percent of the adopter potential.

A similar conceptual framework informs the diffusion research in sociology, closely associated with the Stanford School of sociological institutionalism and its pioneering work on the global diffusion of Western rationality (e.g., Meyer, Boli, Thomas, Ramirez 1997; Meyer, Frank, Hironaka et al. 1997; Thomas, Meyer, Ramirez, and Boli 1987; see also Finnemore 1996). This line of research demonstrates the global spread of ideas, policies, and economic and social practices from a variety of theoretical and methodological perspectives (e.g., Holzinger, Jörgens, and Knill 2007; Simmons, Dobbin, and Garret 2008). Diffusion research has traditionally emphasized the convergence of ideas and practices despite vastly different socioeconomic and cultural contexts. Only very recently has this research started emphasizing the causal mechanisms by which ideas diffuse, such as coercion, the manipulation of utility calculations, socialization, persuasion, or emulation.

In the legal sciences, Harold Koh (1996) has stressed the importance of interaction, interpretation, and internalization and has argued in favor of a theory of transnational legal process. Such a perspective is nontraditional in breaking down the strict distinction between domestic and international realms of action; nonstatist in focusing also on nonstate actors; and dynamic in pointing to vertical (both upward and downward) as well as horizontal processes connecting different areas and types of actors (see also Dezalay and Garth 1996).

We will return to these different aspects of rule of law dynamics in the concluding chapter; on the basis of the information provided in this volume, we will ask what changes have occurred and what challenges remain. Next, however, we provide detailed synopses of the chapters.

3. CHAPTER SYNOPSES

Part I. Rule of Law at the International, National, and Transnational Levels

The chapters in the first part of the book explore the diffusion of rule of law standards across states as well as to new transnational and international levels of government.

The chapters aim at grasping the dynamics of rule of law norms. Has rule of law promotion been successful in the sense that more states have internalized the rule of law? Does international law obligate states to abide by rule of law principles in their internal matters? What dynamic processes have contributed to the increasing pressure on IOs to themselves comply with rule of law principles? Do new modes of governance in which private and nonstate actors play an important role challenge traditional conceptions of rule of law and require modification of rule of law principles?

In Chapter 1, Wolfgang Merkel summarizes what we know about the state of rule of law globally and regionally on the basis of a survey of five well-known rule of law indices: Freedom House Civil Rights; World Bank World Governance Indicators for Rule of Law; the Bertelsmann Transformation Index for Rule of Law; the Democracy Barometer Rule of Law Index; and the World Justice Project Rule of Law Index. Actors in the rule of law field – whether international development agencies, domestic policy makers, or academics – rely heavily on these indicators in developing strategies and evaluating progress toward the goal of implementing rule of law globally. To what extent, though, is our understanding about the current state of rule of law and historical trends in rule of law development well founded? Evaluating the indices in terms of concept, validity, reliability, and aggregation rules, Merkel concludes that each falls short of social science requirements for reliable measurement. Most problematically, most indices are not based on a clear conception of rule of law.

Given the conceptual limitations of the indices, Merkel is careful in drawing strong inferences from this survey. Nevertheless, some reasonably well-supported findings do emerge. First, on the whole, these indices do not show a significant overall improvement in rule of law globally. Only the Freedom House rule of law index points to slight improvements. In the most developed countries, there is even a clear downward trend after 9/11, as the Democracy Barometer shows. However, the measurement of the rule of law in these indices is a relatively recent phenomenon. Most of them begin after 2000, including the Freedom House rule of law index (from 2005 on). The Freedom House civil liberties index shows that the most significant changes on the aggregate level may have occurred between 1990 and 1995, a time not covered by the more refined rule of law indices.

Second, some regions do better than others, depending largely on the nature of the measure; not surprisingly, regions with a large number of authoritarian regimes do less well when measured by thick liberal-democratic rule of law indices. Similarly, regions where liberal values and civil and political rights are assigned a lower priority, including parts of Asia and the Middle East, do less well on some of the measures that emphasize the protection of such rights. Nevertheless, and again as expected given the close relationship between rule of law and wealth, the Organization for Economic Cooperation and Development does relatively well on all standards, whereas sub-Saharan Africa does relatively poorly.

Third, rule of law and democracy do not necessarily go hand in hand; some authoritarian states do well on thin rule of law measures, whereas some democracies fare poorly. More importantly, the indices show that emerging electoral democracies in which the rule of law is weak often fail and revert to authoritarianism.

In short, although the indices do not show a significant diffusion of the rule of law across states on the aggregate level in the past decades, there seem to be numerous dynamics within regions and in specific countries.

We undoubtedly live in an age where rule of law has become a much trumpeted ideal in United Nations (UN) General Assembly resolutions and the policy documents of a variety of international institutions. Nevertheless, doubts remain, in the face of widespread violations of rule of law principles, as to what extent different states are genuinely committed to the noble ideals expressed in these generally nonbinding declarations.

In Chapter 2 Helmut Philipp Aust and Georg Nolte explore the extent to which rule of law requirements have become incorporated into international law binding on states. They conclude that compliance with basic rule of law principles is not a requirement for formal state recognition, although regional organizations have relied on rule of law principles to condition a country's admission, as in the EU, or to justify suspension, as in Africa. They claim, however, that there is a growing normative expectation that states will comply with basic rule of law principles. This emerging standard of rule of law is reinforced by the traditional international law notion of a "minimum standard of justice" applicable to aliens, foreign investment law, and human rights law. The unlikelihood that these three disparate and at times conflicting areas of law will lead to a coherent concept of rule of law suggests the need for a more comprehensive and theoretically informed foundational multilateral treaty (or treaties) of the sort that have underpinned the international human rights movement, although the authors themselves do not discuss the possibility of such treaties or advocate this approach.

Whereas Chapter 2 focuses on the requirements that international law formulates for the introduction of rule of law norms and principles into domestic legal systems, the next two chapters examine rule of law at the international level.

Tim Gemkow and Michael Zürn ask in Chapter 3 to what extent and why the diffusion of the rule of law concept to the international level has occurred. They argue that the rise of political authority beyond the nation-state and the increased intrusiveness of international regulations form the decisive process underlying this development. Because political authority requires legitimacy, the incorporation of the rule of law concept may help international institutions to enhance their legitimacy.

This is, however, mainly a functional argument. Gemkow and Zürn therefore go on to ask to what extent and through which causal mechanisms institutional rules that derive from the rule of law concept have developed in the past decades. Thus the chapter inquires why rule of law norms diffuse across international and national levels. In looking at one component of the rule of law concept – the protection of individual rights – Gemkow and Zürn identify mechanisms through which the rule of law concept has diffused to the international level. Discussing some recent cases in which IOs have introduced compliance review mechanisms that allow groups of people to complain about violations of the respective organization's own standards and policies, they argue that a combination of learning processes within IOs and political pressure from outside are the most important mechanisms. In rarer cases, emulation processes and the competition between IOs play a role as well.

In a third step, they aim at identifying the conditions under which such causal mechanisms are triggered. They set out several hypotheses that derive from the guiding hypothesis: The more IOs are exercising authority and are active in the field of rule of law promotion, the more likely is the introduction of rule of law components in IOs. These hypotheses may guide future research in a field in which future research is urgently needed.

In Chapter 4, Gunnar Folke Schuppert examines how new governance, by shifting responsibilities or functions of the government to private actors, is challenging traditional notions of rule of law that emphasize government legality, such as limited government, government accountability, administrative law, and judicial review. Schuppert focuses on one of the challenges from the growing role of private actors: the rise of transnational rule making. Transnational rule making comes in a variety of forms, from standard setting, to societal self-regulation, to World Trade Organization trade rules, to rule making in the shadow of the law, to transgovernmental networks for regulating financial markets. However, transnational rule making generally exhibits four main characteristics: the deterritorialization of rule making; the blurring of the traditional borderline between binding and nonbinding norms; a change from top-down rule making to a bottom-up system; and a trend toward informality. Schuppert suggests that rule of law principles drawn from a relatively thin or procedural conception of rule of law (as opposed to thicker conceptions that incorporate substantive values such as democracy and human rights) can provide a normative yardstick to guide and evaluate transnational rule making. At the same time, he also suggests that these procedural requirements for transnational rule making should be combined with liberal democracy and the right to participate in the rule-making process and that the rules should be implemented in ways that ensure equality before the law. However, the next crucial step is to transform these general rule of law requirements into area-specific requirements and to develop rules for rule making that have the capability to govern different rule-making processes in particular areas.

Part II. Actors: Strategies and Responses

The chapters in Part I show that the rule of law concept has developed and diffused quite dynamically. Whereas the immediate goals of rule of law promotion have been achieved at best partially, there are nonintended and unforeseen effects, especially on the international and transnational level, that have occurred. Against this background, the second part of the book focuses on the major actors in the field of rule of law dynamics. It analyzes their strategies and how they have adapted to the new dynamics.

In Chapter 5, Frank Schimmelfennig analyzes the rule of law policies and methods of promotion of major Western powers – the United States, the EU, Great Britain, Germany, and France. He finds some general similarities: Rule of law is part of broader democracy promotion and good governance agendas; their policies focus on formal and institutional aspects and emphasize the independence and efficiency of the judicial system; all use mixed approaches that combine top-down with bottom-up programs, though the emphasis has been on top-down methods; and most combine socialization (persuasion) with positive and negative conditionalities and in some cases coercion (imposition through military means), although coercion is rare and conditionality has remained contested and inconsistent. Notwithstanding these general similarities, there are many differences in content, namely concepts and components of the rule of law; organizational setup and institutional context; strategies and instruments; budgets and expenses; and target regions and countries.

Whereas rule of law promotion in the United States is highly decentralized, highly specialized, and fairly fragmented, French rule of law promotion is highly centralized, concentrated, but with low specialization, with the other powers falling in between. The amount of money spent on rule of law promotion as a percentage of official development aid varies widely, though comparisons are difficult because different countries use different categories and there have been variations in spending over time. Although the end of the Cold War led to an increase in rule of law funding, 9/11 led to a reallocation toward security concerns including policing and law enforcement.

All major powers provide global assistance, but they tend to concentrate on regions where their interests are most directly affected. The United States historically focused on Latin America, before turning to Eastern Europe after the fall of the Berlin Wall, and more recently to Iraq and Afghanistan. In Europe, patterns reflect colonial legacies as well as geographical proximity. Interestingly, most funds go to states that have made some progress on political and legal reforms rather than to the worst offenders.

In general, Schimmelfennig does not see significant strategic adaptations to the dynamics just identified. Although there seems to be an increasing recognition of the need to involve local actors, this has yet to be really reflected on the strategic level. Moreover, major states seem to pay little attention to the rule of law quality of international institutions in designing their rule of law promotion strategies.

Turning from states to IOs and NGOs, Monika Heupel finds in Chapter 6 that IOs and NGOs rely on similar approaches for promoting rule of law. Drawing on the literature, she finds that IOs and NGOs adopt a broad array of strategies depending on whether they attribute shortcomings in rule of law to the lack of political will, capacity, or knowledge. To address the lack of political will, IOs and NGOs rely on exposure – explaining the benefits of rule of law and shaming and blaming governments for failing to abide by rule of law standards. They may also rely on positive and negative conditionalities, though in general NGOs are not in a position to impose conditionalities on governments. To address lack of capacity, IOs and NGOs rely on nonhierarchical (noncoercive) or in some cases more hierarchical (coercive) capacity building and technical assistance, including training for legislators, judges, lawyers, police, and other legal complex actors; programs to improve the criminal justice system and management of detention facilities; and programs to improve access to justice and the protection of human rights. To address lack of knowledge, they rely on nonhierarchical or hierarchical diffusion of knowledge and beliefs by collecting and disseminating information in print and online, for example via the UN's online Rule of Law Document Repository or the UN Department of Peacekeeping Operations' online Peacekeeping Resource Hub. Much of this information is in the form of reports summarizing international best practices or "lessons learned" from the organization's experiences in various rule of law promotion initiatives.

Although the number of actors and activities is impressive, Heupel suggests several reasons why the results have been disappointing. First, knowledge deficits remain, particularly regarding why some attempts to promote rule of law succeed whereas others fail. Second, reforms have been too top down, with the agenda driven by foreign actors often lacking in local knowledge, and with insufficient participation and empowerment of local actors. Third, efforts to promote rule of law have been undermined by the failure of international actors themselves to abide by rule of law principles. NGOs have taken note of these shortcomings, and they seem to adapt to the changing rule of law dynamics more swiftly than state actors. For instance, NGOs increasingly work to incorporate local actors in rule of law promotion and are among those who demand the rule of law on the international level as well.

The next three chapters adopt case studies to explore in greater detail the role of powerful states, IOs, NGOs, and the military. In Chapter 7, Paulette Lloyd, Beth Simmons, and Brandon M. Stewart use human trafficking to illustrate the diffusion of norms and policies to address transnational crime as part of a broader global effort to establish the rule of law at the national level. They find that concern for domestic rule of law, hegemonic pressures, and negative externalities all play a role in the recent transnational rule of law wave against crime and human trafficking in particular. The battle to combat human trafficking was led by the United States and other powerful Western states committed to rule of law domestically. However, developing countries that suffered the negative externalities of trafficking – either states with internal human trafficking problems or destination states – also actively participated in the process. Although many states had their own reasons for criminalizing human trafficking in national law, Western powers, particularly the United States, also sought to pressure them, mainly through "shaming and blaming" and other forms of persuasion rather than through denial of material benefits, the imposition of sanctions, or other more coercive means.

In Chapter 8, Linn Hammergren examines the evolving strategies of one of the major IOs, the World Bank, for promoting rule of law in middle-income countries (MICs). One of the criticisms of the rule of law promotion industry has been the heavy reliance on one-size-fits-all solutions that failed to distinguish between post-conflict situations and different stages of development. In low-income countries, the main obstacles to effective governance are the lack of resources and weak or nonexistent institutions. By definition, MICs have some, albeit limited, resources, and most MICs have established the usual institutions that are associated with modern states and found in high-income countries. Thus political resistance and opposition tend to become more important. Reforms produce winner and losers. Unfortunately, as Hammergren notes, the World Bank and other international donors are not well positioned to address these types of local political contests, in some cases because of limited mandates and in other cases because of the lack of local knowledge and other restraints pointed out by Heupel.

The wide diversity among MICs presents another challenge. Indeed, it is highly unlikely that MICs as currently defined (i.e., countries with per capita income from $900 to $12,000) will emerge as a useful category for analysis or a useful basis for rule of law programming. Further disaggregation is required, not only by levels of wealth but along other dimensions as well. Hammergren begins that process by distinguishing on functional grounds between four different types of MICs and then offering more tailored reform proposals for each.

In Chapter 9, Tilmann J. Röder discusses the recent emergence of the military as an important actor in rule of law promotion. He notes that the need to establish order in postconflict situations has forced the military to cooperate with civilian organizations in a range of activities to establish legal institutions and the rule of law. Although the North Atlantic Treaty Organization (NATO), the EU, and the UN use slightly different terms to describe the interaction between military and civil organizations, their policies and strategies share several main features. First, the United States, NATO, and the EU (though not the UN) all conceive of rule of law promotion primarily as a tool to achieve military objectives rather than long-term humanitarian goals, economic development, the consolidation of democracy, or the protection of human rights, even though all also emphasize the importance of rule of law to these larger goals. Second, the emphasis has generally been on security and the "law and order" aspects of rule of law, which are colloquially referred to as the three Cs (courts, cops, and corrections) or the three Ps (police, prisons, and prosecutors). Third, all civil–military cooperation operations to date have suffered from coordination problems, even though they have adopted a variety of approaches to counter such problems. Fourth, all missions have encountered local resistance and produced less than satisfactory results in establishing the rule of law.

Although there are many reasons for the disappointing results, one is the lack of legitimacy. In some cases, the lack of legitimacy derives from the nature of the intervention, as when NATO intervened in Kosovo and Iraq without UN approval and a clear mandate under international law. In other cases, it results from the narrowness of the mission with its emphasis on military objectives. In still other cases, it results from how the mission is carried out. All too often there is inadequate consultation with local leaders and citizens. In many cases, citizens have different needs and priorities than the military. Although citizens no doubt value security, they complain most about public administration, poor governance, procedural violations, and the inability to resolve civil disputes, including conflicts over land rights. At times, the emphasis of international actors on formal institutions has undermined local institutions, which although far from perfect may be more effective than the newly created court system. Similarly, laws modeled on Euro-American precedents are frequently out of step with the level of development of the local economy or include norms at odds with local values and practices. Finally, reinforcing the need for international actors to be accountable and comply with rule of law standards, citizens have expressed outrage over the immunity of foreign military personnel for violations of local and international law.

Whereas the previous chapters focused primarily on the policies, strategies, and incentives of the main promoters of rule of law, the remaining chapters shift the focus to the recipient perspective. The identification of the sources of resistance to rule of law diffusion and the study of the dynamics of rule of law conversion capture an important aspect of the process, and they point to important fields for future research.

In Chapter 10, John Gillespie introduces the theme by discussing the different ways in which the role of recipient countries affects rule of law promotion. He emphasizes first the regulatory capacity of local institutions to adopt and implement rule of law. He notes that countries at different levels of economic and institutional development have different types of demand for rule of law, and they often lack the capacity to implement "international best practices" modeled on institutions in Euro-America and other developed countries. Moreover, he uses sociological theory to point to different mechanisms through which social actors in the recipient countries respond to the import of rule of law concepts. The theory of social subsystems on the one hand is used to explain how social systems try to incorporate external demands without changing their practice significantly. On the other hand, constructivist theorizing points to the need for legitimacy before externally induced changes can achieve the desired results. Gillespie concludes by proposing a new research agenda that does not focus on supply-side failures but attends to capacity issues and the willingness of recipients to change, and that pays particular attention to various sources of local legitimacy among different epistemic communities or constituencies.

In Chapter 11, Richard Zajac Sannerholm discusses the trials and tribulations in promoting rule of law in Kosovo, providing a cautionary tale of how things can go radically wrong when international actors fail to take into account local circumstances and the needs and desires of citizens in the recipient country. Despite the expenditure of considerable sums of money and the vast amount of technical assistance, the general consensus is that Kosovo still falls far short of any reasonable standard of rule of law. The list of maladies is long, including but not limited to lack of respect for constitutional authority, judicial corruption, ethnic discrimination, and weak implementation of newly passed laws.

The reasons for the failures are equally long, and they point to many familiar weaknesses in rule of law promotion: the rapid, top-down introduction of laws modeled on laws in high-income countries, while failing to attend to levels of development and institutional capacity; the failure to consult and empower local actors, resulting in prioritization of reforms not emphasized by citizens while the demands of citizens for other reforms were not met; the lack of understanding of local social practices; the conflict between international best practices and local norms and institutions; the failure to take advantage of existing institutions; the lack of legitimacy of the military operations; and anger over the immunity of foreign actors. Indeed, Kosovo stands for how *not* to promote rule of law, as acknowledged by a former UN Human Rights Commissioner who characterized the international community's approach as benevolent despotism.

In Chapter 12, Sarah M. H. Nouwen investigates the newly established ICC's role in rule of law promotion through a case study of Uganda. Officials and academics alike have assumed that the ICC will strengthen the rule of law. Against this background, Nouwen critically examines how the ICC's intervention has affected the rule of law, in its various aspects, in Uganda, the first country that came within the Court's jurisdiction. The conclusion is mixed. Nouwen demonstrates that although the ICC has strengthened the rule of law in some respects, its promotion of the rule of law can sometimes clash with other elements of the rule of law, which were safeguarded at the national or local level. She concludes that the ICC's intervention has unleashed dynamics in Uganda that are in synergy with some aims of the rule of law (supremacy of law and accountability) but in tension with others (equality before the law, separation of powers, fairness, and legal certainty). Once again, the external intrusion of fundamental norms creates unanticipated consequences when they collide with existing rule of law norms at the national level.

4. PROVISIONAL CONCLUSION

In sum, although rule of law promotion may have produced deficient results so far, it has also triggered dynamics that have led to a diffusion of the rule of law concept to new fields and levels. Rule of law dynamics are an ongoing process, calling for constant reflection and appraisal. By seeking to understand these recent developments and the dynamics of change, this volume aims at moving beyond the perspective of rule of law promoters. Only if we understand these distinct yet interrelated processes can the lack of knowledge in this field be significantly reduced. There are many dedicated people trying their best to make things work, and many individuals whose lives would be immeasurably better were they to live in a state governed by the rule of law. It is therefore worthwhile to address these issues and point to areas in which further research is needed. We do this in the concluding chapter, where we summarize the main developments in the three areas of promotion, diffusion, and conversion; the causes of these developments; and issues for further investigation.

PART I

Rule of Law at the International, National, and Transnational Levels

1

Measuring the Quality of Rule of Law

Virtues, Perils, Results

Wolfgang Merkel

This chapter surveys trends and developments in rule of law globally and regionally, based on five well-known democracy and rule of law indices: Freedom House; World Bank Worldwide Governance Indicators; the Bertelsmann Transformation Index; the Democracy Barometer; and the World Justice Project.

Although indices of rule of law are increasingly used by academics, politicians, and practitioners of good governance aid, they rarely meet standard social science requirements for reliable measurement. Therefore, I first critically review the five indices according to the four "classical" evaluative standards: root concept, validity, reliability, and aggregation rules. I also report on the scope and time period covered. All of these indices have their shortcomings. It is particularly striking that most rule of law indices do not follow Sartori's (1970: 1038) iron rule: "Concept formation stands prior to quantification."

Notwithstanding their limitations, these five indices do shed light on several key issues: whether rule of law is increasing globally, regional variations in rule of law, and the much discussed relationship between rule of law and democracy. The major trends and findings for each indicator are set out in the relevant section and then summarized in the conclusion.

1. THE CONCEPT OF RULE OF LAW

Rule of law is a notoriously contested concept. In general, rule of law conceptions may be classified along a thin (procedural) to thick continuum. Schematically and reductively, one can distinguish among three different concepts of rule of law (i.e., Lauth and Sehring 2009; Møller and Skaaning 2010a; Skaaning 2010; Tamanaha 2004, 2007), although many would distinguish between rule *by* law and rule *of* law (Peerenboom 2002). However, one can also place the different types of rule of law on a continuum ranging from minimalist to maximalist concepts (see Table 1.1). In addition, the midrange version could also come in nonliberal democratic variants

TABLE 1.1. *Three concepts of rule of law*

Minimalist	Midrange	Maximalist
Rule by law	Liberal Democratic rule of law	Social Democratic rule of law
Power executed by positive law: • Maintaining order and regulating political and civic transactions	Rule by law plus: • Law is public, prospective, certain • Equality before the law • Guarantee of human and basic rights • Lawmaking by democratically legitimized bodies • Power is controlled by checks and balances • Independence of the judiciary	Democratic rule of law plus: • Social universal rights institutionalized in a welfare state • Legal regulation to reduce socioeconomic inequality to a minimum

Source: Adopted and modified from Møller and Skaaning (2010a: 15).

(as in Hong Kong, Singapore, and other East Asian states, and arguably in some of the Middle Eastern states), with corresponding differences in terms of civil and political rights and institutions (Peerenboom 2005).

Although most of the indices do not make the root concept of their measurement indicators explicit with the critical review of them, it becomes clear that they rely implicitly on different understandings of the rule of law. This heavily influences the measurement results. All of the rule of law indices reviewed in this chapter rely on a midrange concept, although the World Bank's Good Governance Indicators are the most minimalist. The reasons for the predominance of the midrange concept are namely normative reasons and reasons that are rooted in the character of comparative empirical research: The minimalist concept would not generate much variance between most democracies and even many of the semi-authoritarian regimes. The maximalist concept is seen by most theorists as overextending the core understanding of rule of law. Furthermore, even among maximalist theorists there is no consensus regarding the extent to which socioeconomic inequality should and could be diminished without constraining liberty and property rights whose protection is seen as a core function of the rule of law in the Western liberal tradition.

2. A SURVEY OF FIVE RULE OF LAW INDICES

2.1. *Freedom House: Civil Rights*[1]

Since 1972, *Freedom in the World*, a survey by Freedom House, has offered an annual evaluation of the global state of freedom, which is defined as "the opportunity to

[1] I am thankful to R. Andrew Gómez and Dag Tanneberg for collecting information on all the indices under review concerning the Freedom House.

act spontaneously in a variety of fields outside the control of government and other centres of potential domination."[2] Largely derived from the *Universal Declaration of Human Rights*, freedom is thought to find expression in two broad categories: political rights and civil liberties. Whereas the former addresses the capacity to "participate freely in the political process," the latter incorporates "freedoms of expression and belief, associational and organizational rights, rule of law and personal autonomy."[3] Both dimensions are ranked on a scale from 1 to 7, where 1 is the best possible and 7 the worst possible rating.

Questions on the rule of law first address the existence of an independent judiciary, which is (second) capable of prosecuting criminal behavior. Third, the questions turn to the absence of war, insurgencies, and state-organized terror. Fourth, the checklist pays attention to equal treatment under the law.

2.1.1. Concept

Freedom House has never built its components and subcomponents (i.e., indicators) on an explicit root concept of democracy or freedom. Although it has an implicitly thick understanding of democracy, which goes far beyond free and fair elections, the subcategory of rule of law is rather thin. Nevertheless, it covers substantial defining elements such as equality before the law and the independence of the judiciary. It also adds data on the effectiveness of the state in guaranteeing the security of citizens against war, insurgencies, crime, and terror. However, the more fine-grained subquestions signal that the experts do not evaluate just pure "technical" effectiveness; they always have to take into account whether this effectiveness is generated within the boundaries of rule of law.

2.1.2. Scope

The scope of the Freedom House data is impressive. It covers 193 countries and 15 so-called territories. The data begin in 1972 and are collected on an annual basis. However, the subscores have been made available to the public only since 2005. Therefore, separate data on rule of law exist for just a few years.

2.1.3. Validity

Because there is no clear root concept of the constructs of freedom or rule of law, the validity of the indicators and the subsequent questions cannot really be

[2] Freedom House, "Methodology 2005 Edition." Accessed November 18, 2009 at http://freedomhouse.org/template.cfm?page=351&ana_page=354&year=2009.

[3] Ibid.

judged with regard to validity. They are not systematically derived from any explicit theoretical concept. Instead, they follow a plausible but thinner understanding of rule of law. The reason is not that Freedom House has a thin concept of constitutional democracy in general, but that the guarantees of civil rights or checks and balances are subsumed under different subcategories and not under the explicit label "rule of law." Therefore, the data presented here reflect a "thin" understanding of rule of law.

2.1.4. Reliability

The reliability of the data is low. There is a team of changing experts that distributes scores along the outlined questions. However, the codebooks of Freedom House consist of little more than a simple "checklist defining the parameters of the indicators with no description of how to interpret the numerical scores assigned to the attributes or their components" (Møller and Skaaning 2010a: 454; see also Lauth 2004; Thiery, Sehring, and Muno 2010). Additional problems derive from incremental changes to the methodology, most notably seen in 1989. Since Freedom House did not make the subscores public until 2006, the transparency of the single scores that lead to the aggregate index is particularly low. Freedom House aims to ensure the comparability of ratings from year to year; nevertheless, caution is advised when one is comparing ratings over longer periods, especially because changes are not revised retroactively. Furthermore, the rating process opens up into a joint review and discussion of results during which – in certain cases – minor changes are made. Thus, the whole process becomes somewhat nontransparent.[4] "In the end the aggregate data offered by Freedom House has to be accepted largely on faith" (Munck and Verkuilen 2002: 21). Consequently, Freedom House has made the subscores, including the one for rule of law, public since 2006.

2.1.5. Aggregation Rules

As with most of the other indices, Freedom House uses the simple average of data at the indicator level (questions) without any weighting. Each of the indicators is considered to have equal weight for the rule of law, regardless of whether it concerns the core principle of "equality before rule of law" or the government's effectiveness in guaranteeing law and order. This is understandable: Even if Freedom House had a theoretically elaborated concept and argued that some elements are more relevant than others, which is indeed the case, each precise weighting would have an arbitrary character.

[4] For more details, see Hadenius and Teorell (2005: 15 et seq.).

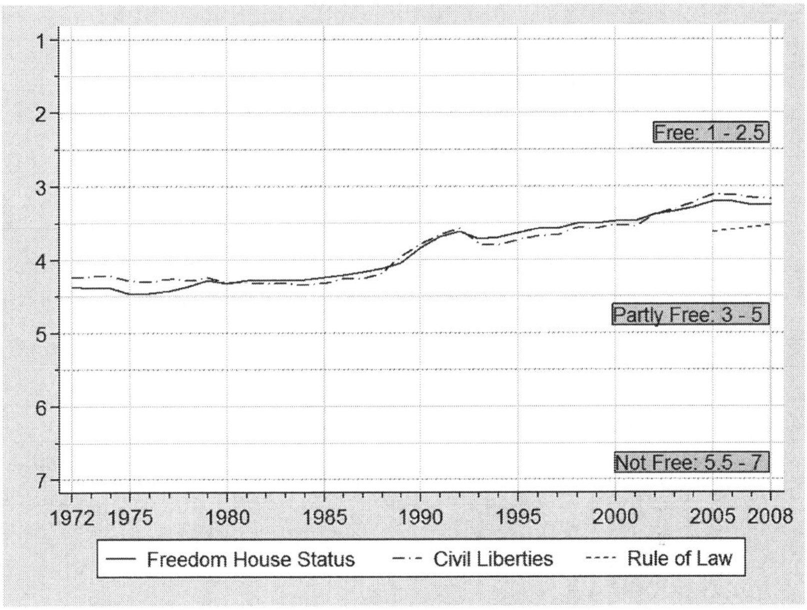

FIGURE 1.1. Freedom House: Deviations between freedom, civil liberties, and rule of law.

2.1.6. Trends

With all cautiousness taken as a result of the theoretical and methodological shortcomings of the Freedom House indices, some trends can be observed (see Figure 1.1).

The overall state of civil liberties rose by approximately 1 point between 1972 and 2008. Civil liberties took root throughout the world even though their general state remained within the gray zone of partial compliance with the Freedom House checklist. Most significant was the period from 1988 to 1992, when the collapse of the Soviet communist regimes took place. The mostly peaceful transitions from socialism to democracy in Central and Eastern Europe clearly show their imprint on the Freedom House Index, with an associated half-point increase – the strongest single change over the whole observation period. Before 1988, changes remained marginal and civil liberties stayed close to 4.25 points. From 1990 on, civil liberties experienced further proliferation, lowering the mean of the scale from around 3.6 to around 3.2 points. However, the post-1992 slope does exhibit more moderate growth than before and even shows civil liberties in retreat from 1992 to 1994 and 2005 to 2008. Although there was a recent marginal decline of civil liberties and political rights, which caused a series of articles about "freedom in retreat" or "the democratic rollback" (i.e., Diamond 2008; Puddington 2008), the subscore of rule of law points in a different direction. According to Freedom House, the quality of rule of law slightly increased as an aggregate in the 193 countries between 2005 and 2008. This trend continued during the following two years.

2.2. *World Bank Worldwide Governance Indicators: Rule of Law*

The latest Worldwide Governance Indicators (WGI) cover the years 1996 through 2008 and have the promotion and measurement of so-called good governance as their overarching goals. Governance is defined as follows:

> [T]he process and institutions by which authority in a country is exercised: (i) the process by which governments are selected, held accountable, monitored, and replaced; (ii) the capacity of governments to manage resources efficiently, and to formulate, implement, and enforce sound policies and regulations; and, (iii) the respect for the institutions that govern economic and social interactions among them.[5]

The working definition of good governance is further broken down into six subcomponents through which the definition is operationalized: voice and accountability, political stability and absence of violence, quality of the regulatory framework, government effectiveness, control of corruption, and rule of law. Rule of law is defined as "the extent to which agents have confidence in and abide by the rules of society, including the quality of contract enforcement and property rights, the police, and the courts, as well as the likelihood of crime and violence."[6] The purpose is to "measure the success of a society in developing an environment in which fair and predictable rules form the basis for economic and social interactions and the extent to which property rights are protected."[7] Interestingly enough, neither the separation of power nor equality before the law nor the democratic legitimacy of the legislating bodies is mentioned. There can be no doubt: The definition is based on a thin concept of rule of law, has a technical governance bias, and resembles the minimal definition of a legal state, that is, rule *by* law. As is evident from its position within the good governance framework, rule of law is only one of six aspects of good governance. This is one reason why rule of law is reduced to a thin concept, as is the case with rule of law within the Freedom House index. However, rule of

5 See World Bank, "Governance & Anti-Corruption." Accessed November 18, 2009 at www.worldbank.org/wbi/governance/.

6 See World Bank, "Worldwide Governance Indicators: Links to the Individual WGI Sources." Accessed November 18, 2009 at http://info.worldbank.org/governance/wgi/sources.htm.

7 See World Bank site. Accessed November 18, 2009 at www.worldbank.org/wbi/governance/pubs/govmatters4sra.html.

law is further broken down into two key areas. They also reflect the more formal and technical conceptualization:

- The effective use of public resources (control of corruption);
- The shaping and implementation of rules, regulations, and policies of the state.

2.2.1. Scope

One of the WGI project's biggest strengths is its sheer mass of data, which is used in measuring the indicators. As the WGI Web site states, the "aggregate indicators combine the views of a large number of enterprise, citizen and expert survey respondents in industrial and developing countries. The individual data sources underlying the aggregate indicators are drawn from a diverse variety of survey institutes, think tanks, non-governmental organizations, and international organizations."[8] They cover 212 countries and territories for 1996, 1998, 2000, 2002, and subsequent years on an annual basis. The scope of the countries surveyed is impressive and the period of nearly 15 years is significantly longer than the Freedom House rule of law subscore (which has existed since 2006).

2.2.2. Concept and Validity

Beyond the just cited definition, Kaufmann and his collaborators from the World Bank have never developed a clear theoretical concept. The definition is more a "summary description of the many indicators that are bundled together as an expression of Kaufmann, Kraay and Mastruzzi's non-articulated personal ideas" (Skaaning 2010: 452). The collected data reflect more in a plausible than in a systematic manner the six subdimensions of the good governance definition. In addition, the subdimensions, including rule of law, are not based on a theoretically elaborated and transparent concept. The question of validity, therefore, cannot be seriously answered; in a strict methodological sense it does not exist. However, the more formal and technical understanding of the thin rule of law concept is reflected in the selection of the data.

2.2.3. Reliability

The WGI are no primary data collected by the Kaufmann team. Rather, they are a huge collection of secondary data. The "WGI 2007" are based on 340 single

[8] See World Bank, "Worldwide Governance Indicators: The Worldwide Governance Indicators (WGI) project." Accessed November 18, 2009 at http://info.worldbank.org/governance/wgi/index.asp.

indicators drawn from 35 different sources generated by 32 different organizations (Kaufmann and Kraay 2008: 8). However, the indicators differ from year to year and from country to country. This cast doubts on the reliability of the data in time-series analyses and has provoked criticism from different sides (Iqbal and Shah 2008: 25 et seq.; Knack 2006: 20–21). Kaufmann et al. acknowledged the theoretical core of the criticism, but they argued that inconsistencies in the data do not show up in the empirical results because of the sheer amount of data used (Kaufmann, Kraay, and Mastruzzi 2007a: 3 et seq.). Nevertheless, the problem remains that the WGI team is unable to control for various theoretical and methodological problems that arise from how its sources collect their data.[9] Although one may argue that the sheer mass of data will naturally correct for some of the problems inherent with aggregating data from a plethora of sources,[10] this approach nevertheless inevitably distorts the data and leaves the WGI open to criticism. The WGI team, therefore, does not hide this fact and has published its equation for calculating error; it has also constructed a system in which weighting of the various inputs is supposed to reduce systematic error.[11]

2.2.4. Trends

The WGI rule of law indicator, as measured from 1996 through 2008, has a global average of 0.00, with the 2008 world average serving as the standard by which previous years are then measured. This mechanism allows for temporal comparisons across regions and individual countries. Changes in the scores of each region are only scored relative to the rest of world. Therefore, the changes in Eastern Europe and the former USSR from 1996 to 2000 (−0.261 to −0.401) could be attributed to either a worsening of the state of the rule of law in those countries, an increase in the rest of world's scores relative to Eastern Europe and the former USSR, or a combination of both. It is therefore impossible to state that, for example, the *absolute* state of the rule of law in Eastern Europe and the former USSR decreased between 1996 and 2000; it can only be stated that the development of the rule of law in these countries decreased vis-à-vis the rest of world in this period (see Figure 1.2).

But Kaufmann et al. regularly make claims about global trends in rule of law: For example, in 2005, the authors of the World Bank's ongoing study of good governance cautiously concluded that there is no evidence of "any significant improvement in governance worldwide, and if anything the evidence is suggestive of a deterioration,

9 See the section on the Bertelsmann Transformation Index concerning problems with its collection of the aggregate rule of law indicator as one example of the problems of a survey becoming problems for the WGI's aggregate indicator.

10 For a list of sources, see World Bank, "Worldwide Governance Indicators: Links to the Individual WGI Sources." Accessed November 18, 2009 at http://info.worldbank.org/governance/wgi/sources.htm.

11 See World Bank, "Weights Used to Construct the Worldwide Governance Indicators for 1996–2008." Accessed November 18, 2008 at http://info.worldbank.org/governance/wgi/resources.htm.

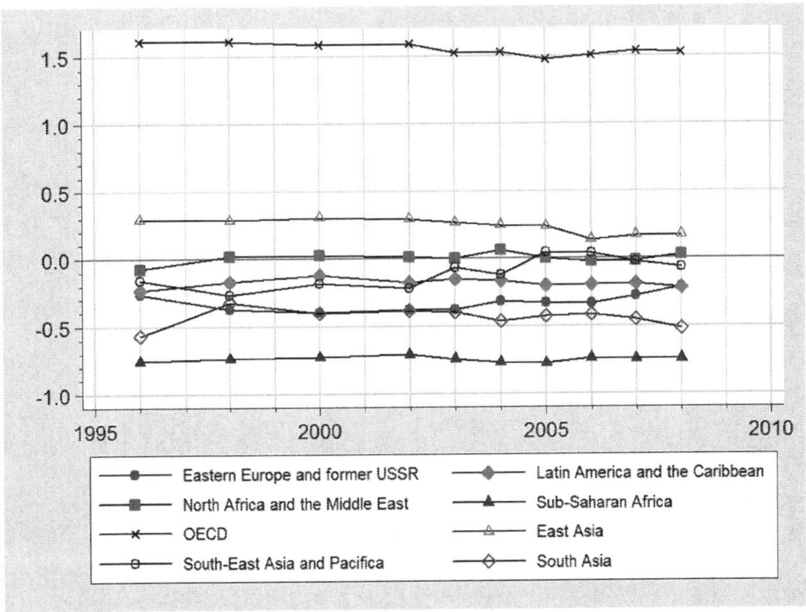

FIGURE 1.2. Development of rule of law by regions. (*Note*: Mexico is included in "Latin America and the Caribbean." The figures plot regional means relative to the global average of "rule of law." For example, the OECD was 1.5 points above the global average in 2008. *Source*: Kaufmann, Kraay, and Mastruzzi 2009, own figures.)

at the very least in key dimensions such as rule of law, control of corruption, political stability and government effectiveness" (Kaufmann and Kraay 2008: 14).

Unsurprisingly, the Organization for Economic Cooperation and Development (OECD; here, without Mexico) is far above the world average for the entire time period although its overall score has suffered since the so-called War on Terrorism began (its effects were first noticeable almost immediately in 2002). Although the rule of law in the OECD countries fell by more than 0.1 points in this period vis-à-vis the rest of world, it was nearly back to its 1996 level by 2007.

Latin America and the Caribbean exhibit the second-best figures when it comes to the quality of rule of law from 1996 to 2008. However, in 2003 the region was surpassed by Southeast Asia and the Pacific. Latin America had no major shift over the period concerned although there has been a slight decline from its peak in 2000, at which point the region sat just below the world average.

The difference between Africa's component subregions is striking and obvious at first glance. Although as a whole Africa seems to be doing quite poorly relative to the rest of world, North Africa and the Middle East actually scored slightly better than the world average over the entire period under investigation, whereas Sub-Saharan Africa performed the worst and is mainly responsible for Africa's low overall rating. Surprisingly, North Africa and the Middle East are performing visibly better when

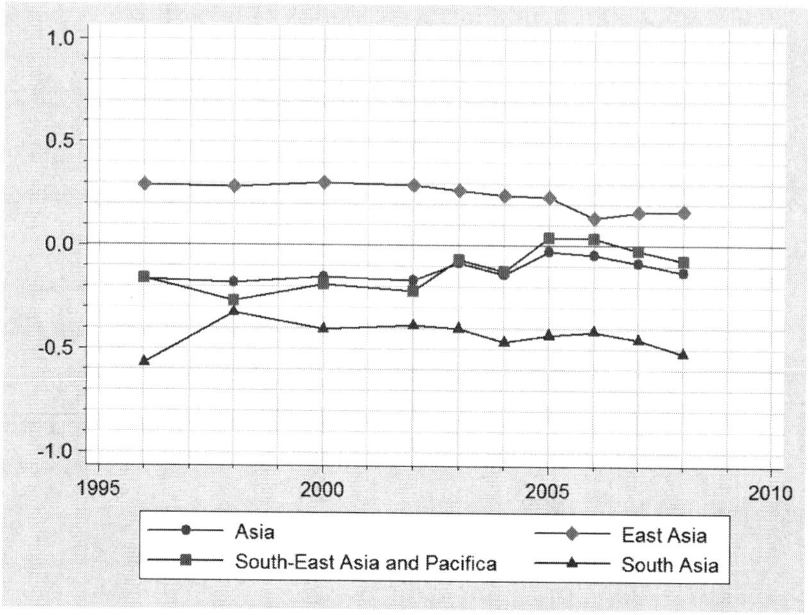

FIGURE 1.3. Development of rule of law in Asia. (*Note*: The figures plot regional means relative to the global average of "rule of law." For example, the whole region of Asia was 0.1 points below the global average in 2008. *Source*: Kaufmann et al. 2009, own figures.)

it comes to the rule of law indicators than one might otherwise assume, given that almost all indices of democracy consider it to be one of the most autocratic regions in the world. If one compares the region's rule of law scores with data from Freedom House and the Bertelsmann Transformation Index (BTI), it is clear that the Middle East and North African (MENA) countries perform much better on the World Bank's rule of law index. The major reason for this striking difference is that the WGI have a bias toward the technical side of effective governance and the formal legal state. The comparatively low figures of crime and violence – compared with those of Latin America or South Asia – contribute to this surprising performance. The WGI do not reflect a thick understanding of rule of law, which would be more sensitive to those elements that go beyond the formal legal state and are particularly sensitive to the workings of democracy, namely the legal and actual guarantee of human and civic rights and the constitutional checks and balances of horizontal accountability (see Figure 1.3).

Asia is the most diverse continent in terms of the quality of rule of law, with South Asia scoring well below the world average and higher only than Sub-Saharan Africa; Southeast Asia and the Pacific stay slightly below the world average for most of the time period until exceeding it in 2005; and East Asia ranks well above the world average for the entire period although it has seen a slight decline in recent years.

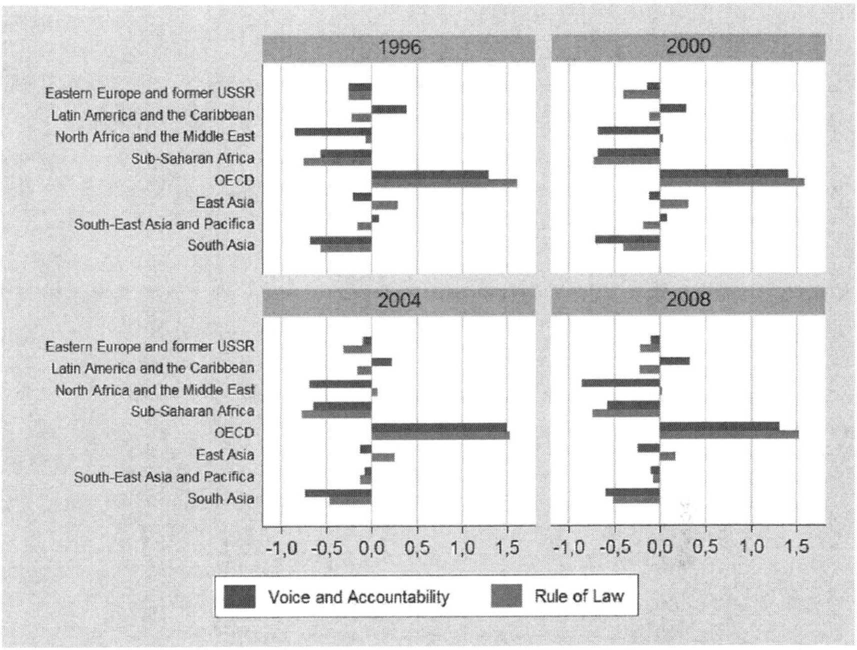

FIGURE 1.4. Gap between democracy and rule of law by regions. (*Note*: Mexico is included in "Latin America and the Caribbean." The figures depict the gap between the mean of "voice and accountability" and "rule of law" over regions as offered by the good governance indicators. Every bar is relative to the global average of good governance. For example, North Africa and the Middle East ranked close to the global average of "rule of law" in 2008, but in terms of "voice and accountability" those countries performed the worst. *Source*: Kaufmann et al. 2009, own figures.)

2.2.5. The Gap Between Voice and Accountability and Rule of Law

What do the WGI tell us about the relation between democracy and rule of law? Only if one conceptualizes both democracy and rule of law in a minimalist way, do they not overlap. On the other, thicker index, constitutional democracy and rule of law become an integral component. The WGI have indeed embarked on such a minimal conceptualization. Democracy understood in the minimalist sense of Schumpeter (1942) or Dahl (1971) is subsumed under "voice and accountability," which offers information on the "perceptions of the extent to which a country's citizens are able to participate in selecting their government, as well as freedom of expression, freedom association, and a free media" (Kaufmann et al. 2009: 6). The indicator relates closely to Dahl's minimalist definition of polyarchy. It justifies its utilization as an estimate of democracy.

The bar charts in Figure 1.4 offer information on the regional averages of the "rule of law" and the "voice and accountability" indicators in 1996, 2000, 2004, and 2008. Considering the interaction of minimal democracy and the rule of law, one can see that most regions of the world perform in a clearly different fashion on the two indicators.

Expectedly, the OECD countries rank well above the global average of rule of law as well as voice and accountability. Even so, only in 2004 did both dimensions come equally close to being 1.5 points above the global average. In 1996, 2000, and 2008, the rule of law slightly outranked the possibilities of political participation in the OECD countries. Sub-Saharan Africa is an example of the opposite. In 1996 as well as in 2000, 2004, and 2008, this region trailed most other parts of the world on both accounts – democracy and the rule of law – with ratings about 0.5 points below the global average. Despite the slightly better performance of rule of law compared with democracy, both spheres appear to be grossly but equally underdeveloped. The disastrous complementary interrelation between rule of law and voice and accountability is largely due to the fact that many states are failing or close to failing.

Things become more puzzling when we turn our eyes to Latin America and the Caribbean as well as North Africa and the Middle East. Whereas the former is currently considered to be at least mostly inhabited by electoral democracies, the latter may be said to be the world's stronghold of autocracy. Not only do both regions show divergent rankings on the two dimensions, as did the OECD and Sub-Saharan Africa, but the scores even point in opposite directions. Thus, Latin America and the Caribbean performed above the global average of voice and accountability by approximately 0.3 points, but rule of law, in contrast, consistently ranked below that average in 1996, 2000, 2004, and 2008. The particular weakness of the rule of law and governmental inefficiency (e.g., with regard to law and order) is typical for mere electoral "defective democracies." Their main characteristic is the discrepancy between fairly well-established pluralist democratic elections but severe deficits in civic rights and a highly deficient regime of horizontal accountability (Merkel, Croissant, Puhle, and Thiery 2006; Merkel 2004).

North Africa and the Middle East display divergence on the two dimensions as well, albeit in the opposite direction. Although this region consistently remained more than 0.5 points below the global voice and accountability average and has indeed shown the worst performance on this index, its rule of law ratings stayed close to the global average, and from 2000 onward even slightly surpassed it. This reflects the minimalist and formal rule of law concept of the WGI, which is in fact compatible with authoritarian regimes too.

2.3. *The Concept of Rule of Law in the Bertelsmann Transformation Index*

First published in 2003, the BTI attempts to evaluate the democratic quality of political regimes beyond the established democracies of the OECD world. The BTI aims to bridge the gap between scientific research and politics while underscoring the importance of democracy's being anchored by the rule of law and by a market economy, which is flanked by sociopolitical safeguards. By evaluating the rule of law, the BTI puts forward a broader concept of democracy than is usual in the measurement of the quality of democracy. It is based on a midrange concept of democracy (free elections plus rule of law). Accordingly, it includes indicators for the rule of law as well as social and political integration (Bertelsmann Stiftung 2003).

The index is organized into two subindices: One measures the management of transformation through the actions of relevant actors (management index); the other, a two-dimensional subindex, points out the status of the market-based economy as well as democracy (status index). The latter is the decisive one for our purpose. It differentiates among five criteria, each with between two and five aspects. It is here, among the criteria of statehood, political participation, the stability of democratic institutions, and political and social integration, that the BTI places the criterion of rule of law.

At the indicator level, the rule of law criterion is assessed by four indicators, which are rated on a 10-point scale:

- Effective horizontal separation of powers;
- Independence of the judiciary;
- Prosecution of the abuse of public authority;
- Protection of civil rights.

The overall status of the rule of law is calculated by averaging all of the indicators.

2.3.1. Scope

First published in 2003, the BTI covers the years from 2000 onward on a biannual basis. At present, 131 countries are evaluated, excluding all established democracies of the OECD world and countries with fewer than 1.5 million inhabitants. The intent is to measure the development or transformation of non-OECD countries toward market economies.

2.3.2. Concept

Although the BTI does not present a clear conceptual tree as recommended by Munck and Verkuilen (2002), there are some basic conceptual documents (Bertelsmann Stiftung 2003; Merkel 1998; Merkel and Puhle 1999) that clearly lay out the normative foundation and the core elements of democracy. Democracy is understood as an *embedded democracy* (Merkel 2004) based on general, free, and fair elections, permeated by the rule of law, and embedded into a socially regulated market economy and a vital civil society. This is a thick understanding of democracy and a thick concept of democratically legitimized rule of law, including the control dimension of horizontal accountability. Despite the thickness of the concept, rule of law is measured by only four indicators. However, these four indicators or questions are quite encompassing (see earlier list), in that many more detailed aspects are included in the expert judgments or answers. Regardless of the more encompassing nature of the questions, the rule of law subindex lacks a certain depth of sharpness. There is a certain bias in favor of horizontal accountability while other aspects such as the ban on retroactivity or equality before the law are only implicitly included.

2.3.3. Validity

The validity of the indicators–questions measured against the proposed thick concepts of democracy and rule of law as outlined in the aforementioned documents is higher than in all the other indices (Müller and Pickel 2007). Still lacking, though it is planned for the 2012 edition, is a stepwise and transparent derivation of the indicators–questions from the fundamental core dimensions of democracy, respectively rule of law.

2.3.4. Reliability

Regarding the reliability of the data, the BTI stands out because of its multilayered procedures. The numerical scoring is based on a precise and systematically structured narrative report of approximately 20 pages. The rule of law subscore encompasses approximately 2 pages. The codebook is very detailed and provides a solid support to the coders. There is an original report and numerical coding by an expert from the respective country, which is reviewed by a German expert on this country. Following the communications of the two individual experts, the scoring is reviewed and recalibrated by a commission of regional experts, and the review process is concluded in a final round by the BTI Board which consists of approximately 15 experts on comparative research of democracy and market economy. The detailed codebook, the first report, and the following three rounds of discursive reviews examine the degree of subjectivity that is immanent to all expert judgments.

2.3.5. Trends

On a global scale, rule of law has seen an uneven development since 2003. Whereas democracies[12] covered by the BTI witnessed a visible increase between 2003 and 2006, from about 6 to nearly 7 points,[13] ratings dropped marginally from 2006

[12] The BTI separates democracies from autocracies on a numerical basis. Each country receiving fewer than 3 points in one criterion is rated as an autocracy.

[13] Figures from 2003 have to be interpreted very cautiously. Because the BTI was originally based on a scale from 1 to 5, the given information is barely comparable to succeeding rounds. To avoid inflated values, the 2003 round does not receive further attention.

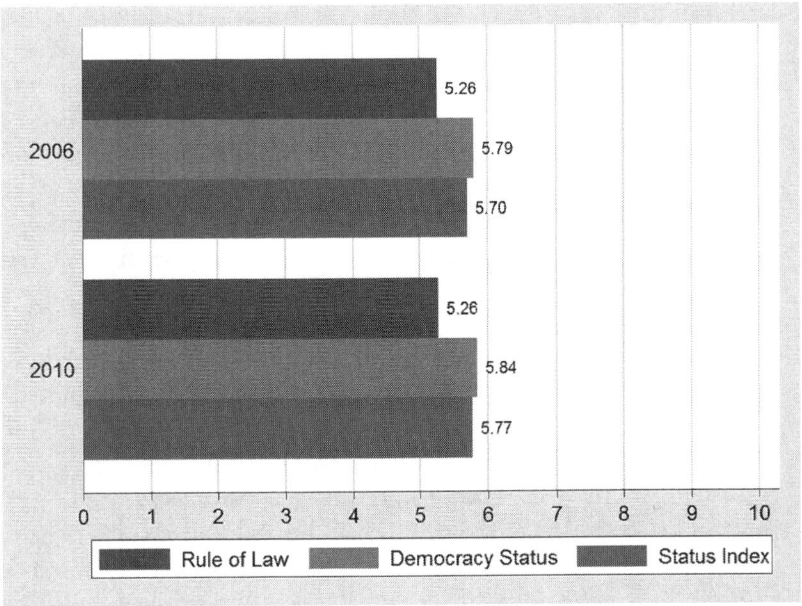

FIGURE 1.5. Overall Development of Rule of Law in the BTI, 2006, 2008, and 2010. (*Source*: Bertelsmann Transformation Index 2006, 2008, and 2010; own figures.)

to 2008. Autocracies, in contrast, showed a steady increase from about 3 to 3.5 points from 2003 to 2008. The overall index for democracy rose from about 5.5 (2003) points to about 5.8 in 2008, even though democracies stagnated between 2006 and 2008 (about 7.2), after a swift increase between 2003 and 2006 (about 6.8 to 7.2).

Only 13 of 75 democratic states exhibited stable levels of the rule of law category. At the same time, 23 of 75 democracies suffered from severe defects. In 2008, rule of law was the second-worst performing category of all democracies, trailed only by social and political integration. Corruption in fragile states is emphasized as one of the major causes.

The aggregate status of rule of law did not change from 2006 to 2010 (see Figure 1.5). Neither the overall status of democracy nor the status of rule of law showed substantial variation. Stagnation of democracy and thereby rule of law is caused by the largely successful transformation of the Central and Eastern European countries, most of which entered the European Union (EU) in 2004 or 2007. Their achievements, however, were countered by autocratic setbacks in countries such as Russia and Venezuela. With a value of 5.3 (on a scale from 1 to 10), rule of law remained stable on average but at a low level.

If we compare the quality of rule of law with the quality of democracy (which includes rule of law as one of its five dimensions), then we can discover a significant difference: Rule of law performs significantly worse than democracy. If we compare the dimension rule of law with the participatory and electoral dimension of democracy (close to Robert Dahl's polyarchy), we find that the gap between rule of law and the polyarchical elements of democracy becomes even more significant. To simplify this finding, we can say that the essential problem of young democracies, or all political regimes outside the OECD world, is less one of electoral and political participation than of severe defects within rule of law. Moreover, research on young democracies (Merkel, Puhle et al. 2003; Merkel, Puhle et al. 2006) has shown that the grave deficiencies of rule of law, in particular of horizontal accountability, turn out to be the entry point for severe defects in other partial regimes of democracy, such as civil and political rights.

In general, the status of rule of law as assessed by the BTI remained stable throughout the years and regions, with the sole exception of Central, Eastern, and Southeastern Europe. Institutions of separation of power and independent judiciaries are present, but their viability remains on a low to very low level.

The comparison of rule of law among world regions shows expected patterns. As in 2006, states in North Africa and the Middle East ranked lowest in this dimension in 2008 as well as in 2010, even though their rating increased from 3.8 to 4.0. This finding clearly deviates from the WGI, which see the rule of law quality of the Sub-Saharan countries as clearly below that of the North Africa–Middle East "region." The poor rule of law performance of the mostly autocratic states is largely due to the elements of horizontal accountability and civic liberties, which form definitional parts of the rule of law subindex.

Best performances were achieved in Central, Eastern, and Southeastern European countries – most of which either entered the EU or achieved candidate status (e.g., Croatia). In addition, this group advanced further from 8.2 points in 2006 to 8.4 points in 2010. Speaking in terms of rule of law, these states come close to being considered fully consolidated democracies. All other regions stagnated, showing only marginal changes of 0.2 points in the rule of law. No global trend is obvious (see Figure 1.6).

The same is true also for the development within connected regions. For example, the overall status of democracy in Asia increased by 0.1 points. The rule of law criterion, however, remained stable with 4.6 points. A slight decrease of 0.1 points may be marked for the states of Asia and Oceania. Citizens of the Commonwealth of Independent States (CIS) and Mongolia, on the contrary, saw no improvement. With a value of 4.4 points, this region ranks quite low. Only the Middle East and North Africa, as well as West and Central Africa, trail it. Even though institutions to guarantee the rule of law are present in both these regions, they are often disregarded. A predictable and democratic formulation of political will is barely possible.

African regions form a mostly heterogeneous group in the 2006, 2008, and 2010 rounds of the BTI. In line with the global development of the status of democracy and the rule of law, aggregate numbers within Africa remain stable. Although democracy

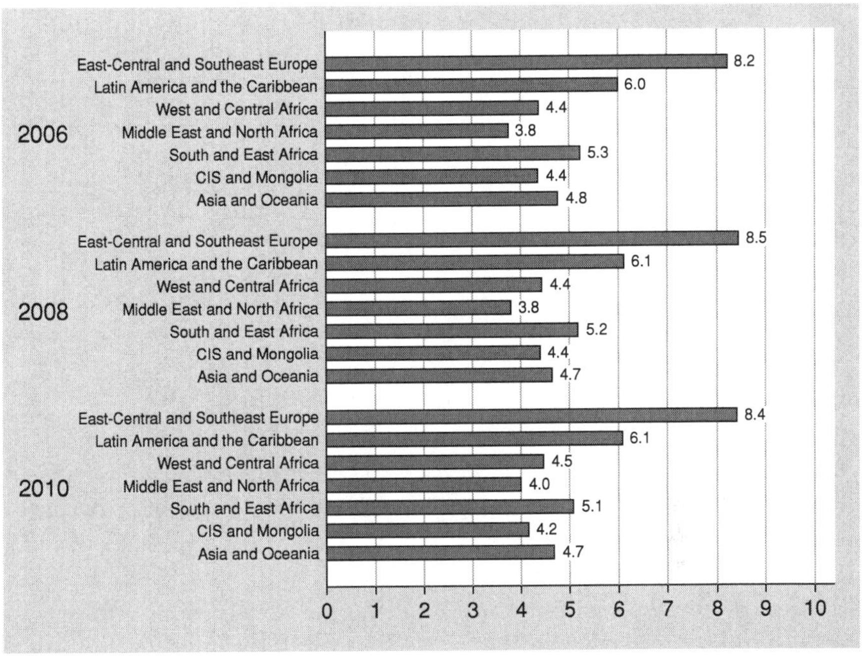

FIGURE 1.6 Rule of law in different regions of the world, 2006, 2008, and 2010. (*Note*: Only countries from all three rounds of the BTI were included for the sake of comparability over time. *Source*: Bertelsmann Transformation Index 2006, 2008, and 2010; own figures.)

receives 5.0 points, the rule of law remains at 4.5 points. Obviously, corruption, a weak civil society, and the imperfect enforcement of the separation of powers slow the progress of other, better developed aspects of democracy. States of Eastern and Southern Africa, however, perform far better than the other African regions, leading by nearly 1 point in the rule of law. The Middle East and North Africa account for the BTI's lowest rankings in terms of rule of law. This result differs significantly from the surprisingly good rule of law score showed for this region by the WGI, but it demonstrates the affinity of polyarchy. The reason certainly lies in the different concepts of rule of law: The BTI has a thick concept of democratic rule of law, whereas the WGI have a thin concept that is closer to a formal legal state where law and order dominate, civic rights play a minor part, and horizontal accountability has no role.

2.4. *Democracy Barometer: Rule of Law*

Learning from all the conceptual deficiencies and the methodological shortcomings of most of the other indices, there is a new index on the market, namely the Democracy Barometer. It measures the quality of democracy in the "best"

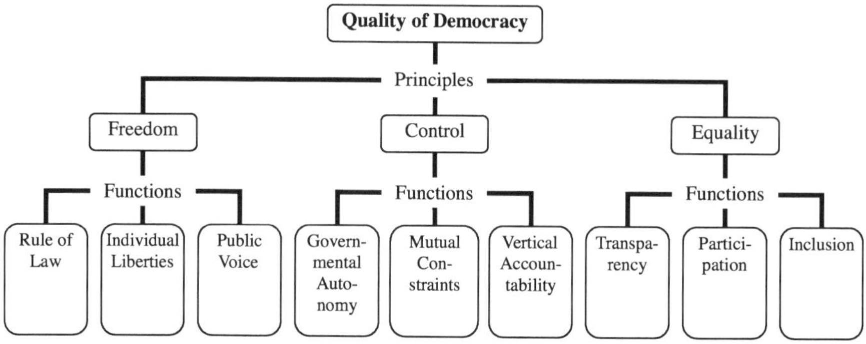

FIGURE 1.7. The concept tree of the Democracy Barometer. (*Source*: Bühlmann et al. 2011a.)

30 democracies during the past two decades.[14] It is capable of measuring variance between those established democracies where Freedom House and Polity do not see any differences,[15] such as between Berlusconi's Italy, the United States after 9/11, and Poland on the one side and Sweden, Finland, or Switzerland on the other. The index is overwhelmingly built on secondary data, which are selected out of an impressive array of existing sources. The selection of the data is made on the basis of theoretical arguments and specific methodological criteria (Bühlmann et al. 2011a). The scores given to the indicators reflect neither optima nor maxima, but relative differences[16] between the countries based on best practice.

2.4.1. Concept

The Democracy Barometer is firmly anchored in a midrange concept of democracy. It develops its final indicators step by step from 3 core principles (freedom, equality, and control), to 9 core functions, to 18 components, to 36 subcomponents, and, finally, 90 indicators. Rule of law is one of the nine core functions of democracy as seen in Figure 1.7.

Rule of law is more thinly defined than it is within the BTI, because "mutual constraints" of the constitutional powers and "individual liberties" are summarized as core functions in their own rights (see Figure 1.8).

Rule of law designates the independence, the primacy, and the absolute warrant of and by the law. This requires the same prevalence of rights as well as formal and

14 The 30 best democracies, which comprise the "old" OECD countries and a few other democracies from Latin America and Eastern Europe, are those countries that have performed best in a so-called blueprint period from 1995 to 2005 according to the combined index of Freedom House and Polity.

15 With regard to civil liberties and political rights, these countries have always received the optimal score of 1; only Berlusconi's Italy received, for two years, the second-best grade of 1.5.

16 For the complex and sophisticated rules of measurement in general and aggregation in particular, see Bühlmann et al. (2011b).

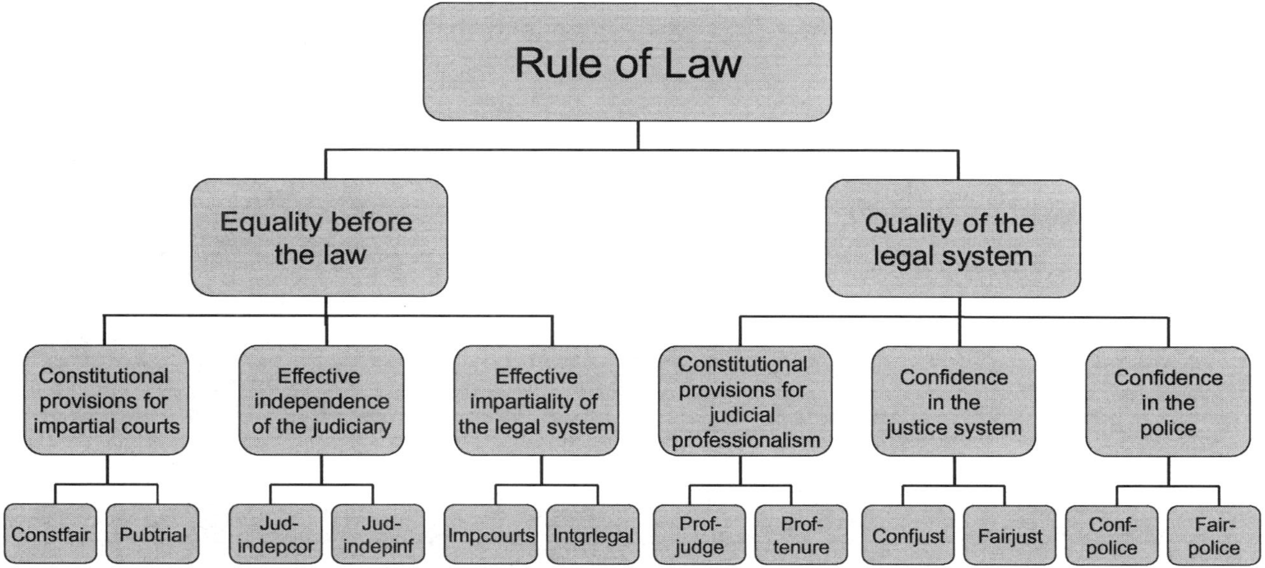

Note: Constfair = Constitutional provisions for fair organization of the court system (no exceptional courts and hierarchical judicial system).
Pubtrial = Constitutional provisions guaranteeing a public trial.
Judindepcor = Level of independence of the judiciary (no inside corruption or outside influence).
Judindepinf = Level of independence of the judiciary from political influences of members of government, citizens, or firms.
Impcourts = Legal framework is not inefficient and subject to manipulation.
Intgrlegal = Integrity of legal system.
Profjudge = Professionalism (law degree, professional experience) is a precondition for appointment of judges to highest courts.
Proftenure = Professionality of judges concerning length of tenure. Professionality is high; if tenure is not restricted, i.e., it is lifelong.
Confjust = Shate of citizens with confidence in the legal system.
Fairjust = Assessment of the confidence in the fair administration of justice in society.
Confpolice = Share of citizens with confidence in the police.
Fairpolice = Assessment of reliability/effectiveness of the police services.

FIGURE 1.8. The concept tree of rule of law.

procedural justice for all individuals (Beetham 1994; Rawls 1971). Respecting these thoughts, the "function" rule of law is split into two main components: equality before the law (Component 1) and quality of the judicial system (Component 2). Equality before the rule of law means that the impartiality of courts must be constitutionally provided and that judicial proceedings are not selectively or deliberately restricted by public policy, political pressures, or prevailing social practices. The quality of the judicial system depends on constitutionally guaranteed judicial professionalism and effective independence of the judges from social or political influences. Additionally, because the only political capital for courts is legitimacy, the quality of the judicial system also depends on diffuse support or institutional trust (Gibson 2008).

2.4.2. Scope

The sample of the countries comprises 30 countries. These are those countries that proved to be most democratic between 1995 and 2005 according to the combined index of Freedom House and Polity (so-called blueprint countries). The data collection is going to be extended to approximately 50 more democracies in Eastern Europe, Latin America, and Asia. The sample of countries will be limited to political regimes that can be minimally classified as "electoral democracies." The covered period spans from 1990 to 2010.[17]

2.4.3. Validity

The two components of the validity function are each measured by four different indicators.

Equality before the law first must be guaranteed by the constitution. Bühlmann et al. (2010) argue that equality in terms of impartiality is best reflected by the existence of constitutional provisions stating that there must be no exceptional courts in a hierarchical judicial system. Additionally, impartiality is strengthened when trials are public. Thus, the explicit mention of public trials in the constitution is seen as an important condition for equality before the law. The two indicators are merged into a subcomponent that constitutes one part of the equality before the law component.

The second part of this component is built by two further indicators. As already argued, not only does democracy consist of constitutional guarantees but *Verfassungswirklichkeit* (constitutional reality) matters too. Therefore, a measure that captures the degree of effective impartiality of the courts as rated by people from the

[17] The data are available on the following Web site: http://www.democracy barometer.org.

respective countries is included. The first assessment measures to what degree the legal framework in a country is subject to manipulation or whether it follows a clear and neutral process. The second indicator estimates the degree to which the judiciary in a given country is exposed to political or societal interference.

The second component of the rule of law reflects the quality of the judicial system. Again, the indicators measure both constitutional provisions and effective impact. On the one hand, a constitutional provision that increases judicial autonomy and strengthens the professionalism of the judges by guaranteeing lifelong tenure and the impossibility of dismissal is taken into account.

On the other hand, the quality of the judicial system depends on its ascribed legitimacy, which is reflected by the confidence that people have in it. Confidence in the legal system – as reported in representative surveys – and an assessment of the perceived fairness of judicial processes measure this aspect.

2.4.4. Reliability

The reliability of the Democracy Barometer is ensured by means of different strategies: (1) different types of data are used ("hard" data, aggregated survey data, and expert judgments); (2) a broad set of sources as well as own calculations are used; and (3) the final set of indicators was derived on theoretical and empirical grounds from a much larger set of indicators (all in all, 300 for the whole Democracy Barometer).

Although the first two strategies significantly reduce the probability of systematic errors related to the type of data or the source, the usage of a large number of indicators is a reasonable method to reduce random measurement error. In regard to the rule of law function, all in all, 12 indicators are used to measure the concept, which ensures not only a valid score but also one that is less prone to measurement error.

2.4.5. Aggregation Rules

The Democracy Barometer is a complex measure that starts from indicators which are aggregated to subcomponents, components, functions, principles, and finally the overall score.[18] Because indicators and subcomponents are not considered necessary and sufficient conditions, the aggregation rule is a mere calculation of the mean.[19] Components, in contrast, are considered to be of a different nature: Equality before the law (Component 1) and quality of the judicial system (Component 2) are both

[18] This section draws heavily on the "Methodological Explanatory Note" of the Democracy Barometer project. For details see Bühlmann, Merkel, Müller, et al. (2011).

[19] As a result of different measurement levels and in accordance with the basic concept of the Democracy Barometer, all indicators are standardized to a scale from 0 (worst practice) to 100 (best practice) in advance.

necessary to ensure rule of law. Nonetheless, because the project deals with established democracies, a strict rule of necessary condition is not applied. Instead, a modification, which allows for compensation for poor quality in one element by better quality in another element, is introduced. Compensation, however, is not full compensation (substitutability). The larger the disequilibrium, the smaller the compensation. Thus, disequilibrium has to be "punished" by the aggregation formula relative to equilibrium, and the more so the larger the disequilibrium is.[20]

2.4.6. Trends

Ranking the countries according to the quality of the rule of law function as measured by nine indicators shows the order given in Table 1.2.

The top three Scandinavian countries are no surprise. Their rule of law index correlates perfectly in Denmark and Finland, and to a lower – but still high – degree with the overall democracy index. The fourth rank of Austria surprises in particular if we consider Rank 17 of the overall democracy index. The U.S. aggregate rule of law index for the period between 1995 and 2005 is still high (Rank 7). However, if we compare the starting year 1995 with the end year 2005, we can observe a significant decline of the rule of law quality. The last three countries, namely Poland, Italy, and Costa Rica, are also not at odds with other indices. The Berlusconi years certainly did harm to the quality of the rule of law, but the quality was not that high even before Berlusconi's advent to power.[21]

2.4.7. Rule of Law and Democracy

If we compare the aggregate rule of law index (one function) with the overall Democracy Barometer index (nine functions), we can observe an almost similar development. Nevertheless, the democracy index performs slightly better than the rule of law index. However, a drastic divergence became visible after 9/11, when particularly the United States but also the United Kingdom and other well-established democracies rapidly installed security laws that partly overstretched the sensitive limits of rule of law in fields such as citizen's surveillance, privacy, and imprisonment on remand, which were extended in favor of police at the cost of civil liberties and judicial assessment. After a few years, the quality of rule of law improved, and both developments again began their mutual rapprochement which characterizes well-established and consolidated liberal democracies (see Figure 1.9).

[20] The formula can be found in Appendix 3 of the "Methodological Explanatory Note" (see Bühlmann, Merkel, Müller, et al. 2011).

[21] However, one has to note that the strongest interference into legal matters occurred during Berlusconi's third tenure in power since 2008.

TABLE 1.2. *Rule of law: Countries (ranked according to mean of rule of law compared to quality of democracy)*

	Equality before the law		Quality of legal system		Mean	
Country	1995	2005	1995	2005	Rule of law (1995–2005)	Quality of democracy (1995–2005)
Denmark	92.55	91.46	94.05	97.30	94.34	1
Sweden	95.13	87.61	80.61	81.78	87.96	6
Finland	95.00	88.32	78.03	84.23	87.62	2
Austria	79.73	79.49	82.11	87.70	82.91	17
Luxembourg	87.95	81.82	77.43	78.98	82.38	13
Canada	88.72	79.38	75.88	73.29	80.51	5
United States	84.41	73.67	74.88	73.76	77.62	12
New Zealand	80.83	74.38	72.42	69.81	75.92	8
Norway	63.62	60.24	94.91	89.47	75.30	3
Netherlands	79.67	77.13	73.99	68.51	74.82	4
Australia	79.43	75.62	69.58	69.08	74.30	10
Ireland	75.69	68.94	73.55	73.37	72.52	14
Japan	78.56	73.98	73.85	70.01	72.13	21
Germany	74.88	70.36	64.45	69.69	68.81	11
Portugal	80.11	70.49	61.98	61.72	67.90	19
United Kingdom	74.18	67.50	62.99	57.49	66.60	24
Switzerland	69.25	81.05	52.31	51.88	64.82	15
Belgium	71.96	70.57	55.19	54.81	61.98	9
Iceland	57.34	60.09	62.17	64.88	61.42	7
Hungary	67.08	51.84	59.36	61.68	59.23	18
Slovenia	71.90	59.01	51.77	50.16	58.77	20
Cyprus	61.48	72.21	45.46	46.13	55.43	23
Spain	66.94	53.37	47.75	49.44	53.67	16
Czech Republic	66.00	44.58	49.04	45.74	52.44	22
France	47.19	46.71	58.29	55.78	51.33	27
South Africa	56.56	57.28	48.17	44.13	50.90	29
Malta	60.93	53.91	31.33	42.33	47.64	26
Poland	55.22	37.78	48.00	53.92	46.06	30
Italy	43.61	27.12	41.58	42.13	42.52	25
Costa Rica	50.81	58.62	16.12	18.11	35.31	28

Source: Bühlmann et al. (2010); Adopted and modified from Møller and Skaaning (2010a: 15).

2.5. *World Justice Project: Rule of Law Index*

2.5.1. Concept

Only in 2008 did the World Justice Project (WJP) come up with the broad-based WJP Rule of Law Index. As the project itself is a "multinational and multidisciplinary initiative to strengthen the rule of law" (Agrast, Botero, Ponce-Rodríguez, and Dumas

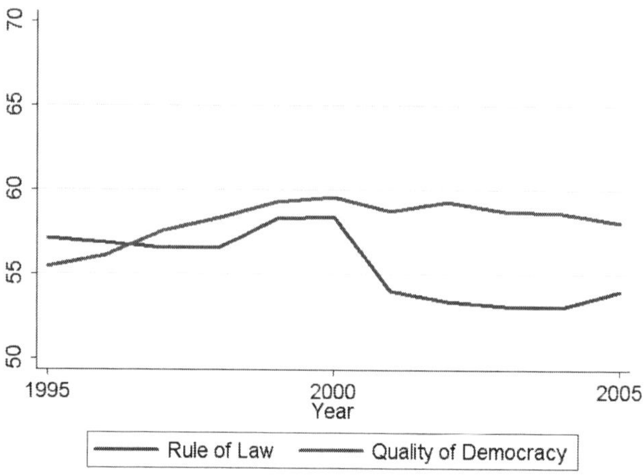

FIGURE 1.9. The rule of law and quality of democracy over time.

2008: 4) worldwide, it regards the WJP Rule of Law Index as a quantitative tool to assess not only de jure but also de facto government adherence to the rule of law. The index is thereby dedicated to providing a "road map" (Agrast, Botero, and Ponce-Rodríguez 2009: 7) for "identifying strengths and weaknesses and promoting specific, targeted reforms in a variety of dimensions that are relevant to the rule of law" (ibid.: 12).

The WJP bases the rule of law on four principles:

I. The government and its officials and agents are accountable under the law.
II. The laws are clear, publicized, stable, and fair, and protect fundamental rights, including the security of persons and property.
III. The process by which the laws are enacted, administered, and enforced is accessible, fair, and efficient.
IV. Access to justice is provided by competent, independent, and ethical adjudicators, attorneys, or representatives, and judicial officers who are of sufficient number, have adequate resources, and reflect the makeup of the communities they serve (ibid.: 13).

These principles are further broken down into 16 factors and 68 subfactors. Thus, the editors address the extent of fair participation and even constitutional checks and balances without demanding democracy. They capture the protection of human rights most significant for the rule of law and established under international law. Finally, attention is paid to access to justice without including legal empowerment of the poor and disfranchised (ibid.). In sum, the index is based on a thick concept of rule of law, incorporating both substantive and procedural elements but no social measures in order to enable people from the lower classes equal access to law, judiciary, and justice (Agrast et al. 2008: 6). The concept is thick but not maximalist.

2.5.2. Scope

Starting with six pilot countries in 2008 (Colombia, Argentina, Australia, Spain, Sweden, and the United States), the WJP Rule of Law Index had already covered 35 countries by 2009, namely 45.6 percent of the world's population. By the end of 2010, the country coverage was set to rise to 70. In 2011, the WJP covered 65 countries with subsequent expansions until global coverage is achieved. However, there seems to be no comprehensible plan for the selective inclusion of countries. Except for the pilot countries, neither functional nor regional arguments account for the inclusion of states. Therefore, until truly global coverage is achieved, the case-selection methods of the WJP remain rather cloudy, and as a consequence, the index is skewed or even unrepresentative for regions or otherwise defined groups of countries. This overshadows the self-set objectives of cross-country comparison and the tracking of trends over time (Agrast et al. 2009: 9).

2.5.3. Reliability

An outstanding feature of the WJP Rule of Law Index is its reliance on exclusively self-generated data combining triannual general population polls with yearly qualified respondents' questionnaires. For each survey, a total of 1,000 persons from three major metropolitan areas are randomly selected. Equally divided by gender and 18 years of age or older, the respondents were presented with a uniform questionnaire. Expert interviews relied on legal practitioners, such as attorneys and judges, and academics with expertise in at least one of the four areas: civil and commercial law, criminal justice, labor law, and public health. For each field, a separate questionnaire was developed that included both open- and close-ended questions as well as several highly detailed hypothetical scenarios. Internal cross-check mechanisms and external local and cross-country data comparisons ensure the accuracy of the country reports (Agrast et al. 2009: 9 et seq.).

2.5.4. Aggregation Rules

The index builders shied away from a sole aggregate figure representing a country's adherence to the rule of law in a single numeric value. Instead, the WJP provides detailed country profiles on factor and subfactor levels to control for the problem of unidimensionality of the index (for discussion, see Agrast et al. 2008: 13). Figures for subfactors are drawn from a simple average of the corresponding questions in the survey and the experts' questionnaires. To ensure comparability across scale levels, each variable contributing to the score of a subfactor was rescaled to a range between 0 and 1, with the former representing the lowest and the latter representing the highest possible value. The average scores of the variables are again standardized following the Min-Max method to have an identical range from 0 to 1 (Agrast et al. 2009: 47). On which level best and worst performers are identified, however, is not clear from the 2009 report. Whether factor scores of a single country or factor scores of all countries are compared remains an open question. Only the latter would allow for cross-country comparisons.

2.5.5. Validity

Although the WJP's principles and factors may soundly be interpreted as comprehensively capturing the rule of law, the overall concept lacks an elaborated theoretical basis. Neither a justification of the four principles nor their components are given. Furthermore, the measurement by polls suffers from a regional bias. Interviews are conducted in the three largest urban areas. Rural areas, however, remain out of focus for now (ibid.: 30). Thus, the measured perception of the rule of law may be representative for larger cities, but for the infrastructurally weak and remote rural areas, especially common in less developed countries, this is not the case. Even though the experts' questionnaires might account for this lack of regional representativeness, this possibility is lost through the aggregation of variables using nonweighted averages. An expert's possibly higher knowledge of the de facto rule of law is subdued by the more numerous general public's perceptions. Therefore, the WJP Rule of Law Index runs the risk of not measuring the rule of law on the country level, but primarily measuring the rule of law as perceived by the population in metropolitan areas. This may not make such a difference in Denmark, but in India, Indonesia, and Pakistan it does.

2.5.6. Reliability

This anchoring of expert evaluations in public perceptions and experiences also poses a severe problem for the reliability of the measurement. Although on the one hand the qualified respondents' perceptions may not reflect actual conditions faced by the general population (Agrast et al. 2009), the public, on the other hand, may not have an accurate perception at all if respondents do not have previous experiences with factors of the rule of law (ibid.: 29). How the combination of both methods should be able to compensate for either bias remains unclear. The plausible but methodologically problematic answer may be that it is exactly the combination of the elite and mass biases that evens out the final product.

3. CONCLUSION

Rule of law indices are younger than most democracy indices and *grosso modo* theoretically and methodologically still less developed. They appear mostly as rule of law subdimensions of wider democracy indices. Consequently, they tend to be normatively rather minimalist instead of maximalist, because potential elements of a thicker rule of law concept, such as civil rights or horizontal accountability, are mostly subsumed under other dimensions, or are constructed as separate dimensions in their own right. The rule of law subscore of the Bertelsmann Transformation Index with its thick normative approach represents an exception. Normatively close to it, but more sophisticated on the indicator level, is the World Justice Project's Rule of Law Index. It is an index in its own right rather than a mere subdimension of a democracy index. This contributes to its comparative advantage, specifically that it is based on the broadest set of indicators of all rule of law indices under review here. The main problem is that it does not yet provide time-series data and a systematic sample of many countries, reducing its scientific value.

Common to almost all indices is a lack of both theoretical justifications of the concept and aggregation rules. None of the indices provides a long time series of data. The most extended ones are provided by the Democracy Barometer (since 1990) and the World Governance Indicators (since 1996); the shortest one is provided by the World Justice Project (since 2008). The intercomparability of the rule of law indices is relatively low, lower than between the democracy indices as simple bivariate correlations demonstrate (Skaaning 2010: 456). This does not come as a surprise, because at the level of the core elements of the rule of law constructs, it is already evident that the indices simply measure different things. The continuum of the constructs reaches from thin "technical" concepts such as found in the WGI to the "substantial" thick concepts presented by the BTI and WJP.

The correlation between rule of law and democracy depends on the thickness of the conceptualization of the former. Minimalist concepts of rule of law do not correlate strongly with democracy. If the concept of rule law is based on a thick and substantial understanding of rule of law, it correlates highly with the quality of democracy. However, there is a strong risk of collinearity involved. This holds true even if one excludes indicators of liberal rights or horizontal accountability from the democracy index to avoid overlapping, that is, if one defines democracy in a thin, polyarchical manner.

Except for Freedom House, which sees a slight tendency toward an improvement of the rule of law, the diagnosed trend of the other indices is stagnation. But the time series of indices are too short, and the fact that particularly the "oldest" rule of law index from the World Governance Indicators has changed so often its constitutive indicators does not base Freedom House's predication on solid empirical ground. However, in most of the indices, rule of law performs worse than democracy. This confirms previous analyses that argue that weak rule of law is the main entrance point for authoritarian viruses into democracy (Merkel, Puhle, et al. 2003; Merkel, Puhle, et al. 2006; Merkel 2004); it is the major reason for the mushrooming of defective democracies in the wake of the third wave of democratization. Therefore, strengthening rule of law based on a thicker understanding can also be considered an effective investment to improve democracy, whereas the promotion of free elections does not necessarily lead to an improvement of rule of law.

2

International Law and the Rule of Law at the National Level

Helmut Philipp Aust and Georg Nolte

1. INTRODUCTION

The role of international law with respect to the rule of law at the national level can be conceived in different ways. Here, we want to focus on expectations by international law that domestic legal systems respect certain features of the rule of law.

We will look first at some international practice with a view to the question of whether the concepts of statehood and sovereignty have changed as a result of an increased significance of the idea of the rule of law in international law. We will conclude that a fundamental change of the *lex lata* has not occurred (Section II), but this is not the end of the matter. We can identify an emerging normative expectation that states organize their public powers in conformity with a certain understanding of the principle of the rule of law. We will argue that this normative expectation can be conceived as a contemporary expression of the traditional international "minimum standard of justice" (Section III). We will conclude that there is an incremental change toward an international legal expectation to respect the rule of law, albeit in a form that has not yet fundamentally altered the vision of the state and its sovereignty in international law.

This incremental change is a facet of the rule of law dynamics to which this volume is devoted. These dynamics comprise processes of promotion, diffusion, and conversion.[1] This chapter is limited to such processes of promotion, diffusion, and conversion that determine whether international law provides for rules on certain aspects. Suffice it to say that all three modalities of the rule of law dynamics have a role to play in the identification of new international legal rules: The promotional perspective is about how and by whom a claim about a new rule is introduced into

We are grateful to Thomas Kleinlein (Frankfurt/Main), Isabelle Ley, and Alejandro Rodiles (both Berlin) for helpful comments and discussion. Any mistakes are our own.

[1] See the introduction to this volume by Michael Zürn, André Nollkaemper, and Randall Peerenboom.

the legal discourse. How this claim and its resulting rule are then received by other relevant actors concerns its diffusion. Finally, we can only speak of conversion in terms of public international law when we can affirm that a given rule has sufficiently taken root in international practice.

We will not discuss definitional questions with respect to the rule of law (formal v. material, thin v. thick, procedural v. substantive).[2] In this connection we just want to note that although a global understanding of the rule of law will necessarily be more formal than one flowing from a particular cultural, legal, and political tradition (Chesterman 2008a: 342; 2008b: para. 14), this does not rule out that we may come across more embellished ("thicker") emanations of the rule of law at the universal level in specific areas or that more encompassing standards of the rule of law may develop over time.

2. INTERNATIONAL PRACTICE ON THE RULE OF LAW

The establishment of the rule of law as a core principle for the organization of state powers is a challenge to the traditional understanding of statehood and sovereignty. According to the traditional view, states were free to organize their internal powers as they saw fit.[3] In addition, it was out of the question to deny an entity the hallmark of statehood by invoking deficiencies with respect to the rule of law. Rather, effective government was the main criterion for determining whether an entity qualified as a state.[4]

2.1. *Declarations on the Rule of Law and Good Governance*

This view has been challenged in recent years. Effectiveness is no longer considered to be the sole criterion for determining statehood. Rather, considerations of legality and legitimacy have been introduced. These apply, first and foremost, to the issue of whether statehood is qualified by a principle of democratic governance. In 1992, Thomas Franck postulated an emerging right to democratic governance (Franck 1992: 46–91). Although it is still premature to hold that international law only recognizes democratically organized states as full-fledged members of the

[2] For issues of history, theory, and definition see, e.g., Tamanaha (2004). For studies from the viewpoint of international law, see Watts (1993: 15–45); Crawford (2003: 3–12); and Corten (2009: 11–40).

[3] Declaration on Principles of International Law concerning Friendly Relations and Co-Operation among States in Accordance with the Charter of the United Nations, UNGA Resolution 2625 of 24 October 1970, UN Doc. A/RES/2625; *Case Concerning Military and Paramilitary Activities in and against Nicaragua* (*Nicaragua* v. *United States of America*), International Court of Justice, Merits, Judgment of 27 June 1986, ICJ Reports 1986, 14, para. 258: "(e)very State possesses a fundamental right to choose and implement its own political, economic and social systems."

[4] *Island of Palmas Arbitration*, Award of Sole Arbitrator Max Huber, 4 February 1928, RIAA Vol. II, 821: 838–839; for an overview of the relevant criteria and their role in contemporary international law see Crawford (2006: 37–95) and Krieger (2000: 82 et seq.).

international community, it is also apparent that there is an ongoing discussion about the preferred model of statehood in contemporary international law.[5] This debate has been spurred, to a large degree, by conceptions of so-called good governance that define characteristics of statehood that international actors wish to see fulfilled.[6] The rule of law is frequently included among the features of good governance.[7] Evidence for this development ranges from the 1997 United Nations (UN) Development Programme report on sustainable development[8] and the European Union's Cotonou Agreement for Development Cooperation with the African, Caribbean, and Pacific Group countries[9] to the criteria set forth for the granting of loans by the African Development Bank[10] or its counterpart in the Americas, the Inter-American Development Bank.[11] The rule of law has also been included in declarations of regional organizations that defined the relationship between their constituent principles and good governance, as has been the case, for example, for the Organization of American States (OAS)[12] or the Economic Community of West African States (ECOWAS).[13] However, the rule of law does not figure in all definitions of good governance. For example, it is neither included in the definition drawn up by the Asian Development Bank[14] nor was it expressly mentioned in the work of the UN Commission on Human Rights (UNCHR) on good governance.[15]

5 For recent views see Fox (2008: 154–155) (liberal democracy as the preferred international model of governance) and Petersen (2008: 33–84) (obligation to develop toward democracy).

6 For an overview see Dolzer (2004: 533–546).

7 For a survey of existing definitions of good governance see, European Commission for Democracy through Law ("Venice Commission"), "Draft Report on the Notion of 'Good Governance' on the basis of comments by O. Kask and A. Eide." Study no. 470/2008, CDL(2008)091 (8 October 2008).

8 United Nations Development Programme, "Governance for Sustainable Development." Accessed 28 March 2010 at http://mirror.undp.org/magnet/policy/.

9 Partnership Agreement between the Members of the African, Caribbean and Pacific Group of States, of the one Part, and the European Community and its Member States, of the Other Part ("Cotonou Agreement") (2000), Official Journal L317/3 of 15 December 2000, as revised (2005) Official Journal L209/27 of 11 August 2005, Article 9 ("essential elements"); see also the second revision, signed on 19 March 2010 but not yet entered into force, available at http://ec.europa.eu/development/icenter/repository/second_revision_cotonou_agreement_20100311.pdf (last accessed 28 March 2010).

10 See the fact sheet of the African Development Bank. Accessed 28 March 2010 at www.afdb.org/en/topics-sectors/sectors/economic-financial-governance/overview/.

11 Inter-American Development Bank, "Modernization of the State Report," July 2003: 15 et seq. Accessed 28 March 2010 at http://idbdocs.iadb.org/wsdocs/getdocument.aspx?docnum=1441783.

12 OAS, "Declaration of Santiago on Democracy and Public Trust: A New Commitment to Good Governance for the Americas." Adopted on 10 June 2003, OAS Doc. AG/DEC.31 (XXXIII-O/03); Article 3 of the Inter-American Democratic Charter of 11 September 2001.

13 ECOWAS, Protocol on Democracy and Good Governance, Protocol Supplementary to the Protocol Relating to the Mechanism for Conflict Prevention Management, Resolution, Peacekeeping and Security. Adopted on 10 December 1999.

14 Asian Development Bank, "Governance: Sound Development Mechanisms," August 1995. Accessed 28 March 2010 at www.adb.org/Documents/Policies/Governance/default.asp.

15 See "The Role of Good Governance in the Promotion of Human Rights," UNCHR Resolutions 2000/64, 2001/72, 2002/76, 2004/70, and 2005/68. Accessed 28 March 2010 at www2.ohchr.org/english/bodies/chr/regular-sessions.htm.

We can find many governmental statements and declarations on the rule of law as being an essential principle for the organization of public powers in the current debate in the Sixth Committee of the UN General Assembly (UNGA) on the rule of law at the international and national levels.[16] It emerges from that discussion that a large number of states are of the view that the rule of law is a central principle for the organization of public powers.[17] The commitment of UN member-states to the rule of law has also been expressed in the 2005 World Summit Outcome Document.[18]

It is more difficult, however, to identify the concrete normative relevance of these statements. States, after all, do not commit themselves very specifically when they recognize that the rule of law is an important principle for the organization of public authority.[19] It is nonetheless hard to ignore that states at least purport to view the rule of law as a central principle for the organization of state powers. This verbal practice is not limited to Western states and organizations. Documents by the OAS, ECOWAS, and the development banks in Africa and the Americas testify to this (Rudolf 2006: 1017).

2.2. *Recognition of States*

The traditional field for the determination of what constitutes statehood in international law is the granting or withholding of recognition to and from states and governments. In 1992, the European Community (EC) and its then twelve member-states formulated Guidelines on the Recognition of New States in Eastern Europe. In these guidelines, the EC and its member-states

> adopt a common position on the process of recognition of... new States, which requires: respect for the provisions of the Charter of the United Nations and the commitments subscribed to in the Final Act of Helsinki and in the Charter of Paris, *especially with regard to the rule of law*, democracy and human rights.[20]

These guidelines have sometimes been interpreted as implying that a shift has taken place away from the traditional discretion that governments exercise when they recognize states toward a recognition that is based on legal principles.[21] Other states have, however, not followed suit. Even the practice of the European Union (EU)

[16] See "The Rule of Law at the National and International Levels," UNGA Resolution 64/116 of 15 January 2010, UN Doc. A/RES/64/116.

[17] See "The Rule of Law at the National and International Levels: Comments and Information Received from Governments," Report of the Secretary-General of 11 July 2007, UN Doc. A/62/121.

[18] 2005 World Summit Outcome, UNGA Resolution 60/1 of 24 October 2005, UN Doc. A/RES/60/1: para. 134.

[19] For skeptical remarks by a close observer and participant of the discussions at the UN level, see Fitschen (2008: 379–380).

[20] Guidelines on the Recognition of New States in Eastern Europe and the Soviet Union of 16 December 1991, reprinted in *International Legal Materials* 31 (1992): 1485–1487, emphasis added.

[21] See, e.g., Hillgruber (1998: 492–493).

and its member-states has not always been faithful to this declaration. A mixed picture emerges if we consider the attitude of the EU and its member-states in the aftermath of the Kosovo Declaration of Independence on February 17, 2008. The European Council held that the EU member-states would "decide in accordance with national practice and international law on their relations with Kosovo."[22] Although a number of issues are emphasized in the declarations accompanying the respective national decisions, the rule of law is not always among them. Where the rule of law *is* mentioned, this occurs in a rather ambiguous way that does not allow one to infer *opinio juris* on the side of the respective EU member-state that respect for the rule of law was an indispensable element for its decision to recognize Kosovo.[23] The declaration of Sweden provides a particularly striking example. When recognizing Kosovo as an independent state, Sweden affirmed that "a difficult and demanding process is now being started to build a Kosovar state that meets international requirements." In this respect, the international community would need to supervise "the development of Kosovo in the direction of a modern society based on the rule of law."[24] Apart from the fact that this statement can even be read to imply that Sweden has recognized an entity that is not yet in possession of the relevant criteria for statehood, it at least makes clear that, for Sweden, compliance with the rule of law was not a necessary criterion for the granting of recognition. The German Foreign Minister also emphasized that it was a goal to help Kosovo develop toward a democratic state governed by the rule of law (*demokratischer Rechtsstaat*).[25]

If we look beyond the EU member-states, we see that the picture does not change. In the cases of Kosovo, South Ossetia, and Abkhazia, states granting or withholding recognition have emphasized "traditional" issues of international law: the role of self-determination, the consequences of the unlawful use of force, respect for decisions of the UN Security Council, and the like.[26] Especially in the case of Kosovo, a major issue was whether or not Kosovo was a "special case"[27] or whether it would lend itself

[22] See the Statement of the Council of the European Union of 18 February 2008: 2851st External Relations Council Meeting, Brussels, 6496/08 (Presse 41). Accessed 13 March 2010 at www.consilium.europa .eu/uedocs/cms_data/docs/pressdata/en/gena/98818.pdf.

[23] One finds references to the rule of law, for example, in the Statement of Finland of 7 March 2008. Accessed 28 March 2010 at http://formin.finland.fi/public/default.aspx?contentid=123797&nodeid= 15146&contentlan=2&culture=en-US. Hungary stressed that the rule of law needs to be respected by the newly recognized state; see Statement of Hungary 19 March 2008. Accessed 28 March 2010 at www.mfa.gov.hu/kum/en/bal/actualities/spokesman_statements/Kosovo_recognition_080319.htm.

[24] "Sweden Recognizes the Republic of Kosovo," Press Release of 4 March 2008. Accessed March 13, 2010 at www.sweden.gov.se/sb/d/10358/a/99714.

[25] Speech by Mr. Frank-Walter Steinmeier, the German Foreign Minister to the German Federal Parliament, 20 February 2008. Accessed 13 March 2010 at www.auswaertiges-amt.de/diplo/de/Infoservice/ Presse/Reden/2008/080220-Steinmeier-BT-Kosovo.html.

[26] For further information, see Borgan (2009).

[27] This was the formulation of the U.S. Secretary of State, Condoleeza Rice. See Statement by Condoleeza Rice on Recognition of Kosovo as Independent State of 18 February 2008. Accessed 10 March 2010 at www.america.gov/st/texttrans-english/2008/February/20080218150254bpuh5.512637e-02.html.

to generalizations.[28] At least for those states that argued that the case of Kosovo could not be compared to other situations in international law, it must have been difficult to explain their decisions in terms of principled arguments. In sum, the most recent cases of recognition marked a "return to pragmatism after years of insistence on questions of principle" (Gioia 2008: 5). This does not bode well for a development that wishes to challenge the traditional predominance of factual categories for the determination of statehood.[29]

2.3. SECURITY COUNCIL PRACTICE IN THE CONTEXT OF STATES WITH WEAK GOVERNMENTAL AUTHORITY

Another source for relevant practice consists of the Security Council (SC) resolutions with respect to states with weak governmental authority. We do not need to enter the debate on the normative status of so-called failed states here.[30] The practice of the SC can generally be described as following the premise "we *need* states with adequate powers to do what only they are capable [of]" (Krygier 2004: 260). This practice demonstrates that, in the context of weak states, it is this enabling function of the rule of law and not its constraining function[31] that is emphasized (Magen 2009: 72). It also demonstrates that different ends pursued by rule of law promotion may well conflict: Establishing law and order may come at a price with respect to human rights protection (Kleinfeld 2006: 59).

The SC frequently refers to the rule of law when dealing with destabilized states. The council almost routinely calls for a return to the rule of law (Farrall 2009; Stromseth, Wippman, and Brooks 2006: 98 et seq). In the case of Somalia, the prime example for a "failed state," the SC has from the start emphasized that a return to law and order is necessary.[32] The rule of law has also often been mentioned with respect to other states with a weak governmental structure.[33] What is primarily aimed for is the (re-)creation of state structures. Deficits with respect to the rule of law are thus addressed with a view to the international security issues that arise from the widespread collapse of governmental authority in Somalia. Thus, the SC has

28 Against the special-case argument, see Corten (2008: 758).

29 This emphasis on the traditional criteria was also emphasized by the Independent International Fact-Finding Mission on the Conflict in Georgia. See "Report of the Independent International Fact-Finding Mission on the Conflict in Georgia," Part II: 127. Accessed 9 May 2010 at www.ceiig.ch/Report.html.

30 Instead see Thürer (1999) and Nolte (2007).

31 On the two functions of the rule of law and constitutionalism, see Kleinfeld (2006: 59) and Möllers (2006: 193).

32 UNSC Resolution 897 of 4 February 1994, UN Doc. S/RES/897: para. 5.

33 See, on the Cote d'Ivoire, UNSC Resolution 1739 of 10 January 2007, UN Doc. S/RES/1739: para. 2 (m); UNSC Resolution 1880 of 30 July 2009, UN Doc. S/RES/1880: para. 27; on Liberia, UNSC Resolution 1750 of 30 March 2007 UN Doc. S/RES/1750: preamble; on Haiti, UNSC Resolution 1892 of 13 October 2009, UN Doc. S/RES/1892: preamble.

intrinsically linked the rule of law situation and the problem of piracy by this reminder to the Transitional Federal Government of Somalia:

> [T]he strengthening of State institutions, economic and social development and respect for human rights and the rule of law are necessary to create the conditions for a full eradication of piracy and armed robbery at sea off the coast of Somalia.[34]

Some SC resolutions are more ambitious. A straightforward formulation of the rule of law as a key element of statehood can be found in a resolution on the situation in Haiti: "respect for the rule of law and human rights are vital components of democratic societies."[35] This statement can be read as an expression of a normative preference on the side of the SC that states should organize their public powers in conformity with the rule of law. In 2003, the SC also used the rule of law as a shorthand to describe the goal toward which the (then still occupied) Iraq should develop.[36]

A chain of resolutions concerning the situation in the Democratic Republic of Congo (DRC) is noteworthy in this regard. There, the council has emphasized the "primary responsibility" of the government of the DRC "for ensuring security in its territory and protecting its civilians with respect for the rule of law, human rights and international humanitarian law."[37] The reference to the primary responsibility of the DRC could be read in the light of the discussion about the "responsibility to protect."[38] This concept, which was launched in 2001 by the International Commission on Intervention and State Sovereignty in the aftermath of the 1999 Kosovo intervention,[39] has since undergone various transformations. Its most authoritative formulation in the 2005 World Summit Outcome Document[40] conceives it as a shared responsibility of individual member-states and the organized international community to prevent mass atrocities (genocide, crimes against humanity,

[34] UNSC Resolution 1838 of 7 October 2008, UN Doc. S/RES/1838: preamble; see also UNSC Resolution 1846 of 2 December 2008, UN Doc. S/RES/1846: preamble; UNSC Resolution 1897 of 30 November 2009, UN Doc. S/RES/1897: preamble; UNSC Resolution 1918 of 27 April 2010, UN Doc. S/RES/1918: preamble.

[35] UNSC Resolution 1658 of 14 February 2006, UN Doc. S/RES/1658: preamble.

[36] UNSC Resolution 1483 of 22 May 2003, UN Doc. S/RES/1483: preamble.

[37] UNSC Resolution 1756 of 15 May 2007, UN Doc. S/RES/1756: preamble; UNSC Resolution 1794 of 21 December 2007, UN Doc. S/RES/1794: preamble; UNSC Resolution 1807 of 31 March 2008, UN Doc. S/RES/1807: preamble; UNSC Resolution 1856 of 22 December 2008, UN Doc. S/RES/1856: preamble; UNSC Resolution 1857 of 22 December 2008, UN Doc. S/RES/1857: preamble; UNSC Resolution 1896 of 30 November 2009, UN Doc. S/RES/1896: preamble.

[38] See also UNSC Resolution 1265 of 17 September 1999, UN Doc. S/RES/1265: preamble.

[39] International Commission on Intervention and State Sovereignty, "The Responsibility to Protect." Accessed 12 March 2010 at http://www.iciss.ca/report-en.asp.

[40] 2005 World Summit Outcome, UNGA Resolution 60/1 of 24 October 2005, UN Doc. A/RES/60/1: paras. 138–139.

war crimes, and "ethnic cleansing") from happening.[41] This responsibility rests primarily with the respective state whose population is subject to such dangers. Only if the respective state cannot live up to its responsibility to prevent atrocities from happening can the organized international community step in. The repeated references by the SC to the primary responsibility of the DRC to uphold the rule of law imply that a secondary responsibility rests with the UN. In that sense the SC expresses a normative expectation that states respect the rule of law.

What follows from this normative expectation for the level of enforcement is quite another matter. The case of the DRC is illuminating in this regard. Here, the council at one point included the rule of law as one of the aims of the resolutions that authorized the UN Organization Mission in the DRC (at the time known as MONUC) to take enforcement measures.[42] In a subsequent resolution, however, the authorization to enforce no longer extended to the realization of the rule of law. Although the rule of law was still included in the list of goals of MONUC, it now figured in a subparagraph that was not linked to enforcement powers of the international presence.[43] This is no coincidence, because a direct authorization for a multinational force, for example, to implement the rule of law *tout court* would be too broad and indeterminate. It is therefore not surprising that the SC mostly refers to the rule of law in the preambular paragraphs of its resolutions. Such resolutions will then focus on specific aspects of the rule of law, mainly in the field of legal reform. The variety of orders and recommendations of the SC in this area is impressive. They include demands concerning the restructuring of the security sector,[44] calls to cooperate with international tribunals to end impunity,[45] capacity building in the judicial sector,[46] 10-year programs of judicial reform,[47] the review of "all relevant legislation,"[48] the "rapid identification and implementation of mechanisms to address prison overcrowding,"[49] training in human rights standards,[50] and the fight against corruption.[51] Because these measures cover a wide field, it is, however, doubtful whether they portray a coherent vision of the rule of law on the part of the SC. Rather, they appear to be adopted in an ad hoc manner, according to the specific situation and, of course, depending on the constraints imposed by the different kinds of mandates that the UN missions fulfill.

41 For an overview of the evolution of the concept, see Peters (2009: 513–544).
42 UNSC Resolution 1756 of 15 May 2007, UN Doc. S/RES/1756: paras. 3 and 4.
43 UNSC Resolution 1856 22 December 2008, UN Doc. S/RES/1856: para. 4.
44 UNSC Resolution 1605 of 17 June 2005, UN Doc. S/RES/1605: para. 2 (w); UNSC Resolution 1739 of 10 January 2007, UN Doc. S/RES/1739: para. 2(m).
45 UNSC Resolution 1610 of 30 June 2005, UN Doc. S/RES/1610: preambular paragraph.
46 UNSC Resolution 1620 of 31 August 2005, UN Doc. S/RES/1620: para. 1(v).
47 UNSC Resolution 1662 of 23 March 2006, UN Doc. S/RES/1662: para. 11.
48 UNSC Resolution 1702 of 15 August 2006, UN Doc. S/RES/1702: para. 14.
49 ibid.
50 UNSC Resolution 1778 of 25 September 2007, UN Doc. S/RES/1778: para. 2(f).
51 UNSC Resolution 1806 of 20 March 2008, UN Doc. S/RES/1806: para. 4(e).

2.4. POSTCONFLICT ADMINISTRATION

The SC has an institutional window of opportunity to exercise more influence on the development of the rule of law on the ground in situations of postconflict UN administration or UN-authorized forms of administration. Here we are faced with a considerable amount of international practice.[52] The models for international influence on postconflict societies vary in terms of their institutional setup and depending on the intensity with which the organized international community is influencing the local processes of state building. Whereas the cases of Kosovo[53] and East Timor[54] saw direct UN administrations, UN practice has, for different reasons, subsequently shifted to "the lighter footprint" (Stahn 2008: 350–351),[55] which does not involve direct administrative competences of the UN.[56] In virtually all cases it has been a priority of the relevant international actors to promote the rule of law (Stromseth et al. 2006: 4). This is understandable in view of the often desolate situation of the legal sector in postconflict situations. Security and stability are among the priorities of any actor involved in postconflict administration (Stromseth et al. 2006: 134). These goals are frequently framed in terms of the rule of law.[57]

It has been remarked that in this field the focus on the rule of law has been a mixed blessing. In East Timor and Kosovo, in particular, efforts of the UN to promote the rule of law were perceived as exhibiting double standards because the UN itself was not eager to be subject to judicial scrutiny or other legal accountability for its actions (cf. Stahn 2008: 309). What is more, the general conditions for rule of law promotion were not always encouraging. In East Timor, for example, there was a general distrust of law, and the legal establishment as law had always been viewed as an instrument of Indonesian rule. When the UN Transitional Administration in East Timor established its presence in East Timor, there was not a single trained East Timorese jurist who was able to work in the framework of the international administration. Candidates had to undergo training on the job (see Strohmeyer 2001a: 50). Also, in East Timor and Kosovo the applicable law was not entirely clear (Matheson 2001: 80). In both situations, the UN administration issued declarations at the outset concerning the applicable law, which consisted of a combination of local law and international human rights law.[58] Accordingly, it was not overly clear

[52] For a presentation of the pertinent cases see Fox (2008: 41–111).

[53] UNSC Resolution 1244 of 10 June 1999, UN Doc. S/RES/1244.

[54] UNSC Resolution 1272 of 25 October 1999, UN Doc. S/RES/1272.

[55] On the situation in Kosovo in particular, see Nolte (2006: 245–258).

[56] In some situations, this move toward the so-called lighter footprint of the UN could also be ascribed to a lack of willingness on the part of other actors to involve the UN in the actual decision-making processes.

[57] See also the section on the rule of law and peace building in the Statement by the President of the Security Council, "The Promotion and Strengthening of the Rule of Law in the Maintenance of International Peace and Security," 29 June 2010, UN Doc. S/PRST/2010/11.

[58] See UNMIK Regulation 1999/1 on the Authority of the Interim Administration in Kosovo of 25 July 1999, para. 3; UNTAET Regulation 1999/1 on the Authority of the Transitional Administration in East Timor of 27 November 1999, section 2.

what the law in force actually was – at least not to the local population and for their sense of "local ownership."

Local ownership has been seen as increasingly important in rule of law promotion.[59] It was also reflected in the UN's move toward more cooperative rather than coercive forms of postconflict administration. However, this lighter footprint comes at a price. It has been argued that a focus on local ownership prevents the international actors from exerting the necessary influence to actually get rule of law reforms on the way. Especially in the case of Afghanistan, this led to delays in the provision of justice and to a bad record in terms of human rights protection (Stahn 2008: 361–362). Here is a veritable dilemma: If international administration becomes too imposing, it is criticized for disrespect of local ownership and resemblance with forms of imperialism. If it respects local preferences, it gets caught up in protests against a lack of effectiveness.

2.5. THE RULE OF LAW AND REGIONAL INTEGRATION

One would expect less ambiguity in the practice of regional organizations, because such organizations are usually embedded in a higher degree of overlapping mutual expectations among their members. These organizations usually define common values in their constituent instruments or related agreements. Among these values one frequently finds the rule of law. This holds true for the EU,[60] the Council of Europe,[61] the OAS,[62] the African Union,[63] the Association of Southeast Asian Nations,[64] and the International Conference on the Great Lakes Region.[65] Taken together, these organizations represent a formidable share of all states members of the international community and testify that, again on a normative level, the principle of the rule of law is almost universally considered to be central to the organization of public authority.

However, the crux lies with specification and implementation. In this respect, we need to distinguish among the various organizations and also among different contexts in which respect for the rule of law has a role to play. Whereas "(m)ost clubs set explicit conditions for joining" (Smith 2003: 106), these rules are complied with to a varying degree.

The EU rules on the accession of new member-states are probably the most detailed in this regard (Ruffert and Walter 2009: 91). However, the picture is also mixed in practice here: "The difference between how enlargements are regulated

59 See, e.g., UNSC Resolution 1806 of 20 March 2008, UN Doc. S/RES/1806: para. 4.

60 Article 2 of the Treaty on the European Union, (2008) *Official Journal C/115*.

61 Article 3 of the Statute of the Council of Europe of 5 May 1949, ETS no. 1.

62 Protocol of Washington of 1991, reprinted in *International Legal Materials* 33 (1994), 1005.

63 Article 4, lit. m) of the Constitutive Act of the African Union of 11 July 2000.

64 Article 2, lit. h) of the Charter of the Association of Southeast Asian Nations of 27 November 2007.

65 ECOWAS, Protocol on Democracy and Good Governance, Protocol Supplementary to the Protocol Relating to the Mechanism for Conflict Prevention Management, Resolution, Peacekeeping and Security, adopted on 10 December 1999; Article 6 of the Pact on Security, Stability and Development in the Great Lakes Region, reprinted in *International Legal Materials* 46 (2007), 173.

in practice and what can be found in the Treaty is striking" (Kochenov 2008: 14). Moreover, it seems that the EU enlargement round in 2004 was particularly difficult in this regard, because the commission did not follow a consistent approach with respect to human rights, democracy, and the rule of law. Rather, these three notions had been conflated, which makes it difficult to identify the exact contours of the rule of law element (Kochenov 2008: 117–121).

So far, the EU has not made use of the mechanism to suspend membership rights if a member-state violates the fundamental principles of the Union. When the "XIV" adopted sanctions against Austria in 2000 over concerns regarding possible authoritarian tendencies of a newly elected right-wing government, the mechanism of Article 7 of the Treaty on European Union was not applicable because it did not permit sanctions for future violations.[66] This possibility was only introduced by the Treaty of Nice in 2001 and has not been used since.

In comparison, the Council of Europe has actually halted an accession process because of concerns over the rule of law when it withdrew the special guest status of Belarus in 1997. Belarus had applied for Council of Europe membership in 1992. In the view of the Parliamentary Assembly of the Council of Europe (PACE), the announcement of a plan for constitutional reforms by the president of Belarus would have diminished "the role of the parliament to a degree which would call into question its ability to function as an independent legislature and to exercise democratic control over the executive" and would have led to problems with the rule of law.[67] So far, however, the mechanism for suspension of member-states in Article 8 of the council's statute has never been used. The organization came very close to making use of it after the usurpation of power by a military regime in Greece in 1967. Before a suspension could take place, however, Greece withdrew from the organization.[68] After the increase in Council of Europe membership in the 1990s, the issue of a possible suspension of membership rights arose with greater frequency. PACE reminded member-states of their commitment to the central values of the organization as set out in Article 3 of the statute and the related enforcement mechanism in Article 8.[69] A particularly challenging case in this regard was Russia, whose conflicts in Chechnya provoked criticism in the Parliamentary Assembly. A recommendation by PACE to initiate proceedings to suspend Russia's membership rights over its alleged violations of Council of Europe core principles in Chechnya was ultimately unsuccessful.[70]

[66] On these measures and their legal basis see Schorkopf (2002: 61 et seq.).

[67] PACE Resolution 1102 (1996)1 of 7 November 1996: para. 2; see most recently PACE Resolution 1727 (2010) of 29 April 2010.

[68] For a detailed description of the Greek case, see Magliveras (1999: 80–83).

[69] PACE Order No. 488 (1993), on the honoring of commitments entered into by new member-states, 26 June 1993; see also PACE Order No. 508 (1995) of 26 April 1995.

[70] PACE Recommendation 1444 (2000) of 27 January 2000 (see para. 4 for the reference to the rule of law); PACE Recommendation 1456 (2000) of 6 April 2000: paras. 2, 25; in response to the lack of compliance with these recommendations by the Committee of Ministers, see PACE Resolution 1221 (2000) of 29 June 2000.

Other regional organizations have a more active practice with respect to suspending member-states in situations in which unconstitutional changes of government have occurred. This is the case for the OAS, which suspended the membership rights of Honduras after the coup d'état against President José Manuel Zelaya Rosales in June 2009. The violation of the rule of law through the unconstitutional change of government played a prominent role in the OAS resolution. The legal basis for the resolution was Article 21 of the Inter-American Democratic Charter, which allows for sanctions based on the violation of the principles of democratic order – a notion that includes the rule of law (Article 3 of the charter).[71] In the months after the suspension of the membership rights, unity among the OAS members on this question vanished,[72] and on June 1, 2011, Honduras was formally readmitted to the OAS.[73]

The African Union also frequently suspends membership rights in similar situations. In its recent practice, we find such reactions by the Peace and Security Council of the AU after the coup d'états in Guinea in 2008[74] and in Madagascar in 2009.[75] In these cases, however, the Peace and Security Council has not mentioned the rule of law as a motive for its sanctions, but has merely demanded the restoration of constitutional government.[76] Other African organizations such as ECOWAS have followed suit in this regard, suspending the membership rights of Niger.[77]

3. THE RULE OF LAW AS MINIMUM STANDARD

Does our inquiry lead to the conclusion that the rule of law, although being generally recognized on the global level as a normative expectation, ultimately lacks much specific legal content and is context dependent? We think not. We do think, however, that such specific legal content is not to be found in developments at the macro level of the conditions for the coming into existence of states or general blueprints

[71] Resolution on the Suspension of the Right of Honduras to Participate in the OAS. Adopted at the second plenary session (held on 4 July 2009) and reviewed by the Style Committee, Organization of American States General Assembly, AG/RES.2 (XXXVII-E/09): paras. 2–4.

[72] See "Clinton Presses Region to Recognize Honduras," *The New York Times*, 6 March 2010. Accessed 28 March 2010 at http://www.nytimes.com/2010/03/06/world/americas/06clinton.html.

[73] Participation of Honduras in the Organization of American States. Adopted at the Plenary Session held on June 1, 2011 and reviewed by the Style Committee, Organization of American States General Assembly, AG/RES.1 (XLI-E/11).

[74] See "African Union Bars Guinea on Coup," *BBC News*, 29 December 2008. Accessed 28 March 2010 at http://news.bbc.co.uk/go/pr/fr/-/hi/africa/7802803.stm.

[75] See "African Union Suspends Madagascar After 'coup'," *The Guardian*, 20 March 2009.

[76] See Peace and Security Council decision adopted at the 216th meeting of 19 February 2010, PSC/PR/COMM.1(CCXVI) on Madagascar; and Peace and Security Council decision adopted at the 216th meeting of 19 February 2010, PSC/PR/COMM.2(CCXVI) on the Republic of Niger.

[77] See "Niger's Military Coup Criticized by France and Africa," *BBC News*, 19 February 2010. Accessed 28 March 2010 at http://news.bbc.co.uk/2/hi/8523573.stm.

for the organization of public power. We rather suggest that the core legal content of the rule of law develops out of a traditional area of international law concerning the standards of judicial protection. There is substantial practice with respect to minimum standards in this field. These standards originally developed with respect to the treatment of injuries to aliens. Today they can be found in modern international economic law as well as in human rights law.

In this section, we argue that a modern version of the minimum standard of justice can be identified as an element of the international rule of law that is binding upon states. This minimum standard gives more specific content and meaning to the general expectations we have presented so far. International lawyers have so far mostly neglected the relationship between the general and broad affirmations of the rule of law and the more concrete and modest steps to establish a minimum standard in specific subject areas of international law (for an exception see Schill 2009: 79-81; Schill 2010: 154). It is, however, only through a combined reading of these two developments that the existing dimension and the future potential of the international rule of law can be fully grasped.

3.1. *The Traditional Minimum Standard Pertaining to Injuries to Aliens and its Emanation in Contemporary International Economic Law*

The minimum standard of justice was developed in the 19th century – in a previous era of globalization that witnessed an enormous increase of foreign investment. As U.S. Secretary of State Elihu Root remarked in 1910,

> (a)ll these forms of peaceful interpenetration among the nations of the earth naturally contribute their instances of citizens justly or unjustly dissatisfied with the treatment they receive in foreign countries and calling upon their governments for protection. (Root 1910: 519)

Protection of these citizens took various forms. Outright armed intervention was one means and was resorted to, in the words of Root, "by strong countries" in situations in which control by foreign governments was "inadequate for the preservation of order" (Root 1910: 520). As Root observed, this was problematic for the sovereignty of the state in which intervention was carried out. A more lenient approach, therefore, was to call on the respective governments to observe "the established standard of civilization" with respect to foreigners (Root 1910: 521). What denial of justice effectively meant was always a matter of debate: A narrow understanding of the term limited it to the express denial of justice, meaning that there was simply no avenue at all by which foreigners could challenge infringements upon their property rights. Another narrow view would also include unreasonable delays of justice (Freeman 1938: 116–132). There were, however, also more substantive conceptions of denial of justice. In its 1927 resolution on the matter, the Institut de Droit International offered the following definition of denial of justice:

Art. 5 – L'Etat est responsable du chef de déni de justice:

(1) Lorsque les tribunaux nécessaires pour assurer la protection des étrangers n'existent ou ne fonctionnent pas.
(2) Lorsque les tribunaux ne sont pas accessibles aux étrangers.
(3) Lorsque les tribunaux n'offrent pas les garanties indispensables pour assurer une bonne justice.[78]

Obviously, the third criterion makes denial of justice in part a substantive criterion. The members of the institute debated whether this paragraph should be included in the provision.[79] Ultimately, the issue boiled down to the proposition that "what the international legal order demands is a minimum degree of judicial organization, on a scale comparable with that found in a normally constituted State" (Freeman 1938: 135). This was opposed by those international lawyers, especially from Latin America, who adhered to the so-called Calvo Clause, according to which foreigners were entitled to the same benefits of protection as the citizens of the given state (see Paulsson 2005: 20 et seq.).[80] From the perspective of Latin American countries, the whole regime pertaining to the minimum standard of justice and denials of justice were thus instruments of the capitalist European and North American states to protect their economic interests. This was openly admitted by authors from these regions as well. Frederick Sherwood Dunn, for example, wrote:

> we find that this minimum standard of justice is nothing more nor less than the ideas which are conceived to be essential to a continuation of the existing social and economic order of European capitalistic civilization. . . . In other words: legal justice in this sense calls for nothing more than a continuation of the basic ideas of existing social order. . . . As long as these states remain dominant in international society, it is the fundamentals of their civilization which will determine the content of the standard of justice in the international legal system. (Dunn 1928: 175–176)

In our days Gerry Simpson has put the matter in the following terms:

> One attribute of civilization was the possession of a liberal or at least pseudo-liberal legal order in which alien (read Western) nationals would be afforded full liberal rights. Those entities excluded from the system were thought incapable of ensuring this level of protection and were thus deprived of certain sovereign rights and jurisdictional immunities in "unequal treaties" and capitulations. (Simpson 2004: 234)

In view of this background, it may appear counterintuitive to recycle the traditional minimum standard as a point of departure for the concretization of the modern international rule of law. However, a closer look at the philosophical underpinnings

78 Résolution de l'Institut de Droit International, XXXIVe session, *Annuaire de l'IDI* 1927, tome III, 331.
79 Ibid., at 121 et seq.
80 It should be noted that the Calvo Clause remains binding constitutional law in several Latin American countries; see, e.g., Article 27, para. 1 of the Constitution of the Mexican United States.

of this minimum standard gives reason for reflection. This minimum standard, Dunn said, related to the "natural rights of man" and was to be found in "every bill of rights and in nearly every constitution that was adopted in the period following the decline of absolutism" (Dunn 1928: 176). At the time Dunn was writing, this argument rang hollow because the international legal system still allowed for outright discrimination among states. Also the bills of rights to which he referred were arguably concentrated in only a few states and did not necessarily apply to everyone within those states.

Today, the picture is different. The human rights treaties at the universal and regional level have universalized the "natural rights of man." With this universalization the legal context for the minimum standard of justice has changed. Just as Root, Freeman, and Dunn attempted to reconcile the European standards of civilization and the universal minimum standard at their time of writing, it is possible today to relate the minimum standard of justice to the broader picture of human rights as protected in today's international legal system.[81]

This emerging convergence was already foreshadowed by the unfortunate start of the long drafting history of the International Law Commission's Articles on State Responsibility. In 1956, F. V. García Amador, the first Special Rapporteur on the topic, tried to reconcile the antagonism between the rights of aliens and of citizens.[82] He wished to turn the International Law Commission project on state responsibility into a great reform project that would have integrated human rights considerations into the regime for the protection against injuries to aliens. With his fervor he could only fail at the time, as the emerging Cold War was not the right environment in which consensus on a matter that was contested between the different sides could be reached. However, the reasons he gave for his approach resonate today:

> (B)oth the "international standard of justice" and the principle of equality between nationals and aliens, hitherto considered as antagonistic and irreconcilable, can well be reformulated and integrated into a new legal rule incorporating the essential elements and serving the main purpose of both. The basis of this new principle would be the "universal respect for, and observance of, human rights and fundamental freedoms" referred to in the Charter of the United Nations and in other general, regional and bilateral instruments. The object of the "internationalization" (to coin a term) of these rights and freedoms is to ensure the protection of the legitimate interests of the human person, irrespective of his nationality. Whether the person concerned is a citizen or an alien is then immaterial: human beings, as such, are under the direct protection of international law.[83]

[81] This claim is, of course, exposed to its own critique concerning the debate about universality and particularity in human rights law; for further discussion see Nolte (2008).

[82] Also see the earlier work by Lauterpacht (1950: 121).

[83] Report on the International Responsibility by Mr. F.V. Garcia Amador, Special Rapporteur, UN Doc. A/CN.4/96, YBILC 1956, Vol. II: at 194, para. 111. See also Lauterpacht (1950: 202, para. 156). For a rather critical view see Simma (1985: 361).

A tendency has been identified in international practice according to which the minimum standard in customary international law and the more specific standards under various bilateral investment treaties (BITs) and multilateral treaties as well as under human rights law begin to benefit from cross-fertilization (Paulsson 2005: 66–67; Schill 2010: 176).[84] The traditional boundary between the protection of aliens and human rights of citizens is becoming blurred (Francioni 2009: 732). The fact that international investment law is no longer a one-way street has contributed to this development.[85] The United States and Canada have changed their model BITs to provide for regulatory leeway for incoming investment. The understanding that the United States puts forward in their new model BIT now approaches the fair and equitable treatment standard with the minimum standard of justice.[86] This is also the leading interpretation in the framework of the North American Free Trade Agreement (NAFTA; see Dolzer and Schreuer 2008: 125; Schill 2010: 154).[87]

There is now also some support in international investment law practice for the view that the minimum standard of justice could be an authoritative emanation of what can currently be understood by the rule of law.[88] If the alleged cross-fertilization between international investment law and human rights law succeeds, we could be in the presence of an emerging and legally binding universal standard for the international rule of law (see also Schill 2010: 176). This would not only benefit investments. If understood in this way, the rule of law would benefit in turn from the customary law status of the minimum standard.[89]

3.2. *The Minimum Standard in Human Rights Law*

The connection between a minimum standard of procedural justice and the rule of law is recognized in virtually all instruments of international human rights protection.[90] In its General Comment No. 29, the UN Human Rights Committee has underlined that procedural guarantees are central provisions to the International

[84] See also Francioni (2009: 731–732) and Petersmann (2009).

[85] See Thilo Rensmann, "Nationales Verwaltungsrecht und internationaler Investitionsschutz," forthcoming (manuscript on file with the authors).

[86] For critical remarks see Schwebel (2009: 519–521).

[87] The change in U.S. practice followed an interpretive note of the Free Trade Commission of NAFTA on the meaning of "fair and equitable treatment" in Article 1105, para. 1 of NAFTA, entered into force on 1 January 1994. This interpretive note identified the standard with the customary law minimum standard.

[88] For example, Mexico has affirmed in an arbitration as a third-party intervener that the core idea behind the international minimum standard would be "arbitrary action being substituted for the rule of law," *Mondev International Ltd v. United States of America*, Award of 11 October 2002, 6 *ICSID Reports* 19: para. 108. See further Kingsbury and Schill (2009).

[89] On this status see Tomuschat (2009: § 178, para. 18).

[90] For a concise overview see Weissbrodt (2009: 62–69).

Covenant on Civil and Political Rights.[91] The committee has also found that basic elements of the right to a fair trial may not be derogated from, even in times of emergency.[92]

In the *Golder* case, the European Court of Human Rights has emphasized the connection between access to court and the rule of law. The European Court underlined that the reference to the rule of law in the preamble of the European Convention[93] is not a "more or less rhetorical reference," devoid of relevance for the interpretation of the Convention.[94] The European Court also stressed that the procedural rights embodied in Article 6 of the Convention need to be read in the light of the international law principle of denial of justice.[95] Finally, the court affirmed that it would follow automatically from the object and purpose of Article 6, paragraph 1 of the Convention that "access to court" is a right of fundamental importance: "The fair, public and expeditious characteristics of judicial proceedings are of no value at all if there are no judicial proceedings."[96]

The Inter-American Court of Human Rights has followed this reasoning. It identifies a connection between procedural rights and the rule of law on the basis of Articles 8 and 25 of the American Convention on Human Rights.[97] Article 8 provides that "(e)very person has the right to a hearing, with due guarantees." Article 25 holds in its paragraph 1 the following:

> Everyone has the right to simple and prompt recourse, or any other effective recourse, to a competent court or tribunal for protection against acts that violate his fundamental rights recognized by the constitution or laws of the state concerned or by this Convention, even though such violation may have been committed by persons acting in the course of their official duties.

In a manner comparable to the approach of the European Court of Human Rights, the Inter-American Court has found that these two provisions may not be derogated from in times of emergency, because this would render meaningless other nonderogable rights of the Convention.[98] The jurisprudence of the Inter-American Court is anchored in the understanding that the rights set forth by the Convention

[91] International Covenant on Civil and Political Rights of 16 December 1966, entered into force on 23 March 1976, 999 UNTS 171.

[92] UNCHR, General Comment No. 29 on States of Emergency (Article 4), UN Doc. CCPR/C/21/Rev.1/Add.11 of 31 August 2001: para. 16.

[93] Convention on the Protection of Human Rights and Fundamental Freedoms of 4 November 1950, entered into force on 3 September 1953, ETS no. 5.

[94] See *Golder* v. *United Kingdom*, European Court of Human Rights, Application No. 4451/70, Judgment of 21 February 1975, Series A no. 18, para. 34.

[95] Ibid., para. 35.

[96] Ibid.

[97] American Convention on Human Rights of 22 November 1969, entered into force on 18 July 1978, OAS Treaty Series No. 36.

[98] See "Advisory Opinion on Judicial Guarantees during States of Exception," Inter-American Court of Human Rights, Series A No. 9, 6 October 1987: paras. 29, 30, and 38.

must be guaranteed effectively and that it would amount to a denial of justice if that were not the case.[99] In an advisory opinion on the status of undocumented migrant workers, the Inter-American Court has come very close to affirming that the due process rights belong to the peremptory norms of international law.[100]

The Southern African Development Community Tribunal has also drawn an explicit connection between the minimum standards of due process and the rule of law in its 2008 decision in a case concerning land-reform projects of the Zimbabwean government. There, the tribunal found the following:

> It is settled law that the concept of the rule of law embraces at least two fundamental rights, namely, the right of access to the courts and the right to a fair hearing before an individual is deprived of a right, interest or legitimate expectation. . . . Article 4 (c) obliges Member States of SADC to respect principles of "human rights, democracy and the rule of law."[101]

These examples show that the notion of a minimum standard of justice is accepted at the universal level as well as by different regional systems of human rights protection. Both the European and the Inter-American Court of Human Rights have acknowledged the connection between this human rights standard and the standard of denial of justice as it can be found in general international law.

3.3. *A Converging Minimum Standard?*

It would be premature to argue that a uniform minimum standard has already emerged that would apply across general international law, the law of investment protection, and human rights law (similarly Schill 2010: 176). Nevertheless, there is a tendency that the standards in these fields are converging.[102] In all three fields, the respective minimum standard is developed by having recourse to the rule of law as the underlying rationale. What are we to make of this?

99 *Las Palmeras* v. *Colombia*, Merits, Inter-American Court of Human Rights, Judgment of December 6, 2001. Series C No. 90: para. 58. In a dissenting opinion, two judges have postulated that Article 8, para. 1 of the Convention "is the guarantee, *par excellence*, of all human rights and a requirement *sine qua non* for the existence of a State in which the rule of law prevails": *Claude-Reyes et al.* v. *Chile*, Merits, Reparations and Costs. Inter-American Court of Human Rights, Judgment of September 19, 2006. Series C No. 151, dissenting opinion Judges Alirio Abeu Burelli and Cecilia Medina Quiroga, para. 1. The former president of the court, Judge Cançado Trindade, has commented that the court has developed the guarantees of Articles 8 and 25 of the Convention into a "veritable right to have rights," which include the right to a legal system, national or international in scope (Cançado Trindade 2008: 81–82).

100 See "Juridical Condition and Rights of the Undocumented Migrants," Inter-American Court of Human Rights, Advisory Opinion OC-18 of September 17, 2003. Series A No. 18: para. 122.

101 *Mike Campbell (Pvt) Ltd and Others* v. *Republic of Zimbabwe*, Southern Africa Development Community Tribunal, Decision of 18 November 2008, reprinted in *International Legal Materials* 48 (2009): 540.

102 For the further development of this standard, a useful approach is suggested by Teitel and Howse (2009).

The interrelationship between the rule of law and the notions of a minimum standard blesses the rule of law with a hallmark of approval in the traditional sources of international law. This gives the rule of law legal significance beyond its appeal as an aspirational principle. It is also imaginable that a cross-fertilization is taking place between the different minimum standards that would help to cure deficiencies in the respective fields. In investment protection, bridges to human rights law can help to foster greater respect for the consideration of public policy issues such as health, environment, and participation issues (cf. Hirsch 2008). This does not follow from the minimum standard as such, but from a dialogue between these fields. From the perspective of human rights law, anchoring the minimum procedural standards in different legal regimes may help to overcome the criticism that views human rights law as being nothing more than an appeal to lofty principles. If the same minimum standard plays a role in a regime as crucial to international economic governance as the law of investment protection, it cannot be an irrelevant nicety. Cross-fertilization need not be limited to interaction between these two fields. We also find recourse to the rule of law and the minimum standard in domestic constitutional law[103] or in the jurisprudence of the World Trade Organization (WTO) dispute settlement mechanism.[104] Article X:3(b) of the 1947 General Agreement on Trade and Tariffs already provided that "(e)ach contracting party shall maintain, or institute as soon as practicable, judicial, arbitral or administrative tribunals or procedures for the purpose, *inter alia*, of the prompt review and correction of administrative action relating to customs matters."[105] When the WTO Appellate Body analyzed a similar provision under the Trade-Related Aspects of Intellectual Property Rights agreement, it found that these review procedures "provide for an internationally-agreed minimum standard which Members are bound to implement in their domestic legislation."[106]

A converging minimum standard could also be a cure for problems of fragmentation in the system of international protection for procedural rights. Individuals, be they foreigners or citizens, may find themselves exposed to different standards of protection, depending on the regime under which they fall. A common standard of denial of justice that derives its content from a multitude of sources – human rights law, investment protection, world trade law, domestic constitutional law – could provide them with guidance for their minimum level of protection. This movement against a fragmentation of the available levels of protection would also connect with another idea that is frequently considered to be a consequence of the rule of law: that a system of law shall not be self-contradictory (cf. Raz 1979: 213). A certain harmonization of standards of protection and differing procedural avenues would thus represent a major step forward for the idea of an international rule of law.

[103] See, e.g., *Zondi* v. *MEC for Traditional and Local Government Affairs and Others*, Constitutional Court of South Africa, 2005 (3) SA 589 (CC), Ngcobo J: para. 82.

[104] See further Buiyan (2007: 42 et seq.).

[105] General Agreement on Trade and Tariffs of 1 January 1948.

[106] United States – Section 211 Omnibus Appropriations Act of 1998, WTO Appellate Body, WT/DS176/AB/R of 2 January 2002: para. 206.

4. CONCLUSION

The rule of law is becoming an increasingly relevant reference point against which the behavior of states is assessed under international law. We have tried to show, however, that the rule of law has not, as such, led to a redefinition of statehood at the international level. There is certainly a growing normative expectation that states respect the rule of law. It is also obvious, however, that this expectation cannot be satisfied in a schematic fashion. Nonetheless, we hope to have shown that the international expectations concerning the rule of law at the national level rest on a substantial legal foundation.

This legal foundation implies a change of perspective. Instead of the macro level of statehood, it is the perspective of the individual that takes center stage. However, the two perspectives are not unconnected. Already Article 16 of the Declaration of the Rights of Man and of the Citizen of 1789 held the following: "Toute Société dans laquelle la garantie des Droits n'est pas assurée, ni la separation des Pouvoirs déterminée, n'a point de Constitution." Mutatis mutandis, we can say that the core international legal expectations for the rule of law at the national level must be derived from the minimum procedural guarantees of individuals.

3

Constraining International Authority through the Rule of Law

Legitimatory Potential and Political Dynamics

Tim Gemkow and Michael Zürn

1. INTRODUCTION

Rule of law standards have traditionally been applied to states. For a long time, the respective demands were also put forward mainly within the domestic realm. Helmut Aust and Georg Nolte show in Chapter 2 of this volume that there is now a growing normative expectation on the international level as well that states will comply with basic rule of law principles. In addition, recent years have seen the development of new and urgent questions about the applicability of rule of law prescriptions to international and transnational actors. This latest shift is best illustrated by comparing the statement by the president of the United Nations (UN) Security Council in 2006 with the one in 2010. In the 5474th meeting of the Security Council held on June 22, 2006, the president stated that the "Security Council attaches vital importance to promoting peace and the rule of law, including respect for human rights, as an indispensable element of lasting peace."[1] Four years later, the respective opening of the paragraph reads as follows: "The Security Council expresses its commitment to ensure that all UN efforts to restore peace and security themselves respect and promote the rule of law."[2] This remarkable shift from the promotion of the rule of the law to promoting and respecting the rule of law indicates a double dynamic across different political levels. In the first place, international actors and institutions promoted the rule of law principle on the national level. Meanwhile these demands came back: Rule of law standards are now addressed to international institutions as well. It is this double dynamic that is analyzed in this chapter. That rule of law principles have traveled to the international level, we argue, is causally linked to the rise of international authority. In addition, we explore whether or not the use of rule

We are grateful to Monika Heupel, Nico Krisch, George Nolte, and Randall Peerenboom for their helpful comments on earlier drafts of this chapter.

[1] Statement by the President of the Security Council, 22 June 2006, UN Doc. S/PRST/2006/28.

[2] Statement by the President of the Security Council, 29 June 2010, UN Doc. S/PRST/2010/11.

of law principles can improve the legitimacy of authority-exercising international institutions. After briefly outlining the general dynamics, we focus in this chapter on the element of rule of law for which the analogy to domestic rule of law norms seems particularly strong: decision making in international organizations directly addressing specific individuals.

The rising relevance of rule of law norms in the international sphere is intricately linked to changes that undermined Westphalian sovereignty in the past two to three decades. International institutions nowadays play an active and often crucial role in many policy areas. They make decisions in a majoritarian mode in such important organizations as the World Bank, the International Monetary Fund, and the European Union (EU), thus canceling the vetoes of individual states and overcoming blockades. They adjudicate in cases of diverging interpretations of the rules and expect states to follow such rulings, as in the case of the World Trade Organization Dispute Settlement Body. We can even observe an increased readiness for actions of international institutions in response to a violation of international rules. Implementation committees, liability regimes, legal sanction mechanisms either as part of the constitutive treaty (Kyoto Protocol) or as part of contracts (World Bank), and even a preparedness to authorize the use of force – especially since 1989, cases of gross violation of human rights have increasingly been responded to with military force and economic sanctions. International institutions thus have become a site of political authority. Moreover, international organizations have greatly expanded the scope of their commands: From state interactions at the borders, they have moved to regulate behind the border issues that require states to regulate societal actors, and they have even begun to directly address individuals and other societal actors by their decisions in a relevant number of cases.

This raises the issue of legitimacy of international institutions. The stronger the role that international institutions play in policy making and the less mediated their power over individuals is by state institutions, the stronger demands for their legitimacy can be expected to arise. The rule of law is one of the conceivable sources for the legitimation of political authority. Against this background, we try to answer two questions in this chapter. First, is it possible to improve the legitimacy of international public authority through the establishment of institutional procedures that introduce components of the rule of law – and in particular protection of individual rights – at the international level? In doing so, we focus on international organizations as public forms of international authority. Although similar considerations will probably be relevant for powerful forms of private transnational authority as well, this contribution focuses on the exercise of *public* authority on the international level. Second, even if rule of law procedures were capable of increasing the legitimacy of international authority, they could be seen as a utopian demand without any grounding in real-world developments. Therefore, in a second step, we ask this: Are there any mechanisms discernible through which an establishment of an international rule of law encompassing individual rights protections can take place? With respect to this second question, we will argue that a number of such processes exist, including feedback processes from the promotion of rule of law norms by international organizations that generate pressure on international organizations themselves to conform to rule of law ideals. In this sense, the rule of law movement has created an internal dynamic through which the rule of law promotion by international institutions may lead to an increased relevance of the rule of law in international institutions as a result of diffusion.

2. POLITICAL AUTHORITY BEYOND THE NATION-STATE AND SOURCES OF LEGITIMATION

The modern institution of international law defined states as the constitutive actors of international society and the basic parameters of rightful action for them (see Reus-Smit 2004: 34). The most fundamental principle of this order was the Westphalian notion of sovereignty emphasizing the principle of nonintervention into domestic affairs. This notion involved three norms: first, that a state exercises sole authority over its territory; second, that all states are judicially equal; and third, that state parties are not subject to any law other than their own – with state obligations in international law being ultimately derived, at least hypothetically, from the respective state's consent.

With the rise of interdependencies and the growing need to coordinate actions between states, the consent principle for international institutions emerged as a logical corollary to the principle of sovereignty. Because sovereign states would not accept any law besides their own, international norms and rules required the consent of all parties to an agreement. As long as all the states concerned have agreed to international norms, the principle of sovereignty is upheld and the legitimacy of international law is thus ensured. In this view, international institutions are considered to be instruments of the territorial state, without possessing a political authority in their own right.

Since the end of World War II and especially since the mid-1980s, however, the design of international institutions and the process of international policy making have increasingly undermined the consent principle. Three institutional developments are responsible for this move. First, states have increasingly delegated autonomous power to make decisions to international institutions. The secretariat of the International Atomic Energy Agency, for instance, is monitoring regulations and their domestic implementation, and the World Bank and many other international organizations implement policies autonomously. The most significant development in this respect is, however, the rise of international dispute settlement bodies. Given the moment of lawmaking that is involved in any case of adjudication, the increase in international judicial bodies is especially remarkable (see Bogdandy and Venzke 2010). In 1960, there were only 27 quasi-judicial bodies worldwide; by 2004, this number had grown to 97. If we narrow the definition and include only those bodies that meet all of the prerequisites for formal judicial proceedings, then only 5 such bodies existed worldwide in 1960, climbing to 28 by 2004.[3] A specific look at international environmental regimes shows that about 30 percent of all policy functions are delegated to international organization. Given the rise of international treaties, the absolute number of such policy functions autonomously performed by international organizations has grown significantly (Green and Colgan 2010: 7).

Second, international institutions without such a formal delegation of power can undermine the consent principle as well, when decisions are made on the basis of some form of majority voting. Majoritarian decision making increases the ability of international institutions to act by canceling the vetoes of individual states and overcoming blockades. Today, roughly two-thirds of all international organizations with the participation of at least one great power have the possibility to decide by majority (see Blake and Payton 2008). A detailed investigation of international environmental regimes reveals a similar but more differentiated picture. In the area of international environmental policy, there are also many cases of decision by majority that have been stipulated by agreement. In practice, however, states are actually more strongly consensus oriented in their approach to international environmental problems. In only 20.2 percent of the cases investigated were consensus decisions prescribed; in practice, however, 58.4 percent of all decisions were arrived at through consensus (see Breitmeier, Young, and Zürn 2006: 125). Even if decision by majority is employed far less often than it is formally available to be used, it still exerts pressure on veto players and increases their readiness to seek compromise.

Third, international organizations have substantially expanded the scope of their regulations as well as the actors addressed by them. Unlike the traditional image of international law as rules delimitating sovereign borders and interaction at those borders, modern international institutions often prescribe behavior – such as emissions reduction or the enforcement of intellectual property rights – that states can meet only by extensively regulating the behavior of societal actors within their territory. In addition, more international organizations have become involved in decisions about individual acts of public authority, rather than just in general rules: Examples are decisions by the UN Security Council to include specific named individuals in its sanctions lists or decisions by the UN High Commissioner for Refugees (UNHCR), pursuant to treaties with a substantial fraction of its member-states, determining whether specific individuals do or do not fall under the international refugee classification.

Through the delegation of policy functions to international organizations, the pooling of decision making (see Hawkins, Lake, Nielson, et al. 2006 and Moravcsik 1998: 67 for this distinction), and the increasing intrusiveness of their regulations (see Kahler 1995), international institutions have become a site of political authority.

[3] See Project on International Courts and Tribunals, "Material and Publications," available at http://www.pict-pcti.org/matrix/matrixintro.html. See also Alter (2009).

International institutions have political authority when states recognize, in principle or in practice, their ability to make binding decisions on matters relating to a state's domestic jurisdiction, even if those decisions are contrary to a state's own policies and preferences (Cooper, Hawkins, Jacoby, et al. 2008: 505). This type of public or political authority, however, requires political legitimacy.

Political (or public) authority is more than social authority based on credibility and reputation for expertise and integrity (see Raz 1990). To the extent that social authority is based on credibility and reputation, legitimacy is built in (see Hurd 2007: 3 and Ruggie 1998: 64 for an understanding of authority along these lines). Political authority, in contrast, not only requires the general willingness to obey instructions fostering the common good even if they are perceived to go against one's own immediate interests, but also a belief in the rightful exercise of this authority. Political authority therefore requires legitimation. *Political authority* in modernity is never granted unconditionally and can therefore be conceived as a social contract (see Lake 2010).[4] An international institution has political authority when the direct and indirect addressees recognize, in principle or in practice, its right to make binding decisions.[5] In return, the addressees will expect that the ruling institutions act in a way that achieves joint goals – some vision of the common good – that compensates them for the loss of freedom.

Political authority relationships are therefore embedded in certain beliefs of legitimacy on the side of the ruled about how the ruling institution has to act in order to credibly advance the common good. Of course, these criteria need not always be met, and political authority can be exercised without being fully legitimate. In this case, one would speak of a legitimacy deficit. However, in the long run, authority will indeed only be accepted if it is successfully legitimated by reference to prevailing conceptions of the common good.[6]

What then causes actors to consider an (international) political authority legitimate? The concept of legitimacy has two sides (cf. also Bodansky 1999). From a normative perspective, it refers to the normative validity of a political order and its justificatory claims (see Habermas 1976: Part III). From a descriptive perspective, in contrast, the focus is on the societal acceptance of political decisions and political orders and the belief in legitimacy.

There are two important arguments for including both aspects in our analysis. First, a purely descriptive account of legitimacy strips the social scientist of any

4 Although also bound to shared notions of the common good, traditional authority relationships are based on tradition and divinity rather than on a social contract conceived as an exchange between common good provision and individual freedom.

5 Barnett and Finnemore (2004: 5) similarly define authority in general terms as the ability to use institutions and discursive resources to induce deference from others. See also Rittberger, Nettesheim Huckel, et al. (2008) and Bogdandy, Dann, and Goldmann (2010).

6 See Zürn, Binder, and Ecker-Ehrhardt (2011) for a more encompassing conceptualization of international political authority.

competence to make judgments about legitimacy, because she or he is compelled to do no more than report data about the beliefs of actors. This is unfortunate because we would also want to be able to predict acceptance of different institutional arrangements and normative orders, and to recognize patterns and causes of people's decisions to confer or withdraw beliefs of legitimacy. Second, a merely behavioralist definition of legitimacy shifts the most relevant questions about the relationship between different normative principles and societal support out of the spotlight. In other words, "a given power relationship is not legitimate because people believe in its legitimacy, but because it can be justified in terms of their beliefs" (Beetham 1991, 11). We therefore follow an empirical understanding of legitimacy that is based on normatively grounded justifications of rule.

Given these conceptual clarifications, we can state that if international institutions exercise political authority, then they must appeal to some valid notion of legitimacy to remain effective in the long term. Authority needs legitimacy if it is to avoid appearing arbitrary and creating resistance. Indeed, with the rise of political authority on the international level, in recent years there has been increasing resistance to international organizations and their policies. This growing need to legitimate international institutions is evidenced by the unwillingness of national publics, parliaments, and transnational civil society to accept without further ado the outcomes of major international negotiations as urgently necessary achievements of international cooperation. It is also evident in the resistance organized at the national level to the perceived undermining of democratic sovereignty, for example in referendums on European integration. Rising powers also critique, and dissent from, intrusive international institutions as a means of prolongation of Western dominance (Zürn and Ecker-Ehrhardt 2011).

Can this growing demand for legitimation be met? As we already mentioned, in general, the content of the rules produced by political authorities must be justifiable in terms of prevalent beliefs about the common good. Obviously, these belief systems vary immensely across space, time, and different types of political authority (Beetham 1991: chapter 3) and therefore create particular legitimation problems for international institutions.

On the domestic level, there are different *sources* for the legitimation of modern political orders available. Good outcomes based on expertise, fostering a sense of community, acceptance of individual rights and legality, accountability of the power holders, participation in the selection of decision makers and in the decision-making process, public debates, and contestation are certainly among them (see Avant, Finnemore, and Sell 2010; Beetham 1991; Halberstam 2011; Zürn and Stephen 2010). Most of these types of justification for political authority become to some extent problematic when we leave the realm of national societies (see also Bodansky 1999). Expertise, for example, is not accepted by all concerned societies to the same extent; when it is used on the international level it is seen by many to emanate from pro-Western bias. Broad societal participation and representation in international decision-making are institutionally hardly developed. They take place mainly informally by means of nongovernmental organizations (NGOs), interest groups, and multinational corporations, most of them based in the Western world and, in so doing, further increase the general suspicion of Western bias. Public debates over international issues across borders are up to now extremely rare and are at best beginning to emerge. Moreover, although the construction of an insider–outsider distinction can foster a sense of imagined community at a regional level (as indicated, e.g., in some justifications of the strengthening of the EU), this source of legitimacy is unable to be exploited by those international institutions with a global reach.

3. THE RULE OF LAW, LEGALIZATION, AND CONSTITUTIONALISM AS SOURCES OF LEGITIMACY FOR INTERNATIONAL AUTHORITY

A greater convergence of beliefs seems to exist concerning the rule of law. Thomas Carothers (2006c: 7), among others, has pointed out that the general concept of rule of law is almost universally accepted. Outside the Western world it is less contested than the notion of democracy, and in the West it is seen to remove the chief obstacles to democratization. Accordingly, Brian Tamanaha (2004: 2) has listed a set of citations in favor of the rule of law, some of which shall be cited here. He writes,

> Support for the rule of law is not exclusive to the West. It has been endorsed by government heads from a range of societies, cultures, and economic and political systems. Russian "President Putin continue(d) to place judicial reform and the full implementation of the principles of the rule of law among the country's highest priorities." China recently signed a UN pact for cooperation and training to develop the rule of law. "Chinese leaders say they . . . support the establishment of the rule of law," a commitment underscored by the highly publicized attendance of President Jiang Zemin at a seminar on the rule of law. His successor as President, Hu Jintao, observed following his selection that "We must build a system based on the rule of law and should not pin our hopes on any particular leader." . . . Seven months after taking office, Indonesian President Abdurrahman Wahid identified as one of his major achievements: "we are beginning the rule of law." Mexican President Vicente Fox Quesada declared that the lack of the rule of law is "the theme that worries Mexicans most."

Looking at these statements, we can conclude with Thomas Carothers (2006c: 10): "Around the world the movement toward rule of law is broad but shallow."

Given this widespread support for the rule of law as a source of legitimacy for the exercise of political authority, the concept has potential to support the legitimacy not only of domestic but also of international public authority. It is a form of "legitimation through procedure" (Luhmann 1969) that guarantees impartial and even-handed decision making. In this sense, it would weaken the suspicions according to which international authority permanently uses double standards, applies rules selectively, and is a modern form of Western dominance.

Nevertheless, the statements just cited also make clear that there are still different understandings of the meaning of the rule of law. In a minimalist understanding, rule of law refers only to legal certainty, whereas in a maximalist version, the process of lawmaking needs to follow democratic procedures (Casper 2004) or even adds social rights (Møller and Skaaning 2010b: 15). The most expansive conceptions certainly go beyond the international consensus outlined here. In contrast, the most reductive concepts offer little credible guarantee to be beneficial for the subjects of authority, codifying a "rule by law" more than anything else. For our purposes, hence, we follow an understanding that lies in between those two extremes that we believe captures important elements of the legitimatory power of rule of law ideas in the contemporary world. It consists of the following four components (see, e.g., Carothers 2006c, 4; Cass 2001; Waldron 2008, 2009).

- The rule of law first of all implies *authority of law and not of people*. Therefore, people in positions of authority should exercise their power within a constraining framework of public norms that includes limitations on the abuse of public power for private gain. No one is above the law.
- Second, the rule of law requires *legal certainty and predictability*. This is the requirement that norms and rules be laid down clearly in advance and are accessible to all, including the adjudication procedures and possible repercussions in case of charges about norm violation.
- Third, our concept of rule of law includes *legal equality*, ensuring that the law is the same for all concerned actors and contains no arbitrary distinctions or special personal prerogatives for those in a position of social or political power.
- Finally and partially implied in the first three components, the rule of law implies the *recognition of some basic individual rights*. This is particularly crucial when we consider those cases in which international decisions directly address individual cases, in which the legitimate interests of the affected people need some kind of institutionalized protection.[7]

If a political authority accepts such a rule of law, it can claim much more forcefully that it fosters the common good than in the absence of these principles. This is not to say that those who endorse the rule of law always act in favor of the common good. Our argument is, however, that those who purport to act according to the rule of law can make a more appealing justification of their political authority (see also Waldron 2008: 32). Our suggestion, therefore, is that to the extent that international institutions

7 Overall, this understanding comes very close to the "consensual rule of law definition" of the Venice Commission of the Council of Europe. See European Commission for Democracy through Law ("Venice Commission"), Report on the Rule of Law, adopted by the Venice Commission at its 86th plenary session, Venice, 25–26 March 2011, CDL-AD(2011)003rev.

adopt these components of the rule of law, they can increase their legitimation. Moreover, we argue that the conception of the rule of law outlined herein can capture its legitimatory potential better than two familiar concepts often used in international law and international relations research in this context: constitutionalization and legalization.

First, in international relations, the concept of legalization has been introduced to capture new features of international institutions and to explain improved compliance with international norms. Legalization refers to a process by which it is ensured that regulations fulfill certain criteria, such as clarity, pertinence, stringency, adaptability, and a high degree of consistency, both within themselves and in relation to other laws. Abbott, Keohane, Moravcsik, et al. (2000: 401) identify three elements in this process: "obligation," meaning that states or other actors are bound by a rule or a commitment; "precision," meaning that the rules accurately and unambiguously define the conduct that they require, authorize, or proscribe; and "delegation," meaning that authority has been granted to third parties to implement the rules, including their interpretation, application, dispute settlement, and further rule making. Whereas this concept of legalization has created a fruitful research program about why and when these institutional features are chosen, the concept is normatively thinner than that of the rule of law. It emphasizes the first two components of our rule of law conception and is essentially built on a notion of "rule by law." As already mentioned, although a rule by law may certainly be more beneficial than an arbitrary exercise of political power, it is hard to see how it, in itself, would be enough to convince the ruled of the legitimacy of an authority not otherwise bound to respect their will and their conceptions of the common good. Only legal equality, as the absence of arbitrary distinctions and privileges *within* the law, and the protection of individual rights can provide these assurances. Therefore, legalization alone is hardly able to legitimize international authority. For the legitimation of international authority, the components of legal equality and individual rights seem to be of special interest.

Our notion of rule of law is, however, thinner than most understandings of constitutionalization. Constitutionalization in general describes a process in which different legal orders are integrated by the establishment of an ultimate legal authority in the form of a (written or unwritten) constitution that serves as higher law and is bound to fundamental values (see Krisch 2010; Kumm 2009). Although this vision is intimately bound to the concept of rule of law, it goes further by prescribing the legal means through which it can be achieved. Given that the concept of constitutionalism involves a "limitational" (circumscribing the powers of public authorities) and a "foundational" (the ability of the constitutionalized community to govern itself) aspect, this project contains a strongly utopian flavor. As long as there is no common understanding of the community that needs to be constitutionalized, the lack of consensus may lead to fundamental conflicts and any step toward strong constitutionalization may be read as an instrument of power. As John Dryzek has put it, in some circumstances, "the peace is disturbed only by philosophers who believe a constitutional solution is required" (quoted after Krisch 2010: 64).

Against this background, legal pluralists therefore argue against the constitutionalist point of view and suggest that major components of an international rule of law can be established in the absence of a global constitution. According to this view, a world in which different political authorities exist without being integrated in a hierarchical order must not be detrimental to the rule of law. To be sure, one of the major objections to such a notion of legal pluralism or cosmopolitan constitutionalism (Kumm 2009) is that it cannot guarantee a stable rule of law and therefore cannot tap on its legitimatory potential. This seems to be a very strong statement, however, given a number of possibilities and mechanisms of how conflicts between different legal orders can be resolved. This may happen by means of mutual acceptance of general legal principles (Bogdandy 2010; Kumm 2009). There are also good arguments that these collisions have to be solved outside of the legal sphere, because they point to political matters (Waldron 1999). As Nico Krisch writes,

> The rule of law critique of pluralism in the postnational order is thus ultimately unconvincing. It overstates the degree to which law typically achieves certainty and predictability, and it exaggerates the place of the rule of law and integrity relative to other political values. As we have seen, important values in postnational politics – the need to reflect multiple competing polities and to enable strong contestation – can serve to justify compromises with rule of law ideals. (Krisch 2010: 250)

Moreover, law is always shaped to a large degree by the most powerful actors of the day. This is also true for constitutions that limit the possibility of future legal change and contestation. Given the enormous differences in power in the international system, a full process of constitutionalization may therefore reduce, rather than enhance, legitimacy. This is especially the case for weak states from the Southern hemisphere, which often indeed perceive constitutionalization as a project of prolonging Western dominance (see, e.g., Rajagopal 2003).

Against this background, we argue that the four components of the rule of law can display their advantages and create a legitimatory potential at the international level even in the absence of a global constitution – and possibly even better so. Moreover, the establishment of the components of the rule of law as just discussed can also be seen as a process that does not necessarily contradict the utopian ideal of constitutionalization. As Dieter Grimm (2009: 599) has recently argued forcefully, the constitutionalist state has developed in stages and needs to develop in stages. A single-minded focus on the rule of law sacrificing or at least subordinating all other sources of legitimacy, especially democratic participation and public contest, may in effect undermine the legitimatory force of the rule of law at the international level. Although the rule of law cannot function as the sole source of legitimacy for international public authority, we maintain that it could provide an anchor or a coral reef for international political legitimacy that would allow other sources of legitimacy to develop alongside it.

Therefore, in the remainder of this chapter, we focus on causal mechanisms that can create a dynamic as a result of which the growing authority of international organizations leads them to accept the rule of law as their guiding principle. We do this by focusing on individual rights. Although it has been argued elsewhere that other components of the rule of law are part of an emerging global administrative law (see Kingsbury, Krisch, and Stewart 2005) or general principles of international public authority (Bogdandy 2010), the obligation for international organizations to institutionalize protection of individual rights is a new and counterintuitive development that is in need of explanation and yet crucial to any international rule of law.

To sum up this section, we have argued that the introduction of an international rule of law – especially when it includes the components of legal equality and individual rights – can contribute to the urgently necessary legitimation of international institutions. This is, however, mainly a functional argument. The question, to be tackled in the next section, arises whether there are any developments in the real world that would make this possible. To do so, we focus on one area where the analogy between domestic and international rule of law norms seems particularly strong: We ask to which extent and through which causal mechanisms institutional rules for the protection of individual rights and equal implementation have developed in international organizations in the past decades. Let us put it differently: Through which mechanisms can the diffusion of the rule of law concept from the national to the international level take place?

4. INTERNATIONAL ORGANIZATIONS AND INDIVIDUAL RIGHTS

The very idea of law beyond the nation-state as a form of binding obligation is not easily accepted by many authors.[8] Most of their objections focus on a single dominant problem: As a defining criterion, any form of law requires legal certainty and neutral and impassionate application and, in this sense, equality before the law; its enforcement cannot accept any differences between actors not provided for by the law itself. This, in turn, requires that law meets with substantial overall compliance, for anything else would amount to arbitrary application and inequality before the law. In the international realm, however, widespread compliance can be guaranteed neither by an overarching monopoly of force nor by a strong sense of community, and it is for this reason that many authors contend that law beyond the nation-state

[8] Within the international relations literature, this is most prominently articulated by realists such as Mearsheimer (2003) and Waltz (1979). Nonetheless, even prominent legal theorists such as Hart (1961) often see at least the need to discuss doubts about the legal nature of international law and international obligations, even if only to argue against them.

as a form of binding obligation independent of the immediate exercise of power is impossible.

However, research in both international law and international relations has shown that this general position does not adequately capture the role of law beyond the nation-state. In fact, a considerable number of international norms achieve substantial degrees of compliance among their addressees, even though incentives to defect exist, and at times they even outperform the success of national norms in soliciting compliance (Zürn and Neyer 2005). Nor is this outcome surprising theoretically: There are a variety of alternative mechanisms that can explain the power of international law to induce compliance. The literature on legalization and the rational design of international institutions has convincingly shown that international law can be part of self-sustaining international institutions that benefit all members, even if they occasionally have to accept compliance with unwanted decisions (Abbott, Keohane, Moravcsik, et al. 2000; Koremenos, Lipson, and Snidal 2001); constructivists and international lawyers have likewise shown that internalized norms and even some bonds of community do exist in the international realm and help substantiate the role of law (cf. Byers 1999; Finnemore and Toope 2001; Franck 1988, 1990). Its role is certainly more tenuous in the international sphere than in well-established national legal systems, but the law is a relevant force in international life nonetheless.

This does not suffice, however, to ensure that international organizations can fully benefit from the legitimatory potential of the rule of law. As outlined before, the rule of law requires besides legal certainty and legal equality the protection of some individual rights. Only this leads to public norms that include limitations on the abuse of public power and thus display those features of fairness and impartiality that create legitimacy.[9] Given the current state of legalization in international affairs, among these components of the rule of law, it is probably the institutionalized protection of individual rights against international political authority that is the most remote from their traditional form of organization and hence the greatest political challenge for international organizations. It has also become an important issue of political contestation, and has thus considerable potential to advance – or to undermine – the legitimacy of international public authority. For these reasons, we focus in the remainder on concrete mechanisms that permit individuals to challenge violations of their individual rights. This includes rights to a process that meets the core principles of the rule of law, and to obtain redress and reparation when their rights have been violated. In accordance with this focus, we concentrate on international organizations because demands for the institutionalization of protection at the international level necessarily require at least some organizational capacity on this level.

9 See Finnemore and Toope (2001: 749), who refer back to the "internal morality of law" exposed by Fuller (1969).

At first, the development of such effective institutional mechanisms may seem unlikely. Processes of state-driven legalization of international institutions have usually been dominated by functional concerns to make these institutions more effective, which may not necessarily coincide with the best protection of individual rights.[10] Likewise, the invisible college, or the global community of international law, retains a strongly state-centric outlook. Although it attaches strong importance to the protection of individuals rights within international law, it does not consider issues of individual standing and individual access to legal remedies against international acts as a particularly high priority compared to other crucial contemporary dilemmas of international law, as evidenced by the fact that the International Law Commission's work on the responsibility of international organizations focuses on their responsibility toward states, not individuals (Hafner 2003: 236). Is there, then, any reason to expect institutional change in the direction of individualized human rights protections against international organizations and hence toward a meaningful form of a rule of law governing their actions?

Recent years have in fact seen a variety of developments in this direction. Several important international organizations, such as the regional development banks, have created compliance review mechanisms that allow groups of people to complain about violations of the respective organization's own standards and policies (cf. Suzuki and Nanwani 2005). UN and EU sanctions procedures against individuals have introduced limited possibilities to initiate review of an individual's inclusion in the respective sanctions lists (see Heupel 2009). Several organizations within the UN with direct political authority over individuals, such as UNHCR or the international transitional authority in Kosovo, have introduced or strengthened internal oversight mechanisms to prevent rights violations and have also opened up some channels for formalized complaints from individuals (cf. Pallis 2005 on UNHCR and Zajac-Sannerholm, this volume, on Kosovo). These developments are often hesitant and partial, reflecting the political difficulties of institutionalizing rights protections that we have discussed earlier, but they are still too broad and relevant to be ignored. Even more importantly, they are highly uneven: Some organizations adopt rights protection mechanism faster than others, and some do not adopt them at all; some organizations move closer toward the ideal of an individualized form of legal redress whereas others seem to stabilize at lower levels of protection. It is important to understand the nature and causes of this variation, and we maintain that the best way to do so is to look at the processes that may, or may not, bring about institutional change in international organizations.

10 See, e.g., Smrkolj (2008), who argues that some member-states' governments profit from limited protection of individual rights with respect to oversight mechanisms at UNHCR, and Suzuki and Nanwani (2005) concerning member-state interests in restrictions of inspection functions at multilateral development banks.

We are therefore concerned with the diffusion of rule of law norms to international organizations. Heupel and Zürn (2010) suggest that there are several alternative processes or mechanisms that might bring about a spread of institutional rules for the protection of individual rights among international organizations, and that these can be conceptualized along the lines proposed by studies about the diffusion of policies and political concepts among states (see, e.g., Simmons, Dobbin, and Garrett 2006). We follow this suggestion and adopt these mechanisms – learning, emulation, coercion, and competition – here, but we modify them as needed to account for the specificities of international organizations.[11]

First, it is possible that international organizations adopt individual rights protections because of *learning processes* that lead them to change their beliefs about the best means to achieve their objectives (tactical learning) or their beliefs about appropriate ends (deep learning; see Simmons et al. 2006: 795). Learning processes can follow from internal debates or research within an organization. Very often, however, they result from the interaction with outside experts or policy makers (Böhling 2001) or from the observation and analysis of other international organizations and their experiences.[12] Monika Heupel (2010), for example, argues that the UN Security Council increasingly relied on targeted rather than comprehensive sanctions during the 1990s in part because of tactical learning: Council members came to question the efficacy of comprehensive sanctions in obtaining regime change, and were at the same time confronted with expert advice by academics and NGOs that informed them about the possibility and promise of more specific targeted sanctions. Both contributed substantially to the ensuing policy change.

Learning implies a rational process of acquiring and processing new information. However, it is also possible that decision makers in international organizations simply copy practices from other organizations without analyzing in detail why these were introduced, what their costs and benefits are, and whether they would have similar effects in other organizations. This second mechanism may be labeled *emulation* (see also Mayer 1959 and Powell and DiMaggio 1991 on related concepts of isomorphism). A plausible example is the rapid spread of inspection mechanisms across multilateral investment banks. After lengthy debate, the World Bank introduced its Inspection Panel in late 1993, which allowed, for the first time, complaints to an independent body by people affected by a Bank project who allege violation of the World Bank's own policies. This represented a sharp departure from earlier practice at the World Bank and other multilateral development banks. Nevertheless, it rapidly gained followers: The Inter-American Development Bank established an inspection mechanism in 1994 and the African Development Bank in 1995 (Suzuki and Nanwani

[11] See Heupel and Zürn (2010) for a broader explication of this conceptual framework.

[12] This is in analogy to the argument of Simmons et al. (2006: 795) concerning the cross-national observation of policy effects.

2005: 188f.), at a time when it was still too early to have much information about the practices and success of the World Bank's Inspection Panel.

A third possible mechanism for the spread of individual rights protections is *coercion*, understood as the direct manipulation of incentives. The most obvious form of coercion is the use of material power, which has traditionally been the realm of powerful nation-states. In this perspective, it is governments that confront an international organization with demands linked to direct coercion. An interesting example is again the creation of the World Bank Inspection Panel. Within the World Bank group, the International Development Association facility gives out grants and subsidized loans and therefore regularly needs new capital. During negotiations with member-states on the periodic replenishment of the International Development Association, powerful members such as the United States conditioned approval of new funds on the creation of an inspection function, thereby using material power to add considerable momentum to the existing proposal of an inspection mechanism (Shihata 2000: 4f.; Suzuki and Nanwani 2005: 187).

Governments, however, are not the most likely candidates to impose individual rights protections. As already outlined here, they are first and foremost concerned with monitoring international organizations that act on their behalf and with minimizing agency slack. Thus, they may press for administrative law elements that strengthen the rule by law and reduce discretion by the international organization, but they are less likely to press for individual rights protections that might reduce an international organization's effectiveness. The World Bank's Inspection Panel, for example, ultimately reports noncompliance with World Bank policies to the member-state representatives that oversee its work, but it has no powers to grant individual redress or protection to the individuals who handed in a complaint in the first place (cf. Suzuki and Nanwani 2005). Where international organizations require the active cooperation of national authorities, however, national courts may also sometimes be in a position to coerce reforms if they are able to hinder national authorities from cooperating. In this vein, for example, the German Constitutional Court exerted pressure on the European Court of Justice (ECJ) in the 1970s and 1980s to expand the protection of individual rights in the European Community (EC) legal order by threatening to block the recognition of the supremacy of EC law in German courts (Slaughter 1994: 109, cf. concerning this conflict also Schimmelfennig 2006). Likewise, the ECJ recently annulled the implementation of UN Security Council sanctions against individuals in community law on grounds of individual rights violations (De Sena and Vitucci 2009: 221 et seq.; Heupel 2009: 314).

Moreover, coercion can also come from societal actors that directly oppose an international organization on the ground. In some cases – such as when implementing development projects – international organizations may also depend directly on the cooperation of local populations and hence be, to some degree, exposed to direct pressure on their part for greater procedural fairness and protection of individual rights. However, unlike state coercion from powerful states, affected societal actors will often lack the power to ultimately impose themselves on international organizations. A recent example is a prolonged sit-in by several thousand migrants in Egypt protesting against UNHCR practices and demanding, among other things, faster and fairer decisions about individual applications for refugee status. Despite repeated attempts, negotiations with UNHCR ultimately failed, and dozens of people died when the Egyptian state forcibly removed the protesters (Smrkolj 2008).

Societal actors, however, may also resort to more indirect forms of coercion, also referred to as soft coercion or as "blaming and shaming" (Keck and Sikkink 1998; Liese 2006), by publicly censuring international organizations. Again, this is not open to the most disadvantaged actors for lack of media access and public relations capabilities, but it is open to many transnational actors, such as international NGOs[13] and even particularly prominent individuals (on the role of such individuals in international relations, see Cooper 2007; Stein 2008). Public pressure from NGOs and media criticism were instrumental in bringing about a large-scale public investigation of allegations of abuse in UNHCR camps in West Africa, for example, while similar allegations of abuse in Nepal that did not arouse international media attention led only to a confidential internal investigation of uncertain outcome (Pallis 2005: 909).

Soft coercion thus can operate on two different levels. Public criticism can bring direct pressure on an international organization to change. In the case of blacklisted terrorist suspects, for example, transnational actors such as Human Rights Watch and Amnesty International criticized the UN Security Council directly for violations of due process, and they demanded change through their access to a variety of media and public forums, even though powerful member-state governments in the UN were slow to adopt the criticism themselves (cf. Heupel 2010). But public criticism can also mobilize domestic publics in powerful states, which in turn leads governments in these states to use more direct forms of material coercion to bring about change in an international organization. As mentioned earlier, for example, member-state threats to withhold funding were an important factor in reform debates at the World Bank. Lori Udall (1997) maintains that pressure by the U.S. Congress, in particular, was in return the result of NGO criticism against the World Bank that targeted U.S. lawmakers directly, thus leveraging U.S. national power to promote institutional change (Shihata 2000: 1). Thus, material coercion and blaming and shaming are not necessarily competing mechanisms but can also form part of a causal chain.

The final mechanism of diffusion identified by Simmons and her collaborators (Simmons et al. 2006) is *competition*, which would seem to be less suited to account for the introduction of individual rights protections in the practice of international organizations. International organizations do often have partly overlapping areas of activity, and can therefore find themselves in a competition for donor funds, projects, competences, and prestige. However, they generally compete for the approval of (certain crucial) member-states or donor states, not for the direct approval of societal

[13] See, e.g., Keck and Sikkink (1998) on their ability to censure national governments.

actors. Therefore, competition could create pressures for individual rights protections only if member-state governments consider the issue to be an important concern. Given that individual rights protection may hinder the direct implementation of international organization policies or conflict with national policies in host states, however, it is even possible that member-state governments may in some cases see strong rights protections as a comparative disadvantage, rather than an asset, of a certain international organization.[14]

Nevertheless, matters may change when international organizations depend on the cooperation of private actors and these actors can choose between different organizations to work with. Examples are those international dispute settlement mechanisms that allow direct access for private parties. In these cases, the role and relevance of the institution depend, among other things, on the willingness of private parties to bring their claims in this particular forum, which in turn depends on their evaluation of the institution. Here, it is quite plausible that private actors will often favor mechanisms that guarantee rule of law characteristics. Moreover, in those instances in which disputes are between states and individuals, the latter will also prefer institutions that adopt more expansive definitions of individual rights and are thus more likely to decide against a state party's public policies on grounds of individual rights. It would seem, for example, that the ECJ managed to attract many references initially through its aggressive stance on the assertion of the four freedoms in the internal market of the EC that led plaintiffs to favor national court referrals to Luxembourg (Stone Sweet and Brunell 1998; Stone Sweet and Sandholtz 1997). Similarly, in those instances where international organizations depend on diffuse support in broad publics in ascertaining their authority against competing institutions, they may also leverage individual rights protection as an issue strongly resonating with many national publics. Schimmelfennig (2006), for example, describes how both the ECJ and the European Court of Human Rights used the protection of individual rights provided by them as a key argument in attempts to assert judicial supremacy in Europe.

In this section, we have identified some of the mechanisms that point in favor of the diffusion of the rule of law norm. In doing so, we do not claim that the rule of law on the international level is already consistently present or necessarily coming. We deliberately focused on diffusion mechanisms that have created a certain dynamic; we did not systematically analyze the interests that work against such a diffusion, possible counterforces, and problems of conversion of the rule of law concept to the international level. Indeed, all the identified cases of movements toward institutionalized procedures for the protection of individual rights (with the possible exception

[14] As already mentioned, Smrkolj (2008), for example, makes the argument that member-state governments may have an active interest in UNHCR refugee status determinations that do not fully conform to due process standards for several policy reasons.

of the highly particular European cases) still have serious shortcomings. In addition, the development toward greater and more reliable protection of individual rights has often been slow and uneven, and other international organizations have not seen any significant change at all. There remain thus serious doubts whether this is a general movement that will go on and lead to a meaningful version of the rule of law concept. Understanding these problems and variations, and the causes behind them, is the major task ahead.

5. MOVING FROM CAUSAL MECHANISMS TO HYPOTHESES

The four mechanisms outlined herein provide four possible pathways to institutional change and seem to have been present in at least some important processes of international reform. In this sense, we can state that indeed some institutional mechanisms for the protection of human rights have developed in recent times. These processes are, however, obviously highly conditional. There is a need to better understand the conditions under which these causal mechanisms lead to the establishment of mechanisms for the protection of individual rights and thus a strengthening of the rule of law on the international level. Although definitively answering this question exceeds the scope of the present chapter, we want to make a first step in this direction by formulating testable hypotheses about the empirical implications of these four mechanisms. We do this by building on these causal mechanisms and asking which features of international organizations and regulations are most likely to trigger such mechanisms.

As we have already outlined, a first *general* hypothesis – applying to all causal mechanisms – underlying the present analysis is the idea that demands for increases in the rule of law, and in particular for institutionalized mechanisms to protect individual rights, will be addressed primarily at international organizations that exercise direct authority over individuals, whether they be development agencies implementing infrastructure projects on the ground, international courts for individuals and international transitional administrations exercising powers of police and criminal justice, or international organization officials deciding about the legal status of individual migrants. We do not generally expect such claims to be directed against international organizations that exercise political authority indirectly by crafting rules binding on their members. Of course, decisions by the World Trade Organization in dispute settlement or by the World Bank in setting structural adjustment conditionalities for loans have sparked political contestation and have led to serious opposition in many countries. However, we argue that these protests usually do not focus on improving mechanisms for the protection of individual rights; rather, they attack either policies as such or demand institutional reform in the direction of greater democratization (where they accept the need for international authority on the subject as such) or of renationalization of decisions. This is very distinct from demands to provide individualized justice through court-like procedures resembling administrative law.

> H1: *International organizations are more likely to face demands to institutionalize individual rights protection if they exercise direct authority over individuals.*

Change dynamics can arise through *learning processes* internal to an international organization, but this requires that the institution has sufficient capacities to reflect on its own practices and to discuss possible deficiencies openly. This is true even when expert advice from the outside can identify problems and provide suggestions for possible solutions, for even then the organization needs the necessary capacity to listen to, understand, and evaluate this advice. Consequently, the possibility of learning strongly depends on the devotion of resources to it.

> H2: *International organizations are more likely to institutionalize the protection of individual rights the more resources they devote for learning and reflection processes concerning their own practices.*

Moreover, in many fields of international relations, different international organizations overlap to some degree in their activities, but some institutions – often those with global reach as opposed to smaller regional institutions – will be larger, more visible, and more renowned than others. Where such hierarchies of prestige exist, the institutional setup of the lead institution(s) may provide a sort of focal point or standard for appropriate institutional settings. If the lead institution changes, therefore, others are likely to follow suit, *emulating* the leader.

> H3: *International organizations are more likely to introduce institutionalized protection of individual rights when a prominent international institution in their field has already done so.*

Exercising pressure or *coercion by nonstate actors* is contingent on certain conditions as well. Nongovernmental actors usually have to rely on media access if they want to expose and criticize individual rights violations by international organizations in a way that generates political momentum. Obtaining this access, however, depends on the media's own calculations about the relevance of certain news to their audience; this relevance increases as more members of this audience know of the organization and consider its work relevant and important. Consequently, nongovernmental actors have an easier time exposing wrongs committed by large, well-known international organizations than by more obscure organizations that may seem marginal to the casual media consumer.

> H4: *International organizations are more likely to face demands to institutionalize individual rights protection if they are more visible to and more well known by the general public in national forums.*

Moreover, the world media system is still dominated by news corporations based in major industrialized countries and with particular focus on the respective industrialized country markets. Likewise, media consumers in industrialized countries still tend to pay particular attention to the fates of their own nationals (as is reflected, for example, in the general media practice to report the number of affected nationals of one's own country when one is reporting about catastrophes occurring abroad). This bias suggests that the logic of the media system not only devotes more attention to some international organizations than to others but also to some victims of rights violations than to others. In particular, abuses by international political authority of nationals from industrialized countries are more likely to trigger public protests amplified through international media than abuses of authority affecting others.

> H5: *International organizations are more likely to face international demands to institutionalize individual rights protection the more they exercise direct political authority over nationals of industrialized countries.*

Blaming and shaming strategies (*coercion by nonstate actors*) are particularly powerful if they can confront an international organization with proof that it violates its own professed principles. This creates the interesting possibility of a so-called boomerang effect: International organizations that engage in the active promotion of rule of law ideas and in the dissemination of best practices in legal reform obviously commit themselves strongly to due process and human rights norms, even when it is not evident that they, themselves, always conform to these norms. In turn, they become particularly vulnerable to public criticism on these grounds and may experience particularly strong pressure to institutionalize protection of individual rights. In fact, even international law arguments about the responsibility of international organizations to respect human rights – despite the fact that they are not and generally cannot be members of most human rights treaties – often focus precisely on the legal prohibition to act inconsistently with their own public support for these norms.

> H6: *International organizations are more likely to face demands to institutionalize individual rights protection if they are engaged in rule of law promotion or in international mechanisms for the protection of human rights.*

The use of *coercion by states*, in turn, depends on two crucial factors: disposition of sufficient coercive powers and willingness to use them to create institutional change. As already explained, member-state governments and parliaments – at least in some states – will have the greatest access to coercive resources. Nonetheless, they will often lack the will to use it because they are afraid that institutionalized mechanisms to protect individuals may compromise effective policy action by the respective organization. However, governments do face problems of controlling actions by international organizations and have incentives to use outsider information to monitor whether international organizations, as their agents, comply with the instructions they give them. We therefore expect governments to take a more narrow view of an international rule of law that focuses on compliance review rather than individual protection and redress.

> H7: *International organizations are more likely to institutionalize compliance review procedures (as pure oversight mechanisms without a mandate to use judicial remedies) when there is otherwise greater scope for them to deviate from member-state instructions.*

Finally, societal actors will often hold strong preferences for greater institutional safeguards protecting their rights, but they will be unable to force the issue. Sometimes, however, and in particular in legal disputes, they may have some liberty to chose among alternative forums to bring their claims, and it may be in the institutional interest of each forum to be attractive to complainants or plaintiffs. In this case, different dispute resolution mechanisms or courts may indeed compete on the extent that they credibly safeguard individual rights (*competition*).

> H8: *International organizations charged with dispute resolution or adjudication are more likely to institutionalize the protection of individual rights when they depend on the forum choice of societal actors.*

6. CONCLUSION AND THE BLACK SPOTS

The protection of individual rights from any kind of political authority, including that of international organizations, always involves difficult and contentious conflicts. This holds even more true in those instances in which the objective is not only to redress individual wrongdoings, but also to induce institutional changes to prevent or correct further rights violations in the future. Nevertheless, our chapter has shown that there is nothing per se utopian about institutionalized protection of individual rights against international authority: There are a variety of mechanisms that can potentially bring about the political momentum for such legalized forms of rights protection, and there are considerable signs of movement in this direction among important existing international organizations. What we now need is a more comprehensive empirical investigation that ascertains whether these mechanisms are valid beyond individual examples, whether the hypotheses derived from these four mechanisms do account for the variation to be observed, and whether some of them are more powerful in explaining institutional changes than others. Only then will we be able to comprehensively assess the scope and depth of the creation of individualized rights protection mechanisms, and see more clearly where they are or are not likely to arise.

But to the extent that such reform does occur, we can also see now that it raises important questions about the possibility, or impossibility, of separating legal redress from democratic forms of accountability. International organizations increasingly rule directly or indirectly over individuals and are thus expected to follow the standards of due process and fundamental rights. Nevertheless, although the rule of law contributes to the promotion of political legitimacy, it is not itself sufficient to guarantee it. International authorities, while getting more influential in determining political outcomes, also generally lack democratic accountability and participatory mechanisms ensuring a voice for all those affected by their decisions. Instead, their decision-making setting is still most often characterized by executive multilateralism premised on diplomatic deal-making behind closed doors. This raises empirical and normative challenges even beyond an international rule of law, two of which shall be mentioned here.

Empirically speaking, powers of legal redress have a polyvalent use not limited to individual rights protection: True, often enough, court filings against public action seek to prevent or undo direct harm to individual human rights. In many cases of administrative law, though, as in actions against planning processes for public infrastructure projects such as roads and airports, the issue is less clear-cut, and the plaintiff rather seeks to obtain a say in the public decision process. Here, the threat of legal obstruction provides it with the necessary bargaining chip to obtain access to administrative decision-making forums that would otherwise not be open to it. Will we see similar developments in the case of international organizations? Will local populations, for example, demand and perhaps obtain a greater voice in the planning of development programs through the threat of Inspection Panel action if the World Bank should fail to incorporate them into the process?

Normatively, the authority of international organizations is not limited to cases of direct individual authority but extends much further by affecting major general policy decisions, and this leaves us with important cases of probable nonreform. Structural adjustment programs and other loan conditionalities, for example, can undoubtedly have strong implications for individual human rights, yet they are both mediated through the implementing national government and largely unsuited to traditional forms of legal control guaranteed by the rule of law. In domestic settings, the only solution to this dilemma has been the reinforcement of democratic control over decisions of this magnitude. Can we expect similar changes in international organizations? If not, what will be the consequences for their legitimacy?

4

New Modes of Governance and the Rule of Law

The Case of Transnational Rule Making

Gunnar Folke Schuppert

The aim of this chapter is to discuss new modes of governance from a constitutional law perspective. This endeavor implies the following three assumptions: First, it makes sense to speak of new modes of governance; second, if we can identify new modes of governance then it is to be expected that they raise questions in terms of principles of constitutional law; and third, rule of law principles can be introduced as a normative yardstick in the discussion about the general problem of constitutionalizing transnational rule making as one of the most prominent examples for new modes of governance.

1. TRANSNATIONAL RULE MAKING AS A NEW MODE OF GOVERNANCE

1.1. *Identifying New Modes of Governance*

For our understanding, the concept of governance is a "dynamic concept" (Botzem, Hofmann, Quack, Schuppert, and Strassheim 2009); that is to say, we are confronted with an ongoing process of change in the field of governance, with changing governance arrangements emerging as a response to changing challenges in societal and economic development on a daily basis (Kempa, Sheering and Burris 2006). Therefore, we do not belong to the friends of the narrative of "new" governance, and we would prefer to speak of "changes in governance." Despite this skepticism in regard to the "new" governance label, it is useful and, for further analysis even necessary, to identify those areas of changes in governance where theses processes are so dynamic and so visible that it makes sense to speak of new modes of governance. For identifying such areas of change I recommend a methodological approach, which has been developed in a working group on governance at the Social Science Research Centre Berlin (see Botzem et al. 2009). This approach can be called the four-headlamps or four-spotlights model, and it consists of the following four guiding questions:

1. Do we meet (in a certain policy field) new actors or new actor constellations?
2. Can we observe new institutional arrangements or new modes of regulation?
3. Are we witnessing the blurring of traditional borderlines – between public and private, national and international, formal and informal?
4. What do these new actor constellations, new institutional arrangements, and especially the blurring of borderlines mean in terms of democratic legitimacy and the rule of law principles?

These four questions should enable us to identify significant areas of change.

If we looked for policy fields that could serve as the proverbial proof of the pudding of this headlamp model, several areas of changes in governance would come to mind. An extremely prominent candidate would certainly be the governance of financial markets with new actors (rating agencies, hedge funds), hybrid forms of regulation (Basel I and II), and the mushrooming of new institutional arrangements in the field of financial oversight and the restructuring of collapsed banking systems another candidate would be the process of decoupling of state and law, characterized by an increasing hybridization and privatization of lawmaking. "Our" candidate that I want to discuss in this chapter is transnational lawmaking as the core of transnational governance, because I think that this candidate best illustrates the relationship between a new form of governance and the necessity to conceptualize constitutional principles such as the rule of law for developments beyond the nation-state.

2. TRANSNATIONAL GOVERNANCE BY TRANSNATIONAL RULE MAKING AS A NEW MODE OF GOVERNANCE

The governance area or governance realm that is referred to as transnational governance (Djelic and Sahlin-Andersson 2006) is a space located somewhere beyond the reach of the nation-state and below the legal regime of international law and the authority of international organizations. In this space without clear-cut frontiers there seems to be a need for transnational rules and transnational governance structures, a finding that has been put by Dieter Grimm (2003) as follows.[1]

> But beyond the nation state and the reach of international organizations modes of law making come into being, which cannot be influenced by states and international organizations. Global markets create regulations by themselves – independent of politics. In case of conflict courts of arbitration are the conflict-solving actors, applying a transnational law, which is to a large degree shaped by themselves and which is used as a template in similar cases thus spreading all over the world.

Taking these findings as a starting point, we can now try to describe the phenomenon of transnational governance in terms of the aforementioned four-headlamps model.

[1] I translated this quote.

First, thinking in the category of new actors or new actor constellations, not only do we find a lot of them in the transnational realm but this space seems to be a perfect environment for the mushrooming of the type of actors that are characteristic of governance beyond the nation-state. We meet transnational standards setters such as "standard-setting committees" in the field of accounting standards, transnational norm-building networks (Mückenberger 2008) such as stewardships in different policy fields, transgovernmental networks as institutional backbones of a new world order (Slaughter 2004), and – last but not least – actors such as rating agencies that are of the utmost importance for the governance of financial markets.

Second, if we look for new modes of regulation, we have to explore – in comparison with the legal system of the nation-state – a different world of rules, characterized by the growing importance of standards created, for instance, by the International Standards Organization (ISO); codes of conduct of international corporations such as Shell or BP; and transnational contracts that are part of a new branch of governance labeled "contract governance" (Schuppert 2010a).

Third, the most striking and – in terms of legitimacy and the rule of law – most challenging finding is the observable blurring of traditional borderlines, especially between public and private, formal and informal, and national and international. The examples of this erosion of borderlines in the transnational realm are so numerous that it might indeed be helpful to develop a "theory of hybridity" (Gillespie 2009; Trubek, Cottrell, and Nance 2005). Only one example shall be mentioned here: the erosion of the classic borderlines between binding and nonbinding norms by the process referred to as "the hardening of soft law" (for more information see Schuppert 2010b).

Fourth, it is more than obvious that new actor constellations, new modes of rule making, and the blurring of traditional borderlines raise a lot of questions in terms of legitimacy and accountability. The accountability problem is especially difficult to solve now that traditional chains of accountability become less omnipresent: How do we hold a network responsible, and how shall we deal with hybrid organizations? These questions are often addressed but rarely answered, and if progress is to be made in this difficult area a rethinking of the concepts of accountability and legitimacy is needed (Scharpf 2005). However, it is not only and not primarily the problem of so-called democratic governance that I want to discuss in this chapter; we are rather focusing on the rule of law principles, and we want to find out how rule of law becomes the normative yardstick in this field of transnational governance. Before we ask the hopefully correct questions in this regard, it might be useful to reassure ourselves what we mean when talking about transnational governance.

3. TRANSNATIONAL GOVERNANCE AS REGULATORY GOVERNANCE

Transnational governance is about rule making (Schuppert 2010b), mainly by non-state actors, but also by transgovernmental networks as the typical mode of coordination in the architecture of transnational governance (Slaughter 2000). Both types

TABLE 4.1. *Modes of global standard setting*

	Actors	Address	Enforcement	Accountability
Private standardizing	Standard setters, standard users, enforcement agents	Best practice for many: "to whom it may concern"	Legal, market exit, evaluation by information intermediaries	Low
Committee standardizing	Transnational committee of regulators, private lobbying, and consulting	Best practice for public administration	Peer review, market pressure	Medium
Network standardizing	Transnational committee of regulators supervising national self-regulation of public and private actors	Identity of regulator and regulatee: rolling best-practice rules for the regulators	Peer review	High
Organizational standardizing	Decision making supervised by members	Standards for members	Compulsory for members	High, similar to directives

of actors replace and substitute for the nonexisting world legislator: It is their "job" to fill the "regulatory gap" that is characteristic of the transnational governmental space. In this sense, transnational governance can be understood as "regulatory governance" (Schuppert 2006). Three examples may illustrate transnational regulatory governance at work.

3.1. *Standard Setting as Regulatory Governance*

Standards are rules enacted by standard-setting bodies, which are nonbinding in a legal sense but in practice can claim a high degree of compliance. From a functional perspective, standardization is perhaps the most important mode of regulatory governance, a judgment made by Niels Brunsson and Bengt Jacobson (2000) in the introduction to their book *A World of Standards* as follows: "To regulate is, in our view, to create and propagate rules. We do not view regulation as something narrow and largely technical, although some standardisers would have us believe that it is. On the contrary, regulation should be seen as rule-making in a broad sense, as a form of organized governance."

Within this broad field of governance by standard setting, we can discern different modes of transnational standards brought into being by different types of standard setters; Dieter Kerwer (2005: 626) suggests the useful typology shown in Table 4.1.

Standard setting is, under the condition of globalization, a "transnational business" performed mainly by nonstate transnational actors as a private-sector alternative to what were formerly state activities; in the words of Bridget Hutter (2006: 73), "Ericson, Doyle, and Barry (2003) explicitly link the growth of insurance to governance beyond the state and the need for private sector alternatives to formerly state activities. And the alternatives which emerge are often transnational with their institutional territories transcending state boundaries."

3.2. *Setting up Codes of Conduct as Transnational Rule Making*

3.2.1. Codes of Conduct and International Business

The phenomenon of codes of conduct as a mode of self-regulation is closely related to the increasing globalization of economic activities on the one hand and the simultaneously starting career of the concept of corporate social responsibility on the other. U.S. companies began introducing such codes in the early 1990s, and the practice spread to Europe in the mid-1990s. Voluntary codes of conduct range from vague declarations of business principles applicable to international operations to more substantive efforts as a mode of effective self-regulation. They tend to focus on the impact of transnational corporations (TNCs) in two main areas: social conditions and the environment. A variety of stakeholders, including international trade union organizations, development and environmental nongovernmental organizations (NGOs), and the corporate sector itself, have played a role in the elaboration of codes of conduct for international business.

According to a classification of codes of conduct suggested by the report of the United Nations Research Institute for Social Development (Jenkins 2001), the following five types of codes of conduct could be distinguished:

- Company codes, mainly by TNCs. A famous example is Shell's Revised Statement of General Business Principles.
- Trade association codes, adopted by a group of internationally acting firms in a particular industry. Examples are the Bangladesh Garments Manufacturers and Exporters Association code and the Kenya Flower Council code.
- Multi-stakeholder codes, adopted as a result of negotiations between industry, NGOs or trade unions, and governments. A well-known example is the United Kingdom's Ethical Trade Initiative Base Code.
- Model codes, designed to provide a benchmark of what a particular organization regards as good practice in terms of codes of conduct.
- Intergovernmental codes, negotiated at an international level and agreed to by national governments. Examples are the Organization for Economic Cooperation and Development's Guidelines for Multinational Enterprises and the International Labour Organization's Tripartite Declaration of Principles Concerning Multinational Enterprises.

3.2.2. Contextual Factors in Favor of the International Career of Codes of Conduct

In his report written for the United Nations Research Institute for Social Development, Rhys Jenkins (2001) has identified several contextual factors that contributed to the impressive international career of codes of conduct; I pick up three of them that are, from my point of view, the most important.

The first aspect I want to highlight is the obvious relationship between codes of conduct and "governance by reputation." Especially TNCs in the field of extractive industries are under close observation by NGOs, which are professionalized in "naming and shaming" as a mode of immense public pressure. However, a company such as Nike, which spends heavily on advertisement and promotion to establish a corporate image, is also highly vulnerable to a loss of reputation and therefore willing to set up and comply with a code of conduct.

The second factor consists of changing public attitudes; in particular, the awareness of environmental issues has increased significantly. Companies in the North can no longer ignore the impact of their activities on the environment with impunity.

Last but not least, changes in the world of communication have to be taken into account. The developments in global communication have not only enabled corporations to control production activities on an ever-widening scale but they have also facilitated the international transmission of information that companies would prefer not to have widely disseminated. The speed with which information about working conditions in a subsidiary or subcontractor of a multinational corporation somewhere in Asia can be made available to NGOs and consumers in North America is unprecedented (Jenkins 2001: 8).

3.3. *Some Short Interim Remarks*

After these short visits to the world of standards and the world of codes of conduct, we can summarize that classic lawmaking by statutory law enacted and passed by parliament as the prototype of a legitimate lawmaking body gets more and more accompanied by other modes of rule making with other types of rules, other rule-making bodies, and other forms of sanctions. These findings seem to be especially true for the transnational sphere, and these modes of rule making can be regarded as a typical instrument of transnational governance.

Therefore, it seems to be a good idea to look for a conceptual umbrella for these new modes of rule making in the transnational realm, and my chapter would perhaps be regarded as incomplete if we did not take a look – at least a very short one – at a phenomenon that has been labeled "transnational law."

3.4. *Regulatory Governance by Transnational Law?*

Some scholars in the field of legal theory have identified a "new" type of law that they call "transnational law" and that can be understood through a "post-etatistic

TABLE 4.2. *Tetra lemma of global law*

(4) Neither–nor: transnational	(2) The other: international
(1) The one: national	(3) Both: supranational

approach" (Calliess 2006) as an alternative to traditional, state-centered law, enacted by the regulatory power of a transnational civil society. Alongside the domestic–international dichotomy that marked international law for a very long time, transnational law offers itself as a supplementary and challenging category within interdisciplinary research on globalization and law. Transnational law "breaks the frames" (Teubner 1997a) of traditional thinking about interstate relationships by pointing to the myriad forms of border-crossing relations among state and nonstate actors.

Gralf Peter Calliess (2006: 218), who presented the most elaborated theoretical concept of transnational law, explains the peculiarity of this type of law by drawing our attention to the tetralemma of global law, shown in Table 4.2. In this definition, transnational law is neither national nor international law, and also the in-between category of supranational law is not appropriate: "transnational law is a new category of law beyond the traditional state law."

Transnational law is rooted in a global civil society, based on general principles, and it offers private actors alternative forms of dispute settlement by courts of arbitration that implement and shape this transnational law. The main example for this new type of law is the *lex mercatoria*, going back as Ancient Law Merchant to medieval times; other examples referred to are the regulation of the Internet – *lex informatica* – and the very tight regulation of sports – *lex sportiva*.

I personally doubt very much that these interesting modes of self-regulation deserve the label of a new type of law. There is no empirical proof for the existence of *lex mercatoria* – the main example for transnational law – (Ipsen 2009) and the *lex sportiva* is a regulatory regime with all the qualities of a hard-law regime set up by professional sports organizations within an elaborated quasi-judicial system of conflict solving with a Court for Arbitration for Sport (CAS) in Lausanne at the very top. A civil society inspired self-organizing law seems to be more of a myth than a phenomenon within the actually existing world of rules.

Let us therefore leave aside the trendy category of transnational law and proceed to this question: What is special and what is problematic about transnational rule making?

3.5. *What Is Special about Transnational Rule Making and What Is Problematic in Terms of Constitutional Law?*

3.5.1. Peculiarities of Transnational Rule Making

If we look back to the examples for transnational rule making, it is quite obvious that all these modes of rule making are so different in origin and character – from security standards to hybrid rule making by state-approved corporate governance codices – that they do not fit into a passé-partout. Despite all these differences, some common features can however be found; following the observations of Stefan Oeter (2008) and Christian Tietje (2001, 2002), we can identify four peculiarities of transnational rule making:

1. The first point is the deterritorialization of lawmaking. Although the concept of law of the modern state is an etatistic and territorial one (Sassen 2006), lawmaking under the conditions of globalization is a complex arrangement of territorial and deterritorialized law structures.
2. The second characteristic feature is the blurring of the traditional borderline between binding and nonbinding norms. Lawmaking in a globalized world is a complex mix of nonbinding, semibinding, and legally binding norms, a mix of soft and hard law, and – to make it even more complicated – processes of hardening of soft law.
3. The third aspect is an observable change from top-down lawmaking to a bottom-up system. Although traditional lawmaking was a state-centered top-down process, modern transnational rule making is a process in which different actors and mechanisms are involved in network-style "law production."
4. Above all – and that is the fourth point – we witness a common trend to informality (Oeter 2008); informal rule-making is not only a way to regulate when a legislative power is missing (for the role of soft law, see Senden, 2004) it also seems to have many advantages in terms of flexibility and effectiveness which make it become more and more popular.

3.5.2. The Problem of Transnational Rule Making: It Is Not Lawmaking, but It Looks Like Lawmaking

The paradox of transnational rule making is rooted in the fact that these rules are generally nonbinding in a legal sense, meaning that they do not belong to the world of hard law, however they do look like and function equally as law. The best example is again the business of standard setting; Harm Schepel (2005) has pointed out quite clearly that, from a functional perspective, standard setting is lawmaking:

> In reality, of course, it is very seldom that standards are derived from the customs and practices of social life or deduced from the immutable laws of nature. Standards are products of discussion, negotiation, deliberation and compromise between engineers, manufacturers, academic experts, professionals, trade unionists, representatives of consumer organisations and public officials meeting in boards, committees, task forces and working groups in associations and other organisations. They bring to the table economic, political, moral and technical arguments and ultimately arrive at a solution that will to some extent hurt some groups and in some degree benefit others – consumers or producers, importers or domestic manufacturers.

> Standardisation is a microcosm of social practices, political preferences, economic calculation, scientific necessity, and professional judgement. Standardization looks a lot like lawmaking.

If these findings are right, then questions of constitutional law come in automatically: How do we deal with a growing industry of lawmaking that is not governed by constitutional guidelines which normally have to be applied to the procedures of statutory law? Lothar Michael (2005: 449) has put these questions as follows: "If private standards have to be legitimized and if they are – as it is the case here – incompatible with the tenants of democratic legitimacy, new ways of input-legitimation have to be found. The aim cannot be a comprehensive democratization which transforms society into a state-like phenomenon. The task is to set up a minimum of procedural requirements which ensure an input-legitimacy of private standards."

If we follow the arguments, that on the one hand transnational rule making needs to be legitimized and that – on the other hand – this mode of law production is, for structural reasons, not directly guided by constitutional law, then the solution could probably be found in the idea of constitutionalization as a way to foster the guiding force of constitutionalism in areas beyond the nation-state. We should therefore have a closer look at the popular narrative of constitutionalization.

4. CONSTITUTIONALIZING TRANSNATIONAL RULE MAKING?

4.1. *The Popular Narrative of Constitutionalization*

The project of constitutionalization is "in" and the number of books and essays on the subject is increasing rapidly (see De Wet 2006; MacDonald and Johnston 2005; Peters 2006). Within the project of constitutionalization we should distinguish between two phases of development: The first phase we can call "Constitutionalization I" as a reaction to the processes of privatization, outsourcing and the like – processes that endangered the capacity of the constitution to fulfill its claim of establishing and regulating all public power that has an impact on the territory where the constitution is in force. This phase titled Constitutionalization I can be understood as an answer to an internal erosion of the steering capacity of the constitution.

Now the perspective shifts from the internal to the external erosion of the constitution's regulatory claim by processes of internationalization and transnationalization. With regulatory powers being transferred to international and transnational governance actors, those actors' activities escape the scope of national constitutions. This Constitutionalization II project has recently been described by Dieter Grimm (2010a: 2) as follows:

> One response to this development has been the attempt to elevate constitutionalism to the international level. The recent boom of the term "constitutionalization"

is an indicator of this tendency. Different from traditional constitution-making, it describes not an act by which a constitution takes legal force, but a process which eventually ends up in a constitution. Such processes are already underway. The Charter of the United Nations as well as the statutes of other international organisations such as the World Trade Organisation are interpreted as constitutions. Even global public policy networks and self-organisation processes of private global actors are discussed in terms of constitutionalism – all objects which were not regarded as constitutions just a few years ago.

Despite the fact that this concept of constitutionalization is booming, I am skeptical that this really is the appropriate wording for the endeavor of fostering the guiding power of constitutional principles. If we take constitutionalization seriously and if we stick to the concept of constitutionalism as it has developed since the terms of enlightenment (see Grimm 2010a: 8–9) with its basic elements of

- being a set of legal norms,
- regulating the establishment and the exercise of all public power, and
- originating from the people being the only legitimate source of power,

then this concept is comprehensive and ambitious, leading at its very end to worldwide governance structures reigned by constitutional principles (of a Western type). I do think that calling the intended upgrade of law in the context of global governance "constitutionalization" is misleading; what the "friends of constitutionalization" have in mind is not the establishment of a global constitution, but the fostering of processes of legalization or juridification, in German *Verrechtlichungsprozesse* (Zangl and Zürn 2004) – based on – and that is the close relation to constitutionalism – *general legal principles*.

What, from my point of view, is really going on and should be going on are processes of fostering the guiding force of general legal principles based on and routed in the concept of constitutionalism. If these processes, which we can name with Bernhard Zangl (2010) a way to the international reign of law,[2] are the very heart of the project of constitutionalization, then we have to answer two questions: What are these general legal principles? What is their constitutional source? If we conceptualize the problem of constitutionalization like this, then the rule of law steps in automatically. The rule of law not only constitutes the backbone of constitutional thinking but it can also be split up – and that is an important comparative advantage with regard to other general concepts such as democracy or welfare – into a set of core elements agreed upon by a worldwide law community and can – as I will show – serve as a normative framework for rule making beyond the nation-state.

[2] The German title of the book recently edited by Bernhard Zangl is *Auf dem Weg zu internationaler Rechtsherrschaft*.

Before I start to develop some thoughts in this direction, I present and discuss two ongoing processes of *Verrechtlichung* that can be understood as inspired by the principle of rule of law.

4.2. *Two Rules of Law-Inspired Projects as Modes of Constitutionalizing Rule Making Beyond the Nation-State*

In contrast to the national level, where the constitution provides guidelines for the process of lawmaking – see Chapter X of the German Grundgesetz dealing with *Gesetzgebung* – actors at the transnational level have to operate without constitutional guidelines. Obviously, however, there is a need for rules, which offer constitution-like guidance for rule making, rules act as a functional equivalent, filling this so-called regulatory gap. Indeed, in the transnational sphere we do find some initial stages in the development of a framework for governing nonstate rule making, stages that can be regarded as modes of constitutionalization in a broader sense; I introduce two of these briefly.

4.2.1. Rules for Rule Making

It is not even a new or revolutionary idea to develop rules for rule making. Some scholars in the field of lawmaking theory proclaim the necessity of a general code for the "production" of laws as being a part of a comprehensive *Gesetzgebungslehre* (Lücke 2001). Others suggest a checklist as a guiding framework for "good legislation," but all these ambitious efforts have had no real success because they collided with the reality of the political process of lawmaking, which follows its own rules and logic (Schuppert 2003).

However, what does exist on the national level is a body of rules for appropriate lawmaking, incorporated in a procedural code for ministries as the decisive units in terms of preparing and drafting laws. This code – which is not very well known by social scientists – is called "Gemeinsame Geschäftsordnung der Bundesministerien, GGO" and the addressees of this code are not the citizens and the general public but the ministries being the very heart not only of the bureaucratic but also the legislative state: More than 80 percent of all law drafts are – before reaching the parliamentary arena – worked out by ministries, which should have the necessary expertise for that job (for the increasingly popular trend of outsourcing drafting laws, see Schuppert 2010b). This code, which can be characterized as a form of inner-state law, claims that every draft law has to be based on written reasoning, must discuss the possible regulatory alternatives, and should inform the members of parliament and the public about the costs to be expected and recently – as part of policies fighting bureaucracy – the "administrative burdens" for citizens and entrepreneurs.

In the transnational arena other ways of setting up rules for rule making must be found; again, the example of standardization is very helpful. As Harm Schepel (2005) has observed, nearly all big standard setters have set up "standardization standards," laying down minimal standards including the following requirements:

1. Elaboration of draft standards in technical committees with a balance of represented interests (manufacturers, consumers, social partners, public authorities);
2. A requirement of consensus on the committee before the draft goes to
3. A round of public notice and comment, with the obligation on the committee to take received comments into account, and
4. A ratification vote, again with the requirement of consensus rather than mere majority, among the constituency of the standards body, and
5. The obligation to review standards periodically.

As an example of this mode of self-regulation, I quote from the *Code of Good Practice for Standardization* (ISO/IEC Guide 59, first edition 1994), which contains, among others, the following general provisions:

> 3.1 This code is intended for use by any standardizing body, whether governmental or non-governmental, at international, regional, national or sub-national level.
>
> 4.1 Written procedures based on the consensus principle should govern the methods used for standards development. Copies of the procedures of the standardizing body shall be available to interested parties in a reasonable and timely manner upon request.
>
> 4.2 Such written procedures should contain an identifiable, realistic and readily available appeals mechanism for the impartial handling of any substantive and procedural complaints.
>
> 4.3 Notification of standardization activity shall be made in suitable media as appropriate to afford interested persons or organizations an opportunity for meaningful contributions.
>
> 4.6 All standards should be reviewed on a periodic basis and revised in a timely manner. Proposals for the development of new or revised standards, when submitted according to appropriate procedures by any materially and directly interested person or organization, wherever located, should be given prompt consideration.
>
> 6.1 Participation in standardization processes at all levels shall be accessible to materially and directly interested persons and organizations within a coherent process as described in this clause.

But scholars working in the field of standardization have also presented principles for the organization of standard setting. Kristina Tamm Hallström (2006) – one of the leading experts in this field – has identified four such principles, which should be taken into account by standard-setting organizations (see Figure 4.1). Summing up these findings, they show a very clear effort to constitutionalize a certain mode of rule making by developing a framework of general principles that would be a prominent candidate for drafting a transnational constitution.

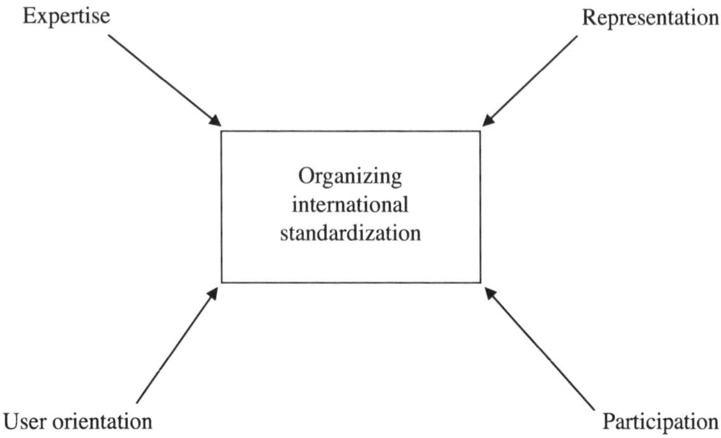

FIGURE 4.1. Four principles of organization for an international standardization body.

4.2.2. The Project of a Global Administrative Law

If we start again with the nation-state, administrative action is framed by an "administrative procedure act" (*Verwaltungsverfahrensgesetz*) and by general principles of administrative law (*Allgemeines Verwaltungsrecht*). This is a common standard in continental Europe, and these general principles – including traditional administrative law rights such as participation, transparency, reasoned decision, proportionality, and reasonableness (Cassese 2005: 691) – can be regarded as basic norms in the field of public administration and by their character of being *Grundlagengesetze* (Hufen 1998) as a mode of constitutionalization in a broader sense.

Switching from the national to the transnational level, we meet a field of public administration, which is not ordered and structured as well as it is the case in the national context, but consisting of a variety of governance actors including nonstate actors and hybrid institutional arrangements. The Global Administrative Law (GAL) Project of the New York University Law School[3] suggests that we distinguish the following five types of transnational administration:

- International Administration, by formal international organization;
- Network Administration, based on collective action by transnational networks of cooperative arrangements between national regulatory officials (such as the Basel Committee of national bank regulators);
- Distributed Administration conducted by national regulators under treaty, network, or other cooperative regimes;
- Hybrid Administration, by hybrid intergovernmental-private arrangements (such as ICANN); and

[3] Information is available at http://iilj.org/GAL.

- Private Administration, by private institutions with regulatory functions (such as the ISO).

Although these types of administration are mainly performing what we have called regulatory governance, their addressees are not only the state and other public entities – like in the traditional international law – but – as a consequence of their "behind the border issues" (Zürn 2006) – individuals, corporations, or even NGOs. Kingsbury, Krisch, and Stewart (2005: 23) summarize these findings as follows:

> Traditionally understood, the subjects of international law are states. . . . Increasingly however, regulatory programs agreed to at the international level by states are effectuated through measures taken by governments at the domestic level to regulate private conduct. . . . But the real addressees of such global regulatory regimes are now increasingly the same as in domestic law: namely, individuals (as both moral agents and economic and social actors), and collective entities like corporations and, in some cases, NGOs.

If these findings are right – and we have no reason to doubt them – a legal framework of the administrative law type is urgently needed. This is the convincing starting point of the GAL Project (Kingsbury et al. 2005; Krisch and Kingsbury 2006), which aims to "constitutionalize" transnational public administration by general legal principles of administrative law rooted deeply in the rule of law. Therefore – this is my reading of the project – the GAL Project is in its essence a rule of law project. The text on the homepage of the project is quite clear in this respect:

> Much of global governance can be understood as regulatory administration. Such regulatory administration is often organized and shaped by principles of an administrative law character. Building on these twin ideas, we argue that a body of global administrative law is emerging. This is the law of transparency, participation, review, and above all accountability in global governance. . . . Exercises of public power in the global administrative space are increasingly channelled, and controlled, by mechanisms of an administrative law type. These include rules requiring greater transparency, adoption of notice-and-comment procedures in rule-making, and the opening of new or strengthened avenues of judicial and administrative review.

Reading this project's statement reminds us very much of the project discussed before, the development of a guiding framework for standardization; both projects are normative projects aiming at a consensus about general principles applicable for all regulatory activities beyond the nation-state. Going back again to the statement of the GAL Project, it is clearly spelled out: "We describe this field of law as 'global' rather than 'international' to encompass the enmeshment of national and intergovernmental regulation, the increasing roles of private regulators and public-private hybrid bodies, the wide array of informal institutional arrangements that now operate alongside formal institutions, and the foundations of the field in normative practices, and normative sources, that extend beyond international law sources."

5. CONCEPTUALIZING THE RULE OF LAW AS A NORMATIVE FRAMEWORK FOR RULE MAKING BEYOND THE NATION-STATE

5.1. *The Rule of Law Principles as a Set of Second-Order Principles*

I cannot discuss all the competing definitions of the rule of law here (see Kleinfeld 2006); I also want to leave aside the interesting and politically important question of whether a "thinner" or a "thicker" concept of the rule of law would be appropriate (for the main arguments in favor and against, see Schuppert 2008). What I can do, however, is to build on the observable consensus in the literature to find elements of the rule of law that can be regarded as a minimum concept of it, paying particular attention to including all those elements that are indispensable for a working concept in the reality of statehood (for the changing world of statehood, see Schuppert 2010c).

Looking for a list of such widely agreed elements of the rule of law I came across the following table (Table 4.3), presented in an article by Hans-Joachim Lauth and Jennifer Sehring (2009) dealing with the realities of *Rechtsstaatlichkeit* all over the world; I do find this list quite useful and suggest that it be taken as a common ground because of the following reasons.

If we go through this representative list of rule of law principles, it is obvious that those criteria are not dealing with the substance of the norms in question, but relate to certain requirements of laws in terms of their "production," their quality in guiding the behavior of their addressees (clear, nonreactive, certainty of law), and their implementation by trained law professionals and independent courts. This direction of the rule of law is pointed out by Robert S. Summers (1999: 1692), suggesting to pick up a well-known distinction in legal theory, the distinction of first- and second-order principles:

> The principles of the rule of law differ from principles of ordinary "first order law." Principles of ordinary first order law apply directly to determine legal relations between immediate addressees of such law. . . . Unlike such "first order" principles, the principles of the rule of law are what might be called "second order" principles. . . . Principles of the rule of law are about first order law in the sense that they are general norms that direct and constrain how first order law is to be created and implemented.

I do find this distinction extremely useful as a starting point for our reflections on the rule of law as a normative framework for transnational rule making, but before continuing I would like to clarify that these second-order rules should by no means be understood as purely formal or technical requirements; they do serve the substantive goals of the rule of law, and it is important to notice this indispensable close relationship between the elements "des formalen und des materialen Rechtsstaats"

TABLE 4.3. *Principles of the rule of law*

1. The universality of the law (framing laws while unaware of the specific cases in which they will be applied, not ad personam).
2. The knowledge of the law among those concerned.
3. The prohibition of retroactive laws.
4. The clear and comprehensible formulation of laws.
5. The absence of contradictory laws (in and of themselves, with regard to other laws, and with regard to the constitutional norms).
6. The absence of behavioral requirements that are impossible to meet (unfair laws).
7. Relative stability of the laws (changes not made too often – legal certainty).
8. The prohibition of excesses (proportionality of ends and means).
9. Equality before the law, general application of the law independent from the social status of those concerned (fairness imperative, impartiality of the law).
10. The application of the law to the state and all its institutions (legal liability of the government, all are subject to the law, an explanation of the areas of legal basis for action, primacy of the law, caveats).
11. Independency and effective controlling competence of the courts (effective legal protection from the state, protection of the courts).
12. Adequate procedural and process law (no sentencing or imprisonment without a trial, time limits for processes, accessibility for all, legal counsel, professional judges, penalties that fit the crime, the chance to appeal, fairness, transparency and public nature of the process, equal treatment of equal cases).
13. Right to compensation payments, if and to the extent applicable; government liability.
14. Realization of legal justice (relinquishment of arbitrariness and contribution to justice).

Note: The original title of the table is "Principles of the (Formal) Rechtsstaat."

(Böckenförde 1969: 1703). Summers (1999: 1693) has put this important argument as follows:

> The main functions of the principles of the rule of law are threefold. The formal, second order principles of the rule of law are indirectly instrumental in serving the substantive policies and principles embodied in first order law. Formal principles of the rule of law also define what constitutes law-like form in the content of first order law, as well as law-like creation and implementation of such law. Beyond these two major forms of significance, adherence to formal principles of the rule of law also distinctively serves fundamental political values and general legal values.... Among the foremost fundamental political values so served are the legitimacy of governmental action, the freedom and dignity of citizen self-direction under limited government, and procedural and certain other forms of justice and fairness.

5.2. *The Requirements of the Second-Order Rule of Law Principles at Work*

The requirements for making and practicing laws – which follow from the discussed rule of law principles – are threefold, and I therefore suggest distinguishing the following three branches of requirements:

- production requirements
- quality requirements
- implementation requirements

To formulate requirements for the production of laws means to combine formal legality with the principle of liberal democracy, a relationship that has been pointed out by Brian Tamanaha (2004: 99) as follows:

> A common refrain in Western political thought, initiated by the Athenian democrats and repeated by Rousseau and Kant, among many others, is that freedom is to live under laws of one's own making. This is the notion of political liberty. According to the philosopher Jürgen Habermas, who has provided the most sophisticated account of the link between formal legality and democracy, "the modern legal order can draw its legitimacy only from the idea of self-determination: citizens should always be able to understand themselves also as authors of the law to which they are subject as addressees" (Habermas 1996: 44).

Insofar as quality requirements are concerned, we speak of qualities that are related to legal certainty and to the claimed capability of laws to steer and guide individual behavior. Again I quote Tamanaha (2004: 119), who is pointing out the close relation between rule of law and liberalism:

> The second cluster of meaning revolves around the construal of the rule of law as formal legality. The rule of law in this sense entails public, prospective laws, with the qualities of generality, equality of application, and certainty. As indicated earlier, these formal qualities are characteristic of rules as such. Formal legality emphasizes a rule-bound order established and maintained by government. The fullest procedural sense of formal legality also includes the availability of a fair hearing within the judicial process.

Last but not least, we have to think of implementation requirements, their core element being equality before the law, an important point that Rachel Kleinfeld (2006: 38) has pointed out as follows:

> Equality before the law ensures that all citizens – no matter how well-connected, rich, or powerful – are judged for their actions by the same laws, equally applied. Equality before the law is onc of the core ways in which citizens can ensure that government officials, the rich, the powerful, and the well-connected do not become a caste apart. It is also essential for upholding the rights of marginalized groups, such as women and racial and religious minorities.

5.3. *From General Rule of Law Principles to Area-Specific Requirements*

As we have seen and as I have discussed in this chapter, there exists a great variety of modes of rule making beyond the nation-state – from standard setting to societal self-regulation by stewardships, from the Kyoto Protocol to rules for international trade (World Trade Organization), from rule making in the shadow of the law (the German Corporate Governance Codex) to transgovernmental networks for regulating financial markets. Therefore the decisive step is to transform the aforementioned general rule of law requirements into area-specific requirements and to develop specific rules capable of governing rule-making processes in specific areas for instance in rule-making by standard setting or in rule-making by international organizations or TNCs. This is to be done in a future project. I, however, cannot develop these area-specific requirements here. What I can do is develop some general ideas that could guide the development of area-specific requirements of rule-making, for instance – in a very first approach – by formulating the following "rules":

1. The more the rule-making looks like state lawmaking, the more should the so-called normal standards in terms of democratic legitimacy and rule of law principles be mandatory. This means in particular that the requirements for the deliberate production of such norms should be high.
2. The more the rule-making affects the rights and interests of the individual addressees, the more should the user orientation of such norms be taken seriously. The requirements regarding democratic representativeness should thus be high.
3. The more the rule-making affects vested interests, the more should the balancing of these interests as well as the institutional arrangements ensuring the just representation of all affected interests in the procedure be taken into account the balancing of these interests and institutional arrangements that ensure that all affected interests are represented in the rule-making procedure.
4. The more the rule-making touches upon the public interest as a whole, the more should its procedure ensure an appropriate representation of all relevant stakeholders.

If we go further in this direction, we should be able to develop area-specific rules for rule-making; if this is done successfully, then it might be appropriate to call this endeavor the constitutionalization of rule making beyond the nation-state.

PART II

Actors

Strategies and Responses

5

A Comparison of the Rule of Law Promotion Policies of Major Western Powers

Frank Schimmelfennig

1. INTRODUCTION

The international promotion of the rule of law has become a cottage industry of global public policy. Starting with the dissemination of the Napoleonic *Civil Code* across continental Europe, there have been several historic waves of international rule of law promotion, often linked to war, colonialism, and occupation. It was only after the end of the Cold War, however, that it became truly global: The promoters comprise a large number of countries (mainly from among the group of highly developed democratic countries) as well as regional and global international organizations, and the recipients can be found in all parts of the world.

The rule of law thus appears to have become part of the world culture that governs the contemporary international system. Like the state, the market, and the bureaucracy, with which it is closely linked, the rule of law is an institution based on Western, rational values, backed by the authority of international organizations, and disseminated across the globe.[1] Some authors point more specifically to a change in transnational economic and development paradigms occurring at the turn of the 1980s to the 1990s. In this perspective, the emergence of the rule of law paradigm resulted from the shift from "embedded liberalism" to "neoliberalism," the upsurge of democracy promotion after the end of the Cold War, and "global neoconstitutionalism" (Rodríguez-Garavito forthcoming; Trubek 2003).

In addition, there seems to be widespread agreement regarding the desirability and policy relevance of the rule of law. According to Amichai Magen and Leonardo Morlino (2009b: 7), "more so than the term 'democracy' even . . . the ideal of the rule of law is advocated nearly universally and, just as importantly, never seriously rejected." Thomas Carothers (2009b: 51) finds the "degree of apparent international

[1] This perspective is based on the Stanford School's institutionalist model of a "world polity." For an overview, see Finnemore (1996).

consensus on the value and importance of the rule of law . . . striking" – and again more pronounced than in other areas of development or democracy promotion policy.

There are, however, good theoretical reasons to assume that the consensus may be limited. First, judicial systems and legal codes differ among Western countries. Whereas all of them subscribe to the rule of law in principle, concrete institutions and practices vary, and this variation is likely to influence their rule of law promotion policies. Second, rule of law promotion is institutionally embedded in existing structures of foreign and development policies. These structures differ among Western countries and this difference can be assumed to affect rule of law promotion as well. Finally, just as democracy promotion and political aid in general are integrated in (and often compromised by) general foreign policy and its economic and strategic objectives, so is international rule of law promotion. As a consequence, rule of law promotion policies may vary with the different economic and strategic objectives of foreign policy actors.

In this chapter, I seek to probe into the apparent rule of law consensus and the potential sources of variation. To what extent and why do the rule of law promotion policies of relevant players in the field converge or diverge? How do the differences in domestic rule of law institutions, the organization of foreign and development policy, and general foreign policy orientations affect their rule of law promotion policies? To answer these questions, I compare the rule of law promotion policies of major Western foreign policy actors: the United States of America (United States), the European Union (EU), and its three largest member-states – Britain, France, and Germany.[2] In addition, I disaggregate these policies according to content, organization, instruments, funding, and targets.

This endeavor is fraught with methodological problems. Much of the literature on rule of law promotion is normative and prescriptive. Analytical work is rare. Comparative analysis of rule of law promotion policies is virtually nonexistent. Whereas there are a few (comparative) studies of democracy promotion that contain useful data and treat the rule of law as a subfield of democracy, it is extremely difficult to distinguish specific data and findings on the rule of law from general data and findings on democracy promotion. To a large extent, this chapter therefore had to be based on the assumption that rule of law promotion (and differences in rule of law promotion policies) behaved similarly to general democracy promotion. A more reliable analysis would have to be based on a primary analysis of raw project and budget data.

The chapter is organized around the core dimensions of rule of law promotion policies: (1) content, that is, concepts and components of the rule of law;

[2] Here and there, I include other countries in the analysis as well. In a division of labor, the chapter by Monika Heupel in this volume will deal with international organizations. There is a slight overlap regarding the EU, which is treated as a quasi-state actor here.

(2) organizational setup and institutional context; (3) strategies and instruments; (4) budgets and expenses; and (5) target regions and countries. The final section draws conclusions on the similarities and dissimilarities.

I argue in this chapter that there are indeed significant similarities and parallel developments in rule of law promotion policies among the actors studied here. The promotion of the rule of law has become a persistent issue in their foreign policies since the early 1990s. It is part of their democracy promotion and governance agendas, focuses on formal and institutional aspects, and emphasizes the independence and efficiency of the judicial system. In addition, all countries have focused on top-down capacity-building and training (socialization) activities, whereas conditionality has remained contested and inconsistent. Beyond this general international consensus, however, differences abound regarding specific legal rules and judicial institutions, the organization of rule of law promotion, the budgets allocated, and the regions and countries targeted. These differences can be explained by domestic institutions as well as institutional and foreign policy legacies.

2. WHAT IS BEING PROMOTED? CONCEPTS AND COMPONENTS OF THE RULE OF LAW

The same authors who marvel at the global consensus on the rule of law hasten to add that it masks an "extraordinary divergence of understandings" (Magen and Morlino 2009b: 8). In this section, I therefore explore how far the international rule of law consensus goes and to what extent it is undermined by diverging domestic understandings and solutions. To answer this question, the literature proposes several classifications of rule of law promotion policies.

A widespread categorization distinguishes between formal, institutional, or "thin" definitions, on the one hand, and substantive, ends-based, or "thick" ones, on the other (e.g., Brooks 2002: 2283–2284; Kleinfeld 2005; Magen and Morlino 2009b: 8–9). Whereas the formal or institutional definition focuses on constitutions, laws, courts, and law enforcement agencies, the substantive definition includes legal culture (the values and attitudes of the judiciary) and substantive outcomes (in terms of individual human rights, equality, and justice). Second, rule of law promotion policies might vary according to the substantive domain (economic, criminal, or political) and the context in which rule of law promotion is embedded: This could be (1) economic reform, development or liberalization; (2) democratization and human rights; (3) good governance; or (4) postconflict state building.

Generally, the literature suggests (and often criticizes) that international rule of law promotion has been based on the thin definition, that is, the formal dimension and legal and institutional reform (Brooks 2002: 2284–2285; Carothers 1999: 165–167; Kleinfeld 2005). First, rule of law promotion is seen as a sectoral policy focusing narrowly on the justice sector. Second, it focuses on the institutions in this sector. Third, the independence and effectiveness of the justice sector institutions as well as improved access to justice are the core objectives.[3] According to U.S. General Accounting Office figures for the region of Latin America (the most important recipient region) in the 1990s, 57 percent of rule of law funding went into "criminal justice and law enforcement," and another 21 percent was dedicated to judicial and court operations.[4] Thomas Carothers (1999: 168) detects a "standard menu" of rule of law promotion including reforming institutions, rewriting laws, upgrading the legal profession, and improving legal access and advocacy. Regarding the ingredients of this menu, qualitative differences between the rule of law promotion policies of major Western actors are hard to find.

In addition, Thomas Carothers (2009b) suggests that there has been a shift in the domains of rule of law promotion over time: from a narrow understanding in the context of economic reform and liberalization in the early period to an inclusive conceptualization in the context of democratization in the 1990s, and back to a detachment from democratization and a focus on postconflict state building and good governance more recently. The current programmatic and organizational context of rule of law promotion policies, however, suggests that "democracy," "human rights," and "governance" are still the relevant domains in all major donor countries today. In the United States, the Office of Democracy and Governance of USAID (U.S. Agency for International Development) deals with rule of law promotion. In the EU, the "programmatic trinity" is democracy, human rights, and the rule of law. The relevant thematic financing instrument is the *European Instrument for Democracy and Human Rights*. In France, rule of law promotion is grouped under "democratic governance"; in Germany's Federal Ministry for Economic Cooperation and Development (BMZ), the relevant unit is "Governance, Democracy, and Rule of Law." Finally, the British Foreign and Commonwealth Office includes a "Human Rights, Democracy, and Governance Group."

Domains rather vary along functional and organizational lines. Whereas the actors of international development cooperation appear to emphasize the democracy and human-rights context of the rule of law, foreign and security policy actors tend to focus more strongly on postconflict state building and crisis prevention. This is true, for instance, for the German foreign ministry, which subsumes rule of law promotion under crisis prevention, the consolidation of peace, and state building, and highlights the establishment of police structures in Afghanistan in its Web presentation.[5] It is equally true for the EU in which the Council – composed of the member-state

3 See U.S. Agency for International Development, "USAID Primer: What We Do and How We Do It." Revised January 2006. Accessed 20 July 2010 at http://www.usaid.gov/about_usaid/PDACG100.pdf. See also the descriptions provided by EuropeAid, "Democratic Governance." Accessed 20 July 2010 at http://ec.europa.eu/europeaid/what/governance/index_en.htm.

4 United States General Accounting Office, "Foreign Assistance. Rule of Law Funding Worldwide for Fiscal Years 1993–98." Washington, D.C., June 1999 (GAO/NSIAD-99–158): 11.

5 See http://www.auswaertiges-amt.de/DE/Aussenpolitik/Friedenspolitik/Krisenpraevention/Massnahmen/Uebersicht_node.html. Accessed 22 July 2010.

governments – is dominant in foreign and security policy and is responsible for such postconflict missions as EULEX (the EU's rule of law mission in Kosovo) or the EU Monitoring Mission in Georgia.

Whereas the principles of rule of law promotion are an internationally shared concern and objective, national solutions and peculiarities come to the forefront once we move down to the level of specific laws and institutions. At this level, the dominant pattern is the externalization of domestic solutions. Countries tend to advocate and export their own legal models, codes, and laws. Whereas continental European rule of law promoting agencies advocate the continental models of civil law and bench trials, the United States promotes jury trials, and the United Kingdom (UK) praises the virtues of common law systems (Carothers 2004: 128). Furthermore, whereas the abolition of the death penalty is an important issue in European rule of law promotion, it is absent from U.S. promotion programs. This is not only true of big countries. Case studies show that Dutch agencies promoted the Dutch civil code (Smits 2003) and Swedish agencies advocated the ombudsman institution, a Swedish "invention" (Reitz 2003). Finally, the EU bases its promotion activities on its *acquis communautaire*.

Rule of law promotion in Georgia is an instructive example of national solutions and international competition. According to a representative of USAID in Tbilisi, rule of law promoters pursue different approaches depending on their respective legal traditions: "Everybody's pushing their system." The pre-Soviet legacy of German law in Georgia initially provided an opening for German agencies to assist with legal reform in the post-Soviet period. The Rose Revolution of 2003, however, brought to power those elites who orient themselves more strongly toward the United States. As a consequence, the jury trial was written into the new constitution, German agencies abandoned the field of criminal law, and the United States took over. Both defend the virtues of their systems. According to USAID, the jury trial system is less conducive to political influence and corruption, whereas the German GTZ (*Deutsche Gesellschaft für Technische Zusammenarbeit*) considers the bench trial system to be less costly.[6]

The externalization of domestic solutions can be explained both in a rational and in an institutional perspective. In a rational perspective, an international environment that mirrors domestic institutions is in the best interest of state actors. It creates a legal environment that they are familiar with and know to use to their benefit. This reduces adaptation and information costs and gives them a potential advantage over other actors (Peters and Wagner 2005: 216). This is true for business actors that can operate under familiar legal conditions. It may also be true for law firms and legal experts whose services will be in higher demand if they know the laws and legal institutions from their home country. It is certainly true for law enforcement

[6] Author interviews of USAID and GTZ staff, Tbilisi, June 2010. See also Maisuradze (2006).

agencies combating globalized crime. Few actors are as outspoken as the German Ministry of Justice in this respect:

> In the age of globalisation, law has also become the subject of competition. Nowadays, Anglo-American common law and continental European codified law compete with one another. Germany must seek to play a more active role in this competition, as the spreading of our system of law represents much more than a scientific and cultural exchange. It also facilitates international activities of German companies, offers German law firms new perspectives and increases foreign companies' willingness to invest in a country with a familiar legal system. This is why Federal Minister of Justice Brigitte Zypries formed the "Alliance for German Law" on 27 October 2008 with the big German organisations operating within the administration of justice. The players involved aim to work together to spread German law abroad.[7]

The externalization of domestic solutions may also have to do with internalized values and norms as well as established routines and templates. Regarding the EU, for instance, Federica Bicchi (2006: 287) suggests that EU external policy can "be seen as unreflexive behaviour mirroring the deeply engrained belief that Europe's history is a lesson for everybody." Rule of law promoters often lack training in comparative law or in the legal systems (and general conditions) of the countries they assist. Thus they simply promote what they know: their national legal systems and laws (Reitz 2003: 462). Even though the externalization of domestic solutions is generally criticized as neglecting the (national) cultural and institutional contexts in which the rule of law is embedded – and donor organizations regularly profess to have overcome the tendency to transplant legal codes and institutions – it appears to be a stable pattern of rule of law promotion.

Another clear difference in rule of law promotion has to do with the diverging U.S. and European attitudes toward international, multilateral rule of law institutions. In contrast to European countries, the United States has traditionally been wary of adopting legally binding human-rights conventions and accepting the jurisdiction of international courts. Correspondingly, support for the international rule of law, including the International Criminal Court and the implementation of relevant United Nations (UN) conventions, features on the priority list of European rule of law promotion but is weak or absent on the U.S. agenda.

In sum, then, the Western rule of law consensus extends to general principles (such as the independence of the judiciary and the principle of legality) that are common to all liberal democracies. It also holds for the predominantly formal, institutional focus of rule of law promotion. When it comes to concrete legal norms

7 See http://www.bmj.de/DE/Recht/Justizverwaltung/InternationalerechtlicheZusammenarbeit Rechtsstaatsdialoge/_doc/Das_Buendnis_fuer_das_deutsche_Recht.html?nn=1471926 Accessed 12 July 2010.

TABLE 5.1. *Organizational dimensions of rule of law promotion*

	Centralization	Concentration	Specialization
High	Predominantly ministerial level (EU, France, UK)	1–2 organizations (France)	Rule of law unit (US)
Medium	Roughly balanced (Germany)	3–4 organizations (United States, UK)	Democracy, human rights, or governance unit (EU, Germany, UK)
Low	Predominantly agency level (US)	5 or more (EU, Germany)	General-purpose unit (France)

and institutions, however, the externalization of domestic solutions brings national differences to the fore.

3. WHO PROMOTES THE RULE OF LAW? ORGANIZATIONS AND INSTITUTIONAL CONTEXT

This section analyzes the organizational structure of rule of law promotion in the United States, the EU, France, Germany, and the UK. The organization can be described in three major dimensions: centralization, concentration, and specialization. Centralization refers to the level of government predominantly dealing with international rule of law promotion; concentration refers to the dispersion of authority across agencies; and specialization refers to the degree to which these agencies and their relevant units specialize in rule of law promotion. For each dimension, I propose to specify a high, medium, and low value (Table 5.1).

As Table 5.1 shows, the United States and France represent the extreme cases in the sample. Whereas the rule of law promotion in the United States is organized in a highly decentralized, highly specialized, and fairly fragmented way, French rule of law promotion is characterized by high centralization and concentration as well as low specialization. In between, we find the cases of Britain, the EU, and Germany.

3.1. *United States*

A 1999 report by the General Accounting Office identified at least 35 entities from various government departments and agencies as being involved in rule of law promotion and assistance activities during the years 1993 through 1998. According to the report, most of these entities, however, are "law enforcement agencies providing training and technical assistance to their counterpart overseas."[8] In terms of funding

[8] United States General Accounting Office, "Foreign Assistance. Rule of Law Funding Worldwide for Fiscal Years 1993–98." Washington, D.C., June 1999 (GAO/NSIAD-99-158): 36.

and actual implementation of rule of law assistance, however, the organizational field is more concentrated. During the 1990s, USAID conducted almost half of all activities (measured as share of funding), followed by the Department of Justice with just over 20 percent (currently focusing on training programs for criminal investigators and prosecutors) and the Departments of State and Defense with roughly 10 percent each. Funding is even more concentrated and underlines the core position of USAID. Over 90 percent of funding was provided by USAID, the State Department, and the U.S. Information Agency (with a focus on visits and exchange programs). USAID provided the lion's share of funds – including interagency transfers to other departments for their rule of law assistance activities.

USAID is an "independent federal government agency that receives overall foreign policy guidance from the Secretary of State."[9] It is headed by an administrator who is appointed by the president and confirmed by the Senate. USAID is a general-purpose agency providing development assistance globally. It has a specialized Rule of Law Division, which belongs to the Office of Democracy and Governance, which was established in 1994. The office is part of the Bureau for Democracy, Conflict and Humanitarian Assistance, one of the functional bureaus of USAID. Concrete rule of law promotion projects are conducted by public and private contractors on the basis of USAID calls.

In the Department of State, rule of law is one issue of many for which the Bureau of Democracy, Human Rights, and Labor is responsible. The bureau is led by an Assistant Secretary of State and currently does not have any specialized subunit for rule of law promotion. The Department of Justice has two specialized agencies, namely the International Criminal Investigative Training Assistance Program and the Office of Overseas Prosecutorial Development, Assistance, and Training.

Given the central role of USAID, I classify centralization in U.S. rule of law promotion as low. Ministries have limited budgets or receive their funding predominantly from the agency. The main organizations of general rule of law promotion are USAID and the Departments of Justice and State. This is a medium concentration. Finally, specialization is relatively high. Both USAID and the Department of Justice have specific rule of law units.

3.2. *European Union*

In the EU, the promotion of the rule of law is also distributed across various institutions. Whereas the European Commission manages rule of law promotion in the context of the EU's external assistance programs, the Council is responsible for activities in the context of the EU's Common Foreign and Security Policy. This division of labor is a legacy of the EU's (now officially abolished) "pillar structure," which assigned the Common Foreign and Security Policy to the intergovernmental

9 See USAID, "This is USAID." Accessed 20 July 2010 at http://www.usaid.gov/about_usaid/.

pillar and development and external assistance policies to the supranational pillar. Whereas, however, the Council is involved in only a few (albeit highly visible) rule of law missions, general international rule of law promotion is provided by the Commission.

Depending on the addressees, three Directorates-General are involved in rule of law promotion: Development, Enlargement, and External Relations. DG Enlargement deals with candidate countries and potential candidate countries, focuses on the police and the judiciary, and has a unit on institution building. DG Development manages relations with Africa, the Caribbean, and the Pacific (the ACP countries that have a special status in EU development policy) but has no thematic office for issues of democracy, governance, and the rule of law. DG External Relations deals with the rest of the world, in particular with the European Neighbourhood Policy covering Eastern Europe, Northern Africa, and the Middle East. It has two thematic units on human rights as well as democratization and elections in its Directorate for Multilateral Relations and Human Rights.[10] The assistance programs are managed by EuropeAid, the EU's development agency. Just as in the case of USAID, funding for concrete projects is awarded to contractors on the basis of calls. Moreover, DG Justice, Freedom, and Security[11] has overall thematic responsibility for the external aspects of internal justice and home affairs policies such as asylum, police cooperation, and the fight against organized crime and terrorism. Whereas this DG has run its own support program for activities in different domains of law, which can also involve nonmember countries, there are no specific administrative units dealing with the international promotion of the rule of law.

If we treat the European Commission's Directorates-General as equivalent to ministries, centralization is high in the EU. The competences of EuropeAid are clearly weaker than those of USAID. At the same time, fragmentation is more pronounced. With three relevant Commission DGs dealing with different parts of the world, two DGs for Justice and Home Affairs, and the Council, concentration can be classified as low. So is specialization. Whereas there are no specific rule of law units in the organizations involved, all (except DG Development) have units dealing with human rights or governance.

3.3. *France*

In France, the ministries of foreign affairs and development cooperation were merged in 1999 into what is currently called the Ministry of Foreign and European Affairs. The promotion of the rule of law is institutionally located in the Democratic Governance Mission, which is part of the Global Economy and Development

[10] This information is based on current organizational charts of the Directorates-General.

[11] In July 2010, this Directorate-General was split into two new Directorates-General, namely one for Justice and the other for Home Affairs.

Strategies Directorate of the Directorate-General for Global Affairs, Development, and Partnerships. Formerly, democracy and rule of law promotion had been entrusted to a Sub-Directorate for Governance. By contrast, the French Development Agency, founded in 1992 as the successor organization of the *Caisse française de développement* and the principal project operator of France, does not list the promotion of the rule of law or democratic governance among its sectors of activities.[12] According to its Web site, the Ministry of Justice does not have any dedicated international rule of law promotion programs either.

Organizationally, French rule of law promotion policy can therefore be characterized as highly centralized and concentrated. Although there is a democratic governance unit in the Ministry of Foreign and European Affairs, this unit is clearly less prominently positioned than similar units in other foreign ministries and belongs to a higher-level unit without reference to democracy, human rights, or governance (Youngs 2006: 16). To clearly mark the difference to other countries in the sample, I therefore classified specialization as low.

3.4. *Germany*

In contrast to France, German development policy is run by a separate ministry, namely the BMZ. The BMZ has a unit dealing with "governance, democracy, rule of law" in a division of the ministry that combines a geographical focus on Asia, Europe, and Latin America with a thematic focus on issues of peace and democracy.

The practical work on the ground is conducted by a large number of implementing organizations. In the field of rule of law promotion, GTZ is the most important one. It is a private enterprise that is, however, fully owned by the federal government. It has a thematic "governance and democracy" unit. In addition, the foundations of German political parties receive money from the BMZ. Among the party foundations, the Konrad Adenauer Foundation of the center-right Christian Democratic Union as well as the Friedrich Naumann Foundation of the liberal Free Democratic Party put a special emphasis on rule of law promotion and run specific programs in this field. Whereas the GTZ focuses on technical assistance for governments, the party foundations play a more political and educational role.

Rule of law promotion is, however, not only a domain of development cooperation actors. The foreign ministry runs its own assistance programs focusing on postconflict peace building and state building. Accordingly, the relevant administrative unit is entitled "crisis prevention, peace consolidation, and state-building." The ministry of justice provides external assistance primarily in the writing of laws. It does not have a specific administrative unit dedicated to rule of law promotion but mainly works through the German Foundation for International Legal Cooperation, which it supports financially.

[12] See http://www.afd.fr/jahia/Jahia/home. Accessed 20 July 2010. See also Youngs (2006: 87).

Germany's rule of law promotion policy is primarily located at the ministerial level but independent agencies such as GTZ and the party foundations play an important role as well. Centralization should therefore be classified as medium. The distinctive feature of the organization of Germany policy in this area is its high fragmentation. Not only do three ministries run significant rule of law promotion programs, but the BMZ (and, to a much lesser extent, the Ministry of Justice) additionally delegate the implementation of their policies to further organizations with significant autonomy. Specialization is medium in general. Rule of law promotion is taken care of in units dealing with broader questions of democracy, governance, or both.

3.5. *United Kingdom*

In the UK, two ministries are mainly involved in rule of law promotion: the Foreign and Commonwealth Office (FCO) and the Department for International Development (DfID). In contrast to France, the DfID was separated from the FCO in 1997 and became an independent ministry under the Labour government. The FCO has a thematic unit, the Human Rights, Democracy, and Governance Group in the Political Directorate, which covers rule of law issues. Funding for rule of law promotion comes from the Strategic Programme Fund for Human Rights and Democracy, which replaced the Global Opportunities Fund, in operation from 2003 to 2007. The DfID does not have any directorate or division dealing specifically with issues of governance, democracy, human rights, or the rule of law, even though it provides funding in these areas. In addition, the Ministry of Justice is engaged in international rule of law promotion. In this respect, the British Council and the British Institute of Comparative and International Law play a similar role to the German Foundation for International Legal Cooperation (Reitz 2003: 458). Similar to France, international rule of law promotion is located at the ministerial level in the UK – but less concentrated. The degree of specialization is medium.

It is clear from the overview that the international promotion of the rule of law is not a strong policy in organizational terms. There are no specialized rule of law (promotion) organizations and, with the partial exception of the United States, there are not even specialized administrative units and programs. Rather, international rule of law promotion is normally subsumed under democracy and human-rights promotion or governance assistance. In addition, rule of law promotion is a cross-cutting issue of foreign, development, and judicial policy. Thus, the ministries and agencies involved in these policies will also be to some extent involved in international rule of law promotion. The conceptualization of organizational structures proposed here was designed to maximize variation. On the whole, however, the organization of rule of law promotion can be characterized as weakly specialized and highly fragmented.

Finally, the centralization and concentration of international rule of law promotion policy mainly follow national institutional legacies of development policy. Centralization is high where development policy is mainly made in ministries and

TABLE 5.2. *Strategies of rule of law promotion*

	Imposition (coercion)	Conditionality (incentives)	Socialization (knowledge building and capacity building)
Top-down (intergovernmental)	Rare: protectorates	Secondary, mostly inconsistent strategy	Dominant strategy
Bottom-up (transnational)	None	None	Subsidiary strategy: autocratic systems

it is low where it is delegated to agencies (the U.S. case). Concentration is high where development cooperation is integrated into the foreign ministry (France), and it is low where development policies are institutionally fragmented as well (as in the EU and Germany). At a more general level, the centralized and concentrated organization of French rule of law promotion is typical for the centralized French state, whereas the more decentralized and fragmented character of U.S. and German policies can be related to their decentralized, federal political systems. Furthermore, there may be a correlation between specialization and relevance of rule of law promotion policies. The high degree of specialization in the U.S. case appears to be indicative of the high emphasis the United States puts on promoting the rule of law, whereas the marginalized position of the Democratic Governance mission in the French foreign ministry bespeaks the French skepticism toward democracy promotion.

4. HOW IS THE RULE OF LAW PROMOTED? INSTRUMENTS AND STRATEGIES

This section analyzes the instruments and strategies of rule of law promotion. In line with the general literature on democracy and human-rights promotion, I will use a two-dimensional classification of strategies based on the mode of interaction, on the one hand, and the channel of rule of law promotion, on the other hand (see, e.g., Magen and McFaul 2009; Schimmelfennig, Engert and Knobel 2006). Table 5.2 illustrates the matrix.

Regarding modes of interaction, we can distinguish imposition, conditionality, and socialization.[13] The coercive mode of imposition generally requires the military occupation and international administration of the target country. By contrast, conditionality works through the manipulation of incentives in negotiations between the rule of law promoting actors and the target country actors. Conditionality comes in two main varieties. In negative conditionality, the external actor punishes the

[13] See the chapter by Monika Heupel in this volume.

target actor's violation of rule of law conditions by imposing costs on the target actor. In contrast, positive conditionality rewards the target actor for fulfilling rule of law conditions. Otherwise, the reward is withheld. Finally, socialization is based on providing the target state with the attitudes, the knowledge, and the capacity to implement the rule of law.

Regarding the channel of rule of law promotion, the main distinction in the literature is between top-down (intergovernmental) and bottom-up (transnational) channels. In the top-down, intergovernmental channel, rule of law promotion agencies interact directly with target governments and try to induce them to respect the rule of law and make the appropriate legal and institutional changes. Transnational or bottom-up strategies seek to teach, train, and empower civil society organizations and raise societal awareness in general. In the case of rule of law promotion, specifically, it targets lawyers and lawyers' associations as well as journalists reporting on legal affairs. Although, theoretically, channels and modes of interaction can be combined in various ways, for practical purposes, imposition and conditionality generally use the top-down, intergovernmental channel, whereas socialization is more open. The first thing to emphasize is that actors usually pursue mixed strategies. They combine conditionality and socialization (and, in rare circumstances, imposition) as well as top-down and bottom-up strategies. The differences are thus differences in degree rather than kind.

One commonality that one finds in various policy documents of rule of law promotion is the priority given to working with the state and the government. Because rule of law promotion is primarily targeted at formal, institutional change, this change has to be effectuated in laws, state institutions (such as courts and the police), and relations between state institutions (such as the judiciary and the executive). Bottom-up strategies are seen as subsidiary. On the one hand, they are designed to train the nongovernmental actors in the legal system (above all, lawyers). Moreover, they serve as alternative strategies. If the state is unwilling to cooperate and to enter into reforms of the judicial system, international rule of law promotion targets civil society – either to protect it from an autocratic state or to empower it to bring about changes in government from below (see Huber 2008: 48).[14]

For both the United States and the EU (and its member-states), imposition is an exceptional strategy limited to the establishment of international protectorates or quasi-protectorates such as Bosnia–Herzegovina, Kosovo, Afghanistan, Iraq, and Haiti. These are cases of military intervention in which the baseline strategy of cooperation with the government did not work but, in contrast to other such cases, they also presented a real (Afghanistan) or constructed (Iraq) security threat to the West or a breakdown of the state, civil war, and massive human-rights violations. State building and the promotion of good governance including the rule of law

[14] For the German BMZ, see http://www.bmz.de/de/was_wir_machen/themen/goodgovernance/rechtsstaatlichkeit/index.html?follow=adword. Accessed 20 July 2010.

were important rationales in all of these cases. In addition, imposition is regularly associated with high amounts of rule of law and governance funding.

Explicit democratic and rule of law conditionality is a post–Cold War invention. Implicit political conditionality existed before but was tied to a country's position in the East–West conflict rather than its domestic political system. Whereas some sort of political conditionality was introduced in all Western countries at the beginning of the 1990s, donors differed to the degree that they embraced it. Whatever the programmatic or rhetorical status of conditionality, however, studies generally find that negative conditionality and positive conditionality have not been applied consistently by donor countries (see, e.g., Hook 1998; Zanger 2000) – with the exception of EU accession conditionality (Schimmelfennig 2003; Vachudová 2005). Rather, economic and strategic concerns as well as traditional, often colonial, foreign policy ties have tended to confound the use of political criteria for aid allocation. These general considerations suggest that top-down socialization has been the default strategy of Western rule of law promotion.

4.1. *United States*

In a study of democracy promotion in the Middle East and Northern Africa, Daniela Huber (2008: 48) comes to the conclusion that U.S. democracy promotion is more bottom up than European democracy promotion. Between 1990 and 2003, 42 percent of all democracy and governance aid went into civil society assistance (Finkel, Pérez-Liñán, Seligson, and Azpuru 2006: 34). These figures, however, cannot be easily extrapolated to the field of rule of law promotion. In the USAID categorization, "rule of law" is a separate category (distinct from "civil society," "governance," and "elections"), and there are no data available that break down rule of law assistance according to state or civil society recipients. Based on general policy statements that rule of law funding is primarily targeted at state institutions (see earlier text) and the clear distinction between "civil society" and "rule of law" funding categories, it is therefore safe to conclude that rule of law promotion has been primarily top down and not significantly less so than that of other Western donors.

The traditional and most widespread approach to rule of law assistance can be classified under "socialization." USAID awards contracts and resources to actors that help build institutional rule of law capacities and teach and train professionals working in the legal sector. USAID does not list conditionality in its principles of foreign aid. The clearest example of rule of law conditionality in U.S. foreign aid is the Millennium Challenge Corporation (MCC), which was founded in 2004 and manages the Millennium Challenge Account (MCA). The MCC selects countries for multiannual "compacts" on the basis of several indicators in the categories "ruling justly," "investing in people," and "economic freedom." The rule of law is one item in the ruling-justly category and is measured with World Bank indicators (Worldwide Governance Indicators). Thus, rather than trying to improve the rule of law ex post by specific assistance programs, the MCC takes into account the rule of law as one among several ex ante conditions for the allocation of foreign aid. It thus creates incentives to improve the rule of law ahead of the receipt of funding. The MCA has, however, been much smaller than USAID funding. During 2004–2008 the MCA amounted to $7.5 billion (U.S. dollars) as compared to $52 billion for USAID. In addition, the MCC has suffered from political change. Introduced by the Bush administration as a flagship project for the reorientation of foreign aid, its budget was scaled back under the Obama administration.

4.2. *European Union*

The EU has a pronounced mix of strategies and instruments (see Baracani 2009), but has embraced conditionality more than any other actor. The unique feature of EU rule of law promotion is accession conditionality. Together with democracy and respect for human rights, the rule of law is one of the EU's political membership conditions. The EU's accession conditionality is primarily positive: European countries that meet the EU's political conditions are rewarded with the opening of accession negotiations if they wish to become members. On the basis of close monitoring and regular reports, the European Commission assesses the progress potential member-states have made toward meeting the EU's conditions and makes a recommendation concerning the opening and conclusion of accession negotiations and further improvements to be made by the candidate. Accession conditionality is accompanied by socialization and capacity-building instruments. The best example of the EU's socialization efforts are the Twinning programs in which officials from member-state administrations are seconded to non-member-state administrations to help with administrative reforms – including the areas of justice and home affairs. The EU also funds rule of law reform projects in its neighboring countries. These socialization and capacity-building instruments, however, have a conditionality component as well: the closer neighboring countries are to membership, the higher are the designated financial means.

Outside the group of (potential) candidate countries for membership, the EU still employs conditionality nominally. It offers conditional incentives such as market access and financial assistance depending on a country's willingness to move toward democracy and the rule of law. In addition, most of its agreements with third countries have a human-rights clause, which allows the EU to suspend the agreement in cases of systematic and massive human-rights violations by the partner country. Nonetheless, the EU uses the human-rights clause and sanctions based on it rarely and inconsistently (see, e.g., Schimmelfennig 2009; Warkotsch 2008; Youngs 2001). This leaves the EU with Political Dialogue, a socialization instrument that is a regular part of the EU's agreements with third countries, and financial and technical assistance. For bottom-up rule of law promotion, the EU uses the European Instrument for Democracy and Human Rights (EIDHR), which can operate without the consent of the third-country government. EIDHR funding is, however, much below intergovernmental funding, which gives EU rule of law promotion a predominantly top-down character.

4.3. *France*

According to a survey of European democracy promotion policies, "France was certainly one of Europe's 'back-markers' on investing democracy policies with meaningful substance. Where it did address issues of political liberalization in the developing world it sought to do so within the framework of long-standing paternalistic approaches to key partner states, and conceived desirable reform as a more state-led process than any other European Union (EU) member state" (Youngs 2006: 82). French policy focused on top-down, government-to-government relations, largely ignored civil society, and did not use conditionality (ibid.: 83, 86).

4.4. *Germany*

For Germany, the same survey reports variation over time and across actors. During the 1990s, under the Kohl government, there was a tendency toward conditionality. In 1991, development assistance became formally conditional upon several criteria, one of them the rule of law (Youngs 2006: 118). In contrast, the subsequent red–green Schröder government returned to a more socialization-based strategy. It seems, however, that aid conditionality had not been implemented coherently anyway (Youngs 2006: 122). The more persistent pattern is due to the variety of actors in German development policy. The division of labor between the Foreign Office and BMZ appears to have been between short-term and long-term policies, and that between GTZ and party foundations is between top-down and bottom-up strategies. Because of its variety of actors, German democracy and rule of law promotion have consisted of parallel strategies (Youngs 2006: 114, 131).

4.5. *United Kingdom*

Similar to Germany, the British government introduced "good government" in the early 1990s as a condition for development aid and reduced allocations to some of the worst perpetrators (Crawford 2001: 60–61). Among the EU leaders of the past decade, Tony Blair was arguably the most outspoken in favor of assertive democracy and rule of law promotion and conditionality. This stance, however, was not shared uniformly in the Labour Party and the British government. Rather, organizational conflict lines were similar to those in Germany, with the development ministry (DfID) being more in favor of long-term, socialization-based strategies, whereas the foreign ministry FCO engaged in more short-term, conditionality-based policies (Youngs 2006: 213–214, 233).

This comparative overview shows that socialization strategies focusing on capacity-building and training activities enjoyed the support of traditional development bureaucracies. With the exception of the special case of EU association and accession conditionality, more strongly conditionality-based policies met with skepticism in the development community. They found stronger institutional support in foreign ministries or new agencies such as the MCC. In contrast, there is no clear partisan pattern. It is true that the center-right political groups in Germany and the Republicans in the United States pushed an assertive, conditionality-based agenda, which was downscaled by their center-left successors. British Labour Prime Minister Blair, however, sided with the Republican agenda (even though Labour was divided on this issue), whereas the French right remained skeptical of democracy promotion and political conditionality (see also Youngs 2006: 14). Traditional foreign policy orientations appear to have been more relevant than partisan cleavages.

5. WHICH RESOURCES FOR RULE OF LAW PROMOTION? BUDGETS AND EXPENSES

Regarding budgets and expenses for rule of law promotion, it is notoriously difficult to find reliable data. For one, this has to do with the organizational fragmentation of rule of law promotion. Whereas budget figures exist for some organizations individually, country-wide sums are rare. In addition, rule of law promotion budgets are sometimes drawn up separately but are often hidden in larger categories such as democracy promotion. Furthermore, the definition of rule of law promotion may vary between organizations and countries. The best one can come up with are rough variations over time and across countries. Finally, these figures refer to socialization instruments mainly. Rule of law conditionality is not captured by budgets for democracy promotion activities.

Table 5.3 shows how much countries spent relative to overall official development aid (ODA). These data are not specific to rule of law but cover all democracy and governance aid according to the donor's specifications. Data are for 2003 or 2004, depending on availability. For illustrative purposes, data on additional countries are added.

These data must be interpreted with extreme caution because aid categories are not necessarily consistent and do not represent overall democracy and governance assistance (the EU's EIDHR, for instance, is only one of many assistance programs, and not the largest one). Moreover, they represent a snapshot for one year only. However, the data do show a basic pattern of variation. Sweden has the strongest democracy promotion profile, followed by the UK, Denmark, Spain, and Germany, with a share of roughly 10 percent. France is clearly the country that attaches the least relative importance to democracy promotion. U.S. and Dutch shares are in between the top and the bottom group.

Which share of total democracy and governance aid was allocated to rule of law promotion? In 2003, USAID rule of law promotion funding accounted for roughly

TABLE 5.3. *Relative share of democracy and governance aid*

State	Aid category	Percent of total ODA
UK	Governance	11 (2004)
Germany	Democracy, Civil Society and Public Administration	9 (2004)
United States	Democracy and Governance	5 (2003)
EU	European Instrument for Democracy and Human Rights	2 (2004)
France	Governance	1 (2004)
Sweden	Democratic Governance	17 (2003)
Denmark	Human Rights and Democratization	11 (2004)
Spain	Democracy and the Rule of Law	9 (2003)
Netherlands	Good governance, human rights, and peace building	4 (2004)

Source: Youngs (2006: 20) for all countries except the United States. U.S. data are based on Finkel et al. (2006: 35) and OECD data for ODA.

12 percent of total funding – rising to over 40 percent if taken together with the governance category (Finkel et al. 2006: 35). In the EU, 11 percent of funding was allocated to rule of law promotion as narrowly defined and almost 30 percent when the categories of torture, justice, and death penalty were included (Youngs 2006: 66). In France, justice and police funding also amounted to almost 30 percent of the governance assistance budget (Youngs 2006: 88).[15] Thus, the rule of law shares of overall democracy and governance promotion were roughly similar across state actors.

Which temporal trends can we detect in spending? U.S. data show an increase of funding during the first half of the 1990s (Finkel et al. 2006: 36).[16] During the second half of the decade, USAID democracy and governance aid stagnated and those sums dedicated to the rule of law even decreased. At the same time, however, "governance" aid expanded dramatically and may well have subsumed some rule of law promotion activities. This interpretation is supported by the fact that, overall, rule of law expenses increased during the second half of the 1990s.[17] After 2001, USAID democracy and governance aid increased sharply again. The same is true for German BMZ funding and British DfID funding (Youngs 2006: 120, 216). In France, in contrast, the allocations decreased from an already very low base (Youngs 2006: 88).

Although the figures must be interpreted with considerable caution, they appear to confirm the view that Nordic countries attach comparatively high importance to democracy promotion, whereas France's "realist" stance in development policy

15 No thematic breakdown was available for the UK and Germany.

16 United States General Accounting Office, "Foreign Assistance. Rule of Law Funding Worldwide for Fiscal Years 1993–98." Washington, D.C., June 1999 (GAO/NSIAD-99-158): 4.

17 Ibid.

is reflected in relatively minor funding. Longitudinal trends appear to have been shaped by two historic events: the end of the Cold War and 9/11. Whereas the end of the Cold War provided a window of opportunity for disseminating the rule of law across the globe, the 9/11 terrorist attacks demonstrated the need for international legal and police cooperation and improving law enforcement in third countries.

6. WHERE IS THE RULE OF LAW PROMOTED? TARGET REGIONS AND COUNTRIES

Although the rule of law promotion of all major Western countries has a global reach in principle, their regional foci and priorities are marked. In U.S. rule of law promotion, Latin America was the almost exclusive target region in the 1980s. During the 1990s, however, the regional focus shifted from Latin America to Central and Eastern Europe. Between 1993 and 1998, the relative share of Latin America declined from 44 to 19 percent and that of Central and Eastern Europe increased to 31 percent.[18] For democracy promotion in general, the picture is similar. Between 1990 and 2003, Latin America and the Caribbean received relatively more funding than other world regions. In addition, rule of law promotion has absorbed a much higher share of overall democracy and governance assistance in Latin America than in any other region. In Latin America, it received the largest relative share of funds compared with "elections," "civil society," and "governance," whereas in other regions it has ranked last or second to last (Finkel et al. 2006: 35–36).

In contrast, European democracy promotion focused strongly on sub-Saharan Africa during the early 2000s. This regional focus was strongest in France, with over 80 percent of political aid going to this region, and less pronounced in the UK, which split its governance aid almost evenly between Africa and Asia (Youngs 2006: 216). The only European exception was Spain, with roughly 50 percent of its funding going to Latin America (Youngs 2006: 22). This exception points to another pattern in European assistance: colonial legacies. Whereas "French governance aid remained heavily oriented toward Francophone states," "the UK carried out distinctively strong engagements in Sierra Leone, Nigeria, Pakistan and post-invasion Iraq" (Youngs 2006: 23). In sum, it appears as if democracy and rule of law promotion conforms to traditional geographic patterns of foreign and development policy rather than to an issue-oriented functional logic (Crawford 2001: 106). Investments in democracy and rule of law promotion follow general development cooperation.

This regional view masks considerable variation across countries within the regions. There are two general patterns that appear to hold for all rule of law promoting countries. First, the worst rule of law offenders receive the least assistance (Youngs 2006: 64). In contrast, funding seems to be concentrated on countries that have already gone some way in conducting democratic and rule of law reforms

[18] Ibid: 4–5.

(Crawford 2001: 120). Accordingly, U.S. assistance has partially shifted from Latin America to Central and Eastern Europe when this region democratized in the 1990s. This distribution appears natural, given the donors' focus on formal and institutional reform, which presupposes a "willing state" (in the absence of direct imposition). Second, assistance varies with strategic importance for Western donors. Postinvasion Iraq and Afghanistan as well as the Palestinian Territories have consistently been among the largest recipients of Western assistance in the Middle East (Huber 2008: 50, 57). In the case of the EU, proximity to accession is another factor of differentiation. Candidate countries receive more funding than potential candidate countries, and potential candidate countries obtain more assistance than European Neighbourhood countries (Baracani 2009: 81).

7. CONCLUSIONS

Here I summarize the commonalities and differences among Western rule of law promotion policies, give a tentative explanation, and finally comment on the policy implications.

At the end of the Cold War, international rule of law promotion became a standard item on the global foreign and development policy menu of all Western countries. Based on a consensual view that the rule of law was a good thing and an indispensable ingredient of the economic and political transition to liberal democracy, the rule of law has indeed become an uncontested norm in Western policy. The analysis of the international rule of law promotion policies of the United States, the EU, Britain, France, and Germany has revealed many commonalities that point to the international origins and structuring of rule of law promotion.

First, and following the lead of the United States and its experience in Latin America in the 1980s, all Western countries introduced rule of law promotion simultaneously at the beginning of the 1990s. The 9/11 event generated another impetus for rule of law promotion across most actors. Second, the actors adhered to a similar set of rule of law principles; embedded rule of law promotion in the programmatic and organizational contexts of democracy, governance, and human rights; promoted formal and institutional changes in the laws and judicial systems; and pursued the goals of judicial independence, efficiency, and legitimacy based on fundamental human rights. Third, they did so with a similar set of strategies and instruments. Rule of law promotion has been predominantly a top-down, intergovernmental socialization policy, focusing on projects of institutional capacity building and of training public officials and legal professionals. This socialization strategy was complemented by bottom-up socialization, intergovernmental conditionality, and – under special circumstances – imposition. Fourth, aid has focused on liberalizing and democratizing countries.

These commonalities can be accounted for by political commonalities as well as systemic changes and opportunities. All Western countries adhere to the rule of law domestically and value the rule of law as a fundamental principle of good government. The end of the Cold War and the simultaneous wave of democratization provided a unique opportunity to assert this and other liberal principles on the international scene and to find many new and willing cooperation partners. In addition, 9/11 posed a common challenge to Western countries.

This broad Western policy consensus was confronted, however, with the diversity of national organizational structures and national policy traditions. It was embedded in diverse legal and judicial systems, foreign and development policies, and organizational competences and divisions of labor. This diversity produced variation in the specific objectives and contents, the organization, the instruments, the budgets, and the recipients of rule of law promotion. On closer observation, the apparent consensus on the rule of law principles, and the relevance and instruments of rule of law promotion, gives way to nuances and varieties. First, each actor promotes its own legal and judicial rules, procedures, and institutions. Second, each actor inserted the promotion of the rule of law in its existing foreign and development policy and used existing organizations to implement it. This resulted in weak specialization and high fragmentation as a common feature but otherwise different degrees of centralization, concentration, and specialization across actors. It also resulted in rule of law promotion following traditional geographic and implementation patterns of foreign aid.

Variation is predominantly but not exclusively national. Within each polity, we find differences in rule of law promotion policies between ministries, agencies, and parties. Typically, development ministries and agencies put rule of law promotion in the service of development and favor long-term socialization strategies, whereas foreign ministries are more concerned with crisis prevention and general foreign policy strategy, and they are more inclined to use conditionality (and imposition, under exceptional circumstances).

There are no consistent patterns across the dimensions of rule of law promotion policies. In other words, organizational structures, strategies, budgets, and recipients do not seem to be systematically correlated. Whereas the miniscule French democracy promotion budget fits well with its marginal organizational status, this does not hold for the other countries under investigation.

Are the differences in Western rule of law promotion policies a problem? Answering this question would require an analysis of effectiveness, which this chapter does not provide. In general, though, it seems that problems rather result from what Western rule of law promotion policies have in common than what distinguishes them from each other. As already pointed out, many observers emphasize and criticize the widespread focus on a thin definition of the rule of law, the pervasive inconsistency of rule of law conditionality, and the subordination of democracy promotion to traditional geographic, strategic, and economic foreign policy priorities. Whereas the tendency to externalize domestic solutions is generally criticized as well, the competition between Western countries at least gives the recipient countries a modicum of choice. Absent the rare cases of imposition – and given that Western rule of law promotion policy focuses on intergovernmental socialization and "willing partners" – it is ultimately the target governments that get to select from the menu of rule of law institutions and legal codes on offer from international donors.

6

Rule of Law Promotion through International Organizations and NGOs

Monika Heupel

1. INTRODUCTION

Rule of law promotion has experienced a tremendous boost since the end of the Cold War. Not only states but, to an increasing degree, also international organizations (IOs) and transnational nongovernmental organizations (NGOs) have made use of their new scope of action to diffuse the rule of law around the globe, especially to less developed countries.[1] The emergence of the rule of law promotion "enterprise" (Faundez 2005: 567) or "industry" (Peerenboom 2009: 9) reflects a broader trend of international and transnational actors intervening ever more deeply in states and engaging in social engineering with regard to formerly domestic matters (Zürn 2004). It is also indicative of good governance standards becoming ever more authoritative for states that are increasingly expected to orient their domestic legislation and institutions to such standards (Nanda 2006).

Despite an ever-increasing amount of literature on rule of law promotion, we know relatively little regarding the commonalities in and differences between the approaches to rule of law promotion of IOs and transnational NGOs.[2] Do IOs and NGOs apply the same strategies to diffuse the rule of law? Alternatively, do they hold different assumptions as to what the causes of rule of law deficits are and orient their strategy choices accordingly? Or do IOs and NGOs dispose of different institutional, material, and reputational resources and strive to bring them

[1] For an analysis of rule of law promotion through states, see the chapter by Schimmelfennig in this volume.

[2] For helpful directories that provide on overview of different rule of law promotion activities by IOs and NGOs, see the International Development Law Organization (IDLO), "Rule of Law Assistance Directory." Accessed 20 April 2010 at www.idlo.int/english/Resources/ROL/projectandiniziatives/Pages/home.aspx. Also see the International Bar Association, "International Rule of Law Directory." Accessed 20 April 2010 at www.roldirectory.org/index.htm.

to bear when promoting the rule of law? For instance, is there a "good cop, bad cop" type of division of labor between IOs and NGOs in the sense that the former apply more confrontational strategies and the latter more cooperative ones or vice versa?

Nor do we have a clear understanding of what the specific challenges are that IOs and NGOs are confronted with when they engage in rule of law promotion. It is apparent from the literature that actors taking part in rule of law promotion face several challenges: They lack the solid knowledge that is needed to devise effective rule of law promotion strategies. They must ensure the participation and empowerment of local stakeholders to facilitate rule of law conversion and reach sustainable outcomes. In addition, to be credible, they have to live up to rule of law standards themselves. Are IOs and NGOs affected by these challenges in a similar manner, or do they face a differing set of challenges?

This chapter intends to address these gaps. On the basis of a review of documents focusing on the rule of law originating from relevant IOs and NGOs and of existing research on the topic, I will arrive at the following conclusions: The approaches of IOs and NGOs to rule of law promotion are strikingly similar. Both IOs and NGOs use a broad array of different rule of law promotion strategies that are based on different assumptions on the causes of rule of law deficits. The conjecture that IOs and NGOs hold diverging assumptions on the causes of rule of law deficits and adjust their choice of strategies accordingly can therefore not be confirmed. There are, however, differences between the approaches of IOs and NGOs. With respect to some strategies, NGOs differ from IOs in that they do not dispose of the necessary prerequisites to deploy the strategies on their own. NGOs therefore sometimes act as junior partners and support IOs in the application of rule of law promotion strategies. This lends at least some support to the conjecture that the comparative advantages of rule of law promoters predict their choice of strategies. Finally, although challenges to rule of law promotion, as presented in the literature, apply to both IOs and NGOs, IOs seem to face a greater degree of challenge than NGOs.

The chapter is structured as follows: I start out by presenting different assumptions on the causes of rule of law deficits; I then assign different diffusion strategies that correspond with them, and I briefly outline the prerequisites that actors need to dispose of to apply each strategy (Section 2). I proceed to examine the commonalities in (Section 3) and differences between (Section 4) the approaches to rule of law promotion of IOs and NGOs. Next, I distill from the literature the common challenges to rule of law promotion and assess them in light of their implications for the activities of IOs and NGOs (Section 5). In the conclusion, I summarize the findings and suggest issues of specific interest for future research. I also touch on the interrelationship between the rise of rule of law promotion efforts by IOs and NGOs, and the corresponding rise in expectations that IOs and NGOs themselves abide by rule of law standards (Section 6).

2. ASSUMPTIONS, STRATEGIES, AND PREREQUISITES

It is well known that most states suffer from some level of rule of law deficit (e.g., Kaufmann, Kraay, and Mastruzzi 2009).[3] Nonetheless, in line with different strands of compliance theory (Chayes and Chayes Handler 1995; Downs, Rocke, and Barsoom 1996), there are differing assumptions as to what the causes of these deficits are. One assumption is that a lack of *will* among the political elite lies at the heart of rule of law deficits. According to this, political actors take decisions based on instrumentalist logic and, correspondingly, introduce rule of law reforms only if the benefits of doing so outweigh the costs. Frequently, however, this is not the case. Another assumption is that rule of law deficits occur as a result of *capacity* shortcomings. Hence, local actors especially in less developed countries may well have the will to introduce rule of law reforms but lack the necessary capacities to realize their intent. Another assumption is that rule of law deficits can be traced back to a lack of *knowledge* with respect to how the rule of law can be strengthened and a limited *belief* in the value of the rule of law. States with weak rule of law records usually do not have the capacity to systematically gather information themselves and learn from the experience of others. They are therefore dependent on external actors that transfer the experiences of other states to them.

Different assumptions on the causes of rule of law deficits suggest the application of different rule of law promotion strategies (Morlino and Magen 2009). Actors that hypothesize that lack of political will is the central obstacle are likely to choose strategies that alter the cost–benefit ratio of local actors vis-à-vis rule of law reforms. One way to do this is public *exposure* not only of good but also, and even more importantly, of bad rule of law performance. The rationale behind this is that states, groups, and individuals care about their reputation. Another way to influence the cost–benefit calculation of actors in target states is *conditionality*. When applied to rule of law promotion, conditionality implies linking material rewards – such as accession to an IO – or retributions – such as cancellation of development aid – to the introduction of rule of law reforms or, conversely, the failure to do so. In contrast, actors that assume that a lack of the relevant capacities is the main cause of rule of law deficits tend to engage in *capacity* building and the provision of technical assistance. To this end, they can ensure the consent of key political and societal actors and enter into *nonhierarchical* relationships. They can also try to impose institutions and capacities on local actors if they are authorized to administer the respective territory for a given time in a *hierarchical* setting. Furthermore, actors that assume that it is lack of the necessary knowledge and a limited belief in the value of the rule of law that give rise to rule of law deficits will engage in the diffusion of

[3] For a presentation of the most relevant rule of law indices, see the chapter by Wolfgang Merkel in this volume.

TABLE 6.1. *Assumptions, strategies, and prerequisites*

Assumptions	Lack of political will		Lack of preconditions as regards capacities, knowledge, and beliefs	
Strategies	Exposure	Conditionality	*Nonhierarchical* diffusion of capacities, knowledge, and beliefs	*Hierarchical* diffusion of capacities, knowledge, and beliefs
Prerequisites	Capacity to gather and process information Ability to attract attention	Availability of carrots and/or sticks	Availability of expertise Access based on attractiveness	Availability of expertise Access based on UN mandate

knowledge and will make efforts to persuade actors in target states of the value of the rule of law and thus alter their *beliefs*. Again, they can do this based on consent or by the imposition of knowledge and beliefs on local actors.

To be able to apply any of the aforementioned rule of law promotion strategies, IOs and NGOs need to dispose of specific prerequisites. External actors who want to have an impact on local actors by exposing their good or bad rule of law performance (or both) need to have the capacity to gather and process relevant *information*. They also need to be visible and credible to make sure that they attract *attention* so that their assertions are noticed and have weight. External actors who want to use conditionality as a strategy to promote the rule of law must possess valuable material resources that they can use as either a *carrot* or a *stick*. To be able to build capacities and diffuse knowledge and beliefs, rule of law promoters obviously need to dispose of respective *expertise*. If they want to diffuse capacities, knowledge, and beliefs in the context of a nonhierarchical setting, they need to be perceived of as a sufficiently *attractive* cooperation partner to be granted access. If they want to impose capacities, knowledge, and beliefs on local actors in the framework of international transitional administrations, they need a *mandate* of the United Nations (UN) Security Council (see Table 6.1).

3. COMMONALITIES IN THE APPROACHES TO RULE OF LAW PROMOTION OF IOs AND NGOs

There are striking commonalities in the approaches to rule of law promotion of IOs and NGOs. Both types of institutions are involved in the application of each of the rule of law promotion strategies highlighted herein. It is thus erroneous to suppose that IOs and NGOs consistently hold diverging assumptions on the causes of rule of law deficits and adjust their choice of strategies accordingly. This does not mean that IOs and NGOs take on the same roles when it comes to the application of a strategy. Rather, as I show in Section 4, IOs and NGOs assume different roles when using conditionality as a rule of law promotion strategy and when imposing the rule of law on local actors in the framework of transitional administrations. Nevertheless, when it comes to exposure and the diffusion of capacities, knowledge, and beliefs in nonhierarchical settings, there are remarkable similarities between IOs and NGOs in their approaches to rule of law promotion.

3.1. *Exposure*

As regards exposure, both IOs and NGOs have in recent years drawn on their reputational resources to put pressure on states to agree to rule of law reforms. Indeed, more and more IOs and NGOs have developed indicators and published rankings that juxtapose states' rule of law records. The World Bank's Country Policy and Institutional Assessments, for example, which have been publicly disclosed since 2005, rate recipient countries according to various criteria, among them criteria related to rule of law such as "rule-based governance," "property rights," and "transparency, accountability, and corruption in the public sector."[4] Researchers affiliated with the World Bank and the Brookings Institution run the Worldwide Governance Indicators project that ranks countries according to various governance indicators, one of them being the rule of law (Kaufmann, Kraay and Mastruzzi 2009). Transparency International has developed the Corruption Perceptions Index that classifies countries according to perceived levels of corruption in the public sector.[5] Finally, Freedom House publishes Freedom in the World, a comparative assessment of state performance with respect to protection of political rights and civil liberties.[6]

In contrast to rankings that expose bad and good performance as regards conformity with rule of law standards, shaming, another form of exposure, is more confrontational because it concentrates on singling out and showcasing only bad performance. Of the various components of the rule of law, bad performance with regard to compliance with human rights standards is most frequently framed as unacceptable or even scandalous. Indeed, various NGOs make efforts to expose states' poor human rights records to put pressure on those states and shame them into greater compliance with human rights standards. Amnesty International and Human Rights Watch, for instance, are well known for their role in drawing attention to human rights abuses and pillorying states that flagrantly violate international

4 International Development Association, "Country Policy and Institutional Assessment (CPIA)." Accessed 9 April 2010 at http://web.worldbank.org/WBSITE/EXTERNAL/EXTABOUTUS/IDA/0,,contentMDK:20941073~pagePK:51236175~piPK:437394~theSitePK:73154,00.html.

5 Transparency International, "Corruption Perceptions Index (CPI)." Accessed 9 April 2010 at www.transparency.org/policy_research/surveys_indices/cpi/2009.

6 Freedom House, "Freedom in the World." Accessed 9 April 2010 at www.freedomhouse.org/template.cfm?page=15.

human rights law. By publishing reports on human rights abuses and staging well-publicized campaigns, these organizations aim to make human rights abuses more costly and, in so doing, to induce officials to take steps to ensure the protection of human rights (Hafner-Burton 2008).

IOs also have established bodies that expose noncompliance with international human rights law. The UN Human Rights Council, for instance, publishes assessments of compliance by UN member-states with international human rights law on the Web site of the Office of the High Commissioner for Human Rights (OHCHR).[7] The UN Human Rights Committee that monitors implementation of the International Covenant on Civil and Political Rights (ICCPR) by member-states also publishes its assessments on the OHCHR's Web site.[8] Finally, international courts regularly issue judgments that determine whether states have violated the human rights of their citizens or residents and, in so doing, blemish the public record of such states by labeling them human rights violators. In Europe, the European Court of Human Rights and the European Court of Justice can render judgments that determine whether signatories to the European Convention on Human Rights, in the former case, or European Union (EU) member-states, in the latter, have violated fundamental rights of their citizens and residents. In the Americas, the Inter-American Court of Human Rights can render such judgments for the signatories to the American Convention on Human Rights that formally accept the court's jurisdiction (Forsythe 2006).

3.2. *Nonhierarchical Diffusion of Capacities*

Both IOs and NGOs have in recent years gone to great lengths to provide technical assistance and build capacities relevant to the rule of law in the beneficiary states that formally consent to these activities. In this context, there are various forms of cooperation between IOs and NGOs, with both types of actors being donors and implementers of specific programs. Among the IOs that take an active part in capacity building related to rule of law, the UN, the World Bank, the EU, the Council of Europe, and the Organization for Security and Cooperation in Europe (OSCE) stand out. The UN Development Programme, for instance, has developed programs to facilitate rule of law related capacity building in conflict, postconflict, and noncrisis countries.[9] The UN Office on Drugs and Crime assists states in ratifying drug control and crime prevention conventions and in adopting

7 OHCHR, "Universal Periodic Review." Accessed 20 April 2010 at www.ohchr.org/EN/HRBodies/UPR/Pages/Documentation.aspx.

8 OHCHR, "Human Rights Committee." Accessed 20 April 2010 at www2.ohchr.org/english/bodies/hrc/index.htm.000.

9 United Nations Rule of Law, "United Nations Development Programme (UNDP)." Accessed 13 April 2010 at www.unrol.org/article.aspx?article_id=13.

relevant legislation.[10] Moreover, UN peace-building missions are usually mandated to engage in rule of law promotion in states emerging from violent conflict alongside other activities.[11] UN peace building certainly involves power asymmetries and is thus in a strict sense not entirely nonhierarchical. Nevertheless, as opposed to UN-led transitional administrations (see Chapter 4), it presupposes the formal consent of local stakeholders. The UN has also established a Rule of Law Coordination and Resource Group to harmonize the numerous capacity-building and technical assistance activities carried out by different UN entities.[12]

The World Bank also makes efforts to support states in introducing legal and judicial reforms that it considers to be prerequisite for economic growth and poverty reduction. It provides financial and technical assistance for the implementation of rule of law reforms through its International Bank for Reconstruction and Development and through the International Development Association. In some cases, the World Bank funds stand-alone rule of law projects; in other cases, it integrates rule of law components into more comprehensive projects.[13] Such activities either serve to help states meet conditions imposed on them by the World Bank (see Section 4) or are implemented irrespective of other programs.[14] The EU also puts an emphasis on capacity building and the provisions of technical assistance. To help states that want to accede to the EU comply with the so-called Copenhagen criteria, the EU developed assistance mechanisms, such as the PHARE[15] program, which states were entitled to apply for, once they had committed themselves to the rule of law and other good governance standards. The EU European Neighbourhood Policy and the EU's broader development policy also involve capacity building and the provision of technical assistance for legal and judicial reforms (Börzel and Risse 2004). Finally, the EU has established several field missions in the framework of its Common Security and Defence Policy (CSDP) that engage in rule of law related capacity building. Among them are broad rule of law missions such as EUJUST THEMIS/Georgia[16] (2004–2005) and EUJUST LEX/Iraq[17] (since 2005), and more

[10] UN Office on Drugs and Crime, "Legal Tools." Accessed 14 April 2010 at www.unodc.org/unodc/en/legal-tools/index.html?ref=menuside.

[11] For the mandates of UN peace-keeping missions, see the UN, "United Nations Peacekeeping." Accessed 20 April 2010 at www.un.org/en/peacekeeping/.

[12] United Nations Rule of Law, "Rule of Law Coordination and Resource Group." Accessed 21 April 2010 at www.unrol.org/article.aspx?article_id=6.

[13] World Bank, "Law and Justice Institutions." Accessed 13 April 2010 at http://web.worldbank.org/WBSITE/EXTERNAL/TOPICS/EXTLAWJUSTINST/0,,contentMDK:20746118~menuPK:1980807~pagePK:210058~piPK:210062~theSitePK:1974062,00.html. See also Barron (2005).

[14] For an analysis of the World Bank's approach to rule of law promotion in middle-income countries, see Chapter 8 by Hammergren in this volume.

[15] This stands for Poland and Hungary Assistance for the Restructuring of the Economy.

[16] This is the EU Rule of Law Mission to Georgia.

[17] This is the EU Integrated Rule of Law Mission for Iraq.

specialized police missions such as EUPOL PROXIMA/FYROM[18] (2003–2005) and EUPOL AFGHANISTAN[19] (since 2007).[20]

For the Council of Europe and the OSCE, rule of law related capacity building among their member-states is part of their core mission. The Council of Europe's Directorate of Co-operation implements joint projects in the council's member-states in various areas related to rule of law, such as advanced vocational training of legal professionals, dissemination of legislative expertise, and management of detention facilities. The Council of Europe has also established the European Commission for the Efficiency of Justice to help states improve the functioning and efficiency of their justice systems and to help them comply with relevant standards set by the council.[21] The OSCE has set up a Rule of Law Unit in the Democratization Department of the Office for Democratic Institutions and Human Rights that focuses on issues such as criminal justice reform, independence of the judiciary, and public law.[22] At the same time, rule of law capacity building is a cross-cutting theme that forms part of the work of other units and departments. Furthermore, many OSCE field operations such as the missions to Georgia (1992–2008), Serbia (since 2001), and Montenegro (since 2006) are mandated to provide technical assistance with regard to rule of law matters.[23]

Rule of law promotion through capacity building is not the exclusive domain of IOs but has also been adopted as a strategy by a vast number of NGOs with specialized expertise. The American Bar Association (ABA) is a major actor in the field and engages in rule of law related capacity building around the globe. Its extensive Rule of Law Initiative (ABA ROLI) comprises seven programs, namely Access to Justice and Human Rights, Anti-Corruption and Public Integrity, Criminal Law Reform and Anti-Human Trafficking, Judicial Reform, Legal Education Reform and Civic Education, Legal Profession Reform, and Women's Rights. Each program aims at developing local capacity and expertise to anchor the rule of law in local societies.[24] The Open Society Institute & Soros Foundation Network also runs an extensive

[18] This is the EU Police Mission in the former Yugoslav Republic of Macedonia.

[19] This is the EU Police Mission in Afghanistan.

[20] For the mandates of EU rule of law and police missions, see Council of the European Union, "EU Common Security and Defence Policy (CSDP), Overview of the Missions and Operations of the European Union April 2010." Accessed 22 April 2010 at www.consilium.europa.eu/showPage.aspx?id=268&lang=EN.

[21] Council of Europe, "Directorate of Co-operation." Accessed 14 April 2010 at www.coe.int/t/dghl/overview_cooperation_en.asp. See also Council of Europe Committee of Ministers, "The Council of Europe and the Rule of Law – An overview, Ministers' Deputies CM Documents." CM(2008)170, 21 November 2008. Accessed 20 April 2010 at www.coe.int/t/e/legal_affairs/legal_co-operation/fight_against_terrorism/3_codexter/working_documents/2008/CM%282008%29170%20en.pdf.

[22] OSCE, "Office for Democratic Institutions and Human Rights." Accessed 14 April 2010 at www.osce.org/odihr/13479.html. See also Evers (2010).

[23] OSCE, "Field Operations." Accessed 14 April 2010 at www.osce.org/about/13510.html.

[24] ABA, "ABA Rule of Law Initiative." Accessed 12 April 2010 at www.abanet.org/rol/?gnav=global_publicresources_rol.

rule of law promotion program that builds on capacity building and the provision of technical assistance. It has launched the Open Society Justice Initiative, which engages in capacity building as regards legal reform, criminal justice reform, and anti-corruption policies.[25] It has also developed the Human Rights & Governance Grants Program, which awards grants to NGOs that work on human rights, the rule of law, and accountability issues in Europe and Central Asia.[26] Academic institutions are involved in capacity building too. Georgetown University's International Law Initiative, for example, provides rule of law related training and technical assistance to public officials and the private sector in various developing countries.[27]

3.3. *Nonhierarchical Diffusion of Knowledge and Beliefs*

As regards nonhierarchical diffusion of knowledge, again, both IOs and NGOs are heavily involved in producing and disseminating knowledge that is relevant to rule of law. The same IOs that are strongly involved in capacity building and the provision of technical assistance also play a major role in putting together and publicizing available relevant knowledge. The UN has established an online Rule of Law Document Repository, which contains lessons-learned documents that draw on the experience of various rule of law promotion initiatives of UN bodies.[28] In addition, the UN Department of Peacekeeping Operations has set up an online Peacekeeping Resource Hub that provides information on lessons learned in peace-keeping operations in terms of promoting the rule of law and other matters.[29] The World Bank has sponsored research on the determinants for rule of law promotion effectiveness, and it has posted numerous publications on law and justice reform on its Web site.[30] The EU Institute for Security Studies, the EU's think tank on security issues, likewise publicizes research on rule of law and other security-related matters on its Web site.[31] The Council of Europe's Directorate of Standard Setting drafts binding and nonbinding legislation such as conventions and so-called recommendations that the council members are expected to comply with. Moreover, the Venice Commission – the

[25] Open Society Institute, "Open Society Justice Initiative." Accessed 12 April 2010 at www.soros.org/initiatives/justice/focus.

[26] Open Society Institute, "Human Rights & Governance Grants Program." Accessed 14 April 2010 at www.soros.org/initiatives/hrggp.

[27] International Law Institute (ILI), "About the International Law Institute." Accessed 12 April 2010 at www.ili.org/ms/ili_mission.htm.

[28] UN Rule of Law, "United Nations Rule of Law Depository." Accessed 13 April 2010 at www.unrol.org/dr.aspx.

[29] UN, "Peacekeeping Resource Hub." Accessed 13 April 2010 at www.peacekeepingbestpractices.unlb.org/PBPS/Pages/Public/Home.aspx.

[30] World Bank, "Law and Justice Institutions." Accessed 13 April 2010 at http://web.worldbank.org/WBSITE/EXTERNAL/TOPICS/EXTLAWJUSTINST/0,,contentMDK:20813872~menuPK:2260959~pagePK:210058~piPK:210062~theSitePK:1974062,00.html.

[31] EU Institute for Security Studies, "Publications." Accessed 13 April 2010 at www.iss.europa.eu/publications/.

council's think tank on legal issues, composed of academics, senior judges, and members of national parliaments – produces studies and conducts seminars on constitutional matters.[32] The OSCE has established Legislationline, a voluminous database that enables access to national legislation of OSCE member-states, and to international norms and standards related to issues such as human trafficking, police, and citizenship. The database is supposed to help lawmakers align national legislation with relevant international human rights standards.[33] Moreover, the OSCE's Strategic Police Matters Unit has collected and documented a number of good practice measures and published a guidebook on democratic policing.[34]

NGOs also go to great lengths to produce and diffuse knowledge on how rule of law promotion can yield sustainable results. It even seems that, although the generation and diffusion of knowledge are undertaken equally by IOs and NGOs, it is the NGOs – especially policy think tanks and academic institutions – that put a greater emphasis on it.[35] The Carnegie Endowment for International Peace, for example, recently published a book titled *Promoting the Rule of Law Abroad: In Search of Knowledge* that tries to take stock of current knowledge on the challenges to effective rule of law promotion. This work, edited by a leading expert in the field, Thomas Carothers, has received wide notice; it brings together chapters by distinguished scholars and practitioners, and it provides a critical assessment of the underlying assumptions and the main goals and methods of current rule of law promotion efforts (Carothers 2006a). Many other NGOs have focused on producing knowledge on specific features of current rule of law promotion efforts. The International Commission of Jurists, for instance, has published a report that investigates the impact of counterterrorism measures on the rule of law and human rights, and it develops policy recommendations.[36] The International Peace Institute releases books and policy papers on best practices for rule of law promotion in fragile, postconflict states (e.g., Hurwitz 2008). Finally, the International Legal Assistance Consortium, a grouping of more than 40 NGOs, helps governments in postconflict states to rebuild judicial institutions by assessing the status quo of the institutional setup and making tailored recommendations.[37]

[32] Council of Europe, "Human Rights and Legal Affairs." Accessed 14 April 2010 at www.coe.int/t/dghl/default_en.asp.

[33] OSCE, "Office for Democratic Institutions and Human Rights, Legislationline.org." Accessed 21 April 2010 at www.osce.org/odihr/13462.html.

[34] OSCE, "Secretariat – Strategic Police Matters Unit," Accessed 14 April 2010 at www.osce.org/spmu/publications.html.

[35] See International Development Law Organization, "Rule of Law Inventory Report, Practice Part: 'The IDLO Rule of Law Portal'," 20 April 2007. Accessed 22 April 2010 at www.idlo.int/ROL/ROLcv/Inventory_Report_Practice_Part_by_IDLO1.pdf.

[36] International Commission of Jurists. "Assessing Damage Urging Action, Report of the Eminent Jurists Panel on Terrorism, Counter-terrorism and Human Rights," 2009. Accessed 14 April 2010 at http://ejp.icj.org/IMG/EJP-Report.pdf.

[37] International Legal Assistance Consortium, "About ILAC." Accessed 12 April 2010 at www.ilac.se/about.

IOs and NGOs also both make efforts to persuade local actors of the value of the rule of law. Efforts to substantiate the value of the rule of law can be found in speeches of IOs and NGO spokespersons, as well as in the programmatic documents and mission statements of both types of organizations. Some statements appeal to the logic of appropriateness and provide reasons as to why it is normatively correct for states to adhere to rule of law standards. The Council of Europe, for instance, states on its Web site that the rule of law, like human rights and democracy, is a value that forms the "foundation of a tolerant and civilised society."[38] The UN states on its Web site that the rule of law concept is embedded in the Charter of the United Nations, according to which the UN is mandated inter alia to create the conditions under which justice and respect for international obligations can prevail.[39] Other statements use causal arguments that explicate the rationale behind the promotion of specific components of the rule of law. The OSCE explains, for instance, that an independent judiciary is the precondition for the right of accused persons to a fair trial and for cases being adjudicated in a just manner.[40] In addition, the ABA declares that access to equal justice presupposes a public defender system.[41]

Some statements frame the rule of law as a means to achieve other important ends. The ABA frames it as a panacea, arguing that promotion of the rule of law is "the most effective long-term antidote to the most pressing problems facing the world today."[42] A more specific line of reasoning is that the rule of law and democracy are inextricably tied together. Accordingly, the rule of law is either portrayed as the component of democracy upon which all other components are built (Diamond and Morlino 2005), or the rule of law and democracy are depicted as mutually reinforcing entities (e.g., Peerenboom 2009). A particularly prominent line of reasoning that is frequently put forth especially in World Bank publications is that the rule of law is a prerequisite for economic development. Based on new institutional economics, it is argued that economic growth presupposes legal norms and infrastructure that guarantee the protection especially of property rights and the enforcement of contracts. Accordingly, the protection of property rights and the enforcement of contracts are important for investment and trade because they constrain actors' behavior and thus reduce uncertainty and risk. Although, in recent years, the assumption has been challenged that there is a linear causal relationship between the rule of law and economic development, and that the rule of law is a necessary precondition for

38 Council of Europe, "Our Objectives." Accessed 15 April 2010 at www.coe.int/aboutCoe/index.asp?page=nosObjectifs&l=en.

39 United Nations Rule of Law, "What is the Rule of Law?" Accessed 15 April 2010 at www.unrol.org/article.aspx?article_id=3.

40 OSCE, "Office for Democratic Institutions and Human Rights, Independence of the Judiciary." Accessed 15 April 2010 at www.osce.org/odihr/36363.html.

41 ABA, "Rule of Law Initiative, Criminal Law Reform and Anti-Human Trafficking Programs." Accessed 15 April 2010 at www.abanet.org/rol/programs/criminal-law.html.

42 ABA, "Rule of Law Initiative, About the ABA Rule of Law Initiative." Accessed 15 April 2010 at www.abanet.org/rol/about.shtml.

economic growth, it is still widely accepted that the rule of law is at least conducive to economic development (e.g., Dam 2006; Posner 1998).

4. DIFFERENCES BETWEEN THE APPROACHES TO RULE OF LAW PROMOTION OF IOS AND NGOS

The preceding section has shown that there are large commonalities in the approaches to rule of law promotion of IOs and NGOs. Nevertheless, there are also differences that derive from the unequal prerequisites of IOs and NGOs. As has been shown, both IOs and NGOs dispose of the necessary prerequisites to expose good or bad rule of law performance of states and to engage in capacity building and the diffusion of knowledge and beliefs in nonhierarchical settings. However, when it comes to conditionality as well as capacity building and the diffusion of knowledge and beliefs in hierarchical settings, NGOs lack the necessary prerequisites to take an active part independent of the engagement of IOs. Only when IOs provide the appropriate framework can NGOs at least act as junior partners and support IOs in using conditionality to put pressure on local actors or hierarchically imposing the rule of law on them.

4.1. *Conditionality*

In light of the various material rewards and retributions they can apply, major IOs are in a far better position than NGOs to use conditionality as a strategy to promote the rule of law. Especially the EU relies heavily on conditionality to promote the rule of law in third countries. In fact, the Maastricht Treaty that went into force in 1993 stipulated that political conditionality was compulsory in every agreement between the EU and a third state. On the one hand, the EU ties accession to the union to compliance with the rule of law and other good governance standards (e.g., Schimmelfennig and Sedelmeier 2004). The association agreements the EU signed with prospective candidate countries required such countries to comply with the Copenhagen criteria according to which states were to establish stable institutions that guarantee, among other things, the rule of law.[43] The EU never actually suspended an association or accession agreement as a result of insufficient progress in establishing the rule of law or other good governance related reforms. However, it did invoke negative conditionality by delaying the conclusion of accession agreements in some cases – such as Romania and Bulgaria – in order to provide incentives for intensified efforts to implement the rule of law and other reforms (Börzel and Risse 2004).

On the other hand, the EU makes preferential trade agreements, trade liberalization, and development aid dependent on rule of law reforms. The Lomé IV

[43] European Council in Copenhagen, "Conclusions of the Presidency," 21–22 June 1993: 12–16. Accessed 20 April 2010 at www.consilium.europa.eu/uedocs/cms_data/docs/pressdata/en/ec/72921.pdf.

Convention of 1990, for instance, which the EU concluded with the African, Caribbean, and Pacific Group of States, made compliance with rule of law related provisions a condition for nonreciprocal preferential trade relations.[44] In this case, the EU did not hesitate to invoke the built-in suspension clause and consequently interrupted development cooperation with several African states that failed to conform to the agreed upon provisions. The Cotonou Agreement, which replaced the Lomé Convention in 2000 as the basis for development cooperation between the EU and the African, Caribbean, and Pacific Group of States, also relies on political conditionality.[45] This agreement provides for greater local ownership and enhanced dialogue between the EU and state and society actors in recipient countries, but the suspension clause was not scrapped and aid is still tied to performance based on specific indicators such as the rule of law (Börzel and Risse 2004). Finally, the European Neighbourhood Policy of 2004, which provides the framework for cooperation between the EU and neighboring states by land or sea that have not been accorded the option of accession, relies equally on conditionality (Kelley 2006). Partner countries are granted a "privileged relationship" if they commit to "common values" such as the rule of law, human rights, and good governance more generally.[46]

Other IOs also rely on conditionality to make states commit to rule of law reforms. For example, in the 1990s the World Bank began to make the disbursal of loans and aid subject to commitment to rule of law reforms specifically or to good governance reforms more broadly. At first, the World Bank tried to encourage good governance reforms in recipient countries by disbursing funds and, at the same time, attaching political conditionality to them. When the bank realized that the strategy proved less effective than initially hoped for, it switched from conditionality to selectivity – that is, it only disbursed funds to states that had already made progress vis-à-vis good governance reforms. The World Bank Group's International Development Association, for instance, which lends to the world's poorest countries, decides how funds are to be allocated by using a performance-based system that takes compliance with good governance standards into account (Hout 2007; Nanda 2006).

NGOs tend to lack sufficiently conducive carrots and sticks to effectively put pressure on states through conditionality. Needless to say, NGOs cannot dangle accession as a carrot. Moreover, although some NGOs, for instance the Bill & Melinda Gates Foundation, are able to distribute vast sums of money, normally NGOs can offer or withhold significantly fewer resources to states than colossal

44 Lomé IV Convention, signed in Mauritius on 4 November 1995.

45 Partnership Agreement Between the Members of the African, Caribbean and Pacific Group of States, of the one Part, and the European Community and its Member States, of the Other Part ("Cotonou Agreement") (2000), Official Journal L317/3 of 15 December 2000, as revised (2005) Official Journal L209/27 of 11 August 2005, Articles 9 and 96.

46 Commission of the European Communities, "European Neighbourhood Policy, Strategy Paper," COM (2004) 373 final, 12 May 2004: 3. Accessed 20 April 2010 at http://ec.europa.eu/world/enp/pdf/strategy/strategy_paper_en.pdf.

organizations such as the World Bank. This does not mean that NGOs completely shun conditionality as a means of providing incentives for local actors to agree to rule of law reforms. NGOs instead tend to enter this framework as junior partners in partnerships with IOs that use conditionality as a strategy to promote the rule of law. Indeed, NGOs on numerous occasions implement projects that are funded by IOs that make aid dependent on certain conditions. This way, NGOs indirectly endorse the strategy to pitch rule of law reforms to reluctant local stakeholders through conditionality.

4.2. *Hierarchical Diffusion of Capacities, Knowledge, and Beliefs*

The UN is the only actor that has the authority to formally authorize transitional administrations. Since the end of the Cold War, it has authorized four UN-led transitional administrations, namely UNTAC[47] (Cambodia, 1992–1993), UNTAES[48] (Eastern Slavonia, 1996–1998), UNTAET[49] (East Timor, 1999–2002), and UNMIK[50] (Kosovo, since 1999). The transitional administration in Bosnia and Herzegovina (since 1995) came into being on the basis of a peace treaty and is not led by the UN but by representatives of the UN and all of the other major IOs involved.

Rule of law promotion has been and continues to be an important component of the mandates of the UN-led transitional administrations in Cambodia, Eastern Slavonia, East Timor, and Kosovo and of UNMIBH,[51] the UN mission that formed part of the transitional administration in Bosnia and Herzegovina. UNTAC was tasked to supervise the local police and conduct a human rights education campaign. It was also commissioned to write an electoral law and to supervise further law enforcement and judicial processes in consultation with the Cambodian interim government. UNTAES was instructed to monitor compliance of local parties with human rights standards. It was also assigned the task of establishing a temporary international police force, developing a training program for a local police force, and monitoring the treatment of offenders and the prison system. UNTAET was mandated to train local police forces and deploy an international police force until training was completed. In addition, it was given full legislative powers and was responsible for the administration of all law enforcement services. UNMIK was likewise tasked to set up local police forces and, in the short term, to deploy international police personnel. Moreover, it was consigned the responsibility to protect and promote human rights. UNMIBH was mandated to monitor existing law enforcement activities, train and advise law enforcement personnel, and support the reform of

47 UNTAC is the UN Transitional Authority in Cambodia.
48 UNTAES is the UN Transitional Administration for Eastern Slavonia, Baranja, and Western Sirmium.
49 UNTAET is the UN Transitional Administration in East Timor.
50 UNMIK is the UN Interim Administration Mission in Kosovo.
51 UNMIBH is the UN Mission in Bosnia-Herzegovina.

the criminal justice system. The mission was also charged with amending laws that were inconsistent with the constitution.[52]

When it comes to carrying out the various rule of law related functions that transitional administrations are mandated to perform, the UN normally works alongside, cooperates with, or delegates specific tasks to other IOs. In Kosovo, the EU Rule of Law Mission in Kosovo is mandated to support the local authorities with regard to police, justice, and customs matters, and thus complements UNMIK's rule of law promotion activities.[53] Moreover, the OSCE dispatched a mission to Kosovo that was tasked with monitoring the compliance of the police, courts, and local municipalities with the rule of law, especially human rights standards.[54] The OSCE also sent a mission to Bosnia and Herzegovina that was to engage in judicial and legal reform, and to support the local authorities in promoting and protecting human rights and developing democratically accountable institutions that respect the rule of law.[55]

NGOs have never been given formal responsibility for the interim administration of territories. Nevertheless, they are, again as junior partners, involved in implementing rule of law reforms in the context of transitional administrations that are formally led by IOs. In East Timor, for instance, UNTAET invited the International Centre for Not-for-Profit Law to provide technical assistance with a view to establishing a legal framework for the operation of civil society groups.[56] With regard to Bosnia–Herzegovina and Kosovo, the influx of transnational NGOs involved in the implementation of rule of law promotional activities has been so great that it has been characterized as an "invasion" (Pouligny 2003: 363).

5. CHALLENGES

The extensiveness of rule of law promotion efforts and the vast number of different IOs and NGOs involved in this enterprise are impressive and unprecedented when compared with earlier waves of the same. Nevertheless, the literature abounds with criticism concerning the lack of effectiveness of efforts by IOs, transnational NGOs, and other external actors to promote the rule of law (e.g., Carothers 1998). To systematically assess the effectiveness of the various strategies and activities that IOs and NGOs apply is obviously far beyond the scope of this chapter. What I try to do

52 For the mandates of UNTAC, UNTAES, UNTAET, UNMIK, and UNMIBH, see the UN, "United Nations Peacekeeping." Accessed 20 April 2010 at www.un.org/en/peacekeeping/.

53 EULEX Kosovo, "European Union Rule of Law Mission." Accessed 20 April 2010 at www.eulex-kosovo.eu/?id=1.

54 OSCE, "OSCE Mission in Kosovo." Accessed 7 April 2010 at www.osce.org/kosovo/.

55 OSCE, "OSCE Mission in Bosnia and Herzegovina." Accessed 7 April 2010 at www.oscebih.org/oscebih_eng.asp.

56 "Country Reports: Asia Pacific," *The International Journal of Not-for-Profit Law* 2(3) (2000). Accessed 22 April 2010 at www.icnl.org/knowledge/ijnl/vol2iss3/cr_1.htm#easttimor.

instead is to outline the main challenges with which IOs and NGOs are confronted and touch on some of their attempts to come to terms with these challenges. I also show that IOs and NGOs are, at least to some extent, in different ways affected by these challenges.

5.1. *Lack of Solid Knowledge*

Solid knowledge is a necessary condition of successful rule of law promotion. However, a pivotal challenge that applies to all rule of law promotion strategies and that affects IOs and NGOs alike is the lack of solid knowledge. Many scholars have drawn attention to the fact that IOs, NGOs, and other external actors do not have sufficient knowledge to devise effective strategies (see, e.g., Carothers 2003). Veronica Taylor even refers to a "knowledge vacuum" and argues that it is "alarming to observe this level of spending... on the basis of relatively superficial information" (Taylor 2009: 46). Indeed, many reasons that are provided as justification for the value of the rule of law are disputable. Although the positive effect of the rule of law on democracy and economic development is often presented as a proven fact, reality often reveals otherwise: The actual interrelationship between the concepts seems to be far more complex than is frequently and readily assumed. Moreover and more importantly for the day-to-day work of IOs and NGOs engaging in rule of law promotion, there is clearly a knowledge deficit in terms of why some attempts to promote the rule of law promotion succeed while others fail (Krygier 2009).

Carothers and others have identified various factors that can account for the absence of reliable knowledge. The intricacy of rule of law promotion and the vast differences between legal systems make the generation of generalizable knowledge a formidable task. Furthermore, IOs and NGOs involved in rule of law promotion tend to have few incentives, or they lack the necessary resources to rigorously evaluate the effectiveness of their own activities, possibly also exposing glaring failures. In recent years, awareness of the need for self-evaluation has risen, and lessons-learned units have mushroomed among many IOs and NGOs. Nevertheless, the evaluations were often superficial and, even if they yielded practicable results, this did not necessarily invoke operational change. Scholars to date have also not done much in the way of systematic empirical research on the determinants for effectiveness and sustainability of different rule of law promotion strategies applied by IOs and NGOs. In fact, most academic research tends to concentrate on aid, regrettably to the detriment of other activities. Finally, the present body of knowledge is characterized by fragmentation: Practitioners and scholars have only splintered knowledge, and they frequently fail to exchange and integrate their ideas. Jurists, development economists, political scientists, sociologists, anthropologists, and other specialists often rely solely on knowledge generated in their own respective disciplines and fields, tending to neglect the insights of others in other areas (e.g., Carothers 2003; Magen and Morlino 2009b).

5.2. *Participation and Empowerment of Local Actors*

A second challenge for IOs and NGOs, and a second condition of successful implementation of any rule of law promotion strategy, is to ensure the participation and empowerment of local stakeholders.[57] There is wide consensus in the literature that a simple top-down transfer of legislation and institutions from external actors to recipient states will not do. Sustainable outcomes are unlikely if local actors only agree to rule of law reforms because they are pressured to do so or if efforts at capacity building fail to take local culture and institutions into account. Nor is a simple transfer of uniform knowledge likely to yield long-term results. Rather, to facilitate rule of law conversion, efforts at capacity building and knowledge diffusion have to adjust to the local context. Moreover, activities that rely on the manipulation of incentives must be complemented by softer activities that aim to contribute to a better understanding of the value of the rule of law (see Mani 1998; Pouligny 2003).

The need to involve and empower local stakeholders and to adjust the different components of the rule of law to local culture is most acute when it comes to the most top-down and intrusive strategy, namely the imposition of the rule of law in the context of transitional administrations. The demand to provide for the participation and empowerment of local stakeholders is therefore addressed primarily to IOs whereas NGOs are less affected. In responding to these concerns, IOs are normally mandated to consult local stakeholders. This can be framed in general terms, for instance, as in the case of East Timor, where UNTAET was mandated to consult closely with the local population. Mandates can also be more specific, for instance, as in the case of Eastern Slavonia, where UNTAES was to consult with local actors with respect to specific governmental appointments. In many cases, however, failure to involve local actors led to their frustration. In East Timor, for example, local NGOs complained that funding was predominantly channeled to transnational NGOs. In Bosnia and Herzegovina, the widespread use of rule by decree and dismissal of local officials engendered opposition. In Cambodia, the transferal of responsibility to local actors was bumpy, and efforts at local capacity building frequently encountered obstacles (Chesterman 2004; Richmond and Franks 2007).

5.3. *Observation of Rule of Law Standards*

A third challenge is for the actors that engage in rule of law promotion to live up to rule of law standards themselves.[58] This applies particularly to IOs that try to impose the rule of law in hierarchical settings. Again, especially IOs that take responsibility in transitional administrations in particular have been frequently charged with violating

[57] See also the chapters by Röder, Gillespie, and Zajac-Sannerholm in this volume.

[58] See also the chapter by Röder in this volume.

the very rule of law standards that they try to promote. They have been accused of exceeding their powers and violating fundamental rights of individuals. There has also been clear condemnation of the absence of mechanisms to enable those whose rights have been thus abused to hold the responsible transitional administrators to account. In Kosovo, for instance, UNMIK has been accused of using excessive force, ordering extrajudicial detentions, extending pretrial custody, and depriving defendants of legal assistance. It has also been accused of inequitable treatment of ethnic minorities and failing to guarantee the protection of such individuals more broadly. In East Timor, the UN was also accused of prolonging pretrial detention (Caplan 2005; Chesterman 2004; Mégret and Hoffmann 2003).

In all cases, opportunities for individuals to hold IOs or their personnel (or both) accountable for wrongdoings have been limited. In response to criticism, many IOs that were involved in the execution of transitional administrations did establish some accountability mechanisms – albeit modest ones. The World Bank, for instance, set up an Inspection Panel that accepts complaints from individuals alleging that a specific World Bank project has failed to live up to the bank's own good governance standards. In Kosovo, an ombudsperson was established by the OSCE, who was mandated to investigate complaints brought forward by local citizens against UNMIK and other international personnel. In East Timor, an ombudsperson with similar competences was established. In addition, an Inspector General's Office was set up that operates under the responsibility of local actors and was tasked with monitoring the use of World Bank funds. What is more, UNTAET's human rights unit was also charged with receiving and investigating complaints against the transitional administration personnel in East Timor. Despite these efforts, however, widespread doubt remains that existing mechanisms can effectively guarantee that international actors abide by rule of law standards. This is evidenced inter alia by the World Bank Inspection Panel, which is little known among local populations. Further, ombudspersons are authorized to issue recommendations only: They have no power to take binding decisions or to enforce binding legislation, and they are frequently plagued by resource shortages (Chesterman 2004; Mégret and Hoffmann 2003).

6. CONCLUSION

The purpose of this chapter has been, first, to ascertain the commonalities in and differences between the approaches to rule of law promotion of IOs and NGOs and, second, to assess common challenges to effective rule of law promotion in terms of their implications for IOs and NGOs. I have shown that, overall, the approaches to rule of law promotion taken by IOs and NGOs are remarkably similar: Both IOs and NGOs are involved in all of the rule of law promotion strategies explicated in the second section, namely exposure, conditionality, and the diffusion of capacities, knowledge, and beliefs in hierarchical and nonhierarchical settings. Hence, both types of actors not only apply strategies that are based on the assumption that a lack of political will among local stakeholders can explain rule of law deficits but also strategies that derive from the assumption that lack of preconditions as regards capacity, knowledge, and beliefs is the key obstacle.

The conjecture that IOs and NGOs hold different assumptions regarding the causes of rule of law deficits and that they devise their rule of law promotion strategies accordingly can, therefore, not be confirmed. This finding is further corroborated by the observation that in some cases one and the same actor simultaneously applies different strategies that relate to different assumptions on the causes of rule of law deficits. The EU, for instance, relies heavily on conditionality. At the same time, however, it also engages in capacity building to help states fulfill the conditions imposed on them and other forms of socialization to encourage local stakeholders to commit to the rule of law. Similarly, the World Bank works with conditionality and exposure on the one hand, and, on the other, makes efforts to help states meet the conditions. In contrast, the empirical findings of the chapter lend more support to the conjecture that the choice of any strategy is to a high degree determined by the prerequisites of the actors that engage in rule of law promotion. Both IOs and NGOs dispose of the necessary technical and reputational resources to influence local actors by exposing good or bad rule of law performance and to provide technical assistance and diffuse knowledge and beliefs. Nonetheless, when it comes to the use of conditionality and the imposition of institutions, capacities, knowledge, and beliefs in hierarchical settings, NGOs clearly lag behind IOs and are therefore limited to acting as junior partners.

This chapter has juxtaposed IOs and NGOs and did not attempt to expose and analyze variance within the group of IOs, on the one hand, and variance within the group of NGOs, on the other. It might be worthwhile for future research to address intragroup differences and examine whether there is a division of labor within both groups. At least with regard to the group of NGOs, the empirical findings of this chapter suggest that there are indeed the contours of such a division of labor in which different NGOs play off their specific strengths and draw on their comparative advantages vis-à-vis other NGOs. NGOs such as Transparency International and Freedom House compile rankings that classify states according to the quality of the rule of law. Advocacy groups such as Amnesty International and Human Rights Watch publish incriminating reports to shame bad rule of law performers. A plethora of service NGOs such as ABA and The Open Society Institute & Soros Foundation Network focus on capacity building and the provision of technical assistance. Finally, research-oriented nonprofit organizations such as the Carnegie Endowment for International Peace and the International Peace Institute engage in the diffusion dissemination of knowledge and beliefs. With regard to IOs, it is more difficult to assign specific strategies to individual organizations or types of organizations, especially as vast organizations such as the EU and the World Bank apply a variety of different rule of law strategies simultaneously. Future research may look into this issue more closely and systematically compare different IOs involved in rule of law promotion according to their choice of strategies, their assumptions, and their institutional, material, and reputational resources.

Whether rule of law promotion efforts by IOs and NGOs will lead to more favorable results in the future depends on the extent to which they address the three challenges set out in this chapter. At the same time, the future will also show in what way the dynamics sparked by IO and NGO rule of law promotion efforts will have a reciprocal effect on IO and NGO compliance with rule of law standards (see the chapter by Tim Gemkow and Michael Zürn in this volume). There are already indications that IOs and NGOs that promote the rule of law trap and expose themselves as regards their own commitment to this institution and expectations that rule of law standards apply to them as well (see, e.g., Woods and Narlikar 2001). As mentioned earlier, some IOs that are strongly involved in rule of law promotion have already responded to criticisms and tried to meet expectations by establishing accountability mechanisms to ensure conformity to some basic rule of law standards. The World Bank's Inspection Panel and the human rights ombudspersons in transitional administrations are cases in point. Moreover, some degree of spillover could also result, in the sense that IOs promoting the rule of law are also increasingly expected to make other policies conform to rule of law standards. In some cases these IOs have already taken steps in this direction: Although moderate, initial measures undertaken by the UN and the EU to ensure due process and to protect the rights of individuals singled out for targeted sanctions suggest that IOs do indeed try to meet expectations (Heupel 2009). Some NGOs engaging in rule of law promotion have also established accountability mechanisms to answer complaints against illegitimate behavior by their staff. The efforts made by Amnesty International in this regard are a telling example.[59] Rule of law promotion by IOs and NGOs, despite persistent shortcomings, thus not only has an effect on the state of the rule of law at the nation-state level. Rather, it seems that it already feeds back to the international and transnational level and, in so doing, indirectly advances the internationalization of the rule of law as well.

59 Amnesty International, "Making a Complaint." Accessed 19 April 2010 at www.amnesty.org/en/who-we-are/accountability/making-a-complaint.

7

Combating Transnational Crime

The Role of Learning and Norm Diffusion in the Current Rule of Law Wave

Paulette Lloyd, Beth A. Simmons, and Brandon M. Stewart

1. INTRODUCTION

One of the defining aspects of the end of the 20th century was the turn to market liberalization and political democracy as twin organizing principles for human societies in many parts of the world (Simmons, Dobbin, and Garrett 2008). Practically every region of the world has participated to some degree in these twin liberalizations, although there are still stark differences among countries in the extent and enthusiasm of their participation. Some of the primary explanations for the globalization of liberalization have been new and intensified forms of economic competition on the one hand, and the spread of normative commitments to human rights and democratic participatory forms of governance on the other. Spurred by the foreign policies of major powers, the programs of major financial institutions, and a proliferating set of civil society actors, the second half of the 20th century might aptly be termed "an era of liberalization."

What, however, have these twin liberalizations meant for the broadening and deepening of the rule of law within and across countries? On the one hand, liberalization seems to assume the strengthening of domestic rule of law institutions, such as transparent decision making, independent judiciaries, professionalized law enforcement, and competent regulatory bureaucracies.[1] On the other hand, abrupt marketization and economic liberalization have also created opportunities for the transnationalization of crime. As transaction costs have fallen, there are ever-greater opportunities for illicit traders to operate in an unrestricted fashion across borders. Transnational crime in turn creates growing challenges for national authorities

We thank our team of research assistants: Joe DiGrazia, HuiGuo Liu, and Leigh Wilson at Indiana University, and Iza Ding, Marina Ivanova, and Trung Nguyen at Harvard University. We also thank Yuri Zhukov for helpful suggestions.

[1] See the various essays in *The Hague Journal of the Rule of Law* 1, 2009: Peerenboom (2009); Nollkaemper (2009); and Trubek (2009).

at all levels, from foreign policy and security establishments, to law enforcement authorities, to border control officials, to local courts. In some ways, transnational crime has become a threat to "good governance" and even state sovereignty globally.

This chapter focuses on the global diffusion of norms and policies to address transnational crime, with a focus on human trafficking. Global anti-crime efforts are a transnational extension of efforts to establish the rule of law at the national level.[2] We argue that (1) countries that evidence a commitment to the rule of law domestically have led the international campaign and set the example for how to counter transnational human trafficking; (2) the wave of activity has been fueled by largely nonmaterial pressure from powerful and highly committed states, especially the United States of America; and (3) countries that experience the negative externalities from trafficking are most likely to adopt legal measures to counter it. We will show that concern for the domestic rule of law, hegemonic pressures, and negative externalities all play a central role in the recent transnational rule of law wave against crime and human trafficking in particular.

The argument presented here may very well generalize to all kinds of transnational criminal activities, but our focus here is on human trafficking. This choice reflects a pragmatic way to limit the inquiry while concentrating on one of the fastest growing transnational crime sectors. Trafficking in human beings has certainly become easier as transactions costs associated with travel, communication, and trade have fallen (Ebbe and Das 2008; Kapur and McHale 2005; Kara 2009; Turner and Kelly 2009; Maltzahn 2008; Von Struensee 2000). Human trafficking is also connected to other transnational crimes and crime networks involving narcotics, small arms, and other contraband (Thachuk 2007) and to many other related crimes, including identity fraud, threats, abuse, bribery, and money laundering (Curley and Wong 2008). By supplementing a largely qualitative, ethnographic literature, our focus on human trafficking will allow for reflection on how norms against the buying and selling of human services into nearly slave-like conditions diffuse internationally and are connected to global currents in the rule of law more generally.

2. BACKGROUND: TRANSNATIONAL CRIME IN CONTEXT

One of the most difficult problems associated with studying transnational crime is that no one has a good handle on the dimensions or the geography of the problem worldwide. Hard data are notoriously difficult to come by because many of these crimes are not detected, reported, or prosecuted. Havocscope.com, an independent online database that aims to quantify black market activities, estimates world illicit trade to be almost $730 billion per year, with counterfeiting and piracy to be between $300 billion and $1 trillion; the global drug trade about $321 billion; trade in environmental goods, $69 billion; human trafficking, $44 billion; and illicit

[2] Rule of law countries are more resistant to, and less tolerant of, the organization and activities of criminal organizations within their jurisdictions in the first place. See, e.g., Shelley (1999).

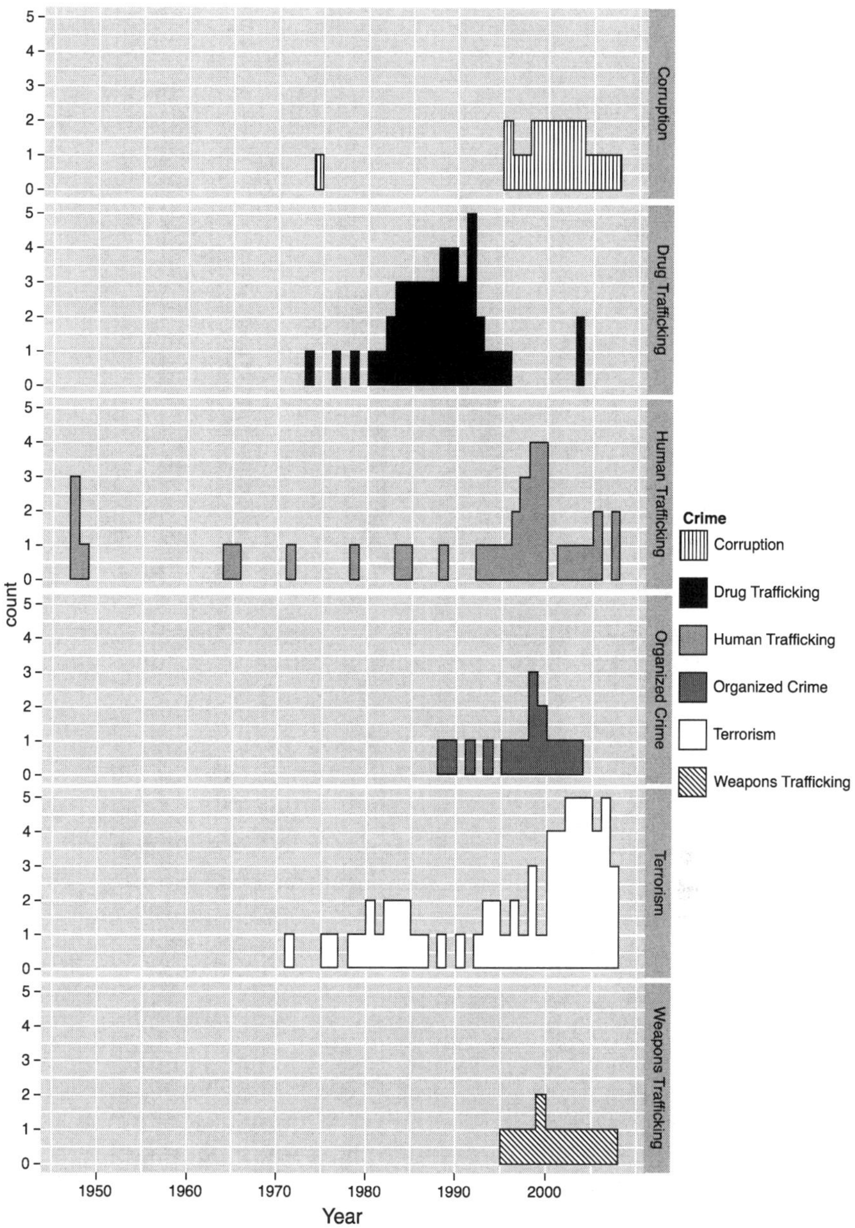

FIGURE 7.1. Adopted UN resolutions by transnational crime.

weapons trade, $10 billion.[3] It is easy, however, to document the waxing and waning of global *attention* to various transnational crime issues. Figure 7.1 illustrates the

[3] The Millennium Project, "Global Challenges Facing Humanity," available at http://www.millennium-project.org/millennium/Global_Challenges/chall-12.html.

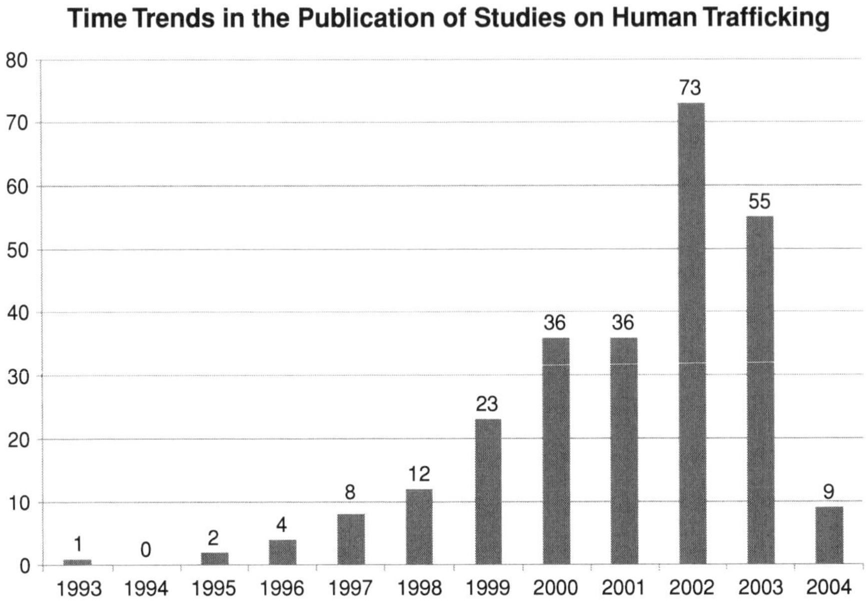

FIGURE 7.2. The increase in academic interest in human trafficking. (*Source:* Farquet, Romaine, Heikki Matilla, and Frank Laczko, "Human Trafficking: Bibliography by Region." *Data and Research on Human Trafficking: A Global Survey*, 2005.)

waves of attention, as measured by the number of United Nations (UN) resolutions on transnational crime adopted each year over the course of the past several decades. Human trafficking was one of the earliest crime sectors to get any attention at the UN. Drug trafficking was the primary agenda item in the 1980s, whereas resolutions on terrorism received a big boost in the time period after 9/11. Resolutions addressing corruption, weapons smuggling, and transnationally organized crime in general round out the crime focus of the past two decades. Collectively, it is fair to say, there has been a significant upsurge in international interest in *transnational* rule of law problems worldwide.

Human trafficking in particular has recently become much more prominent in the academic and popular press. Figure 7.2 demonstrates that there has been a recent upsurge in studies of human trafficking, although the total numbers are small and appear to be in decline. Figure 7.3 illustrates the number of hits per year for searches on "human trafficking" and "sex trafficking" with the use of the LexisNexis database of international English-language newspapers. At a minimum, we can assert with reasonable confidence that awareness of the problem associated with human trafficking has likely increased over the past decade.

The problem of *addressing* the transnational crime remains a serious one, however. For one thing, transnational crime statistics are largely guesswork when it comes to human trafficking. A recent report by the United States Government Accountability

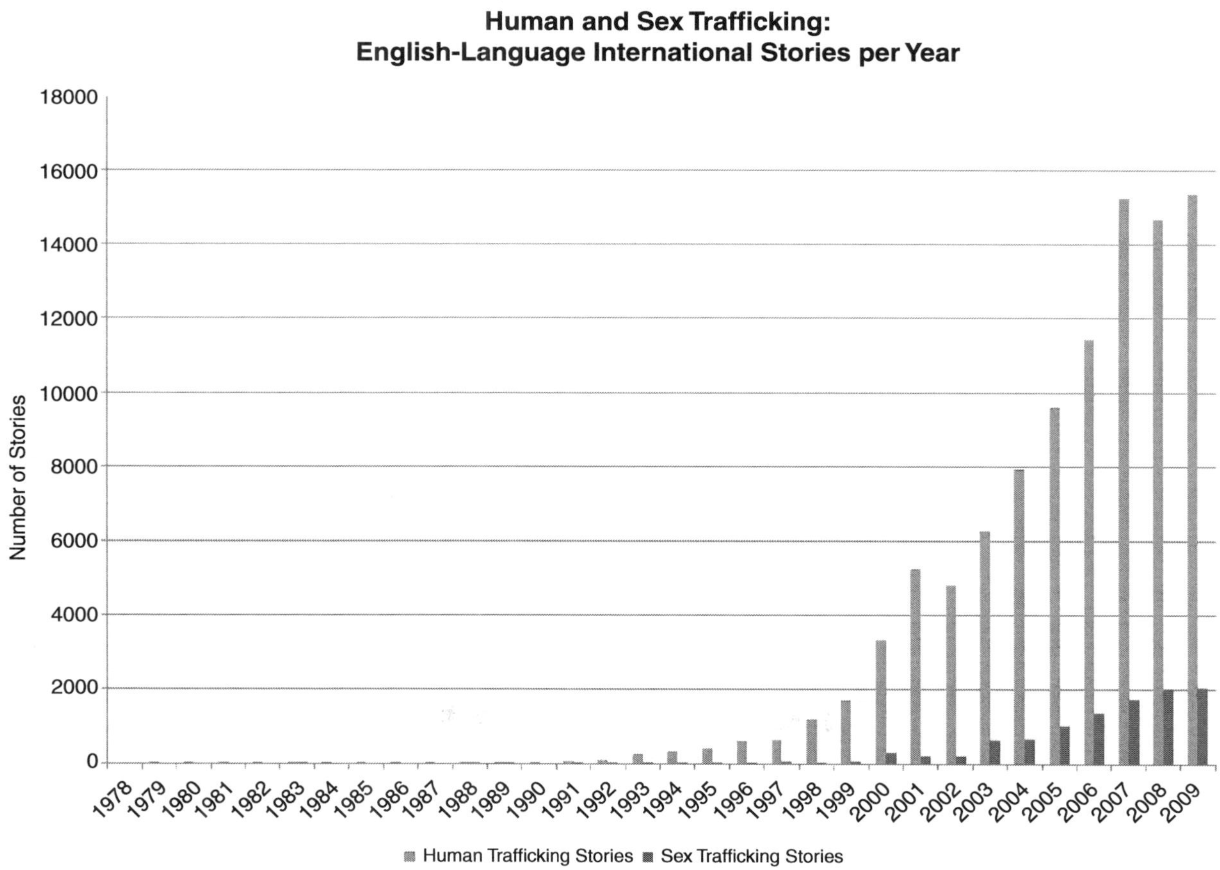

FIGURE 7.3. The increase in public awareness of human trafficking. (*Source:* LexisNexis, current as of December 2009.)

Office (U.S. GAO) stresses the utter uncertainty about the scope of the problem worldwide, largely as a result of different ways of measuring and reporting the crime, the unavailability and incomparability of trafficking numbers across countries, and the huge gap between observed (or reported) cases and estimates.[4] The difficulty of formulating a coherent policy response is compounded by hard-to-change structural and cultural conditions in which human trafficking has flourished. Economic desperation, demeaning cultural attitudes toward women (Dewey 2008; Parrot and Cummings 2008; William 2008), and diaspora networks have been cited as conditions facilitating human trafficking (Turner and Kelly 2009). Normative denunciation is not a given; some studies emphasize that various forms of bonded labor are in some societies widely accepted (Dewey 2008; William 2008). Corruption adds to the problem when local officials accept bribes to turn a blind eye (Abadeer 2008; Dewey 2008). Cooperation among nations and national law enforcement agencies is further complicated by different incompatible legal systems, inconsistent definitions of what constitutes a crime, and varying interests in and capacities to enforce whatever patchwork of law may exist in this area (Jonsson 2009; Maltzahn 2008; Ross 2004).

3. INTERNATIONAL CRIMINAL LAW COOPERATION

The history of international efforts to address human trafficking spans more than a century (see Locher 2007). Nineteenth-century campaigns focused on what was generally referred to at the time as the "white slave trade," by which was meant the international trade in women and girls, especially for prostitution. By 1902, 13 European countries had negotiated and ratified an International Agreement for the Suppression of White Slave Trade.[5] In 1921 the League of Nations sponsored a conference on trafficking, which led later that year to the 1921 Convention for the Suppression of the Traffic in Women and Children.[6] World war brought these efforts to a standstill, and it was not until 1949 that the UN General Assembly (UNGA) passed a resolution that formed the basis of the 1950 Convention for the Suppression of the Traffic in Persons and of the Exploitation of the Prostitution of Others.[7] This treaty was the first to call for the criminalization of the act of

4 The GAO terms the U.S. government's own estimate of some 600,000 to 800,000 persons trafficked annually across borders as "questionable." See U.S. GAO, "Human Trafficking: Better Data, Strategy, and Reporting Needed to Enhance U.S. Antitrafficking Efforts Abroad" in Report to the Chairman, Committee on the Judiciary and the Chairman, Committee on International Relations, House of Representatives, Washington, DC: 2.

5 International Agreement for the Suppression of White Slave Traffic, 18 May 1904, 35 Stat. 426, 1 LNTS 83.

6 Convention for the Suppression of the Traffic in Women and Children, signed in Geneva on 30 September 1921, entered into force on 15 June 1922.

7 Convention for the Suppression of the Traffic in Persons and of the Exploitation of the Prostitution of Others, approved by UNGA Resolution 317 (IV) of 2 December 1949, entered into force on 25 July 1951.

exploiting others for prostitution, but it did not extend to trafficking in human beings for other purposes. In a series of debates and resolutions over the course of the 1990s, the international community tried to address this shortcoming. This effort culminated in an international framework for law enforcement and judicial and technical cooperation embodied in the 2000 UN Convention against Transnational Organized Crime (UNCTOC) and the Protocols on Trafficking in Persons and Smuggling of Migrants.[8] Ratification of the UNCTOC obligates states parties for the first time to criminalize a range of transnational activities, including participation in a transnational organized crime group (Article 5), money laundering (Article 6), and various forms of corruption (Article 8). The protocol addresses human trafficking specifically, defining it in Article 3a as relating to exploitation, and not limiting it to prostitution.[9] The protocol also calls on state parties to criminalize trafficking in persons in Article 5.

This chapter asks, most broadly, *how was this possible?* How did the international community reach normative agreement on the criminalization of human trafficking? What explains states' willingness to become formal parties to these agreements, and (moreover) to change their own national penal codes to conform to this now predominant international standard, which puts criminalization and international cooperation at the center of the effort? The answers to these questions are not at all obvious. Although human trafficking may seem to some to be an egregious evil, attitudes vary among and within states about how to respond. Leaders in countries that are primarily sources of trafficked persons may have concerns that leaders in destination countries want to control immigration generally. There may even be fiscal concerns relating to this issue. Governments such as Moldova's encourage migration to secure remittance-based tax revenues, whereas countries such as Indonesia and the Philippines have explicit policies of increasing human "exports" to support their balance of payments and inward remittance flows. Because it is difficult at times to distinguish voluntary smuggling from involuntary and exploitative trafficking (Zhang 2007), some developing countries worry that the effort to criminalize the latter reflects a broader motive to control migration more generally. Kara's research in South Asia, for example, revealed attitudes among the Nepalese that anti-trafficking awareness campaigns were "nothing more than anti-immigration propaganda" (Kara 2009).

8 Convention against Transnational Organized Crime (UNCTOC) and the Protocols on Trafficking in Persons and Smuggling of Migrants, by UNGA Resolution 55/25 of 15 November 2000.

9 The protocol states the following: "'Trafficking in persons' shall mean the recruitment, transportation, transfer, harbouring or receipt of persons, by means of the threat or use of force or other forms of coercion, of abduction, of fraud, of deception, of the abuse of power or of a position of vulnerability or of the giving or receiving of payments or benefits to achieve the consent of a person having control over another person, for the purpose of exploitation. Exploitation shall include, at a minimum, the exploitation of the prostitution of others or other forms of sexual exploitation, forced labour or services, slavery or practices similar to slavery, servitude or the removal of organs . . . ".

How to handle human trafficking is not exclusively a North–South issue; it is potentially a divisive cultural and ideological issue as well. There are divides, on the one hand, between religiously conservative groups and nations who think that a ban on trafficking should focus on the sexual exploitation of women and children (the approach of the 1949 Treaty, subsequently discussed); and, on the other hand, between feminists who may either join with conservatives in viewing prostitution as inherently exploitative or embrace a more liberal approach that views it as "sex work" (Scarpa 2008). The latter emphasize the exploitative nature of human trafficking for *all* kinds of labor and denounce the emphasis on female sexual exploitation as a patronizing limitation on women's autonomy of movement and career choice (Kempadoo and Doezema 1998). Ostensibly liberal countries make different choices about prostitution: The Netherlands has legalized it whereas Sweden has criminalized it (Di Nicola 2009). Even if countries can agree that particular kinds of trafficking constitute egregious exploitation and should be criminalized, it is harder to get agreement on the boundaries of the exploitative activities in question.

Finally, there is the question as to whether criminalization is the right approach to human trafficking at all. Nongovernmental organizations (NGOs) and human rights activists hardly speak with a single voice on this question. On the one hand, some use the framework of cost–benefit analysis and argue that by raising the price of "doing business" the criminalization and enforcement of the law – with financial penalties sufficient to cut significantly into profits – are the best ways to reduce the problem of human trafficking (Kara 2009). On the other hand, a plethora of analyses emphasize the structural nature of the trafficking problem and warn against too much emphasis on a law enforcement approach (Cameron and Newman 2008).

These points are important, because they highlight the range of disagreements among governments and NGOs that profess to oppose human trafficking. Nevertheless, most of the key international resolutions addressing human trafficking were passed not by transparent voting, but by "consensus." If we look carefully, however, it is possible to understand the interests and actors that were at the forefront of the most recent efforts to criminalize human trafficking, at least as these have played out in the UN.

4. THE GLOBALIZATION OF ANTI-TRAFFICKING RULE OF LAW

4.1. *Initiators: Norm Origination*

In a deep sense, the roots of today's global anti-trafficking efforts were laid by Europeans. The first-ever international agreement in 1902 was among 13 European states, and the diplomats of Europe continued to dominate official discussion of the issue during the interwar years. However, geographical participation expanded considerably in the postwar UN. This is in part, of course, a natural reflection of the rise of newly independent states after decolonization, but it is also consistent with a concern that human trafficking posed a real problem to the sovereignty, security, and development objectives of nations of the global South.

The end of the Cold War presented a new opportunity to address human trafficking in the context of the UN. Meanwhile, the breakup of the Soviet Union and the new freedom to cross borders as well as the economic turmoil it unleashed made the problem of trafficking more urgent over more of the globe than ever before. In 1994, the UNGA approved the Naples Political Declaration and Global Action Plan against Organized Transnational Crime, which had been introduced by a diverse coalition of countries including Costa Rica, the Dominican Republic, Guinea-Bissau, Myanmar, Panama, the Philippines, and the Russian Federation.[10] Two years later, representatives from the Polish government submitted the first draft of the UNCTOC to the General Assembly.

We want to stress that the mechanisms for shaping this resolution into a treaty were quite inclusive. The UNGA created an Ad Hoc Committee on the Elaboration of the Convention against Transnational Organized Crime, which was open to all countries, to develop a comprehensive convention against organized crime. This committee operated out of Vienna from the UN Office on Drugs and Crime.[11] Eleven sessions over a two-year period were dedicated to incorporating the international community in the effort to reach consensus on how to confront transnational crime. Representatives from a wide range of countries representing all regional groups, plus representatives from UN organizations, representatives of the Missions of Permanent Observers, Intergovernmental Organizations, Nongovernmental Organizations, and Institutes of the UN Crime Prevention and Criminal Justice Program network participated in these sessions. The Ad Hoc Committee elected the Italian representative, who served in his personal expert capacity, as chair.[12] The convention addressed a range of transnational crimes including corruption, organized crime, terrorism, and money laundering. Separate protocols were created to address trafficking in persons, smuggling of migrants, and weapons trafficking. It was clearly a significant effort to include a wide swath of the global community in the creation of policy solutions to address common problems.

As already noted, it was the United States, Italy, Austria, and to a certain extent Argentina that took the lead on efforts to create the Human Trafficking protocol to the UNCTOC. By the end of 1998, American officials had led the completion of a first draft of the protocol, and representatives of the major industrialized countries signed a resolution in Vienna in 1998 committing themselves to work collaboratively on the trafficking protocol. In March of 1999, this proposal was introduced at one

[10] Naples Political Declaration and Global Action Plan against Organized Transnational Crime, UNGA Resolution 49/159 of 23 December 1994, UN Doc. A/RES/49/1590.

[11] We thank Delphine Schantz, UN Office on Drugs and Crime, for her insights on the development of the UNCTOC.

[12] See UNGA Resolution 55/383 of 2 November 2000, UN Doc. A/55/383 for a summary report on each session and key statements by state leaders.

of the first sessions of the broadly inclusive Ad Hoc Committee, and it formed the basis for the proposal that would be introduced at the UN Third Committee in 2000. The draft protocol was proposed to the Third Committee by a coalition of states, including 22 from Western Europe, 7 from Eastern Europe and the Former Soviet Union, 11 from the Americas, 9 from Asia, 7 from Africa, and 1 from the Middle East. Reflecting their respective priorities, drafts left the Argentines' hands with references to women and children; American pens tended to broaden coverage to "persons." According to one account, "Because it combined the initial work of Argentina and the U.S., the proposal alternately defined victims as 'persons' or 'women and children'" (DeStefano 2007: 20).

A series of controversies marked the early discussion of the protocol. One emerged between destination countries and those with significant amounts of legal outmigration. The latter were concerned largely about provisions that persons found to be trafficked would be returned to their country of origin. Sending countries such as Pakistan, China, and India did not want this to be part of the formal agreement. (These states as well as Japan, Egypt, Thailand, and Ukraine abstained from signing the protocol, very possibly over this issue.) Another controversy emerged among the destination countries at the forefront of the drafting process. Conservative constituencies influenced the United States to take a harder line against prostitution than did several other leading industrialized countries, which "raised the hackles of a number of western countries, including Canada and the Netherlands" (DeStefano 2007: 26).

However, before concluding that a handful of wealthy industrialized countries were the sole supporters of resolutions and treaties to control human trafficking, we find it instructive to examine exactly what took place over the course of the past decade and a half at the UN. Human Trafficking resolutions were introduced, debated, and revised in the Third Committee (the Social, Humanitarian, and Cultural Committee). Between 1994 and 2008, at least ten resolutions were introduced relating to human trafficking (including the series of resolutions in 2000 referred to earlier that became the Human Trafficking Protocol). In this forum, developing countries took an especially active role, both as the initial sponsors of resolutions as well as the relatively small cluster of countries to subsequently join in sponsoring resolutions well before consensus was reached on its passage (as already mentioned, no formal votes were taken). Table 7.1 lists the most active participants on the record in the UN Third Committee, from 1995 onward with respect to the major human trafficking resolutions. This is hardly a list dominated by the wealthy first world. Costa Rica, Panama, and the Philippines initiated more resolutions on human trafficking than any other countries in this forum. African nations played a clear supporting role as "joiners," eventually sponsoring resolutions introduced by others. Seven out of 13 of the top joiners over the past decade and a half were from Africa.

What the most active participants have in common is not so much their developmental status or their culture but rather how they experience the externalities

TABLE 7.1. *Most active participants in sponsoring the major human trafficking resolutions in the UN Third Committee, 1995–2009*

Most active initiators	No.	Most active joiners	No.	Most active overall	No.
Costa Rica	8	Liberia	4	Costa Rica	9
Panama	8	Ethiopia	4	Philippines	9
Philippines	7	Tanzania	4	Panama	9
Bangladesh	5	Norway	4	Argentina	8
Dominican Republic	5	Paraguay	4	Dominican Republic	7
Ecuador	5	Indonesia	4	Ecuador	7
Argentina	4	Namibia	4	Belgium	7
Chile	4	Ghana	4	Bangladesh	6
France	4	Argentina	4	Paraguay	6
Germany	4	Azerbaijan	4	Thailand	6
Greece	4	Belgium	4	Liberia	6
Italy	4	Madagascar	4	Mongolia	6
Luxembourg	4	Malawi	4	Ukraine	6
Mongolia	4			Luxembourg	6
Nigeria	4			Cote d'Ivoire	6
South Africa	4			Austria	6
				Lithuania	6
				El Salvador	6
				Greece	6
				Indonesia	6

Note: The table shows the number of resolutions initiated or sponsored.

associated with human trafficking. By gathering data on whether a country is a country of origin, a destination, a transit country, or one with a significant internal trafficking problem (these are not mutually exclusive categories; countries can be in more than one or even all four, as in the case of India), we find that destination countries (see Figure 7.4) introduced and joined significantly more anti-trafficking resolutions in the Third Committee than did countries that are not major trafficking destinations. On average, destination countries introduced or joined almost three resolutions between 1994 and 2008, whereas nondestination countries sponsored slightly over two. The difference in means is statistically different from zero at the 90 percent level. The same is true for countries with significant internal trafficking problems: They were far more active in advancing the anti-trafficking agenda than were countries that have no such problems. In contrast, the difference in anti-trafficking activity in the Third Committee did not differ much based on whether a country was a country of origin or a transit country.

These patterns persist if we look at the evidence in a different way. Table 7.2 looks at the factors that influence the likelihood that a country will initiate or join one of the major anti-trafficking resolutions in the UN Third Committee in any year in

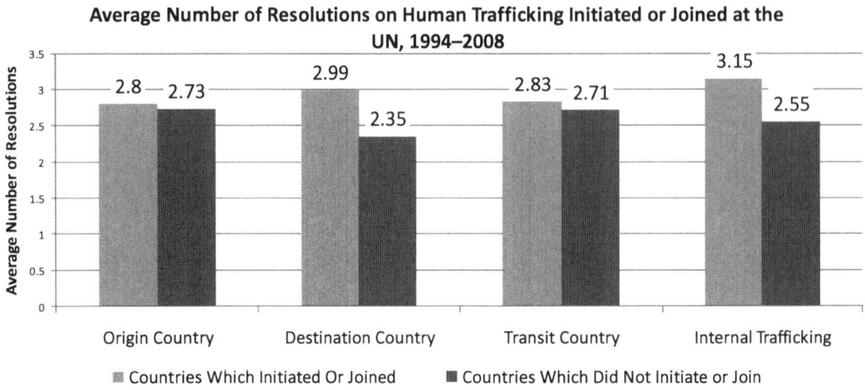

FIGURE 7.4. Resolutions on human trafficking. (*Note:* Countries can be in more than one category. Number of origin countries = 110; nonorigin countries = 45; destination countries = 104; nondestination countries = 51; transit countries = 89; non-transit countries = 66; internal trafficking countries = 59; noninternal trafficking countries = 96.)

which one of those resolutions was introduced at all. (That is, we have eliminated the large numbers of years in which no resolutions were introduced for purposes of this analysis.) There is a strong and consistent correlation with having experienced the externalities associated with human trafficking and sponsoring leadership in the Third Committee. The most striking result is that countries that have internal trafficking problems are among the most likely to introduce or join a major anti-trafficking resolution in this forum. This is true even when we control for the developmental or income level (which never seems to have a systematic impact on anti-trafficking norm development) and when we control for child labor (which probably does affect such activity, negatively). The results also suggest that countries reputed to have the strongest commitment to the rule of law domestically are leaders in developing anti-trafficking norms in the UN. Moreover, the table suggests that normative convergence increases over time: The positive and highly significant coefficient on the year variable indicates that more and more countries chose to co-initiate and join these resolutions over time. Overall, Table 7.2 provides an interesting picture of who most actively supported anti-trafficking norm development: It appears to have been spearheaded by the countries most affected, and those with the strongest (reputed) commitment to furthering the rule of law.

4.2. *Norm Diffusion*

Although leadership in UN forums indicates a strong interest in a particular set of norms, it does not create legal obligations to implement or to adhere to them. Indeed, norm development, though crucial, is only a first step in the globalization

TABLE 7.2. *Influences on anti-trafficking activity in the UN Third Committee*

Explanatory variables	Model 1	Model 2	Model 3
Country of origin	.105* (p = .085)	.136** (p = .038)	.138** (p = .032)
Transit country	.001 (p = .977)	.002 (p = .962)	.0005 (p = .992)
Destination country	.102* (p = .052)	.035 (p = .521)	.102* (p = .069)
Internal trafficking	.125** (p = .011)	.127** (p = .012)	.133*** (p = .008)
Rule of law	.093*** (p = .000)	.098*** (p = .001)	.061 (p = .104)
Year	.046*** (p = .000)	.048*** (p = .000)	.045*** (p = .000)
Child labor	–	−.003 (p = .107)	–
Low income			−.012 (p = .902)
Lower-middle income			.061 (p = .479)
Upper-middle income			.019 (p = .780)
High income			.145 (p = .101)
constant	−91.69*** (p = .000)	95.94*** (p = .000)	−90.28*** (p = .000)
No. of observations	1085	1008	1085
R^2	.128	.138	.131

Dependent variable: initiation or joining of anti-trafficking resolutions.
Note: Table includes years in which resolutions were introduced only. Results are of a logistic regression with robust standard errors, clustered by country.
* Significant at the .10 level; ** significant at the .05 level; *** significant at the .01 level.

of the rule of law. We have discovered that governments of societies affected by transnational crime were active in formulating anti-trafficking norms, but how do we explain the *diffusion of these norms in a legally binding form?* In this section we develop two possible mechanisms of normative diffusion: diffusion that results from experience with the externalities (and anticipated externalities) associated with the cross-border movement of coerced human labor, and diffusion via hegemonic pressure.[13]

[13] No doubt other factors are at work, such as the use of powerful frames that define human trafficking as a human rights issue, making it harder to oppose criminalization and punishment, but we reserve analysis of that and cognate processes to another paper.

4.2.1. Negative Externalities

To appreciate the role that externalities potentially play in the global diffusion of law aimed to combat human trafficking, one must appreciate the potential threat posed by these practices to the health of societies in which trafficking flourishes, and to the authority of the state itself, especially to those states that have struggled to develop and maintain institutions of fair, transparent, and legitimate governance. The challenge to state authority starts at the national borders: Trafficking potentially corrupts immigration and border control officials. Kara estimates that trafficking was so heavy and bribery so common at the border between Nepal and India that it drove the illicit price of entry to a mere 2–5 percent of the final price of the trafficked individual (Kara 2009). Trafficking not only corrupts officials of the state but it also means a loss of sovereign control over the territory of the state itself.

Governments also have to worry about the negative externalities associated with criminal economies of scale. Even if a government has no particular sympathy for modern-day slaves, traffickers are increasingly linked to broader criminal networks that operate by using similar transit routes and networks. Traffickers in human beings often use the same connections as do smugglers of weapons, drugs, and other contraband. There is also the potential for organized crime and terrorist organizations to join forces, a potential that is increasingly being realized in various parts of the world (Jonsson 2009). Evidence suggests that terrorist organizations from the FARC guerrillas in Colombia to the Wa State army in Burma, and from the PKK in Turkey to the ETA in Spain, have used narcotics smuggling as a source of income (Cornell 2009); human trafficking, using the same channels, is potentially an additional income stream.

Finally, human trafficking can result in a whole range of consequences that could be socially or politically destabilizing. Among these are the spread of violence, communicable diseases, and severe psychological and physical damage to victims. Where human exports consist mainly of large numbers of young women, it can contribute to processes of demographic decline already underway, as in the case of Russia, Ukraine, and Moldova (Shelley 2009). Because trafficking numbers are unavailable, it is impossible to quantify these impacts with any precision. But the point is this: Human trafficking is a violent and socially corrosive activity, typically connected with broader networks and almost inevitably conducive to corruption of public officials. Although it may line the pockets of perpetrators and some officials, it is generally detrimental to public health, political stability, and the domestic rule of law in both sending and receiving countries (Jonsson 2009). For these reasons, "It would seem to be in the interest of most states to cooperate with other states in the fight against trafficking. The only exception would be if the state itself somehow makes a profit on the trafficking in persons directly or indirectly[,] which may very well be the case" (Österdahl 2009).

New information is often critical to the policy choices states make and, as we have illustrated in Figures 7.2 and 7.3, there has been a huge increase in information relating to the human trafficking problem over the past decade.[14] Indeed, it is possible that policy makers are becoming more aware of trafficking and its consequences in their own jurisdictions than they were only a few years ago. As information increases about the range and nature of the problem, we might expect governments self-interestedly to embrace anti-trafficking norms. In addition, governments are increasingly likely to anticipate the consequences of policies designed to clamp down on human trafficking elsewhere. The flexible and ad hoc nature of trafficking networks means that criminalization and law enforcement decisions in Country A can block and rechannel criminal activities in ways that negatively affect nearby countries. Patrick Keenan (2006) gives the example of how the more vigorous prosecution of sex trafficking in the United States has likely led to an increase in sex tourism to other jurisdictions. Similarly, when the United States cracked down on Puerto Rico's participation in drug transit between South America and the United States, drug traffickers descended on Haiti (Gros 2003). Governments sensitive to negative externalities are likely to anticipate the consequences if other countries in their neighborhood criminalize human trafficking, and they do not. Anticipation of spillover effects could cause governments to update their expectations about the relative costs and benefits of criminalizing trafficking and enforcing the law within their own jurisdiction. The very fluidity of transnational crime provides strategic incentives to harmonize policies with neighbors to avoid becoming the weak link in the law enforcement chain.

If the current wave of transnational criminal law can be explained at least in part by a growing appreciation of the negative externalities associated with human trafficking, several patterns should be observable in state behavior. First, we would expect states that experience the trafficking problem to be among the first to accept stronger anti-trafficking norms embodied in legally binding treaties and domestic criminal law reform. Countries of origin, those plagued by internal trafficking, and destination countries should all be far more eager to criminalize and commit to international agreements than their relatively unaffected counterparts. Second, the externality argument can be tested by looking at the response of so-called Country A to the policies of other countries within its region. Specifically, we expect that if nearby countries criminalize human trafficking, expectations of spillovers as criminal networks set up shop in lower risk jurisdictions will encourage others to criminalize as well. We use the density of criminalization events in the region as a reasonable proxy for updating information about negative externalities.

4.2.2. Hegemonic Pressure

Coercion is a mechanism that is central to much of the literature on policy diffusion (Simmons et al. 2008), and it is a possibility in the areas of transnational crime

[14] We are unable to formally test this proposition in the models that follow, because the distribution of the data does not permit the calculation of hazard ratios in plausible specifications.

and human trafficking as well. Unlike some normatively laden issue areas, such as (domestic) human rights practices, the nature of externalities provides strong motives for powerful actors to marshal resources to coerce others into their conceptions of appropriate transnational law enforcement. Because the cross-border consequences of transnational crime are potentially severe, powerful states (especially destination states) have motives to use whatever leverage they can marshal – including economic or even security pressures – to encourage others to criminalize unwanted activities and to enforce the law.

Theories of acculturation by means of various forms of social pressure, including hegemonic pressure, are also central to much of the literature on norm cascades and policy diffusion. Ryan Goodman and Derek Jinks (2004) define acculturation as the "general process by which actors adopt the beliefs and behavioural patterns of the surrounding culture." It includes a number of microprocesses such as mimicry, status maximization, and identification. Acculturation is effective when groups generate varying degree of cognitive and social pressures, real or imagined, to conform. This is a process that borders on coercion, except that there need not be explicit material incentives to alter behavior or policies. The line between coercion and acculturation is not always a bright one, but both involve outside pressures as the primary mechanism of diffusion.

Just how might we expect powerful states to influence others to get serious about human trafficking? Material pressure can be exerted through the use of economic or security threats, as the Bush administration did, to try to force its views regarding the International Criminal Court on other countries (Kelley 2007). One measure of the potential for such pressures is the extent of trade dependence a country has on the United States or the European Union (or both). As the major destination countries, these two entities have both the motive and the means to use trade to influence the effort others make to suppress human trafficking. We think it is much more likely, however, that powerful states will attempt to pressure others to accept international anti-crime norms at minimal cost to themselves. One way to do this is through shaming. Fortunately, excellent evidence is available of hegemonic attempts to shame other countries regarding their human trafficking efforts. Every year, the U.S. Department of State issues reports on human trafficking and literally rates countries on their efforts to control it. We have read all of those reports, and where a country rates as making "no effort," or is on the "watch list" for making no effort, we have coded that as "U.S. pressure."[15] If the shaming tactic is effective,

[15] The U.S. Department of State, "Trafficking in Persons Report" (2009): 51, says the following: "Tier 2 Watch List: (2WL): Countries whose governments do not fully comply with the TVPA's minimum standards but are making significant efforts to bring themselves into compliance with those standards AND: (a) The absolute number of victims of severe forms of trafficking is very significant or is significantly increasing; or (b) There is a failure to provide evidence of increasing efforts to combat severe forms of trafficking in persons from the previous year; or (c) The determination that a country is making significant efforts to bring themselves into compliance with minimum standards was based

we expect a low rating by the U.S. Department of State to lead to a tougher policy stance on criminalization in the following year.

How plausible is this shaming mechanism, and how appropriate the measure? First, it is noteworthy that the U.S. GAO itself admits that the State Department ratings are not scientific and are used primarily to try to influence others' policies.[16] Thus we argue that although it would hardly be appropriate to use the U.S. tier ratings as objective measures of actual policies, they constitute reasonable evidence of efforts on the part of the United States to lean on other countries to tighten up their policies. Furthermore, the secondary literature sometimes makes explicit reference to U.S. Trafficking in Persons reports as being especially embarrassing and responsible for policy review in some countries (Fein 2007). Research by DeStefano reveals how upset countries get when they are not happy with their rating, and how this displeasure sometimes translates into policy change. He notes, "A number of nations, including South Korea, Israel, and Saudi Arabia, complained publicly about their Tier 3 ranking [in 2001]." By 2002, South Korea "had moved to protect victims, created a task force, and coordinate more than 1000 prosecutions" (DeStefano 2007: 121). If this anecdote can be generalized, we should expect a low rating to correlate with policy improvements on average in the following year or years.

We examine two outcomes that reflect states' legal commitment to counter transnational crime. First, we model one important aspect of the emerging international consensus regarding human trafficking: that it should be criminalized in domestic law. In fact, criminalization is required by Article 5 of the Human Trafficking Protocol. Second, we model the factors that increase the likelihood of ratifying the Human Trafficking Protocol of 2000 itself. This protocol to the 2000 Transnational Organized Crime Convention constitutes the most explicit and legally binding commitment states can currently make to cooperate to counter international human trafficking. It is the source of international rule of law norms that define state obligations to one another internationally. Together, these two policy choices – ratification of international rules and adaptation of domestic law to their requirements – constitute important evidence of the "interface" between the rule of law at the domestic and international levels (Nollkaemper 2009).

We use statistical methods that focus on the period of time until the events of interest occur (in this case, domestic criminalization of human trafficking and ratification of the protocol). Widely used in epidemiological studies that seek to understand factors that affect mortality rates, this technique can be used analogously to test for the conditions associated with a greater "risk" of these policy changes

on commitments by the county to take additional future steps over the next year. Tier 3: Countries whose governments do not fully comply with the minimum standards and are not making significant efforts to do so." Tier 2WL and Tier 3 are combined to form our indicator of "U.S. pressure."

16 U.S. GAO, "Human Trafficking: Better Data, Strategy, and Reporting Needed to Enhance U.S. Antitrafficking Efforts Abroad," in Report to the Chairman, Committee on the Judiciary and the Chairman, Committee on International Relations, House of Representatives, Washington DC.

occurring (given that they have not yet occurred yet).[17] We are interested in exploring whether systematic influences associated with domestic commitments to the rule of law, negative externalities, and hegemonic pressures influence the rate of ratification and criminalization. These influences should show up in statistically significant *hazard ratios* that, if greater than 1, signify a positive influence and if smaller than 1 signify a negative influence.

4.3. *Findings: Criminalization*

Table 7.3 provides some preliminary evidence on these mechanisms. The dependent variable in this case is *criminalization of human trafficking in national law*. We have two definitions of criminalization, reflecting different levels of stringency. The strictest definition implies that the country has brought itself into compliance with international treaty standards, making trafficking of persons illegal and defining trafficking broadly. Definition 1 comprises those cases in which a country has enacted specific anti-trafficking legislation, with broad coverage admitting of no important exceptions. The second definition is more lax. It includes all cases under the first definition, but it also adds countries who have partially criminalized trafficking or who have criminalized with some exceptions.[18]

First, it is fairly clear that countries with stronger reputations for adherence to the rule of law as measured in surveys by the World Bank are more likely to have criminalized human trafficking since 1990 than those that rate lower. A shift of 1 point (on a World Bank rule of law scale that ranges from −2.3 to 2) is associated with anywhere between a 47 and 67 percent increase in the probability of criminalizing trafficking in a given year, given that a country has not done so already. Moreover, the reputed strength of the rule of law in a country is apparently slightly stronger

[17] Specifically we employ a Cox proportional hazard model to examine the effects of a number of continuous and categorical predictors, and because some of these vary over time, the tests presented here use time-varying covariates. The Cox model estimates a "hazard rate," which is defined as follows:

$$h(t) = \frac{\text{probability of ratification between times } t \text{ and } t \pm 1}{(t+1)\,(\text{probability of ratification after time } t).}$$

The hazard rate is then modeled as a function of the baseline hazard (h_0) at time t – which is simply the hazard for an observation with all explanatory variables set to zero – as well as a number of explanatory variables, the estimates of which indicate proportional changes relative to this baseline hazard. The null hypothesis is that the proportionate hazard rate for any given explanatory variable of interest is 1 (it has no effect on the baseline hazard rate).

[18] Countries that are included in Definition 3 that are NOT included in the most stringent definition include Bangladesh, Benin, Bulgaria, Burkina Faso, Cambodia, Chile, Costa Rica, Ecuador, Egypt, Eritrea, Gabon, Guatemala, Iraq, Israel, Mali, Mauritius, Mexico, Morocco, Nepal, Pakistan, Panama, Serbia, Singapore, South Africa, Togo, Turkmenistan, Turkey, the United Kingdom, Venezuela, and Zambia. Coding is based on descriptions available in the UN's *Global Report on Trafficking in Persons*. See United Nations Office on Drugs and Crime, *Global Report on Trafficking of Persons*, February 2009.

TABLE 7.3. *Criminalization of human trafficking in national law*

Explanatory variables	Model 1a	Model 1b	Model 2a	Model 2b	Model 3a	Model 3b	Model 4a
Rule of law	1.64***	1.43***	1.52**	1.48***	1.67**	1.47**	1.76***
	($p = .005$)	($p = .005$)	($p = .031$)	($p = .009$)	($p = .024$)	($p = .020$)	($p = .001$)
Ratification of the 2000 agreement	1.37**	1.48***	1.28	1.41***	1.33*	1.38***	1.46***
	($p = .028$)	($p = .001$)	($p = .110$)	($p = .006$)	($p = .089$)	($p = .008$)	($p = .008$)
Density of criminalizations in region ($t - 1$)	6.98***	4.04***	9.77***	4.65***	4.23**	2.64	9.17***
	($p = .000$)	($p = .005$)	($p = .000$)	($p = .004$)	($p = .035$)	($p = .142$)	($p = .000$)
U.S. pressure ($t - 1$)	2.20***	1.80***	2.38**	1.90***	1.82*	1.79**	2.46***
	($p = .009$)	($p = .008$)	($p = .016$)	($p = .009$)	($p = .089$)	($p = .024$)	($p = .003$)
Prevalence of child labor	.978**	.976***	.983	.976	.967***	.974**	–
	($p = .047$)	($p = .013$)	($p = .222$)	($p = .035$)	($p = .010$)	($p = .021$)	
Low- and middle-income category	2.50**	1.89**	1.95	2.05**	3.02**	1.99**	2.18**
	($p = .024$)	($p = .038$)	($p = .150$)	($p = .054$)	($p = .016$)	($p = .050$)	($p = .031$)
Country of origin			.531	1.28			–
			($p = .160$)	($p = .498$)			
Transit country			.974	1.04			–
			($p = .922$)	($p = .873$)			
Destination country			.534*	1.41			–
			($p = .056$)	($p = .171$)			
Internal trafficking			1.36	.830			–
			($p = .311$)	($p = .375$)			
U.S. aid/GDP	–	–	–	–	608.02**	81.73	–
					($p = .011$)	($p = .189$)	
U.S. trade/total trade	–	–	–	–	.487	1.02	–
					($p = .521$)	($p = .879$)	
EU trade/total trade	–	–	–	–	1.39	1.15	–
					($p = .618$)	($p = .779$)	
No. of news stories	–	–	–	–	–	–	1.0002**
							($p = .040$)
No. of countries	134	132	116	114	121	120	138
No. of criminalizations	76	107	63	90	63	90	78
No. of obs.	2126	1918	1882	1692	1715	1586	2137
Prob. > χ^2	0.000	0.000	0.000	0.0001	0.000	0.000	0.000

Note: Results are of a Cox proportional hazard model with robust standard errors, clustered by country. Hazard ratios and probability values are shown. The "a" models have a strict definition; the "b" models have a lax one.

* Significant at the .10 level; ** significant at the .05 level; *** significant at the .01 level.

when we use the stricter definition of criminalization. This suggests that the wave of attention given to transnational crime is related to the recent status of a country's rule of law generally.

Second, it appears that countries on average implement their commitments under the 2000 UNCTOC and its Human Trafficking Protocol. Ratification of one of these agreements increased the probability of subsequently criminalizing human trafficking by between 28 and 48 percent. (As we will see, it is more likely that ratification of one of these treaties increases the probability of criminalization, rather than the other way around.) Unsurprisingly, the treaty ratification effect may be slightly stronger when the weaker definition of criminalization is employed; more states are likely to make minimal rather than maximal changes to implement their treaty obligations.

There is some fairly consistent evidence of hegemonic pressures at work in explaining criminalization, at least of a shaming sort. Across each of these models, if the U.S. State Department has put the country in the "no effort" or "watch list" categories in its human trafficking reports, chances *just about double* that that country will criminalize human trafficking in the following year. This comports with what we have read in the secondary literature, which sometimes refers to the embarrassment of government officials in particular countries when the United States criticizes their efforts so publicly (Fein 2007).

To further explore the possibility of pressures from the United States, we collected data on aid and trade dependence for each country. Because the U.S. Tier system was designed specifically to allow for the possibility of tying aid to improvements in human trafficking policies, we should expect that the higher the dependence of a country on U.S. bilateral aid, the more likely that country would be to criminalize human trafficking. This in fact appears to be the case, especially for more stringent definitions of criminalization. For every 1 percentage point increase in the proportion of a country's aid as a share of its gross domestic product (GDP), there is an estimated sixfold increase in the probability that a country will adopt strict laws criminalizing human trafficking. The result for the more lax definition is not as clear, but it is also in the expected direction.

Trade with the United States or with Europe is not plausibly correlated with criminalization policies, however. We collected data on the share of each country's trade with the United States and with Europe as a share of its total trade, but this measure failed to explain criminalization. This finding is consistent with the literature that emphasizes the difficulties of using trade as a sanctioning weapon for human rights or other purposes. Nonetheless, it also supports the intended purpose of U.S. legislation: to pressure countries to criminalize and to use the threat of reducing or eliminating U.S. *aid* to do so.

There is also evidence consistent with the anticipation of negative externalities associated with criminalization in a neighboring jurisdiction. The growing density of criminalizations within a country's region is associated with strong pressures to change one's national criminal code in similar ways. One way in which the transnationalization of criminal law has taken place, apparently, is through the anticipation of the negative spillovers associated with being one of the few remaining jurisdictions in a region that does not take trafficking seriously. Such a stance is likely to make one's own jurisdiction even more attractive to transnational criminal elements.

One might object to our interpretation of the effect of the density of criminalization in the region as a reaction to potential negative externalities. Arguably, a possible interpretation that is more common in sociology is some form of mimicry, based on a less rational explanation of state behavior. We think this interpretation is less plausible than an anticipated response to externalities. Note that the hazard ratio is one-third to one-half again as strong in the case of countries implementing the strictest definition of criminalization. These are precisely the cases in which strong enforcement could be expected to divert criminal activities to other jurisdictions. A strong response in kind under these conditions is likely to represent quite meaningful criminal legal reform. In contrast, the hazard ratios are convincing but smaller for the more lax definition of criminalization. Were nonrational mimetic processes at work, we might expect the strength of the hazard ratios to be reversed.

The likelihood of criminalizing human trafficking in domestic law also seems to increase with the exposure of trafficking issues in the international media. Model 4 shows that there is a strong positive relationship between stories in the global press (data are those plotted in Figure 7.3) and the probability of criminalization. With reasonable precision, the model suggests that every 1,000 stories to be found in LexisNexis is associated with a 20 percent increase in the likelihood that a country will criminalize, according to the stricter of the two definitions.[19] This could support our claim about the importance of negative externalities: As information increases describing the extent and the nature of human trafficking, more countries may be likely to take the move to criminalize.

Surprisingly, however, we found no evidence that jurisdictions in which trafficking was a severe problem were more likely to criminalize, at least not with a rather strenuous set of control variables. Especially difficult to understand is that the only statistically significant result was in the unexpected direction: Destination countries were apparently *less likely* to criminalize human trafficking than were nondestination countries. One possibility is that the data we have are incapable of establishing the direction of causation. The categories do not vary over time; in fact, they are gleaned from fairly recent NGO assessments. It is possible that destination countries are in that category because they have refused – for whatever reason – to criminalize human trafficking. Because we cannot disentangle cause and effect with the categorical, unchanging data available to us at this point, we simply note that these results do not comport well with how we originally formulated our argument about negative externalities.

We included a few other controls that bear some discussion. We expected a country's developmental level to have some influence on criminalization and found

[19] We could not estimate a confidence interval by using the lax definition. Moreover, it was only possible to calculate confidence intervals at all when we increased observations by removing the child labor variable.

that, indeed, the biggest shifts in this direction were to be found in the low- and low- to middle-income categories as defined by the World Bank. As a group, these countries were just about twice as likely to criminalize compared with the upper-middle and upper-income categories. It is interesting that some of the poorer countries have been most ready to criminalize human trafficking. Note that this is the case even when we control for U.S. pressure as already described. On the assumption that it is more difficult to alter practices if they are broadly sewn into the fabric of a culture and an economy, we further controlled for child labor, and as expected found that the greater the economic activity of 10- to 14-year-old children in an economy, the less likely a country is to criminalize human trafficking. Child labor practices, although not themselves immutable to change (Simmons 2009), likely contribute to the social and political resistance that makes criminalization of human trafficking more difficult.

We checked for the robustness of these results by controlling for other conditions that for purposes of saving space are not reported in the tables. For example, we found no evidence for the proposition that ratification of human rights treaties – a proxy for the appeal of the human rights frame in addressing human trafficking – has anything to do with the national criminalization of human trafficking. Countries that ratify lots of human rights treaties are no more likely to criminalize human trafficking than those that tend to stand aloof from such obligations. (We will see this is clearly not the case for ratification of the protocol, as discussed later.) Nor is there any evidence that membership in regional, subregional, or cultural organizations contributes to an increased probability of criminalization, which is suggestive of the weakness or possible irrelevance of organizations such as the Council of Europe, the Association of Southeast Asian Nations, the Organization of American States, the African Union, and the Organization of Islamic Conference in socializing states toward criminalization of human trafficking. (This is another contrast with our findings regarding protocol ratification.) In some specifications, we found membership in these organizations was associated with a very slight negative likelihood of criminalization, but these results were not very robust, and they do not change the findings discussed herein. We also found a decreased likelihood to criminalize human trafficking in countries that are predominantly Islamic (when we used the more lax definition of criminalization), but we do not have a strong theoretical explanation for this finding, which in any case does not alter our main findings. Although we think it likely that culture matters in the formulation of criminal law provisions,[20] we cannot think of a coherent theoretical argument for the negative association between Islam and criminalization of human trafficking.

[20] Culture may influence governance more broadly; for example, it may influence attitudes toward and tolerance of the rule of law, corruption, and accountability. See, e.g., Licht, Goldschmidt, and Schwartz (2002).

Overall, these results suggest that the most promising avenues for understanding the diffusion of criminalization lies in a combination of not-so-subtle social pressure by the United States, concerns about negative spillovers when others criminalize, growing information in the media about problems associated with human trafficking, and a desire to maintain the rule of law by combating activities that can lead to the corruption of public officials and denigrate human dignity.

4.4. *Findings: Ratification of the 2000 Human Trafficking Protocol*

In the earlier section we tested for influences on the decision to change national laws. In this section we turn to the ratification of international law. What factors make it more or less likely that a country will ratify the Human Trafficking Protocol within the year, if it has not already done so? Our efforts to answer this question are displayed in Table 7.4. The first point to make is that despite the fact that the protocol takes a prosecute-and-punish approach to human trafficking, very different explanations seem to apply to treaty behavior compared to national penal policies. Models 1a and 1b import most of the variables from the national criminalization models of Table 7.3, but find them wanting in the context of treaty ratification. In particular, there is practically no relationship between a country's rule of law status and its propensity to ratify the Human Trafficking Protocol. Interestingly, whether or not a country has already criminalized human trafficking in national law also has no systematic bearing on the willingness to ratify these agreements. Moreover, the density of ratifications in the region in the previous period loses its explanatory power in a specification that takes membership in regional organizations and a country's broader patterns of treaty ratification into account (Model 4). Developmental indicators are no longer linearly related to the outcome of interest; it is not the lower-income but the middle-income countries that are more likely to be at the forefront of treaty ratification. Nor does the prevalence of child labor help to explain the willingness or reluctance to ratify. Pressure from the United States has no discernible effect on ratification. The weak results for U.S. pressure might also be due to the fact that – judging from its own record of multilateral treaty ratification – the United States puts more stock in changes in *national* laws than in *international* law.

There is some evidence that the nature of externalities influences states' ratification decisions. The strong positive influence (with the exceptions of Model 4) associated with the density of regional ratification is again consistent with concern about spillover effects if other states decide to toughen their enforcement of anti-trafficking norms. Countries of origin are reluctant to ratify the Human Trafficking Protocol: They are almost 42 percent less likely to ratify than are countries that are not significant sources of trafficked persons. There is good evidence that transit countries and countries with internal trafficking problems are more likely to ratify the

TABLE 7.4. *Ratification of the Human Trafficking Protocol, 2000*

Explanatory variables	Model 1 (Protocol)	Model 2 (Protocol)	Model 3 (Protocol)	Model 4 (Protocol)
Rule of law	1.12	1.09	1.08	.053
	($p = .335$)	($p = .413$)	($p = .434$)	($p = .636$)
National criminalization	1.01	–	–	–
	($p = .971$)			
Density of ratifications in region ($t - 1$)	4.64***	2.85**	4.99**	1.83
	($p = .005$)	($p = .035$)	($p = .016$)	($p = .250$)
Ratification of 1949 Treaty	1.31	1.36	1.26	1.07
	($p = .140$)	($p = .3087$)	($p = .205$)	($p = .688$)
Prevalence of child labor	.994	–	–	–
	($p = .579$)			
Middle-income categories	1.56**	1.68***	1.39*	1.60***
	($p = .046$)	($p = .003$)	($p = .081$)	($p = .007$)
Country of origin	–	.577***	–	–
		($p = .006$)		
Destination country	–	.977	–	–
		($p = .912$)		
Transit country	–	1.34	–	–
		($p = .119$)		
Internal trafficking	–	1.64**		–
		($p = .011$)		
U.S. pressure ($t - 1$)	–	–	1.19	–
			($p = .541$)	
U.S. aid/GDP	–	–	15.35	–
			($p = .310$)	
U.S. trade share	–	–	.776	–
			($p = .612$)	
EU trade share	–	–	2.04	–
			($p = .115$)	
No. of human rights treaties ratified	–	–	–	1.16***
				($p = .000$)
Membership in regional organization	–	–	–	1.28*
				($p = .098$)
No. of countries	137	155	160	184
No. of ratifications	104	112	103	129
No. of observations	1031	1202	1114	1454
Prob. > χ^2	0.024	0.000	0.0038	0.000

Note: Results are of a Cox proportional hazard model with robust standard errors, clustered by country. Hazard ratios and probability values are shown.

* Significant at the .10 level; ** significant at the .05 level; *** significant at .the 01 level.

protocol. Countries with severe internal human trafficking problems are estimated to be about 64 percent more likely to ratify than those without an internal trafficking problem, whereas transit countries are (somewhat less) likely to be about 34 percent more likely to ratify than are those for whom human trafficking transit is not an issue. We note, though, that this result is just slightly below well-accepted standards of statistical significance ($p = .119$). It is surprising that status as a destination country apparently does not influence ratification, however.

In sharp contrast to domestic legal changes, international legal commitments are much more influenced by regional associations and ratification patterns with respect to human rights agreements. Membership in regional associations had limited explanatory power with respect to domestic criminal law reform (and possibly, as already mentioned, a negative association on criminalization), but a significant and positive influence on the ratification of the Human Trafficking Protocol. Membership in a regional, subregional, or cultural organization (Council of Europe, Association of Southeast Asian Nations, the African Union, Organization of American States, and the Organization of Islamic Conference) was associated with a 28 percent increase in the probability of ratifying the trafficking protocol. Certainly, it appears that the human rights frame has had some influence on the decision to ratify. The number of human rights treaties ratified by a country is a strong, positive predictor; indeed, it is one of the few reliable indicators associated with ratification of the human trafficking protocol. Each human rights treaty ratified is associated with about a 16 percent increase in ratifying the Human Trafficking Protocol. This means that once a state has ratified about eight human rights treaties, the likelihood of ratifying the protocol has about doubled. We tentatively conclude that in addition to states' interests in avoiding the negative externalities associated with human trafficking, strong socialization forces may be at work when it comes to ratifying formal human trafficking agreements.

5. CONCLUSIONS

The rule of law has proved to be an attractive way to put many issues of good governance squarely on national and international agendas, from Afghanistan to Zimbabwe, from the World Bank to the United Nations. Globalization has raised the issue of the transnationalization of good governance, especially in the interstices of national legal systems. International institutions and major destination countries have worked hard to convince governments that trafficking in persons represents a threat not only to some abstract goal of "good governance" but also to economic development itself. The UN has further asserted that there is a link between addressing transnational crime, establishing the rule of law, and supporting economic development. Speaking before the UN Third Committee in 2008, just as they took up the problem of formulating a global action plan to implement the Human Trafficking Protocol, UN officials warned that governments who cannot enforce the law find their countries are "trapped in a malign spiral of underdevelopment leading to violence that feeds back into an even greater degree of poverty."[21] The European Union takes a similar position.[22] It is quite natural, therefore, that national authorities have approached the problem of transnational crime as an extension of the project of good governance and the domestic rule of law. There is what one might term a "functional logic" that is touted to encourage the criminalization of human and other forms of trafficking: The problem is illicit trade in persons; the solution is better and more universal law enforcement. At stake may very well be the ability of national authorities to maintain control over their jurisdiction and, it is often claimed, over the future trajectory of their development.

The effort to establish international understandings and cooperation to deal with the rise in transnational crime associated with globalization is a reflection of this development. If the last quarter of the 20th century can be characterized by a wave of interest in not only liberalization of markets and polities but also the "good governance" of these institutions, then the attention that transnational crime has received in national and international forums can be readily understood.

This chapter has advanced several arguments about the diffusion of transnational criminal law norms internationally. There is some evidence that ideas about what is a transnational crime and how to deal with it have diffused through subtle and not so subtle pressures by the United States, but there is also evidence that countries with a strong reputation for the rule of law domestically have seen value in developing global norms and criminalizing human trafficking, before it can have a corrupting influence that will be difficult to reverse. There is also some evidence that countries at risk for severe negative externalities from trafficking have been willing participants in the process, especially in fashioning resolutions in the UN and ratifying the resultant treaty. After all, transnational crime potentially threatens their own developmental plans, corrupts the local rule of law, and can interfere with other programmatic goals of the state. Future research should probe these processes further, and in particular assess the extent to which the use of human rights frames may have added a strong normative component to the arguments in favor of criminalizing trafficking, despite any initial misgivings about a prosecutorial approach to these matters.

One of the most interesting findings is the evidence that states seem to anticipate the spillover effects of their neighbors' enforcement efforts: One of the strongest and most consistent predictors of the adoption of a criminal approach to human trafficking is the density of law enforcement policies in the region. Some may believe this reflects normative socialization, but we believe it is at least as likely to represent the problem of negative externalities associated with being the most lax jurisdiction in the neighborhood.

[21] See "Strengthening Rule of Law 'Key' to Unlocking Millennium Development Goals, Head of United Nations Office on Drugs and Crime Tells Third Committee," *States News Service*, October 9, 2008.

[22] Ibid.

Surprisingly, the factors that are most strongly associated with treaty ratification do not directly predict criminalization of human trafficking. This is true despite the fact that ratifying the Human Trafficking Protocol obligates states parties to make such trafficking a crime in domestic law. When we compare the models closely, it appears that treaty ratification is most persuasively explained by participation in international agreements and organizations in general, such as ratification of human rights agreements and membership in various regional organizations. These factors do not, however, move a state to criminalize trafficking in persons in domestic law. A strong commitment to the rule of law, concerns about externalities when neighbors criminalize, as well as a strong dose of U.S. pressure seem the most likely explanations for actual changes in national law. Nonetheless, international law appears to play an important role in the acceptance of the law enforcement model to human trafficking. Although states were no more likely to ratify the Human Trafficking Protocol by virtue of having already criminalized human trafficking in national law, we have found some suggestive evidence that ratification is associated with national criminalization at a later point in time. This may be evidence that ratification is in many cases followed by implementation rather than, as some assume, the ratification of agreements that merely reflect what states are doing anyway (Downs, Rocke, and Barsoom 1996).

Of course, we have not been able to show that implementation will lead to effectiveness on the ground, any more than domestic rule of law reformers have been able to demonstrate the effectiveness of reforms inspired by Western models and institutions (Krygier 2009; Taylor 2009). Such a project will inevitably be frustrated by a lack of reasonably good data on transnational crime in general and human trafficking in particular. However, if it is true that success is more likely to follow from an approach "that recognizes a greater role and responsibility for target countries and is more open-ended and tolerant of institutional innovations and differences in norms, practices and outcomes" (Peerenboom 2009), then *domestic* criminalization rather than *external* enforcement would seem a reasonable approach to take. Moreover, the latest wave of rule of law stresses partnership between states and private actors (Trubek 2009). The Human Trafficking Protocol reflects this trend, especially in its call for states to work toward the protection of trafficking victims, in cooperation with NGOs and other elements of civil society.[23]

Speculation about effectiveness aside, this research suggests some clear drivers in the spread of anti-trafficking norms worldwide. As evidence gathers of the negative consequences of unchecked human trafficking – threats to law and order, risks of corrupting government officials, and undermining public health, not to mention perverting the rights and well-being of the trafficked victim herself – states have

[23] See Section II, Article 6, paragraph 3 and subclauses of the Protocol to Prevent, Suppress and Punish Trafficking in Persons, especially women and children, supplementing the United Nations Convention against Transnational Organized Crime (UNCTOC).

come to see this issue as standing at a unique intersection of human rights and state sovereignty. With some pressure from powerful players such as the United States, and, we suspect, some skillful framing by human rights advocates, this has proven to be incentive enough for some states to alter their laws and ratify a major international agreement to cooperate in international efforts to define and control transnational crime.

8

Rule of Law Challenges in Middle-Income Countries and Donor Approaches to Addressing Them

Linn Hammergren

1. INTRODUCTION

This chapter serves several purposes: to introduce the issue of rule of law (RoL) reforms in middle-income countries (MICs); discuss how donors have dealt with them; and identify some problems, lessons, and areas for further investigation. It is developed in four parts: first a brief history of World Bank RoL policies; then a discussion of MICs as a category for RoL promotion; an analysis of the World Bank programs as applied to MICs; and finally a review of the lessons and unanswered questions. Because this is a huge topic I have been selective in my focus, not only in using the World Bank as a proxy for donor efforts but also in the choice of countries and regions with which I am most familiar.

2. THE WORLD BANK'S EVOLVING APPROACH TO RoL REFORM

Technically, the World Bank is predominately a lender, not a donor; it has, as subsequently explained, a number of additional constraints on what it can do arising in its Articles of Agreement, its membership composition, and its need to work directly with governments or with their explicit approval. However, even with these limitations the evolution of its RoL programs is not that different from that of other "donors," whether lenders or grant givers. Two further points are worth noting: first, the World Bank, like most donors, treats RoL as an area of operations, not a specific model it is advancing; and second, it promotes RoL reform (often under other names) as an instrumental goal, a means to advance its primary objectives of promoting economic growth and poverty reduction. This instrumental view of RoL reforms is common to other donors although the primary objectives may be different – for example democracy promotion in the U.S. Agency for International Development (USAID).

The World Bank's approach has gone through three stages (and various name changes), all applied to MICs and lower-income countries (LICs) alike, but only in the last stage explicitly trying to tailor programs to these different categories. However, much of its most innovative work is still targeted at developing programs addressed to other categories – fragile, conflict-afflicted states; states characterized by legal pluralism; LICs; and so on. This section addresses these changes, with some references to their application to MICs, although that issue is addressed in more detail later.

2.1. *The First-Stage Bank Program – Pre-Judicial Reform*

Law reform has been a standard World Bank activity almost since the bank's inception. Early work focused on other sectors (e.g., finance, transportation, energy), and only occasionally on laws (bankruptcy, secured collateral) with a greater relevance for justice operations. Much of this predated the Bank's discovery that "institutions matter," and thus its impact was limited by this oversight. Laws adopted without attention to institutional capacity to apply them frequently remained laws only on the books. Drop-in experts often applied their models in complete disregard of local conditions, did not speak the local language, had little or no knowledge of the court system, and possessed an understanding of the issues limited to the "lack of a modern law." This was not an MIC-specific strategy as the term had yet to be invented, and given the insertion of these activities in larger operations of various types (infrastructure, energy, finance, and so on) it is difficult to identify them with any certainty, let alone evaluate their impact.

Law reforms were applied indiscriminately across regions and countries, often using the same model law for all comers. Nonetheless they played a particularly important role in one MIC-dominated region, Europe and Central Asia (ECA), not because these were MICs but because of the emphasis on restructuring the legal framework to accommodate a transition to market-based development. Efforts were less intensive in other regions, whether they were MIC dominated or not. In Latin America and the Caribbean (LCR), another MIC-intensive region, law reform was carried out, but with no greater emphasis than in Africa, where MICs are relatively rare.

In the beginning, the approach was enthusiastically adopted by many countries in the belief that it was a quick route to improving their economic performance or because it was part of a package featuring larger investments in other areas (infrastructure, financial reforms, and broader public- or private-sector development). Over time, the enthusiasm has waned as the World Bank and its partners discovered that enacting a new law was at best a first step toward changing behaviors and results. The template laws were frequently inappropriate for the specific cultural setting, faced institutional blockages, and sometimes produced perverse results. A study by the bank's independent evaluation group (Gupta, Kleinfeld, and Salinas 2002) made just these points about the massive law reform effort in Eastern Europe. Although not so systematically studied, it was immediately apparent that new bankruptcy laws introduced in Latin America would face similar challenges. Bankruptcy proceedings in these countries traditionally served other purposes (in Brazil, constituting an extreme form of debt collection, as the creditor can ask a judge to declare a company insolvent on the basis of any unpaid debt). In much of Latin America, the notion that bankruptcy could be used to eliminate or restructure inefficient firms conflicted with the value judges placed on preserving jobs. The massive, efficiency-driven restructurings anticipated by the laws' authors did not occur. Another example, albeit largely aimed at African LICs, was a project to harmonize the commercial laws of francophone countries (see Walsh 2010 for details). The participants of these countries did develop a set of framework laws, but for the most part they have not been adopted in the countries they represented.

The World Bank and local participants ran into other setbacks. Some involved conflicts with other donors as regards the "correct" model law. Although the bank's staff is multinational and a large portion comes from civil law countries, the bank tends to promote common law norms – possibly because they are more compatible with its market-based economic models, or because many of its economists received their degrees in U.S. universities. This bias has been perpetuated by the World Bank's "Doing Business" program and publications,[1] which have argued that common law practices are more business friendly.[2] Ideological battles aside, the more important impediment to legally induced change is the ease with which countries enact a law to meet conditionality, and then either ignore or reverse it once the World Bank releases the funds or begins the program that was contingent on this step. The bank's experience with promoting privatization and reductions in force in Argentina is a case in point. The privatizations did occur once the necessary laws were enacted, but they were conducted in a secretive and relatively corrupt fashion. The country is still paying the price for those actions. Reductions in force were still easier to counteract. The Argentine federal government dismissed public employees and replaced them with contractors or passed the responsibility for service delivery along with the service deliverers to the provinces.

The bottom line on legal reform as a RoL strategy is fairly easy to draw. Changing laws (or even constitutions) is hardly a sufficient means of inducing behavioral change. New laws, like new policies, are a convenient way to announce an intent to change things, but those changes will occur only with additional actions to

[1] *Doing Business in 2005: Removing Obstacles to Growth.* The World Bank, the International Finance Corporation, and Oxford University Press, 2005.

[2] This position has provoked a series of articles and books by continental lawyers and economists criticizing the Doing Business methodology. See the Independent Evaluation Group (IEG), "Development Results in Middle-Income Countries: An Evaluation of the World Bank's Support," The World Bank, 2007 for the bank's own evaluation and a list of related critiques, and Fauvarque-Cosson and Kerhuel (2009) for a review of French reactions.

facilitate and encourage their realization. Although the World Bank's early experience was largely directed at creating a "market enabling environment," donors more interested in promoting a respect for due process in criminal cases (USAID), judicial independence, or the recognition of international human rights standards had similar results. Throughout Latin America, the new criminal procedures codes supported by USAID included provisions to criminalize gender violence and encourage its prosecution. Nonetheless judges, prosecutors, and police continue to discredit the complaints of victims and encourage mediation where it is both illegal and inappropriate.[3] Despite these lessons, the emphasis on law revision continues as an important element of World Bank and other donor programs. Their economists have not helped much with their frequent insistence that justice reform is essentially a question of "enacting better laws and enforcing them."[4]

2.2. *The Second-Stage Programs – The Justice Reform "Template"*[5]

In the early 1990s, the World Bank began to move into direct work with the justice sector. Its focus was largely on the judiciary and on civil cases, areas that its lawyers determined were "less political" and thereby not in conflict with its Articles of Agreement (Decker 2010; Hammergren 2010; Santos 2006) but rather supportive of its mandate to encourage economic growth. The underlying logic was that the courts' more efficient handling of civil and commercial cases would strengthen property rights and juridical security, thus creating a "market enabling environment." This coincided with the thrust of the Washington Consensus's second-generation (i.e., institutional) reforms and was supported by a somewhat truncated reading of North's (1990) work on institutions (overlooking his emphasis on informal rules, mental models, and incentive systems).[6] North did see the courts and what he called the rule of law as essential to encouraging investment, but he had a more sophisticated vision of what it took for this to occur.

Despite this justification, the World Bank's subsequent justice or judicial reform programs would be hard to consider strictly "pro-business," but for better or worse, the label has stuck. This continues to arouse charges that it aims at creating a beachhead for multinational corporations (Cavalcanti 2003, responding to a summary of bank

[3] Vera Institute of Justice, Draft Report of the Review of the IADB Citizen Security Program in Nicaragua. No. 1590/SF-NI, December 2009. Interviews with feminist lawyers from Chihuahua, Mexico, 2010 also support this statement.

[4] The author was told this by World Bank economists on two separate occasions, admittedly several years ago, but the point is that the lawyers and economists for once reach agreement, unfortunately on a dubious conclusion.

[5] The term "template" was introduced by Thomas Carothers (2003) to describe what he perceives as the single recipe or formula used by nearly all donors for their justice work.

[6] See Williamson (1990) for a discussion of the first-generation Washington Consensus reforms, largely focused on reducing governments' direct economic role, cutting public expenditures, and eliminating deficit spending.

programs in Dakolias 1996[7]). However, as attorneys working with international firms have suggested (Hewko 2002), foreign and local entrepreneurs neither need nor have benefited from the bank's work in these areas. The quality of a country's justice system may be much overrated as an incentive for investors who are perfectly capable of circumventing any legal obstacles they encounter.

At face value, the new "template" programs seem fairly innocuous from any standpoint. The term "rule of law" was rarely used; the World Bank instead referred to its programs as judicial reforms or modernization. The typical operation, a medium-sized loan comprising substantial expenditures on infrastructure, equipment, and training, was first developed in LCR and ECA and largely aimed at medium-income countries, but only because it was easier to work with them.[8] Despite criticisms of the amount of infrastructure in an early Venezuelan operation[9] and its redesign to pass courthouse construction to the government counterpart, infrastructure continued to constitute a significant portion of World Bank financing, partly because governments wanted it and partly because it allowed larger loans. Programs were usually designed on the basis of minimal assessments of even the judiciary's situation, let alone that of the rest of the sector, and typically responded to what high-ranking judges and other government officials said was needed to allow the courts to function better.

As for the rest of the programs' content, much of it built on work introduced on a pilot basis by other donors – court administration, automation, and training – things requiring loan funding for nation-wide replication. In ECA, work with law reform continued, expanding to laws specific to the sector (civil, civil procedures, and commercial codes, for example). Given Latin America's region-wide emphasis on criminal justice (financed by other donor programs), there was less local demand for changing noncriminal laws. As the decade wore on, the bank began to conduct more research on justice or RoL, albeit always with an emphasis on civil disputes and juridical security. The World Bank's RoL component of its governance indicators, for example, purports to capture "perceptions of the extent to which agents have confidence in and abide by the laws of society, and in particular the quality of contract enforcement, property rights, the police and the courts, as well as the likelihood of crime and violence" (Kaufman, Kraay, and Mastruzzi 2007b). Crime and violence were a relatively late addition to the index, and the bank still does little with them in its operational work.[10] The equally famous *Doing Business*

7 In effect it would be hard to pull Cavalcanti's interpretation out of the Dakolias paper, which speaks of many reform objectives and benefits. His is a very selective reading.

8 Africa, for example, just got its first stand-alone project, in 2010.

9 *Halfway to Reform: The World Bank and the Venezuelan Justice System.* Lawyers Committee for Human Rights and the Venezuelan Program for Human Rights Education and Action, New York, 1996.

10 The bank's recent entrance into these areas still avoids the criminal justice system and instead works with community prevention programs.

studies[11] do not refer to "rule of law"; their section on the legal system measures judicial performance (duration, steps, and costs) in resolving typical commercial disputes. Although by the end of the 1990s the bank's themes for its overall governance work included "corruption" (which has its own governance indicator) and access, these were generally given short shrift in its judicial reform programs and research.

The program's justifications drew on econometric analysis establishing positive correlations between RoL as defined herein and not only economic growth but also poverty reduction, education, and health. However, the relationships between a so-called well-functioning RoL system or judiciary and the template programs were never adequately tested. Some heroic (and disputable) assumptions instead informed the work: Automation would speed up processes; training would enhance quality of judgments; new courthouses were needed for "dignification" of justice, to allow automation, or because the existing ones were in bad shape. Because few statistics were available, there was no baseline against which to measure progress, and often none was subsequently created. The size of loans and thus of programs generally depended on the willingness of the ministries of finance to accrue more debt and not on a prior needs assessment (which, when done, was usually fairly generic, coming up with similar findings everywhere). MICs were frequent candidates because they had more space for borrowing. LICs got very little, not for lack of need but because they had other more urgent priorities.

The template programs were enthusiastically received by judiciaries because they got the benefits (equipment, training, and infrastructure) and if to a lesser degree by ministries of finance because (1) they believed the arguments about better judiciaries attracting investment; (2) this often fulfilled conditionality for other operations; (3) judicial reform was part of a "democratic" or good governance agenda (especially in ECA and LCR); and (4) no one was yet worried about accruing too much debt. The World Bank in fact has a goal of positive cash flow – more loans going out than being repaid. The programs did provide a quick means for equipping and housing courts that had suffered years of neglect; helped expand court services geographically (countries only needed to provide staff); and introduced modern management tools (whether they were used or not is another question). However, happy judges are not necessarily more productive or more honest judges, and even when they are, many problems remained unresolved.

Although the World Bank's standard evaluation mechanism (the Implementation Completion Report or ICR) rated most of these projects as satisfactory, both the ratings and the self-assessment process have been questioned by outsiders.[12] The bank

[11] The Doing Business report comes out annually, and while since 2005 there have been changes in the test case used for contract enforcement, the three criteria – duration, number of steps, and costs – have not been altered, nor, according to critics has the pro-common law bias.

[12] Insiders, and especially the Bank's IEG, have also begun to question them, in some cases insisting that ratings be lowered. Because the manager in charge of the project writes or supervises the ICR's

and other lenders have been reluctant to judge their work more harshly, because this could damage relationships with the borrower and might reflect poorly on the project managers. Like Lake Woebegon's children, all projects are "above average." For example, the initial $58 million loan program in the Russian Federation was rated "satisfactory," although as the World Bank admits, "set against the entirety of the legal and judicial system, the project's contributions must be seen as somewhat marginal."[13] The ICR did, however, rate the accomplishments as of "questionable sustainability."

There is sufficient external criticism to create internal concerns. The bottom line on the template model can be summarized as follows: It eliminated many excuses for poor performance, but it rarely succeeded in improving output by any measure. Corrupt courts remained corrupt; citizen confidence did not improve; efficiency was not noticeably increased; and although courthouse construction may have facilitated physical access, many citizens stayed away when they could because of the multiple problems associated with using the courts. However, because all did not or could not avoid going to court, a further development of this period was an expansion of the supply–demand gap. More cases meant more congestion and thus threatened to eliminate any minimal improvement in overall efficiency.

2.3. *The Third Stage – Tailoring Programs to Incorporate New Themes and Different Needs*

The World Bank's approach to what it still called judicial or justice reform began to evolve significantly during the past five years. This evolution is due to a series of influences.

- There have been changes in what its client countries are demanding, especially regarding entrance into the Bank's forbidden areas such as criminal justice, citizen security, police, and prisons.
- There has been a gradual recognition that its universal template is potentially less suited to many countries, and moreover has not been that effective in any of them.
- There has been a growing impression within the bank and especially among those who control the money (e.g., "Country Directors" – those in charge of the entire lending program for a given country) that justice projects are poor performers in both their ability to expend their budgets and to produce visible impacts on the problems they were to address.

drafting, there are clearly perverse incentives involved. Typically, negative ratings only occur when a new manager does the ICR, and even then, country directors might insist that scores be raised.

13 World Bank, "Implementation Completion Report on a Loan in the Amount of US$ 58 Million to the Russian Federation for a Legal Reform Project." Report No: 36549, June 28 2006.

- There have been similarly negative views from ministers of finance, who are questioning the justification for taking out loans that produce few improvements but increase operating costs.
- There has been competition from other donors, potentially making the bank's loans less attractive. There is no question as to counterpart preference for grants, but even compared with other lenders, the bank's preparation of loan operations takes an extremely long time. Some projects stay in the planning stage for years. Other multilateral banks (e.g., the Inter-American Development Bank, IADB) start projects more rapidly, although afterward they run into the same problems.
- There have been internal and external pressures from socially concerned groups that believe the operations offer few if any benefits to the majority of the population.[14] Although the bank has responded with more emphasis on pro-poor and access programs, its reputed pro-business bias and excessive focus on efficiency are more questioned than ever (Faundez 2010; Tshuma 2000).

The most important internal reaction may be the declining interest of the World Bank's money movers. By the middle of the past decade, the expansion of conventional judicial reforms appeared to have ended in most regions, and staff specializing in them began to turn to other activities. LCR's projects appeared at a standstill, with new operations in Venezuela and Guatemala effectively canceled and a program in Mexico reduced to an operation in one state. Activities in ECA were slowing down, while the bank never had been able to start anything significant in the big MICs – China, India, and Brazil – except for Russia, where it was trying again. An entrance into criminal justice might have saved the day, but this remained a forbidden area. Work on citizen security had been taken over by the bank's social network, which stressed preventive actions (social services, community mobilization, and programs with youth at risk).

As this last comment indicates, there has been a simultaneous proliferation of groups within the bank working on justice-related themes, and if not in control of, then at least represented in the design of operations. Many of them advocated greater attention to basic human rights, pro-poor activities, and less-favored ethnic minorities (and majorities). It does not appear that their contributions have been any more effective in achieving their goals than were those of the "efficiency and juridical security" crew.[15] Most commonly, the newcomers' work has been channeled through

[14] These groups have already scored a coup against two World Bank instruments used to assess justice performance, the World Bank Institute's governance indicators and the Doing Business rankings. Both are currently used very gingerly, and Doing Business's labor rights section is now not to be referenced inasmuch as its explicit and implicit recommendations are seen as violating international standards and conventions.

[15] The IADB, which has been quicker to leap into the citizen security gap, has done this through large loans stressing service provision to conflict-prone communities. It remains to be seen (and many within the IADB have expressed doubt) whether this really deceases crime rates, but it at least gets poor communities the government services to which they are legitimately entitled.

small grants (up to $1.5 million) to social-interest nongovernmental organizations (NGOs) and government organizations working with the poor. This trend seems most pronounced in the LICs and in the Latin American region. Whether as grants or loan components, these new themes have not altered the template but rather modified it around the edges. Among donors, this is known as mission creep, a proliferation of objectives served by any project that virtually guarantees none of them will be advanced satisfactorily.

A final consequence has been for the World Bank's mainstream justice reform groups (largely in its legal and public sector units) to begin their own evaluative and strategic work. So far none of this has produced changes in operations, but the ECA has announced a new stage of programming specifically tailored, it claims, to the distinctive needs of the countries covered. By proposing strategies focused on MICs, the bank has acknowledged that levels of development matter, and that LICs and MICs have different needs and face different challenges.

3. MICs AS A CATEGORY AND THEIR DEVELOPMENTAL CHALLENGES

3.1. *Toward a Definition*

The division of the world's nations into LIC, MIC, and high-income (HIC) countries is based solely on economic criteria and specifically on their per capita gross national income (p.c. GNI). Economists usually recalculate the p.c. GNI in terms of purchasing power parity (PPP). This adjusts nominal incomes against what they really buy in different countries and so facilitates comparison.[16] The MICs are the largest of the three groupings (86 nations in 2007, comprising just under half of the world's population; by 2011,[17] there were an estimated 100 nations). They are extraordinarily diverse, even in terms of the basic economic criterion. In 2008, members' per capita GNI, adjusted for PPP, ranged from $975 to $11,455.[18] Despite their relative wealth, the MICs included one-third of the world's poor in 2007 (World Bank, IEG, 2007) and over half by 2010 (Sumner 2010), and they often demonstrate extreme levels of inequality.

[16] With its tongue only partially in cheek, *The Economist* has invented the "Big Mac Index" – which illustrates the PPP logic or, as it says, makes it "more digestible." Once annually, the journal publishes the nominal prices (in local currency and in dollars) of a Big Mac in a variety of countries, thereby demonstrating the overvaluation or undervaluation of the currencies covered. See, for instance, "McCurrencies: Happy 20th birthday to our Big Mac Index," *The Economist*, 25 May 2006. Accessed 11 July 2011 at http://www.economist.com/node/6972477?story_id=E1_GJSNQSS.000.

[17] Part of the change is due to the addition of countries to the list. In 1990, only 166 were included. The figures for 2011, based on 2009 data, were 220. However, the only category losing size was LICs, which went from 48 in 1990 to a high of 61 in 2000 to 39 in 2011. The number of MICs increased by 31 and that of HICs by 30 over the 11-year period (Sumner, 2010).

[18] It should be noted that both the cutoff points and the nations included vary slightly from year to year.

MICs are found in all of the developing regions: LCR, ECA, East Asia–Pacific, South Asia, sub-Saharan Africa, and the Middle East–North Africa. By number of countries (not population), the regions with the highest concentration of MICs are Latin America and ECA with, in 2007, 28 and 22 nations, respectively. (By population, China alone won the placement for East Asia in 2007; with the 2008 inclusion of India and of Pakistan a year later, South Asia now leads.) At the upper and lower edges, placements are in constant fluctuation, with LICs rising to MIC status, or former MICs graduating to HICs, or dropping to the LIC category. Because only per capita income counts, there is considerable variation within the group on other economic characteristics. In several countries, including some high-end MICs, inclusion is the result of primary resource wealth unaccompanied by much further economic development. In others, a moderate to high per capita income is a consequence of more balanced economic growth. Even in the latter group, levels of inequality frequently remain high, and wealth and economic modernization may be geographically concentrated. In short, graduation to the middle-income category has not necessarily benefited the entire population. This seems to be a particular problem for Latin America, many of whose countries evince some of the highest levels of inequality in the world.

3.2. *Treating MICs as a Category for Further Analysis*

The MICs are important as a group, but how helpful it is to deal with them as such to explore other development issues? Part of the answer has to do with donor programming. A more fundamental reason is that "the legitimate MICs" (not those included by virtue of a backyard oil deposit or diamond mine) have come a certain way toward developing their economies, polities, and societies, but now face some common impediments to further advancement – many of them institutional, but others arising in the negative wages of progress (increasing inequality, escalation of internal conflicts, and even disputes about the models being followed, implicitly or explicitly). The World Bank (World Bank, IEG, 2007) notes that progress has been especially slight on the quality of "governance" as measured by a variety of international indices. More generally, although MICs will have to find their individual solutions, their "glass half-full or half-empty" status suggests the need for more intensive focus on the available alternatives for moving ahead. Much of the development advice informing programs funded by donors or by countries themselves arose from experience with LICs and so may be less appropriate for more advanced societies and the changing conditions they face. Not all MICs may aspire to become HICs (at least not if that only means increasing p.c. GNI), but most of their citizens do want the wider benefits that status implies – a better life for them and their families, less violence and crime, greater security and stability, and a more just society.

The benefits of investigating MIC problems are not limited to MICs. They may also serve those exploring generic economic, political, and RoL models. If development advice has been based on LIC experience, our notions of where things should be heading and how they will get there draws largely from HICs, and for the most part those following a Western European cultural tradition. Here the very diversity of the MIC class, the different mix of obstacles they face individually, and their often unconventional approaches to the project of constructing better societies can help the model makers expand their own notions about the necessary means–ends relationships. Doing this well will require taking the category apart, which is a project not feasible in this short chapter but one that is left for the research agenda of a proposed second-stage volume.

3.3. *Developmental Challenges*

In economic terms, the MICs as a whole face two principal challenges, namely increasing growth and spreading its benefits. They have done better on the former than the latter goal. The expansion of their numbers is more indicative of progress in the LICs (as well as additions to the list of those covered), but MICs have been growing more rapidly than the LICs and the HICs – at least until the post-2008 worldwide economic crisis, whose results have not been fully analyzed. Unfortunately, during the period (2001–2007) when two-thirds of the MICs were increasing per capita income at over 2 percent annually, more than half were also increasing their rates of inequality (World Bank, IEG, 2007). The World Bank, unsurprisingly, credits the growth rate to a greater role for the private sector and the expansion of market economies. The downside of the picture may well be the unequal distribution of benefits.

MICs face other challenges, albeit in different dimensions according to their individual circumstances. Many of these involve increasing access to basic services – health, education, and security – and to commodities such as potable water, energy, communication, and transportation infrastructure for more of their populations. Access to credit, other financial services, identification documents and property titles, and of course, justice also requires attention. Other challenges revolve around global issues – environmental safety, food security, fluctuating commodity prices and terms of trade, international crime and terrorism, and the difficulties of setting national priorities and policies in an increasingly interconnected world.

MICs share the challenge of improving institutional quality, in both the public and private sectors, to confront these problems. With few exceptions (again the resource-rich nations), recent graduates to the HIC category generally have one common characteristic – a better quality of institutions, and especially of those in the public sector. Their forms of government do differ. Those with a slight predisposition to more centralized control, if not to say authoritarianism, often figure among recent graduates from LIC to MIC, or MIC to HIC status. Still, given the gravity of the other challenges, stronger institutions – with a capacity for monitoring their own performance, increasing efficiency and efficacy, controlling corruption, enhancing public confidence, and planning reforms in their internal operations and service delivery – would benefit all of them.

Counties in all three categories need work here, but the nature of the challenges is different. Whereas the LICs' public sector is often nearly dysfunctional (for reasons of internal disorganization, rampant corruption and politicization, or vastly insufficient resources), the HICs are currently seeking ways to rationalize and redistribute services to make their already high budgets go further. The HIC issues are more political than technical, requiring the redefinition of benefits from and beneficiaries of publicly funded programs in the context of resistance from complex, interlocking vested interests. The MICs face comparable challenges, but they still have room for technical solutions, replacing antiquated rules and practices with something more compatible with mass-based, if heterogeneous and constantly changing, societies. Common problems affecting public institutions include corruption (and related vices such as politicization, clientelism, and penetration by criminal organizations); a poorly trained if often overly large workforce; insufficient or poorly applied modern technologies; a process rather than results orientation (bureaucratization); inefficient organizational engineering; and perverse internal incentives. Whether the public sector absorbs 10 or 60 percent of the gross domestic product, funds could inevitably be used more effectively; the challenge is how to effect that change in the face of considerable institutional, political, and cultural obstacles.

3.4. *Rule of Law in MICs*

Generalizing about the justice sector in MICs is no easier than generalizing about the group itself. Nearly all MICs suffer from weaknesses in the sector, but specific problems vary considerably from case to case. The problems are not limited to patent (operational) shortcomings in fulfilling normal functions. MICs, like the wealthier HICs, also confront more political issues concerning what the sector ought to do and how it ought to do it.

3.4.1. Operational Issues

Operationally, MICs demonstrate the problems typical to a not entirely functional public sector in their justice institutions as well – corruption, inefficiency, delays, unequal access and treatment, excessive bureaucratization, and a consequent emphasis on form over substance. However one defines RoL (thick or thin, process or outcome focused, an emphasis on conflict resolution or enforcing a basic set of rights[19]), the sector as a whole and the courts in particular suffer from a series of characteristics that impede their ability to uphold it.

19 Although many readers may believe there are no choices here and that there is only one model, as elaborated here, this position does not characterize donor interventions. Within and among donors, there is considerable disagreement on priorities in general and as applied to specific countries. See Kleinfeld (2005) and Santos (2006).

Situations vary, obviously. At the low end (Albania and Paraguay, for example), justice institutions are often riddled with corruption, politically controlled, staffed with excessive numbers of inefficient and inadequately prepared personnel, poorly directed and monitored, and largely operating according to legal frameworks, practices, and procedures more suited to the 19th than the 21st century. At the higher end, corruption and politicization are usually diminished or reasonably "controlled" (which is to say not running rampant); organizational governance exists and has some means of monitoring internal performance and extraorganizational relationships; and efficiency-enhancing programs may already be underway. At the high end, modern technology has usually been introduced with some impact on performance. At the low end, often as a result of donor financing, it may be present but with no impact on the quantity or quality of outputs. In extremely concrete terms, the difference is that between courts whose judges and staff must be paid small bribes to do their normal work and who for larger sums will alter judgments, and a judiciary in which what corruption occurs is the product of large, targeted bribes (as it is in Organization for Economic Cooperation and Development, or OECD, countries). "Honest" courts are not necessarily efficient or easily accessible, but whereas at the low end the problems tend to coincide, in the more developed MICs the courts usually are making progress, if unevenly, in all these areas. There are a number of further observations that might be made with regard to regional trends and variations. They cannot be covered in this chapter but are rather left for a future research agenda.

3.4.2. The Political Side of MIC RoL Issues

Unfortunately, the MICs' justice challenges are not limited to these relatively simple (albeit difficult to resolve) operational issues. The other side of the coin involves some highly charged questions, many of which also plague HICs. The difference is that the latter have usually resolved the basic operational concerns. Worth noting here are the following questions.

- What is the desired level of independence for sector organizations and the means by which it is best attained? Although these questions are usually directed only at the judiciary, they also apply to other sector members – defense, prosecution, and even police.
- What is the balance of power between the judiciary and other branches of government, how should the determination be made, and what is the means by which the desired equilibrium is best attained?
- What is the extent to which judges should intervene in policy decisions, and what is the basis on which they can do so?
- What is the role of the constitution and the constitutional jurisdiction, not only in limiting abuses but also in directing and defining the content of government programs?

The operational issues may strike rule of law advocates as mere technical details; these new questions may impress them as irrelevant, because the answers are provided in a universal RoL model. Unfortunately, that model today seems less universal and more contestable than they believe, and whether or not they regard alternative answers as valid, many developing nations are pursuing them.

On the issue of organizational and especially judicial independence, the positions taken by entire nations or groups within them vary widely. On the one hand, the so-called Asian RoL model (comparable to Asian democracy) is not only on the thin side but also sets constraints on sector independence from governmental and political authorities (Peerenboom 2005). Singapore, with its highly paid, probably very honest but nonetheless politically compliant judiciary, is one example, but there are others, and not only in Asia. Two non-MIC African examples are Rwanda and Ethiopia; Ethiopian judges are required to be "loyal to the Constitution," but loyalty is clearly tied to their positions on a few controversial political themes, and increasingly it is said, to support for the ruling party (Hammergren 2009). For Latin Americans, in contrast, judicial independence, although honored in the breach in the most problematic nations, has been pushed in unusual directions by judges and jurists in Colombia and Brazil in particular. Following a line of thought developed by a few Spanish constitutionalist scholars and called neoconstitutionalism or new law (López Medina 2006; Uprimny, Rodríguez, and Garcia 2006), proponents argue that judges will enforce constitutionally guaranteed rights *and* use the contents of aspirational constitutions to direct government policy. One variation, popularized in Brazil where it is called the Robin Hood Thesis (Ribeira 2006), advises any judge confronted with a law that does not protect the weaker party to circumvent the law and apply social justice.

This line of thought also affects the answers to the remaining questions and at least in Latin America is proving very divisive and producing conflicts among the branches of government, especially between the judiciary and the executive. It is not only judges, and not only countries with more sophisticated jurists, that are using the new law to reshape the courts' role. In Ecuador and Bolivia, these discussions have called into question a number of international standards, with arguments that indigenous tradition should stand on equal footing with "Western law." Bolivia is preparing to recreate a Constitutional Court composed of an equal number of Western jurists and representatives of indigenous communities. In Bolivia, Ecuador, Honduras, Paraguay, and Venezuela, executives have used similar arguments to oust or attempt to oust high courts or entire benches. Whether one regards this as a poorly disguised reassertion of executive control or a sincere attempt to create (as it was called in Peru in the 1970s[20]) a new judicial mentality, the trend appears to be gaining ground.

[20] The military government controlling Peru between 1969 and 1980 claimed the need to create a "revolutionary" judge who would recognize social justice and make his or her decisions accordingly. See Hammergren (1998) for a discussion of the outcomes, most of them not very positive.

These arguments have not attracted the same attention in other regions. When they do, additional issues (ethnic, partisan, and religious schisms) often explain their appearance. In Africa, the region most fraught by ethnic conflicts, these only seem to involve the judiciary when religious divisions pose the question of "whose law?" Otherwise, the multiplicity of ethnic groups seen in most countries seem content with the usual international standard of recognition of their homegrown systems so long as they do not conflict with other international rights. Otherwise, balance of power debates take the more conventional form of executive efforts to control the judges, often by manipulating the appointment system. If for different reasons, the ECA region saw fewer debates over balance of power and related judicial-political issues at least until recently, as rulings of constitutional courts begin to vie with preferences of political leaders and, to some extent, ordinary citizens. For European Union (EU) aspirants or members, accession criteria defined most of the earlier answers, and those left unresolved were left for EU discussion and decisions.

4. APPLICATION AND IMPACTS OF THE BANK'S THREE STAGES IN MICS

The World Bank may have had more success in applying the two first stages of its justice reforms to MICs than it will obtain through the proposed efforts to tailor programs to country needs. Contextual conditions that facilitated the acceptance of the earlier work have either disappeared or are unlikely to function for any new model. Especially in ECA, the carrot of EU accession spurred many countries to make legal and structural changes. Latin America lacked this incentive, but arguments about impacts on economic growth and improved access bolstered both legal reform and investments in court operations. In Africa, although justice was a priority for few governments, legal reforms were little resisted and concessional loans to finance infrastructure, equipment, and training were usually accepted, especially when they figured as part of larger multisector programs. However, application does not guarantee impacts, and in all three regions the disappointing effects on performance underlie the interest in reshaping programmatic approaches. Although this chapter does not attempt to assess work in other regions, it is likely that the experience was similar there as well: acceptance of the programs for a variety of reasons, delivery of the "inputs" and production of the immediate outputs (the better infrastructure and equipment, new training programs, drafting and passage of new laws), but little impact on performance or on the resolution of the problems used to justify the efforts. For MICs in the three regions surveyed, the accomplishments of the first two stages can be summarized as follows.

- There has been modernization of the legal frameworks, especially in ECA. This did not always bring the anticipated benefits, but it was arguably moving in the right direction despite inattention to the need for contextual adjustments and possibly a surfeit of new laws. Laws alone may not change much, but the revised legal framework could facilitate direct improvements in outputs.

- Both in ECA and LCR, and to a lesser extent in Africa, there have been the provision of improved infrastructure and the introduction of automation, at least in theory, building local capacity for self-monitoring, upgrading performance, and providing greater transparency.
- There have been financing of judicial training programs and the encouragement of adjustments to appointment systems (merit criteria, some inputs from other stakeholders, greater transparency) and the terms of employment for judges (higher salaries, fixed terms, or lifelong tenure allowing dismissals only for cause), thus contributing to the recruitment and retention of better-quality professionals in all three regions.
- There has been the introduction, usually on an experimental or pilot basis, of a variety of mechanisms intended to expand access to state or alternative conflict-resolution mechanisms for the poor and other nontraditional clients. These mechanisms include paralegals (especially in Africa and LCR), mobile courthouses and "circuit-riding" judges, public defense offices, legal representation and advisory services provided by local NGOs, programs to provide interpreters and translate legal texts and explanations of state justice into the vernacular, a variety of forms of alternative dispute resolution, and policies to recognize traditional dispute-resolution mechanisms. A few donors did push these experiments further, for example USAID's work with public defense in Colombia, which supported the creation of a nationwide service.[21]

Collectively, these accomplishments could be regarded as laying the foundation for more fundamental improvements; the World Bank, as it moves into its third-stage programs, increasingly depicts them as such. The new efforts (in ECA, possibly in LCR and elsewhere) to track performance and even tie it to budgets may be considered the logical follow-up, building on the organizational infrastructure and capacity that the first stages created. However, there are caveats. First, the third-stage logic requires a reinterpretation of the earlier programs and may not lie well with ministries of finance that will now be told that they "bought" only part of the package and that the promised improvements will require further investments. Second, the third-stage programs are likely to be less popular with sector institutions because they will require radical changes in business as usual. Now rather than passively receiving new investments, they will be expected to use these to increase their efficiency, reduce corruption, and broaden access. Third, the ability of the third-stage programs to produce these improvements is still only hypothetical, even should the other parties be willing to adopt them.

The bottom line on past World Bank and other donors' support is that it failed to halt the continued, often growing public dissatisfaction with the quality of "justice"

[21] USAID's programs in Colombia supported the development of a public defense office over a period of more than a decade, during which time the quality of services improved considerably and the office grew from 400 to the current 2,000 defenders, arguably the largest such program in Latin America.

provided. In LCR and ECA, and conceivably in other MIC-dominated regions (as well as in some poorer regions and countries), many local stakeholders (including, most importantly, their ministries of finance) show a decreasing interest in putting still more funds into judicial reforms. The World Bank's efforts to design programs for LICs and conflict-afflicted countries will continue and include some interesting innovations (especially efforts to work with traditional dispute resolution, which in Africa is likely to constitute the default justice system for some time to come). However, for the more numerous (and more profitable) MICs, the obstacles facing the bank, other lending institutions, and the grant-giving donors are considerable:

- There is reform fatigue within the donor community and among country counterparts based on the difficulties posed by past projects, their questionable results, and the increased costs of operating the "semi-reformed" systems.
- For the World Bank in particular, there is internal resistance to the use of medium-sized loans whose preparation and supervision costs are the same as those for much larger operations.
- There is a need to develop a better repertoire – a different set of offerings with a better match to varying country needs – and to convince both the bank and the borrowers that this is worth the investment.
- There are changing country priorities for justice as seen in their requests for help in new areas (criminal justice, prisons, prosecution) and the bank's continuing failure to define what it can do (according to its Articles of Agreement).

The World Bank's response to these challenges is still a work in progress. It also varies substantially by region, with consequent implications for how it will affect work with MICs. In the MIC-dominated ECA, the proposed new strategy[22] promises an emphasis on empirics, efficiency and productivity, and attacking country-specific bottlenecks. As a first step, the regional unit commissioned work to develop indicators for measuring progress in various RoL goals. Some of the candidate indicators suggest an interest beyond sheer efficiency, but it remains to be seen which will be selected and applied. Because efficiency is the easiest dimension to measure, it will continue to be stressed, but perhaps this time with more impact on programming and, one hopes, results. This does not mean a "pro-business" focus. Courts' efficiency in disposing of cases is equally a concern in criminal, administrative, constitutional, and noncommercial civil cases. Obviously, disposing of cases quickly has no necessary relation with quality or with who or what gets there to be judged. However, even before this officially announced sea change, some of the smaller ECA operations were taking this line – for example a $5 million project to improve the handling of bankruptcy cases in Croatia, where the emphasis was not only on timeliness but also consistency of outcomes.

22 Europe and Central Asia Region Justice Reform and the World Bank: Status, Trends, and Strategic Directions: Briefing Note. Draft on file with author, 2009.

In Latin America, the Middle East and North Africa, and East and Southeast Asia, the other regions with a significant proportion of MICs, the transition seems far off, and operations still pursue the generic goals of efficiency, access, and "quality" (predictability of outputs) through the conventional inputs – infrastructure, automation, training, some law revision, and a soupçon of access-enhancing activities to benefit the poor. Despite considerable diagnostic work, in Africa the first two large ventures (Kenya and Senegal, the latter having recently graduated to MIC status) seem to follow the old template.

Ironically, the template seems alive and well in MIC-rich LCR, the region potentially most receptive to a broader approach to RoL reform, one stressing a wide variety of internationally recognized rights, an attack on government abuses, and services to the poor. Instead, a very recent World Bank venture in LCR appears to advance the efficiency model one step further, by advocating "results-based budgeting" in the justice sector.[23] In Latin America, World Bank and most donor projects have turned their back on the politically charged debates over balance of power and related themes, preferring to focus on less explosive issues that also match their policy concerns. USAID continues working on criminal justice, stressing both due process rights and an attack on crimes of interest (terrorism and drugs among others). The EU whose government programs traditionally stressed training increasingly prefers to work with NGOs and grassroots organizations to help protect the poor from rights violations or to advance the recognition of their own dispute resolution forums. The IADB increasingly emphasizes citizen security as a locally based and locally soluble phenomenon (in apparent disregard of organized and internationally based crime).[24]

RoL advocates may find this completely irrelevant, but it is important to recognize that the donors are increasingly trying to engage with problems prioritized by citizens of the countries where they work. Whether they are doing so effectively is another issue. Despite the various regional efforts, the World Bank still lacks an overall RoL strategy, and given the proliferation of interested internal groups, it seems unlikely to develop one over the short term. For the World Bank in particular, two fundamental questions have never been answered, at least not since the Washington Consensus days: Why is it working in justice reform? What is it attempting to promote through this work? Within the bank the answers vary widely – from the thinnest to the thickest of models. It is not just two ships but several entire armadas that are passing each other in the dark. Of course, for the cynical observer, the answer is obvious; the World Bank pursues this work because it is a way to make loans (Easterly 2010). However, it would be unfair to apply this response to many bank employees, most of

[23] The paper is still in draft, but it comes out of the Public Sector Group (which in LCR dominates justice programming) and builds on OECD experience in improving court efficiency and on the group's current emphasis on the new public management.

[24] For additional analyses of other donor programs, see the chapter by Schimmelfennig in this volume.

whom would prefer that the situation be changed, albeit usually to favor whatever model or perspective they believe is most important.

For other donors, internal disagreements may be less extreme, but they all face a similar disconnect between what they do, why they say they are doing it, and the results they are likely to produce. Moreover, virtually all programs work on only part of what could be considered a RoL model, and any attempt to measure their impacts, even in this restricted sense, is still more limited. Head counts (for numbers of trainees), laws enacted, and percentage of courts with automation equipment still prevail as the indicators of progress.

5. CONCLUSION: LESSONS LEARNED AND DIRECTIONS FOR FUTURE WORK

5.1. *What Do MICs Need and Can the Donors Provide It?*

As discussed in earlier in this chapter, the MICs are a highly diverse group, and it is thus impossible to provide a single answer to either question. However, a little disaggregation facilitates the task and allows some tentative responses. In very broad terms, the MICs can be divided into several categories as regards their RoL operational shortcomings. Although the political issues are also important, development agencies are less well equipped to deal with them, and thus for current purposes they are included only implicitly.

1. There are countries (either low-end MICs or MICs by virtue of a rich primary resource endowment) with dysfunctional systems largely because of internal disorganization, few curbs on external interference of all types,[25] low budgets and small size, and a mass of citizens physically far removed from the reaches of the state system.
2. There are countries (usually low- to mid-range MICs) with larger but still dysfunctional systems because of systematic political penetration, rampant but often more organized corruption, and inaccessibility to most citizens as a result of costs, cultural factors, and simple distrust.
3. There are countries (usually mid-level MICs) with more orderly and usually larger state systems that are nonetheless unsatisfactory performers because of lingering but more targeted political interference, significant but not rampant corruption, often overly complex but poorly engineered organizations, or (characteristic of LCR) an independence–accountability gap (courts and other sector actors have achieved sufficient independence to function in

[25] By this is meant not only interference from above but also the uncontrolled ability of system users to strike their own bargains with judges, staff, and other judicial operators, as well as the latter's ability to initiate negotiations.

relative disregard of user needs and sometimes to strike their own bargains with political authorities).

4. There are higher-end MICs characterized by inefficiency, some outmoded practices, and a rising supply–demand gap for sector services.

Although there is some regional correspondence with these categories, examples of each can be found in nearly all of the World Bank regions. Regional characteristics are important as regards additional exogenous constraints – ethnic pluralism and interethnic conflicts (including those involving religious differences), certain idiosyncratic organizational and operational traditions (path dependencies[26]), and other values shaping elite and popular expectations. However, in very general terms, the four situations suggest different priorities as regards where reform programs should start and how far they can go. Countries at the low end, of which there are relatively few among the MICs, face a larger governance problem whose solution will be constrained by limited resources or (for the MICs by virtue of a resource windfall) a lack of political interest. Given the relative nonimportance of state institutions, donor efforts could focus on improving their performance while recognizing that, over the short to medium term, the majority of the population will at most receive indirect benefits from these reforms. Instead, to counter this limitation, more efforts might go to citizen education in basic rights, building bridges with traditional dispute resolution mechanisms, and the development of paralegals and other nontraditional service providers.

A similar approach might apply to the second, far larger category of MICs, but with emphasis on enhancing access to state services for poorer citizens by attacking obstacles posed by costs and distrust – physical distance being less important here. This also implies more concerted efforts to attack formal system vices and the use of many second-stage, "template" activities targeted to the visible resolution of specific problems. Better human resource management, rudimentary monitoring systems, and efforts to impede petty corruption through some process reengineering are key lines of action. Issues of judicial independence would not be attacked head on, but rather through the efforts to improve the quality and incentives of sector staff.

For countries in the third category, where many MICs sit, donor programs can follow several parallel tracks. One of the most important is the construction of a management information system (MIS) for the courts and all other sector institutions, something conventional automation programs have usually left on the back burner.[27]

[26] "Path dependency" is a term introduced by Douglass North (1990) to explain countries' predilections for certain organizational arrangements. Examples might include the more independent role of police investigators in common law as opposed to civil law countries (based in the Anglo common law system on the traditional entrustment of both investigation and prosecution to the police) or the variety of ways countries handle administrative cases. A path dependency does not signify an inferior system, but it does limit the types of changes that can be made.

[27] It is advisable, however, not to attempt to construct one system for the entire sector – an undertaking that even far more developed countries have found nearly impossible (Reiling 2009).

Without such systems, any further reform, whether technical or political, becomes a stab in the dark, and contrary to the usual excuses for not creating an MIS, it is not inherently costly and can often be mounted on whatever automation has already been installed. (Of course, if one is automating from scratch, this should be a first priority.) An MIS, even in a fairly rudimentary form, can help plan and implement remedies for other common problems – improved appointment and career systems more impervious to political interference, evaluation systems as an incentive to employee performance, improvements to workload and work unit distribution, internal reorganizations to promote efficiency and more attention to high-priority services, identification of problem areas and bottlenecks and development of remedies, further legal change and tracking of its effects, strengthening of the monitoring and policy-making capabilities of governance bodies, and so on.

For the high-end MICs, the former steps, if not already taken, are essential, but the usual focus is on reducing the supply–demand gap through more sophisticated, information-based remedies. Some of these may also require purely political decisions, as regards filtering mechanisms (which cases will be assigned higher priorities, not attended, or diverted to other forums), development of alternative mechanisms and means for collective resolution of common complaints (possibly the introduction of class actions, but also the more direct approach of penalizing the abuses that give rise to them[28]), and entrance into balance of power and intergovernmental relations debates. Donors would be ill advised to propose solutions for the latter, but they can help explore the issues and familiarize decision makers with alternative approaches.

In all four levels of programming, tailoring programs to different needs requires more sophisticated donor skills – both in recognizing what is required and being able to point counterparts toward appropriate sources of technical expertise – as well as an ability to recognize a political issue for what it is and thus avoid imposing answers. Traditionally donor programs have relied on well-meaning generalists, sometimes entrusting program development and management to individuals with only a rudimentary knowledge of the justice sector. In the current era, MICs' needs have transcended the capabilities of this group. Although more specialized expertise (in building a judicial MIS, or designing criteria for judicial appointments or training programs) will rarely reside with the donors, RoL staff must be knowledgeable enough to engage with counterparts on the general issues. Unfortunately, for many donors, and not only the World Bank, public sector, governance, and RoL positions are often filled by staff who lack more specialized qualifications (in public health, economics, or transportation) and thus are assigned to these jobs absent other

[28] In Latin America, and quite probably elsewhere, many common abuses by public and private sector organizations (e.g., unfair dismissals, denial of guaranteed services, overcharging by banks and utilities) currently carry very low civil or administrative penalties, making it worthwhile to continue them. Access to justice could involve facilitating individual claims, but it may be more effective to raise the penalties or criminalize the offenses.

options. Some rise to the challenge and develop the appropriate skills and knowledge, but for many these are temporary resting places while waiting for a promotion to management. If this situation continues, it is unlikely that donors can respond to the third-stage challenges. That is one reason why they remain stuck with the second-stage programs – because it does not take much experience to "recommend automation" or design a project in response to a judicial wish list. It also explains the lack of consensus among donor RoL officers as regards the objectives being pursued because they come from disparate backgrounds, bringing many different perspectives to their work. Whatever donors are attempting in their RoL programs, these techniques will not get them any further in advancing those aims.

5.2. *Is the World Bank's ECA Approach or the Possible LCR Variation Sufficient?*

It is always easier for the World Bank to work with a country or judiciary that knows what it wants to do, and only lacks financing. This simple fact goes a long way toward explaining both the successful application and the limited impact of the second-stage programs, but in a few cases it has produced successes on both counts. One MIC example, albeit not from the World Bank, is the IADB's court reform program in Costa Rica, which, because the court knew what it wanted, successfully put it in place. A non-MIC World Bank project in Ethiopia likewise adopted a model developed by the Ethiopians and the Canadian International Development Agency and is currently expanding it throughout the country. Both programs have their critics, but they clearly produced significant changes in court operations rather than just delivering the goods. USAID's two decades of experience supporting criminal justice reforms throughout Latin America are another example. The agency built on a regional movement to shift to more accusatory procedures. Again, many observers (including the author) have criticized the approach for its exaggerated reliance on legal change and consequent neglect of fundamental institutional problems. Still, there is no denying its impact on criminal justice operations and the reduction of some traditional vices, especially as regards the violation of due process rights. Nonetheless, as the World Bank and other donors introduce programs to attack long-standing performance problems, they confront a situation in which many prospective partner countries seem to lack ideas (or political will) for further reforms and may well have exhausted their appetite for "building more capacity" in the abstract.

In this context, if the donors intend to continue their work, they will need to revisit three critical foundational elements: their definition of what judicial, RoL, or justice reform entails; their systems for diagnosing country shortcomings (beyond just asking judges what they want); and the set of specific remedies they propose to apply. Their initial formulations, the basis on which they conducted their past programs, are no longer adequate either for their own purposes or those of their clients. They also increasingly expose them to external criticism.

For the World Bank and other multilateral institutions, dealing with the first two elements may be extremely difficult because of the inevitable political content of the answers and the likelihood that any response will provoke a backlash from one of their members. However, these difficulties confront all donors. Despite their emphasis on good governance, over the past few years, donors have become noticeably reluctant to criticize "system flaws." This partly explains a renewed interest in performance indicators – as an effort to tie any such criticism to an external rating system and so avoid having to forward one's own appreciations.[29] It may also push them toward an adoption of some sort of universal RoL model, based on standards incorporated in international conventions and so bring what they say they are doing into closer conformity with what external RoL experts see as their logical objectives.

Nonetheless, efforts to operationalize (give concrete content to) that model risk conflicts with governments that prefer their own versions, and they will hardly make the third element – the selection of remedies – any easier. It is one thing to say that judges should be independent, another to determine the extent of their independence in any given country, and still another to devise recommendations as to what changes will augment their independence there. Although international standards sometimes try to combine the two last steps by stipulating the structural conditions for independence, a quick review of the results of their application in any number of countries suggests the limitations of the approach.[30]

Conceivably, the donors might be better off leaving the broader debates on whither justice (Element 1) to the politicians, advocates, and academics and instead focusing on building their technical expertise in tracking (Element 2) and providing remedies (Element 3) for a series of more concrete, lower-order problems related to their former vague objectives of enhancing efficiency, quality, and access. This does not preclude avoiding certain actions because of the perverse political ends to which they may be put, but it does suggest not attempting to give advice on constructing political utopias of whatever stripe. Thomas Carothers (2009a), in a review of USAID programs, recently made a similar suggestion with regard to efforts to promote democracy, participation, or civil society development. His argument and the recommendations here as to donor RoL work do not discount the importance of these larger projects, but they do recognize that defining and advancing solutions

[29] Such systems are again proliferating. For examples see Vera Institute of Justice and Altus Global Alliance, "Developing Indicators to Measure the Rule of Law: A Global Approach." Report to the World Justice Project, July 2008, which also contains links to alternative approaches.

[30] On this point, note Fritz, Kaiser, and Levy (2009: 16) on the risks associated with first-best solutions, that is, of what happens to ideal legal and policy reforms when the institutional environment does not support them. See also Heyland, Morne, and Willumsen (2008) on problems associated with adopting *Doing Business* recommendations.

are far beyond the donors' limited expertise. It is also probably beyond the advice counterparts and MICs in particular will welcome because they too recognize the donors' limitations.

In this context, internal discussions of Element 1 would be ratcheted down a few notches to define the donors' role as supporting the solution of certain common problems, not the construction of ideal systems. In this, the ECA and LCR initiatives could be a place to start, but only for MICs that define their problems in efficiency terms. The World Bank's proposals to turn to new public management and results-based budgeting are more dubious, first because their application to justice is already questioned in the OECD "model" countries, and second because although ECA and LCR countries do show some interest in augmenting efficiency, the remedies are probably too radical for acceptance. Moreover, it would be unwise for the bank, even given its traditional biases, to disregard other priorities – increasing the quality of outputs and expanding access. Here it could do much more in developing approaches for diagnosing problems and creating alternative remedies. Much the same can be said of other donors – that also could benefit from enhancing their technical expertise in these areas. Finally, there is the question of the World Bank's reluctant entrance into citizen security, but if it does wish to engage here, it needs not only its lawyers' permission but also know-how. Obtaining the former may be far easier than getting the latter, but that is also a concern. Well-intentioned amateurs working on civil justice or access will at most waste funds; those working in criminal justice could have lethal affects.

Even with this less ambitious agenda, there is a good deal the World Bank and the broader donor community could contribute to helping the MICs improve their justice systems. Realizing this contribution will require an ability to distinguish political from technical issues, develop sufficient technical expertise to address the latter, and, to the extent they wish to help advance solutions to the former, provide counterparts with a range of alternative answers. Donors, especially donors such as the World Bank, are in a privileged position with regard to their ability to canvass the alternatives and provide a wide variety of options to countries attempting to construct their own RoL models. That said, there are members of donor organizations who could contribute to the politicized discussion of RoL alternatives, either as technical experts or as well-prepared advocates, but for that to happen another donor obstacle would have to be overcome: a reluctance to recognize internal disagreements and to permit the expression of opinions diverging from the politically correct line of the moment.[31] In short, the donors, in order to help reform "justice systems," will also

[31] I say this because I have been a participant in World Bank discussions on the UN Legal Empowerment of the Poor initiative and have heard bank staff express doubts about the UN committee's overwhelming endorsement of land titling as a benefit to the poor. Technical experts can shed light on ideological debates, but most donors are extremely reluctant to let their staff diverge very far from the official line. This is unfortunate inasmuch as these individuals could certainly improve the quality of these discussions.

have to reform some of their internal biases and procedures. The MICs can provide some useful lessons here so long as donors are willing to transcend the simple clichés and engage with the broader problems – justice in the 21st century may not coincide with 20th-century models, and the donors can provide an extremely useful role in facilitating dialogue rather than restricting themselves to the acceptable answers to extremely complex questions.

9

Civil–Military Cooperation in Building the Rule of Law

Tilmann J. Röder

1. INTRODUCTION

Building the rule of law during or after an armed conflict poses complex challenges to the involved institutions and organizations. Recent experiences in war-torn countries such as Liberia, Somalia, Bosnia, Kosovo, Timor-Leste, Sierra Leone, Afghanistan, and Iraq have shown that success cannot be easily reached. Particular problems faced by domestic state institutions are the demolition of physical infrastructure and the lack of educated law professionals, threats to government staff by conflict parties, the rapid spread of crime and corruption facilitated by insecurity and low law enforcement capacities, prevalent reliance on informal forms of dispute resolution, and difficulties in identifying and implementing adequate responses to human rights violations that may have occurred in the course of the conflict (transitional justice). The involvement of international military forces in this domain, which has traditionally been regarded as strictly civilian, is a new and still surprising phenomenon.

Since the mid-1990s, the United States and allied forces have endeavored to rebuild the judicial institutions and influence legal developments in their operational areas in order to contribute to the stabilization of fragile states. In the process, they have had to cope with problems similar to those of civilian organizations, a situation that poses specific challenges to the military. One of the greatest difficulties is the fact that, time and again, the "international community" on the ground reveals itself as a chimera. In most cases, confusing diversities of civilian and military actors with diverging mandates and capacities try to implement their own rule of law strategies. The need for some bilateral consultation with domestic institutions is widely accepted and reasonably met, but comprehensive, multilateral coordination

The author would like to thank all those who contributed to this research with their valuable comments and suggestions. Gary Peters, Leo Vester, and the editors deserve particular recognition.

remains a general deficiency. The varying approaches taken to solve this core problem include the coordination through transitional administrations led by the United Nations (UN) in the cases of Kosovo (Carlowitz 2003) and Timor-Leste (Coning 2000: 83), the streamlining of diverging strategies through one dominating foreign actor such as the United States in the case of Iraq (Pregent 2010a; Tripp 2004), and the appointment of "lead nations" as sector coordinators in the case of Afghanistan, where Italy took responsibility for the judicial sector and Germany for the police.[1] However, none of these strategies has resulted in visible, sustainable success in establishing the rule of law.

At the same time, "CIMIC" has been systematically developed as a management tool on the operational level and as a doctrine for complex crises on the strategic level by a diversity of military and civilian bodies. Whereas the North Atlantic Treaty Organization (NATO) terminology speaks of "civil–military *cooperation*," the UN and other international organizations (IOs) prefer the more distanced term "civil–military *coordination*," and some nongovernmental organizations (NGOs) try to avoid any sign of shared goals by using the distinctly neutral expression "civil–military *interaction*." Notwithstanding these terminological and conceptual differences, the acronym "CIMIC" prevails and will be used in this chapter to denote the phenomenon.

The chapter begins with some historical observations (Section 1) before explaining the underlying CIMIC concepts that form the framework for contemporary military rule of law promotion in more detail (Section 2). A complementary, no less important context is 21st-century counterinsurgency doctrine, "COIN" in military language, which is introduced in the same part of this chapter. The main arenas of military involvement in rule of law assistance are Iraq, where the new counterinsurgency doctrine was shaped, and Afghanistan, where CIMIC rule of law activities take place in the most complex conflict scenario of today (Section 3). Subsequently, theoretical issues raised in the course of the analysis are discussed (Section 4). The first issue concerns the legitimacy of military involvement in building the rule of law. It implies, among others, questions regarding the mandate of the foreign military forces and their capacity to promote the rule of law, the legitimacy of the supported regime, and the popular acceptance of both the foreign military and the institutions assisted by them. The second, associated issue is the extremely narrow notion of the rule of law that military forces involved in the interventions in Iraq and Afghanistan have. The chapter ends with some conclusions reflecting my position on the issue.

For two reasons, NATO and especially the U.S. forces stand in the center in this analysis. First, the doctrine incorporating rule of law promotion was originally

[1] Further "lead nations" that committed themselves to specific areas of the Security Sector Reform (SSR) in Afghanistan include the United States with responsibility for the Afghan Army, the United Kingdom for Counter Narcotics, and Japan for Disarmament, Demobilization, and Reintegration (later called the Disbandment of Illegal Armed Groups). See Sedra (2006: 96).

developed by the U.S. military. Other NATO members have only partly adopted and translated it into practice. For instance, British, Italian, and Australian forces have been to some extent involved in rule of law promotion in Iraq and Afghanistan, whereas French and German forces have refrained from such activities and have left them to specialized civilian organizations that they would, however, at times support in the implementation of rule of law programs; and the armed forces of non-NATO countries have never immersed themselves in legal matters apart from operational law[2] for ideological reasons. In particular, there is no known evidence of any involvement of the Soviet Army, the later Russian armed forces, or the Chinese armed forces in the domestic judicial sector in any of their military operations. Their mission objectives naturally never comprised building the rule of law; if at all, they may have interfered in alien judicial affairs for other ideological purposes.

The second reason why the focus of this chapter is directed toward the U.S. and other NATO forces in the early 21st century is the more trivial fact that sources from other historical phases such as the 1950s and 1960s when the late colonial powers tried to hand over not only political but also judicial power to newly formed domestic institutions are difficult to trace and would go beyond the scope of this chapter.

The following brief historical review is therefore not meant to be exhaustive.

2. HISTORICAL DEVELOPMENT TOWARD MILITARY INVOLVEMENT IN RULE OF LAW ACTIVITIES

The involvement of international military forces in rule of law activities such as institution building and legal reform can be traced back to the end of World War II. Earlier efforts to establish functioning, legitimate governance structures in overseas territories were primarily instruments of colonial rule. Discussing them as rule of law efforts would mean ignoring this historical context. Despite the statement of U.S. President William McKinley during the Spanish-American War (1898) that the United States was obligated not only to liberate the former colonies but also to guide them toward self-governing, democratic society (Offner 2004: 50), the activities of army lawyers in these territories cannot be referred to as the beginning of the U.S. forces' efforts to promote the rule of law.[3] The same is valid for the French, English, German, or any other colonial powers' imposition of justice and administrative structures in territories controlled by them.

[2] This is the body of domestic, foreign, and international norms (including international humanitarian law and rules of engagement) that affect the activities of armed forces in and outside of war.

[3] The U.S. military governments in Cuba, Puerto Rico, the Philippine Islands. and Guam primarily aimed at replacing the existing Spanish-based institutions and legal systems with American-style government structures. To this end, judge advocates drafted and enacted legislation such as the Criminal Code of the Philippines (1899), filled important positions in supreme courts, and acted as legal advisors to American-sponsored governments even after these territories had gained formal independence. See Birtle (1998: 99–100). Borch (2008: ix) argues that these activities constitute the beginning of the U.S. Army's involvement "in rule of law programs."

In the aftermath of World War II, U.S., British, and French military lawyers not only operated military courts in Germany and Japan but also implemented their governments' policies designed to integrate these countries into the bloc of the Western democracies that was sliding more and more into a confrontation with the Soviet Union and its satellite states (Ziemke 1984: 59).[4] These policies were fundamentally different from those designed for colonies or mandate territories because they aimed at establishing full-fledged democracies. The historical circumstances also proved to be more promising: Both countries had well-educated elites and Germany had experienced democracy during the Weimar Republic (1919–1933). Therefore, the establishment of the rule of law was more realistic an aim than anywhere else. The consequent success in Germany, Japan, and other formerly totalitarian countries marked the beginning of the era of rule of law assistance in general and the involvement of military forces in these efforts in particular. In Japan, U.S. army officers and judge advocates[5] even dominated the drafting of the new constitution, which did, not quite surprisingly, depart from the U.S. concept of the rule of law (Koseki 1998).

The next noteworthy rule of law operation of the U.S. military took place in Vietnam. In 1964, the Staff Judge Advocate for Military Assistance Command, Colonel George S. Prugh (1975: 13), argued in a report that judge advocates should begin using the law to enhance mission success, as "there cannot be a successful counterinsurgency program until there is established a respect for law and order." These words demonstrate a change of paradigm. Whereas establishing the rule of law constituted the core of a democratization strategy in Germany and Japan, it was reduced to a tool for military success in Vietnam. Prugh was the first to propose the inclusion of the rule of law as an element in a counterinsurgency strategy. He was predominantly a soldier and from this perspective analyzed the complex circumstances of a war as a combination of a domestic and international war, insurgency, and nation-building, without failing to notice the rapid disintegration of the remnants of the colonial French legal establishment (Prugh 1975: v). Over the following two years, Prugh established a Law Society that organized lectures and talks on different aspects of U.S. jurisprudence for Vietnamese lawyers and launched an advisory program for the military lawyers of the South Vietnamese Army. All of these efforts were intended to promote loyalty among the Vietnamese law community to the government supported by the U.S. forces. After their withdrawal in 1973 and the collapse of the South Vietnamese government in 1975, the remains of these rule of law efforts were wiped away and the experience was lost in the military's "collective amnesia regarding its rich history in [stability and reconstruction] operations" (Schultz and Merill 2007:

4 See also the report of the Army Reserve Judge Advocate who served as Chief of the German Courts Branch of the Office of Military Government for Bavaria: Nobleman (1950: 37).

5 These are officers of the Judge Advocate Generals' Corps primarily serving as legal advisors to the command to which they are assigned, but also as military prosecutors.

116). The U.S. forces went as far as to expunge any counterinsurgency, postconflict stabilization, and transformation elements from their doctrine. Consequently, rule of law issues did not appear as an element of any formulated U.S. or NATO military strategy.[6]

In 1993–1995, the U.S. forces experienced another failure in Somalia, where they used pure warfare doctrine in a mission aimed at creating an environment that was safe enough for humanitarian operations, the disarmament of militias and the beginning of a nation-building process (Schultz and Merill 2007: 118). Under this impression, the U.S. military began to develop a new doctrine for stability operations, a process that was still evolving during the Bosnia and Kosovo operations (Olsen and Davis 1999: 2).

Rule of law promotion, however, did not appear as an element of any military strategy until 2003.[7] When the question of whether nation-building was a military task was controversially discussed in the U.S. presidential election campaign in 2000, the chairman of the Joint Chiefs of Staff, Army General Henry Shelton, clearly stated, "We can provide a safe and secure environment, but we don't do the law enforcement, and don't do the court system, we don't get commerce going again. That's, in my definition, what you do when you get into nation building."[8]

Change of mind came about when the United States and its coalition partners faced massive insurgencies in Afghanistan and Iraq. Afghanistan had experienced two relatively calm years after the defeat of the Taliban in 2001. The insurgencies in both countries erupted shortly after the 2003 invasion of Iraq. Relief and development work proved to be extremely dangerous, and civilian rule of law organizations were unable to take effective measures to restore the rule of law in large parts of the country. Judge advocates and civil affairs officers[9] who came to Iraq as operational law advisors observed a rapidly disintegrating domestic judicial system and tried to counter this development with whatever means they had at hand. Their reports contributed to the renovation of the U.S. military's counterinsurgency doctrine that brought the rule of law into the prominent place it holds today. However, like in Vietnam, building the rule of law does not constitute an end in itself in today's theaters of war; for the

[6] The only exception before the late 1990s was the counterinsurgency theory drawn up by the British colonial administrator Sir Robert Thompson from his experiences during the so-called Malayan Emergency (1948–1960) and the Vietnam War, where he served an advisor to the South Vietnamese government. Thompson (1966) outlined five "Basic Principles of Counter-Insurgency," which included adherence to the law to win the trust of the population. However, he did not propose taking active measures for a general reform of the state supported by foreign forces.

[7] In 2003, a new field manual explicitly addressed the rule of law as being "fundamental to peace and stability," adding that "civilian organizations are responsible for civil law and order. However, Army forces may need to provide limited support." Department of the Army, "FM 3–07 – Stability Operations and Support Operations" (2003): 4–26.

[8] See "Bush Aide Hints Police Are Better Peacekeepers than Military," *New York Times*, 17 November 2000.

[9] Civil Affairs Officers act as a liaison between the armed forces and civilian authorities and populations of the nation in which their units are operating.

military, it remains a tool to ensure a mission's success. In this spirit, the then-Chief Strategist of the Office of the Coordinator for Counterterrorism of the U.S. State Department, David J. Kilcullen (2006: 5), stressed the importance of increasing the legitimacy of the supported government in September 2006. For this purpose, he included a new element into the security pillar of his theory: "building a framework of human rights, civil institutions and individual protections." His and other theorists' proposals were not only heard but embraced by the U.S. military leadership. The rule of law finally gained its central role in the counterinsurgency doctrine of the U.S. forces with the publication of the field manual *FM 3-24, Counterinsurgency* in December 2006.[10] This manual was developed under the auspices of U.S. Army Commander David H. Petraeus and U.S. Marine Corps Commander James F. Amos, who forthrightly state in the foreword, "'Soldiers and Marines are expected to be nation builders as well as warriors. They must be prepared to help re-establish institutions and local security forces and assist in rebuilding infrastructure and basic services. They must be able to facilitate establishing local governance and the rule of law.'"[11]

The objective of *FM 3–24* has been to define a basic common understanding of counterinsurgency for the Army and Marine Corps. Commanders in the field are tasked to adapt its principles and translate them into clear operational and tactical guidance. This is what General Petraeus tried to do in Iraq[12] and, as a successor to General Stanley McChrystal, also in Afghanistan. *FM 3–24* is not the only relevant manual of the U.S. forces; it must be read in the context of the doctrine elaborated in the field manual *FM 3–0, Joint Operations* of September 2006, which constitutes the strategic update for the U.S. forces in the post-September 11 world.[13] The *Rule of Law Handbook: A Practitioner's Guide for Judge Advocates*, developed by The Judge Advocate General's Legal Center and School as a response to the expectation that it was "highly likely that the Global War on Terror (GWOT) will require the US military to engage in operations that include rule of law operations as an essential part of the overall mission," followed in 2008.[14]

The official recognition since 2006 that rule of law activities should form an integral part of U.S. military doctrine has institutionalized the approach masterminded

[10] Rule of law promotion was given a lesser role in an earlier version, Department of the Army, "FMI-3–07.11, Counterinsurgency Operations" (2004), where the focus was rather directed at restoring law and order. Regarding the pre-history of Department of the Army: Department of the Army, "FM 3–24, Counterinsurgency" (2006), see (Schultz and Merill (2007: 131 et seq.).

[11] Petraeus, David and Amos, James. "Foreword" in Department of the Army, "FM 3–24, Counterinsurgency" (2006).

[12] See, e.g., Petraeus (2008: 2–4); International Security Assistance Force, "ISAF Commander's Counterinsurgency Guidance" (2009), available at. http://smallwarsjournal.com.

[13] The authors called this field manual "a revolutionary departure from past doctrine." See Wallace, William, "Foreword" in "FM 3–0, Operations" Department of the Army (2008). Emphasis in original.

[14] See "Preface" in Gorove and Nachbar (2008: i).

by Colonel Prugh during the Vietnam War between 1964 and 1966. Even though the influence of his ideas on 21st-century doctrine may have been marginal, they have been at last remembered.

After having been tested in Iraq, rule of law as a military strategic tool is today firmly established in the world's most complex counterinsurgency operation in Afghanistan. Other countries' armed forces have not gone that far and remain more reluctant to get involved in rule of law activities. The German Bundeswehr, for instance, has no military lawyers tasked with rule of law promotion at all; institution building, justice reform, and related activities are exclusively left to civilian organizations funded and coordinated by the Ministry for Economic Cooperation and Development and the Federal Foreign Office.

Turning back to the wider scope of this chapter, the military involvement in (post-)conflict rule of law assistance is only one aspect of civil–military cooperation. "CIMIC" as a term and concept came to be known to a wider public during the 1990s, when the international community began to interfere in violent domestic conflicts to an increasing degree all over the world. The new reality of a global interventional policy led to more and closer contact between international armed forces and civilian actors.[15] Situations such as the First Liberian War (1989–1996) with a joint military intervention by the Economic Community of West African States and a UN Observer Mission; the UN-authorized Gulf War (1990–1991) waged by an international coalition led by the United States against Iraq; and the Bosnian War (1992–1995), which involved UN Protection Forces as well as NATO operations, have revealed the difficulties of coordination between multitudes of civilian and military actors. These include domestic armed forces as well as irregular combatants, international forces frequently under common command (e.g., by NATO), civilian and armed UN peace-keeping units, humanitarian relief bodies such as the International Committee of the Red Cross and Red Crescent (ICRC), and numerous government-sponsored organizations and NGOs. Forms of closer cooperation emerged in practice and were described as civil–military cooperation, which has consequently become a key policy term and operational reality. Although they recognize the need to find methods of cooperation and coordination, the different actors hold various views on how to respond to changing circumstances.

3. CIMIC STRATEGIES OF NATO, THE EUROPEAN UNION, AND THE UN

The numerous actors in recent and ongoing missions have developed a wide range of diverging CIMIC concepts. A universally accepted definition has not emerged. However, there seems to be growing consent that the term "CIMIC" should be used for activities during a military intervention in a foreign country.

[15] This notion includes domestic state institutions and NGOs as well as IOs, international or foreign donor agencies, implementing agencies, and foreign NGOs.

The CIMIC concepts of NATO, the European Union (EU), and the UN can be considered most influential because of the immense policy-shaping and implementing power of these organizations. Until about 1995, CIMIC was not seen as very important by any of them. Then, the experiences of the Implementation Force (IFOR) and Stabilization Force missions in Bosnia-Herzegovina led to the evolution of NATO's CIMIC doctrine. IFOR's major responsibility was the implementation of the military elements of the Dayton Agreement.[16] At first, the relations with nonmilitary organizations were merely supportive; IFOR assisted the United Nations High Commissioner for Refugees and the ICRC. By the spring of 1996, IFOR had succeeded in establishing a secure environment. This paved the way for the implementation of the civilian parts of the peace agreement. Nonmilitary organizations could begin with their work. From this moment on, IFOR got increasingly involved in humanitarian support, national elections, longer-term projects, and infrastructure reconstruction (Phillips 1998: 23). This shift in IFOR's responsibility raised the awareness for the necessity of a coherent CIMIC policy and special CIMIC units.

NATO's CIMIC approach is primarily based on the NATO Military Policy on CIMIC of July 2001 (MC 411/1)[17] and the Allied Joint Publication 9 of July 2003 (AJP-9), which provides the actual guiding principles and procedures for the implementation of the CIMIC doctrine.[18] As of May 2011, a revised version named AJP-9(A) has been drafted but not yet promulgated. The draft intends to enable a flexible adaptation of the CIMIC doctrine to operational realities experienced by NATO member forces in Afghanistan, Iraq, and other conflict scenarios.[19]

The AJP-9 subsumes CIMIC tasks according to three core functions:

1. Support to the Force. Any activity designed to create support for the military force from within the indigenous population;
2. Civil-Military Liaison. Coordination and joint planning with civilian agencies in support of the mission;
3. Support to the Civil Environment. The provision of any of a variety of forms of assistance (expertise, information, security, infrastructure, capacity-building, etc.) to the local population in support of the military mission.[20]

It becomes very clear that all coordination and cooperation efforts with the "civil environment" are meant to be a tool to achieve strategic goals. NATO units supporting civilian institutions, organizations, individuals, or the population at large do not act for the sake of humanitarian relief or economic, political, cultural, or any other form of development, but to accomplish their mission. Here lies the root of the

[16] See the General Framework Agreement for Peace in Bosnia and Herzegovina of 21 November 1995, entered into force on 14 December 1995 (GFAP).
[17] NATO Military Council, "MC 411/1 – NATO Military Policy on Civil-Military Co-operation" (2001).
[18] NATO, "Allied Joint Publication 9: NATO Civil-Military Co-Operation Doctrine," AJP-9 (2003).
[19] NATO, "Allied Joint Doctrine for Civil-Military Cooperation (Study Draft 3)," AJP-9(A) (2003).
[20] NATO, "Allied Joint Publication 9: NATO Civil-Military Co-Operation Doctrine," AJP-9 (2003).

long-lasting, fierce debate between NATO on the one hand and humanitarian and development organizations (including those acting in the area of rule of law assistance) on the other, who keep criticizing, among other aspects, that the military units interfering in their fields of activity only seek short-term pacifying effects while ignoring basic principles of sustainable development planning.[21] From a historical perspective, the fact that rule of law assistance by the military primarily serves to achieve its mission goals is not all too surprising. As already described, the activities of the U.S. military during the Vietnam War followed the very same principle.

In current operations, the Provincial Reconstructions Teams (PRTs) play a central role in the realization of CIMIC activities. As of May 2011, NATO member-states operate 27 PRTs in Afghanistan and 15 in Iraq.[22] PRTs typically consist of a military component including CIMIC units, diplomats, police advisors, and development experts who combine their efforts to protect reconstruction works and empower local governance structures. Rule of law activities are regularly part of the portfolio of PRT activities.

Both Afghanistan and Iraq are conflict areas where the international military forces struggle with violent insurgencies. PRTs and other military units therefore combine NATO's CIMIC doctrine with the counterinsurgency doctrine developed by the U.S. military. This does not lead to any noteworthy contradiction in practice, even though both concepts do not aim at entirely congruent objectives at first sight. However, one could easily adapt the phrase from the field manual *Counterinsurgency*, "Establishing the rule of law is a key goal and end state in COIN,"[23] to the NATO–PRT context by exchanging the term "COIN" for "CIMIC." The parallels become even more obvious when reading chapter 8 from the manual:

> 8–42. COIN operations strive to restore order, the rule of law, and civil procedures to the authority of the HN [i.e. host nation] government.[24]
> 8–48. Even when HN authorities have restored judicial functions, counterinsurgents may have to provide logistic and security support to judicial activities. If insurgents continue to disrupt activities supporting the rule of law, the support may be prolonged.[25]

The *Counterinsurgency* field manual further explains why establishing the rule of law is of relevance to the counterinsurgency mission:

> The presence of the rule of law is a major factor in assuring voluntary acceptance of a government's authority and therefore its legitimacy. A government's

[21] See, e.g., the Statement by Médecins Sans Frontières of 28 July 2004, cited in Rana (2004: 565); and Verband Entwicklungspolitik Deutscher Nichtregierungs-Organisationen, "Fünf Jahre Deutsche PRTS in Afghanistan: Eine Zwischenbilanz aus Sicht der deutschen Hilfsorganisationen," VENRO-Positionspapier 1/2009 (2009). Available at http://www.venro.org.

[22] In Iraq, some smaller, functionally equivalent units are embedded in U.S. combat forces.

[23] Department of the Army, "FM 3–24, Counterinsurgency" (2006): D/8.

[24] Department of the Army, "FM 3–24, Counterinsurgency" (2006): 8/14.

[25] Department of the Army, "FM 3–24, Counterinsurgency" (2006): 8/16.

respect for pre-existing and impersonal legal rules can provide the key to gaining it widespread, enduring societal support. Such government respect for rules – ideally ones recorded in a constitution and in laws adopted through a credible, democratic process – is the essence of the rule of law. As such, it is a powerful potential tool for counterinsurgents.[26]

David Kilcullen's and others' emphasis on the importance of legitimacy of the structures that are rebuilt and strengthened also expanded into the counterinsurgency doctrine and parallel CIMIC concepts:

> To establish legitimacy, commanders transition security activities from combat operations to law enforcement as quickly as feasible. When insurgents are seen as criminals, they lose public support. Using a legal system established in line with local culture and practices to deal with such criminals enhances the HN government's legitimacy. Soldiers and Marines help establish HN institutions that sustain that legal regime, including police forces, court systems, and penal facilities.[27]

Meanwhile, the EU has developed its own CIMIC concept for crises operations all over the world. Its definition[28] is, however, close to being a copy of the NATO wording. Most notably, the EU also determines CIMIC to be a military function that serves to achieve the military goals.[29] As a result of their nearly identical wording, the EU and NATO CIMIC concepts have accurately been denoted as "sister doctrines" (Hardegger 2003: 53). It was also to avoid further confusion over terminologies and concepts that the EU has refrained from further elaborating its CIMIC concept.[30]

In most of its missions, the EU focuses on Security Sector Reform (SSR). The EU's holistic and integrative SSR concept includes support to defense, police, intelligence, and judicial reforms as well as the EU's normative commitment to democratic values, human rights, and good governance (Gross 2009: 9–10) and constitutes the main bridge for the EU into the area of rule of law assistance. Current examples are the EU Rule of Law Mission in Kosovo, the EU Police Mission in Afghanistan (EUPOL), and the EU Integrated Rule of Law Mission for Iraq, which do not have military components but closely interact with the international military forces in all three countries.

26 Department of the Army, "FM 3–24, Counterinsurgency" (2006): 1/22.

27 Department of the Army, "FM 3–24, Counterinsurgency" (2006): 1/23–1/24.

28 The U.S. Army states that "Civil-Military Co-operation (CIMIC) is the co-ordination and co-operation, in support of the mission, between military components of EU-led Crisis Management Operations and civil actors (external to the EU), including national population and local authorities, as well as international, national and non-governmental organisations and agencies." See Department of the Army, "FM 3–24, Counterinsurgency" (2006): 20.

29 Department of the Army, "FM 3–24, Counterinsurgency" (2006): 15.

30 This does, however, not mean "an effective abandonment of the concept at the EU level," an assumption expressed in Directorate-General for External Policies of the European Union, "Consolidating the EU's Crisis Management Structures: Civil-Military Coordination and the Future of the EU OHQ" (2010): iv.

The United Nations' CIMIC concept is distinct from those used by NATO and the EU. In 2002, the UN Department of Peacekeeping Operations (DPKO) coined the following definition: "UN Civil-military coordination is the system of interaction, involving exchange of information, negotiation, deconfliction, mutual support, and planning at all levels, between military elements and humanitarian organisations, development organisations, and the local civilian population to achieve UN objectives."[31] Obviously, humanitarian goals form the core of the UN approach to civil–military cooperation. In January 2010, DPKO enacted a consolidated policy for all coordination and cooperation between UN military and UN as well as non-UN civilian personnel, formally introducing the term "UN-CIMIC" for these interrelations.[32] However, the relationship between civilian or military UN mission components and non-UN military forces has not been defined by the UN through a specific policy. The UN's CIMIC policy only states that although it does not apply to military elements that operate outside the UN command and control, "it may provide useful guidance for some missions which are deployed alongside non-UN military partners, in developing local coordination arrangements with them."[33] This is especially relevant for operations that are "hybrid" in the sense that the UN is responsible only for parts of the overall effort, as in the Balkans and Afghanistan, where international military forces including NATO intervened on the basis of UN Security Council Resolutions, or Sudan, where the African Union deployed a peace-keeping mission with NATO assistance.[34]

In practice, UN missions and non-UN military forces only cooperate when such interaction complies with both mandates. A concrete example is the coordination of rule of law activities at meetings organized by the Rule of Law Unit of the UN Assistance Mission to Afghanistan (UNAMA). International Security Assistance Force (ISAF) rule of law officers are invited and take part in these meetings because both sides can only reach a complete picture of what rule of law assistance is provided in the country together.

4. RULE OF LAW EFFORTS IN CIMIC AND COIN OPERATIONS: THE NEW PARADIGM IN PRACTICE

In a typical postconflict situation, a state's ability to maintain peace by enforcing the law has been diminished or destroyed. Police, courts, and detention capacity

31 UN DPKO, "Policy on Civil-Military Coordination" (2002): 2.

32 UN DPKO, "Civil-Military Coordination in UN Integrated Peacekeeping Missions (UN-CIMIC)" (2006). This policy has replaced the DPKO Policy on Civil-Military Coordination of 2002.

33 UN DPKO, "Civil-Military Coordination in UN Integrated Peacekeeping Missions (UN-CIMIC)" (2006): 3.

34 Eide, Espen Barth, Kaspersen, Anja Therese, Kent, Randolph, and Hippel, Karen von, "Report on Integrated Missions: Practical Perspectives and Recommendations." Independent Study for the Expanded UN ECHA Core Group (2005). Available at http://ochanet.unocha.org/p/Documents/Report_on_Integrated_Missions_May_2005_Final.pdf.

are limited or do not exist at all. This was the case in Afghanistan and Iraq after the interventions by international military forces. The original goals of the interventions in both countries therefore included the creation of state structures that would facilitate the transition to a legitimate civil authority operating under the rule of law.

The insurgencies that grew from 2003 onward gave the military another reason to assign rule of law elements a central place in their operations, as these were identified by counterinsurgency experts as being a critical factor in effectively combating the insurgencies. In describing the factors that contributed to the success of the 2007 Iraq "surge," David Kilcullen (2009: 143) later stated that "we conducted operations to support the rule of law, which helped deal with 'accelerants,' and we introduced what we might call 'decelerants' such as political reconciliation and building competent, nonsectarian governance and national institutions, which helped slow and reduce the intensity of the violence."

Looking back, Kilcullen (2009: 126) criticizes the prevalent approach that underpinned the original Operation Iraqi Freedom planning for failing to anticipate the military leverage required to facilitate Iraqi governmental capacity to ameliorate sectarian tendencies: "[B]ecause our focus was on transition rather than stabilization, on getting ourselves out no matter what the situation was on the ground, we lacked the presence or relevance to generate that leverage."

But the problems did not disappear when the rule of law was elevated to one of the core elements of the new counterinsurgency doctrine of the U.S. forces, which was also adopted by the multinational forces in Iraq in their joint campaign and informed the ISAF operations in Afghanistan; the effectiveness of the respective efforts was severely hampered by a lack of coordination. On the one hand, the forces from different nations found it difficult to adapt to the new doctrine and deploy adequate experts, uniformed or not, to implement it. On the other hand, many conflict lines divided the different civilian and military entities involved in building the rule of law. For instance, in Iraq, the responsibilities of the U.S. Department of Defense, Department of Justice, and Department of State were not clearly defined and led to disagreement and contradictory measures.[35] Improvement in internal coordination including between the civilian and military actors was necessary, but only arrived slowly. The importance of civil–military cooperation in rule of law assistance grew but has not been sufficiently met until today. In Iraq, the variety of actors has remained manageable, as the security situation has been prohibitive for most civilian agencies since the early days of the invasion. In Afghanistan, the variety has always been much greater; actors already included the Italian Justice Project, UNAMA's Rule of Law Unit, the World Bank, numerous embassies as donors, and a large community of implementing agencies before the outbreak of the insurgency.

[35] Very informative in this regard is the article of the former judge advocate in the U.S. Embassy in Baghdad, Pregent (2010b: 323 et seq.).

The following sections provide insights into the realities of the involvement of the international military forces and their cooperation with civilian actors in rule of law assistance operations in the two exemplary countries. The instruments they used to promote change in this area can be conceived within a spectrum of different modes of influence, each reflecting different degrees of leverage that is required to achieve it. Taking into consideration the analytical tools developed by Erik Wennerström and Frank Schimmelfennig in this volume,[36] a scale of three levels will be used in the following section. At one end of the spectrum are the most coercive measures, from forthright force to various forms of restriction or punitive pressure. An example would be the detention of justice officials after an invasion. In the middle are measures that are less coercive but based on a similar logic of reward and punishment, aimed at encouraging behavioral changes through offering positive incentives. This mode of influence is more common; not only foreign military forces but also donors typically offer financial or infrastructure assistance under the condition that the beneficiaries comply with predefined strategies. On the other end of the spectrum are noncoercive and nonconditional measures to facilitate change, such as the persuasion of decision makers and capacity building. These instruments are more particularly used by NGOs and other actors that do not have or disapprove of tougher instruments of rule of law promotion.

4.1. *Iraq, 2003–2005: Rule of Law as an Emerging Counterinsurgency Instrument*

The invasion in and occupation of Iraq in 2003 were not sufficiently supported by a UN Security Council Resolution (Litwak 2007: 146; Tomuschat 2003: 41). In particular, NATO members France, Germany, and Canada and non-NATO member Russia were opposed to a military intervention in Iraq and advocated further diplomatic measures to force Iraq to the disarmament required in UN Security Council (UNSC) Resolution 1441. Without the necessary Security Council approval, the military operation of the U.S.-led coalition of 39 states constituted a breach of international law (Grimm 2010b: 263).

This flawed origin affected the coalition's efforts to establish a new political order in Iraq from the beginning onward. The negative impression was aggravated by the rule of the Coalition Provisional Authority (CPA), an interim administration created as a division of the U.S. Department of Defense, in April 2003, which reminded many Iraqis of colonial rule rather than of a trustworthy management of the country's affairs aiming at an early handover of power to elected representatives of the people.

The lack of legitimacy of the foreign presence and rule also compromised the activities of the judge advocates and other legal experts working for the coalition

[36] See Schimmelfennig in this volume. See also Barnes and Griffiths (2008).

forces who began to try to restore the Iraqi justice system soon after the first soldiers entered the country in 2003. They first assessed courthouses and other infrastructures in Basra and other cities of southern Iraq and continued with their evaluation as the war progressed northward. The situations that they found were diverse; some buildings had been burned or looted whereas others were protected by court personnel.

However, no cohesive plan for civil–military interaction with the Iraqi justice institutions was in place. It was also uncertain which law was applicable and which institutions and personnel were authorized to take judicial decisions. To enable the prosecution of criminals, the CPA ordered the application of the 1969 Iraqi Penal Code.[37] It also directed that U.S. forces should not convene occupation courts but rebuild the Iraqi judicial institutions. The interim administration thus tried to comply with the principles of the Fourth Geneva Convention, which, among others, limits the scope of rule of law activities under occupation.[38] However, the CPA also dismissed many of the country's most experienced jurists on the grounds that they had, voluntarily or not, ties to Saddam Hussein's Baath Party. This order of the interim administrators, who had no substantial knowledge of the development and reform of justice systems, was seen as their most fatal decision by many Iraqi lawyers and foreign observers.[39]

U.S. judge advocates, civil affairs officers, and their counterparts from other coalition forces ordered the remaining judges, prosecutors, and other justice personnel by radio and in personal meetings to return to work and tried to overcome practical obstacles such as the payment of salaries to the justice personnel (Warren 2010: 189).[40] However, the activities of the CPA and the judge advocates aiming at a basic rehabilitation of the collapsed judicial institutions were very incoherent. Coordination of their efforts was insufficient, if there was any at all. Common definitions of the rule of law as a notion and concept, operational means to establish it, and common objectives did not exist.[41] Moreover, the judge advocates and CPA lawyers

37 CPA Order Number 7 suspended certain provisions of the 1969 Iraqi Penal Code "that the former regime used... as a tool of repression in violation of internationally recognized human rights standards" and suspended capital punishment. Coalition Provisional Authority, "Penal Code" CPA/ORD/9 Order no. 7 (2003) of June 2003. Penal Code, CPA/ORD/9 June 2003/07.

38 Article 64 of the Fourth Geneva Convention reads, "The penal laws of the occupied territory shall remain in force, with the exception that they may be repealed or suspended by the Occupying Power in cases where they constitute a threat to its security or an obstacle to the application of the present Convention." Article 43 of the Hague Regulations also states, in the pertinent part, that the occupying power shall take measures to restore and ensure public order and safety, "while respecting, unless absolutely prevented, the laws in force in the country."

39 For instance, by two of the leading experts on the rule of law in Arab countries, Bassiouni, Cherif and Abou El Fadl, Khaled, in Hernandez, Nelson, and al-Izzi, Saad, "Iraq's Attorneys Practicing in a State of Fear," *The Washington Post Foreign Service*, 10 June 2006.

40 Warren (2010: 189).

41 Williamson, Clint, "Preliminary Screening Inquiry Report, Investigation of Legal Operations in CJTF-7." End of Mission Report to the Administrator, Department of the Army, CPA (2005): Tab 60.

had no budgets for rule of law activities and depended on their power to persuade their commanders that certain measures needed to be funded and implemented.[42] For these and other reasons, the effectiveness of rule of law promotion was very limited.

In this context, it is important to note that no doctrine was in place that could have given guidance to the judge advocates who were unprepared for the task of rehabilitating the justice system of a country with a culture, language, and legal tradition unknown to them (Stromseth, Wippman, and Brooks 2006: 322–323). The field manuals *FM 3–0, Joint Operations* and *FM 3–24, Counterinsurgency* were published in September and December 2006, and the *Rule of Law Handbook* followed only in 2008.

During the first months of the occupation, coercive measures clearly dominated the relations between the coalition forces and the Iraqi justice institutions.[43] Later, the strategy of the coalition forces in the area of rule of law promotion improved.[44] While the efforts on the national level focused on institutional matters and the problem of judicial corruption, rule of law assistance in the provinces focused on the reconstruction of destroyed infrastructure, training programs, and case management.[45] On this level, relations with the judicial institutions slowly turned from coercion toward the use of incentives and even nonconditional measures.

Even though it was very early understood that rule of law activities could be an essential instrument to reestablish security, order, and public confidence, the CPA and the military commanders limited the scope of activity to criminal matters. In the colloquial army language of the time, the focus was directed toward the "Three Cs" (cops, courts, and corrections) or "Three Ps" (police, prisons, and prosecutors, the latter of which meant to include courts; see Warren 2010: 189).[46] As a consequence, institutions that are essential for a balanced justice system, such as criminal defense organizations, were neglected. In a letter to the U.S. president, the chairman of the Iraqi Bar Association made this criticism:

> America's Rule of Law effort in Iraq has focused almost entirely on training police, building prisons, and supporting prosecutions. This is understandable. These areas are important to security but they represent a policeman's and prosecutor's

42 Depending on the priorities set by their commanders, they received Commander's Emergency Response Program (CERP) funds for rule of law activities. See Department of State Audit, "Inspection of Rule-of-Law Programs, Embassy, Baghdad." ISP-IQO-06–01 (2005): 2.

43 This is also true for the constitution-drafting process in 2005, which was directed by U.S. interests and controlled by high-ranking officials including then-Ambassador Zalmay Khalidzad. See Arato (2009).

44 This occurred in particular through the deployment of a CPA senior advisor to the Ministry of Justice and the creation of Judicial Reconstruction Assistance Teams and Ministry of Justice Offices.

45 Regarding the military rule of law activities, see Rubini (2009: 45).

46 Warren (2010: 189); see also UNAMA and ISAF Southern Region Partners Coordination Board (RC-South), "A Common and Operational Approach to Rule of Law for Southern Afghanistan." (2009), unpublished: 5.

> definition of what Rule of Law means. This definition is limited to law enforcement.... [O]ur legal culture is in need of assistance and America's millions of dollars have done little to assist our institutions.... If you think that "implanting" the Rule of Law in Iraq is limited to your current Rule of Law efforts, then you are receiving poor advice.[47]

This problem of incoherent strategies for the reform of the justice sector was slightly reduced when the U.S. State Department began with basic donor coordination in 2005 through the Bureau of International Narcotics and Law Enforcement Affairs (INL).[48]

The greatest problem, however, remained the lack of legitimacy and credibility. It began with the doubtful legal basis of the invasion and was permanently nourished by other obvious deficiencies such as the lack of familiarity of the military lawyers with the Iraqi legal system, the overwhelming military imprint on all U.S. and coalition activities including rule of law assistance,[49] and many Iraqis' outrage over the fact that foreign military personnel who were breaking Iraqi or international law were immune. The words of an Iraqi judge reflect the aggrieved feelings:

> "Are you familiar with the Code of Hammurabi?" We replied that we knew of the Code of Hammurabi, and he said, "Well, most Americans have never even heard of it. Iraq has an ancient legal culture. We don't need you to come here and tell us about what law is. We invented law. This is the cradle of Western civilization. We are the people who figured law out, thousands of years ago. But now your soldiers are coming in and telling us what to do, and you're not respecting our legal traditions or legal process. The first thing the Americans did after the war was to announce that they were immune from Iraqi legal process. So, if an American commits a crime, they're completely immune, there's nothing that we can do about it. The Americans are unaccountable. How can this be the rule of law?"[50]

U.S. influence on Iraqi politics remained enormous until about 2008, when domestic politicians became more self-confident and regional powers, especially Iran and Saudi Arabia, began to exercise influence more effectively. This change

47 Miranda, Manuel, "Departure Assessment of Embassy Baghdad." Memorandum to Ambassador Crocker, US Embassy, Baghdad, Iraq. Baghdad: Office of Legislative Statecraft, 5 February 2008, quoting a letter from Aswad Al-Minshidi, President of the Iraqi Bar, to President George W. Bush: 9.

48 Department of State Audit, "Inspection of Rule-of-Law Programs, Embassy, Baghdad." ISP-IQO-06-01 (2005): 2.

49 Carlson, Brooks, Nawabi, and Bodansky (2004: 134–135) remark, "This paradox that I have talked about – how to bring the rule of law from the barrel of a gun – partly stems from the fact that in Iraq, the face of the guy with the gun and the face of the guy urging the rule of law are one and the same. With almost all the troops and civilians on the ground operating under the auspices of the American military, most Iraqis unsurprisingly find it difficult to distinguish between our claims about legitimate authority and rights and our sheer power."

50 This anonymous Iraqi judge talking to U.S. judge advocates is quoted in Carlson et al. (2004: 130).

of the political power relations opened the doors for other nonmilitary or military-sponsored organizations' work in the area of rule of law promotion in Iraq.

4.2. *Afghanistan, 2006–2011: CIMIC in the Most Complex Rule of Law Arena*

The conditions for building the rule of law in Afghanistan – regardless of the means, whether they be civilian or military – were fundamentally different from those in Iraq. After more than two decades of war, the country was devastated in every regard. Justice personnel with competent knowledge of the law was scarce. Whereas the institutions had been functioning in Iraq before the invasion – albeit under the conditions of a dictatorship – they had almost totally disintegrated in Afghanistan during the civil war (1992–1996) and Taliban regime (1996–2001). To complicate matters, they had never existed in large parts of the country where tribal forms of conflict resolution had been used from time immemorial. Building the rule of law from the perspective of most external actors meant beginning with laying the most elementary fundaments of a justice system.

In contrast to the Iraq invasion, the ousting of the Taliban regime by U.S. forces and Afghan opposition groups, especially the Northern Alliance, in 2001 (Operation Enduring Freedom–Afghanistan) found some – yet not unanimous – support in the international legal community, mainly as a result of the fresh impression of the September 11 attacks.[51] The ISAF, which was established in December 2001 to secure first Kabul and then wider parts of the country, was based on a UNSC resolution.[52] Soon after the invasion, a multitude of civilian rule of law actors began assisting the Afghan government in the establishment of a justice system.

These included the Italian Justice Project, which was established by the justice sector lead nation Italy for coherent strategic planning and coordination of all efforts; the UN Assistance Mission to Afghanistan (UNAMA), which encompassed Rule of Law as well as Human Rights Units; other UN agencies such as the United Nations Development Program, United Nations High Commissioner for Refugees, and the United Nations Office on Drugs and Crime; the World Bank; embassies as donors; and a large community of implementing agencies including the International Development Law Organization, the U.S. agencies U.S. Agency for International Development and the Bureau of International Narcotics and Law Enforcement

[51] Defenders of the legality and the legitimacy of the U.S.-led military invasion in Afghanistan argue that UNSC authorization was not required because the invasion was an act of collective self-defense provided for under Art. 51 of the UN Charter. Critics hold that the invasion does not fall under Art. 51 because the 9/11 attacks were not "armed attacks" by another state but rather perpetrated by groups of individuals or nonstate actors. Further, even if a state had perpetrated the attacks, no imminent threat of an armed attack on the United States existed after 9/11, and the United States would not have waited three weeks before commencing the bombing campaign against Afghanistan if there had been such a threat: The necessity for self-defense must be instant and overwhelming, leaving no choice of means and no moment for deliberation.

[52] UNSC Resolution 1386 of 20 December 2001, UN Doc. S/RES/1386.

Affairs, the German Gesellschaft für Internationale Zusammenarbeit (GIZ), the Max Planck Institute for Comparative Public Law and International Law, and many other government-funded organizations and NGOs.

The focus of international efforts to stabilize the country was, however, not directed at rule of law issues until about 2006, when the neo-Taliban insurgency became a serious threat to the success achieved until then. Military involvement in rule of law activities also remained very scarce until that time. Meanwhile, the program of the Bonn Agreement of 2001[53] was successfully completed in December 2005 with the establishment of the main state institutions and the opening of Afghanistan's bicameral National Assembly. The living conditions of millions of Afghans had also considerably improved because humanitarian aid could reach almost all parts of the country. However, the Afghan government turned out to be weak and barely capable of developing and implementing sustainable policies. In the justice sector, the lead nation Italy did not meet expectations either (Röder 2007: 308). A widely noted study of June 2007[54] suggested that more than 80 percent of disputes were still settled outside the state courts. The majority of judicial professionals still had not been sufficiently educated, and they lacked access to up-to-date legal resources. Poor salaries led to a rapid spreading of corruption and resulted in diminishing trust in the courts and other institutions among the population.[55] Legal norms had to be described as a patchwork rather than a system. The discrepancy between Islamic and secular provisions remained unresolved and a highly political issue.[56] In addition to the already existing difficulties, new ones resulted from a lack of coherent vision for the development of the judiciary. A National Justice Program did not exist until as late as 2008. To date, all of these problems have not been effectively resolved.

The activities of international military forces in rule of law assistance began in 2006. U.S. forces were the first to take the new direction. Contrary to the initial Iraqi situation, the efforts of judge advocates and civil affairs officers in Afghanistan were not supported but rather ordered by the U.S. military leadership (Tasikas 2007). This strategic adjustment resulted from a combination of three factors. First, insurgent attacks had sharply increased from 2005 to 2006[57] and had drawn the attention of

[53] The agreement aimed at the creation of the Islamic Republic of Afghanistan: Agreement on Provisional Arrangements in Afghanistan Pending the Re-Establishment of Permanent Government Institutions (Bonn Agreement) of 5 December 2001.

[54] Center for Policy and Human Development, "Afghanistan Human Development Report: Bridging Modernity and Tradition: Rule of Law and the Search of Justice" (2007). Available at http://hdr.undp.org/en/reports/nationalreports/asiathepacific/afghanistan/nhdr2007.pdf.

[55] Asia Foundation, "Afghanistan in 2007. A Survey of the Afghan People" (2007). Available at http://asiafoundation.org/resources/pdfs/AGsurvey07.pdf.

[56] For example, in 2007, a group of 200 Afghan clerics from the Western province of Herat argued for the nationwide enforcement of Islamic Shari'a, including punishments such as executions and the stoning of adulterers.

[57] Attacks on the international military almost tripled from over 1,000 in 2005 to almost 2,900 in 2006. Attacks on Afghan forces almost quadrupled from 830 in 2005 to over 3,500 in 2006. Suicide attacks increased by more than six times. UNAMA, "Suicide Attacks in Afghanistan (2001–2007)" (2007). Available at http://www.unhrc.org.

the international community to the fact that neither the state nor the international military forces were in full control of the situation outside of the major cities. Second, the U.S. military capitalized on its experience in Iraq and assigned the rule of law its prominent position in the new counterinsurgency doctrine. Third, as a result of the weakness of the Italian Justice Project and UNAMA in coordinating the justice sector, ISAF began developing its own rule of law capacity. The international military forces may be considered one of the most important actors in law enforcement and judicial reform since about 2008. Civil–military cooperation in building the rule of law can therefore be described as a permanent practice in Afghanistan.

According to the specific guidance developed by the U.S. forces' command from 2006 onward, the judge advocates were directed to identify realistic and affordable judicial sector goals. Capacity building was to be realized in a holistic manner by linking key institutions, including courts, prisons, police, and attorneys. The U.S. military leadership also saw a necessity to indoctrinate both Afghan government officials and the population with the firm belief in the rule of law (Tasikas 2007: 53). At the same time, the Combined Security Transition Command – Afghanistan, a subordinate command to both the command of the U.S. forces and the U.S. Embassy in Afghanistan, developed a strategic plan for the implementation of the U.S. rule of law programs. Judge advocates began drafting laws and regulations believed to be vital to the Afghan government's effectiveness and creating a secure setting, such as the Military Criminal Procedure Code and other criminal legislation for the Afghan National Army and Afghan National Police.[58] Judge advocates discussed the situation in the justice sector with Afghan officials on the provincial and even district levels. The PRTs also played an increasingly important role in identifying possibilities of support. The first provincial justice program that systematically combined civilian and military efforts was launched in Wardak Province in 2006 and became a model for similar strategic experiments (Tasikas 2007: 54).

Since then, judge advocates, other military and civilian, and military-sponsored actors have met local governmental officials, including judges, police, prosecutors, prison wardens, and attorneys, on a regular basis; assessed ongoing developments; and discussed support opportunities in almost all operational areas of the U.S. forces. They organize coordination meetings and so-called Provincial Justice Conferences, assess the infrastructure needs, collect relevant statistical data, and perform other tasks. As in Iraq, judge advocates use Commander's Emergency Response Program (CERP) funds mainly for the rehabilitation and construction of physical infrastructure such as modern courthouses and prisons.[59] Other military-sponsored projects

58 Combined Security Transition Command – Afghanistan, "CSTC-A Fact Sheet" (12 April 2006).

49 See the National Defense Authorization Act for Fiscal Year 2006. Pub. L. No. 109–163, 119 Stat. 3136, 3455–56: para. 1202(a). For a general overview and brief history and purpose of CERP, see Gorove and Nachbar (2008: 273–274), and Martins (2004: 1).

include providing vehicles for the justice institutions, the establishment of defense counsel services, and public awareness campaigns.[60]

The arrival of the Combined Joint Interagency Task Force 435 in 2009 changed the balance between military and civilian actors in rule of law assistance. Although it was originally designed to assume responsibility for U.S. detention operations, this task force expanded its influence to many other areas of the justice system.[61] Despite the presence of an ambassador with exclusive responsibility for rule of law matters at the U.S. Embassy, and despite the fact that, in theory, the U.S. Embassy oversees the aid and development strategy in a foreign country, the U.S. military has become a more significant player in rule of law promotion than the U.S. Embassy. Along with this development, "law" and "order" have become competitive concepts, and the U.S. military has invariably chosen "order" over "law."[62]

Contrary to the Iraqi situation, all external actors including the military in Afghanistan refrained from the use of coercive measures.[63] The main reason is the fact that they did not have to interact with judicial institutions and personnel that had functioned as a constitutive element of a dictatorial system. Under the Taliban, the judiciary had been weak, the police widely replaced by militias, and the prosecution dissolved. When the new government began to rebuild these institutions in 2002, it only had to replace very few remaining officials from the overthrown regime; others were kept not only because of their indispensable knowledge but also because of the convergence of their views with the fundamentalist post-Taliban Chief Justice, Fazl Hadi Shinwari.

In Afghanistan, the main instruments of both civilian and military rule of law promotion are positive incentives, conditionality, persuasion, and capacity-building. Combinations of incentives and conditions are prevalent. The offer of urgently needed financial and technical support for the implementation of openly or not donor-specified reform strategies is very common. This technique does not comply with the proposition that the reform process be "Afghan-owned," but donor representatives customarily justify it with the requirement to use the funds in an effective and transparent manner. Personal advantages offered to Afghan decision makers such as study tours abroad that can be disguised as luxury tours are even less maintainable. Such techniques, and even straightforward corruption, seem to occur with organizations that are under pressure to implement high-budget projects

60 For numerous reports, see the Web sites of ISAF, http://www.isaf.nato.int; the NATO Training Mission Afghanistan, http://www.ntm-a.com; the U.S. Joint Forces Command, http://www.jfcom.mil; the U.S. Department of Defense, http://www.defense.gov; the U.S. Navy Judge Advocate General's Corps, http://www.jag.navy.mil; and the U.S. Army Judge Advocate General's Corps, http://www.jagcnet.army.mil.

61 See the Web site of the U.S. Central Command, http://www.centcom.mil/jtf435.

62 These are views expressed by U.S. Embassy officials in talks with the author.

63 There may have been single cases of detention of Taliban officials who also had had judicial functions, but there is no evidence of cases in which such persons were still in office.

assigned to them while being exempt from all-too-close donor supervision. As to the military, no such cases are heard of. Persuasion and capacity-building are widely accepted by the Afghans as legitimate forms of rule of law promotion. The many meetings and conferences, mentoring programs, and trainings in all kind of legal matters and practical skills organized by judge advocates belong to this category.

The deficiencies of the military rule of law promotion are similar to those in Iraq. Judge advocates are still not sufficiently trained for rule of law operations. Although the U.S. military's *Rule of Law Handbook* has given them some guidance for the work in the field since 2008, the main difficulty continues to lie in understanding the complex religious, cultural, and legal background in Afghanistan. The judge advocates' approach to the rule of law is therefore overly technical and fails to comprehend it as a social and political process.

The lack of coordination is another parallel. In Afghanistan, the work of the judge advocates, civil affairs officers, and their counterparts from other coalition forces is partly coordinated under the common roof of the specialized ISAF units. Civil–military linkages are, however, weak. The U.S. Embassy's Interagency Planning and Implementation Team tries to coordinate the U.S.-funded civilian as well as military rule of law activities, but it faces difficulties caused by, among other reasons, frequent staff changes. UNAMA organizes coordination meetings on issues such as legal training in Kabul, as well as, through its Provincial Justice Coordinators, on the provincial level. Other actors have launched coordination initiatives where they saw the need, such as the Coordination of Police and Prosecutor Training initiative of GIZ and EUPOL, the National Security Prosecutors Training Working Group of the British Embassy, the Inter-Agency Support Group to the Department of Human Rights and Gender of the Police Academy of EUPOL, and so forth.[64] A central coordinating institution is thus lacking.

5. THEORETICAL RULE OF LAW ISSUES AND CHALLENGES RAISED BY CIMIC

The last section of this chapter tries to merge the most important theoretical issues that have been raised in the previous analysis. These are the question of the legitimacy of military rule of law promotion, and the problem of the military's narrow, security-oriented notion of the rule of law.[65]

5.1. *Legitimacy of the Military's Involvement in Rule of Law Promotion*

Any promotion of the rule of law by foreign actors requires substantiated legitimation. Both civilians and the military must be able to answer why they are eligible to take

64 It should be noted that all of these meetings take place in the absence of Afghan officials. The Attorney General's Office has recently started its own series of meetings with donors and implementing agencies in order to be more involved in the decision-making process.

65 Regarding both questions, the author draws on the discussions at the Fourth Meeting of The Hague Rule of Law Network (Utrecht, 23–24 April 2009), which addressed these very issues.

the reform of a state that is not their own into their hands. Considering that the building of the rule of law, by its nature, should be a civilian endeavor,[66] military commanders or civilian authorities mandating the armed forces to get involved in rule of law promotion are expected to present additional arguments. The importance of this matter should not be underestimated. Although the legitimacy discussion may appear theoretical, it directly affects the success of any military activity aiming at building the rule of law. To speak in the words of Isabelle Duyvesteyn, a lack of legitimacy is, in the eyes of the local population, "the ultimate barrier for success."[67]

Differences remain over what constitutes the best source from which to draw such legitimacy. This chapter proposes the consideration of five main sources of legitimacy that need to be discussed individually for every possible mission. These sources include the mandate of the military intervention in general and of the units involved in rule of law promotion in particular; compliance with international legal standards limiting the scope of reform under occupation; the credibility of the international military forces as rule of law advocates in the eyes of the population; the legitimacy of the indigenous government or other institutions supported through the rule of law operations; and the capacity of the military lawyers to trigger processes of change in dysfunctional legal systems.

The first key criterion must always be the legality and legitimacy under international law of the military intervention as such. If the legal grounds of an invasion or occupation are doubtful, the legitimacy of any activity of the foreign forces will be flawed as well. In both exemplary cases used in this chapter, this problem is manifest. Whereas the intervention in Afghanistan has widely been perceived as legitimate, the reasons brought forward for the Iraq war were not accepted to be sufficient by large parts of the international community. This, however, does not necessarily lead to the conclusion that action taken to stabilize law enforcement and judicial institutions in Iraq does not find any legitimization at all; any occupying force is obligated to restore and uphold the law and order in the controlled territory.

The question of the legality and legitimacy of an intervention directly affects the eligibility of the international military forces to change state structures. If armed forces occupy a territory such as in the case of Iraq, they are bound to act within the limits defined in Section III of the Fourth Geneva Convention (Occupied Territories). Article 47 is of particular importance in our context.[68]

> Protected persons who are in occupied territory shall not be deprived, in any case or in any manner whatsoever, of the benefits of the present Convention by *any change introduced*, as the result of the occupation of a territory, *into the institutions or government of the said territory*, nor by *any agreement concluded between the authorities of the occupied territories and the Occupying Power*, nor by any annexation by the latter of the whole or part of the occupied territory.

66 Hague Rule of Law Network, "Final Report: Civil-Military Cooperation in Building the Rule of Law." Report on the Fourth Annual Meeting of The Hague Rule of Law Network (2009): 2.

67 Ibid: 5.

68 Emphasis added.

With regard to the judicial sector, the Geneva Convention determines that the occupying power may not alter the status of public officials or judges if they abstain from fulfilling their functions for reasons of conscience (Art. 54), and it must ensure the effective administration of criminal justice by maintaining the existing tribunals and the penal laws as far as they do not constitute a threat to the security of the occupying power or an obstacle to the application of the convention (Art. 64). In the view of many international lawyers, these lines drawn by the Geneva Convention were crossed by the U.S. government and its allies in Iraq, where they undertook fundamental changes including the de facto imposition of an interim and a permanent constitution (Arato 2009: 136 et seq., 205 et seq.).

Occupying powers may try to create the impression of legality and independence of new indigenous institutions by supporting some cooperative parts of the population of the occupied country who then take over government tasks and change state structures. This practice is, however, incompatible with the traditional concept of occupation as defined in Article 43 of the Hague Regulations of 1907, according to which the occupying authority is considered as merely being an administrator.

This provision protects the separate existence of the occupied state, its institutions, and its laws. However, changes that improve the humanitarian situation of the population are legitimate under the Fourth Geneva Convention, and some measures to strengthen the rule of law, such as enforcement of fair trial rights, may be regarded as compatible with this objective.[69]

The international military forces must further ask themselves whether not only the institutions they support but also the population at large accept them as promoters of the rule of law. Their credibility requires that two preconditions are met. First, they must themselves abide by the rule of law and be seen to do so.[70] In both Iraq and Afghanistan, however, many justice officials and citizens have gained the impression that double standards are applied. In many cases, this impression is understandable; for instance, while judge advocates expect full implementation of fair trial rights according to international standards set by the International Covenant on Civil and Political Rights from local police, prosecutors, and judges, these rights have not been upheld in their own detention facilities such as Abu Ghraib in Iraq, Bagram in Afghanistan, and Guantánamo overseas (Moore 2003). The reputation of the international military forces in the local population is further damaged if civilians are affected by military operations and the responsible personnel are not punished, or information about their prosecution at home is not conveyed to the population. Immunity of members of armed forces under local law is easily taken for impunity

69 International Committee of the Red Cross, "ICRC Commentary on the Convention (IV) relative to the Protection of Civilian Persons in Time of War," Geneva (1949).

70 This argument is also shared by military officers, e.g., Lieutenant Colonel A. Goshi (U.S. Army). Hague Rule of Law Network, "Final Report: Civil-Military Cooperation in Building the Rule of Law." Report on the Fourth Annual Meeting of The Hague Rule of Law Network (2009): 6.

by the population.[71] The phenomenon that local institutions and populations expect the external actors to adhere to rule of law principles that they themselves promote resembles the "boomerang effect" known from other areas of rule of law promotion.[72] Second, serious partnership respecting the local ownership of legal developments is of great importance for the effectiveness of all planned measures. Civilian as well as military actors sometimes tend to misunderstand or ignore the agendas of the "partner institutions" of their "host nation" and thus impair entire rule of law programs.[73]

The third aspect affecting legitimacy of military involvement in rule of law promotion is the legitimacy of the supported government and other indigenous institutions. Particularly in the situation of an insurgency, both sides fight over the acceptance and support of the population that will ultimately determine the outcome of the war. Accordingly, civil–military operations form the core of counterinsurgency operations because they aim at building the indigenous government's legitimacy.[74] Thus, if this government is regarded as illegitimate by the population, the counterinsurgency efforts will go astray.[75] The negative impact can, however, also take the opposite direction if the counterinsurgency does not meet local acceptance and affects the supported government.[76]

Finally, the capacity of the military lawyers to stimulate change is important in order to produce positive feedback from the legal community and the general population, which should ultimately profit from their activity. As already demonstrated here, the judge advocates had and still have today considerable difficulties in understanding the complex normative orders of Iraq and Afghanistan, and in developing and implementing strategies for their improvement. This is not all too surprising given the, at least for outsiders, inscrutable relations among secular, Islamic, and customary law, the cultural and linguistic barriers, and other difficulties. Judge advocates are primarily trained in operational and armed-conflict law. Even though their training has been adjusted over the past years, it does not sufficiently prepare them for

71 The bombing of two fuel tankers close to Kunduz City (Afghanistan) on 4 September 2009 is such an example.

72 See, e.g., Gemkow and Zürn, in this volume.

73 The Research, Reporting, and Donor Relations Coordinator of the Afghanistan Independent Human Rights Commission, Musa Sultani, argued at a conference that the Afghan ownership was "an empty word" because the justice sector reform strategies are authored, laws drafted, and project funds allocated by the donors. In his view, CIMIC activities aimed at "bribing the community" with projects. Hague Rule of Law Network, "Final Report: Civil-Military Cooperation in Building the Rule of Law." Report on the Fourth Annual Meeting of The Hague Rule of Law Network (2009): 7.

74 Department of the Army, "FM 3–24, Counterinsurgency" (2006).

75 Crane, Conrad, "COIN of the Realm?: The Role and Importance of Legitimacy in Counterinsurgency." Presentation at the Future Defense Dilemma Seminar of the 21st Century Defense Initiative and the Strategic Studies Institute, 2 April 2008. Available at http://www.povertyfrontiers.org, 2008: 2.

76 View of Duyvesteyn, quoted in Hague Rule of Law Network, "Final Report: Civil-Military Cooperation in Building the Rule of Law." Report on the Fourth Annual Meeting of The Hague Rule of Law Network (2009): 5.

the task with which they are faced in the field. Because their assignments are short – rarely more than six months – they do not have a real chance to learn enough in practice before being replaced.[77] Wisely, they mainly implement infrastructure projects by themselves and entrust civilian, local or international, organizations with the realization of legal trainings and other activities that demand a high level of expertise.

The legitimacy of military rule of law promotion certainly has to be answered on a case-by-case basis. All things considered, however, it seems to be difficult to meet the criteria introduced in this section. This analysis certainly does not disprove the skeptical views on military rule of law promotion. Proponents of the military involvement argue that there may be places where only the military can operate as a result of a bad security situation; but there, the international armed forces do not reconstruct courthouses but are intent on clearing and holding the fought-over area.

5.2. *The Military's Narrow Notion of the Rule of Law*

The second theoretical issue of relevance in the context of this volume is the extremely narrow notion of the rule of law proposed and practiced by the international military forces. Their rule of law concept focuses almost entirely on criminal justice reform. As a consequence, large areas including private law, administrative law, and constitutional law are widely ignored, except for cases in which they indirectly affect the criminal justice sector. For instance, land disputes are only seen as relevant because they regularly turn violent,[78] and administrative reform is considered only as far as it is a tool for the improvement of the performance of the law enforcement and justice institutions.[79] Human rights are accepted to be an important issue, but the establishment of law and order is given priority. For this reason, U.S. military lawyers in Afghanistan tend to plead for a greater role of non-state justice panels (so-called *shuras* or *jirgas*), which function as platforms for the resolution of disputes but are also known to frequently violate human and especially women's and children's rights. The very much institution- and infrastructure-oriented approach to judicial reform is also striking.

All this may result from the short time frame of military presence compared with the time frame that civilian organizations dispose of.[80] However, the typical rule of law activities of the military only produce sustainable results if they are embedded in a comprehensive project that addresses legal and judicial reform

77 These problems are not totally unknown in the civilian rule of law organization community, but in general, the level of understanding and the development capacity are better.

78 See, Colin Deschamps and Alan Roe, "Land Conflict in Afghanistan," in Whit Mason (ed.), *The Rule of Law in Afghanistan – Missing in Action*, Cambridge University Press, p. 211.

79 The relevance of the rule of law for public administration reform is highlighted by Bergling, Wennerström, and Zajac-Sannerholm (2010).

80 This argument was proposed by Vester in an e-mail to the author (26 October 2010).

in a holistic manner. On the institutional level, it is not sufficient to build up functioning police, prosecution, and courts; in addition, it is necessary to develop a proper system of prisons and detention centers, sufficient numbers of defense counsels protecting the fair trial rights of accused persons and representing the citizens in civil and administrative matters, government and parliament lawyers capable of drafting sound laws, law schools and training centers educating students and professionals according to the needs they are faced with, and so forth. It must also be kept in mind that the rule of law is also a matter of habits, commitments, and trust of the people in the legal and judicial system. Creating it must therefore include tools for cultural change, which is more difficult to achieve and implies a much longer-term engagement than the technical and institutional improvements advised by the military. After all, "[p]romoting the rule of law requires interveners to keep many balls in the air at once" (Stromseth, Wippman, and Brooks 2006: 310), and the military certainly does not have the empty hands for this juggling in all current theaters of war. However, the solution to this dilemma cannot be to ignore the essential elements of the rule of law, as this will prevent success from the very beginning.

6. CONCLUSIONS

Civil–military cooperation was of great importance in Vietnam as an instrument in a counterinsurgency war. Already at that time, rule of law promotion was sporadically utilized in this very context by military lawyers. After the withdrawal of U.S. forces from the Indochinese peninsula, however, all of these elements were eliminated from military doctrine, only to return in the mid-1990s. Since about 2006, they have gained an importance that was heretofore unthinkable in the entire military history to date. Building the rule of law with CIMIC means is a core element in the counterinsurgency strategy developed for the most grueling conflicts of the time in Afghanistan and Iraq, and they play a similarly important role in other ongoing stabilization missions.

However, all pendula swing back, and it is not unlikely that the role assigned to building the rule of law by the U.S. armed forces and some of their allies will lose importance again in the near future. This reason is based on the assumption that the military as an actor and CIMIC as an instrument will not produce the effects hoped for, mainly as a result of the legitimacy gap and the narrow and short-termed engagement described in the last section of this chapter.

The norms governing a society are a highly sensitive area; this is especially true for Muslim societies, where law is closely interwoven with religion. Particularly in countries such as Afghanistan and Iraq, the military should therefore be the very last resort for any rule of law activities. Whenever a civilian solution is available, it should prevail. This means that the military's involvement in rule of law activities should be widely limited to its primary role of providing security, which is one of the indispensable preconditions of the work of civilian actors.[81]

Three areas remain where military assistance to judicial sector reforms is certainly necessary. The first area is support to judicial institutions in places that civilian organizations cannot access for geographical or security reasons. Here, the military should assume the role of a facilitator and enable civilian organizations, for example with logistical support to fulfill their mandate. The second area is legal training and mentoring of military staff of the supported government. No civilian organization can teach operational law and similar topics better than judge advocates. These contributions are more likely to produce sustainable and durable positive outcomes than more overt approaches. Third, the military may be legally obligated under international humanitarian law to perform certain basic functions for the benefit of the local population. These functions can include elementary activities related to the judicial sector such as assistance to the police, prosecutors, and courts to restore and uphold the law and order in a territory they control.

For the political leadership, giving the pendulum of military doctrine a push in the right direction should not be all too difficult; the right measure is to reallocate the hundreds of millions of dollars spent by the military on rule of law and other development projects[82] to the civilian organizations and limit the military activity to the three areas just mentioned, where it is undoubtedly useful.

[81] Musa Sultani (Afghanistan Independent Human Rights Commission) recommends engaging local, civilian actors in the process of building's Afghanistan's rule of law and to a far greater scope, and to avoid entrusting the same people that are responsible for security with the civilian-by-nature responsibility of constructing Afghanistan's rule of law. Hague Rule of Law Network, "Final Report: Civil-Military Cooperation in Building the Rule of Law." Report on the Fourth Annual Meeting of The Hague Rule of Law Network (2009): 7.

[82] For CERP alone, 3.8 billion in U.S. dollars was spent from 2004 until 2010. "Where the Money Goes," *The Washington Post*, 4 January 2011.

10

Developing a Theoretical Framework for Evaluating Rule of Law Promotion in Developing Countries

John Gillespie

1. INTRODUCTION

Rule of law (RoL) promotion proceeds on the belief that particular regulatory techniques associated with effective development in developed countries ("international best practice") are broadly applicable in less-developed countries (Rodrik 2006). However, one of the few areas of agreement in a field that attracts so much controversy is that the expenditure of billions of dollars on promoting reforms based on international best practice has produced mixed results (Trebilcock and Daniels 2008: 37–42). Country studies discussed in this volume (see, e.g., Zajac-Sannerholm) reveal complex reception patterns where RoL principles and practices provoke different responses among disparate social groups within the same country. RoL ideas may initially be rejected or ignored by recipients, only to reemerge decades later in highly contextualized reformulations.

Widespread disappointment with RoL projects suggests the need to look beyond RoL promotion (the promoter perspective) and diffusion (the modalities that disseminate RoL ideas) to examine the underresearched and theorized RoL conversion (the recipient perspective; see the Introduction to this volume). Many commentators attribute RoL failures to a lack of focus and coordination among donors, an inability or unwillingness to learn from mistakes, as well as inappropriate modes of promotion such as imposition and incentives (Morlino and Magen 2009).

This chapter argues instead that international donors need to rethink their approach to understanding RoL promotion. It posits that the ideas underlying RoL promotion have little intrinsic meaning and they are reinterpreted and given contextually relevance by recipients. It is consequently important for donors to understand and recalibrate their projects to accommodate the factors that motivate recipients in developing countries to adopt, resignify, or reject RoL promotion.

The author gratefully acknowledges the useful comments by reviewers of this chapter and the financial support from ARC Grant DP0985927.

2. MEASURING THE SUCCESS AND FAILURE OF ROL PROMOTION

Before discussing at more length the factors that might motivate recipients to adopt RoL reforms, it is necessary to consider what is meant by program failure. As Merkel notes in this volume, the way actors evaluate RoL promotion depends to a large extent on their mode of assessment (also see Taylor 2007: 87–88; Trebilcock and Daniels 2008: 12–29). The central questions to consider are: Must RoL promotion induce behavioral change of the kind contemplated by donors or recipient lawmakers? Or is it sufficient for RoL promotion to act as a catalyst that stimulates behavioral modifications in ways that may be unforeseen by lawmakers? If this latter definition is accepted then any response to RoL promotion constitutes success.

The idea of success or failure assumes that laws have measurable goals. For Alan Watson, most RoL promotion is successful simply because legal borrowing is a major source of law reform around the world (Watson 1983: 1121). Pierre Legrand (2001), in contrast, argues against an instrumental understanding because it conveys the misapprehension that RoL promotion is about social engineering. Though reaching different conclusions about the role of legal transfers, both theorists agree that success must refer in some way to changing normative behavior in the recipient country. This in turn suggests that where RoL programs are designed to realize some specified goal, the degree to which the programs achieve that goal – the behavioral effectiveness – is measurable.

A related issue is determining from whose perspective behavioral effectiveness should be measured. RoL promotion might appear useful for one social group but useless or even socially disruptive for another. By challenging established patterns of behavior, RoL promotion has the capacity to create winners and losers. As Roger Cotterrell (2001: 79) observed, "the way law is conceptualized colours the way that the success (indeed, the very possibility) of legal borrowing is judged."

Further complicating this assessment is the lack of coordination among international donors regarding the content of RoL promotion. This sometimes results in the situation in which developing countries are exposed to different messages. Even so, with the possible exception of RoL promotion by Japan (Taylor 2005), most projects advocate a standard range of ideas that fit comfortably within a minimalist or a full-blown liberal democratic version of the RoL (see Merkel, in this volume).

The next section briefly reviews the literature dealing with donor explanations for RoL failures, and then it examines in more depth what recipients think about RoL promotion.

3. ROL PROMOTION AND DONOR EXPLANATIONS FOR FAILURES

Much of the Law and Development (L&D) literature searches for RoL failures in the conception and delivery of donor projects (see Heupel and Schimmelfennig in this volume). This focus on donor perspectives is found in the earliest writing about

RoL promotion. Trubek and Galanter (1974) famously blamed the failures of the U.S. efforts to promote the RoL in South America during the 1960s and early 1970s on shortcomings in the project design; development programs were considered in a top-down fashion, lacking empirical grounding and being ethnocentric. As Trubek and Galanter explained, L&D practitioners were strongly influenced by modernization theory, then in vogue among development theorists, which drew on a reductive reading of Weber that stripped away the nuance and focused on his pronouncements about the role of "rational" legal systems in the emergence of modern capitalism. In this view, the RoL could be instrumentalized by transplanting U.S. institutions and substantive law ("international best practice"). Law became a positivist instrument to engineer social change.

International donors during the 1980s and 1990s sought to correct earlier failures, which they believed had underestimated the self-interest of recipient states. For example, the 1981 World Bank's report "Accelerated Development in Sub Saharan Africa"[1] depicted the state as the source of all economic problems. Instead of an instrumentalized Weber, they prescribed neoliberalism. They aimed to roll back the state and placed their faith in markets to produce development objectives. John Williamson (1990) labeled the neoliberal policies that flowed from this approach the "Washington Consensus." These policies advocated streamlined regulatory procedures, small budget deficits, broad tax bases, few state subsidies, market-determined interest rates, liberalized trade and foreign investment, privatization of state-owned enterprises, few impediments to foreign direct investment, and guaranteed and secure property rights.

When deregulation did not produce the desired economic growth, donors turned to New Institutional Economics (discussed later), which offered a more nuanced account of development without fundamentally disrupting neoliberal objectives and reforms based on a predetermined set of international best practices. By the mid-1990s, the state was no longer considered predatory and venal, but "the key institution to ensure that the market functions properly" (Harrison 2004: 19). Donors ceased talking about macroeconomic fundamentals and instead spoke of "governance" and the importance of "good governance." They advocated post–Washington Consensus reforms in which the private economy no longer entirely dominated and other objectives such as human rights and poverty alleviation gained prominence (Harvey 2005; Newton 2008).

Reflecting on 30 years of RoL promotion, Trubek and Santos (2006: 86) opined that "L&D veterans could only sigh as they saw many of the errors of the past being repeated. For them, the emphasis on top-down, one size fits all reform, suggested that little had been learned from prior experiences." What they were alluding to is the search by donors for RoL failures in the design and delivery of projects. With few exceptions, they considered debates among donors about improving the

[1] World Bank, "Accelerated Development in Sub Saharan Africa: An Agenda to Action," 1981.

delivery of projects self-referential and reflecting developmental fashions in donor countries more than developmental concerns in developing countries (Newton 2008; Trubek 2006). A central assumption underlying much deliberation was that donors could engineer more effective RoL projects by learning from past mistakes. In other words, rather than considering what recipients thought about RoL promotion, donors sought to improve the modalities of communicating "international best practice."

One explanation for this preoccupation with the delivery of the RoL message is the previously discussed instrumental positivism that underpins donor thinking. Donors treat "international best practice" as an exogenous variable – a "thing out there" – that can communicate norms, understandings, and processes across geopolitical and cultural boundaries. It is assumed to have an inherent and ahistorical meaning that can be decoded by appropriate trained technicians in recipient countries. International donor agencies acknowledge that misinterpretations of RoL messages routinely occur. However, they usually attribute miscommunication to a lack of skills and knowledge on the part of recipients to *correctly* interpret RoL projects (Trebilcock and Daniels 2008: 281–282). To minimize misunderstandings, many RoL projects use legal education and training to ensure that recipients have the appropriate linguistic and legal skills to decode the RoL message.

Although research shows a strong interchange in conversations among lawmakers educated in similar legal systems (Gordley 1995: 561), evidence considered in this volume (see Zajac-Sannerholm) and elsewhere (Bui 2010) suggests that legal training and education may familiarize recipients with the precepts and language of RoL promotion, and yet not necessarily induce them to follow the RoL message. Recipients may operate in a conceptual environment that makes the RoL message appear inefficient, unsuitable, or imposed. Rather than recognizing such cognitive constraints to RoL promotion, some international donors are quick to accuse reticent lawmakers of lacking the political will for reform or, even worse, of immorality (i.e., corruption).

Also attributable to positivism is the belief held by many donors that legal change is primarily imposed from above through top-down chains of command (Vanderlinden 1989: 149). One consequence of this thinking is the reluctance of many, but certainly not all, donors to meaningfully inquire into nonstate or hybrid regulatory practices that interact with and shape sovereign power. Scoping studies that precede the project-design phase generally search for domestic institutional partners and overlap with other donor programs, rather than examining in depth the attitudes, demand, and capacity for change. "Most significant change analysis," a review process favored by many donors, assembles stories about transformative change from relevant stakeholders (Davies and Dart 2005). Although well suited to capturing the intangible and unintended consequences of RoL projects, this type of review does not study the legal landscape before the intervention. It searches for reasons why RoL projects fail to produce desired outcomes, without fundamentally reappraising the use of legal transfers to effect change or the underlying demand for change.

In an industry as large and varied as RoL promotion, naturally some research sponsored by international donors examines the recipients' perspective (see Wojkowska 2006; also see Heupel, this volume). Much of this work is informed by attempts by practitioners on the ground to reconcile donor projects with local institutional and regulatory conditions (Hammergren 2003). However, as Trubek and Santos (2006) observed, too often this work is reinterpreted by donors to support a predetermined "international best practice" approach to development. This disconnect between project design and country-specific research is recognized by prominent Law and Development commentators (Berkowitz, Pistor, and Richard 2003; Dezalay and Garth 2002) who encourage donors to use social science methods to more firmly ground project designs on the underlying capacity and demand for change in recipient countries.

Taking up this challenge, the remainder of this chapter looks for RoL failures, first in the regulatory capacity of recipient institutions to adopt and implement the RoL, and then in the cognitive assumptions circulating in recipient countries.

4. THE REGULATORY CAPACITY FOR ROL REFORMS

4.1. *Stages of Economic Development*

Peerenboom (2007) and Hammergren (in this volume) link RoL development with overall levels of economic development in recipient countries. The argument goes something like this: If economic conditions in developing countries can restrict the regulatory options available to recipients, and if all developing countries are not at similar levels of development, then donors should adjust RoL promotion to suit the developmental stages of individual countries and not uniformly rely on international best practices reforms.

This notion that donor projects should reflect the stages of economic development in recipient countries is now examined in the context of a core donor trope – court reform should everywhere focus on promoting judicial independence (Jensen 2003: 345–349; Trubek 2006: 277–286). A brief study of judicial reforms complicates this proposition by suggesting a close nexus between the stages of economic development and the regulatory capacity to sustain politically neutral courts.

In premodern England and America, the judiciary was the main constitutional agency used to formulate regional policies (Skowronek 1982). The legislature and executive lacked the organizational power to gather information and formulate regulatory policies at the provincial level; their power was remote from the everyday decisions made by most people. The absence of central power, coupled with judicial powers to draw from historical cases – the precedent powers – gave courts an unparalleled capacity to develop policy and regulate local affairs in areas left unregulated by the central state (Dowdle 2009: 24–6). During this period, courts were not politically neutral and actively engaged in policy development.

The politically neutral courts, promoted by international agencies today, only began to emerge with the creation of the welfare state and administrative bureaucratization in post–World War I Europe and America (Majone 1994). To meet the enlarged state responsibilities, central administrative organs needed to expand in size and competency and began to more actively oversee local governance. At the same time, industrialization and marketization increasingly harmonized and standardized markets (Jessop 2001). This in turn increased the capacity of bureaucrats to apply central regulations uniformly across the nation – a development that is now termed the "regulatory state." As integrated markets flattened regional difference, there was less need for courts to flexibly apply policy at the local level. The preferred role of courts changed from active policy making to politically neutral agencies applying legislative rules – this is the international best practice model advanced in RoL promotion.

What this brief history suggests is that international donor agencies treat a particular type of judicial regulation – politically neutral courts – that evolved in response to specific administrative and economic conditions as a universally applicable model. The history of judicial development also suggests that this type of court is not necessarily the most effective way of resolving disputes in developing countries (Friedman 1998: 333, 394–395). Court judgments create losers. Attacks on courts are inevitable, especially during their vulnerable inception period. Because judges lack the "purse and the sword" to defend themselves, to some extent courts must rely on politics to defend themselves from powerful state and private actors. Although political intervention threatens judicial independence, it is needed sometimes to protect embryonic courts in developing countries (Gillespie 2007).

This discussion illustrates some of the problems international donor agencies face in relying on international best practices as models for RoL reforms, without adequately taking into account the economic and regulatory conditions in recipient countries. These observations support the argument that RoL promotion should be carefully sequenced to match the stages of development in recipient countries (Mansfield and Snyder 2007; Peerenboom 2007). New Institutional Economics (NIE) theorists take this argument further by closely linking the global diffusion of RoL ideas with the institutional structures in recipient countries.

5. INSTITUTIONAL STRUCTURES IN RECIPIENT COUNTRIES

The NIE literature suggests that institutions are another independent variable that influences the capacity of recipients to adopt RoL projects. Douglass North (1991: 97), a leading exponent of NIE, explained that institutions "are the humanly devised constraints that structure political, economic and social interaction. They consist of both informal constraints (sanctions, taboos, customs, traditions, and codes of conduct), and formal rules (constitutions, laws, property rights)." He acknowledges the complex interaction between law and economic relationships and argues that institutions influence economic growth through their capacity to manage social expectations about norms and preferences (Daniels and Trebilcock 2008; Nabli and Nugent 1989). Nevertheless, North contends that property rights, above all else, order economic behavior. For North (1990: 54), "the inability of societies to develop effective, low-cost enforcement of contracts is the most important source of both historical stagnation and contemporary underdevelopment in the Third World."

By the early 1990s, international donors seized on NIE theory to stress the importance of institutions – especially stable property rights – in correcting the failures of the neoliberal reforms they had promoted in socialist transitional Europe. China's transition, which flourished with ambiguous property rights, high levels of corruption, and weak rule of law, complicates the reliance on property rights in NIE theory (Upham 2009). The "essential institutions" were not in place and yet China continued to grow. To explain this apparent anomaly, Rodrik (2003, 2007), building on the work of China specialists, argues that neoclassical economic principles are institution free. Protection of property rights and appropriate competitive incentives are *functions* of institutions, none of which map into particular institutional forms. "Unorthodox institutions work precisely because they produce orthodox results" (Rodrik 2003: 9). Through trial and error, China has managed to engineer alternative institutional structures that nevertheless generate the appropriate market functions. For Rodrik, there are varieties of institutional forms, but a similarity of functions. A close reading shows that North also supports this view, arguing that "the key is to create the necessary incentive structure, not slavishly to imitate the institutions of developed countries" (North 2005: 51). Critics, however, argue that donors ignored this aspect of North's writings in formulating RoL projects that focused almost exclusively on property rights and courts (Manders 2004; Upham 2009).

Other critics (Dowdle 2011) challenge the assumption in NIE theory that only domestic institutional structures constrain RoL reforms, arguing instead that regulatory capacity is also shaped by transnational factors that operate outside the reach of domestic institutions. External factors can limit not only regulatory capacities in particular industries (Krugman 1998), but even a country's overall regulatory capacity. Studies have found, for example, that a country's economic growth and associated regulatory capabilities correlate quite significantly with economic growth in neighboring countries; with geographical distance from core consumer regions (Schwartz 2007); and with cultural distance from core financial and technological regions (Clark 2005; Saxenian 2004).

This body of research calls into question the assumption that institutions modeled on international best practice can perform equivalent regulatory functions in every country. It suggests that the capacity of some countries to adopt RoL programs is affected by spatial disparities, such as proximity to markets, access to knowledge, and other comparative competitive advantages that lie outside the country and beyond the power of political rulers to control. This sobering insight implies that there are geographical constraints to the spread of RoL. For instance, the inherent regulatory capacity of Malaysia, with its geographical proximity to international markets and its cultural connections through the Chinese Diaspora to capital and know-how, is significantly higher than the capacity of Timor Leste.

The next section moves from considering regulatory constraints to RoL projects to discussing the demand for reforms. It examines the norms and tacit understanding, such as personal devotion, altruistic behavior, nationalism, and religious beliefs, that research in this volume and elsewhere demonstrates shape perceptions about RoL projects.

6. THE RECIPIENTS' PERSPECTIVE ABOUT ROL PROMOTION

The discussion so far has examined how markets and other institutions affect RoL promotion. Although this inquiry conveys a general sense that regulatory capacity limits the ability of countries to absorb RoL reforms, it is difficult to say anything more specific without focusing at close range on the factors that induce recipients to follow RoL ideas.

6.1. *Decentering the Research Focus*

It is methodologically impossible to determine what all recipients in developing countries think about RoL promotion. Researchers need to ascertain whether certain key recipients shape the way others interpret RoL reforms.[2] Unsurprisingly, many studies take domestic lawmakers as their starting point because this is where donors locate most RoL programs and where decisions are made about the selection and adoption of RoL principles and practices. Halliday and Carruthers, (2007) study about insolvency reforms in East Asia illustrates this type of inquiry. By focusing on the dialogical interaction between international donor agencies and local government elites, they showed how coalitions of like-minded international consultants and local lawmakers pushed through legislative reforms. What this study does not explain is why the new insolvency laws have rarely been used by the domestic business communities in East Asia.

Sociolegal and regulatory theory suggests the need to refocus the analysis beyond governing elites and examine what nonstate actors think about RoL promotion (see Schuppert in this volume). International donor agencies have only recently come to recognize that states do not monopolize regulation, but rather are one of many regulators. [3] For decades, law and society theorists have observed plural legal subsystems – state, hybrid, and nonstate – flourishing in the same geopolitical

[2] Nicos Poulantzas (1973) hypothesized that certain clusters of ideals (which he termed "regions") consistently influenced ruling elites, state institutions, and economic behavior more powerfully than others.

[3] Commission on Legal Empowerment of the Poor, *Making the Law Work for Everyone. Volume 1.* Commission on Legal Empowerment of the Poor and UNDP, 2008.

space. In fact, efforts by states to impose new legal orders under RoL programs rarely seem to displace preexisting legal and regulatory orders entirely (Benda-Beckmann and Benda-Beckman 1994). One postulated explanation is that state law exists in a mutually constituted and often dependent relationship with hybrid and nonstate legal systems.

Regulatory theorists offer complementary insights (Hancher and Moran 1989). To explain regulatory pluralism, they use the notion of "regulatory space" – an arena in which different regulators – state, nonstate, and hybrid – variously compete and cooperate to control particular types of behavior. This conceptualization suggests that what we recognize as the RoL – sets of state-based rules, norms, and practices – does not so much control behavior directly as it coordinates and interacts with other regulatory orders. This decentered understanding of regulation suggests that research must look past central lawmaking elites and examine what people embedded in nonstate regulatory regimes think about RoL programs.

Another reason for decentering the analysis is that by shifting responsibilities or functions of the government to private actors, new governance (see Schuppert in this volume) has proliferated nonstate RoL principles and practices. For example, transnational nongovernmental organizations (NGOs), standards organizations, and commercial transactions have created a kind of global regulation that is independent from the hierarchical forms of state law and bypasses states, interacting directly with nonstate actors (Black 2008; Teubner 1997b). The Forest Stewardship Council provides an interesting example, because it formulates standards governing the sustainable exploitation of timber that are binding on members but have no relationship with domestic law (Cashore 2002). In another example, the International Standards Organization promotes ISO 9000:2000 protocols that contain corporate governance norms and processes that resemble, but have no formal connection with, provisions in corporate legislation. In each case, globally disseminated RoL ideas are interpreted and implemented by recipients that operate outside the state orbit.

All this suggests that an inquiry into what recipients think about RoL promotion should examine the dialogical and regulatory processes that exist beyond the realm of central state elites. The question then becomes this: How is RoL promotion understood in particular environments or subsystems of meaning? This inquiry probes the subdivision of knowledge and interpretive practices within recipient societies. It asks, What reservoirs of knowledge and cognitive assumptions are needed for RoL ideas to function? Are only technical legal skills required or are certain normative and cognitive preferences also needed?

7. THE DIALOGICAL CONVERSION OF ROL IDEAS

The Introduction to this volume conceptualizes the interplay between RoL ideas and recipients as a process of "translation." The authors acknowledge that this involves much more than a merely a linguistic or textual change; it is a "cultural practice, a category of action itself." They go on to say that "the starting point of the translation concept is not the assumption of two separate, unconnected contexts but the interpenetration and entanglement of different contexts, discourses, and social fields."

Taking this discussion further, it is argued that the diffusion of RoL ideas and norms is primarily (although not entirely) cognizable and effectuated through communication, because the interpretation, selection, adaptation, and implementation of RoL projects involve discourse. Moreover communicative acts do not just passively reflect what people think about RoL projects; they also actively shape behavior – they have a regulatory function (Black 2002).

7.1. *Systems Theory*

Systems theorists (Luhmann 1992; Teubner 1998) advance this discussion by explaining how communicative acts regulate legal and regulatory systems. They begin with the observation that legislatures cannot simply import RoL principles and expect that they will translate into laws that produce predetermined behavioral changes. Systems theorists explain uneven reception patterns by arguing that recipient countries are divided into different social subsystems (including the state legal system) that interpret RoL ideas according to internal normative logics. According to Teubner (1998: 12), RoL promotion acts like "legal irritants in host-country legal systems; they interpret laws on their own terms. They unleash an evolutionary dynamic in which the external rule's meaning will be reconstructed and the internal context will undergo fundamental change."

He attributes this "irritation" to dialogical exchanges between legal and other social subsystems. Although subsystems are self-constituting, self-organizing, and self-reproducing, they coexist and coevolve in complex ways with each other. The negotiations and discussions that promote coevolution require the development of effective interpersonal networks that extend social relationships and deliberative forums among different subgroups.

Provided the subsystems share common epistemic assumptions, over time discourse reconciles differences and identifies common objectives (Post 1991). Teubner calls this coevolution "structural coupling." If the legal, political, and social subsystems are normatively aligned with each other, then "structural coupling" ensures that most people are receptive to state legal norms and precepts (Scott 2004). Conversely, where RoL principles are imported from regulatory systems with different norms and operational logics, they are unlikely to generate deep "structural coupling" or fundamentally reorder preexisting social subsystems. Not only do RoL programs fail in these circumstances, but, as Upham (2005) and Merry (2006a) have shown, if implemented too quickly they may disrupt preexisting regulatory systems without providing a workable alternative system of governance.

Systems theory recognizes the central role played by epistemic communities in interpreting and localizing RoL projects; they provide the conceptual framework through which rules, norms, and tacit understandings are constructed and interpreted. However, systems theory does not clearly explain what promotes dialogue and negotiation among different epistemic communities. This is a serious omission, because epistemic communities are primarily concerned with their own self-reproduction and are difficult to steer toward unified normative systems such as the RoL. Systems theory connects here to more middle-range research on organizational and institutional governance that offers ways to understand what stimulates coevolution and convergence among different state and nonstate epistemic communities.

8. THE ROLE OF SOCIALLY CONSTRUCTED LEGITIMACY IN SHAPING ATTITUDES TO ROL PROMOTION

Work by scholars in a wide range of fields that include law and society (Silbey 2005), sociology (Berger and Luckman 1967), economics (Greif 2006), and neoinstitutional theory (Frank and Meyer 2002) offers a more fine-grained understanding of what shapes attitudes to RoL ideas. They argue that the deep beliefs in society form a network or web that determines what ideas, arguments, and facts people find compelling. As Sally Engle Merry (2006b: 991) put it, communities make sense of global ideas by referring to "local webs of meaning based on religion, ethnicity, or place." These webs of meaning provide a conceptual framework that makes particular types of regulation, such as RoL, appear to be the natural and logical way to order the world.

This social constructionist theory also offers insights into why there are different responses to RoL promotion within particular countries. Sociologists have long recognized that diverse educational, economic, and social experiences generate major differences in the distribution of knowledge within societies (Berger and Luckman 1967). Especially in rapidly transforming societies (DiMaggio 1997: 263–287), there are pronounced differences in knowledge that generate different social subgroups. Each subgroup (or epistemic community) makes sense of the world from different conceptual perspectives. These networks of abstract social relationships have the potential to generate cooperation and shared responses to RoL promotion.

Work by organizational sociologists on legitimacy theory (Scott, Ruef, Mendel, and Caronna 2000: 237) posits that individuals assess the legitimacy and desirability of external norms and rules from the "web of meaning" in which they are embedded (Levi and Sacks 2009: 313–315). As Mark Suchman (1995: 574) put it, "Legitimacy is a generalized perception or assumption that the actions of an entity are desirable, proper, or appropriate within some socially constructed system of norms, values, beliefs, and definitions." The socially constructed systems to which Suchman refers are, of course, epistemic communities.

Legitimacy can be analyzed from two distinct but interrelated dimensions (Zürn 2004). In much of the political science literature, legitimacy is treated like a resource that regulators use to claim authority and promote particular regulatory policies. However, legitimacy also acts like an endowment; that is, it is something that cannot be possessed or exchanged, but rather something that is conferred (Scott 2003: 213–214). It is this second understanding that is used in this discussion.

Mark Suchman (1995) identified three types of legitimacy – pragmatic, normative, and cognitive – that are likely to influence perceptions about RoL promotion.

8.1. *Pragmatic Legitimacy*

Interdisciplinary research shows that people confer pragmatic legitimacy on RoL ideas that convey, or appear to convey, some material benefit (Bernstein and Cashore 2007; Suchman 1995: 578–579). For example, in weighing up the relative benefits of legal and relational contracting, traders in China see costs associated with using courts to enforce agreements, but little cost in maintaining the family hierarchies and friendships that cement informal trading networks.

A growing body of empirical studies (Abbott and Snidal 2000; Black 2008) shows that members of epistemic communities critically evaluate cost–benefit transactions according to the norms and tacit assumptions in which they are embedded (Levi-Faur 2005: 25–27). This may, and often does, result in outcomes that cannot be predicted by a single-minded calculation of economic interests (Finnemore and Toope 2001: 742–745).

8.2. *Normative Legitimacy*

Social constructivists argue that what constitutes a material benefit is socialized by understandings of the collective good. This in turn is assessed by reference to a deeper, moral base – to normative legitimacy (Esty 2006). Norms provide shared understandings about what a regulatory regime can and should do. People make reflective moral judgments about regulators, processes, and the norms embedded in particular regulatory modes. For example, empirical studies (Berkowitz et al. 2003; Merry 2006b) show that recipients take the origin of laws into account when conferring legitimacy. They give legitimacy to laws drawn from prestigious legal systems and withdraw consent to laws that are considered alien and imposed (Ajani 1995).

Research also shows that recipients are more likely to recognize the authority of imported norms where they are tied to preexisting local concepts – or, one could say, new wine in old bottles (Merry 2006a). For example, Sally Engle Merry (2006b: 984–989) shows how social activists from one country transferred methods to reduce domestic violence against women across geopolitical and culture boarders. In one case, a coalition of international and domestic NGOs persuaded Indian lawmakers to incorporate provisions from the United Nations (UN) Convention on the Elimination of All Forms of Discrimination against Women into the Indian domestic violence law enacted in 2001. Many of those provisions in the UN Convention were originally derived from U.S. domestic law.

Merry (2006b: 991) insists that the values underlying the RoL ideas "grew out of a vision of the good and just society that emphasises autonomy, choice, equality, secularism, and protection of the body." This system of knowledge developed in a particular type of Western society that held the state responsible for securing personal values. To convince Indian lawmakers, who did not widely accept state responsibility for such values, to extend legislative protection, the NGOs linked the global ideas to corresponding, but slightly different, domestic norms and assumptions about protecting women. Once tied to familiar idioms and concepts, the new ideas changed the way lawmakers thought about domestic violence.

Recipients may also evaluate the legitimacy of RoL promotion by assessing its perceived social impact. One important variable is whether the law achieved the predicted objectives – the instrumental effectiveness of regulation (Wendt 2001). Another variable is whether it enhances community notions of equity and justice (Black 2008). For example, many Thai farmers resisted RoL programs aiming to introduce intellectual property protection for plant varieties (Kuanpoth 2009: 200–201, 207–209). They claimed that intellectual property rights conveyed exclusive control over naturally occurring organisms to foreign investors, overriding community norms of public access and eroding community solidarity and identity. They were not simply concerned about the economic impact of the reforms; in fact, farmer associations conceded that new rice varieties might increase prices for farmers. The overriding objection was that by controlling seed supply, multinational companies would disrupt village trading and community networks.

In other cases, the normative content of RoL reforms may not be an issue, but the procedures implementing the norms might affect perceptions of legitimacy. For example, the legitimacy of RoL norms may become tainted by their association with discredited processes or predatory state officials. Halliday and Carruthers (2007) provide a clear example from Indonesia. To bail Indonesia out of the Asia financial crisis, the International Monetary Fund (IMF) extended a loan in 1998 on the condition that Indonesia enact a new bankruptcy law and establish a bankruptcy court. Despite a broad consensus that bankruptcy provisions introduced during the Dutch colonial period were unsuited to a modern global economy, the new law and court encountered considerable domestic resistance. Both state and private lawyers questioned the legitimacy of the conditions attached to the IMF bailout. They thought the conditions were tainted by duress, because the government accepted them when Indonesia faced bankruptcy and could not effectively protect its domestic interests.

Röder (in this volume) also shows that RoL reforms may lack normative legitimacy when the nature of the intervention by international donors lacks legal consent by international or domestic authorities. He has in mind the RoL projects in Kosovo and Iraq, supported by the North Atlantic Treaty Organization, that were initiated without UN approval and a clear mandate under international law.

Conversely, research in China (Fishkin, He, Luskin, and Siu 2006) and the Philippines (Golub 2000) demonstrates that the participation of nonstate actors in RoL projects promoting public accountability increased the legitimacy of these reforms. For example, public forums that allowed citizens to decide which infrastructure projects Wenling City (China) should fund, resulted in measurable increases in public compliance with the projects (Fishkin et al. 2006). This deliberative polling project was supported by researchers from Stanford University.

8.3. *Cognitive Legitimacy*

Cognition also shapes perceptions of legitimacy. It is closely allied to ideology, because it builds consensus or resistance to particular norms (such as RoL principles) by creating an evaluative frame of reference (Tyler 2006). It coordinates members of epistemic communities to act collectively, carry out joint tasks, and construct community cohesion. It also acts as the interface between individual practices and collective action, compelling people to regard a regulator and its procedures and outcomes as inevitable and necessary (Bernstein and Cashore 2007).

In general, religious groups or those guided by self-referential ideologies such as Marxism–Leninism are the most resistant to external ideas. However, as some commentators have shown in the context of socialist-transforming China (Dowdle 2002) and Vietnam (Gillespie 2006: 286–287), some degree of cognitive confusion and discord may actually create space for RoL ideas. For example, the party in these socialist-transforming countries uses some ideological precepts such as party paramountcy and democratic centralism to instill coherence and stability into existing institutional structures. But these political concepts, which aim to preserve party power, conflict with RoL imagery used by the state to increase public compliance with legislation. Reformers have been able to capitalize on the ensuing ideological uncertainty by smuggling RoL ideas into public discourse. This would not have been possible during the high socialist period when the dominant Marxist–Leninist ideology actively blocked RoL ideas.

Cognitive legitimacy is also closely associated with perceptions of identity and tradition because it is based on underlying tacit assumptions about how individuals see their role in the world. As James March and Johan Olsen (1996: 251) observed, "identities define the nature of things and are implemented by a cognitive process of interpretation." Identities and traditions are difficult to change because they are often associated with categorical thinking and habits that are taken for granted. The norms and cognitive assumptions associated with identities and traditions build up legitimacy over time. In these circumstances, RoL promotion must attract high levels of legitimacy if it is to change existing regulatory thinking (DiMaggio 1988).

For example, sunglass manufactures and traders, who are closely connected to a village in northern Vietnam, are highly resistant to legal reforms introduced by the state (Gillespie 2012). They strongly identify with village traditions and have developed a robust relational trading network that coexists with state-backed legal regimes. Their visceral rejection of RoL reforms contrasts with the more receptive responses of city-based traders who identify more closely with the cosmopolitan global trading networks ordering domestic markets.

8.4. *How Do the Different Modes of Legitimacy Interact with Each Other?*

Pragmatic, normative, and cognitive understandings are always at play in shaping people's attitudes to other regulatory subsystems. Although there is no strict hierarchy ordering their interaction, studies show (Gillespie 2012) that pragmatic legitimacy is shaped by the normative and cognitive frameworks operating within particular epistemic communities. As previously mentioned, insolvency reforms promoted by the IMF as a condition for bailing Indonesia out of the East Asian financial crisis in 1998 lacked moral legitimacy in the eyes of many Indonesians, because the government accepted them in humiliating circumstances (Halliday and Carruthers 2007). Government officials acknowledged the utility of the reforms in improving the efficiency of managing private debt, but they could not bring themselves to support morally questionable processes.

Changes in normative and cognitive understandings can shift the way self-interest is conceptualized. Members of epistemic communities do not all think alike, because they are each influenced by different sets of epistemic communities (Lessig 1995: 958–961). For example, judges in developing countries are simultaneously members of families, local communities, and court-based communities, each of which may adopt different sets of assumptions about the pragmatic, normative, and cognitive legitimacy of court-based RoL reforms (Gillespie 2011). They are not entirely creatures of habit unthinkingly reproducing received norms and beliefs. Rather they reflectively apply ideas, arguments, and facts contained in one epistemic community to reinforce or discredit beliefs and practices privileged in another epistemic community. Over time the dominant ideas, which are often based on taken-for-granted traditions or cultural identities, win out.

8.5. *Shaping Legitimacy at a Societal Level*

Research suggests the need to look beyond individual epistemic communities and examine how society as a whole comes together and acquires a relative unity in responding to RoL promotion (Jessop 2001: 222–223). Epistemic communities do not only respond to RoL projects according to their own narrow sectional interests; they also respond in the name of the general interests of society as a whole. The type of state organization – liberal democracy, communist, or illiberal East Asian developmental state such as Singapore – plays a critical role in shaping how epistemic communities come together to dialogically construct the legitimacy of RoL projects (Suchman 1995: 584–585). Habermas (1987: 164–197) showed that, in liberal democratic societies, governments make decisions on behalf of nonstate epistemic communities, but through elections and public discourse nonstate communities have some leverage over the government and each other. More recent neo-Habermasian scholarship suggests that effective deliberation does not necessarily need liberal democracy to flourish; it can take place in semipublic spaces such as workplaces, Internet sites, and other social gatherings (Neblo 2005). Even in authoritarian countries such as China where the state actively controls public discourse, state-owned enterprises, business associations, mass organizations, and unions play a limited role in shaping societal responses to RoL projects (Potter 2006; Tsai 2007). In contrast, authorities in tightly controlled theocratic societies can hold pragmatic, moral, and cognitive legitimacy in close alignment and present a united resistance to RoL ideas.

9. SKETCHING A RESEARCH AGENDA FOR ROL PROMOTION

9.1. *Researching Dialogical Development*

What emerges from this discussion is the need to rebalance donor research. The search for RoL failures from the donor perspective – the conception and delivery of RoL projects – should be informed by the recipient perspective – the capacity and willingness of recipients to change. Stages of development, NIE, and spatial disparity approaches offer promising ways to move the analysis beyond the consideration of material constraints to legal reforms, such as inadequate legal training and lack of resources. They shed light on how institutional, geographical, and cultural factors influence the capacity of recipients to implement RoL reforms. For example, differences in the proximity to markets and technology suggest reasons why countries at similar stages of economic development may have different capacities to absorb RoL reforms.

A shortcoming with the stages of development and NIE approaches is their assumption that efficient program delivery is objectively knowable and largely a product of regulatory, institutional, and market conditions in recipient countries. For example, they claim that the delivery of RoL projects is more efficient in middle-income rather than low-income economies because there are fewer constraints on program delivery. In addition, countries that protect property and contractual rights are more likely to move up the income scale and adopt RoL reforms. China arguably fits the stages-of-development thesis but not the NIE approach, whereas Malaysia does not support either proposition.

Socially constructed legitimacy, as outlined in this chapter, offers a corrective to these approaches. It suggests that program delivery is also profoundly influenced by perceptions about what constitutes an effective regulatory system and what are the best ways of realizing it. It enables researchers to determine why different epistemic communities (state and nonstate) conceptualize RoL projects in different ways. In addition, it offers insights into the dynamic interaction and cooperation among epistemic communities in developing society-wide responses to RoL projects.

Although perceptions of legitimacy are a potent force in shaping attitudes to RoL ideas, there are undoubtedly other factors at play. For example, a growing body of research suggests the importance of emotion in shaping regulatory preferences (Lange 2002). In view of its contingent status, legitimacy is best thought of as a heuristic (rather than a causal factor) that guides research toward the norms, ideals, and assumptions that shape attitudes to RoL promotion.

9.2. *Constructing a Research Program*

To understand the dynamics of the RoL from a recipient's perspective requires a comprehensive approach to law and development. Research not only has to map the formal and informal institutional structures, since perceptions about legitimacy rest heavily on communication; it also has to explore the dialogical exchanges that order responses to RoL initiatives.

Experience shows that researching discourse within epistemic communities is difficult, not just because this type of communication is often unrecorded and secretive but also because the tacit assumptions that play a major role in ordering epistemic communities are by their nature taken for granted and thus subconscious. Time-consuming observational research is sometimes required to fathom these subverbal assumptions and precepts. In contrast, dialogical exchanges among epistemic communities about RoL reforms are usually more clearly articulated and conducted in the public domain.

Because in-depth analysis across a large number of epistemic communities is difficult, researchers generally select one of two alternatives. They use an in-depth qualitative analysis of a small number of representative cases, or they use a quantitative analysis that examines a large number of cases, but by necessity more superficially, with the risk of losing the insights provided by in-depth analysis. Some commentators (Arvind and Stirton 2010; Markovits 2004: 57) caution that there are simply too many variables involved in measuring RoL promotion for quantitative analysis to produce meaningful results. They advocate a middle path in which researchers combine in-depth techniques with systematic analysis that aims to identify what combination of variables shapes the capacity and willingness of recipients to follow RoL reforms.

9.3. *Researching Legitimacy*

It is argued that socially constructed legitimacy provides a heuristic guide to the factors that shape recipients' perceptions about RoL projects. As we have seen, reforms are more likely to proceed in societies that are normatively and cognitively open to RoL ideas and least likely in societies tightly ordered by religion, ideology, or traditional concepts of identity. In rapidly transforming developing countries where norms and cognitive assumptions are in a state of flux, research must explore the multiple perspectives of the main epistemic communities that influence dialogical exchanges about RoL projects.

RoL reforms are most likely to attract legitimacy where they appear to provide pragmatic benefits that conform with existing normative and cognitive orders and present few challenges to established regulatory logics. In countries where the normative and cognitive order is fragmented, some epistemic communities may support particular aspects of RoL programs while others resist some or all reforms. In these circumstances, researchers may need to investigate the hegemonic visions and associated strategic capacities of the competing communities to assess the prospects for RoL reform.

Legitimacy research offers international donor agencies the tantalizing possibility of reconfiguring their message to appeal to, or form alliances with, key epistemic communities. It is possible for state and nonstate regulators to create and manage their own legitimacy. This concept may appear alien to legal scholarship, which has traditionally evaluated legitimacy by assuming that regulators are the passive object of evaluation. However, donors can increase the legitimacy of their message by conforming to normative claims by making their projects more transparent or by allying themselves with an existing regulator that possesses these qualities (Suchman 1995; also see Heupel in this volume). In most cases the donors are required to work with state agencies, but in some cases it is possible to team up with political parties, NGOs, or mass organizations that are considered more legitimate than the state.

In an interesting example the United Nations Development Programme in Vietnam abandoned conventional institutional-strengthening projects with the courts and instead supported dialogical forums between the party and international and domestic lawyers and academics (Nicholson and Pitt 2012). The courts follow party leadership and respond more positively to initiatives emanating from the party than to reforms promoted by state agencies such as the National Assembly and Ministry of Justice.

Donors can also manipulate expectations by pretending to conform while actually perusing other objectives or by switching from one objective to another, more favorably perceived objective. In addition, they can disseminate information that highlights aspects of their projects that they think will attract acceptance by key epistemic communities. In short, they may become active agents in enhancing the legitimacy of the RoL project. And yet if there is one clear message from legitimacy research, it is that attempts to generate legitimacy are complex because donor agencies have little control over how their message is interpreted. Recipients in developing countries are very sensitive to domination, hypocrisy, and manipulation.

11

Rule of Law Promotion after Conflict

Experimenting in the Kosovo Laboratory

Richard Zajac Sannerholm

1. INTRODUCTION

Only a few weeks before Kosovo declared its independence from Serbia on February 17, 2008, the Council of the European Union established the European Union Rule of Law Mission in Kosovo (EULEX), the largest European Union (EU) mission thus far under the framework of European security and defense policy.[1] With the establishment of EULEX, the main responsibility for rule of law promotion in Kosovo shifted from the United Nations Mission in Kosovo (UNMIK) to the EU. The transfer of responsibility marked the closing of a unique and nearly a decade-long United Nations (UN) executive mission in which rule of law promotion had been in focus, involving a vast range of activities in the regulatory experimentation of Kosovo – for example, legislation on license plates, casino gambling and political parties; the establishment of war-crimes tribunals; and ad hoc and hybrid national and international bodies to deal with property rights, judicial reform, vetting and screening of legal professionals, and infusion of international norms and standards in the (still) emerging domestic legal corpus of Kosovo.

With the establishment of EULEX as a watershed, this chapter looks to the efforts of international actors to strengthen the rule of law in Kosovo from the perspective of the types of rule of law model that the UN, EU, and Organization for Security and Co-operation in Europe (OSCE) have promoted. It also includes a discussion of some of the most salient areas of reform, the methods employed, and the diffusion dynamics between international actors as promoters on the one hand, and the conversion perspective of the recipient domestic institutions on the other.[2] It is argued in this chapter that the rule of law promoted in Kosovo has been centralistic and top down, and it has primarily taken the promoter's perspective. Moreover, rule of law models

[1] Council of the European Union, "Council Joint Action 2008/124/CFSP of 4 February 2008 on the European Union Rule of Law Mission in Kosovo, EULEX KOSOVO."

[2] See the Introduction by Zürn, Nollkaemper, and Peerenboom in this volume.

have by and large dealt with criminal law and security and have failed to influence the broader administrative and regulatory environment, despite the fact that it is in the everyday regulatory practices and interactions between civil servants and citizens (registering births, deciding in urban planning, inspecting compliance with labor regulations) that a majority of essential tasks are dealt with that are important for rule of law development, and for postwar recovery.

The question of what type of rule of law model international actors have promoted is important for three reasons. First, for rule of law practitioners, policy makers, and decisions makers, there are lessons to learn from Kosovo that should inform future engagements in complex environments. Vast amount of resources (human, material, and financial) are invested toward the elusive goal of strengthening the rule of law, yet there seems to be agreement among most observers that the legal and administrative system in Kosovo still falls far short of a rule of law standard, however vaguely or sector defined. A long list of rule of law constraints and problems in Kosovo can be composed. Just in relation to the judiciary, the International Crisis Group states that "Kosovo's judiciary has deteriorated to the point that many, perhaps most citizens lack genuine access to justice.... There is no effective management or oversight; judges and prosecutors are largely left alone to work as they can, in inadequate facilities and without recourse should help or protection be required."[3] The challenges facing many central legal and administrative institutions in Kosovo after nearly a decade of international rule of law promotion merit further examination.

Second, EULEX has assumed responsibility for rule of law promotion. The EU is in a unique position with future membership negotiations as a stick and carrot, and it is important that EULEX be adaptive and reflective in the implementation of its monitoring, mentoring, and advising (MMA) mandate to rule of law problems experienced by Kosovar institutions and citizens. In the 2010 EULEX Programme Report, the only sector to receive a mark of progress was the border security. Other sectors and institutions, such as the Kosovo Judicial Council, public prosecutors, ministry of justice, and the integration of government strategies into operational plans, are described as slow in progress or problematic with very limited or no progress.[4]

Third, international actors, such as the UN, EU, and the OSCE, act both as "norm entrepreneurs" or "teachers of norms" in Kosovo and as enforcers of norms (Morlino and Magen 2009: 36). State and nonstate actors in Kosovo are under pressure to implement norms and adopt new policies, often based on international standards and benchmarks (Schimmelfennig 2002: 1). Having a clear conception of the rule of law goal that international actors promote allows for the elaboration of indicators by which reforms can be implemented and measured, for international and national

[3] International Crisis Group, "The Rule of Law in Independent Kosovo," 19 May 2010: 12.

[4] EULEX Kosovo, "Programme Report 2010: Building Sustainable Change Together" (2007). Available at http://www.eulex-kosovo.eu/docs/tracking/EULEX%20Programme%20Report%202010%20.pdf: 7.

actors alike. Moreover, clarity of communication on what the rule of law means can increase the normative force behind the concept. From regulatory theory, the assumption that a precise and clear conception of what is promoted provides for an easier understanding and compliance, with breaches more clearly observed, brings to the fore the importance of looking into the rule of law "message" conveyed by international actors in Kosovo.[5]

This chapter starts by looking into the mandate of the international presence in Kosovo, and how the three dominant actors involved in rule of law promotion use and refer to the concept on policy and operational levels. The following sections focus on some of the most significant rule of law reforms undertaken in Kosovo in the areas of law reform and institutional reform. This is followed by an examination of international control and local ownership, and a discussion of how the model or models of rule of law that are being promoted relate to rule of law challenges and obstacles. The final section examines the different approaches and methods in rule of law reform, and it discusses the type of rule of law model or models that international actors have promoted in Kosovo.

2. MODELS, MANDATES, AND MISSIONS: UN, EU, AND OSCE RULE OF LAW PROMOTION IN KOSOVO

It is possible to outline some general background principles that are common in most discussions of the rule of law. The rule of law is typically seen as having two primary attributes (or functions): (1) protection against arbitrary rule by imposing certain limitations and procedural checks and balances,[6] and (2) the capacity to guide human conduct – that is, by providing a framework of law that facilitates human interaction in terms of protecting against arbitrary interference from the state, and predictability of a system of rules in order to calculate the legal consequences of one's actions (Krygier 2006: 133). Both of these attributes are desirable for their enhancement of predictability, certainty, and legal security, both between state and individuals, and between individuals. Both attributes also depict the rule of law as a systemic concept applicable to all state and individual interactions resting on a set of principles such as legality, legal equality, due process, and legal certainty. Putting

[5] See, e.g., "the more sweeping an intervening authority's objectives, the more resisted its efforts are likely to be" (Dobbins, Jones, Crane, and Degrasse 2007: 4); and "rule of law is almost never carefully defined as a concept; users of the expression allude to meanings they assume to be clear and objective but that are not so . . . naturally, this would be a perfectly innocent and common phenomenon, not worth an inquiry, were it not for the weighty political implications of the phrase in different contexts" (Mattei and Nader 2008: 10). See also Abbott and Duncan (2000: 427).

[6] In a European context, see case law from the European Court of Human Rights where the principle of legality and supremacy of law has been frequently reaffirmed, e.g., *Winterwerp v. the Netherlands*, European Court of Human Rights, Judgement of 25 October 1979, A33 and *Malone v. the United Kingdom*, European Court of Human Rights, Judgement of 2 August 1984, A/82.

the rule of law concept and the constituting principles into effect, however, has proven to be a daunting and challenging task in rule of law promotion.

One reason for this is that, for a long time, rule of law promotion has lacked guiding operational and practical frameworks. Absence of clear guidelines on what the concept means for rule of law officers and related staff on the ground is illustrated in a survey conducted by the Centre for OSCE Research. The survey targeted 18 field missions of the OSCE, asking questions to their personnel such as whether they based their activities on any particular rule of law definition or if they had criteria for distinguishing rule of law tasks from those of human rights and democratization (Evers 2010: 9). The results from the survey describe the absence of rule of law guidance in the field and, one can assume, are not limited to the perceptions of OSCE staff but are rather symptomatic for most actors involved in rule of law reform:

> The field operations have no recourse to a standardized, conclusive definition of the rule of law or rule of law promotion. A number of field operations (30 per cent) work without any definition whatsoever. The majority, however, define the rule of law or rule of law-promotion, some with reference to Kofi Annan's report for UN rule of law promotion, the Copenhagen Document (1990), or the Ljubljana decision . . . , and others according to their own preferences. In conversations, field mission staff identified the lack of clear definitions and conceptual frameworks as a definite handicap. They indicated a need for material that would provide a survey of the field and give definitions of terminology. (Evers 2010: 9–10)

What the Centre for OSCE Research survey reveals is that, for some rule of law practitioners in the field, there is a lack of a comprehensive understanding of what is meant by rule of law or rule of law promotion. For some organizations, such as the UN, the question of rule of law models being promoted in missions such as that in Kosovo becomes even more pertinent, considering that it was not until 2004 that the organization attempted to establish a common and authoritative definition of its own.[7] Other organizations, such as the EU or the OSCE, as discussed later, have no coherent definition of what the rule of law means for their operational activities, relying instead on a combination of policies and standards in their respective *acquis*.

The general vagueness on what the rule of law means is not matched by vagueness in the mandate given to international actors to promote it. In Kosovo the international presence is founded on UN Security Council Resolution 1244, which established UNMIK as the executive, legislative, and judicial authority in theater.[8] This also added another legal source to the fledging system in Kosovo – the regulations enacted by UNMIK.[9] The UN Security Council directed UNMIK to "the immediate

7 Report of the Secretary-General on the Rule of Law and Transitional Justice in Conflict and Post-Conflict Societies, 23 August 2004, UN Doc. S/2004/616: 4.

8 UNSC Resolution 1244 of 10 June 1999, UN Doc. S/RES/1244.

9 See the first UNMIK regulation, Regulation No. 1999/1 of 25 July 1999, UN Doc. UNMIK/REG/1999/1.

re-establishment of an independent, impartial and multi-ethnic judiciary" and to "re-establish and reform the correctional system in Kosovo."[10]

Through Resolution 1244, the Security Council also established a "pillar" structure in an attempt to create a clear division of labor and avoid a scenario of overlapping mandates and turf wars that had been plaguing the past experience of complex state building.[11] This represented an idea of effective resource management – the organ most competent to deal with a specific subject matter was given a lead role – and in Kosovo, the division of responsibilities originally consisted of four pillars: civil administration (UN), economic reconstruction (EU), human rights and democratization (OSCE); and humanitarian affairs (UN High Commissioner for Refugees). UNMIK also sought to establish co-administration early on in the mission through the establishment of the Kosovo Transitional Council (Bull 2008: 128).

The strong mandate and pillar structure established by the UN Security Council Resolution 1244 should have provided opportunities for a concerted, clear, and unified rule of law reform promotion in Kosovo. What unfolded, however, was a problematic working relationship between different international actors. The UN was primarily responsible for setting up and administering the justice sector, and in the overall administration of justice, whereas the OSCE was appointed the responsibility of supervising and monitoring the functions of the justice system (Narten 2006: 158). This meant, in effect, that one international organization was responsible for monitoring the work of another. For example, UNMIK Department of Judicial Affairs (later the Department of Justice) was responsible for inter alia creating and administering judicial and penal institutions, while assisted but also monitored by the OSCE (Marshall and Inglis 2003). Moreover, the division of powers established through the pillar structures seems equally to have been about international politics rather than an actual reflection of each organization's capacity and competence (Stromseth Wippman, and Brooks 2006: 360). In relation to emerging national authorities, cooperation was often put on hold, or severely restricted, and UNMIK kept control over many of the substantial reform areas long into the mission.[12] In relation to civil society organizations, UNMIK and now EULEX lacked a coherent plan for cooperation and support. EULEX in its MMA mandate does not include civil society organizations, and there is no separate funding for support and joint initiatives with nongovernmental organizations.[13] This is problematic from the point

[10] Report of the United Nations Secretary-General on the United Nations Interim Administration in Kosovo, 12 June 1999, UN Doc. S/1999/799: paras 66 and 72.

[11] Five years after the Dayton Agreement, the lack of effective coordination led the High Representative to conduct an internal audit to determine precisely what international participants actually did in Bosnia and Herzegovina. See International Crisis Group, "Bosnia: Reshaping the International Machinery," Balkans Report No. 112, 29 November 2001: 29.

[12] International Crisis Group, "The Rule of Law in Independent Kosovo," 19 May 2010: 2.

[13] EULEX Kosovo, "Programme Report 2010: Building Sustainable Change Together" (2010). Available at http://www.eulex-kosovo.eu/docs/tracking/EULEX%20Programme%20Report%202010%20.pdf: 65–68.

of view of checking and restraining arbitrary uses and abuses of power. It is generally perceived that checking the abuse of power is best achieved through "complex plurality of many separate powers," including executive, judicial, and administrative oversight bodies as well as civil society organizations (Braithwaite 2006: 885).

2.1. *UN Rule of Law Values and Definitions*

In the comprehensive mandate for UNMIK, rule of law reform became a centerpiece component and also a reform area directly linked with the future status question.[14] At the time of the inception of UNMIK, however, rule of law as a constituent and essential part of peace-keeping and peace building was a relatively new phenomenon.

A first attempt from the UN to provide some form of operational guidelines for rule of law promotion came in a report from the UN General Assembly in 1994. Enhanced activity in the UN's technical assistance program to developing countries and transition economies led to a compelling need to attend to the questions of what the rule of law meant in the context of technical support.[15] Then, in 2004, as a reflection of the increased commitment and responsibility to rule of law reform in war-torn societies, the UN Secretary-General launched a common UN rule of law definition. Following the UN's responsibility as an international administrator in Kosovo and East Timor, the need grew for a more comprehensive definition that would also provide certain normative boundaries. The concept of the rule of law is described as follows:

> a principle of governance in which all persons, institutions and entities, public and private, including the State itself, are accountable to laws that are publicly promulgated, equally enforced and independently adjudicated, and which are consistent with international human rights standards. It requires, as well, measures to ensure adherence to the principle of supremacy of the law, equality before the law, accountability to the law, fairness in the application of the law, separation of powers, participation in decision-making, legal certainty, avoidance of arbitrariness and procedural and legal transparency.[16]

[14] See Kosovo Standards Implementation Plan, 31 March 2004.

[15] The UN General Assembly's report brings to the fore certain key legal and institutional constructions, such as a strong constitution and legal framework; national human rights institutions, including independent commissions on human rights and ombudsman offices; a strong judiciary; and an adequate national training regime for lawyers, judges and prosecutors, police, and prison officials, which includes attention to their role in the protection of human rights. Report of the Secretary-General on the Strengthening the Rule of Law to the UNGA, 20 July 2000, UN Doc. A/49/512: 5–8.

[16] Report of the Secretary-General on the Rule of Law and Transitional Justice in Conflict and Post-Conflict Societies, 23 August 2004, UN Doc. S/2004/616: 4. The normative foundation for the UN's rule of law assistance is also set out in the same report. Apart from the UN Charter, the normative foundation is said to consist of international human rights law; international criminal law; international refugee law; and international humanitarian law.

This definition summarizes current policy toward the concept within the international community, in particular by stating its compliance with international human rights standards. Putting this policy into effect, the UN approach in the field seems to be more informed by past practice than recent conceptual developments.[17] The practice of peace-keeping and state-building missions in the early 1990s on legal and judicial reform was undertaken with no explicit reference to a comprehensive rule of law ideal, and overall responsibility for coordinating and implementing rule of law mandates in peace-keeping operations resides with the Department for Peace-keeping Operations. To put into effect the rule of law concept, this department has a practice of focusing on four core areas: police, prisons, courts, and human rights.[18] This is emulated in corresponding departments and units within the field of a peace-keeping mission. Thus, when the 2004 UN common rule of law definition was introduced as an all-embracing imperative, the policy had to relate to nearly two decades of established practice in the field (Farrall 2009).

2.2. *The European Union and the Rule of Law*

The EU, originally responsible for economic reconstruction in Kosovo, has similarly to the UN been forced to conceptualize an ongoing practice and commitment to rule of law in its field operations. In the Treaty of the European Union, the concept of the rule of law is inserted together with liberty, democracy, human rights, and fundamental freedoms as the guiding values upon which the common European security and defense policy is built.[19] Since then, the concept has been repeatedly referred to in political commitments and declarations by European Community institutions.[20]

[17] Several of the early UN missions in the first half of the 1990s stated the need to work with judicial reform, police restructuring, penal reform, and human rights promotion. UNSC Resolution 865 of 22 September 1993, UN Doc. S/RES/865 on Somalia noted that the reestablishment of the Somali police force was essential for the maintenance of peace, stability, law, and order. The resolution also stated that the reestablishment of the judicial and penal system was critical for instituting security and stability.

[18] Uniting our Strengths: Enhancing United Nations Support for the Rule of Law, Report of the Secretary-General of 14 December 2006, UN Doc. S/2006/980: 5. See also UN Approach to Rule of Law Assistance, Guidance Note of the Secretary-General, April 2008.

[19] Treaty on the European Union (2008), Official Journal C/115.

[20] Respect for the rule of law is also a condition of membership. The criteria elaborated by the European Council in its Copenhagen Meeting in 1993 asserted each candidate country to have achieved stability of inter alia the rule of law. See European Council in Copenhagen, "Conclusions of the Presidency," 21–22 June 1993: 12–16. Accessed 20 April 2010 at www.consilium.europa.eu/uedocs/cms_data/docs/pressdata/en/ec/72921.pdf: Art. 7 (iii). See also Wennerström (2007: 175f). Besides the enlargement process, a material rule of law became an essential condition when human rights became the prevailing trend in EU external relations through the Partnership Agreement between the Members of the African, Caribbean and Pacific Group of States, of the one Part, and the European Community and its Member States, of the Other Part ("Cotonou Agreement") (2000), Official Journal L317/3 of 15 December 2000, as revised (2005) Official Journal L209/27 of 11 August 2005, Art. 9 (1).

The EU has begun to take on a rapidly growing responsibility in relation to state building in war-to-peace transitions. In June 2004 the first EU rule of law mission was launched in Georgia.[21] This mission was followed by the EU Integrated Rule of Law Mission for Iraq.[22] Both of these missions made use of the rule of law concept mostly in criminal justice. The latest EU rule of law mission, EULEX Kosovo, follows a similar line of operationalizing the concept of competent Kosovo institutions "on all areas related to the wider rule of law (including a custom service), whilst retaining certain executive responsibilities."[23] The main areas of support through the MMA mandate are strengthening customs services, contributing to enhancing cooperation and coordination throughout the whole judicial process, particularly in the area of organized crime, and contributing to the fight against corruption, fraud, and financial crime.

The rule of law concept of the EU, it seems, has many aspects and changes form and focus, depending on where it is applied or promoted. Similar to the UN, the EU is not a single normative order but "a set of normative orders or normative sub-orders" (Wennerström 2007: 157). In enlargement processes, the rule of law has come to signify a clear set of necessary marks that candidate countries must achieve, and when put to the test in postconflict and crisis management, as in the rule of law mission to Kosovo, it is translated to take in the concepts of stability, law and order, criminal justice, and security.

2.3. *The OSCE, Human Dimension, and the Rule of Law*

The OSCE, responsible for human rights and democratization in Kosovo and with the largest international civilian presence in theater, has a lesser normative force behind its work than the UN and the EU in the sense that the OSCE *aquis* is not legally binding on its member-states. The OSCE has defined the rule of law as a concept resting firmly on substantive values in terms of "justice based on the recognition and full acceptance of the supreme value of the human personality and guaranteed by institutions providing a framework for its fullest expression."[24] As well as that declaratory definition, the OSCE has also attempted to define the concept on a more operational basis. Similar to the UN and the EU, in the face of a growing responsibility in crisis environments, the OSCE has been seeking

[21] EU Rule of Law Mission to Georgia focuses on three topics: guidance on criminal justice reform; support to the coordinating role of Georgian authorities in the area of judicial reform and anti-corruption; and support planning for new legislation – for example criminal procedure law. See Council of the European Union, "Council Joint Action 2008/124/CFSP of 4 February 2008 on the European Union Rule of Law Mission in Kosovo, EULEX KOSOVO."

[22] Ibid.

[23] Ibid.

[24] Document of the Copenhagen Meeting of the Conference of the Human Dimensions of the CSE (1990): 1(2).

a clearer and more practically attuned rule of law framework. Most notably the OSCE, in addition to its mission in Kosovo where the organization has shouldered a heavy responsibility under the institution-building pillar, also has a vast number of field activities including support to bar associations, trial monitoring, support for legislative initiatives, and a strengthening of the system for the protection of minorities.[25]

In the document *OSCE Human Dimension Commitments*, some of the dominant features of a rule of law definition from the OSCE perspective are stipulated. These include, on a rather detailed and operational level, the following: (1) the supremacy of law and that government, judiciary, and the administration comply with the constitution and act in accordance with the law; (2) the principle of the separation of powers; (3) civilian control over armed forces; (4) human rights and fundamental freedoms guaranteed by law; (5) publicizing and making accessible all legislative acts; (6) administrative decisions must be justifiable and indicate legal remedies; (7) equality before the law and active measures against discrimination; (8) independence of the legal profession; and (9) ensuring fair trial principles in criminal procedures, in particular the right of habeas corpus.[26] No legal obligations stem from OSCE documents, yet they carry significant weight in war-to-peace transitions where the declaratory policy is transformed into practical measures as in Kosovo under the UN Security Council mandate.

The OSCE mandate is broader than rule of law promotion in Kosovo, making it poised to address cross-cutting issues such as municipal governance, protection of community rights, including returns and reintegration of displaced persons, safety and freedom of movement, property rights, nondiscrimination, participation in public life, access to education and other services, and language and culture preservation.

From the brief examination of the three dominant actors involved in rule of law promotion in Kosovo, namely the UN, the EU, and the OSCE, it is possible to observe some commonalities. For all three, the rule of law is only vaguely defined at the policy level as being a holistic and comprehensive concept. The UN is perhaps the exception, with the attempt in 2004 to establish an authoritative definition. Moreover, the rule of law is defined or referred to by all three as a concept closely related to international human rights law, and it is often presented as a concept incremental for human rights protection.

[25] The OSCE mission is derived from UNSC Resolution 1244 of 10 June 1999, UN Doc. S/RES/1244, and the exchange of letters between the OSCE's Chairman-in-Office and the UN Secretary-General, where the division of labor was decided. UN DPKO, "OSCE Permanent Council Decision No. 305 1999 and Letter exchanged between Ambassador Kim Traavik, of the OSCE Department and Bernard Miyet," 19 July 1999.

[26] OSCE, *OSCE Human Dimension Commitments, Volume 1, Thematic Compilation*, 2nd ed. (2005): 88–96. The commitments are derived from seminal meetings (i.e., at Copenhagen in 1990, Moscow in 1991, and in Budapest in 1994).

3. PUTTING POLICY INTO PRACTICE: LEGAL AND INSTITUTIONAL REFORM IN KOSOVO

On the operational level, as illustrated through resolutions and program and project documents, there is sometimes a substantial difference among policy formulations on the rule of law. When policy is put into practice, rule of law is often defined by the institutional setting it is assumed to require, for example, judicial or prosecutorial reform or criminal law reform. In Kosovo, the challenge of operationalizing rule of law policy is evident in legal and institutional reform undertaken by UNMIK, the EU, and the OSCE. Among the first measures UNMIK focused on was the legal framework in Kosovo, and a rather extensive UN legislation evolved. Beyond the reform of the legislative framework, UNMIK, the OSCE, and the EU attempted to improve institutional performance, professionalism, and capacity. Given the unique situation in Kosovo, with the UN as the executive power, much of the international support came to be in the form of an internationalization of institutions – both as temporary measures to alleviate national actors and as more permanent approaches. Among the most salient of institutional and capacity-enhancement reforms are of course those directed at judicial restructuring. Within this gambit the use of international judges stands out. The following sections examine legal and institutional reform in Kosovo from the inception of UNMIK up until the establishment and subsequent handover of rule of law responsibilities to EULEX.

3.1. *Applicable Law and UN Legislation*

The problems UN experienced when attempting to establish a functioning and at the same time legitimate framework of applicable law at the beginning of its mission in Kosovo are well known. The events that unfolded in early 1999 are often used to tell the story of how not to work with law reform in complex war-ravaged societies, particularly centering on the importance of consultation, participation, and local ownership. A lesser discussed aspect, however, is what the initial attempts to establish an applicable legal framework can say about rule of law promotion on behalf of international actors, particularly the UN. The first regulation issued by the Special Representative of the Secretary-General (SRSG) decided the following:

> The laws applicable in the territory of Kosovo prior to 24 March 1999 shall continue to apply in Kosovo insofar as they do not conflict with standards referred to in section 2 [referring to international human rights standards], the fulfilment of the mandate given to UNMIK under United Nations Security Council resolution 1244 (1999), or the present or any other regulation issued by UNMIK.[27]

[27] UNMIK Regulation No. 1999/1 of 25 July 1999, UN Doc. UNMIK/REG/1999/1.

Kosovar Albanian judges and other legal professionals rejected this restatement. The criminal laws of Yugoslavia were seen as instruments of discrimination against Kosovar Albanians by the Milosevic regime from the early 1990s (Strohmeyer 2001b: 12). Only after a legal void of six months did the SRSG amend the regulation and decide that the applicable law was to be the law in force before Milosevic came to power in 1989, even though the pre-1989 law had some clear deficits and weaknesses.[28] The decision on the applicable law was enforced with little consultation with legal professionals and other national actors directly concerned with what type of law to apply.

The choice of applicable law by way of restatement was motivated by practical considerations. It is undeniably less expensive to redesignate a legal framework than starting a process with the aim of creating new structures. At the same time, the choice of applicable law also seems to be motivated by the promoter's perceptions of modernity, rationality, and technicality. Overall, the post-1989 legal framework was more sophisticated and developed than the laws favored by the Kosovar Albanian legal community. Unilaterally siding with the more "modern" and technically advanced framework reveals underlying assumptions on rule of law promotion, at least on behalf of UNMIK, as being founded on technical and rational considerations. The whole process of events also reveals assumptions within the UN that recipients will respond to structural changes based on the same ideals. It also reveals a disregard for general theories on lawmaking and regulation where compliance is assumed to be higher the more legitimate and procedurally fair a law or regulation is seen to be (Braithwaite 2006: 887).

More than eight years after the first regulation on applicable law was enacted, there was still considerable confusion within the Kosovo legal framework. The seventh annual report of the Ombudsperson in 2007 noted that the two fundamental problems with the legal system were still a lack of legal certainty and openness.[29] This legal chaos has had unintended consequences. One of them affects the autonomy and discretion that individual courts retain in the interpretation of applicable law, a discretionary power that encroaches on the authority of the legislative assembly. UNMIK's approach to the question of applicable law has turned the law reform process into a judicially driven process with little overall coordination.

The restatement in Kosovo was not supported with instructions on how to assess the compatibility of existing national laws with international human rights, but left it to judges to interpret compatibility. They therefore faced the difficult task of interpreting the criminal code or the criminal procedure code, for example, in light of international human rights law, UNMIK regulations, and older Yugoslav laws. This amounted to a de facto "re-writing [of] virtually the entire set of previous criminal laws" (Strohmeyer 2001a: 59). The courts in Kosovo could request clarifications from

[28] UNMIK Regulation No 1999/24 of 12 December 1999, UN Doc. UNMIK/REG/1999/24.

[29] Ombudsperson Institution in Kosovo, "Eight Annual Report" (2008): 19.

the SRSG on matters of implementation, but it remained unclear what the status and binding nature of such clarifications were.

Another problem was that of interpretation. A later UNMIK regulation simply declared that if a court was to determine that a subject matter or situation was not covered by the hierarchy of laws put forward in the regulation, but instead covered by a law in force in Kosovo after March 22, 1989, the court should "as an exception apply that law."[30] The decision on applicable law in Kosovo illustrates the dangers of approaching rule of law promotion as being a mere technical legal exercise and as a simple choice between legal regimes where new normative obligations can easily be added or detracted. The regulation, set on amending the legal void created by the first regulation on applicable law, made matters worse; it was roughly criticized by the Ombudsperson in Kosovo. UNMIK and the Legal Office at the UN Headquarters in New York (which assisted in reviewing the "constitutionality" of drafted regulations) were jointly accused of creating "legal chaos."[31]

In general, law reform in Kosovo, from the decision on applicable law and onward, has been marred by a failure to ensure internal legal consistency and establish a hierarchy of norms.[32] Despite the fact that international experts have managed the process of lawmaking, several problems of a formal and procedural nature have persisted that could have been easily avoided. According to the Ombudsperson, UNMIK failed to adequately make new regulations public and to acknowledge the need for a *vacatio legis* – that is, the time between the enactment of a law and when it is entering into effect. Most UNMIK regulations entered into force as soon as they were signed by the Interim Administrator, which allowed for flexible and rapid lawmaking but gave local authorities limited time to adjust and learn about new regulations. Regulations were also for a long time routinely posted

[30] UNMIK Regulation No 1999/24. The following international human rights treaties are listed: *The Universal Declaration on Human Rights of 10 December 1948*; (b) *The European Convention for the Protection of Human Rights and Fundamental Freedoms of 4 November 1950 and the Protocols thereto*; (c) *The International Covenant on Civil and Political Rights of 16 December 1966 and the Protocols thereto*; (d) *The International Covenant on Economic, Social and Cultural Rights of 16 December 1966*; (e) *The Convention on the Elimination of All Forms of Racial Discrimination of 21 December 1965*; (f) *The Convention on Elimination of All Forms of Discrimination Against Women of 17 December 1979*; (g) *The Convention Against Torture and Other Cruel, Inhumane or Degrading Treatment or Punishment of 17 December 1984*; and (h) *The International Convention on the Rights of the Child of 20 December 1989*.

[31] Ombudsperson Institution in Kosovo, "Fourth Annual Report" (2004): 8. The UN Human Rights Committee (HRC) also criticized the confusing and contradictory legal framework and urged UNMIK, in cooperation with Provisional Institutions of Self-Government (PISG), to ensure that any new law or regulation specified which formerly applicable laws or provisions are being replaced, and that laws and regulations are made accessible to the public in all official languages of Kosovo via the Official Gazette and the Internet. Moreover, it was stressed that UNMIK, in cooperation with PISG, should designate a competent body to determine which of the former Yugoslav laws and provisions continue to be applicable. See HRC, Report of 14 August 2006, UN Doc. CCPR/C/UNK/CI/1: 2.

[32] Another aspect, though not explored further in this chapter, is the confusing mix of common law and civil law traditions in Kosovo.

only on UNMIK's Web page.[33] From the perspective of good practices in development cooperation, since 2005 standardized in the Paris Declaration on Aid Effectiveness (and the subsequent 2008 Accra Agenda for Action), the centralized UNMIK approach on applicable law and lawmaking fell far short of adhering to principles of ownership and alignment through broad consultative processes.[34] Through its mandate of MMA, EULEX has retained an active role in legislative drafting, though less direct and executive than UNMIK. EULEX experts have assisted in the drafting of laws on a broad range of topics, including laws on courts, witness protection, criminal code, obligations, juvenile justice, and forensic medicine.[35]

3.2. *Incorporating International Law and Standards in the Domestic Legal Framework*

Beyond direct legislative initiatives, the international community, through UNMIK, attempted various ways of instilling international standards in the fledging legal and administrative framework in Kosovo. A first attempt was by way of making international norms directly applicable in the exercise of public duties in Kosovo. Through UNMIK Regulation 1999/1 it was decided that public officials should observe international standards of human rights in the administration of justice and in their official functions.[36] What the term "observe" means is difficult to assert. It might simply mean a form of guidance and a yardstick for public officials, and does not seem to imply a direct effect of the different international human rights treaties in the respective domestic jurisdiction of Kosovo. The UN Committee on Human Rights, however, argues that it does provide a direct applicability and that the covenant is "binding on all persons undertaking public duties and or holding public office in Kosovo."[37]

Many of the international norms and standards enumerated in the first regulations from UNMIK were later reinforced and given a significant normative weight in the Constitutional Framework for Provisional Self-Governance in Kosovo.[38] The Constitutional Framework also included specific rights of communities and instructions on the responsibilities of Provisional Institutions of Self-Government (PISG). The framework also called for closer integration to EU standards, in essence an obligation

33 Ombudsperson Institution in Kosovo, "Fourth Annual Report" (2004): 9.
34 Organisation for Economic Cooperation and Development's Development Assistance Committee, The Paris Declaration on Aid Effectiveness and the Accra Agenda for Action, 2005.
35 EULEX Kosovo, "Programme Report 2010: Building Sustainable Change Together" (2010). Available at http://www.eulex-kosovo.eu/docs/tracking/EULEX%20Programme%20Report%202010%20.pdf: 46.
36 UNMIK Regulation No. 1999/1 of 25 July 1999, UN Doc. UNMIK/REG/1999/1.
37 HRC, Report of 14 August 2006, UN Doc. CCPR/C/UNK/CI/1: para. 5.
38 UNMIK Regulation No. 2001/9 of 15 May 2001, UN Doc. UNMIK/REG/2001/9.

for Kosovo authorities to harmonize legislation in line with the *acquis communitaire* of the EU. In support of this, the EU provided legislative and technical assistance, for example through the European Agency for Reconstruction (Muharremi, Peci, Malazogu, et al. 2005: 12). The incorporation of international norms and standards, particularly on human rights, is also manifest in the new Kosovo constitution of 2008, drafted under close supervision of international actors. Chapter II of the constitution marks the intention of the drafters to create a "modern" document in line with European standards on human rights. The constitution was also developed in the spirit of the Comprehensive Proposal for the Kosovo Status Settlement, produced by the former president of Finland, Martti Ahtisaari. Thus, the Kosovo constitution includes provisions not typically in line with constitutional traditions of norm hierarchy. Article 143 of the constitution reads as follows:

> Notwithstanding any provisions of this constitution, all authorities in the Republic of Kosovo shall abide by all of the Republic of Kosovo's obligations under the comprehensive Proposal for the Kosovo Status Settlement dated 26 March 2007. They shall take all necessary actions for their implementation.

This means, as addressed in the same article, that in cases of conflict and consistency, the Status Settlement will supersede the constitution.

Another approach was made through the linking of certain standards to the question of status of Kosovo. In 2003 the SRSG issued a blueprint for state building called Standards for Kosovo.[39] The UN Security Council later endorsed these standards, which were a set of objectives that had to be met before talks on future political status could begin and the parallel progress toward EU's Stabilization and Association Process initiated.[40] Rule of law, being one of eight standards, was described in the following way:

> There exists a solid legal framework and effective law enforcement, compliant with European standards. Police, judicial and penal systems act impartially and fully respect human rights. There is equal access to justice and no one is above the law: there is no impunity for violations. There are strong measures in place to fight ethnically motivated crime, as well as economic and financial crime.[41]

The various measures and actions required to reach the standard for rule of law are an extensive catalogue, spanning disparate issues such as a review and amendment of existing witness protection legislation; the implementation of a sustainable system of civil and legal aid compatible with European standards; and gender and human rights education incorporated as core elements in school curricula. It is unclear what influence or effect the importation of international norms and

39 Kosovo Standards Implementation Plan, 31 March 2004.

40 Statement by the President of the Security Council, 12 December 2003, UN Doc. S/PRST/2003/26; Statement by the President of the Security Council, 30 April 2004, UN Doc. S/PRST//2004/13.

41 Kosovo Standards Implementation Plan, Chapter 2, 31 March 2004.

standards has had in Kosovo, in particular international human rights law, where the retaliatory costs of noncompliance are nearly nonexistent. Although several law reform projects founded on international law incorporation have yielded changes, for example in relation to constitutional law, it is uncertain to what extent these changes will "stick" (Magen and Morlino 2009b: 40–43).

In part, the method of incorporating international standards in the domestic law of Kosovo seems to have been applied because it reflects the institutional mandates of international agencies, and political actors in Kosovo have complied in hope of engendering some sense of legitimacy and social good will.[42] Despite the possibility of international law being used as a "Trojan horse," where international laws and standards provide a platform for many issues considered controversial in the national context, once it is incorporated then national actors often find ways of circumventing and undermining its influence. Rule of law reform in Kosovo has faced not only regulatory practices that have watered down imported norms but also an extremely weak capacity with which to implement them, should political commitment actually exist.[43]

Apart from this direct instilling of human rights law in Kosovo to serve as normative guidelines, the UN also provides a general treaty-monitoring function of compliance with international human rights law. In state-building missions, human rights monitoring is often a constituent part of the mandate. In Kosovo, human rights monitoring was in a sense "contracted out" to OSCE. The organization has been responsible for monitoring the legal system in Kosovo, primarily overseeing the criminal justice system, though it recently added superintendence of the administrative law system to its work. The incorporation of international norms and standards in Kosovo has generally followed a top-down approach. The exception is the OSCE, which has more emphasis on local governance and empowerment issues. One example is the 2003 Remedies Catalogue, which the OSCE published early on in its mission with a view to disseminating information on the rights and duties of the emerging state agencies, as well as courses of action people could take if their rights were infringed.[44] The catalogue deals with criminal justice, UNMIK police, Kosovo police forces, and the Kosovo Force (KFOR), as well as nondiscrimination laws and the legal framework available for victims of crime and property rights violations.

3.3. *Judicial Structures, Professionalism, and Accountability Strategies*

The UN initially treated the question of structure and organization of legal institutions as a matter of weak capacity. Thus early on in the UN administration over

[42] One example is the direct incorporation of the UN Convention on International Sale of Goods without substantial harmonization to the legal framework in Kosovo. See Muharremi et al. (2005: 9).

[43] In International Crisis Group, "The Rule of Law in Independent Kosovo," 19 May 2010, it is stated that many observers on Kosovo express a belief that the government prefers a weak judiciary because of corruption and organized crime links.

[44] OSCE, "Human Rights and Rule of Law: Remedies Catalogue" (2003).

Kosovo, for the purpose of putting right the lack of coherent judicial structures, the SRSG issued a regulation establishing two ad hoc bodies – a court of final appeal and an office of the public prosecutor.[45] Parallel to this, the Kosovar judiciary remained with its previous organization. UNMIK also created the Advisory Judicial Commission (AJC) to allow for national ownership in judicial reform by making long-term appointments to the courts of judges and prosecutors. The composition of the commission specifically designated a majority of posts to national experts "to empower them to overrule the international members so as to build a strong sense of ownership over the new judiciaries and to inject as much domestic expertise as possible into the process" (Strohmeyer 2001a: 52). Issues of bias in the appointment of members to serve in the AJC undermined its legitimacy and independence. AJC members lacked qualifications, rendering them susceptible to outside interference and thus operational capacity (O'Neil 2002: 77). Moreover, the appointed members of the commission with a minority background were accused of having collaborated with the Milosevic regime and were thus intimidated (Strohmeyer 2001a: 52).

Reliance on a Kosovar judiciary was both symbolic and practical. After a decade of discrimination under a Serb-dominated judiciary, the legitimacy of the courts had been eroded. The attempt to satisfy local claims for a legitimate court structure and international principles and standards of judicial organization and function proved difficult, with growing accusations of discrimination and failures to provide fair and impartial adjudication. This became manifest in cases in which the alleged offender had belonged to the former Kosovo Liberation Army, or when the accused came from the Serb minority group. The situation eventually prompted the UN administration to adopt a unique measure in state-building missions by introducing international judges and prosecutors to serve within the Kosovo judicial system.[46]

The program for international judges and prosecutors was later expanded through Regulation 2000/64, increasing the number of judges so as to minimize the risk of being "outvoted" when they were sitting with Kosovar judges.[47] The decision to use international judges and prosecutors sparked controversy and criticism from inside and outside Kosovo. The Ombudsperson Institution in Kosovo noted in its 2007 annual report that there was a lack of transparency regarding the appointment of international judges, as well as in case assignment, and argued that the principles applicable to Kosovar judges in respect of merit, appointment, and case assignment should apply equally to international judges.[48] In the EULEX mission, the international presence is still substantial and EULEX experts have continued through a twinning approach of executive functions and MMA.[49]

45 UNMIK Regulation No 1999/5 of 4 September 1999, UN Doc. UNMIK/REG/1999/5.

46 UNMIK Regulation No 2000/6 of 15 February 2000, UN Doc. UNMIK/REG/2000/6.

47 UNMIK Regulation No 2000/64 of 15 December 2004, UN Doc. UNMIK/REG/2000/64.

48 Ombudsperson Institution in Kosovo, "Seventh Annual Report" (2007): 20.

49 EULEX Kosovo, "Programme Report 2010: Building Sustainable Change Together" (2010). Available at http://www.eulex-kosovo.eu/docs/tracking/EULEX%20Programme%20Report%202010%20.pdf: 25.

In many war-torn societies, the low number of educated legal personnel, police, and other public servants is often a problem predating the conflict. In Kosovo, where Kosovar Albanian judges and lawyers were prohibited from practicing law during much of Milosevic regime, lack of experience proved to be just one of many difficulties. Amid growing accusations of biased judges and lawyers toward the Serb minority, the UN authorities in Kosovo deemed it necessary to initiate a review of judges and other legal personnel. Moreover, a survey conducted in Kosovo found that municipal officials, lawyers, and judges were perceived to be among the most corrupt state actors (see Spector, Winbourne, and Beck 2003). Vetting of legal professionals has been built into the selection process of judges in Kosovo. For the AJC, responsible for advising the SRSG on the appointment and removal of judges, the criteria for the selection of candidates insisted (apart from professional skills) that candidates had no criminal record, and furthermore were not registered with any political party or participating in any political activity, and that they had not "participated in discriminatory measures, or applied any repressive law or have implemented dictatorial policies."[50]

The question of disciplinary actions and removal of judges in Kosovo has been addressed on two occasions. The first followed UNMIK Regulation 1999/7 on Appointment and Removal from Office of Judges and Prosecutors. This program of vetting began in the early phase of transition, but it generally fell short of compliance with international best practice – that is, to include reprimands, suspension, and other disciplinary measures that could be employed before a final decision on removal was considered. These disciplinary measures were included following Regulation 2005/25 on the establishment of the Kosovo Judicial Council. Thus, not until five years after vetting was first initiated were provisions established that allowed judges suffering removal the right of appeal. The second vetting program was initiated after UNMIK Regulation 2006/25, which established a comprehensive reappointment process for judges and prosecutors, with the particular aim of ensuring greater participation from minority communities. Since 2008, all judges (and prosecutors) have had to reapply for their position to an international body, the Independent Judicial and Prosecutorial Commission (IJPC).[51]

Considering the experience of the first program and the lack of due process guarantees, it is somewhat surprising that the second program also failed to include proper safeguards. Among other things, the IJPC, charged with responsibility for overseeing reappointments, did not have to explain its reasons when deciding on candidates for the judiciary and prosecutorial offices. Moreover, there were no explicitly mentioned procedures for appealing decisions by the IJPC.[52] For those candidates denied a position, the available option was to file a request for consideration

[50] UNMIK Regulation No 1999/7 of 7 September 1999, UN Doc. UNMIK/REG/1999/7.
[51] UNMIK Regulation No 2006/25 of 27 April 2006, UN Doc. UNMIK/REG/2006/25.
[52] Ibid.

within a reasonable time. Grounds for appeal were also limited to either the material or on grounds that new information had emerged that was unknown to the IJPC when it made its decision.[53] The structure, competence, and function of the IJPC in the second vetting program also went against established best practice for judicial councils, and those deficiencies were attended to eight months later.[54] A new UNMIK directive introduced more extensive grounds for appeal beyond a request for reconsideration, with the possibility open to submit an application to the Supreme Court for a judicial review of the decision.[55] These changes seem to have been successful in creating greater efficiency, openness, and fairness in judicial selection. The Judicial Reform Index, produced by the American Bar Association for Kosovo in 2007, reported significant improvements in judicial reorganization on integrity and impartiality in the procedures on reappointments.[56]

3.4. *International and Hybrid Institutions*

Temporary measures of internationalization of legal and administrative institutions in Kosovo have generally followed two objectives. One is to provide capacity building at the point of operation. This is also a form of socialization, with international actors functioning as "teachers" of norms. The second is to temporarily alleviate national institutions, either from a weak capacity and backlog, or from matters too sensitive to be dealt with impartially within the existing institutional structure.

The employment of interim international experts or institutions in Kosovo has not been without controversy. Besides challenges to national sovereignty and ownership, there are indications that the interim internationalization has postponed the capacity building of local institutions (Bull 2008: 122). Using international experts has also led to the feeling among Kosovar legal professionals of being considered unworthy in professionalism or integrity, or both. Furthermore, when international actors substitute for a weak government or for one yet to be formed, or perform tasks under the guise of assistance by putting in place technical advisors and contractors as staff at ministries and government agencies, there is a risk of a reduction in accountability.

Property rights and land disputes is one area where international bodies assumed responsibility early on in the UN administration. In Kosovo, the Housing and Property Directorate (HPD) and the Housing and Property Claims Commission (HPCC) were set up with jurisdiction over property-related disputes arising between 1989 and

53 UNMIK Administrative Direction No 2006/18 of 28 December 2006, implementing UNMIK Regulation No. 2006/25, UN Doc. UNMIK/DIR/2006/18.

54 That is, "if there are no objective criteria, transferring selection powers to the Judicial Council may only reproduce, or worsen, discretionary and politicized appointments" (Autheman and Elena 2004: 12).

55 UNMIK Administrative Direction No 2007/7 of 3 August 2007, amending UNMIK Administrative Direction No. 2006/18.

56 American Bar Association, "Judicial Reform Index: Kosovo," Volume III (2007): 1.

the 1999 conflict.[57] The HPD had responsibility for providing overall direction on matters concerning property rights in Kosovo and also received residential property claims. The HPCC was given exclusive jurisdiction over deciding claims received by the HPD. The rulings of the HPCC were final and not subject to review or appeal, other than to the commission itself. At the end of 2007 the HPCC had decided on all of the 29,160 cases submitted to the HPD, which formally ended its mandate.[58]

Though the interim internationalization of property management and disputes in Kosovo was successful with regard to the number of claims processed, the relationship between the HPCC and local authorities was always strained and marked by controversies on jurisdictional matters. Despite the finality of the commission's decisions, some aspects were open for court review.[59] Courts receiving cases from the HPCC often arrived at conflicting decisions that competed with HPCC findings, leaving parties without an effective resolution. The situation was further complicated by the fact that courts were unaware of previous decisions of the HPCC (or its predecessor, the Kosovo Property Claims Commission). Moreover, as the OSCE legal monitoring team observed on contested property, even when local courts had been made aware of decisions made by the HPCC or Kosovo Property Claims Commission, they were frequently ignored.[60]

Another important international institution for rule of law promotion is the Ombudsperson Institution in Kosovo, established with support from the OSCE and for the first few years headed by international experts. The Ombudsperson Institution has, however, been more successful in efforts at "localization" and capacity transfer to Kosovar professionals than HPCC and other international bodies. The Ombudsperson quickly gained a more independent status from the OSCE and other pillars of support of UNMIK.[61] In the beginning, the Ombudsperson had the competence to investigate UNMIK, though that competence was the subject of controversy.[62] Nevertheless, the office received more than 900 formal applications between November 21, 2000, and June 30, 2003; in excess of 800 of them concerned alleged violations by UNMIK and KFOR.[63]

Balancing the limited authority of the Ombudsperson Institution, steps were taken toward the establishment of a more comprehensive accountability regime when UNMIK set up the Human Rights Advisory Panel, with competence to accept complaints against actions by UNMIK for failing to comply with the catalogue of international human rights instruments listed in UNMIK Regulation 1999/24.[64]

57 UNMIK Regulation No 1999/23 of 15 November 1999, UN Doc. UNMIK/REG/1999/23.
58 OSCE, "Conflicting Jurisdiction in Property Disputes" (2003): 2.
59 UNMIK Regulation No 2000/60 of 31 October 2000, UN Doc. UNMIK/REG/2000/60.
60 OSCE, "Conflicting Jurisdiction in Property Disputes" (2003): 3.
61 UNMIK Regulation No 2000/38 of 30 June 2000, UN Doc. UNMIK.REG/2000/38.
62 UNMIK Regulation No 2000/6 of 15 February 2000, UN Doc. UNMIK/REG/2000/6.
63 Ombudsperson Institution in Kosovo, "Third Annual Report" (2003).
64 UNMIK Regulation No 2006/12 of 23 March 2006, UN Doc. UNMIK/REG/2006/12.

The Advisory Panel retains jurisdiction over complaints "relating to alleged violations of human rights that had occurred not earlier than 23 April 2005 or arising from facts which occurred before this date where these facts give rise to a continuing violation of human rights."[65] Moreover, the Advisory Panel has the competence to request the participation of UNMIK personnel, and to order the disclosure of its documents, though the SRSG has leave to deny participation or disclosure. The Advisory Panel represents a step toward ensuring accountability of international actors in Kosovo, but the institutional limitations make it generally weak and exclude important issues such as the judicial review of administrative decisions made by UNMIK. The Advisory Panel is also weak in the sense that it can only make findings of a nonbinding character.

4. INTERNATIONAL CONTROL AND LOCAL OWNERSHIP OVER RULE OF LAW PROMOTION

From this review of some of the central rule of law reforms undertaken in Kosovo by the UN, EU, and OSCE, there are several common denominators. One is the internationalization of the rule of law. The transitional legal order created in Kosovo is best described as a form of "hybrid" regime with a mix of international, foreign, and national laws and institutions. Through the employment of various methods – the incorporation of international law in the constitutional arrangement, the establishment of institutions based on international models, the use of international judges and prosecutors, or the employment of standards directly in the legal and administrative framework – Kosovo has been subject to rapid internationalization.

Another common denominator is that the majority of reforms implemented under the heading of rule of law in Kosovo have been primarily concerned with the justice sector. This reflects the institutional mandates and objectives of the international actors involved. Focusing on the justice sector also corresponds with past experience in the field of rule of law reform on behalf of the UN, EU, and OSCE. The predominant focus on justice sector institutions was structurally confirmed through the devolution of powers to Kosovar authorities where the justice sector was exempt and under the responsibility of UNMIK. This has led to a disproportionate legal and institutional development in which certain matters within the justice sector have received substantial international assistance while others have lagged behind. As noted in the International Crisis Group report, "The Rule of Law in Independent Kosovo," "violent crime is relatively rare and the judiciary, weak as it is, can handle criminal cases. But the ineffective civil law system, which includes mainly property rights disputes, leaves society, the economy and the government itself unregulated and open to abuse."[66] The EULEX 2010 program report also states that the massive

[65] UNMIK Regulation No 2006/12 of 23 March 2006, UN Doc. UNMIK/REG/2006/12.

[66] International Crisis Group, "The Rule of Law in Independent Kosovo," 19 May 2010: 12.

number of pending issues of a civil nature indicates a slow progress by local judges and prosecutors to tackle this "urgent problem."[67]

At an early stage in the UN administration it was decided that with a view to preparing for substantial autonomy, the Provisional Institutions of Self-Government (PISG) should be allowed to take a broader responsibility in the administration of the territory, UNMIK distinguished between those matters relating to "core institutions" (judiciary, police, and the rest) and more peripheral institutions such as public administration, administrative law, and other regulatory mechanisms. In the Constitutional Framework for Provisional Self-Government, certain areas were devolved from international control to national authorities, among them a major part of the public administrative system.[68] The SRSG kept core functions within the international domain, in what was called "reserved powers," including the administration of justice – that is, the appointment of judges and control over law enforcement. With the formation of the PISG, UNMIK withdrew from direct management of the administration, including handing over vast responsibilities to the 30 municipalities in Kosovo.[69]

At a cursory glance the devolution of responsibility would meet with approval. The administration of justice is kept within the reserved powers based on the argument that those issues that it includes deal with sensitive questions central to the process of recovery. Commonsensical as this devolution of power might seem, it has constrained possibilities of rule of law reform in matters outside the justice sector, and it fails to recognize that that a rule of law deficit might be caused by circumstances beyond the control of justice sector institutions and others within the reserved powers. That the rule of law model promoted in Kosovo focuses on the justice sector is reinforced by the focus of assessments, evaluations, and ongoing monitoring programs. The OSCE has, from the start of its mission, produced monthly reports monitoring the legal system. With few exceptions, these include a monitoring of the criminal justice sector. Similarly, EULEX in its progress report tracks progress in relation to the justice sector. Other actors, such as the United Nations Development Program, U.S. Agency for International Development, or the American Bar Association, also provide either regular or ad hoc thematic analyses of justice sector institutions, and the latter has for a long time produced reports that track progress in relation to judicial reform, legal education reform, and legal professional reform.

67 EULEX Kosovo, "Programme Report 2010: Building Sustainable Change Together" (2010). Available at http://www.eulex-kosovo.eu/docs/tracking/EULEX%20Programme%20Report%202010%20.pdf: 25.

68 UNMIK Regulation No. 2001/9 of 15 May 2001, UN Doc. UNMIK/REG/2001/9. The Constitutional Framework created 11 ministries; 7 of them came to deal with competences with the civil administrative framework previously belonging to UNMIK.

69 Although the constitutional framework stated that the UN still retained responsibility to ensure that the system of local municipal administration functioned effectively, based on international standards, the actual control was primarily to be within the competence of domestic authorities.

Although assessment and monitoring reports provide valuable and critical information on the state of affairs in the justice sector, which is necessary for sound and well-grounded reform initiatives, they do not encompass rule of law problems outside the justice sector, such as in relation to overall accountability structures of municipal authorities, public administrative agencies, and ministries in Kosovo, and how these institutions treat individuals who rely on their competence and performance for their livelihoods and well-being.

An important exception to the narrow rule of law model promoted by the UN and now EULEX is the OSCE. Through its broad mandate of democratization and human rights, the OSCE, besides rule of law reform, has also worked closely with the Ombudsperson, municipalities, minority returns, civil law, and land and property rights. The OSCE produces analytical reports on a variety of topics highlighting issues pertaining to matters outside the justice sector. The OSCE perspective notwithstanding, there is a limited amount of comprehensive and regularly updated information on how citizens in Kosovo perceive rule of law problems, such as in relation to civil and administrative law. Whereas international actors have undertaken awareness and needs assessments on access to justice, right to a fair trial, and other rule of law principles in relation to the judiciary, little information has been systematically gathered on how citizens perceive these rule of law principles to be handled by, for example, municipalities or administrative agencies.

To portray a fuller picture of rule of law problems in Kosovo, and as a complement to existing knowledge on rule of law deficiencies in the justice sector, one can use grievances and complaints registered with the Kosovo Ombudsperson as helpful indicators (see Table 11.1). Since the inception of the Ombudsperson Institution, a total of 5,962 cases have been registered. The seven most registered claims deal with issues that are primarily handled by other institutions than those within the justice sector.[70]

It is worth noting that the majority of grievances come from interactions with the public administration in which citizens either perceive they are discriminated against, or where their petitions are left without action. The third and fourth most commonly registered complaints deal with civil proceedings. What the numbers from the Ombudsperson Institution bring to the fore is an observation that in relation to crucial state services, whether in civil registration, pensions, employment, health care, or property, a significant number of citizens in Kosovo have felt that their rights have been violated.

Examining the respondent parties to registered complaints supports a view that there are serious rule of law problems outside the justice sector (see Table 11.2). Up until 2006 when the Ombudsperson's authority to investigate UNMIK and KFOR acts was withdrawn, the international actors were the main respondent parties.

[70] There are, of course, considerable overlaps. Property rights is one example, where the registering of property requires filing the record of a deed with a municipal court.

TABLE 11.1. *Ten most registered complaints with the Kosovo Ombudsperson Institution (2000–2009)*

Subject matter	No. of registered complaints
Administrative silence and abuse of authority[a]	1202
Property related issues[b]	931
Issues related to employment[c]	556
Access to court in civil proceedings	493
Procedural and other fair trial issues in civil proceedings, including length of civil court proceedings	456
Housing and Property Directorate and Kosovo Property Agency	448
Economic, social, and cultural rights	445
Failure to investigate a crime and impunity of authorities[d]	328
Fair hearing rights[e]	262
Procedural and other fair trial issues in criminal court proceedings, including length of criminal court proceedings	212
Total number of registered complaints, 2000–2009	5,962

Note: The table shows the 10 most registered complaints per subject matter.

[a] This includes failure of administrative authorities to respond to proper requests, arbitrary or discriminatory administrative decisions, etc.

[b] This includes the taking of property without compensation, damage to property, access to home or other property, nonpayment of pensions, nonremoval of illegal occupant from property, etc.

[c] This includes failure to obtain employment through competitive employment process, dismissals from employment, etc.

[d] This includes failure to adequately investigate alleged inhumane or degrading treatment or violations of the right to life, etc.

[e] Criminal and civil court proceedings were reported in a combined fashion in the annual reports from 2001, 2002, and 2003.

TABLE 11.2. *Respondent parties to registered complaints (2000–2009)*

Respondent parties	No. of complaints
UNMIK	1,244 (until 2006)
Courts	776
Municipal authorities	753
Government ministries	717
Others	530
HPD–Kosovo Property Agency	327
PISG	321
KFOR	178 (until 2006)
Police	87
Kosovo Trust Agency	29
Total	5,962

Apart from international actors (including the Housing and Property Directorate and the Kosovo Trust Agency), the combined categories of municipal authorities, government ministries, and PISG constitute the main bulk of respondent parties.

It is not possible, nor desirable, to quantify and compare grievances. The problems that citizens in Kosovo face, whether in relation to the judiciary or municipalities, are subjective and perceived differently by each individual. Moreover, using complaints filed with the Ombudsperson as a basis of describing problems of rule of law in Kosovo only provides a crude picture, because there might be many situations not covered, and several incidents and violations that are not reported to the Ombudsperson for fear of reprisal, lack of awareness, or trust. With these caveats in mind, what the charts show, however, is that that there are strong indications of rule of law problems in the institutions outside the justice sector.

The fact that international control has remained over judicial and criminal law, first through UNMIK and now through EULEX, despite indications of serious rule of law problems in other areas of the legal and administrative system in Kosovo, is in some part emanating from weak guidelines on what a holistic and comprehensive rule of law concept means in rule of law promotion. Moreover, there are also very limited means of policy mainstreaming within the organizations through unified training and other forms for ensuring policy coherence. Actors such as the UN are organizationally structured in a way that makes policy mainstreaming on the rule of law politically and practically difficult. With weak guidance, rule of law practitioners and experts in the field are left to work with a definition "according to their own preferences," as the OSCE survey put it. Considering that a majority of rule of law promoters are lawyers, judges, and prosecutors in their respective home countries, sometimes seconded by their governments to missions on the basis of their particular expertise, there is a tendency to identify reform issues within the area of familiarity: courts, prosecutorial offices, bar associations, criminal law, and criminal procedural law. Nonetheless, it is by no means certain that this operationalization of rule of law policy responds well to overall rule of law problems in Kosovo (Carothers 2006b: 20).[71]

The rule of law problems that exist outside the justice sector, as illustrated in the statistics from the Ombudsperson Institution, are not unknown to international actors, but they are addressed under different paradigms, for example through that of public administration reform with an emphasis on effectiveness, managerial skills,

[71] See also Channell (2006b: 150): "the legal reform industry regularly recruits and attracts experts and specialists with ten to twenty years of professional experience in both developing and transition countries. This is appropriate. These experts are then expected to report for duty with a full understanding of what needs to be done under their terms of reference and begin doing it. This is inappropriate. Each new assignment should require extensive preparation for the new conditions, cultural variations, and demands on the otherwise qualified specialists who will implement the project. Most will learn on the job, correcting mistakes as they go, but very few will be paid for learning as part of their job."

human resources, and organizational capacities. This is a quantitative paradigm as opposed to the qualitative rule of law paradigm that applies to the justice sector. The OSCE has struggled to build capacity and reform public sector institutions, but it has failed to do so largely as a result of organizational and legislative "semi-chaos" (Bull 2008: 162). In the European Commission progress report from 2009, the problem is noted and described as persisting because of absence of legislation relating to public administration, notably the civil service and on the organization of public administrative institutions.[72]

5. CONCLUSION

The rule of law model promoted in Kosovo is not so different from rule of law models in other peace- and state-building missions, but what makes the situation in Kosovo unique is the executive authority of international actors. This means that the rule of law in Kosovo is not only promoted but also enforced, which also allows for easier identification of the model's typical features.

Generally, the rule of law model promoted in Kosovo, from the inception of the UN mission in 1999 through the transition to EULEX, is inherently an international model. This is reaffirmed in landmark legal developments such as the adoption of the Constitutional Framework in 2001, or in the decision to use international legal professionals and hybrid international and national institutions such as the HPD or Human Rights Advisory Council. The internationalization of the rule of law model pursued by international assistance providers is also likely to have a profound effect on future rule of law development in Kosovo. The constitution adopted in 2008 sets a broad aspirational framework, and it includes provisions that give international law direct applicability and higher status than domestic law (save for the constitution; see Marko 2008). The constitutional court has a composition that allows for six national judges, and three international judges, the latter appointed by the international civilian presence in Kosovo with support from the president of the European Court of Human Rights (Morina 2010: 133).

The internationalization of the rule of law in Kosovo reflects a necessary benchmarking of reforms. Reforms based on international norms and standards are seen as more legitimate, just, and easier to accept than a simple copy-and-paste process from national jurisdictions.[73] The use of international norms and standards, in a sense creating an international rule of law model, represents the striving for modernity and rationality, sometimes expressed in terms of Europeanization or European standards in the context of Kosovo. This also reveals that international actors assume that their counterparts share the same ideologies and convictions. The problems surrounding

[72] European Commission, Kosovo Under UNSCR 1244/99 2009 Progress Report, 2009: 9.

[73] Report of the Secretary-General on the Rule of Law and Transitional Justice in Conflict and Post-Conflict Societies, 23 August 2004, UN Doc. S/2004/616: 5.

the issue of applicable law show that this is not always the case. Moreover, modern and rational laws or institutions cannot solve things on their own, and the direct linking of international laws and standards is not without problems.

Coupled with the international rule of law model pursued by the UN, EU, and OSCE is a preoccupation with security institutions rather than principles or goals. With the noteworthy exception of the OSCE, taking a somewhat broader approach to rule of law through its local governance and democracy focus, the rule of law model promoted (particularly manifest in the EULEX mandate) is an excluding model. Positioning and presenting the rule of law to consist of certain institutions, aimed at addressing a select set of grievances and problems, discards a lot else that look like rule of law problems but that are treated under a different paradigm.

Thus, it is possible to identify a normative approach to rule of law mainly in terms of criminal justice reform through concerted and continued international control by UNMIK and now EULEX, but where civil and administrative law, control, and conversion are less visible. It appears to be the case that rule of law dynamics in Kosovo have been strongest in relation to policy, judiciary, corrections, and customs, and that outside the core functions there is less international control and more responsibility given to national actors. In this sense the rule of law model pursued in Kosovo is a simplification of the concept in tangible institutional terms. Moreover, it is a simplified model based on the assumption that the institutional surroundings outside the justice sector – for example, the parliament, the executive, supervisory accountability institutions, and municipalities – function according to standard. The brief review of rule of law problems in Kosovo, based on the complaints filed with the Ombudsperson Institution as indicators, points toward persisting problems of rule of law outside the justice sector that have been largely left unaddressed, falling outside the rule of law model promoted by international actors. With EULEX now in place, there are few indications that this mission will be interpreted to apply outside the "beaten track" of rule of law reform in Kosovo.

12

The ICC's Intervention in Uganda

Which Rule of Law Does It Promote?

Sarah M. H. Nouwen

Undoubtedly, the most significant recent development in the international community's long struggle to advance the cause of justice and rule of law was the establishment of the International Criminal Court.

UN Secretary-General Kofi Annan[1]

Theoretical approaches have their place and are, I suppose, essential but a theory must be tempered with reality.

Jawaharlal Nehru[2]

1. INTRODUCTION

The former Secretary-General of the United Nations (UN) has not been alone in linking the International Criminal Court (ICC or "the Court") to the rule of law. In a UN debate on the rule of law, 19 of the 29 intervening states explicitly referred to the role of the ICC.[3] The ICC was portrayed as "a symbol for a new world order [that] the UN based on the rule of international law."[4] The ICC Prosecutor, in turn, has advanced the rule of law as "the cornerstone of the international criminal justice system."[5] According to a report commissioned by his office, the Court's

This chapter draws heavily on Nouwen (2011; 2012, forthcoming). Thanks are due to Joe McIntyre and Juliette McIntyre for critical comments on an earlier draft of this chapter.

1 Report of the Secretary-General on the Rule of Law and Transitional Justice in Conflict and Post-Conflict Societies, 23 August 2004, UN Doc. S/2004/616: 49.

2 Jawaharlal Nehru's Speeches 1949–1953, Publications Division, Ministry of Information and Broadcasting, Government of India, 1954: 235.

3 Strengthening International Law: Rule of Law and the Maintenance of International Peace and Security, Security Council Open Debate, 22 June 2006: 1, available at http://www.iccnow.org/documents/UNMemberStates_ExcerptsonInternationalLaw_22June06.pdf.

4 Ibid. 2–3.

5 Keynote Address by Luis Moreno-Ocampo, Prosecutor of the International Criminal Court, Council on Foreign Relations, Washington, DC, 4 February 2010: 4.

Rome Statute[6] "embodies the idea that the rule of law can protect individuals and nations from massive atrocities."[7] A former ICC investigator has explained that "through ratification of the Rome Statute, States bind themselves to enforce the international rule of law within their own borders and agree that, if they fail, the ICC may intervene" (Chung 2007–2008: 229). States Parties to the Statute have "recogni[zed] the noble mission and the role of the International Criminal Court in a multilateral system that aims to end impunity, establish the *rule of law*, promote and encourage respect for human rights and achieve sustainable peace."[8] Scholars, for their part, have argued that international criminal courts "must do more . . . to contribute to strengthening . . . the rule of law on the ground," and they have advocated "outreach," "demonstration," and "capacity-building" as the way to do so (Stromseth 2009: 89; see also Concannon 2000). No matter how wide ranging, these statements linking the ICC to the rule of law appear to be based on two common assumptions: first, that the ICC and rule of law are related; second, that this is a positive relationship.

This chapter reviews these assumptions through an empirical study of rule of law dynamics catalyzed by the ICC's intervention in Uganda.[9] The chapter does not suggest that the ICC intentionally created these dynamics. Nor does it claim that the Court was the only actor in bringing about these developments; some dynamics stem from the actions of others responding to the acts or the mere existence of the Court.

The evaluation of the ICC's contribution to the rule of law in Uganda depends on one's understanding of "rule of law." The first part of this chapter uses the meaning of rule of law that dominates the field of international development

[6] Rome Statute of the International Criminal Court of 17 July 1998, entered into force on 1 July 2002, 2187 UNTS 90.

[7] ICC, "The Importance of Justice in Securing Peace." Review Conference of the Rome Statute, 30 May 2010, RC/ST/PJ/INF.3: 1.

[8] ICC, "Kampala Declaration." Review Conference of the Rome Statute, Kampala, 31 May–11 June 2010, RC-4-ENG-04062010, available at http://www.iccuganda2010.ug/uploads/Docs/The%20Kampala%20Declaration.pdf. Emphasis added.

[9] The data used in this chapter derive from research for Nouwen (2012, forthcoming). For this research over 100 semi-structured interviews were conducted with key actors in the Ugandan legal sector, politicians, army officials, representatives of rebel movements, civil society actors, scholars, journalists, nongovernmental organization (NGO) staff, ICC officials, and representatives of embassies and international organizations in Uganda (August–October 2008 and May and June 2010), The Netherlands, London, New York, and Washington (throughout 2006–2010). Gratitude is due to the Uganda National Council for Science and Technology, which granted permission for research; the Refugee Law Project, which provided an inspiring institutional research home; Célina Korthals and Wendy Hanson, who assisted in reporting and transcribing interviews; Esther Loeffen, for advice and hospitality; Joanna Quinn, for generosity in sharing experiences; and the Gates Cambridge Trust, the Arts and Humanities Research Council, and the Smuts Fund for Commonwealth Studies, which made the research financially possible. In this chapter the interviewees' names and exact locations and dates of the interviews have been replaced by a general description of their positions and a more general indication of the place and date of interviews.

cooperation: a body of legal and judicial instruments and institutions. It then considers the ICC's impact from a more legal-philosophical understanding of the rule of law, namely as a latticework of substantive governance ideals. This chapter argues that, seen through the first lens of "rule of law promotion," the evaluation of the ICC's impact on the rule of law in Uganda can be positive: The ICC's intervention has spurred the creation of laws and courts and has led to an increase in references to international standards. The legal-philosophical lens, however, reveals that these developments have not necessarily enhanced the aims of the rule of law. Moreover, the ICC's intervention has unleashed other dynamics that are in synergy with some aims of the rule of law (supremacy of law and accountability) but in tension with others (equality before the law, separation of powers, fairness, and legal certainty).

Before zooming in on the ICC in Uganda, this chapter's analysis must be located on three theoretical maps of the rule of law: *What* is the rule of law? *Where* does the ICC promote the rule of law? *How* does the ICC promote the rule of law?

1.1. *What Is the Rule of Law that the ICC Is Expected to Uphold or Promote?*

The statements in the opening paragraph do not define the term "rule of law," but their contexts suggest either an overly broad or an overly narrow interpretation. In the former, establishing the rule of law resembles an aim like advancing the cause of justice, ending impunity, promoting and encouraging respect for human rights, and achieving sustainable peace: rich concepts that are as difficult to define as they are to dislike. In these aspirational slogans, "rule of law" and the other concepts are overlapping patches on a neoliberal collage of global well-being: "Peace" is a situation in which the rule of law governs, while the "rule of law" includes an "end to impunity" and compliance with "human rights," which in turn result in "justice". These overlapping meanings, although perhaps sociologically correct, lack the definitional boundaries required for an empirical case study.

In the overly narrow meaning, rule of law is equated with law and courts. According to this reasoning, the ICC is a court, a court applies the law, and in doing so the ICC promotes the rule of law. Put differently, more international law or more international courts result in more rule of law. Lost in this instrumental understanding are the features that distinguish rule *of* law from rule *by* law (Chesterman 2008a: 333).

This chapter takes as its starting point the UN Secretary-General's definition of rule of law:

> [It is] a principle of governance in which all persons, institutions and entities, public and private, including the State itself, are accountable to laws that are publicly promulgated, equally enforced and independently adjudicated, and which are consistent with international human rights norms and standards. It requires, as

> well, measures to ensure adherence to the principles of supremacy of law, equality before the law, accountability to the law, fairness in the application of the law, separation of powers, participation in decision-making, legal certainty, avoidance of arbitrariness and procedural and legal transparency.[10]

The definition aptly describes rule of law as a latticework of ideals (albeit with some tautological elements).

1.2. *Where Does the ICC Uphold or Promote the Rule of Law?*

The statements in the opening paragraph also diverge with respect to the legal order in which the ICC upholds or promotes the rule of law: Is it the international, the domestic, or something in between: the "internationalized"?

The ICC can be seen to uphold the rule of law at the international level: It addresses the impunity of those who violate *international* criminal law, and it can call to account even those who represent sovereign states.[11]

The ICC can at the same time affect the rule of law at the domestic level. An international criminal tribunal that investigates and prosecutes international crimes concerns domestic legal orders, because violations of international criminal law usually also constitute violations of domestic law,[12] differences in legal qualifications (genocide by killing or 500 counts of murder) notwithstanding. The ICC's jurisdiction and that of domestic legal orders are statutorily linked: The principle of complementarity dictates that a case is admissible before the ICC only when the same case is not, or has not been, genuinely investigated or prosecuted in any state.[13] From this perspective of the Court as a backstop of domestic legal systems, the ICC, mirroring Scelle's *dédoublement fonctionnel* (1935: 57), is an administrator of law at both the domestic and international level.

Finally, one can argue that the ICC promotes the rule of law in a sphere that overlaps the international and the domestic level, for which André Nollkaemper has coined the phrase the "internationalised rule of law" (2009: 78). International criminal law is an exemplar of an international legal regime that concerns at the same time horizontal interstate relations and relations between states and international organizations, and vertically penetrates domestic orders, binding individuals irrespective of whether or not their state has incorporated international criminal law into the domestic legal order.

10 Report of the Secretary-General on the Rule of Law and Transitional Justice in Conflict and Post-Conflict Societies 6.

11 Rome Statute, Art. 27(2), but also see Art. 98(1).

12 The most common exceptions are the enlistment, conscription, and use of child soldiers; treatment of prisoners of war; and modes of liability such as command responsibility.

13 Rome Statute, Arts. 17 and 20(3).

Without denying the ICC's relationships with the international and internationalized rule of law, this chapter focuses on the domestic sphere.

1.3. *How Does the ICC Promote the Rule of Law?*

The statements quoted in the opening paragraph also reflect differing visions as to how the ICC upholds or promotes the rule of law. In one view, the ICC does so merely by being part of a regime that embodies the rule of law. This international political regime governed by the rule of law is to a large extent still a sociopolitical aspiration, but the ICC symbolizes part of the ideal. In this view, all the ICC needs to do to promote the rule of law is to comply with its statutory mandate to investigate, prosecute, and try genocide, crimes against humanity, and war crimes.

A more pragmatic view, exemplified by calls for the ICC to engage in "reaching out" to, "demonstrating" to, and "capacity building" of domestic justice systems, is that the ICC should be an actor in technical rule of law promotion. Academics, ICC advocates, and even ICC organs, giving complementarity a meaning beyond that of an admissibility rule in the Rome Statute, have argued that the principle embodies the "primary responsibility" of states to investigate and prosecute crimes within the Court's jurisdiction. In this light the ICC Prosecutor argued in his first statement to the Assembly of States Parties:

> The principle of complementarity . . . compels the prosecutor's office to collaborate with national jurisdictions in order to help them improve their efficiency. That is the first task of the prosecutor's office: make its best effort to help national jurisdictions fulfil their mission.[14]

In this context of rule of law "promotion" or of "strengthening" the rule of law, rule of law is operationalized in accordance with the theories of change, instruments, and jargon of international development cooperation. Rule of law as a latticework of ideals is translated into rule of law programs, the impact of which is measured by indicators such as the number of people "workshopped." In this field, the term "rule of law promotion" is used interchangeably with the term "legal reform" (revising laws) or the term "judicial reform" (strengthening law-related institutions; see Carothers 2006b: 15, 20). In terms of the depth of reform, Thomas Carothers has labeled legal reform as Type I, and judicial reform as Type II. Type III reform, which aims at increasing governmental compliance with law, is more difficult to program because it "depends less on technical or institutional measures than on

[14] Statement by Luis Moreno-Ocampo, "Statement to the Assembly of States Parties to the Rome Statute of the International Criminal Court," New York, 22 April 2003, ICC-OTP-20030502–10-EN, available at http://www.icc-cpi.int/Menus/ICC/Structure+of+the+Court/Office+of+the+Prosecutor/Reports+and+Statements/Press+Releases/Press+Releases+2003/.

enlightened leadership and sweeping changes in the values and attitudes of those in power" (Carothers 2006c: 8).[15]

1.4. *The ICC in Uganda*

Uganda was the first situation ever to be referred to the Court. After 17 years of failed attempts to defeat the notorious Lord's Resistance Army (LRA), the Ugandan government referred the situation to the Court in December 2003. The LRA, under various names, had resisted Ugandan President Museveni ever since he seized power in 1986. The Acholi, an ethnic group in northern Uganda from which many LRA fighters originate, have borne the brunt of the conflict, at the hands of both the LRA and the government. Tens of thousands of people were abducted, at least 200,000 died as a result of conflict-related causes, and, at the height of the conflict, 2 million people were displaced, many of whom were forced by the government into so-called protected camps.

In its letter referring the situation to the Court, the Ugandan government explained that it, "[h]aving exhausted every other means of bringing an end to this terrible suffering . . . turn[ed] to the newly established ICC and its promise of global justice."[16] In July 2005, the Court issued its first ever arrest warrants for five LRA commanders, including LRA leader Joseph Kony, on counts of war crimes and crimes against humanity. Under pressure as a result of changing regional alliances and the ICC arrest warrants, the LRA requested the Government of Southern Sudan to mediate in its conflict with the Ugandan government. The peace talks began in Juba, the capital of Southern Sudan, in June 2006. One and a half years of on-and-off negotiations eventually produced agreements on all agenda items, including "Accountability and Reconciliation."[17] However, LRA leader Kony demanded further clarifications on the relation between the peace agreement and the ICC arrest warrants and has, to the date of this writing, refused to append his signature on the Final Peace Agreement (FPA). The LRA moved to the Democratic Republic of the Congo, the Central African Republic, and Sudan, and reportedly made many more persons their victims. Nonetheless, although the chances that Kony will sign the FPA are slim, the Ugandan Justice Law and Order Sector (JLOS), a coordinating forum bringing together senior officials in government agencies working in the areas of justice, law and order, has begun implementing some provisions of the Accountability Agreements.

15 See also ICC, "The Importance of Justice in Securing Peace." Review Conference of the Rome Statute, 30 May 2010, RC/ST/PJ/INF.3.

16 Government of Uganda, "Referral of the Situation Concerning the Lord's Resistance Army Submitted by the Republic of Uganda," 16 December 2003, on file with author: 6.

17 Agreement on Accountability and Reconciliation Between the Government of the Republic of Uganda and the Lord's Resistance Army/Movement, Juba, 29 June 2007 (Accountability Agreement) and Annexure to the Agreement on Accountability and Reconciliation, Juba, 19 February 2008.

2. THE ICC AND UGANDA THROUGH THE LENS OF RULE OF LAW PROMOTION

Seen through the lens of rule of law promotion, the ICC's intervention in Uganda has produced some visible results.

2.1. *The ICC Act*

The most evident example of Type I rule of law reform that the ICC's intervention has brought about in Uganda is the adoption of the ICC Act of 2010. The Act, adopted to give effect to the Rome Statute, has introduced several novelties to Ugandan law. First, the Act proscribes war crimes, crimes against humanity, and genocide – for almost all crimes, for the first time in Ugandan history.[18] Second, it makes applicable in Ugandan international-crimes proceedings the Rome Statute's "general principles of criminal law,"[19] including the modes of responsibility.[20] Third, it establishes extraterritorial jurisdiction on grounds other than residency or nationality, namely employment by the state of Uganda, passive personality, and universality on the condition of the offender's subsequent presence in Uganda.[21] Finally, it excludes the application of the death penalty for the crimes domesticated under this Act, because otherwise "[p]ersons prosecuted in Uganda under this law will get a harsher punishment than those who will be tried under the Statute."[22] The chairperson of the Legal and Parliamentary Affairs Committee provided an additional reason: The death penalty would be "inconsistent with the Rome Statute."[23]

2.2. *The Special Division of the High Court*

The most evident example of Type II rule of law reform catalyzed by the ICC in Uganda is the creation of the Special Division of the High Court (SDHC), also known as the War Crimes Court (WCC) or War Crimes Division. The SDHC is a product of the Juba peace talks. LRA leader Joseph Kony had informed his delegation

[18] Grave breaches of the 1949 Geneva Conventions had already been criminalized in the Ugandan Geneva Conventions Act (1964).

[19] Ugandan International Criminal Court Act (2010), Art. 19. This chapter uses the term "proceedings" in the meaning of "criminal process," including both investigations and prosecutions.

[20] Not included are those principles that were already part of Ugandan domestic law (most of the *nullum crimen* and *nulla poena sine lege* guarantees) and the principles on the non-applicability of immunities.

[21] Compare Ugandan International Criminal Court Act (2010), Art. 18, with the Ugandan Penal Code Act (1950), Arts. 4 and 5. The Ugandan Geneva Conventions Act (1964), Art. 2, already recognized such broad extraterritorial jurisdiction (even without requiring any link to Uganda) for the grave breaches of the four 1949 Geneva Conventions.

[22] Parliament of the Republic of Uganda, Parliamentary Debates, Hansard Official Report, Wednesday 10 March 2010.

[23] Ibid.

in Juba that he would not sign any agreement if the ICC arrest warrants were not dropped. The only way for the parties to end the ICC's involvement was to challenge admissibility on grounds of complementarity. Both the Ugandan government and the LRA delegation initially took the position that traditional-justice mechanisms could substitute for the ICC.[24] However, over time, the dominant view became that traditional justice would probably not amount to domestic proceedings as envisaged by the ICC's complementarity principle,[25] if only because traditional justice does not include prosecution. The parties agreed that the government would establish a "special division of the High Court" "to try individuals who are alleged to have committed serious crimes during the conflict."[26]

More than two years after the finalization of the Juba peace talks, the chances of Joseph Kony signing the FPA are marginal, but the SDHC is almost up and running. JLOS members presenting the budget for the SDHC argue that the SDHC is for "when" rather than "if" Kony surrenders to Ugandan jurisdiction. Judges, prosecutors, and administrative staff have been assigned, a building has been furnished, budgets have been shared with donors, and senior JLOS officials have visited international(ized) criminal tribunals in The Hague, Bosnia, and Sierra Leone on donor-sponsored study tours. In their view, the SDHC could become a role model for the region, like the Ugandan Commercial Court has become, and could remain operational as a court with jurisdiction over the Great Lakes region.[27]

The SDHC is modeled on the structure of international criminal tribunals. According to the administrative circular, it shall "comprise a bench of at least three judges and a Registry; to which will be attached an OTP [Office of the Prosecutor], and an Office of the Defence Counsel."[28] By reference to the ICC, the International Criminal Tribunal for Rwanda, and the Special Court for Sierra Leone, senior officials in JLOS argue that judges, prosecution, defense, and registry must be part of one court[29] and "under one roof."[30] One of the officials appointed to the WCC explains this mimicry as follows:[31] "If you are driving, you need a driving mirror; the War Crimes Court mirrors the ICC-van."[32] The mirroring goes so far that the

24 Parliament of the Republic of Uganda, Parliamentary Debates, Hansard Official Report, Wednesday 21 February 2007, Statement of the Minister of the Interior; LRA Position Paper on Accountability Truth and Reconciliation in the Context of Alternative Justice System [*sic*] for Resolving the Northern/Eastern Ugandan and Southern Sudan Conflicts, Juba, 19 August 2006: 4.

25 As a prominent Acholi bishop recalled (interview, Kitgum, September 2008), "When we [traditional and religious leaders] were in The Hague, the ICC said that *mato oput* [an Acholi traditional-justice mechanism] is lower than formal justice. They said their benchmarks were higher."

26 Annexure to the Agreement on Accountability and Reconciliation, Juba, 19 February 2008, Clause 7.

27 Meeting of JLOS officials, Kampala, September 2008.

28 Special Division of the High Court of Uganda 2008 Administrative Circular, Clause 2.

29 Meeting of JLOS officials, Kampala, October 2008.

30 Interview with a state attorney, Kampala, September 2008.

31 The term "mimicry" in the legal context is derived from Drumbl (2007: chapter 5).

32 Interview with a person appointed to the WCC, Kampala, September 2008.

proposed WCC budget is long term, given the duration of the cases before the Rwanda Tribunal.[33]

2.3. *Attention to "International Standards"*

There are also modest indications that the ICC's intervention has led to Type III rule of law reform (increasing government compliance with law). The most obvious is the Ugandan authorities' increased attention to international standards. There is a widespread belief among JLOS protagonists that domestic proceedings must meet international standards in relation to the conduct of proceedings and punishments, or even must be like the ICC's for the proceedings to render the ICC's case inadmissible on grounds of complementarity. One senior JLOS official explained this as follows:

> If [the Accountability Agreements are] going to be implemented, complementarity means that there will be two units: one in The Hague and one municipal. These two must not divorce each other. It must be complementary. [The domestic Court] must look like the real thing in The Hague: the benchmarks, the procedure, substantive definitions, what is a war crime, what are massacres, violations of human rights. The Rome Statute has these, ours cannot be different.... We have to be complementary to the ICC, even with sentences, otherwise we have to justify why we differ. If the ICC says 10 years, we cannot say 100 years or 10 days.... Complementary means let us do something they [the ICC] can live with. That is why we are trying to live up to their norms.[34]

The belief that complementarity requires a mirroring of ICC proceedings has also generated greater attention to victim participation and reparations for victims in possible future domestic trials. Ugandan law of criminal proceedings currently does not provide for victim participation with a view to reparations. However, some interlocutors in JLOS now argue that proceedings in the WCC would have to include victim participation and reparations in order to meet the complementarity standard.

The department of prisons also holds a mirror to the ICC. An official in the department stated that he was readying detention facilities that meet "international standards" for the persons sought by the ICC.[35] Some Ugandan actors mention the gym and DVD players in the ICC's detention center in The Hague as representative of "international standards."[36] Another proposes to build "hotels" in Luzira, Kampala's run-down prison, for the Ugandans sought by the ICC.[37]

[33] Meeting of JLOS officials and donors, Kampala, September 2008.
[34] Interview with a senior JLOS official, Kampala, September 2008.
[35] Interview with a senior official in the Ministry of Internal Affairs, Kampala, October 2008.
[36] Interview with a Ugandan government minister, Kampala, October 2008.
[37] Participant observation, official meeting, Kampala, October 2008.

This increased attention given to "international standards" is linked with the ICC's intervention, and in particular with attempts to end it. When domestic proceedings were discussed as an alternative or complement to those of the ICC, Ugandan government ministers, JLOS actors, and judges appointed to the SDHC began to read reports of international nongovernmental organizations (NGOs) on the "benchmarks" that domestic proceedings of international crimes should meet.[38] The Rome Statute, primarily regulating proceedings before the ICC, is relatively silent on domestic proceedings. It provides only that, to render an ICC case inadmissible, domestic proceedings in that case must be genuine. The manifestations of inability and unwillingness that would demonstrate this lack of genuineness are narrowly described.[39] Qualification of crimes, victim participation, reparations for victims, and the quality of detention centers are not part of the definition of inability or unwillingness. However, Ugandan protagonists had hardly studied the Rome Statute when domestic proceedings as an alternative to the ICC were being prepared. This void has been successfully appropriated by international norm entrepreneurs who advocate a human rights agenda far beyond the Rome Statute. Many in the Ugandan government began to refer to the need to comply with "international standards," if not to successfully rely on complementarity, then to secure donor funding.

In sum, if a rule of law promotion practitioner were to be sent to Uganda for monitoring and evaluation, bringing along a checklist of benchmarks and indicators, it is likely she or he would be satisfied. The boxes for a new act, a new court, and more references to international standards can be ticked. However, the picture is murkier when these indicators of rule of law promotion are reviewed from the perspective of the rule of law as a latticework of ideals, and when other dynamics that the ICC has catalyzed in Uganda are considered.

3. THE ICC AND UGANDA THROUGH THE LENS OF RULE OF LAW AS A LATTICEWORK OF IDEALS

3.1. *Reviewing the Rule of Law Promotion Results*

3.1.1. The ICC Act

Uganda's ICC Act could be seen as an instrument that enhances accountability, more specifically, accountability for crimes within the ICC's jurisdiction. Indeed,

[38] See, e.g. Amnesty International, "Uganda: Proposed National Framework to Address Impunity Does Not Remove Government's Obligation to Arrest and Surrender LRA Leaders to the International Criminal Court," 15 August 2007; Human Rights Watch, "Benchmarks for Assessing Possible National Alternatives to International Criminal Court Cases against LRA Leaders," May 2007, accessed 25 February 2008 at http://hrw.org/backgrounder/ij/icc0507/icc0507web.pdf. Also see Human Rights Watch, "Uganda: New Accord Provides for War Crimes Trials; Prosecuting Rights Abusers Will Require Political Will, Legal Reforms," 19 February 2008, accessed 20 February 2008 at http://hrw.org/english/docs/2008/02/19/uganda18094.htm. Further see Keppler (2012, forthcoming: passim).

[39] See Rome Statute, Art. 17.

the Coalition for the International Criminal Court and other "friends" of the ICC have lobbied intensively to convince states to adopt legislation incorporating the Rome Statute crimes into domestic law with a view to combating impunity.

But why would a new act advance accountability if, as in Uganda, the primary cause of impunity is not the absence of legislation? Uganda has had an act criminalizing the grave breaches of the 1949 Geneva Conventions since 1964, but it has never been used, a host of possible violations notwithstanding. Similarly, almost all of the conduct constituting the *actūs rei* of the crimes within the ICC's jurisdiction is criminalized in Ugandan law as ordinary crimes,[40] and yet has not been prosecuted when committed in the context of the conflict in northern Uganda. The cause of impunity in Uganda is more a lack of law enforcement than a lack of laws. Because an absence of legislation has not been the key obstacle to accountability, the adoption of the ICC Act as such does not advance accountability.

The adoption and proposed application of the ICC Act appear to be in tension with other rule of law ideals, for instance the separation and balance of constitutional powers and the principle of legality.

The process by which the ICC Act was adopted formally respected, but substantially undermined, the separation and balance of constitutional powers. Formally, the Ugandan Parliament was in a position to reject and amend the legislation. Substantively, however, there was so much pressure from the executive and international actors on the parliament to adopt this legislation that its adoption was inspired more by this pressure than by any commitment to ending impunity. Whereas in other states ICC legislation was adopted pursuant to, or in preparation for, ratification of the Rome Statute, in Uganda it was spurred by the government's referral of the situation in northern Uganda to the ICC: The OTP required such legislation to facilitate cooperation. For the purpose of facilitating cooperation, it would have sufficed to adopt legislation on cooperation only, but international NGOs recommended and lobbied for legislation that also incorporated the crimes within the ICC's jurisdiction into domestic law. The Ministry of Justice, with influential assistance from the Commonwealth Secretariat, drafted a comprehensive bill on the basis of the Canadian, South African, and New Zealand ICC legislation.[41] After a few months of drafting, the Ugandan ICC Bill was hastily promulgated in May 2004.[42]

40 The Ugandan Penal Code covers almost all of the conduct stated in the ICC arrest warrants against the LRA leaders, with the exception of the enlistment of children. The Ugandan People's Defence Forces Act (2005), Section 52(2)(c) (arguably applicable to the LRA because it applies, according to Art. 119(1)(h), to every person found in unlawful possession of arms), prohibits but does not criminalize, enrollment of persons younger than 18 years of age.

41 E-mail communication with the Department of the First Parliamentary Counsel, Ministry of Justice, Uganda, 3 December 2008; Human Rights Network-Uganda (Hurinet-U), "Analysis of the International Criminal Court Bill (No. 10/2004) in the Context of Uganda's Obligations under the Statute of the International Criminal Court," 17 January 2005, available at http://www.hurinet.or.ug/downloads/Analysis%20of%20the%20ICC%20Bill%20in%20the%20ugandan%20context.pdf.

42 International Criminal Court Bill, XCVII(26), *Uganda Gazette*, 28 May 2004.

In international forums, the executive promised that the bill would soon be adopted.[43] It gave this undertaking to assure the OTP of Uganda's cooperation, but also to be elected to the UN Security Council, and, most of all, to win the bid for hosting the Rome Statute Review Conference in 2010.[44]

Back in Uganda, however, the executive instructed parliament "to go slow" with the ICC Bill.[45] It was thought it would send the wrong message to the Juba peace talks. As it happened, Uganda could cooperate with the ICC, was elected a member of the Security Council, and was chosen to host the Review Conference without having adopted the implementing legislation.

Members of the international criminal justice movement (a loose coalition of mainly Western NGOs and other NGOs funded by Western organizations) organized, with international funding, seminars for parliamentarians and lawyers to keep the legislation on the parliamentary agenda.[46] ICC States Parties told the Ugandan government that it should have its ICC Act adopted before the opening of the ICC Review Conference.[47] In March 2010, three months prior to the commencement of the Review Conference, Ugandan Parliament adopted the ICC Act.[48] JLOS reports:

> As a result the Government of Uganda was able to successfully host the ICC review conference. This could not have been possible since one of the conditions that was set by the ICC to allow the country [to] host the conference was domestication of the Rome statute.[49]

That significant international pressure is brought to bear does not necessarily weaken a parliament's position. In states where democracy is still teething, however, international payment in political or financial perks for the adoption of legislation – whether it concerns the ICC or structural adjustment programs "proposed" by the

43 Khiddu Makubuya, "Uganda's Statement Presented to the Working Group on the Review Conference," Assembly of States Parties, sixth resumed session, New York, 5 June 2008.

44 Ibid. Equally, a senior government representative, asked in an interview in Kampala in October 2008 about the status of the ICC Bill, replied: "We have urged [the legal and parliamentary affairs committee] to consider the Bill as soon as possible." [Interviewer]: *Why?* "Because we are bidding for the 2010 ICC Review Conference. One of the conditions is that we have passed this Bill, even though we should not be put under pressure to pass our own national legislation."

45 Interview with a senior government official, Kampala, October 2008.

46 Interview with former Chairperson of the Legal and Parliamentary Affairs Committee, Kampala, October 2008 and interview with a member of an internationally funded Ugandan NGO, Kampala, September 2008.

47 Uganda's ambassador to the Assembly of States Parties commented on the adoption of the Act a few months before the arrival of the delegates to the Review Conference in Kampala: "It was important to have the bill signed before the review conference took place... [The Assembly of States Parties] wouldn't have cancelled the review conference if it hadn't been, but it was an understanding that we would." See Bill Oketch, "Uganda Set for First War Crimes Trial," Institute for War and Peace Reporting, 14 July 2010.

48 See "MPs Pass ICC Bill," *New Vision*, 10 March 2010.

49 See JLOS, "JLOS Annual Performance Report 2009/2010," September 2010: 65.

International Monetary Fund – makes it difficult for the legislative body not to adopt this (Kleinfeld 2006: 53).

Workshops for parliamentarians organized by international NGOs could enhance, rather than undermine, the critical role of parliament. The Ugandan parliamentary debate on the ICC Act, however, shows a notable confusion between the concepts of, on the one hand, ratification and, on the other, domestication of the ICC Statute, and between Uganda's obligations vis-à-vis the ICC and its obligations to incorporate provisions from the Rome Statute into domestic law.[50] This confusion cannot be attributed to the ICC as such. However, the NGOs that financed, organized, and dominated workshops for Ugandan parliamentarians have not focused on clarifying these matters. Their primary aim is to promote the ICC and other international human rights agendas. Instead of explaining what the Statute actually requires, they explained what, in their view, the Statute *should* require (see also Mégret 2011).

Thus, whereas the Rome Statute requires states to adopt legislation only for cooperation, these NGOs argued that a state *must* domesticate the Rome Statute crimes; whereas the Rome Statute explicitly leaves states to determine the penalties applicable in their domestic proceedings, these NGOs contended that there can be no death penalty for international crimes because the Rome Statute does not apply it (or, countering a reference to Article 80 of the Rome Statute, that donors will not fund any war crimes court with the power to impose the death penalty).[51] Some NGOs come with entire draft ICC Acts, stating that their draft amounts to a "state-of-the-art ICC Act, better than in many western countries."[52] Although the qualification "better" may be correct from the perspective of the NGO's normative agenda, it is not necessarily better from the perspective of the state that would adopt it. Western states may have refrained from adopting such a "state-of-the-art" ICC Act precisely because they balance their interest in a strong ICC with other interests.

Another rule of law aim that may suffer from the ICC Act is the principle of legality, in particular the principle of nonretroactivity. The tension arises as a result of the envisaged application of the ICC Act to crimes committed by the LRA before the adoption of the Act. With the creation of the SDHC, many international advisors have argued that this division should apply the 2010 ICC Act to crimes committed in the conflict between the Ugandan government and the LRA before 2010.

50 See the debate on the ICC Bill, reported in Parliament of the Republic of Uganda, Parliamentary Debates, Hansard Official Report, Wednesday 10 March 2010: 2.56, Minister of State for Justice and Constitutional Affairs, Deputy Attorney-General (Mr Ruhindi): "The purpose of the Bill is to domesticate the statute so that it can be smoothly operationalised in Uganda" and [3.02], the Chairman of the Committee on Legal and Parliamentary Affairs, Mr Tashobya: "the Bill is intended to give the force of law in Uganda to the Rome Statute." See also the quote from the JLOS report given earlier.

51 Of course, NGOs have very legitimate reasons to advocate against the death penalty, but it is misleading to argue in a workshop on the ICC that the Rome Statute prohibits states from applying the death penalty.

52 Discussion with the Director of an American NGO, Amsterdam, June 2009.

The Ugandan constitution provides that "No person shall be charged with or convicted of a criminal offence which is founded on an act or omission that did not at the time it took place constitute a criminal offence."[53] It has been argued that this does not prevent application of the proposed ICC Act:

> The Constitution does not say "constitute a criminal offence under Ugandan law," but leaves it open whether it is restricted to domestic legislation or not. These acts did constitute criminal offences under international law, which is a law binding also on Uganda. Hence, under this reading, there is no obstacle to introducing new legislation which criminalises acts under domestic law that have already been criminalised under international law.[54]

In a state with a dualist approach toward the international order, however, the words in the constitutional provision "constitute a criminal offence" must read "a criminal offence under Ugandan law" (and not, for instance, foreign law), unless the Constitution would make an explicit exception for crimes pursuant to international law, in accordance with Article 15(2) of the International Covenant on Civil and Political Rights, which it does not.

A better way to reconcile the constitutional prohibition against retroactivity with the application of the ICC Act to crimes that have already been committed is to distinguish between "act" and "offence." Wrange has convincingly argued that

> the constitution provides that "[n]o person shall be charged with or convicted of a criminal offence which is founded on an act or omission that did not at the time it took place constitute a criminal offence." Hence, it is not prohibited to introduce new crimes with retroactive application, as long as the acts or omissions in question were criminal at the time of commission. Otherwise the Constitution would have said "[n]o person shall be charged with or convicted of a criminal offence, which is founded on an act or omission that did not at the time it took place constitute that criminal offence."[55]

No matter how this legal question is answered, it should be answered in accordance with constitutional procedures, first by the Ugandan Parliament and, if this is appealed, by the Constitutional Court. International advisors, however, in workshops

53 Constitution of the Republic of Uganda (1995), Art. 28(7).

54 See P. Wrange, "The ICC Bill, Complementarity and 'Retroactivity,'" 30 September 2008, on file with author.

55 Ibid. The argument that, if not the ICC Act, the 1964 Geneva Conventions Act must be applied to prosecute offenses committed during the entire period of the conflict between the LRA and the Ugandan government is also problematic from a legality perspective. The Geneva Conventions Act criminalizes "grave breaches" of the Geneva Conventions, which exist in the context of international armed conflicts only, whereas the conflict between the LRA and the Ugandan government has not at all times been a conflict of an international character. Although sociologically the distinction between international and non-international armed conflicts may no longer be useful, the denial of this distinction in criminal proceedings violates the rule of law element of legality, according to which criminal law shall not be interpreted expansively or *per analogiam*.

lobbying parliamentarians to adopt the ICC Act, have attached more importance to Uganda's prosecuting international crimes in accordance with the ICC Act than to the constitutional procedures being respected.[56]

This prioritization of the Rome Statute to constitutional procedures is all the more noteworthy because the Rome Statute does not oblige states to prosecute the crimes within the Statute. Even for a successful challenge of complementarity it is not necessary to prosecute genocide, crimes against humanity, or war crimes eo nomine. In other words, even if the purpose of Ugandan proceedings is to render the ICC's case against the LRA leaders inadmissible on grounds of complementarity, neither retroactive nor retrospective application of the ICC Act is required – to the extent that all the *conduct* charged by the OTP is covered by Ugandan law, the domestic court could apply its ordinary penal law.[57] However, after several workshops and discussions with so-called international experts, many parliamentarians as well as JLOS officials believe that if Uganda does not charge the conduct in terms corresponding to the crimes provided for in the Rome Statute, the gravity of the offenses will not be accurately reflected and the complementarity criteria not met.[58]

International experts' preference for "international" courts, crimes, and standards can be explained by their background. Most of these experts work at the international level, in international NGOs, courts, and jurisdictions, and have assumed a functional bias toward the international.[59] Their automatic but incorrect assumption is that international laws, standards, courts, and practices are by definition better than domestic ones and that the international is by definition good for the rule of law, at the international *and* the domestic level.

3.1.2. The SDHC

The assumption that the creation of the SDHC by definition promotes the aims of the rule of law is challengeable on a similar ground. The creation of a court, like the adoption of the ICC Act, may seem to enhance accountability. However, the primary cause of impunity in northern Uganda has been a lack of investigations, prosecutions, and arrests, rather than an absence of courts with jurisdiction. The creation of the SDHC has not altered this. The SDHC has investigators, prosecutors, and judges assigned to it, but to date the judges have more actively pursued their work than the investigators and prosecutors. These investigators and prosecutors argue that it

56 Author's participant observation of the symposium "Challenges and Prospects," Entebbe, 5 and 6 September 2008.

57 Compare Rome Statute, Art. 20(3) with Art. 20(2).

58 As was apparent during author's participant observation at the symposium "Challenges and Prospects," Entebbe, 5 and 6 September 2008; and at an official meeting, Kampala, October 2008; and in an interview with JLOS officials, Kampala, October 2008. See also Otim and Wierda (2008: 24–25).

59 On such biases, see Koskenniemi (2005, 600–615).

would be a waste of time and resources to start building cases against persons who may never be arrested.[60]

3.1.3. References to International Standards

Finally, the increased attention paid to "international standards" does not necessarily mean that these standards have "infiltrated" and will be complied with. So experienced at drafting project proposals that at one stage 50 percent of the national budget was externally funded, the Ugandan government knows which jargon is music to the ears of international donors. Once the money has been collected, however, programs are often not implemented in accordance with their purpose, or indeed are implemented contrary to their purpose.[61]

In sum, although laws, courts, and references to international standards are common indicators of rule of law promotion, the ICC's visible results in Uganda (the ICC Act, SDHC, and "international standards" fetishism) do not necessarily enhance (one of) the aims of the rule of law; indeed, they have sometimes been incompatible with some of these aims.

3.2. *Rule of Law Dynamics Catalyzed by the ICC's Intervention in Uganda*

The ICC's intervention in Uganda has catalyzed other developments that are worth considering from the perspective of the rule of law as a latticework of ideals.

3.2.1. Supremacy of Law: A Legal Dimension to the Conflict Paradigm

The expansion of the Ugandan paradigm of the conflict in the north has been the most important contribution of the ICC's intervention in Uganda to the aims of the rule of law. The ICC's intervention and particularly attempts to end it have replaced the until then dominant paradigm that *inter arma leges silent* with a paradigm in which law, in addition to politics and armed force, has a role to play in armed conflict. Even though law is still not considered supreme, the ICC has in this way contributed to the ideal of the supremacy of law.

Before the ICC's involvement, Ugandan officials considered the conflict between the Ugandan government and the LRA an almost exclusively military and at times political issue. The military would work on "neutralizing" the LRA, while religious leaders, civil society actors, and politicians were permitted to attempt to negotiate a peace deal. The Ugandan Police Force, the Office of the Director of Public

[60] Interviews with police investigators and prosecutors, Gulu, September 2008 and Kampala, October 2008 and June 2010.

[61] See, e.g., Omach (2009) on how Uganda received British financial support for programs to reduce its military, but in fact used the programs to expand militarization and "shed off" soldiers who had been integrated into the UPDF from rival armed groups.

Prosecutions (DPP), the Judiciary, or the JLOS did not consider the conflict as within their remit. To the extent that law was involved by means of the Amnesty Act 2000, it was to exclude legal accountability, and hence curtailed the role of the law and of lawyers.[62]

Paradoxically, when in December 2003 the Ugandan government referred "the situation concerning the Lord's Resistance Army" to the ICC,[63] this seemingly judicial move emerged from the prevailing military-political paradigm. The referral could, so it was thought, rally international assistance for the arrest of the government's long-term military opponents and give the government an alternative to declaring war on the Government of Sudan, which it accused of supporting the LRA.[64] The ICC's legal and the Ministry of Defence's military approaches shared the avowed aim of catching the LRA, the former with a view to legal proceedings, the latter in order to defeat the enemy. More than the rule of law, it was law and order that the Ugandan government sought to obtain through the referral.

Although the referral itself fit within the purely military-political paradigm, the subsequent exploration of options to end the ICC's involvement imposed a legal perspective on the Ugandan approach to the conflict with the LRA. This perspective came to the fore only during the Juba peace talks. LRA leader Joseph Kony had informed his delegation that he would not sign any agreement if the arrest warrants that the ICC had issued against him and four other commanders were not lifted. The only sustainable way to end the ICC's involvement in northern Uganda was to challenge admissibility on grounds of complementarity. In Juba, the Ugandan government and LRA thus agreed on Ugandan investigations and prosecutions of serious crimes. Whether the Ugandan government had intended this or not, the involvement of the ICC meant that the quest for resolution of the conflict with the LRA could no longer exclude legal accountability.

The involvement of international legal machinery has, in turn, awoken the domestic legal sector. Before the referral, most Ugandan legal professionals had never considered the LRA as within their remit: It was a military, and, at times, political issue, but not a legal matter. However, during and after the Juba peace talks, Ugandan lawyers became relevant as alternative actors to the ICC. Some key figures in the Ugandan legal scene have seen the space opened up as an opportunity to participate in international advocacy meetings on the ICC, to strengthen the position of JLOS in the administration, to advance their own institution within JLOS, and to acquire

62 In the first years of its existence, the Amnesty Commission did not participate in JLOS meetings. It was considered a commission concerned with military issues (namely demobilization), rather than legal matters.

63 See ICC, "President of Uganda Refers Situation Concerning the Lord's Resistance Army (LRA) to the ICC," 29 January 2004, accessed 29 January 2008 at http://www.icc-cpi.int/press/pressreleases/16.html.

64 Interview with a Ugandan government minister, Kampala, October 2008 and an interview with another Ugandan government minister, Kampala, October 2008. Also see "Uganda: Interview with President Yoweri Museveni," *IRIN*, 9 June 2005.

prestige among national and international colleagues. They have pushed for the adoption of the ICC Act and for the establishment of the SDHC, and are searching cases for the SDHC.

The effect on the domestic approach to the conflict in the north and on the legal sector has to date been professionally and geographically limited, and it may be only temporary. Professionally, this effect has been stronger on the Judiciary, Uganda Law Reform Commission, and JLOS Secretariat than on the police and Office of the DPP. Some in the latter group do recognize the legal dimension to the conflict, but not their own potential role, when they argue that "the ICC now deals with the matter."[65] Particularly those who have assisted the ICC in their investigations in Uganda argue that conflict-related crimes in northern Uganda now "belong to" their "colleagues" at the ICC. They are relieved that they do not have to enter the political minefield, and they look up to ICC staff as more advanced colleagues.[66] Their approach to the conflict in the north has thus expanded to encompass a legal dimension, according to which justice has a role to play, but in their view this role is to be played by the ICC rather than by domestic actors. Geographically, the expansion of the paradigm remains limited in that most law enforcement officials outside Kampala still do not see any role for themselves in conflict-related criminal proceedings. They refer to the army,[67] the SDHC,[68] the ICC,[69] or traditional leaders[70] as more relevant actors and to the applicability of the Amnesty Act[71] as an impediment to successful completion of proceedings. Finally, the inclusion of a legal approach to the conflict may be only temporary, because the Ugandan government's actions in this area have been based primarily on a cost–benefit assessment of political and military interests, rather than on a belief that it is legally obliged or diplomatically compelled to prosecute international crimes domestically. If other options, such as militarily defeating the LRA, providing an amnesty,[72] or handing over the LRA leadership to the ICC,[73] promise to be more convenient, the Ugandan government

65 Discussion with police at the Criminal Investigations Department, Gulu, September 2008.
66 Interview with senior officials of the Criminal Investigations Department, Kampala, October 2008.
67 Discussion with police at the Criminal Investigations Department, Gulu, September 2008.
68 Interview with a senior police officer, Kitgum, September 2008.
69 Discussion with police at the Criminal Investigations Department, Gulu, September 2008.
70 Interview with a senior police officer, Gulu, September 2008.
71 Ibid.
72 In response to rumors that two LRA commanders sought by the ICC were willing to surrender, Museveni repeated the offer of amnesty; see "Odhiambo Won't Face World Court," *New Vision*, 10 February 2009. See also the view expressed in an interview with a senior Ugandan government representative, Voorburg, April 2008: "We [in the GoU] have always said that *we* were willing to give amnesty."
73 In an interview with a Ugandan government minister, Kampala, October 2008, when asked where Kony would go if he were arrested without having signed the FPA, the minister replied, "Why waste our time? We [the GoU] can send him to The Hague. This is the kind of punishment that he does not want."

may simply discard its newfound commitment to domestic legal accountability and leave lawyers without a role to play.[74]

No matter how fragile, the awareness that law has a role to play in armed conflict is revolutionary in Uganda. In advancing this idea, the ICC has advanced a prerequisite for the idea of the supremacy of law, which in turn is a fundamental tenet of the concept of the rule of law.

3.2.2. Accountability to the Law: The Beginning of a Debate

Beyond enhancing the idea of *applicability* of law, the ICC's intervention has also spurred a debate on *accountability* to laws. As a result of the ICC's intervention, it became, paradoxically, in the LRA's interest to insist on accountability – domestic accountability. Amnesty under Ugandan law would not invalidate the ICC arrest warrants. Domestic accountability, however, could be the basis for a successful challenge of the admissibility of the ICC's case. Taking the offensive, the LRA delegation to the Juba peace talks focused not merely on its own accountability but also on the government's, and it insisted on a truth commission, traditional justice, and reparations. The result of the negotiations is a package of transitional-justice mechanisms that is unprecedented in Uganda's transition-rich history. The Juba Agreement on Accountability and the Annexure provide for prosecutions, a body to investigate the past, traditional justice, and reparations; previous peace agreements with other rebel movements had provided only for the transitional-justice mechanism of amnesty, be it de jure or de facto.

Joseph Kony may have refused to sign the FPA that consolidates all agreements reached in Juba, but this has not prevented the Ugandan debate on issues of transitional justice from continuing and expanding. Already before the ICC's intervention, grassroots civil society organizations had been advocating the need for the country to examine its past of human rights violations with a view to reconciliation. However, it was only when the Juba peace talks indicated the need for a domestic alternative to the ICC that the Ugandan government co-opted this agenda, at least rhetorically. Adopting concepts used by international advisors to the peace talks, JLOS created its own Transitional Justice Working Group with subcommittees on formal proceedings, traditional justice, truth telling, integration of the different systems, and the budget. International consultants have flown into Entebbe to advise and "workshop" JLOS and grassroots civil society organizations on what transitional justice encompasses. The efforts of these and domestic norm entrepreneurs have been successful: "TJ" is in vogue. The term's nebulousness, catering as it does to

74 Moreover, what the Ugandan government considers as the legal approach is rather flexible. Interlocutors in the government did not consider the army's killing in 2005 of one of the persons sought by the ICC inconsistent with the legal approach. They argued that it served the same purpose as the arrest warrant and were strengthened in their view by the silence of the ICC in response to the killing (interview with a senior government official, Kampala, October 2008).

diverging (mis)understandings,[75] has allowed everyone to embrace it, while Western donors' interest provides financial incentives not to let go of it. The first person accused of conflict-related crimes is yet to be tried in Uganda, but, in a country characterized by transitions without justice, the discussion of issues of transitional justice in general and of accountability in particular is of itself a revolutionary step toward accountability to law and thus the rule of law.

3.2.3. Entrenching Inequality before the Law

Less positive from the perspective of the ideals of the rule of law is the fact that the ICC seems to have entrenched inequality before the law in Uganda. When the ICC Prosecutor announced that the Ugandan government had referred "the situation concerning the Lord's Resistance Army," NGOs were quick to point out that the referral "concerning the LRA" should not limit the Court's personal jurisdiction to the LRA; the ICC should equally investigate crimes allegedly committed by state actors, in particular the Ugandan Peoples' Defence Forces (UPDF).[76] In response, the OTP changed the name of the situation to "situation concerning northern Uganda" or "situation concerning Uganda."

In practice, however, the OTP has not (yet) opened an investigation into the UPDF. The OTP's primary justification of its decision to start with an investigation of LRA members has been that the LRA's crimes were graver than those committed by the UPDF.[77] Arguably, however, a state's involvement in the commission of crimes against civilians is an independent and sufficient indication of gravity, because of the high risk of impunity for such crimes (see also Schabas 2008: 748). A more pragmatic explanation for the OTP's (hitherto) refraining from opening an investigation into the UPDF can be found in its dependence on cooperation of the Ugandan government for its case against the LRA – had the OTP antagonized the

75 Although transitional justice is generally understood as "the full range of processes and mechanisms associated with a society's attempts to come to terms with a legacy of large-scale past abuses, in order to ensure accountability, serve justice and achieve reconciliation" (Report of the Secretary-General on the Rule of Law and Transitional Justice in Conflict and Post-Conflict Societies: 8), a key actor in the eponymous JLOS working group understood transitional justice to refer to justice involving short punishments (interview, Kampala, September 2008).

76 Amnesty International, "Uganda: First Steps to Investigate Crimes Must Be Part of Comprehensive Plan to End Impunity," 30 January 2004, accessed 30 January 2008 at http://www.amnesty.org/en/alfresco_asset/573bd86a-a3b5–11dc-9d08-f145a8145d2b/afr590012004en.pdf. Also see Human Rights Watch, "ICC: Investigate All Sides in Uganda," 4 February 2004, accessed 30 January 2008 at http://hrw.org/english/docs/2004/02/04/uganda7264.htm; International Crisis Group, "Northern Uganda: Understanding and Solving the Conflict," 14 April 2004, accessed 31 January 2008 at http://www.up.ligi.ubc.ca/ICGreport.pdf: 20.

77 See Statement by Luis Moreno-Ocampo, "Statement on the Uganda Arrest Warrants," The Hague, 14 October 2005, available at http://www.icc-cpi.int/library/organs/otp/speeches/LMO_20051014_English.pdf: 2; Statement by Luis Moreno-Ocampo, "Statement to the Fourth Session of the Assembly of States Parties," The Hague, 28 November 2005, available at http://www.icc-cpi.int/library/cases/ICC-02–04–01–05–67_English.pdf: 2.

Ugandan government by investigating and prosecuting its members or subordinates, chances would have been slim that Uganda would cooperate in the ICC's case against the LRA in the way it has, ranging from providing visas to handing over military intelligence, from accompanying the OTP on investigation missions to, ultimately, chasing the LRA in order to execute ICC arrest warrants.

As a consequence, state officials in Kampala as well as Acholi have seen the ICC as an extension of the executive's instrumentation, rather than an independent court that enforces the law equally. The Ugandan Minister of Defence has guaranteed the Ugandan Parliament that "the number of people to be handled by the ICC does not exceed five,"[78] revealing the government's confidence in its having a firm grip on ICC proceedings. When asked about the absence of plans for domestic proceedings against high UPDF officers for crimes committed on a widespread or systematic scale, army officials feel vindicated by the absence of ICC proceedings and argue that "even the ICC has not found anything."[79] Ugandan officials refer to headlines in a national newspaper that announced that the ICC had "cleared" the UPDF.[80] The article quotes an ICC outreach official to the effect that "the Prosecutor said there was evidence against Kony and not against the UPDF commanders."[81] For the Acholi, the impression of the ICC as Museveni's marionette has been one of the reasons to respond negatively to the ICC's intervention. To many of them, the ICC's selective justice amounts to injustice.[82]

This scenario, also visible in other ICC situation countries (Nouwen and Werner 2010), raises the question of whether a prosecutor who is dependent on the cooperation of one side in a conflict is ever able to enforce the law equally. By not correcting the domestic practice of inequality before the law, the ICC seems to legitimize a violation of a fundamental tenet of the rule of law.

3.2.4. Affecting the Separation of Powers and Discouraging Participation in Decision Making

The ICC's intervention in Uganda has been attended by a strengthening of the executive's position with respect to the legislative and has discouraged the latter's participation in decision making. This has happened in several ways. First, there are strong arguments for the view that the Ugandan executive, representing the state that referred the situation in northern Uganda to the ICC, ratified the Rome Statute in contravention of Ugandan law. In Ugandan law, the executive ratifies treaties, but the Attorney-General must submit a treaty to parliament if ratification requires

78 Statement of the Ugandan Defence Minister Mbabazi, Hansard Official Report, Thursday, 29 July 2004.

79 Interview with a UPDF officer, Kampala, October 2008. See also Lt. Col. Felix Kulayigye, "Otunnu's Notion of Genocide in the North Very Absurd," *The Monitor*, 4 September 2009.

80 Participatory Action Research Focus Group, Gulu, September 2008.

81 A. Mugisa and H. Nsambu, "ICC Clears UPDF in the North," *Saturday Vision*, 30 August 2008.

82 See, *inter plurima alia*, Ogola (2010).

constitutional amendment.[83] The Rome Statute was never submitted to the Ugandan Parliament, even though its ratification may have required amendment of the Ugandan constitution. Some lawyers have raised the alleged unconstitutionality of the ratification in a petition to the Constitutional Court,[84] but the case was discontinued allegedly because of a lack of interest on the side of the petitioners. In fact, the petitioners wished to continue the case despite intimidation, but they did not appear in court on the day of the hearing because they had been made to believe that the Attorney-General would again fail to appear.[85]

A second example of the executive strengthening its position to the detriment of the legislative is the way in which it used the ICC to bypass an act of parliament. In 2000, the Ugandan Parliament adopted an Amnesty Act for persons who had committed crimes during rebellion against the government. President Museveni had wished to exclude the LRA leadership, but Parliament amended the bill into an almost blanket amnesty. By referring the situation to the ICC, an international institution not bound by domestic law, the executive effectively bypassed Parliament and had it its own way.

The government not only undermined the value of the Amnesty Act, it also tried to amend the Act without revealing its motivation. In December 2003, a week after the referral, which at the time was still confidential, the executive announced an Amendment Bill to exclude "leaders of rebellion" as beneficiaries of the amnesty.[86]

In all these areas, parliament could theoretically have opposed the executive's moves; in practice it was hardly aware of what was happening. It was only when the impact of the ICC arrest warrants on the peace process was felt that parliamentarians began to express an interest in the ICC.

3.2.5. Unfairness and Legal Uncertainty

The plans for Ugandan prosecution of LRA members have called into question the legal status of more than 26,000 amnesties granted in accordance with the

[83] Ugandan Ratification of Treaties Act (1998), Section 2.

[84] *John Magezi, Judy Obitre-Gama, Henry Onoria versus Attorney-General*, Constitutional Court (Uganda), Constitutional Petition No. 10, 27 July 2005. The petitioners mentioned four aspects of the Rome Statute that required constitutional amendment. First, the non-applicability of immunities before the Court undermined the president's constitutional immunities. Second, the ICC could retry persons who have been convicted or acquitted in Uganda. Third, the ICC does not respect national pardons, whereas the Ugandan constitution protects them. Finally, Uganda's cooperation with the ICC could violate the right to protection against self-incrimination if Uganda handed over information obtained from persons seeking or benefiting from an amnesty in accordance with the Amnesty Act 2000.

[85] Interview with a person involved in the challenge, Kampala, October 2008.

[86] Ugandan Amnesty (Amendment) Bill (2003). The link between the bill and the referral to the ICC was disclosed only when the ICC press statement announcing the referral publicized: "In a bid to encourage members of the LRA to return to normal life, the Ugandan authorities have enacted an amnesty law. President Museveni has indicated to the Prosecutor his intention to amend this amnesty so as to exclude the leadership of the LRA, ensuring that those bearing the greatest responsibility for the crimes against humanity committed in Northern Uganda are brought to justice."

2000 Amnesty Act, thereby undermining legal certainty and affecting fairness. Legal certainty and fairness as ideals of the rule of law have different meanings in different legal orders, but no matter under which banner, rule of law includes the protection of legitimate expectations and against material retroactivity.[87]

Although the Amnesty Act is still valid, the adoption of the ICC Act has in practice rendered its effect uncertain. This has come to the fore in the case of Thomas Kwoyelo, a senior LRA member who was arrested in a military operation in the Democratic Republic of the Congo in 2009. Kwoyelo was not given an opportunity to apply for amnesty until he had been charged with, among others, kidnapping with intent to murder. The Amnesty Act gives the right to apply for amnesty also to a person charged with crimes, but the DPP must then declare that the person has not been charged with crimes that do not fall under the scope of the act.[88] To date, the DPP has not given such a declaration with respect to Kwoyelo, and hence the Amnesty Commission has not been able to grant his request for amnesty. Instead, Kwoyelo has been committed to be tried by the SDHC.[89]

Legally, there is no apparent reason why Kwoyelo would not be entitled to benefit from the still-applicable Amnesty Act. Persons involved in his prosecution have at different times provided different justifications, illustrating legal uncertainty. A government minister initially explained that Kwoyelo did not qualify for amnesty because he had been arrested before he applied for amnesty.[90] This explanation fails to convince, because the Amnesty Act provides for application for amnesty by detained persons.[91] A prosecutor managing his case argued for his part that the Amnesty Act did not apply because Kwoyelo had been charged with crimes other than "crimes against the state."[92] Bearing in mind the text of the Amnesty Act,[93] this can constitute an explanation only if it is interpreted to mean that Kwoyelo's crimes were not committed "in the cause of" the conflict. Although difficult to maintain,

87 Material retroactivity means the application of a legislative measure to the effects in the future of a situation that has arisen under a former law.

88 Ugandan Amnesty Act (2000), Section 3(3).

89 See Edward Anyoli, "Former LRA Commander Sent to War Court," *New Vision*, 6 September 2010.

90 Discussion with a Ugandan government minister, The Hague, September 2009.

91 Ugandan Amnesty Act (2000), Section 3(2).

92 Telephone interview with a state attorney, September 2009.

93 The 2000 Amnesty Act, Section 2, provides (emphases added):

> (1) An amnesty is declared in respect of any Ugandan who has at any time since the 26th day of January, 1986, engaged in or is engaging in war or armed rebellion against the government of the Republic of Uganda by–
> (a) actual participation in combat;
> (b) collaborating with the perpetrators of the war or armed rebellion;
> (c) committing any other crime *in the furtherance of* the war or armed rebellion; or
> (d) assisting or aiding the conduct or prosecution of the war or armed rebellion.
>
> (2) A person referred to under subsection (1) shall not be prosecuted or subjected to any form of punishment for the participation in the war or rebellion for any crime committed *in the cause of* the war or armed rebellion.

because kidnapping has been one of the main tactics of the LRA rebellion, the position would indicate a revolutionary reinterpretation of the Amnesty Act: In no other case has the DPP argued that crimes committed by an LRA member while part of the rebellion were not covered by the Amnesty Act. One year earlier, the DPP was still explaining the fact that proceedings against members of the LRA were seldom initiated by arguing the exact opposite: that they could *always* invoke the Amnesty Act.[94] Finally, a prosecutor in the team responsible for cases before the SDHC explained that Kwoyelo cannot be granted amnesty now that the ICC Act has been adopted. The ICC Act is silent on amnesties and is, like any other penal code, not by definition incompatible with an Amnesty Act. However, the argument is this: "The framers of the Amnesty Act did not have the ICC Act on the back of their minds. The ICC Act frowns upon immunity. Even constitutional guarantees of immunity may not apply."[95] The interviewed prosecutor argues that the Amnesty Act must be reinterpreted as not to apply to international crimes. This argument founders because the ICC Act has turned international crimes into crimes pursuant to Ugandan law (moreover, if this reasoning is adopted, Kwoyelo would have to be recharged under the ICC Act; he was initially charged with ordinary crimes).

To date the prosecution of Kwoyelo appears to be a one-off case, prompted by opportunism rather than law: Kwoyelo is disliked by the ruling party; Kwoyelo, as a Ugandan "Tadić," can satisfy the SDHC's institutional craving for a first case; and during the ICC Review Conference in Kampala the preparations for his case served to demonstrate the host country's domestic commitment to international justice. As a prosecutor interviewed in Kampala in June 2010 explained, "The DPP has little room to maneuver. Legally, Kwoyelo would qualify for amnesty. Politically, as a country that has committed to the ICC, we must give an example. We don't have a single case before the War Crimes Court. If he gets amnesty it pulls the carpet under our feet and we shall have nobody." With the conference successfully concluded, the pressure is off. In the words of the interviewed prosecutor, "The ICC Review Conference put Uganda in the spot light. Then it is not good to grant an amnesty. Now that we are done with the ICC review conference,"[96] law could prevail over opportunism. A staff member of the Amnesty Commission concurs: Only in "practice, not in law, the Amnesty Act is subjected to the ICC Act."[97]

However, if the Kwoyelo case were to reveal a change in policy, the reinterpretation of the Amnesty Act would violate legitimate expectations. As the interviewed prosecutor acknowledges, in "theory, everybody [i.e., more than 26,000 persons] who has received amnesty could be prosecuted."[98] The ensuing legal uncertainty

94 Interview with the Director of Public Prosecutions, Kampala, October 2008.

95 Interview with a prosecutor involved in the SDHC, Kampala, June 2010. The term "immunity" is used as synonym for "impunity."

96 Interview with a prosecutor involved in the Kwoyelo case, Kampala, June 2010.

97 Interview with a staff member of the Amnesty Commission, Kampala, May 2010.

98 Interview with a prosecutor involved in the Kwoyelo case, Kampala, June 2010.

could be costly. Joseph Kony's refusal to sign the FPA illustrates the price of legal uncertainty. One of his stated reasons for refusing to sign is that he cannot rely on an agreement with the government because such agreements have not saved former Liberian President Charles Taylor from the Special Court for Sierra Leone or Congolese warlord Thomas Lubanga from the ICC. The message has been given that national promises are not worth much in the presence of hovering international courts. Amnesties are hard to reconcile with the accountability element of the rule of law, but disrespecting granted amnesties violates the principle that promises must be kept, which is another fundamental tenet of the rule of law.

3.2.6. Distraction from More Structural, Real Rule of Law Problems

Finally, the international community's myopic focus on the importance of the prosecution of international crimes has distracted attention from more structural rule of law problems in Uganda. While human rights NGOs and donors are busy advising on the new SDHC, the executive continues to use trials to eliminate political foes and fails to give effect to the decisions of the National Human Rights Commission or to implement the recommendations of committees of inquiry according to which senior politicians of the leading party should be prosecuted on counts of corruption.

Worse still, the focus on the prosecution of international crimes deflects attention even from the issue it claims to address: impunity. Impunity in northern Uganda goes far beyond international crimes – until recently, there were hardly any civilian police, prosecutors, or judges in northern Uganda to investigate and prosecute *any* crime. JLOS and international donors have begun to enhance general access to justice in the north, but ever since the idea of an SDHC emerged, agendas, budgets, and attention have been disproportionally tilted toward the functioning of that internationally newsworthy court. Donor agencies from states that are not parties to the Rome Statute have in interviews expressed their reservations about this hype:

> Our concern is that this will affect a very limited group of people and not on the long term. From an international law perspective it is important to get the ICC away, but it is not important from a widespread community level, with which we prefer to work. . . . Why this Special Division [of the High Court] if access to justice in general is so poor in Uganda? . . . It would be a sacrifice of standard justice for special justice.[99]

Whereas Ugandan lawyers working on the SDHC, or the equally donor-driven special Anti-Corruption Court for that matter, see the Court as an opportunity to specialize in an internationally relevant topic, other prosecutors, judges, and clerks fear, like the quoted donor representative, that special courts will undermine the

[99] Interview with an official of a foreign development agency, Kampala, October 2008.

capacity of the ordinary criminal justice system.[100] The risk is that, in mimicking the international focus on ending impunity through "special" justice for those bearing the "greatest responsibility" for war crimes, crimes against humanity, and genocide, the domestic justice system, like the international, turns a blind eye to wider and more structural rule of law problems.[101]

4. CONCLUSION

If one thing is clear from this case study, it is that the relationship between the ICC and the rule of law is more complex than the statements in the opening paragraph acknowledge. Focusing on the relationship between the ICC and rule of law dynamics within Uganda, this chapter has argued that one's evaluation of that relationship depends on one's approach to the rule of law. Seen through the instrument-oriented definition that dominates the field of rule of law promotion, the evaluation can be positive: The ICC's intervention in Uganda led to a new act, a new court, and more references to international standards. It was in this vein that the Ugandan representative in a UN Security Council debate on the rule of law invoked Uganda's ICC Act and the SDHC as evidence of Uganda's "institutionalising the rule of law."[102]

However, as this chapter has illustrated, these instruments do not necessarily promote the aims of the rule of law. In Uganda, a new act and a new court would contribute to addressing impunity if the causes of impunity were a lack of legislation and courts. But they are not.

[100] Interview with a state attorney, Kitgum, September 2008, interview with a judge, Gulu, September 2008, interview with a registrar, Kampala, September 2008.

[101] Citing preambular recitals, the OTP argued in *Prosecutor v. Joseph Kony, Vincent Otti, Raska Lukwiya, Okot Odhiambo and Dominic Ongwen*, Submission of Information on the Status of the Warrants of Arrest in Uganda, International Criminal Court, ICC-02/04–01/05–116, OTP, 6 October 2006: 4 that "lasting peace requires that there be no impunity for crimes of concern to the international community as a whole," suggesting, a contrario, that impunity for crimes with which the international community is not concerned does not affect "lasting peace." For a similar suggestion see ICC, Pre Trial Chamber II, "Situation in the Republic of Kenya, Decision Pursuant to Article 15 of the Rome Statute on the Authorization of an Investigation into the Situation in the Republic of Kenya." See also the dissenting opinion of Judge Hans-Peter Kaul, 31 March 2010, ICC-01/09–19: 8: "As a Judge of the International Criminal Court . . . I would like to ask all in the Republic of Kenya who yearn for justice and who support the intervention of the Court in this country for understanding [sic] the following: there are, in law and in the existing systems of criminal justice in this world, essentially two different categories of crimes which are crucial in the present case. There are, on the one side, international crimes of concern to the international community as a whole, in particular genocide, crimes against humanity and war crimes pursuant to articles 6, 7, and 8 of the Statute. There are, on the other side, common crimes, albeit of a serious nature, prosecuted by national criminal justice systems, such as that of the Republic of Kenya."

[102] Security Council Debate on the Promotion and Strengthening of the Rule of Law in the Maintenance of International Peace and Security, 29 June 2010, UN Doc. S/PV.6347: 11, Mr Rugunda.

If one instead understands the rule of law as a latticework of ideals, the findings are as mixed a bag as the definition of rule of law itself (see also Kleinfeld 2006: 59). The ICC's intervention has unleashed dynamics in Uganda that are in synergy with some aims of the rule of law (supremacy of law and accountability), while in tension with others (equality before the law, separation of powers, fairness, and legal certainty).

Many of these rule of law dynamics have not been brought about by the ICC alone. Contrary to what some advocates say it should be doing, the ICC has refrained from engaging in rule of law promotion activities, for instance "capacity building," in Uganda. Rather, the ICC's involvement has triggered the attention of, and created space for, organizations with normative agendas. Local organizations used the national controversy around the ICC to push for transitional justice in Uganda. International NGOs, in turn, sought and built alliances with Ugandan organizations, which they supported financially in exchange for promotion of their agenda on transitional justice or, more specifically, international criminal justice.

However, hardly any of these norm entrepreneurs aimed at promoting the rule of law in its broad definition. Rather, they emphasized the importance of one element of the rule of law: accountability to law. In fact, their focus was more on the preferred means, namely the ICC regime, than on the aim of accountability itself. For these norm entrepreneurs, the ICC regime is an end in itself and an end that is so important that its pursuit justifies almost all means, even downplaying constitutional provisions.

If it is genuinely desired to enhance synergies and reduce tensions between the ICC's operations and the promotion of the rule of law in the states in which it intervenes, a first prerequisite would be to drop the assumption that ICC intervention by definition enhances the rule of law at the domestic level. A second prerequisite would be to shift the focus from instruments to aims: Rather than assuming that an ICC Act and a new court will address impunity, the first question must be what the real causes of impunity are in the situation concerned. The next question must be how in the situation concerned such impunity is best addressed. Finally, it must be recognized that the promotion of an ideal that in itself contains several ideals may result in the promotion of some ideals to the detriment of others, at least in the short term. This recognition is no apology. It does make the procedure by which rule of law ideals are prioritized all the more important. Because the rule of law is a latticework of ideals that will never be secured if not continuously pursued, the pursuit itself should respect the values embodied in the ideal.

Conclusion

From Rule of Law Promotion to Rule of Law Dynamics

Randall Peerenboom, Michael Zürn, and André Nollkaemper

Rule of law promotion is a dynamic field. There have been significant changes over time in content, strategies, programming, and funding priorities of rule of law promoters (Jensen 2003; Hammergren and Gillespie, this volume). The original law and development movement in the 1960s and 1970s believed the key to be legal education and an instrumental use of law to pursue social change. In the 1980s, the emphasis was on legislative reform and the passage or revision of laws based on foreign models. When that failed to produce the desired results, the attention shifted to institutions under the banner of rule of law and good governance. In practice, rule of law was used interchangeably with legal reform, which in many cases meant judicial reform and the need to establish an independent judiciary. When that approach also came up short, the scope of reform was expanded politically to include democracy, civil and political rights, freedom as an end of development, a robust civil society, increased political participation, and now the new governance of the postregulatory state with its emphasis on private actors and public–private hybrids.

From the perspective of rule of law promotion, these changes are mainly due to frustrated expectations on the side of rule of law promoters and behavioral adaptations in response to obstacles and poor results. In contrast, rule of law diffusion and rule of law conversion provide alternative perspectives that highlight different sources and causes of rule of law dynamics. From these alternative perspectives, rule of law dynamics are at least due to social processes initiated but not foreseen by rule of law promoters and by the reading of and the responses to rule of law in the recipient countries.

When we consider rule of law dynamics from the perspective of diffusion, it can be observed that the rule of law has been disseminated over different levels of government and into new areas, which cannot be explained or captured by processes of rule of law promotion. In particular, there is a growing normative expectation that states will comply with basic rule of law principles. Although compliance with basic rule of law principles is not (yet) a requirement for recognition of states, there seems to be an emerging standard of rule of law in international law, as evidenced by the growing demands to extend the rule of law concept to the transnational and international sphere. International organizations (IOs) involved in the rule of law promotion, exerting pressure on target countries, are themselves increasingly the target of rule of law promotion. Even transnational regulatory institutions are sometimes judged against the criteria of the rule of law.

Also, the outcome of rule of law promotion can only be understood in relation to local responses. Even the most perfect rule of law promotion strategy will lead to a conversion of the original concept when it meets local actors and practices.

To better understand the dynamics of rule of law development, more attention must be paid to the interaction between rule of law promotion, rule of law diffusion, and rule of law conversion. In so doing, we come back to the questions raised in the Introduction to this book. Have the major actors in the rule of law field, including the "great powers" and IOs, altered their strategies, programs, and practices to reflect the shift to new levels and new forms of governance? Do rule of standards apply to new international and transnational forms of regulation? Should they be modified to fit the different context? Can the interactions between national and international levels be structured so that they do not become a new source of rule of law violation? Does international law provide a clear and acceptable set of standards that can form a common baseline for rule of law promotion both in states and for new forms of governance? Finally, how does rule of law promotion, whether or not based on standards of international law, cope with the wide variety of forms of resistance from the targets of rule of law promotion? In this concluding chapter, we address these issues, taking up in turn rule of law promotion, diffusion, and conversion, and summarizing for each the main developments, their causes, and key issues for further research.

1. THE DYNAMICS OF RULE OF LAW PROMOTION DEVELOPMENTS

Notwithstanding the aforementioned significant changes over time, rule of law promotion efforts continue to share certain dominant features and strategies. For most Western state powers and the more influential international development agencies, rule of law promotion is generally seen as part of a broader strategy that emphasizes democracy, good governance, and the independence of the judicial system. Most of the major state powers have chosen a mixed approach that combines socialization (persuasion) with positive and negative conditionalities and in some cases coercion (imposition through military means; see Schimmelfennig, this volume). IOs and transnational nongovernmental organizations (NGOs) rely on similar approaches for promoting rule of law, albeit with less use of coercion (see Heupel, this volume).

While there are successes to be reported, for instance in the area of human trafficking (Lloyd, Simmons, and Stewart, this volume), the failures and problems of rule of law promotion are too striking to be ignored. Most importantly, the significant efforts put into rule of law promotion have produced on the aggregate level mild improvements at best (Merkel, this volume). New developments in response to the poor results are to be expected, including attempts to differentiate the addressees of rule of law promotion, an extension of the scope of actors involved in rule of law promotion activities, and growing awareness of legitimacy issues. Other major developments include the following.

First, while Northern European countries remain committed to democracy promotion, there seems to be a downgrading of it at least in the United States (Carothers 2009a). Increasingly, a significant number of rule of law promoters and rule of law recipients seem to think in terms of a developmental model in which rule of law precedes democracy. In this view, rule of law promotion is a necessary condition for democracy. Also international law, which now poses certain demands on how states provide for a domestic rule of law, falls short of requiring democracy (Aust and Nolte, this volume).

It remains to be seen whether the Arab Spring in the Middle East and North Africa will provide a new boost to democracy promotion, much as the fall of the Berlin Wall in 1989 stimulated democracy promotion throughout the 1990s. Although the international community on the whole celebrated the fall of authoritarian regimes, many commentators cautioned that overturning dictators was only the first step on a long and arduous path toward a functional democracy. Moreover, Europe and America are focused on overcoming the economic crisis and are increasingly preoccupied by the challenges resulting from the rise of China and other emerging countries. They may lack the political will, and the financial and human resources, to support another major democratization effort in the Middle East and North Africa.

Second, rule of law promotion has often been criticized for reliance on one-size-fits-all solutions that failed to distinguish between postconflict situations and different stages of development. Linn Hammergren's analysis of the World Bank's evolving strategies for middle-income countries (MICs) is a response to that. The definition of MICs (i.e., countries with per capita income from $900 to $12,000) still contains huge socioeconomic differences and will require further disaggregation. Nevertheless, a first step has been taken in developing more refined categories that may lead to the design of more tailored and hence effective promotion strategies and reform packages.

Third, the scope of rule of law promotion has expanded to include military cooperation with civilian organizations in a range of activities to establish legal institutions and the rule of law (Röder, this volume). Although the shortcomings of these efforts are substantial and the results less than satisfactory, they point to a broadened understanding of rule of law promotion.

Fourth, the idea of rule of law promotion does not really work for the rule of law at the international level. Because the rule of law at the international level concerns the international community as a whole, there is no obvious distinction between actors who engage in rule of law promotion and recipients of such attempts. For this reason, the development of the rule of law at the international level is better captured by the perspective of diffusion (see subsequent text). However, in a more narrow sense, we can identify a distinct effort of rule of law promotion at the international level within international institutions, notably the United Nations (UN). Such organizations bring a degree of centralization into the otherwise horizontal system of international law. Their institutional context allows for a "vertical dynamic" in which the rule of law can function. Furthermore, because UN membership captures the entire international community, rule of law policies of the UN are the best approximation for rule of law promotion at the international level. For example, the UN Secretary-General stated that "the United Nations must work towards the universal application at the international level of the Organisation's definition of the principle of the rule of law."[1]

Indeed, rule of law promotion efforts of international organizations are now not limited to attempts to improve the rule of law within states (Aust and Nolte, this volume); they are directed to international organizations themselves (Genkow and Zürn, this volume). Such organizations (most notably the UN) have recognized that they should meet the standards that they prescribe for others, if only because the failure to do so undermines the credibility of their external rule of law policies. This has also been shown to undermine the willingness of norm addressees to accept the prescriptions and ambitions of the UN.

Finally, rule of law promoters show a growing awareness of resistance on the receiving side. Any reform produces winners and losers. National and international donors, however, are not well positioned to address these types of local political contests, in some cases because of limited mandates, in other cases because of a lack of local knowledge (see Hammergren and Heupel, this volume).

1.1. *Causes*

In general, the most significant changes in rule of law promotion activities are driven by *perceived problems*, with necessity once again serving as the mother of invention. For instance, civil–military cooperation is the offspring of the military invasion of Afghanistan and Iraq. The downgrading of democracy reflects reform fatigue and disappointment over the enormous human and financial costs of the wars in Afghanistan and Iraq as well as the poor performance of many third-wave democracies and the limitations of democracy promotion (Carothers 2004; Diamond 2008). The recent interest in MICs reflects the fact that today most countries are MICs, which for the World Bank means a very different market for traditional loan

[1] Second Annual Report of the Secretary-General on Strengthening and Coordinating United Nations Rule of Law Activities, 20 August 2010, UN Doc. A/65/318: para. 9

activities as well as a different environment for technical assistance programs. Having focused primarily on low-income countries, often with poor results, donor agencies and academics alike are attracted to the challenges and opportunities presented by MICs. The decision of the UN to address rule of law problems within the organization is a direct result of resistance by states to conform to UN rule of law ideals if the UN itself did not obey such principles.

Although prior failures are often the source of change, the causes of the failures are often deeper and the obstacles to rule of law promotion more fundamental than the modification of policies indicate. These obstacles can be broadly classified as lack of knowledge, market forces, and institutional incentives and culture.

Thomas Carothers (2006a) and other industry actors have highlighted *lack of knowledge* as one of the main reasons for the poor results of rule of law promotion. One aspect of this lack of knowledge refers to different notions about what the rule of law is, and what should be promoted. The concept of rule of law remains unclear and contested. Rule of law serves many masters, and rule of law promotion is aimed at achieving many goals from the more technical enhancing of judicial efficiency and higher levels of professionalism to broader political goals such as economic growth, democratization, human rights, and geopolitical security (see Schimmelfennig, this volume). The relationship between these goals remains unclear; for instance, the relationship of rule of law to economic growth, the consolidation of democracy, and the protection of human rights is still being sorted out (Collier 2009; Peerenboom 2005).

The multiplicity of conceptions, goals, and strategies may lead to conflicting policies and different emphases in different contexts (Kleinfeld 2006). IOs or NGOs generally do not attempt to coordinate their programs with others (Heupel, this volume). The result is that different actors are often working at cross purposes or duplicating efforts. At the very least, given limited resources, the prioritizing of certain goals may hinder progress in realizing other goals. Overloaded governments cannot do everything at once, and yet little is known about the proper sequencing of reforms, which is highly dependent on context.

Our findings support these insights and the importance of improved coordination, but they do not identify this as the most important reason for the poor results to date.

The *lack of knowledge about the recipient countries and appropriate means to exert influence* seems to be more important than different concepts of rule of law. Along this line, many critics correctly attribute the poor results to the emphasis on top-down reforms, the focus on building state institutions, and the mismatch between the attempt to transplant laws and institutions appropriate for economically advanced liberal democracies to radically different contexts. In this view, a greater role for civil society and the private sector is advocated (Channell 2006), with more attention to bottom-up approaches that focus on the immediate needs of citizens for justice, poverty alleviation, legal empowerment, and "rights-based" development

(Banik 2009; Golub 2006; Stephens 2009).[2] Numerous critics have thus pointed out that international actors need to have a better understanding of the legal, political, and economic history of the recipient country (Taylor 2009). The limited and, to some extent, even perverse effect of the International Criminal Court's efforts to strengthen the rule of law in Uganda is largely attributed to a failure to adapt to the local context (Nouwen, this volume).

The chapters in this volume highlight the *lack of legitimacy* as another major reason for the limited success of rule of law promotion. The lack of knowledge about the recipient countries contributes to this legitimacy deficit. Many rule of law promoters are seen as remote external forces pressing societies to change their culture without a deeper understanding of it (Nouwen, this volume). To remedy this, international advisors must work more effectively with local actors, which requires that they have better linguistic skills and greater cultural sensitivity. They also need to tailor their proposals to local circumstances and ensure that reforms meet the needs of local constituencies.

Moreover, rule of law promoters are often seen as acting in their own interest. NGOs and experts, dependent on outside funding or consulting contracts, treat the knowledge gained from projects as trade secrets and are constantly on the lookout for the next "big thing." To secure projects, they promise more than they deliver and they ignore cautionary lessons learned from the past. As with any business concerned with efficiency and economies of scale, they tend to rely on standard prescriptions and reform packages rather than developing programs tailored to the specific context. All of the main parties involved in the project – the donor agency, the subcontracting NGO or expert consultants, the leaders in the recipient country – have an incentive to assess the project in positive terms. As Linn Hammergren wryly remarks in her chapter, the World Bank's internal assessment process concluded that, like the children of the fictional Lake Woebegon, all projects were "above average."

At the same time, national interests still play a role. Not surprisingly, the countries most affected by human trafficking were the biggest supporters of its criminalization (see Lloyd et al., this volume). Major powers promote rule of law not only for altruistic reasons, but out of self-interested concerns for geographical stability or in the belief that rule of law reforms are related to market reforms that will provide new consumers for their products or will provide greater access and a more level playing field for their country's companies. As Schimmelfennig (this volume) notes, major powers have attempted to export their own institutions, practices, and models, not only or necessarily in the belief that these are the best solutions for the target country's problems, but because doing so is in the best interests of important constituencies in the promoting state. Rule of law funding priorities also reflect domestic political

[2] See also Commission on Legal Empowerment of the Poor, *Making the Law Work for Everyone*. Volume 1. Commission on Legal Empowerment of the Poor and UNDP, 2008.

concerns, rather than being rational policies developed on a basis of what works: "As a consequence, rule of law promotion policies may vary with the different economic and strategic objectives of foreign policy actors" (Schimmelfennig, this volume).

The failure of international actors themselves to abide by rule of law principles arguably is the most important source of the legitimacy deficit of rule of law promotion efforts. In some cases, the lack of legitimacy results from the nature of the intervention, as when the North Atlantic Treaty Organization intervened in Kosovo and Iraq without UN approval and a clear mandate under international law. In these cases, the feeling is that like cases are not treated alike. In other cases, it results from how rule of law promotion is carried out. All too often there is inadequate consultation with local leaders and citizens, with citizens most concerned about public administration, poor governance, procedural violations, and the inability to resolve civil disputes while the military emphasizes security and the three Cs: courts, cops, and corrections. In still other cases, the emphasis of international actors on formal institutions undermines local institutions, and laws modeled on Euro-American precedents conflict with local norms and values (Nouwen, this volume).

Although there appears to be a trend toward less coercive modes of transmission, conditionalities and imposition of reforms through force continue to play a prominent role in many contexts (see Heupel, this volume). The incorporation of rule of law principles in international law, although still in its early stages, may have a positive impact in encouraging reforms in domestic legal systems, but it may also legitimate more coercive approaches, including military intervention aimed at regime change, just as the growing body of human rights law has legitimated military intervention in the name of humanitarian intervention (as long as it is approved by the UN Security Council).

1.2. *Future Areas of Research*

The rule of law promotion industry faces many challenges, with many areas in need of further research.

First, recent years have seen the development of a burgeoning literature on issues related to the measurement of rule of law, and the proliferation of new indices in response to claims that existing indices were conceptually or technically flawed (see Merkel, this volume).[3] Unlike many previous indices that included rule of law indicators as part of broader measures of democracy, good governance, political stability, or the business environment, the recently developed index of the World Justice Project (http://www.worldjusticeproject.org/) is solely dedicated to the rule of law, whereas the American Bar Association has developed even more specialized indices such as the Judicial Reform Index, Legal Profession

[3] *The Hague Journal on Rule of Law* has devoted a special issue to the measurement of rule of law.

Reform Index, Prosecutorial Reform Index, and Legal Education Reform Index (http://www.abanet.org/rol/publications.shtml). There are also efforts to create an index that focuses on criminal justice.[4] In response to the concern that most indices focus too much on state institutions, others have sought to develop an index that measures access to justice.[5]

None of the indices is perfect; all suffer from shortcomings in the underlying data and fall short on various technical dimensions; no single index fully captures – or could ever possibly capture – "the meaning" of rule of law. But progress has been made, and further progress can be expected. One example is the role that the World Justice Project attributes to the implementation of international human rights standards, thus in part overcoming the traditional separation between domestic and international conceptions of the rule of law. There is reason to hope, then, that new and improved indices will go a long way toward addressing the challenge that much of what we know or think we know about rule of law is based on flimsy foundations, scientifically suspect data, and poorly conceptualized indicators.

One of the biggest problems with most indices, even many of the new ones, is that they are based on very general rule of law principles. However, it is now widely recognized that basic rule of law principles are consistent with a wide variation in rules, institutions, and practices. This not only makes it difficult to measure rule of law but also affects rule of law promotion (Merkel, this volume), because it leads to confusion for both international donors and domestic policy makers. One possible agenda for the next generation of research would be to attempt to sort out which packages of reforms (rules, institutions, and practices) work in which contexts and at which levels of development. The increasing amount of data now available may allow this to be pursued through quantitative methods. By calling attention to different contexts and dynamics, some of the qualitative work now being done on MICs, postconflict situations (Bergling 2006; Zajac Sannerholm 2007),[6] and legal developments in authoritarian regimes (Ginsburg and Mustafa 2008; Peerenboom 2010a) may also provide guidance.

A second and related area in need of further research concerns the sequencing of reforms. The rise of China and the success of other Asian states have fueled the debate over whether economic growth and the establishment of rule of law should precede democratization or vice versa (compare Carothers 2007 with Peerenboom 2010b). Another macrolevel sequencing debate centers on economic policies and

4 See the United Nations Rule of Law Indicators Project, in conjunction with the Vera Institute of Justice and members of the Altus Global Alliance. Available at http://ar.unrol.org/doc.aspx?n=Newsletter+for+United+Nations+Rule+of+Law+Indicators+Project+June+2009.pdf.

5 See Hague Institute for the Internalisation of Law, "Measuring Access to Justice in a Globalising World." Available at http://www.hiil.org/research/main-themes/rule-of-law/research-project-measuring-access-to-justice-in-a-globalising-world/.

6 See also International Network to Promote the Rule of Law (INPROL). Available at http://www.inprol.org/visitorhome.

models of development, pitting shock therapy, neoliberalism, and the Washington Consensus against gradualism, the developmental state, and the Beijing Consensus, or more accurately, the East Asian Model (Peerenboom 2007). There is also the debate over whether to emphasize aggregate development or promote sustainable rights-based development, which in rule of law programming circles is manifest in the conflict between those who emphasize top-down institutional reforms and those who favor more bottom-up strategies of access to justice and legal empowerment. Another contested sequencing issue involves the need in failed or postconflict states to prioritize peace-keeping, security, and the law-and-order components of rule of law relative to the demands of citizens for improvements in daily public administration and civil dispute resolution mechanisms that address their more immediate needs.

Although judicial independence has been central to rule of law programming, and now is also supported by obligations stemming from international human rights law (Aust and Nolte, this volume), study after study demonstrates that giving more independence and authority to incompetent or corrupt judges does not produce just outcomes or enhance public trust in the judiciary in developing countries.[7] Although the need to sequence reforms in a way that balances judicial independence with judicial accountability is now often acknowledged in theory, how to do so in practice remains elusive.

More fundamentally, judicial reforms have been central to rule of law promotion efforts, but the focus on the judiciary ignores the holistic nature of reforms. Reforms must not only encompass all components of the legal complex (the courts, police, prosecutors, notaries, the legal profession, paralegals, law schools, etc.) but must also be complemented by changes in social norms and practices. Given the prominent role of lawyers in designing programs, reforms are often narrowly conceived in technical terms that ignore the broader social, political, economic, and cultural context. Lawyers tend to have an excessive faith in the power of law to change behavior. The focus on the judiciary also overstates the role of courts in promoting economic growth and resolving civil disputes. Moreover, the proper role for courts is much contested, even in countries known for rule of law (Peerenboom 2010a).

Further research is required to identify which institutions are best suited to resolve different types of disputes in a particular context and how to coordinate the roles of formal and informal institutions. There is also a pressing need for more empirical studies of how laws, including international laws, are implemented and how institutions actually operate in practice. There has also been little systematic study in the rule of law field of how to change social attitudes and norms and build support for rule of law reforms. In short, there is a pressing need for more research on the dynamics of rule of law diffusion.

7 Transparency International, "Global Corruption Report: Corruption and Judicial Systems" (2007). Available at http://www.transparency.org/publications/gcr/gcr_2007#download.

2. THE DYNAMICS OF RULE OF LAW DIFFUSION

2.1. *Developments*

Although rule of law promotion has produced less-than-stellar results in the traditional area aimed at developing states, it has led to a dynamic resulting in rule of law diffusion in unanticipated areas, most notably at the international and transnational levels.

First, rule of law diffusion has followed broader processes of internationalization and globalization. Transboundary investments, migration, and crime often call for parallel processes to strengthen the rule of law. States that are faced with human trafficking, for example, may strengthen law enforcement. Neighboring countries then feel compelled to follow suit to avoid the relocation of the unwanted practices to their less-regulated shores (Lloyd et al., this volume). In general, to the extent that the rule of law has diffused as an organizing principle of nation-states, this is part of the dominance of a Western script of what is modern, which is partially independent from efforts to actively promote rule of law. As the chapter by Merkel shows, rule of law developments and rule of law promotion efforts correlate weakly at best.

Second, rule of law has increasingly become a part of the prescriptions of international law pertaining to the way in which states should organize themselves (Aust and Nolte, this volume). In particular, the justification of strong interventions into war-torn societies on grounds of the rule of law has highlighted the issue of the extent to which states are bound to implement rule of law domestically as a norm of international law. Many governmental statements and declarations purport to view the rule of law as a central principle for the internal organization of states. Although international lawyers may debate to what extent rule of law has become a constitutive norm of sovereignty, there are certainly some signs that it is increasingly accepted as a regulatory norm in international law.

Third, rule of law has increasingly become part of the organization and operation of international institutions themselves (Gemkow and Zürn, this volume). This development is in part fueled by a consistency argument: If international organizations promote the rule of law by means of incentives and coercion, then they should be bound by rule of law principles as well. Although recipient countries that invoke the lack of consistency to justify resistance may be concealing other motivations, the criticism has had enough merit to spur some IOs to adopt rule of law principles embodied in international law. This is more the result of a process of diffusion of rule of law norms from their original domestic context to the international sphere, rather than the result of intentional promotion by the main actors in the rule of law industry.

Fourth, the demand for consistency is aimed not only at international organizations but also nonstate actors in international relations. The concept of rule of law is increasingly applied to transnational rule making and new modes of governance as well as to military actors whose mission is not primarily to establish the rule of law.

To be sure, the results of such developments at the international and transnational level are modest at best. Given the national interests and geopolitical objectives of the major powers, the limited degree to which rule of law standards have been accepted and applied in international institutions, notably the Security Council, is to be expected. Major powers resist rule of law diffusion, just as less developed countries do. Similarly, transnational regulation and the tendency to rely on nonstate actors when intervening in foreign countries are partially driven by the desire to remove these activities from the constraints of national and international law and insulate them from public debate. The incentives to keep such arrangements outside of the realm of the rule of law are strong, and thus the resistance to applying rule of law standards to these areas is equally strong.

2.2. *Causes*

All of these cases of rule of law diffusion involve a number of mechanisms that are interactive in character and cannot be controlled by a small set of actors. Learning and persuasion, mimicry and emulation, and competition may lead to such unforeseen results (Simmons et al. 2008). Rule of law diffusion is therefore not limited to strategically employed coercion and incentives, but is also the result of dynamic processes triggered by rule of law promotion efforts but not intended by the promoters. This is especially true when it comes to the application of rule of law principles to IOs and other international actors and to transnational rule making and governance. As the Schuppert chapter shows, we are only at an early stage in the process of extending rule of law principles to transnational rule making. The same holds for extending the rule of law to the international level generally, and to the operation of international organizations in particular. However, the normative argument that IOs *should* comply with such principles to enhance their legitimacy and the legitimacy of their rule of law promotion activities seems compelling, given the resentment expressed by many over the immunity enjoyed by IOs and the apparent hypocrisy in IOs promoting principles that they themselves do not follow (Gemkow and Zürn, this volume). Research on the dynamics of the evolution of norms in the international realm shows that such dynamics can create significant effects (Finnemore and Sikkink 1998; Risse, Ropp, and Sikkink 1999). The boomerang effect has played a role in many processes. When international actors use norms to justify what they do, the norms are empowered over time and come to apply to those who have invoked them. A number of different causal mechanisms may lead to such a result, although most often a combination of pressure and learning is decisive (see also Lloyd et al. and Gemkow and Zürn, this volume).

Notwithstanding the many obstacles and resistance from interested states and international actors, rule of law diffusion is an observable trend, and there are likely to be further positive developments in the future. The unanticipated results so far of the normative dynamics initiated by rule of law promotion suggest that it may be possible to develop a more universally acceptable conception of rule of law and a set of rule of law principles or standards applicable to all states and transnational actors and activities. The historical development of human rights law provides some basis for optimism. Rule of law appears to enjoy wider acceptance across ideologies, religions, and political regimes than democracy and many allegedly universal human rights, and yet there is no International Bill of Rule of Law comparable to the International Bill of Human Rights (which consists of the Universal Declaration of Human Rights, the International Covenant on Civil and Political Rights, and the International Covenant on Economic, Social and Cultural Rights), much less anything like the dense network of international, regional, and domestic laws and regulations that govern specific human rights. To be sure, for rule of law to retain its appeal and avoid the normative critiques that assert Western bias in the international human rights corpus, the process of incorporation of rule of law principles into international law would have to be based on a more inclusive universalism that includes views and values from other traditions (Otto 2009).

2.3. *Future Areas of Research*

Further research is required to better understand the causal mechanisms that lead states, IOs, and other transnational actors to adopt and comply with rule of law principles, and how that process may be supported. Although rule of law promoters increasingly realize the utility of an emerging international rule of law standard to support their efforts, we now need to identify the causal pathways through which rule of law diffusion takes place and incorporate these insights into a general theory that explains rule of law diffusion across countries and levels of governance (national, transnational, international, and regional).

Rule of law diffusion across levels of governance raises a number of challenging questions about conceptions of world order in which different legal systems based on the concept of rule of law interact with each other. Ultimately, the legitimacy of interventions into societies from the outside depends on such a conception. One response to this challenge is the constitutionalization of world politics. Constitutionalization in this context refers to a process in which different legal orders are integrated by the establishment of an ultimate legal authority in the form of a (written or unwritten) constitution that serves as higher law and is grounded in shared fundamental values (De Wet 2006; Klabbers, Peters, and Ulfstein 2009). Although this vision is intimately bound to the concept of rule of law, it goes further by identifying an overarching authority and prescribing legal means through which it can be achieved. This project therefore contains a strongly utopian flavor. As long as there is no common understanding of the community that needs to be constitutionalized, the lack of consensus may lead to fundamental conflicts and any step toward strong constitutionalization may be read as an instrument of power. Given the enormous differences in power in the international system, a full process of constitutionalization may therefore reduce, rather than enhance, legitimacy – especially in the view of weak states from the southern hemisphere that often perceive constitutionalization as a project of prolonging Western dominance (see, e.g., Rajagopal 2003).

Legal pluralists therefore argue against the constitutionalist approach that major components of an international rule of law can be established in the absence of a global constitution, in a world in which different political authorities exist without being integrated in a hierarchical order. To be sure, one of the major objections to such a notion of legal pluralism (Krisch 2010) or cosmopolitan constitutionalism (Kumm 2009) is that it cannot guarantee a stable rule of law. This may be an overly strong claim, however, given the various possibilities and mechanisms for resolving conflicts between different legal orders, including mutual acceptance of general legal principles (Bogdandy and Venzke 2010; Kumm 2009). Moreover, there are good normative arguments that certain conflicts between legal orders have to be solved outside of the legal sphere anyway, because they involve political matters (Waldron 1999; Zürn et al. 2011). After all, even in domestic systems known for rule of law, many important matters are decided through political channels. If legal pluralism, that is, legal orders that stand in a nonhierarchical relationship with each other, prevails, then the main issue to be resolved is where legal or political mechanisms can be developed to coordinate the different legal orders without generating an excessive amount of legal uncertainty. On this point, more empirical research is needed that would help identify the interacting processes between different (in particular national and international) legal orders. Such research should identify the degree to which international institutions, to the extent that they do not fully conform to external expectations of rule of law compliance, are held in check by national legal (including judicial) and political organs and processes.

In any event, we are at present by all accounts very far from living in a world where international relations are governed by rule of law principles. It is even debatable whether it makes sense to conceptualize "international rule of law" based on an analogy to domestic rule of law given the many structural differences between nation-states and the international legal order (Chesterman 2009). Rather than trying to fit square pegs into round holes, it may be better to try a radically different approach that does not begin with domestic rule of law as the model for rule of law at the international level. This approach would require a thorough analysis of the normative aims of the international legal order and the purposes that international rule of law is meant to serve, as well as the institutions that would be required to achieve it. Although this approach runs the risk of undermining support for efforts to create an international order that comports with the image of domestic liberal democratic rule of law writ large, it need not. It may provide a more realistic framework for pursuing the possibilities and limits of an international rule of law for states that is based on the notion that different forms of political authority require different sources of legitimacy.

Nevertheless, such a differential approach has to take into account that part of international law, notably international human rights law, penetrates domestic legal orders and as such has a dual character – being constitutive of the international and the national rule of law at the same time (assuming that rule of law is conceptualized in thick terms that incorporate human rights notions). There is therefore a strong argument that, at least to the extent that international law is controlling national law, it should satisfy equivalent, not lesser, standards of the rule of law (Bodansky 1999; Crawford 2003).

These different conceptions of international rule of law and their interrelationship are highly complex and may differ between regions and between particular functional areas of international law. More research is needed on the normative, theoretical, and empirical issues relating to the diffusion of rule of law both at the international–transnational level and at the domestic level.

3. THE DYNAMICS OF RULE OF LAW CONVERSION

3.1. *Developments*

One lesson learned over the years is that rule of law principles and practices are likely to be transformed by the recipient actors (Gillespie, this volume). Bringing in the recipient perspective is thus essential to our understanding of rule of law dynamics because the conversion process affects the outcome of rule of law promotion, which in turn leads to further changes in the methods and objectives of rule of law promotion. Three findings are of special importance here.

First, developing countries are now questioning whether rule of law in the form currently promoted is necessary for economic development given the success of China and other Asian states. Their success seems to support a more pragmatic and modest approach aimed at second-best solutions and "good enough institutions" rather than trying to leapfrog ahead through legal transplants of laws and institutions modeled on those in advanced states. More assertive and confident MICs are also decidedly less inclined to accept conditionalities or to bow to the wisdom of foreign powers on key policy issues that no developed country government would dream of ceding to outside actors (except for the EU).

Second, increasing concerns about the legitimacy of rule of law promotion are having a negative impact on rule of law promotion. Recipients are increasingly questioning whether key decisions regarding the strategies and methods of rule of law promotion are the result of a due political process and adequately take their particular needs and circumstances into account. The lack of consistency in these policies, the willingness to subordinate them to considerations based on national interest, and the weakness of rule of law mechanisms on the international level undermine the credibility of rule of law promotion efforts while lending credibility to those who invoke the lack of legitimacy to resist reforms.

Third, the poor record of rule of law promotion over the past several decades is beginning to erode political will for further reforms both among major powers and international institutions involved in rule of law promotion. The reallocation of funding from legal reforms and democracy promotion to security concerns, although partially the result of 9/11 and the ensuing so-called war on terror, also reflects reform fatigue and a growing sense that rule of law and democracy promotion efforts are just not working (Merkel, this volume). To be sure, Western powers have a history of beginning reforms and then not following through when the going gets tough and domestic political winds change. The reformulation of the mission statement from state building and promotion of democracy in Afghanistan and Iraq to the narrower objective of disabling Al Qaeda is only the last in a series that includes the hasty retreat of U.S. forces from Somalia; the withdrawal of UN peace-keeping forces and other personnel when some peace-keepers or UN offices were attacked in Somalia, Rwanda, East Timor, and Iraq; and the failure to adequately fund the International Criminal Tribunal for Rwanda, the International Criminal Tribunal for the former Yugoslavia (Majtenyi 2004), the Sierra Leone special war crimes court, and the Sierra Leone Truth and Reconciliation Commission (Schocken 2002; Udombana 2003). The rule of law field is filled with the carcasses of half-completed projects left to die for lack of funding.

3.2. *Causes*

Rule of law conversion challenges are part of a wider set of challenges that arise when translating concepts across different social contexts. Similar issues occur in the efforts to promote human rights or to persuade countries to adopt (neoliberal) economic policies or to join efforts to deal with nuclear proliferation and climate change. Nevertheless, rule of law has its own dynamic, and recipient-side problems may be more severe than in other areas.

One explanation for the poor results of rule of law efforts emphasizes political economy obstacles and conflicting interests within the recipient state. Trebilcock and Daniels (2008) highlight three types of *interest-based constraints* on the part of the recipients. First is opposition from political leaders in authoritarian states or illiberal democracies who are afraid of establishing alternative sources of power and legitimacy. Second are interest-based conflicts among state organs, between state organs and special interest groups, and within civil society among various interest groups. For example, efforts to enhance the independence and authority of the judiciary may be opposed by the legislature and administrative agencies; the police and prosecutors may oppose attempts to strengthen the defense bar; judges may oppose reforms aimed at enhancing judicial efficiency or ensuring accountability by subjecting the judiciary to supervision by judicial counsels, the media, and citizen groups; and business associations representing heavy industry may lobby against broad standing rules for NGOs favored by environmental activists. Third is the more mundane corruption and rent seeking by individuals or groups of individuals, which cause them to resist welfare-enhancing reforms and to distort the rules.

There is no doubt that all three interest-based obstacles present challenges to successful rule of law promotion. Before assuming that leaders in developing states are inherently opposed to legal reforms or lack the political will to implement reforms in the face of interest group opposition, however, it bears noting that rule of law reform is only one of the many challenges they face. Establishing a functional legal system is a costly business, as the high correlation between wealth and rule of law suggests. Strengthening the legal system may be just one part of a broader effort at state building. The costs of rule of law reforms may outweigh the benefits given a crowded reform agenda in developing states. Failed or low-income states in particular may simply lack the resources and capacity to carry out complex legal reforms.

In any event, many countries, especially MICs, do have the political will and the resources to carry out meaningful reforms. After all, there have been successful cases of rule of law reforms as well – most notably in East Asia but also in Latin America and elsewhere. Thus, interest-based constraints are not insurmountable in all cases.

As noted, two popular explanation of the poor results of rule of law promotion are an overemphasis on top-down reforms and a mismatch between the attempt to transplant laws and institutions appropriate for economically advanced liberal democracies to radically different contexts. A potential corrective would be to pay more attention to bottom-up approaches that focus on the immediate needs of citizens for justice, poverty alleviation, legal empowerment, and "rights-based" development (Banik 2009; Golub 2006). A somewhat broader and more fundamental proposal would be to take more seriously the different cultural contexts and how they require appropriate institutional translation of the rule of law principle, thus modifying not only the mix between top-down and bottom-up approaches but also the mix between formal and informal institutions and the mix between developing new institutions based on foreign models versus adapting existing institutions.

This more fundamental proposal acknowledges that *cultural constraints and normative conflicts* are key barriers to successful adoption of rule of law concepts and implementation of rule of law principles and practices. After all, rule of law reforms do not occur in a vacuum. Reformers are not working on a blank slate. Rule of law reforms often conflict with, and tend to displace, existing normative and governing structures (Upham 2002). Whereas rule of law implies constraints on arbitrary power, rule of law promotion assumes a functional state, with many reforms aimed at creating national laws and strengthening formal state institutions. Reforms alter existing power relationships, including the balance of power between central and local authorities, between local governments and citizens, and between various groups within society. Although that is often the purpose, and may be for the better, sometimes the result is to throw the baby out with the bathwater.

Moreover, most reform projects emphasize the passage of laws that reflect contemporary human rights standards incorporated in international law but mainly implemented in reasonably wealthy Western liberal democracies. Conflicts are more likely in some areas than others. For example, laws that affect religion, gender relations, and minority rights are more likely to encounter local resistance than commercial laws. Criminal law is another contested area, given the high crime rates in many developing countries and the breakdown of order in failed states. Laws that address socioeconomic issues – labor and environmental laws, land titling and government takings, social security (welfare, medical care, and education) – are also likely to be highly dependent on levels of development and to be hotly contested by interests groups based on how they are affected. Administrative law is another area that is very path dependent and subject to wide institutional variation.

One of the most commonly cited "lessons learned" therefore is that reforms must be "country owned and country led." Nonetheless, as the chapters in this volume show, most rule of law promotion strategies are developed by international actors with little input from the recipient countries, and especially from citizens within the recipient countries who will be affected by reforms. The reform agenda is then put to state leaders, often with conditions attached in the form of carrots or sticks or both. The lack of "buy-in" by local stakeholders undermines the legitimacy of efforts to promote rule of law, especially when major powers and international actors themselves often do not comply with rule of law principles.

For reforms to genuinely be country owned and country led would require increased participation of various domestic stakeholders at both the international and domestic levels during all stages of the reform process, from planning, to legislation, implementation, monitoring, and assessment. This shift would greatly increase the role and responsibility of domestic actors for reforms, altering the power dynamics between buyers and sellers. But this is as it should be.[8] Too often local governments cede control over key policy decisions to international actors, with all too predictably poor results.

There is undeniably a greater appreciation that the key to success often depends on the ability to overcome political and cultural obstacles, particularly in MICs. Unfortunately, there is also a growing realization that foreign actors are not well positioned to address such problems, the outcome of which generally depends on political struggle and compromise by domestic stakeholders and interest groups. This is particularly true for problems that result from interest-based conflicts among state organs, between state organs and special interest groups, and within civil society among various interest groups (Zajac-Sannerholm, this volume). However, it also

[8] Country ownership may, of course, have negative consequences in some contexts, for example when leaders are not genuinely interested in reform, when dominant groups use legal reforms to oppress others, or when interest groups take advantage of collective action problems to defeat welfare-enhancing reforms.

applies to cases in which developing country leaders oppose rule of law reforms for fear of losing their grip on power, particularly given that there is now less support for conditionalities, humanitarian intervention, and regime change. Similarly, although corruption is an additional cause of rule of law conversion, and development agencies continue to explore ways to deal with corruption, including judicial corruption, and to promote transparency, the results have been far from ideal.[9] Corruption, like politics, is largely a local phenomenon.

Recognizing the local element of rule of law promotion and diffusion, and thus the crucial role of rule of law conversion, also has major implications for attempts to develop international law requirements for rule of law at the national level. For one thing, it simply hampers efforts to achieve meaningful universally applicable standards, which as a result remain rather minimalistic (Aust and Nolte, this volume). To the extent that such standards do exist, international law inevitably will have to leave room for local adjustment and translation, leading to processes of fragmentation of international law. In view of the impact of international law on domestic law, such translation processes are a central manifestation of the fragmentation of international law (Kunzelmann 2008). Even more than fragmentation between different international legal regimes, the fragmentation caused by divergent national receptions of international law is "an ephemeral reflection of a more fundamental, multi-dimensional fragmentation of global society itself" (see generally Fischer-Lescano and Teubner 2004; Jackson 2010).

Even though fragmentation is generally given a pejorative meaning, a multiplicity of meanings in a domestic context is not necessarily a negative phenomenon. There exists an inescapable tension between the universalist aspirations of much of international law, on the one hand, and, on the other, the need to ground interpretation and application of the law in a localized expression (Adjami 2002).

3.3. *Future Areas of Research*

One of the most important challenges for further research therefore lies in bringing in the recipient perspective. The days of one-size-fits-all rule of law promotion are over. Without a better understanding of which type of societies are conducive to which types of rule of law promotion, externally driven reforms will continue to produce lackluster results. Balancing rule of law principles with local practice (which is not necessarily opposed to the rule of law, but which may simply reflect different aspects of the rule of law; see Nouwen, this volume) will remain a major task of the implementing actors on site. There will never be precise recipes that prescribe the use of strategy A when faced with local constellation X, strategy B when faced with local constellation Y, or strategy C when faced with local constellation Z. However, a better

[9] Again, see Transparency International, "Global Corruption Report 2007: Corruption and Judicial Systems." Available at http://www.transparency.org/publications/gcr/gcr_2007#download.

understanding of different types of political and cultural constellations within the recipient countries would help determine which strategies and substantive reforms are more likely to succeed in the particular context, for instance with regard to sequencing. At the same time, it would help to more accurately assess the success of those efforts by use of more refined indices. There is also a need for a better understanding of how seemingly uniform international standards are received and translated at the national level. Moreover, for typologies to be useful they need to go further than the World Bank notion of middle-income countries, which includes the vast majority of countries today. They need to be more differentiated, and they need to include political and cultural criteria as well as economic criteria.

4. CONCLUSION

The rule of law field is relatively new, as evidenced by the underdeveloped state of rule of law indices relative to democracy indices and the more highly developed state of human rights law. Much remains to be researched and learned. But even with additional knowledge and much good will, the future is likely to contain as many failures as successes. Establishing the rule of law is a long-term process that involves many fundamental and many incremental changes, and many unforeseen dynamics created by interactions between the actors involved. It is the result of protracted political struggle on multiple fronts by multiple actors. Rule of law is also an ideal imperfectly realized everywhere. As such, there will always be new challenges and new struggles, and new dynamics.

For rule of law promotion to be successful a more comprehensive analysis of rule of law diffusion and rule of law conversion is required. Understanding these three processes and the dynamic interrelationships among them is a difficult task. Nevertheless, given the important values served by rule of law, it is a challenge that must be met. We hope that this volume contributes to that worthy goal.

Bibliography

BOOKS AND ARTICLES

Abadeer, Adel, *The Entrapment of the Poor into Involuntary Labor: Understanding the Worldwide Practice of Modern-Day Slavery*. Edwin Mellen Press, 2008.

Abbott, Kenneth, Keohane, Robert, Moravcsik, Andrew, Slaughter, Anne-Marie, and Snidal, Duncan, "The Concept of Legalization." *International Organization* 54(3) (2000): 401–419.

Abbott, Kenneth, and Snidal, Duncan, "Hard and Soft Law in International Governance." *International Organization* 54(3) (2000): 421–456.

Adjami, Mirna, "African Courts, International Law, and Comparative Case-Law: Chimera or Emerging Human Rights Jurisprudence." *Michigan Journal of International Law* 164(24) (2002): 103–167.

Ajani, Gianmaria, "By Chance and Prestige: Legal Transplants in Russia and Eastern Europe." *American Journal of Comparative Law* 43(1) (1995): 93–118.

Alter, Karen, *The European Court's Political Power. Selected Essays*. Oxford University Press, 2009.

Arato, Andrew, *Constitution Making Under Occupation*. Columbia University Press, 2009.

Autheman, Violaine, and Elena, Sandra, *Global Best Practices: Judicial Councils. Lessons Learned from Europe and Latin America*. IFES Rule of Law White Paper Series (2004).

Arvind, T. T., and Stirton, Lindsay, "Explaining the Reception of the Code Napoleon in Germany: A Fuzzy-Set Qualitative Comparative Analysis." *Legal Studies* 30(1) (2010): 1–29.

Avant, Deborah, Finnemore, Martha, and Sell, Susan (eds.), *Who Governs the Globe?* Cambridge University Press, 2010.

Bachmann-Medick, Doris, "Introduction: The Translational Turn." *Translation Studies* 2(1) (2009).

Banik, Dan, "Legal Empowerment as a Conceptual and Operation Tool in Poverty Eradication." *Hague Journal on Rule of Law* 1(2009): 117–131.

Baracani, Elena, "EU Democratic Rule of Law Promotion," in Magen, Amichai, and Morlino, Leonardo (eds.), *International Actors, Democratization, and the Rule of Law. Anchoring Democracy?* Routledge, 2009.

Barnett, Michael, and Finnemore, Martha. *Rules for the World. International Organizations in Global Politics*. Cornell University Press, 2004.

Barria, Lilian, and Roper, Steven, "Judicial Capacity Building in Bosnia and Herzegovina: Understanding Legal Reform Beyond the Completion Strategy of the ICTY." *Human Rights Review* 9(2008): 317–330.

Barron, Gordon, "The World Bank & Rule of Law Reforms." Working Paper Series No. 05–70. Development Studies Institute, London School of Economics and Political Science (2005). Accessed 22 April 2010 at www.lse.ac.uk/collections/DESTIN/pdf/WP70.pdf.

Beetham, David, *The Legitimation of Power*. Humanities Press International, 1991.

Beetham, David, "Key Principles and Indices for a Democratic Audit," in Beetham, David (ed.), *Defining and Measuring Democracy*. Sage, 1994: 25–43.

Benda-Beckmann, Franz von, and Benda-Beckmann, Keebet von, "Property, Politics and Conflict: Ambon and Minangkabau Compared." *Law and Society Review* 28(1994): 589–607.

Berger, Peter, and Luckman, Thomas, *The Social Construction of Reality*. Anchor Books, 1967.

Bergling, Per, *Rule of Law on the International Agenda: International Support to Legal and Judicial Reform in International Administration, Transition and Development Co-operation*. Intersentia, 2006.

Bergling, Per, Wennerström, Erik, and Zajac Sannerholm, Richard, "Rule of Law in Public Administration: Problems and Ways Ahead in Post-Conflict Peace-Building." *Hague Journal on the Rule of Law* 2(2010): 171–202.

Berkowitz, Daniel, Pistor, Katharina, and Richard, Jean Francois, "The Transplant Effect." *American Journal of Comparative Law* 51(2003): 163–203.

Bernstein, Steven and Cashmore, Benjamin, "Can Non-State Global Governance Be Legitimate? An Analytical Framework." *Regulation & Governance* 1(4) (2007): 347–371.

Bhabha, Homi, *The Location of Culture*. Routledge, 2004.

Bicchi, Federica, "Our Size Fits All: Normative Power Europe and the Mediterranean." *Journal of European Public Policy* 13(2) (2006): 286–303.

Bich Lien, Bui Thi, "Legal Education and Legal Profession in Contemporary Vietnam: Tradition and Modification," in Chen, Albert, and Gillespie, John (eds.), *Legal Reforms in China and Vietnam: A Comparison of Asian Communist Regimes*. Routledge, 2010: 299–319.

Birtle, Andrew. *US Army Counterinsurgency and Contingency Operations Doctrine, 1860–1941*. Center of Military History, 1998.

Björkdahl, Annika, "Norm-Maker and Norm-Taker: Exploring the Normative Influence of the EU in Macedonia." *European Foreign Affairs Review* 10(2005): 257–278.

Black, Julia, "Regulatory Conversations." *Journal of Law and Society* 29(1) (2002): 163–196.

Black, Julia, "Constructing and Contesting Legitimacy and Accountability in Polycentric Regulatory Regimes." *Regulation and Governance* 2(2008): 1–15.

Böckenförde, Ernst-Wolfgang, "Entstehung und Wandel des Rechtstaatsbegriffs," in Ehmke, Horst, Schmid, Carlo, and Scharoun, Hans (eds.), *Festschrift für Adolf Arndt zum 65. Geburtstag*. Europäische Verlagsanst, 1969.

Bodansky, Daniel, "The Legitimacy of International Governance: A Coming Challenge for International Environmental Law." *American Journal of International Law* 93(3) (1999): 596–624.

Bogdandy, Armin von, "Prinzipien der Rechtsfortbildung im europäischen Rechtsraum. Überlegungen zum Lissabon-Urteil des Bundesverfassungsgerichts." *Neue Juristische Wochenschrift* 63(1–2) (2010): 1–5.

Bogdandy, Armin von, Dann, Philipp, and Goldmann, Matthias, "Developing the Publicness of Public International Law: Towards a Legal Framework for Global Governance Activities," in Bogdandy, Armin von, Wolfrum, Rüdiger, Bernstorff, Jochen von, Dann, Philipp,

Goldmann, Matthias, (eds.), *The Exercise of Public Authority by International Institutions. Advancing International Institutional Law*. Beiträge zum ausländischen öffentlichen Recht und Völkerrecht Band 210. Springer, 2010.

Bogdandy, Armin von, and Venzke, Ingo, "Zur Herrschaft Internationaler Gerichte: Eine Untersuchung Internationaler öffentlicher Gewalt und Ihrer Demokratischen Rechtfertigung." *Zeitschrift für ausländisches öffentliches Recht und Völkerrecht* 70(1) (2010): 1–49.

Böhling, Kathrin, "Zur Bedeutung von 'boundary spanning units' für Organisationslernen in internationalen Organisationen." *WZB Discussion Paper FS II 01–101*, Wissenschaftszentrum Berlin, 2001.

Borgan, Christopher, "The Language of Law and the Practice of Politics: Great Powers and the Rhetoric of Self-Determination in the Cases of Kosovo and South Ossetia." *Chicago Journal of International Law* 10(2009): 1–33.

Botzem, Sebastian, Hofmann, Jeanette, Quack, Sigrid, Schuppert, Folke, and Strassheim, Holger. *Governance als Prozess: Koordinationsformen im Wandel*. Nomos, 2009.

Braithwaite, John, "Responsive Regulation and Developing Economies." *World Development* 34(5) (2006): 884–898.

Breitmeier, Helmut, Young, Oran, and Zürn, Michael, *Analyzing International Environmental Regimes. From Case Study to Database*. MIT Press, 2006.

Brooks, Rosa, "The New Imperialism: Violence, Norms, and the 'Rule of Law.'" *Michigan Law Review* 101(2002): 2275–2340.

Brunsson, Nils, and Jacobsson, Bengt, "The Contemporary Expansion of Standardization," in Brunsson, Nils, and Jacobsson, Bengt (eds.), *A World of Standards*. Oxford University Press, 2000.

Buden, Boris, and Stefan Nowotny, "Translation Studies Forum: Cultural Translation." *Translation Studies* 2(2) (2009): 196–219.

Bühlmann, Marc, Merkel, Wolfgang, and Wessels Bernhard, *The Quality of Democracy: Democracy Barometer for Established Democracies*. National Center of Competence in Research, NCCR Democracy, University of Zurich, 2010.

Bühlmann, Marc, Merkel, Wolfgang, Müller, Lisa, and Wessels, Bernhard, "The Democracy Barometer: A New Instrument to Measure the Quality of Democracy and its Potential for Comparative Research." European Political Science (2011a): advance online publication, 16 December 2011; doi:10.1057/eps.2011.46, http://www.palgrave-journals.com/eps/journal/vaop/ncurrent/full/eps201146a.html.

Bühlmann, Marc, Wolfgang Merkel, Lisa Müller, Heiko Giebler, and Bernhard Wessels (2011b). Democracy Barometer. Methodology. Aarau: Zentrum für Demokratie.

Buiyan, Sharif, *National Law in WTO Law – Effectiveness and Good Governance in the World Trading System*. Cambridge University Press, 2007.

Bull, Carolyn, *No Entry Without Strategy: Building the Rule of Law Under UN Transitional Administration*. United Nations University, 2008.

Byers, Michael, *Custom, Power and the Power of Rules: International Relations and Customary International Law*. Cambridge University Press, 1999.

Calliess, Gralf-Peter, *Grenzüberschreitende Verbraucherverträge: Rechtssicherheit und Gerechtigkeit auf dem elektronischen Weltmarktplatz*. Mohr Siebeck, 2006.

Cameron, Sally, and Newman, Edward (eds.), *Trafficking in Humans: Social, Cultural and Political Dimensions*. United Nations University Press, 2008.

Cançado Trindade, Antônio Augusto, *Evolution du droit international au droit des gens – L'accès des individus à la Justice internationale – Le regard d'un juge*. Pedone, 2008.

Caplan, Richard, "Who Guards the Guardians? International Accountability in Bosnia." *International Peacekeeping* 12(3) (2005): 463–476.

Carlowitz, Leopold von, "UNMIK Lawmaking Between Effective Peace Support and Internal Self-Determination." *Archiv des Völkerrechts* 41(3) (2003): 336–393.
Carlsnaes, Walter, Risse, Thomas, and Simmons, Beth A. (eds.). *Handbook of International Relations*. Sage Publications, 2002.
Carlson, Scott, Brooks, Rosa, Nawabi, Mariam and Bodansky, Daniel, "From Autocracy to Democracy: The Effort to Establish Market Democracies in Iraq and Afghanistan: Panel 1: Establishing the Rule of Law." *Georgia Journal of International and Comparative Law* 33(2004): 119–142.
Carothers, Thomas, "The Rule of Law Revival." *Foreign Affairs* 77(2) (1998): 95–106.
Carothers, Thomas (ed.), *Promoting the Rule of Law Abroad: In Search of Knowledge*, Carnegie Endowment for International Peace, 2006a.
Carothers, Thomas, "The Problem of Knowledge," in Carothers, Thomas (ed.), *Promoting the Rule of Law Abroad: In Search of Knowledge*. Carnegie Endowment for International Peace, 2006b.
Carothers, Thomas, "The Rule-of-Law Revival," in Carothers, Thomas (ed.), *Promoting the Rule of Law Abroad: In Search of Knowledge*. Carnegie Endowment for International Peace, 2006c: 3–14.
Carothers, Thomas, "Rule of Law Temptations." *Fletcher Forum of World Affairs* 33(1) (2009b): 49–61.
Cashore, Benjamin, "Legitimacy and the Privatization of Environmental Governance: How Non-State Market-Driven (NSMD) Governance Systems Gain Rule-Making Authority." *Governance* 15(2002): 502–529.
Casper, Gerhard, "Rule of Law? Whose Law?" *CDDRL Working Paper No. 10*, Stanford University (2004).
Cass, Ronald, *The Rule of Law in America*. Johns Hopkins University Press, 2001.
Cassese, Sabino, "Administrative Law Without the State? The Challenge of Global Regulation." *New York University Journal of International Law and Politics* 37 (4) (2005): 663–694.
Cavalcanti Melo Filho, Hugo, "A Reforma do Poder Judiciário Brasileiro: motivações, quadro actual e perspectivas." *Revista Centro de Estudios Judiciários*, 21(2003): 79–86.
Chayes, Abram, and Chayes Handler, Antonia, *The New Sovereignty: Compliance with International Regulatory Agreements*. Harvard University Press, 1995.
Chesterman, Simon, *You, the People: The United Nations, Transitional Administration, and State-Building*. Oxford University Press, 2004.
Chesterman, Simon, "An International Rule of Law?" *American Journal of Comparative Law* 56(2008a): 331–361.
Chesterman, Simon, "Rule of Law," in Wolfrum, Rüdiger (ed.), *Max Planck Encyclopedia of Public International Law*, Online ed. Oxford University Press, 2008b.
Chesterman, Simon, "I'll Take Manhattan: The International Rule of Law and the United Nations Security Council." *Hague Journal on Rule of Law* 1(2009): 67–73.
Chung, Christine, "The Punishment and Prevention of Genocide: The International Criminal Court as a Benchmark of Progress and Need." *Case Western Reserve Journal of International Law* 40(2007–2008): 227–242.
Clark, Gordon, "Money Flows like Mercury: The Geography of Global Finance." *Geografiska Annaler, Series B: Human Geography* 87(2) (2005): 99–112.
Collier, Paul. *Wars, Guns, and Votes: Democracy in Dangerous Places*. Harper, 2009.
Concannon, Brian, "Beyond Complementarity: The International Criminal Court and National Prosecutions, a View from Haiti." *Columbia Human Rights Law Review* 32(2000): 201–250.

Coning, Cedric de, "The UN Transitional Administration in East Timor (UNTAET): Lessons Learned from the First Hundred Days." *International Peacekeeping* 6(2000): 83–90.
Cooper, Andrew, *Celebrity Diplomacy*. Paradigm Publishers, 2007.
Cooper, Scott, Hawkins, Darren, Jacoby, Wade, and Nielson, Daniel, "Yielding Sovereignty to International Institutions: Bringing System Structure Back In." *International Studies Review* 10(2008): 501–524.
Cornell, Svante, "The Interaction of Drug Smuggling, Human Trafficking and Terrorism," in Jonsson, Anna (ed.), *Human Trafficking and Human Security*. Routledge, 2009.
Corten, Olivier, "Déclarations unilaterales d'indépenence et reconnaissances prématurées: du Kosovo à l'Ossétie du Sud et à l'Abkhazie." *Révue générale de droit international public* 112(2008): 721–759.
Corten, Olivier, "Rapport General: L'Etat de droit en droit international: quelle valeur juridique ajoutée?," in Société française pour le droit international (ed.), *L'État de droit en droit international*. Pedone, 2009: 11–40.
Cotterrell, Roger, "Is There a Logic of Legal Transplants," in Nelken, David and Feest, Johannes (eds.), *Adapting Legal Cultures*. Hart Publishing, 2001: 71–92.
Crawford, Gordon, *Foreign Aid and Political Reform. A Comparative Analysis of Democracy Assistance and Political Conditionality*. Palgrave Macmillan, 2001.
Crawford, James, "International Law and the Rule of Law." *Adelaide Law Review* 24(2003): 3–12.
Crawford, James, *The Creation of States in International Law*, 2nd ed. Oxford University Press, 2006.
Curley, Melissa, and Siu-lun Wong, *Security and Migration in Asia: The Dynamics of Securitization*. Politics in Asia Series. Routledge, 2008.
Dahl, Robert, *Polyarchy. Participation and Opposition*. Cambridge University Press, 1971.
Dam, Kenneth, *The Law-Growth Nexus: The Rule of Law and Economic Development*. Brookings Institution Press, 2006.
Das, Dilip, and Ebbe, Obi Ignatius (eds.), *Global Trafficking in Women and Children*. CRC Press, 2008.
Decker, Klaus, "World Bank Rule of Law Assistance in Fragile States: Developments and Perspectives," in Perry-Kessaris, Amanda (ed.), *Law in Pursuit of Development: Principles into Practice?* Routledge, 2010: 224–253.
De Sena, Pasquale, and Vitucci, Maria, "The European Courts and the Security Council: Between Dedoublement Fonctionnel and Balancing of Values." *European Journal of International Law* 20(1) (2009): 193–228.
DeStefano, Anthony, *The War on Human Trafficking: U.S. Policy Assessed*. Rutgers University Press, 2007.
De Wet, Erika, "The International Constitutional Order." *International and Comparative Law Quarterly* 55(2006): 51–76.
Dewey, Susan. *Hollow Bodies: Institutional Responses to Sex Trafficking in Armenia, Bosnia, and India*. Kumarian Press, 2008.
Dezalay, Yves, and Garth, Bryant (eds.), *Dealing in Virtue. International Commercial Arbitration and the Construction of a Transnational Legal Order*. University of Chicago Press, 1996.
Dezalay, Yves, and Garth, Bryant, *The Internationalization of Palace Wars, Lawyers, Economists and the Contest to Transform Latin American States*. University of Chicago Press, 2002.
Diamond, Larry, *The Spirit of Democracy: The Struggle to Build Free Societies Throughout the World*. Times Books, 2008.

Diamond, Larry, and Morlino, Leonardo, *Assessing the Quality of Democracy*. Johns Hopkins University Press, 2005.
DiMaggio, Paul, "Culture and Cognition: An Interdisciplinary Review." *Annual Review of Sociology* 23(1997): 263–287.
DiMaggio, Paul, "Interest and Agency in Institutional Theory," in Zucker, Lynne (ed.), *Institutional Patterns and Organizations*. Ballinger, 1988: 3–22.
Di Nicola, Andrea, *Prostitution and Human Trafficking: Focus on Clients*. Springer, 2009.
Djelic, Marie-Laure, and Salin-Andersson, Kerstin, *Transnational Governance: Institutional Dynamics of Regulation*. Cambridge University Press, 2006.
Dobbins, James, Jones, Seth, Crane, Keith, and Degrasse, Beth, *The Beginners Guide to Nation-Building*. Rand Publishing, 2007.
Dolzer, Rudolf, "*Good Governance*: Neues transnationales Leitbild der Staatlichkeit?" *Zeitschrift für ausländisches öffentliches Recht und Völkerrecht* 64(2004): 533–546.
Dolzer, Rudolf, and Schreuer, Christoph, *Principles of International Investment Law*. Oxford University Press, 2008.
Dowdle, Michael, "Of Parliaments, Pragmatism, and the Dynamics of Constitutional Development: The Curious Case of China." *New York University Journal of International Law and Politics* 35(1) (2002): 1–200.
Dowdle, Michael, "On the Regulatory Dynamics of Judicialization: The Promise and Perils of Exploring 'Judicialization' in East and South Asia," in Ginsburg, Tom and Chen, Albert (eds.), *Administrative Law and Governance in Asia: Comparative Perspectives*. Routledge, 2009: 23–37.
Dowdle, Michael, "The Geography of Regulation," in Levi-Faur, David (ed.), *Handbook on Governance*. Oxford University Press, 2011.
Downs, George, Rocke, David and Barsoom, Peter, "Is the Good News About Compliance Good News About Cooperation?" *International Organization* 50(3) (1996): 379–406.
Drumbl, Mark, *Atrocity, Punishment, and International Law*. Cambridge University Press, 2007.
Dunn, Frederick Sherwood, "International Law and Private Property Rights." *Columbia Law Review* 28(1928): 166–180.
Easterly, William, "Foreign Aid for Scoundrels." *New York Review of Books*, 2010: 37–28.
Ebbe, Obi Ignatius, and Das, Dilip (eds.), *Global Trafficking in Women and Children*. CRC Press, 2008.
Ericson, Richard V., Doyle, Aaron, and Barry, Dean, *Insurance as Governance*. University of Toronto Press, Scholarly Publishing Division, 2003.
Esty, Daniel, "Good Governance at the Supranational Scale: Globalizing Administrative Law." *Yale Law Journal* 115(2006): 1490–1561.
Farrall, Jeremy, "Impossible Expectations? The UN Security Council's Promotion of the Rule of Law After Conflict," in Bowden, Brett, Charlesworth, Hilary, and Farrall, Jeremy (eds.), *The Role of International Law in Rebuilding Societies After Conflict*. Cambridge University Press, 2009: 134–156.
Faundez, Julio, "The Rule of Law Enterprise: Promoting a Dialogue Between Practitioners and Academics." *Democratization* 12(4) (2005): 567–586.
Faundez, Julio, "Rule of Law or Washington Consensus: The Evolution of the World Bank's Approach to Legal and Judicial Reform," in Perry-Kessaris, Amanda (ed.), *Law in Pursuit of Development: Principles into Practice?* Routledge, 2010: 180–201.
Fauvarque-Cosson, Bénédicte, and Kerhuel, Anne-Julie, "Is Law an Economic Contest? French Reactions to the Doing Business World Bank Reports and Economic Analysis of the Law." *American Journal of Comparative Law* 57(4) (2009): 811–829.

Fein, Helen. *Human Rights and Wrongs: Slavery, Terror, Genocide*. Paradigm Publishers, 2007.
Finnemore, Martha, "Norms, Culture, and World Politics: Insights from Sociology's Institutionalism."*International Organization* 50(2) (1996): 325–347.
Finnemore, Martha, and Sikkink, Kathryn, "Norm Dynamics and Political Change." *International Organization* 52(4) (1998): 887–917.
Finnemore, Martha, and Toope, Stephen, "Alternatives to 'Legalization': Richer Views of Law and Politics." *International Organization* 55(3) (2001): 743–758.
Fischer-Lescano, Andreas, and Teubner, Gunther, "Regime-Collisions: The Vain Search for Legal Unity in the Fragmentation of Global Law." *Michigan Journal of International Law* 999(25) (2004): 999–1046.
Fishkin, James, He, Baogang, Luskin, Robert, and Siu, Alice, "Deliberative Democracy in an Unlikely Place: Deliberative Polling in China." Stanford University Center for Deliberative Democracy, 2006. Accessed 31 March 2010 at http://cdd.stanford.edu/research/papers/2006/china-unlikely.pdf.
Fitschen, Thomas, "Inventing the Rule of Law for the United Nations." *Max Planck Yearbook of United Nations Law* 12(2008): 347–380.
Forsythe, David, *Human Rights in International Relations*. Cambridge University Press, 2006.
Fox, Gregory, *Humanitarian Occupation*. Cambridge University Press, 2008.
Francioni, Francesco, "Access to Justice, Denial of Justice and International Investment Law." *European Journal of International Law* 20(2009): 729–747.
Franck, Thomas, "Legitimacy in the International System." *American Journal of International Law* 82(4) (1988): 705–759.
Franck, Thomas,. *The Power of Legitimacy Among Nations*. Oxford University Press, 1990.
Franck, Thomas, "The Emerging Right to Democratic Governance." *American Journal of International Law* 86(1992): 46–91.
Frank, David, and Meyer, John, "The Profusion of Individual Roles and Identities in the Post-War Period." *Sociological Theory* 20(2002): 86–105.
Freeman, Alwyn, *The International Responsibility of States for Denial of Justice*. Longmans, 1938.
Friedman, Barry, "The History of the Countermajoritarian Difficulty, Part One: The Road to Judicial Supremacy." *New York University Law Review*, 73(1998): 333–430.
Fuchs, Martin, "Reaching Out; Or, Nobody Exists in One Context Only. Society as Translation." *Translation Studies* 2(1) (2009): 21–40.
Fuller, Lon, *The Morality of Law*. Yale University Press, 1969.
Geroski, Paul, "Models of Technology Diffusion." *Research Policy* 29 (4–5) (2000): 603–625.
Gibson, James, "Judicial Institutions," in Binder, Sarah A., Rhodes, R. A. W., and Rockman Bert A. (eds.), *The Oxford Handbook of Political Institutions*. Oxford University Press, 2008: 514–534.
Gillespie, John. *Transplanting Commercial Law Reform*. Ashgate, 2006.
Gillespie, John, "Rethinking the Role of Judicial Independence in Socialist-Transforming East Asia." *International Comparative Law Quarterly* 56(3) (2007): 837–870.
Gillespie, John, "The Role of State, Non-State and Hybrid Actors in Localizing Global Scripts in East Asia," in Gillespie, John, and Peerenboom, Randall (eds.), *Regulation in Asia: Pushing Back on Globalization*. Routledge, 2009.
Gillespie, John, "Exploring the Limits of Judicial Review in Urban Land Disputes in Vietnam." *Law and Society Review* 45 (2) (2011): 241–275.

Gillespie, John, "Re-Signifying Global Scripts in Networks of Meaning," in Gillespie, John, and Nicholson, Pip (eds.), *Law and Development and the Global Discourses of Legal Transfers*. Cambridge University Press, 2012.

Ginsburg, Tom and Moustafa, Tamir, *Rule by Law*. Cambridge University Press, 2008.

Gioia, Andrea, "Kosovo's Statehood and the Role of Recognition." *Italian Yearbook of International Law* 18(2008): 3–35.

Golub, Jonathan, "Did the Luxembourg Compromise Have Any Consequences?" in Jean-Marie Palayret, Helen Wallace and Pascaline Winand (eds.), *Visions, Votes and Vetoes: The Empty Chair Crisis and the Luxembourg Compromise Forty Years On*. Brussels: P.I.E-Peter Lang, 2006: 279–300.

Golub, Stephen, "A House Without a Foundation," in Carothers, Thomas (ed.), *Promoting the Rule of Law Abroad: In Search of Knowledge*. Carnegie Endowment for International Peace, 2006.

Goodman, Ryan, and Jinks, Derek, "How to Influence States: Socialization and International Human Rights Law." *Duke Law Journal* 54(2004): 621–701.

Gordley, James, "Comparative Legal Research: Its Function in the Development of Harmonized Law." *American Journal of Comparative Law* 43(1995): 555–565.

Greif, Avner, *Institutions and the Path to the Modern Economy*. Cambridge University Press, 2006.

Grimm, Dieter, "Gemeinsame Werte, globales Recht?," in Däubler-Gmelin, Herta, and Mohr, Irena (eds.), *Recht schafft Zukunft: Perspektiven der Rechtspolitik in einer globalisierten Welt*. Dietz, 2003.

Grimm, Dieter, "Stufen der Rechtsstaatlichkeit: Zur Exportfähigkeit einer westlichen Errungenschaft." *Juristenzeitung* 12(2009): 596–599.

Grimm, Dieter, "The Achievement of Constitutionalism and its Prospects in a Changed World," in Dobner, Petra, and Loughlin, Martin (eds.), *The Twilight of Constitutionalism*. Oxford University Press, 2010a.

Grimm, Sonja, *Erzwungene Demokratie. Politische Neuordnung nach militärischer Intervention unter externer Aufsicht*. Nomos, 2010b.

Gros, Jean-Germain, "Trouble in Paradise. Crime and Collapsed States in the Age of Globalization." *British Journal of Criminology* 43 (1) (2003): 63–80.

Gupta, Poonam, Kleinfeld, Rachel, and Salinas, Gonzalo, *Legal and Judicial Reform in Europe and Central* Asia. World Bank Operations Evaluation Department, 2002.

Habermas, Jürgen, *Legitimation Crisis*. Heinemann, 1976.

Habermas, Jürgen, *The Theory of Communicative Action*. Vol. II. Beacon Press, 1987.

Habermas, Jürgen, *Beyond Facts and Norms*. Cambridge University Press, 1996.

Hafner, Gerhard, "Accountability of International Organizations." *Proceedings of the 97th Annual Meeting of the American Society of International Law* (2003): 236–240.

Hafner-Burton, Emilie, "Sticks and Stones: Naming and Shaming the Human Rights Enforcement Problem," *International Organization* 62(2008): 689–716.

Halberstam, Daniel, "Local, Global, and Plural Constitutionalism: Europe Meets the World," in de Búrca, Gráinne, and Weiler, Joseph (eds.), *The Worlds of European Constitutionalism*. Cambridge University Press, 2011.

Halliday, Terence, and Carruthers, Bruce, "The Recursivity of Law: Global Norm Making and National Lawmaking in the Globalization of Corporate Insolvency Regimes." *American Journal of Sociology* 112(4) (2007): 1135–1202.

Hallström, Kristina Tamm, "ISO Enters the Field of Social Responsibility (SR): Construction and Tension of Global Governance," in Schuppert, Gunnar Folke (ed.), *Global Governance and the Role of Non-State Actors*. Nomos, 2006: 117–156.

Hammergren, Linn, *The Politics of Justice and Justice Reform in Latin America: The Peruvian Case in Comparative Perspective*. Westview Press, 1998.
Hammergren, Linn, "International Assistance to Latin American Justice Programs," in Jensen, Erik and Heller, Thomas (eds.), *Beyond Common Knowledge: Empirical Approaches to the Rule of Law*. Stanford University Press, 2003: 290–335.
Hammergren, Linn, "With Friends like These: Can the Multi-Lateral Development Banks Promote Institutional Development to Strengthen the Rule of Law?," in Perry-Kessaris, Amanda (ed.), *Law in Pursuit of Development: Principles into Practice?* Routledge, 2010: 202–223.
Hancher, Leigh, and Moran, Michael (eds.), *Capitalism, Culture and Economic Regulation*. Clarendon, 1989.
Harrison, Graham, *The World Bank and Africa: The Construction of Governance States*. Routledge, 2004.
Hart, Herbert, *The Concept of Law*. Clarendon Press, 1961.
Harvey, David, *A Brief History of Neo-Liberalism*. Oxford University Press, 2005.
Hawkins, Darren, Lake, David, Nielson, Daniel, and Tierney, Michael (eds.), *Delegation and Agency in International Organizations*. Cambridge University Press, 2006.
Heupel, Monika. "Multilateral Sanctions Against Terror Suspects and the Violation of Due Process Standards." *International Affairs* 85(2) (2009): 307–321.
Hillgruber, Christian, "The Admission of New States to the International Community." *European Journal of International Law* 9(1998): 491–509.
Hirsch, Moshe, "Interactions Between Investment and Non-Investment Obligations," in Muchlinski, Peter, Ortino, Federico, and Schreuer, Christoph (eds.), *The Oxford Handbook of International Investment Law*. Oxford University Press, 2008: 154–181.
Holzinger, Katharina, Jörgens, Helge, and Knill, Christoph (eds.), *Transfer, Diffusion und Konvergenz von Politiken*. VS Verlag, 2007.
Hook, Steven, "'Building Democracy' Through Foreign Aid: The Limitations of United States Political Conditionalities, 1992–1996." *Democratization* 5(3) (1998): 156–180.
Hout, Wil, *The Politics of Aid Selectivity: Good Governance Criteria in World Bank, US and Dutch Development Assistance*. Routledge, 2007.
Huber, Daniela, "Democracy Assistance in the Middle East and North Africa: A Comparison of US and EU Policies." *Mediterranean Politics* 13(1) (2008): 43–62.
Hufen, Friedhelm, "Über Grundlagengesetze," in Schuppert, Gunnar Folke (ed.), *Das Gesetz als zentrales Steuerungsinstrument des Rechtsstaates*. Nomos, 1998.
Hurd, Ian, *After Anarchy. Legitimacy and Power in the United Nations Security Council*. Princeton University Press, 2007.
Hurwitz, Agnes and Reyko, Huang, *Civil War and the Rule of Law: Security, Development, Human Rights*, Lynne Rienner, 2008.
Hutter, Bridget, "The Role of Non-State Actors in Regulation," in Schuppert, Gunnar Folke (ed.), *Global Governance and the Role of Non-State Actors*. Nomos, 2006.
Ipsen, Nils Christian, *Private Normenordnungen als transnationales Recht?* Duncker & Humblot, 2009.
ISO/IEC, Code of Good Practice for Standardization, first edition, 1994.
Iqbal, Kazi and Anwar Shah, "How Do Worldwide Indicators Measure Up,?" Internet: http://siteresources.worldbank.org/PSGLP/Resources/Howdoworldwidegovernanceindicators measureup.pdf (World Bank, 2008).
Jackson, Vicki, *Constitutional Engagement in a Transnational Era*. Oxford University Press, 2010.

Jensen, Erik, "The Rule of Law and Judicial Reform: The Political Economy of Diverse Institutional Patterns and Reformers' Responses," in Jensen, Erik and Heller, Thomas (eds.), *Beyond Common Knowledge: Empirical Approaches to the Rule of Law*. Stanford University Press, 2003.

Jessop, Bob, "Regulationist and Autopoieticist Reflections on Polanyi's Account of Market Economics and the Market Society." *New Political Economy* 6(2) (2001): 213–232.

Jonsson, Anna, *Human Trafficking and Human Security*. Routledge Transnational Crime and Corruption Series 4. Routledge, 2009.

Kara, Siddharth, *Sex Trafficking: Inside the Business of Modern Slavery*. Columbia University Press, 2009.

Keck, Margaret, and Sikkink, Kathryn, *Activists Beyond Borders. Advocacy Networks in International Politics*. Cornell University Press, 1998.

Keenan, Patrick, "The New Deterrence: Crime and Policy in the Age of Globalization." *Iowa Law Review* 91(2006): 505–560.

Kelley, Judith, "New Wine in Old Wineskins: Promoting Political Reforms Through the New European Neighbourhood Policy." *Journal of Common Market Studies* 44(1) (2006): 29–55.

Kelley, Judith, "Who Keeps International Commitments and Why? The International Criminal Court and Bilateral Nonsurrender Agreements." *American Political Science Review* 101 (3) (2007): 573–589.

Kempadoo, Kamala, and Doezema, Jo, (eds.), *Global Sex Workers: Rights, Resistance, and Redefinition*. Routledge, 1998.

Keppler, Elise, "Managing Peace and Justice in the Juba Process," in Onyango, J., and Wrange, P. (eds.), *The International Criminal Court and the Juba Peace Process or Global Governance and Local Friction*. Fountain Publishers, 2012, forthcoming.

Kerwer, Dieter, "Rules that Many Use: Standards and Global Regulation." *Governance* 18(2005): 611–632.

Kilcullen, David, *The Accidental Guerilla: Fighting Small Wars in the Midst of a Big One*. Oxford University Press, 2009.

Kingsbury, Benedict, Krisch, Nico, and Stewart, Richard, "The Emergence of Global Administrative Law." *Law and Contemporary Problems* 68(3) (2005): 15–61.

Kingsbury, Benedict, and Schill, Stephan, "Investor-State Arbitration as Governance: Fair and Equitable Treatment, Proportionality and the Emerging Global Administrative Law." *International Law and Justice Working Papers* 2009/6(2009). Accessed 9 May 2010 at. www.iilj.org/publications/documents/2009–6.KingsburySchill.pdf.

Klabbers, Johannes Antonius Maria, Peters, Anne, and Ulfstein, Geir, *The Constitutionalization of International Law*. Oxford University Press, 2009.

Kleinfeld, Rachel, "Competing Definitions of the Rule of Law," in Carothers, Thomas (ed.), *Promoting the Rule of Law Abroad: In Search of Knowledge*. Carnegie Endowment for International Peace, 2006.

Kochenov, Dimitry, *EU Enlargement and the Failure of Conditionality – Pre-Accession Conditionality in the Fields of Democracy and the Rule of Law*. Kluwer, 2008.

Koh, Harold Hongju, "Transnational Legal Process." *Nebraska Law Review* 75(1) (1996): 181–207.

Koremenos, Barbara, Lipson, Charles, and Snidal, Duncan, "The Rational Design of International Institutions." *International Organization* 55(4) (2001): 761–799.

Koseki, Shoichi, *The Birth of Japan's Postwar Constitution*. Westview Press, 1998.

Koskenniemi, Martti, *From Apology to Utopia: The Structure of International Legal Argument* (reissue with a new Epilogue ed.) Cambridge University Press, 2005.

Krieger, Heike, *Das Effektivitätsprinzip im Völkerrecht*. Duncker & Humblot, 2000.

Krisch, Nico, *Beyond Constitutionalism: The Pluralist Structure of Postnational Law*. Oxford University Press, 2010.

Krisch, Nico and Kingsbury, Benedict, "Introduction: Global Governance and Global Administration Law in the International Legal Order." *European Journal of International Law*, 17 (1) (2006): 1–13.

Krugman, Paul, "Ricardo's Difficult Idea – Why Some Intellectuals Don't Understand Comparative Advantage," in Cook, Gary (ed.), *The Economics and Politics of International Trade: Freedom and Trade: Volume II*. Routledge, 1998: 22–36.

Krygier, Martin, "False Dichotomies, True Perplexities, and the Rule of Law," in Sajó, András (ed.), *Human Rights with Modesty – The Problem of Universalism*. Nijhoff, 2004: 251–277.

Krygier, Martin, "Rule of Law: An Abusers Guide," in Sajo, András (ed.), *Abuse: The Dark Side of Fundamental Rights*. Eleven International Publishing Company, 2006.

Krygier, Martin, "The Rule of Law and 'the Three Integrations.'" *Hague Journal on the Rule of Law* 1(2009): 21–27.

Kuanpoth, Jakkrit, "Globalization and Civil Society in Thailand," in Gillespie, John and Peerenboom, Randall (eds.), *Regulation in Asia: Pushing Back on Globalization*. Routledge, 2009: 190–212.

Kumm, Matthias, "The Cosmopolitan Turn in Constitutionalism: On the Relationship Between Constitutionalism In and Beyond the State," in Dunnof, Jeffrey, and Trachtman, Joel (eds.), *Ruling the World: International Law, Global Governance, Constitutionalism*. Cambridge University Press, 2009.

Kunzelmann, Alexander, "An Australian International Law: The Impact of Australian Courts on the Fragmentation of International Law." *Australian Year Book of International Law* 225(27) (2008): 225–256.

Lake, David, "Rightful Rules: Authority, Order, and the Foundations of Global Governance." *International Studies Quarterly* 54(3) (2010): 587–913.

Lange, Bettina, "The Emotional Dimension in Legal Regulation." *Journal of Law and Society*. 29(1) (2002): 197–225.

Langer, Maximo, "From Legal Transplants to Legal Translations: The Globalization of Plea Bargaining and the Americanization Thesis in Criminal Procedure." *Harvard International Law Journal* 45(1) (2004): 1–64.

Lauterpacht, Hersch, *International Law and Human Rights*. Stevens, 1950.

Lauth, Hans-Joachim, *Demokratie und Demokratiemessung. Eine konzeptionelle Grundlegung für den interkulturellen Vergleich*. VS Verlag, 2004.

Lauth, Hans-Joachim, and Sehring, Jenniver, "Putting Deficient Rechtsstaat on the Research Agenda: Reflections on Diminished Subtypes." *Comparative Sociology* 8(2) (2009): 165–201.

Legrand, Pierre, "What 'Legal Transplants,'" in Nelken, David and Feest, Johannes (eds.), *Adapting Legal Cultures*. Hart Publishing, 2001: 55–68.

Lessig, Lawrence, "The Regulation of Social Meaning." *University of Chicago Law Review* 62(3) (1995): 943–1045.

Levi, Margaret, and Sacks, Audrey, "Legitimating Beliefs: Sources and Indicators." *Regulation and Governance* 3(2009): 311–333.

Levi-Faur, David, "The Global Diffusion of Regulatory Capitalism." *Annals of the American Academy of Political and Social Science* 598(2005): 12–32.

Licht, Amir, Goldschmidt, Chanan and Schwartz, Shalom, "Culture Rules: The Foundations of the Rule of Law and other Norms of Governance." *Journal of Comparative Economics* 35(2007): 659–688.

Liese, Andrea, *Staaten am Pranger. Zur Wirkung internationaler Regime auf innerstaatliche Menschenrechtspolitik*. VS Verlag, 2006.

Litwak, Robert, *Regime Change. US Strategy Through the Prism of 9/11*. Johns Hopkins University Press, 2007.

Locher, Birgit *Trafficking in Women in the European Union: Norms, Advocacy-Networks and Policy-Change*. VS Verlag, 2007.

López Medina, Diego Eduardo, *El Derecho de los Jueces*. Legis, 2006.

Luhmann, Niklas, *Legitimation durch Verfahren*. Luchterhand, 1969.

Luhmann, Niklas, "Operational Closure and Structural Coupling: The Differentiation of the Legal System." *Cardozo Law Review* 13(1992): 1419–1455.

Lücke, Jörg, "Die Allgemeine Gesetzgebungsordnung." *Zeitschrift für Gesetzgebung* (2001): 1–49.

Macdonald, Ronald St. John, and Johnston, Douglas, *Towards World Constitutionalism: Issues in the Legal Ordering of the World Community*. Martinus Nijhoff Publishers (Brill Publishers), 2005.

Magen, Amichai, "The Rule of Law and its Promotion Abroad: Three Problems of Scope." *Stanford Journal of International Law* 45(2009): 51–115.

Magen, Amichai, and McFaul, Michael, "Introduction: American and European Strategies to Promote Democracy – Shared Values, Common Challenges, Divergent Tools?," in Magen, Amichai, Risse, Thomas, and McFaul, Michael (eds.), *Promoting Democracy and the Rule of Law: American and European Strategies*. Palgrave (2009).

Magen, Amichai, and Morlino, Leonardo (eds.), *International Actors, Democratization, and the Rule of Law. Anchoring Democracy?* Routledge, 2009a.

Magen, Amichai, and Morlino, Leonardo, "Hybrid Regimes, the Rule of Law, and External Influence on Domestic Change," in Magen, Amichai, and Morlino, Leonardo (eds.), *International Actors, Democratization and the Rule of Law. Anchoring Democracy?* Routledge, 2009b: 1–25.

Magliveras, Konstantinos, *Exclusion from Participation in International Organisations*. Kluwer, 1999.

Majone, Giandomenico, "The Rise of the Regulatory State in Europe." *Western European Politics* 17(1994): 77–101.

Maltzahn, Kathleen, *Trafficked, Briefings*. UNSW Press, 2008.

Manders, Jonathan, "Sequencing Property Rights in the Context of Development: A Critique of the Writings of Hernando de Soto." *Cornell International Law Journal* 37(2004): 177–198.

Mani, Rama, "Conflict Resolution, Justice and the Law: Rebuilding the Rule of Law in the Aftermath of Complex Political Emergencies." *International Peacekeeping* 5(3) (1998): 1–25.

Mansfield, Edward, and Snyder, Jack, "The Sequencing 'Fallacy,'" *Journal of Democracy* 18(3) (2007): 6–22.

Mansfield, Edwin, "Technical Change and the Rate of Imitation." *Econometrica* 29 (4) (1961): 741–766.

March, James, and Olsen, Johan, "Institutional Perspectives on Political Institutions." *Governance* 9(1996): 247–264.

Marko, Joseph, "The New Kosovo Constitution in a Regional Comparative Perspective." *Review of Central and East European Law* 22(2008): 437–450.

Markovits, Inga, "Exporting Law Reform – But Will It Travel?" *Cornell International Law Journal* 37(2004): 95–114.

Marshall, David and Inglis, Shelley, "The Disempowerment of Human Rights-Based Justice in the United Nations Mission in Kosovo." *Harvard Human Rights Journal* 16(2003): 95–146.

Martins, Mark, "No Small Change of Soldiering: The Commander's Emergency Response Program (CERP) in Iraq and Afghanistan." *Army Lawyer* (March 2004): 1–20.

Matheson, Michael, "United Nations Governance of Post-Conflict Societies." *American Journal of International Law* 95(2001): 76–85.

Mattei, Ugo, and Nader, Laura, *Plunder: When the Rule of Law is Illegal*. Blackwell, 2008.

Mayer, Arno, *Political Origins of the New Diplomacy, 1917–1918*. Yale University Press, 1959.

Mearsheimer, John, *The Tragedy of Great Power Politics*. Norton, 2003.

Mégret, Frédéric, "Too Much of a Good Thing? Implementation and the Uses of Complementarity," in Stahn, Carsten, and El-Zeidy, Mohamed (eds.), *The International Criminal Court and Complementarity: From Theory to Practice*. Cambridge University Press, 2011: 361–390.

Mégret, Frédéric, and Hoffmann, Florian, "The UN as a Human Rights Violator? Some Reflections on the United Nations Changing Human Rights Responsibilities." *Human Rights Quarterly* 25(2003): 314–342.

Merry, Sally Engle, *Human Rights and Gender Violence: Translating International Law into Local Justice*. University of Chicago Press, 2006a.

Merry, Sally Engle, "New Legal Realism and the Ethnography of Transnational Law." *Law & Social Inquiry* 31(4) (2006b): 975–991.

Merkel, Wolfgang, "The Consolidation of Post-Autocratic Regimes: A Multi-Level Model." *Democratization* 5(3) (1998): 33–67.

Merkel, Wolfgang, "Embedded and Defective Democracies." *Special Issue of Democratization: Consolidated or Defective Democracy? Problems of Regime Change* 11(5) (2004): 33–58.

Merkel, Wolfgang, and Puhle, Hans-Jürgen, *Von der Diktatur zur Demokratie. Entwicklungspfade erfolgreicher Transformationsprozesse*. Westdeutscher Verlag, 1999.

Merkel, Wolfgang, Puhle, Hans- Jürgen, Croissant, Aurel, Eicher, Claudia and Thiery, Peter, *Defekte Demokratie, Vol. 1: Theorie*. Leske + Budrich, 2003.

Merkel, Wolfgang, Puhle, Hans-Jürgen, Croissant, Aurel and Thiery, Peter, *Defekte Demokratie, Vol. 2: Regionalanalysen*. VS Verlag, 2006.

Meyer, John, Boli, John, Thomas, George, and Ramirez, Francisco, "World Society and the Nation-State." *American Journal of Sociology* 103 (1) (1997): 144–81.

Meyer, John, Frank, David, Hironaka, Ann, Schofer, Evan, and Tuma, Nancy, "The Structuring of a World Environmental Regime, 1870–1990." *International Organization* 51(4) (1997): 623–651.

Michael, Lothar, "Private Standardsetter und demokratisch legitimierte Rechtsetzung," in Bauer, Hartmut, Huber, Peter, and Sommermann, Karl (eds.), *Demokratie in Europa*. Mohr Siebeck, 2005.

Morlino, Leonardo and Magen, Amichai, "Methods of Influence, Layers of Impact, Cycles of Change," in Magen, Amichai, and Morlino, Leonardo (eds.), *International Actors, Democratization and the Rule of Law. Anchoring Democracy?* Routledge, 2009.

Møller, Jørgen, and Skaaning, Svend-Erik, "Beyond the Radial Delusion: Conceptualizing and Measuring Democracy and Non-Democracy." *International Political Science Review* 31(2010a): 261–283.

Möllers, Christoph, "Pouvoir constituant – Constitution – Constitutionalisation," in von Bogdandy, Armin, and Bast, Jürgen (eds.), *Principles of European Constitutional Law*. Hart Publishing, 2006: 183–226.

Moore, Catherine, "The United States, International Humanitarian Law and the Prisoners at Guantanamo Bay." *International Journal of Human Rights* 7(2003): 1–27.

Moravcsik, Andrew, *The Choice for Europe. Social Purpose and State Power from Messina to Maastricht*. Cornell University Press, 1998.

Morina, Visar, "The Newly Established Constitutional Court in Post-Status Kosovo: Selected Institutional and Procedural Concern." *Review of Central and East European Law* 35(2010): 129–158.

Müller, Thomas, and Pickel, Susanne, "Wie lässt sich Demokratie am besten messen? Zur Konzeptqualität von Demokratie-Indizes." *Politische Vierteljahresschrift* 48(3) (2007): 511–935.

Munck, Gerardo, and Verkuilen, Jay, "Conceptualizing and Measuring Democracy: Evaluating Alternative Indices." *Comparative Political Studies* 35(1) (2002): 5–34.

Nabli, Mustapha, and Nugent, Jeffrey, "The New Institutional Economics and Its Applicability to Development." *World Development* 17(1989): 1337–1343.

Nanda, Ved, "The 'Good Governance' Concept Revisited." *Annals of the American Academy of Political and Social Science* 603(2006): 269–283.

Narten, Jens, "Building Local Institutions and Parliamentarism in Post-War Kosovo: A Review of Joint Efforts by the UN and OSCE from 1999–2006." *Helsinki Monitor* 2(2006): 144–159.

Neblo, Michael, "Thinking Through Democracy: Between the Theory and Practice of Deliberative Politics." *Acta Politica* 40(2005): 169–181.

Newton, Scott, "Law and Development, Law and Economics and the Fate of Legal Technical Assistance," in Arnscheidt, Julia, Van Rooij, Benjamin, and Otto, Jan Michiel (eds.), *Lawmaking for Development: Explorations into the Theory and Practice of International Legislative Projects*. Leiden University Press, 2008: 23–52.

Nicholson, Pip, and Pitt, Simon, "Official Discourses and Court Oriented Reform in Vietnam," in Gillespie, John, and Nicholson, Pip (eds.), *Law and Development and the Global Discourses of Legal Transfers*. Cambridge University Press, 2012, forthcoming.

Nobleman, Eli, "American Military Government Courts in Germany." *Annals of the American Academy of Political and Social Science* 267(1950): 87–97.

Nollkaemper, André, "The Internationalized Rule of Law." *Hague Journal on the Rule of Law* 1(2009): 74–78.

Nolte, Georg, "Human Rights Protection Against International Institutions in Kosovo," in Dupuy, Pierre-Marie, Fassbender, Bardo, Shaw, Malcolm, and Sommermann, Karl-Peter (eds.), *Völkerrecht als Wertordnung/Common Values in International Law – Festschrift für Christian Tomuschat*. N. P. Engel, 2006: 245–258.

Nolte, Georg, "'Zerfallende Staaten' und Grundsätze des Völkerrechts," in Beisheim, Marianne, and Schuppert, Gunnar Folke (eds.), *Staatszerfall und Governance*. Nomos, 2007: 174–193.

Nolte, Georg, "Kulturelle Vielfalt als Herausforderung für das Völkerrecht." *Berichte der Deutschen Gesellschaft für Völkerrecht* 43(2008): 1–37.

North, Douglass, *Institutions, Institutional Change and Economic Performance*, Cambridge University Press, 1990.

North, Douglass, "Institutions." *Journal of Economic Perspectives* 5(1991): 97–112.

North, Douglass, *Understanding the Process of Economic Change*. Princeton University Press, 2005.

Nouwen, Sarah, "Complementarity in Uganda: Domestic Diversity or International Imposition?," in Stahn, Carsten, and El-Zeidy, Mohamed (eds.), *The International Criminal Court and Complementarity: From Theory to Practice*. Cambridge University Press, 2011, 1120–1154.

Nouwen, Sarah, *Complementarity in the Line of Fire: The Catalysing Effect of the International Criminal Court in Uganda and Sudan*. Cambridge University Press, 2012, forthcoming.

Nouwen, Sarah, and Werner, Wouter, "Doing Justice to the Political: The International Criminal Court in Uganda and Sudan." *European Journal of International Law* 21(4) (2010): 941–965.

Offner, John, "McKinley and the Spanish-American War." *Presidential Studies Quarterly* 34(1) (2004): 50–61.

O'Neil, William, *Kosovo: An Unfinished Peace*. Lynne Rienner Publishers, 2002.

Orücü, Esin, "Law as Transposition." *International & Comparative Law Quarterly* 51(2) (2002): 205–223.

Österdahl, Inger, "International Countermeasures Against Human Trafficking," in Jonsson, Anna (ed.), *Human Trafficking and Human Security*. Routledge, 2009.

Otim, Michael and Wierda, Marieke, "Justice at Juba: International Obligations and Local Demands in Northern Uganda," in Waddell, Nicholas, and Clark, Phil (eds.), *Courting Conflict? Justice, Peace and the ICC in Africa*. Royal African Society, 2008: 21–29.

Otto, Jan Michiel, "Rule of Law, Adat Law and Sharia: 1901, 2001, and Monitoring the Next Phase." *Hague Journal on Rule of Law* 1(2009): 15–20.

Pallis, Mark, "The Operation of UNHCR's Accountability Mechanism." *International Law and Politics* 37(4) (2005): 869–918.

Parrot, Andrea, and Cummings, Nina, *Sexual Enslavement of Girls and Women Worldwide, Practical and Applied Psychology*. Praeger, 2008.

Paulsson, Jan, *Denial of Justice in International Law*. Cambridge University Press, 2005.

Peerenboom, Randall, *China's Long March toward Rule of Law*. Cambridge University Press, 2002.

Peerenboom, Randall, "Human Rights and Rule of Law: What's the Relationship?" *Georgetown Journal of International Law* 36 (2005): 809–945.

Peerenboom, Randall, *China Modernizes: Threat to the West or Model for the Rest?* Oxford University Press, 2007.

Peerenboom, Randall, "The Future of the Rule of Law: Challenges and Prospects for the Field." *Hague Journal on the Rule of Law* 1(2009): 5–14.

Peerenboom, Randall, *Judicial Independence in China: Lessons for Global Rule of Law Promotion*. Cambridge University Press, 2010a.

Peerenboom, Randall, "The East Asian Model and the Sequencing Debate: Lessons from China and Vietnam," in Gillespie, John, and Chen, Albert (eds.), *Legal Reforms in China and Vietnam*. Taylor and Francis, 2010b.

Peters, Anne, "Comparative Constitutionalism: The Function and Potential of Fundamental International Norms and Structures." *Leiden Journal of International Law* 19(2006): 579–610.

Peters, Anne, "Humanity as the A and Ω of Sovereignty." *European Journal of International Law* 20(2009): 513–544.

Peters, Dirk, and Wagner, Wolfgang, "Die Europäische Union in den internationalen Beziehungen," in Holzinger, Katharina, Knill, Christoph, Dirk, Peters, Rittberger, Berthold, Schimmelfennig, Frank, and Wagner, Wolfgang (eds.), *Die Europäische Union. Theorien und Analysekonzepte*. Schöningh, 2005.

Petersen, Niels, "The Principle of Democratic Teleology in International Law." *Brooklyn Journal of International Law* 34(2008): 33–84.

Petersmann, Ernst-Ulrich, "International Rule of Law and Constitutional Justice in International Investment Law and Arbitration." *Indiana Journal of Global Legal Studies* 16(2009): 513–533.

Petraeus, David, "Multinational Force-Iraq Commander's Counterinsurgency Guidance." *Military Review* (September–October 2008): 2–4.

Post, Robert, "The Relatively Autonomous Discourse of Law," in Post, Robert (ed.), *Law and the Order of Culture*. University of California Press, 1991: vii–ix.
Potter, Pitman, "Legal Reform in China: Institutions, Culture, and Selective Adaptation." *Law & Social Inquiry* 29(2) (2004): 465–495.
Potter, Pitman, "Selective Adaptation and Institutional Capacity: Perspectives on Human Rights in China." *International Journal* 61(2) (2006): 389–410.
Poulantzas, Nicos, *Political Power and Social Classes*. NLB and Sheed and Ward, 1973.
Pouligny, Beatrice, "UN Peace Operations, INGOs, NGOs, and promoting the Rule of Law: Exploring the Intersection of International and Local Norms in Different Postwar Contexts." *Journal of Human Rights* 2(3) (2003): 359–377.
Powell, Walter and DiMaggio, Paul, (eds.), *The New Institutionalism in Organizational Analysis*. University of Chicago Press, 1991.
Pregent, Richard, "Building Rule of Law Capacity in Iraq." *Israel Yearbook on Human Rights* 40(2010a): 159–181.
Puddington, Arch, "Freedom in Retreat: Is the Tide Turning? Findings of Freedom in the World 2008." *Freedom House*, 2008. Available at www.freedomhouse.org/uploads/fiw08launch/FIW08Overview.pdf.
Rajagopal, Balakrishnan, *International Law from Below: Development, Social Movements and Third World Resistance*. Cambridge University Press, 2003.
Rana, Raj, "Contemporary Challenges in the Civil-Military Relationship: Complementarity or Incompatibility?" *International Review of the Red Cross* 86(855) (2004): 565–591.
Rawls, John, *A Theory of Justice*. Belknap Press of Harvard University Press, 1971.
Raz, Joseph, "The Rule of Law and its Virtue," in Raz, Joseph, *The Authority of Law*. Oxford University Press, 1979.
Raz, Joseph (ed.), *Authority*. Blackwell, 1990.
Reiling, Dory. *Technology for Justice: How Information Technology Can Support Judicial Reform*. Leiden University Press, 2009.
Reitz, John, "Export of the Rule of Law." *Transnational Law and Contemporary Problems* 13(2003): 429–486.
Renn, Joachim, *Übersetzungsverhältnisse. Perspektiven einer pragmatistischen Gesellschaftstheorie*. Velbrück Wissenschaft, 2006.
Reus-Smit, Christian, "The Politics of International Law," in Reus-Smit, Christian (ed.), *The Politics of International Law*. Cambridge University Press, 2004: 14–44.
Ribeira, Ivan, "Robin Hood vs. King John Redistribution: How Do Local Judges Decide Cases in Brazil?" Draft paper on file with author (2006).
Richmond, Oliver, and Franks, Jason, "Liberal Hubris? Virtual Peace in Cambodia." *Security Dialogue* 38(1) (2007): 27–48.
Risse, Thomas, Ropp, Stephen, and Sikkink, Kathryn, *The Power of Human Rights: International Norms and Domestic Change*. Cambridge University Press, 1999.
Rittberger, Volker, Nettesheim, Martin, Huckel, Carmen and Göbel, Thorsten, "Introduction: Changing Patterns of Authority," in Rittberger, Volker and Nettesheim, Martin, (eds.), *Authority in the Global Political Economy*. Palgrave Macmillan, 2008.
Röder, Tilmann, "Little Steps Forward: Some Remarks on the Rome Conference on the Rule of Law in Afghanistan." *Max Planck UNYB* 11(2007): 307–312.
Rodríguez-Garavito, César, "Toward a Sociology of the Global Rule of Law Field: Neoliberalism, Neoconstitutionalism, and the Contest over Judicial Reform in Latin America," in Dezalay, Yves, and Garth, Bryant (eds.), *Lawyers and the Transnationalization of the Rule of Law*, forthcoming. Available at http://www.cesarrodriguez.net/docs/articulos/towardsociology.pdf.

Rodrik, Dani, "Growth Strategies." *Working Paper 10050 NBER Working Paper Series*. Cambridge MA USA, October 2003. Accessed 28 May 2011 at http://www.nber.org/~rosenbla/econ302/lecture/rodrick.pdf.

Rodrik, Dani, "Goodbye Washington Consensus, Hello Washington Confusion? A Review of the World Bank's Economic Growth in the 1990s: Learning from a Decade of Reform." *Journal of Economic Literature* 44 (4) (2006): 973–987.

Rodrik, Dani, *One Economics, Many Recipes: Globalization, Institutions, and Economic Growth*. Princeton University Press, 2007.

Rogers, Everett, *Diffusion of Innovations*. Free Press, 1983.

Root, Elihu, "The Basis of Protection of Citizens Residing Abroad." *American Journal of International Law* 4(1910): 517–528.

Ross, Jacqueline, "Impediments to Transnational Cooperation in Undercover Policing: A Comparative Study of the United States and Italy." *American Journal of Comparative Law* 52(3) (2004): 569–624.

Rudolf, Beate, "Is 'Good Governance' a Norm of International Law?," in Dupuy, Pierre-Marie, Fassbender, Bardo, Shaw, Malcolm N., and Sommermann, Karl-Peter (eds.), *Völkerrecht als Wertordnung/Common Values in International Law – Festschrift für Christian Tomuschat*. N. P. Engel, 2006: 1007–1028.

Ruffert, Matthias and Walter, Christian, *Institutionalisiertes Völkerrecht*. C. H. Beck, 2009.

Ruggie, John, *Constructing the World Polity*. Routledge, 1998.

Santos, Alvaro, "The World Bank's Uses of the 'Rule of Law' Promise in Economic Development," in Trubek, David and Santos, Alvaro (eds.). *The New Law and Economic Development: A Critical Appraisal*. Cambridge University Press, 2006.

Sartori, Giovanni, "Concept Misinformation in Comparative Politics." *American Political Science Review* 64(4) (1970): 1033–1053.

Sassen, Saskia, *Territory, Authority, Rights: From Medieval to Global Assemblages*. Princeton University Press, 2006.

Saxenian, Anna Lee, "Taiwan's Hsinchu Region: Imitator and Partner for Silicon Valley," in Bresnahan, Timothy, and Gambardella, Alfonso (eds.), *Building High-Tech Clusters: Silicon Valley and Beyond*. Cambridge University Press, 2004: 190–228.

Scarpa, Silvia, *Trafficking in Human Beings: Modern Slavery*. Oxford University Press, 2008.

Scelle, Georges, "Théorie du Gouvernement International." *Annuaire de l'Institut international de droit public* 41(1935): 41–112.

Schabas, William, "Prosecutorial Discretion v. Judicial Activism at the International Criminal Court." *Journal of International Criminal Justice* 6(4) (2008): 731–761.

Scharpf, Fritz, "Legitimationskonzepte jenseits des Nationalstaates," in Schuppert, Gunnar Folke, Pernice, Ingolf and Haltern, Ulrich (eds.), *Europawissenschaft*. Nomos, 2005.

Schepel, Harm, *The Constitution of Private Governance: Product Standards in the Regulation of Integrating Markets*. Hart Publishing, 2005. University Press 2009.

Schill, Stephan, "Fair and Equitable Treatment, the Rule of Law, and Comparative Public Law," in Schill, Stephan (ed.), *International Investment Law and Comparative Public Law*, Oxford University Press 2010, 151–182.

Schimmelfennig, Frank, "Introduction: The Impact of International Organizations on the Central and Eastern European States – Conceptual and Theoretical Issues," in Linden, Ronald (ed.), *Norms and Nannies: The Impact of International Organizations in the Central and Eastern European States*. Rowman & Littlefield, 2002.

Schimmelfennig, Frank, *The EU, NATO and the Integration of Europe: Rules and Rhetoric*. Cambridge University Press, 2003.

Schimmelfennig, Frank, "Competition and Community: Constitutional Courts, Rhetorical Action, and the Institutionalization of Human Rights in the European Union." *Journal of European Public Policy* 13(8) (2006): 1247–1264.

Schimmelfennig, Frank, "Europeanization Beyond Europe. Living Reviews in European Governance." *Living Reviews in European Governance* (2009).

Schimmelfennig, Frank, Engert, Stefan, and Knobel, Heiko, *International Socialization in Europe. European Organizations, Political Conditionality and Democratic* Change. Palgrave Macmillan, 2006.

Schimmelfennig, Frank, and Sedelmeier, Ulrich, "Governance by Conditionality: EU Rule Transfer to the Candidate Countries of Central and Eastern Europe." *Journal of European Public Policy* 11(4) (2004): 661–679.

Schocken, Celina, "The Special Court for Sierra Leone: Overview and Recommendations." *Berkeley Journal of International Law* 20(2002): 436–461.

Schorkopf, Frank, *Die Massnahmen der XIV EU-Mitgliedstaaten gegen Österreich*. Springer, 2002.

Schultz, Tammy and Merill, Susan, "From Bullets to Ballots," in Brinkerhoff, Derick (ed.), *Governance in Post-Conflict Societies*. Routledge, 2007.

Schumpeter, Joseph, *Capitalism, Socialism and Democracy*. Harper & Brothers, 1942.

Schuppert, Gunnar Folke, "Gute Gesetzgebung: Bausteine einer kritischen Gesetzgebungslehre." *Sonderheft 2003 der Zeitschrift für Gesetzgebung* (ZG) (2003).

Schuppert, Gunnar Folke, "Governance im Spiegel der Wissenschaftsdisziplinen," in Schuppert, Gunnar Folke (ed.), *Governance-Forschung: Vergewisserung über Stand und Entwicklungslinien*. 2nd ed. Nomos, 2006.

Schuppert, Gunnar Folke, "Rule of Law als Grundelement Politischer Kultur," in Schuppert, Gunnar Folke (ed.), *Politische Kultur*. Nomos, 2008.

Schuppert, Gunnar Folke, *Governance und Rechtsetzung: Grundfragen einer modernen Regelungswissenschaft*. Nomos, 2010b.

Schuppert, Gunnar Folke, *Staat als Prozess: Eine staatstheoretische Skizze in sieben Aufzügen*. Campus Verlag, 2010c.

Schwartz, Herman, "Dependency or Institutions? Economic Geography, Causal Mechanisms, and Logic in the Understanding of Development." *Studies in Comparative International Development* 41(1) (2007): 115–135.

Schwebel, Stephen Myron, "The United States 2004 Model Bilateral Investment Treaty and Denial of Justice in International Law," in Binder, Christina, Kriebaum, Ursula, Reinisch, August, and Wittich, Stephan (eds.), *International Investment Law for the 21st Century – Essays in Honour of Christoph Schreuer*. Oxford University Press, 2009.

Scott, Colin, "Regulation in the Age of Governance: The Rise of the Post-Regulatory State," in Jordana, Jacint, and Levi-Faur, David (eds.), *The Politics of Regulation: Institutions and Regulatory Reforms for the Age of Governance*. Edward Elgar Publishing, 2004: 145–174.

Scott, Richard, *Organizations: Rational, Natural and Open Systems*. Prentice-Hall, 2003.

Scott, Richard, Ruef, Martin, Mendel, Peter, and Caronna, Carol, *Institutional Change and Healthcare Organizations: From Professional Dominance to Managed Care*. University of Chicago Press, 2000.

Sedra, Mark, "Security Sector Reform in Afghanistan: The Slide Towards Expediency." *International Peacekeeping* 13(2006): 94–110.

Senden, Linda, *Soft Law in European Community Law*. Hart Publishing, 2004.

Shelley, Louise, "Identifying, Counting and Categorizing Transnational Criminal Organizations." *Transnational Organized Crime* 5 (1) (1999): 1–18.

Shelley, Louise, "Human Security and Human Trafficking," in Jonsson Anna (ed.), *Human Trafficking and Human Security*. Routledge, 2009.

Shihata, Ibrahim, *The World Bank Inspection Panel: In Practice*. Oxford University Press, 2000.

Silbey, Susan, "After Legal Consciousness." *Annual Review of Law and Social Science* 1(2005): 323–368.

Simma, Bruno, "Grundfragen der Staatenverantwortlichkeit in der Arbeit der International Law Commission." *Archiv des Völkerrechts* 24(1985): 357–407.

Simmons, Beth, *Mobilizing for Human Rights: International Law in Domestic Politics*. Cambridge University Press, 2009.

Simmons, Beth, Dobbin, Frank, and Garrett, Geoffrey, "Introduction: The International Diffusion of Liberalism." *International Organization* 60(4) (2006): 781–810.

Simmons, Beth, Dobbin, Frank, and Garrett, Geoffrey (eds.), *The Global Diffusion of Markets and Democracy*. Cambridge University Press, 2008.

Simpson, Gerry, *Great Powers and Outlaw States – Unequal Sovereigns in the International Legal Order*. Cambridge University Press, 2004.

Skaaning, Svend-Erik, "Measuring the Rule of Law." *Political Research Quarterly* 63(2) (2010): 449–460.

Skowronek, Stephen, *Building a New American State: The Expansion of National Administrative Capacities, 1877–1920*. Cambridge University Press, 1982.

Slaughter, Anne-Marie, "A Typology of Transjudicial Communication." *Richmond University Law Review* 29(1994): 99–137.

Slaughter, Anne-Marie, "Governing the Global Economy Through Government Networks," in Byers, Michael (ed.), *The Role of Law in International Politics: Essays in International Relations and International Law*. Oxford University Press, 2000.

Slaughter, Anne-Marie, *A New World Order*. Princeton University Press, 2004.

Smith, Karen, "The Evolution and Application of EU Membership Conditionality," in Cremona, Marise (ed.), *Enlargement of the European Union*. Oxford University Press, 2003: 105–139.

Smits, Jan, "Import and Export of Legal Models: The Dutch Experience." *Transnational Law and Contemporary Problems* 13(2003): 551–573.

Smrkolj, Maja, "International Institutions and Individualized Decision-Making: An Example of UNHCR's Refuge Status Determination." *German Law Journal* 9(11) (2008): 1779–1803.

Stahn, Carsten, *The Law and Practice of International Territorial Administration – Versailles to Iraq and Beyond*. Cambridge University Press, 2008.

Stein, Tine, "Global Social and Civil Entrepreneurs: An Answer to the Poor Performance of Global Governance?" *WZB Discussion Paper SP IV 2008–304*. Wissenschaftszentrum Berlin, 2008.

Stephen, Matthew, and Zürn, Michael, "The View of Old and New Powers on the Legitimacy of International Institutions." *Politics* 30(2010): 91–101.

Stephen, Matthew, "The Commission on Legal Empowerment for the Poor: An Opportunity Missed." *Hague Journal on Rule of Law* 1(2009): 132–155.

Strohmeyer, Hansjörg, "Collapse and Reconstruction of a Judicial System: The United Nations Missions in Kosovo and East Timor." *American Journal of International Law* 95(2001a): 46–63.

Strohmeyer, Hansjörg, "Making Multilateral Interventions Work: The UN and the Creation of Transitional Justice Systems in Kosovo and East Timor." *Fletcher Forum of World Affairs* 107(2001b): 107–128.

Stromseth, Jane, "Justice on the Ground: Can International Criminal Courts Strengthen Domestic Rule of Law in Post-Conflict Societies?" *Hague Journal on Rule of Law* 1(2009): 87–97.

Stromseth, Jane, Wippman, David and Brooks, Rosa, *Can Might Make Rights? Building the Rule of Law After Military Interventions*. Cambridge University Press, 2006.

Stone Sweet, Alec, and Brunell, Thomas,"Constructing a Supranational Constitution: Dispute Resolution and Governance in the European Community." *American Political Science Review* 92(1) (1998): 63–81.

Stone Sweet, Alec, and Sandholtz, Wayne, "European Integration and Supranational Governance." *Journal of European Public Policy* 4(3) (1997): 297–317.

Suchman, Mark, "Managing Legitimacy: Strategic and Institutional Approaches." *Academy of Management Review* 20(3) (1995): 571–610.

Summers, Robert, "The Principles of the Rule of Law." *Notre Dame Law Review* 74(75) (1999): 1691–1712.

Suzuki, Eisuke, and Nanwani, Suresh, "Responsibility of International Organizations: The Accountability Mechanisms of Multilateral Development Banks." *Michigan Journal of International Law* 27(1) (2005): 177–225.

Tamanaha, Brian, *On the Rule of Law. History, Politics, Theory*. Cambridge University Press, 2004.

Tasikas, Vasilios, "Developing the Rule of Law in Afghanistan: The Need for a New Strategic Paradigm." *The Army Lawyer* (July 2007): 45–60.

Taylor, Veronica, "New Markets, New Commodity: Japanese Legal Technical Assistance." *Wisconsin International Law Journal* 23(2005): 251–281.

Taylor, Veronica, "The Law Reform Olympics: Measuring the Effects of Law Reform in Transition Economies," in Lindsey, Tim (ed.), *Law Reform in Developing and Transitional States*. Routledge, 2007: 83–105.

Taylor, Veronica, "Frequently Asked Questions About Rule of Law Assistance (And Why Better Answers Matter)." *Hague Journal on Rule of Law* 1(2009): 46–52.

Teitel, Ruti and Howse, Robert, "Cross-Judging: Tribunalization in a Fragmented but Interconnected Global Order." *New York University Journal of International Law & Politics* 41(2009): 959–990.

Teubner, Gunther, "Breaking Frames. The Global Interplay of Legal and Social Systems." *American Journal of Comparative Law* 45(1997a): 149–169.

Teubner, Gunther, "Global Bukowina: Legal Pluralism in the World Society," in Teubner, Gunther (ed.), *Global Law Without a State*. Ashgate, 1997b: 3–38.

Teubner, Gunter, "Legal Irritants: Good Faith in British Law or How Unifying Law Ends up in New Divergences." *Modern Law Review* 61(1) (1998): 11–32.

Thachuk, Kimberley, *Transnational Threats: Smuggling and Trafficking in Arms, Drugs, and Human Life*. Praeger Security International, 2007.

Thomas, George, Meyer, John, Ramirez, Francisco, and Boli, John (eds.), *Institutional Structure: Constituting State, Society, and the Individual*. Sage, 1987.

Thompson, Robert, *Defeating Communist Insurgency: The Lesson of Malaya and Vietnam*. Praeger, 1966.

Thürer, Daniel, "The 'Failed State' and International Law." *International Review of the Red Cross* 81(836) (1999): 731–761.

Tietje, Christian, *Internationalisiertes Verwaltungshandeln*. Duncker & Humblot, 2001.

Tietje, Christian, "Transnationales Wirtschaftsrecht aus öffentlich-rechtlicher Perspektive." *Zeitschrift für Vergleichende Rechtswissenschaft* 101(2002): 404–420.

Tomuschat, Christian, "Das Völkerrecht ist kein Zweiklassenrecht. Der Irak-Krieg und seine Folgen." *Vereinte Nationen* 51(2) (2003): 41–46.

Tomuschat, Christian, "Der fremdenrechtliche Mindeststandard im Völkerrecht," in Merten, Detlef, and Papier, Hans-Jürgen (eds.), *Handbuch der Grundrechte in Deutschland und Europa, Band VI/2*. C. F. Müller, 2009.

Trebilcock, Michael and Daniels, Ronald, *Rule of Law Reform and Development: Charting the Fragile Path of Progress*. Edward Elgar Publishing, 2008.

Tripp, Charles, "The United States and state-building in Iraq." *Review of International Studies* 30(2004): 545–558.

Trubek, David, "The Rule of Law in Development Assistance: Past, Present, Future." University of Wisconsin-Madison (2003). Available at http://www.law.wisc.edu/facstaff/trubek/RuleofLaw.pdf.

Trubek, David, "The 'Rule of Law' in Development Assistance: Past, Present and Future," in Trubek, David and Santos, Alvaro (eds.), *The New Law and Economic Development: A Critical Appraisal*. Cambridge University Press, 2006: 74–95.

Trubek, David, "The Political Economy of the Rule of Law: The Challenge of the New Developmental State." *Hague Journal on the Rule of Law* 1 (01) (2009): 28–32.

Trubek, David, Cottrell, Patrick, Nance, Mark, "'Soft Law', 'Hard Law' and European Integration: Toward a Theory of Hybridity," in de Búrca, Gráinne, and Scott, Joanne (eds.), *New Governance and Constitutionalism*. Hart Publishing, 2005: 1–41.

Trubek, David and Galanter, Marc, "Scholars in Self-Estrangement: Some Reflections on the Crisis in Law and Development Studies in the United States." *Wisconsin Law Review* (1974): 1062–1083.

Trubek, David, and Santos, Alvaro (eds.), *The New Law and Economic Development: A Critical Appraisal*. Cambridge University Press, 2006.

Tsai, Kellee, *Capitalism Without Democracy: Politics of Private Sector Development in China*. Cornell University Press, 2007.

Tshuma, Lawrence, "The Political Economy of the World Bank's Legal Framework," in Faundez, Julio, Footer, Mary, and Norton, Joseph (eds.), *Governance, Development and Globalization*. Blackstone Press, 2000: 7–27.

Turner, Jackie, and Kelly, Liz, "Trade Secrets: Intersections Between Diasporas and Crime Groups in the Constitution of the Human Trafficking Chain." *British Journal of Criminology* 49 (2) (2009): 184–201.

Tyler, Tom, "Psychological Perspectives on Legitimacy and Legitimating." *Annual Review of Psychology* 57(2006): 375–400.

Twining, William, "Diffusion of Law: A Global Perspective." *Journal of Legal Pluralism and Unofficial Law* 49(1) (2004): 1–47.

Udall, Lori, *The World Bank Inspection Panel: A Three Year Review*. Washington DC: Bank Information Center, 1997.

Udombana, Nsongurua, "Globalization of Justice and Special Court for Sierra Leone's War Crimes." *Emory International Law Review* 17(2003): 56–132.

Upham, Frank, "From Demsetz to Deng: Speculations on the Source." *New York University Journal of International Law and Politics* 41(3) (2009): 522–602.

Upham, Frank, "Who Will Find the Defendant if He Strays with His Sheep? Justice in Rural China." *Yale Law Journal* 114(7) (2005): 1675–1718.

Uprimny, Rodrigo, Rodríguez, Cesar and García, Mauricio, *Justicia para Todos? Sistema judicial, derechos sociales y democracia en Colombia*. Grupo Norma, 2006.

Vachudová, Milada Anna, *Europe Undivided: Democracy, Leverage, and Integration Since 1989*. Oxford University Press, 2005.

Vanderlinden, Jacques, "Return to Legal Pluralism: Twenty Years Later." *Journal of Legal Pluralism and Unofficial Law* 28(1989): 149–152.

Von Struensee, Vanessa, "Sex Trafficking: A Plea for Action." *European Law Journal* 6 (4) (2000): 379–407.
Waldron, Jeremy, *Law and Disagreement*. Oxford University Press, 1999.
Waldron, Jeremy, "The Concept and the Rule of Law." *Georgia Law Review* 43(2008): 1–61.
Waldron, Jeremy, "Representative Lawmaking." *Boston University Law Review* 89(2009): 335–355.
Waltz, Kenneth. *Theory of International Politics*. McGraw-Hill, 1979.
Warkotsch, Alexander, "Non-Compliance and Instrumental Variation in EU Democracy Promotion." *Journal of European Public Policy* 15(2) (2008).
Warren, Marc, "The 'Fog of Law': The Law of Armed Conflict in Operation Iraqi Freedom," in Pedrozo, Raul (ed.), *The War in Iraq: A Legal Analysis*. Naval War College Press, Department of the Navy, 2010: 167–206.
Watson, Alan, "Legal Change: Sources of Law and Legal Culture." *University of Pennsylvania Law Review* 131(1983): 1126–1157.
Watts, Arthur, "The International Rule of Law." *German Yearbook of International Law* 36(1993): 15–45.
Weissbrodt, David, "Due Process, Rule of Law, and Habeas Corpus," in Forsythe, David (ed.), *Encyclopedia of Human Rights*, Vol. II. Oxford University Press, 2009.
Wendt, Alexander, "Driving with the Rearview Mirror: On the Rational Science of Institutional Design." *International Organization* 55(4) (2001): 1019–1049.
Wennerström, Erik, *The European Union and the Rule of Law*. Iustus Förlag, 2007.
William, Thomas, *Child Trafficking: An Unconscious Phenomenon*. Kanishka Publishers Distributors, 2008.
Woods, Ngaire and Narlikar, Amrita, "Governance and the Limits of Accountability: The WTO, the IMF, and the World Bank." *International Social Science Journal* 53(170) (2001): 569–583.
Xu, Zhangrun, "Western Law in China: Transplantation or Transformation – Four Cases and Liang Shuming's Responses," *Social Sciences in China* 25(2004): 134–151.
Youngs, Richard, "European Union Democracy Promotion Policies: Ten Years On." *European Foreign Affairs Review* 6(3) (2001): 355–373.
Zajac Sannerholm, Richard, "Legal, Judicial and Administrative Reforms in Post-Conflict Societies: Beyond the Rule of Law Template." *Journal of Conflict & Security Law* 12(1) (2007): 65–94.
Zanger, Sabine, "Good Governance and European Aid. The Impact of Political Conditionality." *European Union Politics* 1(3) (2000): 293–317.
Zangl, Bernhard, "Judizialisierung als Bestandteil internationaler Rechtsherrschaft: Theoretische Debatten," in Zangl, Bernhard (ed.), *Auf dem Weg zu internationaler Rechtsherrschaft: Streitbeilegung zwischen Politik und Recht*. Campus Verlag, 2010.
Zangl, Bernhard, and Zürn, Michael, "Make Law not War: Internationale und transnationale Verrechtlichung als Baustein für Global Governance," in Zangl, Bernhard, and Zürn, Michael (eds.), *Verrechtlichung: Baustein für Global Governance?* Dietz, 2004.
Zhang, Sheldon, *Smuggling and Trafficking in Human Beings: All Roads Lead to America*. Praeger, 2007.
Ziemke, Earl, "Improvising Stability and Change in Postwar Germany," in Wolfe, Robert (ed.), *Americans as Proconsuls: United States Military Government in Germany and Japan, 1944–1952*. Southern Illinois University Press, 1984.
Zürn, Michael, "Global Governance and Legitimacy Problems." *Government and Opposition* 39(2) (2004): 260–287.

Zürn, Michael, "Global Governance," in Schuppert, Gunnar Folke (ed.), *Governance-Forschung*. 2nd ed. Nomos, 2006.
Zürn, Michael and Ecker-Ehrhardt, Matthias (eds.), *Gesellschaftliche Politisierung und internationale Institutionen*. Suhrkamp, 2011.
Zürn, Michael, and Neyer, Jürgen, "Conclusions – The Conditions of Compliance," in Zürn, Michael, and Joerges, Christian(eds.), *Law and Governance in Postnational Europe*. Cambridge University Press, 2005: 183–217.
Zürn, Michael and Stephen, Matthew, "The View of Old and New Powers on the Legitimacy of International Institutions." *Politics* 30(2010): 91–101.

REPORTS AND INDEXES

Agrast, Mark David, Botero, Juan Carlos, and Ponce-Rodríguez, Alejandro, "The Rule of Law Index: Measuring Adherence to the Rule of Law Around the World. Design and Implementation of the Index Country Profiles for 2009." The World Justice Project. Presented at the World Justice Forum III, Vienna, Austria, 12 November 2009. Available at http://www.worldjusticeproject.org/sites/default/files/World%20Justice%20Forum%20II%20-%20Rule%20of%20Law%20Index%20Report.pdf.
Agrast, Mark David, Botero, Juan Carlos, Ponce-Rodríguez, Alejandro and Dumas, Claudia, "The World Justice Project Rule of Law Index: Measuring Adherence to the Rule of Law Around the World." The World Justice Project. Presented at the World Justice Forum, Vienna, Austria, 3 July 2008. Available at http://www.lexisnexis.com/documents/pdf/20080828015427_large.pdf.
Barnes, Catherine, and Griffiths, Aaron, "Powers of Persuasion: Incentives, Sanctions and Conditionality in Peacemaking." *Conciliation Resources*, Issue 19(2008). Available at http://www.humansecuritygateway.com/documents/Accord_PowersOfPersuasionIncentivesSanctionsConditionalityPeacemaking.pdf.
Bertelsmann Stiftung (ed.), *Bertelsmann Transformation Index 2003. Auf dem Weg zur marktwirtschaftlichen Demokratie*. Bertelsmann Stiftung, 2003. Available at http://www.bertelsmann-transformation-index.de.
Bertelsmann Stiftung (ed.), *Bertelsmann Transformation Index 2006. Auf dem Weg zur marktwirtschaftlichen Demokratie*. Bertelsmann Stiftung, 2006. Available at http://www.bertelsmann-transformation-index.de.
Bertelsmann Stiftung (ed.), *Bertelsmann Transformation Index 2008. Auf dem Weg zur marktwirtschaftlichen Demokratie*. Bertelsmann Stiftung, 2008. Available at http://www.bertelsmann-transformation-index.de.
Bertelsmann Stiftung (ed.), *Bertelsmann Transformation Index 2010. Auf dem Weg zur marktwirtschaftlichen Demokratie*. Bertelsmann Stiftung, 2010. Available at http://www.bertelsmann-transformation-index.de.
Borch, Fred, "The Rule of Law and Judge Advocates: A Short History," in Center for Law and Military Operations, *Rule of Law Handbook: A Practitioner's Guide for Judge Advocates*. The Judge Advocate General's Legal Center & School, U.S. Army, 2008. Available at http://www.loc.gov/rr/frd/Military_Law/pdf/rule-of-law_2010.pdf.
Bühlmann, Marc, Merkel, Wolfgang, Müller, Lisa, Giebler, Heiko, and Wessels, Bernhard, "Democracy Barometer: Methodology. Blueprint Sample. Data for 30 Countries from 1995 to 2005." Version 1, January 2011. Available at http://www.democracybarometer.org/baroapp/files/luw/ore/ika/Methodical_Explanatory_Note_JAN_2011.pdf.
Carothers, Thomas, *Aiding Democracy Abroad: The Learning Curve*. Carnegie Endowment for International Peace, 1999.

Carothers, Thomas, "Promoting the Rule of Law Abroad: The Problem of Knowledge." *Rule of Law Series Working Paper* 34. Carnegie Endowment for International Peace (2003).

Carothers, Thomas, *Critical Mission. Essays on Democracy Promotion*. Carnegie Endowment for International Peace, 2004.

Carothers, Thomas, *Revitalizing Democracy Assistance: The Challenge of USAID*. The Carnegie Endowment for International Peace, 2009a.

Center for Policy and Human Development, "Afghanistan Human Development Report: Bridging Modernity and Tradition: Rule of Law and the Search of Justice" (2007). Available at http://hdr.undp.org/en/reports/nationalreports/asiathepacific/afghanistan/nhdr2007.pdf.

Channell, Wade, "Lessons Not Learned About Legal Reform," in Carothers, Thomas (ed.), *Promoting the Rule of Law Abroad: In Search of Knowledge*. Carnegie Endowment for International Peace, 2006.

Evers, Frank, "OSCE Efforts to promote the Rule of Law." *Working Paper* 20, Centre for OSCE Research (March 2010). Accessed 22 April 2010 at http://www.core-hamburg.de/documents/CORE_Working_Paper_20.pdf.

Finkel, Steven E., Pérez-Liñán, Aníbal, Seligson, Mitchell A., and Azpuru, Dinorah, "Effects of U.S. Foreign Assistance on Democracy-Building. Results of a Cross-National Quantitative Study." Final Report. United States Agency for International Development (USAID), Vanderbilt University and University of Pittsburgh, 2006. Available at http://www.pitt.edu~politicsdemocracydownloadsUSAID_Democracy_Assistance_and_its_Impact_on_Democratization_v34.pdf.

Gorove, Katherine, and Nachbar, Thomas (eds.), *Rule of Law Handbook: A Practitioner's Guide for Judge Advocates*. The Judge Advocate General's Legal Center & School, US Army (2008).

Gross, Eva, "Security Sector Reform in Afghanistan: The EU's Contribution." *European Union Institute for Security Studies Occasional Paper* 78(2009). Available at http://www.iss.europa.eu/uploads/media/op78.pdf.

Hammergren, Linn, "Corruption in Ethiopia's Justice Sector: A Preliminary Overview." Draft report prepared for World Bank Office in Addis Ababa, Ethiopia, 2009.

Hardegger, Sascha, "Cimic-Doktrin im Spannungsfeld zwischen humanitärer Hilfe und militärischer Krisenintervention." *Eidgenössische Technische Hochschule Zürich/ Center for International Studies* 41(2003). Available at http://e-collection.library.ethz.ch/eserv/eth:26228/eth-26228–01.pdf.

Heupel, Monika, and Zürn, Michael, "Internationale Organisationen und der Schutz fundamentaler Rechte von Individuen – Skizze eines Forschungsprojekts." *WZB Discussion Paper SP IV 2010–303*, Wissenschaftszentrum Berlin (2010).

Heyland, Bjorn, Morne, Kalle, and Willumsen, Fredrik, "Be Careful When Doing Business." Report commissioned by the Norwegian Ministry of Foreign Affairs, 2008. Available at http://www.ifiwatchnet.org.

Hewko, John, "Foreign Direct Investment: Does Rule of Law Matter?" Rule of Law Series Working Paper 26. Carnegie Endowment for International Peace, 2002.

Kahler, Miles. *International Institutions and the Political Economy of Integration*. Brookings Institution Press, 1995.

Kapur, Devesh, and McHale, John. *Give Us Your Best and Brightest: The Global Hunt for Talent and its Impact on the Developing World*. Center for Global Development, 2005.

Kilcullen, David, "Three Pillars of Counterinsurgency." Remarks delivered at the U.S. Government Counterinsurgency Conference, Washington, DC, 28 September 2006. Available at http://www.au.af.mil/au/awc/awcgate/uscoin/3pillars_of_counterinsurgency.pdf.

Kleinfeld, Rachel, "Competing Definitions of the Rule of Law. Implications for Practitioners." *Carnegie Papers, Rule of Law Series, No. 55* (2005).

Maisuradze, Tamuna, "People Power: Jury Trials to Come to Georgia." *Caucasus Investigative Reporting Center*, Newsletter May 2006. Available at http://www.circ.ge/news.php?lan=en&newsid=EEuZukkVVpcvRLVrly&pageid=newsletter.

Muharremi, Robert, Peci, Lulcim, Malazogu, Leon, Knaus, Verena and Murati, Teuta, *Administration and Governance in Kosovo: Lessons Learned and Lessons to be Learnt*. Kosovar Institute for Policy Research and Development, 2005.

Mückenberger, Ulrich, "Civilizing Globalism: Transnational Norm-Building Networks – A Research Programme." *GIGA Working Papers* Nr. 90(2008).

Olsen, Howard and Davis, John, *Training U.S. Army Officers for Peace Operations: Lessons from Bosnia*. Special Report. United States Institute of Peace, 1999. Available at http://www.usip.org/files/resources/sr991029.pdf.

Ogola, Florence, "Uganda Victims Question ICC's Balance." Institute for War and Peace Reporting, 14 June 2010.

Pregent, Richard, "Rule of Law Capacity Building in Iraq," in Pedrozo, Raul (ed.), *The War in Iraq: A Legal Analysis*. Naval War College Press, Department of the Navy, 2010b: 323–348.

Prugh, George. *Law at War: Vietnam 1964–1973*. Department of the Army, 1975.

Spector, Bertram, Winbourne, Svetlana and Beck, Laurence, "Corruption in Kosovo: Observations and Implications for USAID." Final Report submitted to the United States Agency for International Development, 10 July 2003.

Sumner, Andy, "Global Poverty and the New Bottom Billion: What if Three-Quarters of the World's Poor Live in Middle-Income Countries?" Working paper in draft (2010). Available at http://www.ids.ac.uk/go/idspublication/global-poverty-and-the -new-bottom-billion.

Thiery, Peter, Sehring, Jenniver and Muno, Wolfgang, "Wie misst man Recht?" Paper presented at the meeting of the DVPW working group "Demokratieforschung," together with the GTZ on "Rule of Law Compliance – Regelbefolgung im Kontext von Kultur, Institution und Akteur," 10–12 June 2010.

Upham, Frank, "Mythmaking in the Rule of Law Orthodoxy." *Carnegie Endowment for International Peace Working Papers*, No. 30, 2002.

Vieira de Mello, Sergio, "How Not to Run a Country: Lessons from Kosovo and East Timor" (2000). UNITAR-IPS-JIIA Conference to Assess the Report on UN Peace Operations, Singapore, February 2001.

Williamson, John, "What Washington Means by Policy Reform," in Williamson, John (ed.), *Latin American Adjustment: How Much Has Happened*. Institute for International Economics, 1990.

Wojkowska, Ewa, *Doing Justice: How Informal Justice Systems Can Contribute*. UNDP, Oslo Governance Centre, 2006.

Youngs, Richard (ed.), *Survey of European Democracy Promotion Policies 2000–2006*. FRIDE, 2006.

TREATIES, CONVENTIONS, AND OTHER LEGISLATIVE DOCUMENTS

Agreement on Provisional Arrangements in Afghanistan Pending the Re-Establishment of Permanent Government Institutions (Bonn Agreement) of 5 December 2001.

American Convention on Human Rights of 22 November 1969, entered into force on 18 July 1978, OAS Treaty Series No. 36.

Charter of the Association of Southeast Asian Nations of 27 November 2007.
Coalition Provisional Authority, "Penal Code" CPA CPA/ORD/9 (2003).
Constitution of the Mexican United States.
Constitution of the Republic of Uganda (1995).
Constitutive Act of the African Union of 11 July 2000.
Convention (IV) Relative to the Protection of Civilian Persons in Time of War of 12 August 1949, entered into force on 21 October 1950, 75 UNTS 287.
Convention Against Transnational Organized Crime (UNCTOC) and the Protocols on Trafficking in Persons and Smuggling of Migrants, by UNGA Resolution 55/25 of 15 November 2000.
Convention for the Suppression of the Traffic in Persons and of the Exploitation of the Prostitution of Others, approved by UNGA Resolution 317 (IV) of 2 December 1949, entered into force on 25 July 1951.
Convention for the Suppression of the Traffic in Women and Children, signed in Geneva on 30 September 1921, entered into force on 15 June 1922.
Convention on the Protection of Human Rights and Fundamental Freedoms of 4 November 1950, entered into force on 3 September 1953, ETS no. 5.
Declaration on Principles of International Law Concerning Friendly Relations and Co-operation Among States in Accordance with the Charter of the United Nations, UNGA Resolution 2625 of 24 October 1970, UN Doc. A/RES/2625.
General Agreement on Trade and Tariffs of 1 January 1948.
General Framework Agreement for Peace in Bosnia and Herzegovina of 21 November 1995, entered into force on 14 December 1995 (GFAP).
Hague Conventions of 18 October of 1907, entered into force on 26 January 1910.
International Criminal Court Bill, XCVII(26), *Uganda Gazette*, 28 May 2004.
Inter-American Democratic Charter of 11 September 2001.
International Agreement for the Suppression of White Slave Traffic, 18 May 1904, 35 Stat. 426, 1 LNTS 83.
International Covenant on Civil and Political Rights of 16 December 1966, entered into force on 23 March 1976, 999 UNTS 171.
Lomé IV Convention, signed in Mauritius on 4 November 1995.
National Defense Authorization Act for Fiscal Year 2006. Pub. L. No. 109–163, 119 Stat. 3136, 3455–56.
North America Free Trade Agreement (NAFTA), entered into force on 1 January 1994.
Partnership Agreement Between the Members of the African, Caribbean and Pacific Group of States, of the one Part, and the European Community and its Member States, of the Other Part ("Cotonou Agreement") (2000), Official Journal L317/3 of 15 December 2000, as revised (2005) Official Journal L209/27 of 11 August 2005.
Protocol of Washington of 1991, reprinted in *International Legal Materials* 33(1994), 1005.
Rome Statute of the International Criminal Court of 17 July 1998, entered into force on 1 July 2002, 2187 UNTS 90.
Statute of the Council of Europe of 5 May 1949, ETS no. 1.
Treaty on the European Union (2008), *Official Journal C/115*.
Ugandan Amnesty Act (2000).
Ugandan Amnesty (Amendment) Bill (2003).
Ugandan Geneva Conventions Act (1964).
Ugandan International Criminal Court Act (2010).
Ugandan Penal Code Act (1950).

Ugandan Peoples' Defence Forces Act (2005).
Ugandan Ratification of Treaties Act (1998).

U.N. DOCUMENTS AND OTHER INTERNATIONAL ORGANIZATION DOCUMENTS

2005 World Summit Outcome, UNGA Resolution 60/1 of 24 October 2005, UN Doc. A/RES/60/1.

Asian Development Bank, "Governance: Sound Development Mechanisms." August 1995. Accessed 28 March 2010 at http://www.adb.org/Documents/Policies/Governance/default.asp.

Commission of the European Communities, "European Neighbourhood Policy, Strategy Paper." COM (2004) 373 final, 12 May 2004: 3. Accessed 20 April 2010 at http://ec.europa.eu/world/enp/pdf/strategy/strategy_paper_en.pdf.

Commission on Legal Empowerment of the Poor, *Making the Law Work for Everyone*, Vol. 1. Commission on Legal Empowerment of the Poor and UNDP, 2008.

Council of Europe, "Directorate of Co-operation." Accessed 14 April 2010 at www.coe.int/t/dghl/overview_cooperation_en.asp.

Council of Europe, "Human Rights and Legal Affairs." Accessed 14 April 2010 at www.coe.int/t/dghl/default_en.asp.

Council of Europe, "Our Objectives." Accessed 15 April 2010 at www.coe.int/aboutCoe/index.asp?page=nosObjectifs&l=en.

Council of Europe Committee of Ministers, "The Council of Europe and the Rule of Law – An Overview, Ministers' Deputies CM Documents." *CM* (2008)170, 21 November 2008. Accessed 20 April 2010 at http://www.coe.int/t/e/legal_affairs/legal_co-operation/fight_against_terrorism/3_codexter/working_documents/2008/CM%282008%29170%20en.pdf.

Council of the European Union, "Council Joint Action 2008/124/CFSP of 4 February 2008 on the European Union Rule of Law Mission in Kosovo, EULEX KOSOVO."

Council of the European Union, "EU Common Security and Defence Policy (CSDP), Overview of the Missions and Operations of the European Union April 2010." Accessed 22 April 2010 at http://www.consilium.europa.eu/showPage.aspx?id=268&lang=EN.

Dakolias, Maria. "The Judicial Sector in Latin America and the Caribbean: Elements of Reform." World Bank Technical Paper No. 319. World Bank, 1996.

Directorate-General for External Policies of the European Union, "Consolidating the EU's Crisis Management Structures: Civil–Military Coordination and the Future of the EU OHQ." (2010).

ECOWAS, Protocol on Democracy and Good Governance, Protocol Supplementary to the Protocol Relating to the Mechanism for Conflict Prevention Management, Resolution, Peacekeeping and Security, adopted on 10 December 1999.

EULEX Kosovo, "European Union Rule of Law Mission." Accessed 20 April 2010 at http://www.eulex-kosovo.eu/?id=1.

EULEX Kosovo, "Programme Report 2010: Building Sustainable Change Together" (2010). Available at http://www.eulex-kosovo.eu/docs/tracking/EULEX%20Programme%20Report%202010%20.pdf.

European Commission for Democracy through Law ('Venice Commission'), Report on the Rule of Law, adopted by the Venice Commission at its 86th plenary session, Venice, 25–26 March 2011, CDL-AD(2011)003rev.

European Commission for Democracy through Law ('Venice Commission'), "Draft Report on the Notion of 'Good Governance' on the Basis of Comments by O. Kask and A. Eide." Study No. 470/2008, CDL(2008)091 (8 October 2008).

European Commission, Kosovo Under UNSCR 1244/99 2009 Progress Report, 2009: 9.
European Council in Copenhagen, "Conclusions of the Presidency." 21–22 June 1993: 12–16. Accessed 20 April 2010 at www.consilium.europa.eu/uedocs/cms_data/docs/pressdata/en/ec/72921.pdf.
Fritz, Verena, Kaiser, Kai and Levy, Brian, *Problem-Driven Governance and Political Economy Analysis*. World Bank, 2009.
HRC, Report of 14 August 2006, UN Doc. CCPR/C/UNK/CI/1.
Inter-American Development Bank, "Modernization of the State Report," July 2003. Accessed 28 March 2010 at http://idbdocs.iadb.org/wsdocs/getdocument.aspx?docnum=1441783.
International Commission on Intervention and State Sovereignty, "The Responsibility to Protect." Accessed 12 March 2010 at http://www.iciss.ca/report-en.asp.
ISAF, "ISAF Commander's Counterinsurgency Guidance" (2009). Available at http://smallwarsjournal.com.
Jenkins, Rhys, "Corporate Codes of Conduct: Self-Regulation in a Global Economy." *United Nations Research Institute for Social Development. Programme Paper* No. 2 (April 2001).
Kaufmann, Daniel, and Kraay, Aart, "Governance Indicators: Where Are We, Where Should We Be Going?" *The World Bank Research Observer* 23(1) (2008): 1–30.
Kaufmann, Daniel, Kraay, Aart, and Mastruzzi, Massimo, "Worldwide Governance Indicators Project: Answering the Critics." World Bank Policy Research Working Paper No. 4149. World Bank (2007a).
Kaufman, Daniel, Kraay, Aart, and Mastruzzi, Massimo, "Governance Matters VI: Governance Indicators for 1996–2006." Policy Research Working Paper. The World Bank Development Research Group (2007b). Available at http://ssrn.com/abstract=999979.
Kaufmann, Daniel, Kraay, Aart, and Mastruzzi, Massimo, "Governance Matters VIII, Aggregate and Individual Governance Indicators 1996–2008." Policy Research Working Paper. The World Bank Development Research Group (2009). Accessed 22 April 2010 at http://papers.ssrn.com/sol3/papers.cfm?abstract_id=1424591.
Knack, Stephen, "Measuring Corruption in Eastern Europe and Central Asia: A Critique of the Cross-Country Indicators." World Bank Policy Research Working Paper No. 3968. World Bank (2006).
Naples Political Declaration and Global Action Plan against Organized Transnational Crime, UNGA Resolution 49/159 of 23 December 1994, UN Doc. A/RES/49/1590.
NATO, "Allied Joint Publication 9: NATO Civil–Military Co-Operation Doctrine." AJP-9 (2003).
NATO, "Allied Joint Doctrine for Civil–Military Cooperation (Study Draft 3)." AJP-9(A) (2003).
NATO Military Council, "MC 411/1 – NATO Military Policy on Civil–Military Co-operation" (2001).
OAS, "Declaration of Santiago on Democracy and Public Trust: A New Commitment to Good Governance for the Americas." Adopted on 10 June 2003. OAS Doc. AG/DEC.31 (XXXIII-O/03).
OECD-DAC, The Paris Declaration on Aid Effectiveness the Accra Agenda for Action, 2005.
OHCHR, "Human Rights Committee." Accessed 20 April 2010 at http://www2.ohchr.org/english/bodies/hrc/index.htm.
OHCHR, "Universal Periodic Review." Accessed 20 April 2010 at http://www.ohchr.org/EN/HRBodies/UPR/Pages/Documentation.aspx.
OSCE, "Conflicting Jurisdiction in Property Disputes" (2003).
OSCE, "Field Operations." Accessed 14 April 2010 at http://www.osce.org/about/13510.html.
OSCE, "Human Rights and Rule of Law: Remedies Catalogue" (2003).

OSCE, "Office for Democratic Institutions and Human Rights." Accessed 14 April 2010 at http://www.osce.org/odihr/13479.html.

OSCE, "Office for Democratic Institutions and Human Rights, Independence of the Judiciary." Accessed 15 April 2010 at http://www.osce.org/odihr/36363.html.

OSCE, "Office for Democratic Institutions and Human Rights, Legislationline.org." Accessed 21 April 2010 at http://www.osce.org/odihr/13462.html.

OSCE, *OSCE Human Dimension Commitments, Volume 1, Thematic Compilation*, 2nd ed. (2005).

OSCE, "OSCE Mission in Bosnia and Herzegovina." Accessed 7 April 2010 at http://www.oscebih.org/oscebih_eng.asp.

OSCE, "OSCE Mission in Kosovo." Accessed 7 April 2010 at http://www.osce.org/kosovo/.

OSCE, "Secretariat – Strategic Police Matters Unit." Accessed 14 April 2010 at http://www.osce.org/spmu/publications.html.

PACE Order No. 488 (1993) on the Honouring of Commitments Entered into by New Member States, 26 June 1993.

PACE Order No. 508 (1995) of 26 April 1995.

PACE Recommendation 1444 (2000) of 27 January 2000.

PACE Recommendation 1456 (2000) of 6 April 2000.

PACE Resolution 1102 (1996) of 1 of 7 November 1996.

PACE Resolution 1221 (2000) of 29 June 2000.

PACE Resolution 1727 (2010) of 29 April 2010.

Pact on Security, Stability and Development in the Great Lakes Region, reprinted in *International Legal Materials* 46(2007).

Peace and Security Council decision adopted at the 216th meeting of 19 February 2010, PSC/PR/COMM.1(CCXVI).

Peace and Security Council decision adopted at the 216th meeting of 19 February 2010, PSC/PR/COMM.2(CCXVI).

Phillips, William, "Civil–Military Cooperation: Vital to Peace Implementation in Bosnia." *NATO Review – Web ed.* 46(1) (1998): 22–25.

Posner, Richard, "Creating a Legal Framework for Economic Development." *World Bank Research Observer* 13(1) (1998): 1–11.

Report of the Secretary-General on the Rule of Law and Transitional Justice in Conflict and Post-Conflict Societies, 23 August 2004, UN Doc. S/2004/616.

Report of the Secretary-General on the Strengthening the rule of law to the UNGA, 20 July 2000, UN Doc. A/49/512.

Report of the United Nations Secretary-General on the United Nations Interim Administration in Kosovo, 12 June 1999, UN Doc. S/1999/799.

Report on the International Responsibility by Mr. F.V. Garcia Amador, Special Rapporteur, UN Doc. A/CN.4/96, YBILC 1956, Vol. II.

Resolution on the Suspension of the Right of Honduras to Participate in the OAS, adopted at the second plenary session, held on July 4, 2009, and reviewed by the Style Committee, Organization of American States General Assembly, AG/RES. 2 (XXXVII-E/09).

Second Annual Report of the Secretary-General on Strengthening and Coordinating United Nations Rule of Law Activities, 20 August 2010, UN Doc. A/65/318.

Security Council Debate on The Promotion and Strengthening of the Rule of Law in the Maintenance of International Peace and Security, 29 June 2010, UN Doc. S/PV.6347.

The Rule of Law at the National and International Levels: Comments and Information Received from Governments, Report of the Secretary-General of 11 July 2007, UN Doc. A/62/121.

UNAMA and ISAF Southern Region Partners Coordination Board (RC-South), "A Common and Operational Approach to Rule of Law for Southern Afghanistan" (2009), unpublished.
UNAMA, "Suicide Attacks in Afghanistan (2001–2007)" (2007). Available at http://www.unhrc.org.
UN Approach to Rule of Law Assistance, Guidance Note of the Secretary-General, April 2008.
UNCHR, General Comment No. 29 on States of Emergency (Article 4), UN Doc. CCPR/C/21/Rev.1/Add.11 of 31 August 2001.
UNCHR Resolution 2000/64. Accessed 28 March 2010 at http://www2.ohchr.org/english/bodies/chr/regular-sessions.htm.
UNCHR Resolution 2001/72. Accessed 28 March 2010 at http://www2.ohchr.org/english/bodies/chr/regular-sessions.htm.
UNCHR Resolution 2002/76. Accessed 28 March 2010 at http://www2.ohchr.org/english/bodies/chr/regular-sessions.htm.
UNCHR Resolution 2004/70. Accessed 28 March 2010 at http://www2.ohchr.org/english/bodies/chr/regular-sessions.htm.
UNCHR Resolution 2005/68. Accessed 28 March 2010 at http://www2.ohchr.org/english/bodies/chr/regular-sessions.htm.
UN DPKO, "Civil-Military Coordination in UN Integrated Peacekeeping Missions (UN-CIMIC)" (2006).
UN DPKO, "OSCE Permanent Council Decision No. 305 1999 and Letter Exchanged between Ambassador Kim Traavik, Head of the OSCE Department and Bernard Miyet," 19 July 1999.
UNDP, "Governance for Sustainable Development." Accessed 28 March 2010 at http://mirror.undp.org/magnet/policy/.
UN DPKO, "Policy on Civil-Military Coordination" (2002).
UNGA Resolution 55/383 of 2 November 2000, UN Doc. A/55/383.
UNMIK Administrative Direction No. 2006/18 of 28 December 2006, implementing
UNMIK Administrative Direction No. 2007/7 of 3 August 2007, amending UNMIK Administrative Direction No. 2006/18.
UNMIK Regulation No. 1999/1 of 25 July 1999, UN Doc. UNMIK/REG/1999/1.
UNMIK Regulation No. 1999/5 of 4 September 1999, UN Doc. UNMIK/REG/1999/5.
UNMIK Regulation No. 1999/7 of 7 September 1999, UN Doc. UNMIK/REG/1999/7.
UNMIK Regulation No. 1999/23 of 15 November 1999, UN Doc. UNMIK/REG/1999/23.
UNMIK Regulation No. 1999/24 of 12 December 1999, UN Doc. UNMIK/REG/1999/24.
UNMIK Regulation No. 2000/6 of 15 February 2000, UN Doc. UNMIK/REG/2000/6.
UNMIK Regulation No. 2000/38 of 30 June 2000, UN Doc. UNMIK.REG/2000/38.
UNMIK Regulation No. 2000/60 of 31 October 2000, UN Doc.
UNMIK/REG/2000/60.
UNMIK Regulation No. 2000/64 of 15 December 2004, UN Doc. UNMIK/REG/2000/64.
UNMIK Regulation No. 2001/9 of 15 May 2001, UN Doc. UNMIK/REG/2001/9.
UNMIK Regulation No. 2006/12 of 23 March 2006, UN Doc. UNMIK/REG/2006/12.
UNMIK Regulation No. 2006/25, UN Doc. UNMIK/DIR/2006/18.
UNMIK Regulation No. 2006/25 of 27 April 2006, UN Doc. UNMIK/REG/2006/25.
UNODC, *Global Report on Trafficking of Persons*, February 2009.
UNODC, "Legal Tools." Accessed 14 April 2010 at http://www.unodc.org/unodc/en/legal-tools/index.html?ref=menuside.
UN, "Peacekeeping Resource Hub." Accessed 13 April 2010 at http://www.peacekeeping bestpractices.unlb.org/PBPS/Pages/Public/Home.aspx.

UN, "United Nations Peacekeeping." Accessed 20 April 2010 at http://www.un.org/en/peacekeeping/.
United Nations Rule of Law, "Rule of Law Coordination and Resource Group." Accessed 21 April 2010 at http://www.unrol.org/article.aspx?article_id=6.
United Nations Rule of Law, "United Nations Development Programme (UNDP)." Accessed 13 April 2010 at http://www.unrol.org/article.aspx?article_id=13.
United Nations Rule of Law, "United Nations Rule of Law Depository." Accessed 13 April 2010 at http://www.unrol.org/dr.aspx.
United Nations Rule of Law, "What is the Rule of Law?" Accessed 15 April 2010 at http://www.unrol.org/article.aspx?article_id=3.
Uniting our Strengths: Enhancing United Nations Support for the Rule of Law, Report of the Secretary-General of 14 December 2006, UN Doc. S/2006/980.
UNSC Resolution 865 of 22 September 1993, UN Doc. S/RES/865.
UNSC Resolution 897 of 4 February 1994, UN Doc. S/RES/897.
UNSC Resolution 1244 of 10 June 1999, UN Doc. S/RES/1244.
UNSC Resolution 1265 of 17 September 1999, UN Doc. S/RES/1265.
UNSC Resolution 1272 of 25 October 1999, UN Doc. S/RES/1272.
UNSC Resolution 1386 of 20 December 2001, UN Doc. S/RES/1386.
UNSC Resolution 1483 of 22 May 2003, UN Doc. S/RES/1483.
UNSC Resolution 1605 of 17 June 2005, UN Doc. S/RES/1605.
UNSC Resolution 1610 of 30 June 2005, UN Doc. S/RES/1610.
UNSC Resolution 1620 of 31 August 2005, UN Doc. S/RES/1620.
UNSC Resolution 1658 of 14 February 2006, UN Doc. S/RES/1658.
UNSC Resolution 1662 of 23 March 2006, UN Doc. S/RES/1662.
UNSC Resolution 1702 of 15 August 2006, UN Doc. S/RES/1702.
UNSC Resolution 1739 of 10 January 2007, UN Doc. S/RES/1739.
UNSC Resolution 1750 of 30 March 2007, UN Doc. S/RES/1750.
UNSC Resolution 1756 of 15 May 2007, UN Doc. S/RES/1756.
UNSC Resolution 1778 of 25 September 2007, UN Doc. S/RES/1778.
UNSC Resolution 1794 of 21 December 2007, UN Doc. S/RES/1794.
UNSC Resolution 1806 of 20 March 2008, UN Doc. S/RES/1806.
UNSC Resolution 1807 of 31 March 2008, UN Doc. S/RES/1807.
UNSC Resolution 1838 of 7 October 2008, UN Doc. S/RES/1838.
UNSC Resolution 1846 of 2 December 2008, UN Doc. S/RES/1846.
UNSC Resolution 1856 of 22 December 2008, UN Doc. S/RES/1856.
UNSC Resolution 1857 of 22 December 2008, UN Doc. S/RES/1857.
UNSC Resolution 1880 of 30 July 2009, UN Doc. S/RES/1880.
UNSC Resolution 1892 of 13 October 2009, UN Doc. S/RES/1892.
UNSC Resolution 1896 of 30 November 2009, UN Doc. S/RES/1896.
UNSC Resolution 1897 of 30 November 2009, UN Doc. S/RES/1897.
UNSC Resolution 1918 of 27 April 2010, UN Doc. S/RES/1918.
UNTAET Regulation 1999/1 on the Authority of the Transitional Administration in East Timor of 27 November 1999.
Walsh, Barry, *In Search of Success: Case Studies in Justice Sector Development in Sub-Saharan Africa*. World Bank, 2010.
World Bank, *Accelerated Development in Sub Saharan Africa: An Agenda to Action*. World Bank, 1981.
World Bank, "Governance & Anti-Corruption." Accessed 18 November 2009 at http://www.worldbank.org/wbi/governance/.

World Bank, "Implementation Completion Report on a Loan in the Amount of US$ 58 Million to the Russian Federation for a Legal Reform Project." Report No. 36549, June 28 2006.

World Bank, "Law and Justice Institutions." Accessed 13 April 2010 at http://web.worldbank.org/WBSITE/EXTERNAL/TOPICS/EXTLAWJUSTINST/0,,contentMDK:20746118~menuPK:1980807~pagePK:210058~piPK:210062~theSitePK:1974062,00.html.

World Bank, "Weights Used to Construct the Worldwide Governance Indicators for 1996–2008." Accessed 18 November 2008 at http://info.worldbank.org/governance/wgi/resources.htm.

World Bank, "Worldwide Governance Indicators: Links to the Individual WGI Sources." Accessed 18 November 2009 at http://info.worldbank.org/governance/wgi/sources.htm.

World Bank, "Worldwide Governance Indicators: The Worldwide Governance Indicators (WGI) Project." Accessed 18 November 2009 at http://info.worldbank.org/governance/wgi/index.asp.

CASES

Agreement on Accountability and Reconciliation Between the Government of the Republic of Uganda and the Lord's Resistance Army/Movement, Juba, 29 June 2007 (Accountability Agreement)

Advisory Opinion on Judicial Guarantees During States of Exception, Inter-American Court of Human Rights, Series A No. 9, 6 October 1987.

Annexure to the Agreement on Accountability and Reconciliation, Juba, 19 February 2008.

Case Concerning Military and Paramilitary Activities in and Against Nicaragua (Nicaragua v. United States of America), International Court of Justice, Merits, Judgment of 27 June 1986, ICJ Reports 1986.

Claude-Reyes et al. v. Chile, Merits, Reparations and Costs. Inter-American Court of Human Rights, Judgment of September 19, 2006. Series C No. 151.

Golder v. United Kingdom, European Court of Human Rights, Application No. 4451/70, Judgment of 21 February 1975, Series A No. 18.

ICC, Pre Trial Chamber II, "Situation in the Republic of Kenya, Decision Pursuant to Article 15 of the Rome Statute on the Authorization of an Investigation into the Situation in the Republic of Kenya." Dissenting Opinion Judge Hans-Peter Kaul, 31 March 2010, ICC-01/09–19.

Island of Palmas Arbitration, Award of Sole Arbitrator Max Huber, 4 February 1928, RIAA Vol. II, 821.

John Magezi, Judy Obitre-Gama, Henry Onoria versus Attorney-General, Constitutional Court (Uganda), Constitutional Petition No. 10, 27 July 2005.

Juridical Condition and Rights of the Undocumented Migrants, Inter-American Court of Human Rights, Advisory Opinion OC-18 of September 17, 2003, Series A No. 18.

Las Palmeras v. Colombia, Merits, Inter-American Court of Human Rights, Judgment of December 6, 2001. Series C No. 90.

Malone v. the United Kingdom, European Court of Human Rights, Judgement of 2 August 1984, A/82.

Mike Campbell (Pvt) Ltd and Others v. Republic of Zimbabwe, Southern Africa Development Community Tribunal, Decision of 18 November 2008, reprinted in *International Legal Materials* 48(2009): 534.

Mondev International Ltd v. United States of America, Award of 11 October 2002, 6 *ICSID Reports* 19.

Prosecutor v. Joseph Kony, Vincent Otti, Raska Lukwiya, Okot Odhiambo and Dominic Ongwen, Submission of Information on the Status of the Warrants of Arrest in Uganda, International Criminal Court, ICC-02/04–01/05–116, OTP, 6 October 2006.

United States – Section 211 Omnibus Appropriations Act of 1998, WTO Appellate Body, WT/DS176/AB/R of 2 January 2002.

Winterwerp v. the Netherlands, European Court of Human Rights, Judgement of 25 October 1979, A33.

Zondi v. MEC for Traditional and Local Government Affairs and Others, Constitutional Court of South Africa, 2005 (3) SA 589 (CC), Ngcobo J.

OTHER DOCUMENTS

"African Union Bars Guinea on Coup," *BBC News*, 29 December 2008. Accessed 28 March 2010 at http://news.bbc.co.uk/go/pr/fr/-/hi/africa/7802803.stm.

"African Union Suspends Madagascar After 'Coup'," *The Guardian*, 20 March 2009.

American Bar Association (ABA), "ABA Rule of Law Initiative." Accessed 12 April 2010 at www.abanet.org/rol/?gnav=global_publicresources_rol.

American Bar Association (ABA), *Judicial Reform Index: Kosovo*, Vol. III(2007).

American Bar Association (ABA), "Rule of Law Initiative, About the ABA Rule of Law Initiative." Accessed 15 April 2010 at http://www.abanet.org/rol/about.shtml.

American Bar Association (ABA), "Rule of Law Initiative, Criminal Law Reform and Anti-Human Trafficking Programs." Accessed 15 April 2010 at http://www.abanet.org/rol/programs/criminal-law.html.

Amnesty International, "Making a Complaint." Accessed 19 April 2010 at http://www.amnesty.org/en/who-we-are/accountability/making-a-complaint.

Amnesty International, "Uganda: First Steps to Investigate Crimes Must Be Part of Comprehensive Plan to End Impunity." 30 January 2004. Accessed 30 January 2008 at http://www.amnesty.org/en/alfresco_asset/573bd86a-a3b5–11dc-9d08-f145a8145d2b/afr590012004en.pdf.

Amnesty International, "Uganda: Proposed National Framework to Address Impunity Does Not Remove Government's Obligation to Arrest and Surrender LRA Leaders to the International Criminal Court." 15 August 2007.

Anyoli, Edward, "Former LRA Commander Sent to War Court," *New Vision*, 6 September 2010.

Asia Foundation, "Afghanistan in 2007. A Survey of the Afghan People" (2007). Available at http://asiafoundation.org/resources/pdfs/AGsurvey07.pdf.

Blake, Daniel. and Payton, Autumn, "Voting Rules in International Organizations: Reflections of Power or Facilitators of Cooperation?" Paper presented at ISA's 49th Annual Convention, San Francisco, CA, 26 March 2008.

Börzel, Tanja, and Risse, Thomas, "One Size Fits All! EU Policies for the Promotion of Human Rights, Democracy and the Rule of Law." Paper prepared for the Workshop on Democracy Promotion, Center for Development, Democracy, and the Rule of Law, Stanford University, 4–5 October 2004. Accessed 22 April 2010 at http://iis-db.stanford.edu/pubs/20747/Risse-Borzel-stanford_final.pdf.

"Bush Aide Hints Police Are Better Peacekeepers than Military," *New York Times*, 17 November 2000.

Carothers, Thomas, "How Democracies Emerge: The 'Sequencing' Fallacy" (2007). Available at http://www.carnegieendowment.org/events/index.cfm?fa=eventDetail&id=953&prog=zgp&proj=zdrl.

"Clinton Presses Region to Recognize Honduras, *New York Times*, 6 March 2010. Accessed 28 March 2010 at http://www.nytimes.com/2010/03/06/world/americas/06clinton.html.

Combined Security Transition Command – Afghanistan, "CSTC-A Fact Sheet" (12 April 2006).

"Country Reports: Asia Pacific." *The International Journal of Not-for-Profit Law* 2(3) (2000). Accessed 22 April 2010 at http://www.icnl.org/knowledge/ijnl/vol2iss3/cr_1.htm#easttimor.

Crane, Conrad, "COIN of the Realm?: The Role and Importance of Legitimacy in Counterinsurgency." Presentation at the Future Defense Dilemma Seminar of the 21st Century Defense Initiative and the Strategic Studies Institute, 2 April 2008. Available at http://www.povertyfrontiers.org, 2008.

Davies, Rick and Dart, Jess, "The 'Most Significant Change' (MSC) Technique: A Guide to its Use." *Version* 1.00, April 2005. Accessed 18 January 2011 at http://www.mande.co.uk/docs/MSCGuide.pdf.

Department of the Army, *FM 3–07 – Stability Operations and Support Operations* (2003): 4–26.

Department of the Army, *FMI-3–07.11, Counterinsurgency Operations* (2004).

Department of the Army, *FM 3–24, Counterinsurgency* (2006).

Department of State Audit, "Inspection of Rule-of-Law Programs, Embassy, Baghdad." ISP-IQO-06–01 (2005).

Document of the Copenhagen Meeting of the Conference of the Human Dimensions of the CSE (1990).

Doing Business in 2005: Removing Obstacles to Growth. The World Bank, the International Finance Corporation, and Oxford University Press, 2005.

Eide, Espen. Barth, Kaspersen, Anja Therese, Kent, Randolph, and Hippel, Karen von, "Report on Integrated Missions: Practical Perspectives and Recommendations." Independent Study for the Expanded UN ECHA Core Group (2005). Available at http://ochanet.unocha.org/p/Documents/Report_on_Integrated_Missions_May_2005_Final.pdf.

EU Institute for Security Studies, "Publications." Accessed 13 April 2010 at http://www.iss.europa.eu/publications/.

EuropeAid, "Democratic Governance." Accessed 20 July 2010 at http://ec.europa.eu/europeaid/what/governance/index_en.htm.

Europe and Central Asia Region Justice Reform and the World Bank: Status, Trends, and Strategic Directions: Briefing Note. Draft on file with author, 2009.

Freedom House, "Freedom in the World." Accessed 9 April 2010 at http://www.freedomhouse.org/template.cfm?page=15.

Freedom House, "Methodology 2005 Edition." Accessed 18 November 2009 at http://freedomhouse.org/template.cfm?page=351&ana_page=354 &year=2009.

Golub, Stephen, "Participatory Justice in the Philippines," in Golub, Stephen, and McClymont, Mary (eds.), *Many Roads to Justice*. The Ford Foundation, 2000: 197–232.

Government of Uganda, "Referral of the Situation Concerning the Lord's Resistance Army Submitted by the Republic of Uganda." 16 December 2003. On file with author.

Green, Jessica and Colgan, Jeff, "Is There Really a Power Shift? Delegating Authority in Global Environmental Politics." Paper presented at SGIR – 7th Pan-European Conference 2010, Stockholm, 2010.

Guidelines on the Recognition of New States in Eastern Europe and the Soviet Union of 16 December 1991, reprinted in *International Legal Materials* 31(1992).

Hadenius, Axel, and Teorell, Jan, "Assessing Alternative Indices of Democracy." *Committee on Concepts and Methods Working Paper Series* (2005).

Hague Institute for the Internalisation of Law, "Measuring Access to Justice in a Globalising World." Available at http://www.hiil.org/research/main-themes/rule-of-law/research-project-measuring-access-to-justice-in-a-globalising-world/.

Hague Rule of Law Network, "Final Report: Civil–Military Cooperation in Building the Rule of Law." Report on the Fourth Annual Meeting of the Hague Rule of Law Network (2009).

Hernandez, Nelson, and al-Izzi, Saad, "Iraq's Attorneys Practicing in a State of Fear." *Washington Post Foreign Service*, 10 June 2006.

Heupel, Monika, "With Power Comes Responsibility. Human Rights Protection in UN Sanctions Policy." Paper presented at SGIR – 7th Pan-European Conference 2010, Stockholm, 2010.

Human Rights Watch, "Benchmarks for Assessing Possible National Alternatives to International Criminal Court Cases against LRA Leaders." May 2007. Accessed 25 February 2008 at http://hrw.org/backgrounder/ij/icc0507/icc0507web.pdf.

Human Rights Watch, "ICC: Investigate All Sides in Uganda." 4 February 2004. Accessed 30 January 2008 at http://hrw.org/english/docs/2004/02/04/uganda7264.htm.

Human Rights Watch, "Uganda: New Accord Provides for War Crimes Trials; Prosecuting Rights Abusers Will Require Political Will, Legal Reforms." 19 February 2008. Accessed 20 February 2008 at http://hrw.org/english/docs/2008/02/19/uganda18094.htm.

Human Rights Network-Uganda (Hurinet-U), "Analysis of the International Criminal Court Bill (No. 10/2004) in the Context of Uganda's Obligations Under the Statute of the International Criminal Court." 17 January 2005. Available at http://www.hurinet.or.ug/downloads/Analysis%20of%20the%20ICC%20Bill%20in%20the%20ugandan%20context.pdf.

International Bar Association (IBA), "International Rule of Law Directory." Accessed 20 April 2010 at http://www.roldirectory.org/index.htm.

International Commission of Jurists, "Assessing Damage Urging Action, Report of the Eminent Jurists Panel on Terrorism, Counter-Terrorism and Human Rights." 2009. Accessed 14 April 2010 at http://ejp.icj.org/IMG/EJP-Report.pdf.

International Committee of the Red Cross, "ICRC Commentary on the Convention (IV) Relative to the Protection of Civilian Persons in Time of War." Geneva (1949).

ICC, "Kampala Declaration." Review Conference of the Rome Statute, Kampala, 31 May–11 June 2010, RC-4-ENG-04062010. Available at http://www.iccuganda2010.ug/uploads/Docs/The%20Kampala%20Declaration.pdf.

ICC, "The Importance of Justice in Securing Peace." Review Conference of the Rome Statute, 30 May 2010, RC/ST/PJ/INF.3.

ICC, "President of Uganda Refers Situation Concerning the Lord's Resistance Army (LRA) to the ICC." 29 January 2004. Accessed 29 January 2008 at http://www.icc-cpi.int/press/pressreleases/16.html.

International Criminal Court Bill, XCVII(26), *Uganda Gazette*, 28 May 2004.

International Crisis Group, "Bosnia: Reshaping the International Machinery." Balkans Report No. 112, 29 November 2001.

International Crisis Group, "Northern Uganda: Understanding and Solving the Conflict." 14 April 2004. Accessed 31 January 2008 at http://www.up.ligi.ubc.ca/ICGreport.pdf.

International Crisis Group, "The Rule of Law in Independent Kosovo." 19 May 2010.

International Development Association (IDA), "Country Policy and Institutional Assessment (CPIA)." Accessed 9 April 2010 at http://web.worldbank.org/WBSITE/EXTERNAL/EXTABOUTUS/IDA/0,,contentMDK:20941073~pagePK:51236175~piPK:437394~theSitePK:73154,00.html.

International Development Law Organization (IDLO), "Rule of Law Assistance Directory." Accessed 20 April 2010 at http://www.idlo.int/english/Resources/ROL/projectandiniziatives/Pages/home.aspx.

International Development Law Organization, "Rule of Law Inventory Report, Practice Part: 'The IDLO Rule of Law Portal'." 20 April 2007. Accessed 22 April 2010 at http://www.idlo.int/ROL/ROLcv/Inventory_Report_Practice_Part_by_IDLO1.pdf.

Independent Evaluation Group (IEG), "Development Results in Middle-Income Countries: An Evaluation of the World Bank's Support." World Bank, 2007.

Independent International Fact-Finding Mission on the Conflict in Georgia. Report of the Independent International Fact-Finding Mission on the Conflict in Georgia, Part II: 127. Accessed 9 May 2010 at http://www.ceiig.ch/Report.html.

International Law Institute (ILI), "About the International Law Institute." Accessed 12 April 2010 at http://www.ili.org/ms/ili_mission.htm.

International Legal Assistance Consortium (ILAC), "About ILAC." Accessed 12 April 2010 at http://www.ilac.se/about.

Jawaharlal Nehru's Speeches 1949–1953, Publications Division, Ministry of Information and Broadcasting, Government of India, 1954.

Justice, Law and Order Sector (JLOS), "JLOS Annual Performance Report 2009/2010." September 2010.

Kempa, Michael, Sheering, Clifford, and Burris, Scott, "Changes in Governance: A Background Review." Paper prepared for the Salzburg Seminar on the Governance of Health, 2006.

Keynote Address by Luis Moreno-Ocampo, Prosecutor of the International Criminal Court, Council on Foreign Relations, Washington, DC, 4 February 2010.

Kosovo Standards Implementation Plan, 31 March 2004.

Kulayigye, Felix, "Otunnu's Notion of Genocide in the North Very Absurd," *The Monitor*, 4 September 2009.

LRA Position Paper on Accountability Truth and Reconciliation in the Context of Alternative Justice System [*sic*] for Resolving the Northern/Eastern Ugandan and Southern Sudan Conflicts. Juba, 19 August 2006.

McCurrencies: Happy 20th Birthday to our Big Mac Index, *The Economist*, 25 May 2006. Accessed 11 July 2011 at http://www.economist.com/node/6972477?story_id=E1_GJSNQSS.

Majtenyi, Cathy, "Rwanda War Crimes Court in Financial Trouble." *VOA News*, 1 July 2004.

Makubuya, Khiddu, "Uganda's Statement Presented to the Working Group on the Review Conference." Assembly of States Parties, sixth resumed session, New York, 5 June 2008.

Miranda, Manuel, "Departure Assessment of Embassy Baghdad." Memorandum to Ambassador Crocker, U.S. Embassy, Baghdad, Iraq. Baghdad: Office of Legislative Statecraft, 5 February 2008.

Møller, Jørgen, and Skaaning, Svend-Erik, "Thin and Thick Definitions of the Rule of Law: An Overview and an Appraisal." Paper presented at the Symposium on The Rule of Law: Concepts, Measures and Theory, Atlanta, 2010b.

MPs Pass ICC Bill, *New Vision*, 10 March 2010.

Mugisa, A., and Nsambu, H. "ICC Clears UPDF in the North," *Saturday Vision*, 30 August 2008.

"Niger's Military Coup Criticized by France and Africa," *BBC News*, 19 February 2010. Accessed 28 March 2010 at http://news.bbc.co.uk/2/hi/8523573.stm.

Oeter, Stefan, "The Openness of International Organizations for Transnational Public Rule-Making." Paper presented on the workshop "The Law beyond the State: Public Governance, Networks and Organizations in the Transnational Sphere," 19–21 June 2008.

"Odhiambo Won't Face World Court," *New Vision*, 10 February 2009.
Oketch, Bill, "Uganda Set for First War Crimes Trial." Institute for War and Peace Reporting, 14 July 2010.
Ogola, Florence, "Uganda Victims Question ICC's Balance." Institute for War and Peace Reporting, 16 June 2010.
Omach, Paul, "Demobilization and Reintegration of Former Combatants in Uganda: The Interplay of Domestic Politics and the International Contexts." Paper Presented at Conference "Rethinking Peacebuilding in Africa," Cambridge, 6 March 2009.
Ombudsperson Institution in Kosovo, "Eight Annual Report" (2008).
Ombudsperson Institution in Kosovo, "Fourth Annual Report" (2004).
Ombudsperson Institution in Kosovo, "Seventh Annual Report" (2007).
Ombudsperson Institution in Kosovo, "Third Annual Report" (2003).
Open Society Institute, "Human Rights & Governance Grants Program." Accessed 14 April 2010 at http://www.soros.org/initiatives/hrggp.
Open Society Justice Initiative. Accessed 12 April 2010 at http://www.soros.org/initiatives/justice/focus.
Open Society Institute, Parliament of the Republic of Uganda, Parliamentary Debates, Hansard Official Report, Wednesday 21 February 2007.
Parliament of the Republic of Uganda, Parliamentary Debates, Hansard Official Report, Wednesday 10 March 2010.
Parliament of the Republic of Uganda, Parliamentary Debates, Hansard Official Report, Wednesday 21 February 2007.
Parliament of the Republic of Uganda, Parliamentary Debates, Hansard Official Report, Thursday 29 July 2004.
Petraeus, David and Amos, James, "Foreword," in Department of the Army, *FM 3–24, Counterinsurgency*. (2006).
Programa Venezolano De Educaci On-Acci O. *Halfway to Reform: The World Bank and the Venezuelan Justice System*. Lawyers Committee for Human Rights and the Venezuelan Program for Human Rights Education and Action. New York, 1996.
Project on International Courts and Tribunals, "Material and Publications." Available at http://www.pict-pcti.org/matrix/matrixintro.html.
Rensmann, Thilo, "Nationales Verwaltungsrecht und internationaler Investitionsschutz," forthcoming (manuscript on file with the authors).
Résolution de l'Institut de Droit International, XXXIVe session, *Annuaire de l'IDI* 1927, tome III.
Rubini, Daniel, "Justice in Waiting: Developing Rule of Law in Iraq." *The Officer* (August 2009): 45–48.
Schuppert, Gunnar Folke, "Contract Governance: Verwaltungsrecht und Verwaltungswissenschaft vor neuen Herausforderungen," in Grundmann, Stefan, Kloepfer, Michael, Paulus, Christoph G., Schröder, Rainer, and Werle, Gerhard (eds.), *Festschrift 200 Jahre Juristische Fakultät der Humboldt-Universität zu Berlin*. De Gruyter, 2010a.
Special Division of the High Court of Uganda 2008 Administrative Circular.
Speech by Mr. Frank-Walter Steinmeier, the German Foreign Minister to the German Federal Parliament, 20 February 2008. Accessed 13 March 2010 at http://www.auswaertiges-amt.de/diplo/de/Infoservice/Presse/Reden/2008/080220-Steinmeier-BT-Kosovo.html.
Statement by Condoleeza Rice on Recognition of Kosovo as Independent State of 18 February 2008. Accessed 10 March 2010 at http://www.america.gov/st/texttrans-english/2008/February/20080218150254bpuh5.512637e-02.html.

Statement of the Council of the European Union of 18 February 2008: 2851st External Relations Council Meeting, Brussels, 6496/08 (Presse 41). Accessed 13 March 2010 at http://www.consilium.europa.eu/uedocs/cms_data/docs/pressdata/en/gena/98818.pdf.

Statement of Finland of 7 March 2008. Accessed 28 March 2010 at http://formin.finland.fi/public/default.aspx?contentid=123797&nodeid=15146&contentlan=2&culture=en-US.

Statement of Hungary 19 March 2008. Accessed 28 March 2010 at http://www.mfa.gov.hu/kum/en/bal/actualities/spokesman_statements/Kosovo_recognition_080319.htm.

Statement by Luis Moreno-Ocampo, "Statement on the Uganda Arrest Warrants." The Hague, 14 October 2005. Available at http://www.icc-cpi.int/library/organs/otp/speeches/LMO_20051014_English.pdf.

Statement by Luis Moreno-Ocampo, "Statement to the Assembly of States Parties to the Rome Statute of the International Criminal Court." New York, 22 April 2003, ICC-OTP-20030502–10-EN. Available at http://www.icc-cpi.int/Menus/ICC/Structure+of+the+Court/Office+of+the+Prosecutor/Reports+and+Statements/Press+Releases/Press+Releases+2003/.

Statement by Luis Moreno-Ocampo, "Statement to the Fourth Session of the Assembly of States Parties." The Hague, 28 November 2005. Available at http://www.icc-cpi.int/library/cases/ICC-02–04-01–05-67_English.pdf.

Statement by the President of the Security Council, 12 December 2003, UN Doc. S/PRST/2003/26.

Statement by the President of the Security Council, 22 June 2006, UN Doc. S/PRST/2006/28.

Statement by the President of the Security Council, 30 April 2004, UN Doc. S/PRST//2004/13.

Statement by the President of the Security Council, "The Promotion and Strengthening of the Rule of Law in the Maintenance of International Peace and Security." 29 June 2010, UN Doc. S/PRST/2010/11.

Strengthening International Law: Rule of Law and the Maintenance of International Peace and Security, Security Council Open Debate, 22 June 2006. Available at http://www.iccnow.org/documents/UNMemberStates_ExcerptsonInternationalLaw_22June06.pdf.

"Strengthening Rule of Law 'Key' to Unlocking Millennium Development Goals, Head of United Nations Office on Drugs and Crime Tells Third Committee," *States News Service*, 9 October 2008.

"Sweden Recognizes the Republic of Kosovo," Press Release of 4 March 2008. Accessed 13 March 2010 at http://www.sweden.gov.se/sb/d/10358/a/99714.

Tamanaha, Brian, "The Good and Bad of the Rule of Law Ideal." Paper presented at the annual meeting of The Law and Society Association, TBA, Berlin, Germany, 2007. Available at www.allacademic.com/meta/p177729_ index.html.

The Millenium Project, "Global Challenges Facing Humanity." Available at http://www.millennium-project.org/millennium/Global_Challenges/chall-12.html.

Transparency International, "Corruption Perceptions Index (CPI)." Accessed 9 April 2010 at http://www.transparency.org/policy_research/surveys_indices/cpi/2009.

Transparency International, "Global Corruption Report: Corruption and Judicial System" (2007). Available at http://www.transparency.org/publications/gcr/download_gcr#download.

Uganda: Interview with President Yoweri Museveni, *IRIN*, 9 June 2005.

United Nations Rule of Law Indicators Project, in conjunction with the Vera Institute of Justice and members of the Altus Global Alliance. Available at http://ar.unrol.org/doc.aspx?n=Newsletter+for+United+Nations+Rule+of+Law+Indicators+Project+June+2009.pdf.

USAID, "This is USAID." Accessed 20 July 2020 at http://www.usaid.gov/about_usaid/.
USAID, "USAID Primer: What We Do and How We Do It." Revised January 2006. Accessed 20 July 2010 at http://www.usaid.gov/about_usaid/PDACG100.pdf.
United States Department of State, "Trafficking in Persons Report" (2009).
United States General Accounting Office, "Foreign Assistance. Rule of Law Funding Worldwide for Fiscal Years 1993–98." Washington, DC, June 1999 (GAO/NSIAD-99–158).
United States Government Accountability Office, "Human Trafficking: Better Data, Strategy, and Reporting Needed to Enhance U.S. Antitrafficking Efforts Abroad," in Report to the Chairman, Committee on the Judiciary and the Chairman, Committee on International Relations, House of Representatives, Washington, DC (2006).
Vera Institute of Justice and Altus Global Alliance, "Developing Indicators to Measure the Rule of Law: A Global Approach." Report to the World Justice Project, July 2008.
Vera Institute of Justice, Draft Report of the Review of the IADB Citizen Security Program in Nicaragua. No. 1590/SF-NI, December 2009.
Verband Entwicklungspolitik Deutscher Nichtregierungs-organisationen, "Fünf Jahre Deutsche PRTS in Afghanistan: Eine Zwischenbilanz aus Sicht der deutschen Hilfsorganisationen." VENRO-Positionspapier 1/2009 (2009). Available at http://www.venro.org.
Wallace, William, "Foreword," in *FM 3–0, Operations*. Department of the Army (2008).
"Where the Money Goes," *Washington Post*, 4 January 2011.
Williamson, Clint, "Preliminary Screening Inquiry Report, Investigation of Legal Operations in CJTF-7." End of Mission Report to the Administrator, Department of the Army, CPA (2005): Tab 60.
Wrange, P., "The ICC Bill, Complementarity and "Retroactivity." 30 September 2008.
Zumbansen, Peer. Transnational Law. CLPE Research Paper No. 09/2008. Osgood Hall Law School, Toronto, 2008.
Zumbansen, Peer, "Governance: An Interdisciplinary Perspective," in David Levi-Faur (ed.), *Oxford Handbook on Governance*. Oxford: Oxford University Press, forthcoming.
Zürn, Michael, Binder, Martin, and Ecker-Ehrhardt, Matthias, "Political Authority beyond the Nation State and Its Politicization." Paper presented at the International Studies Association, Montreal, March, 2011.

Index

Explanatory variables	Model 1a	Model 1b	Model 2a	Model 2b	Model 3a	Model 3b	Model 4a
Rule of law	1.64*** ($p = .005$)	1.43*** ($p = .005$)	1.52** ($p = .031$)	1.48*** ($p = .009$)	1.67** ($p = .024$)	1.47** ($p = .020$)	1.76*** ($p = .001$)
Ratification of the 2000 agreement	1.37** ($p = .028$)	1.48*** ($p = .001$)	1.28 ($p = .110$)	1.41*** ($p = .006$)	1.33* ($p = .089$)	1.38*** ($p = .008$)	1.46*** ($p = .008$)
Density of criminalizations in region ($t - 1$)	6.98*** ($p = .000$)	4.04*** ($p = .005$)	9.77*** ($p = .000$)	4.65*** ($p = .004$)	4.23** ($p = .035$)	2.64 ($p = .142$)	9.17*** ($p = .000$)
U.S. pressure ($t - 1$)	2.20*** ($p = .009$)	1.80*** ($p = .008$)	2.38** ($p = .016$)	1.90*** ($p = .009$)	1.82* ($p = .089$)	1.79** ($p = .024$)	2.46*** ($p = .003$)
Prevalence of child labor	.978** ($p = .047$)	.976*** ($p = .013$)	.983 ($p = .222$)	.976 ($p = .035$)	.967*** ($p = .010$)	.974** ($p = .021$)	–
Low- and middle-income category	2.50** ($p = .024$)	1.89** ($p = .038$)	1.95 ($p = .150$)	2.05** ($p = .054$)	3.02** ($p = .016$)	1.99** ($p = .050$)	2.18** ($p = .031$)
Country of origin			.531 ($p = .160$)	1.28 ($p = .498$)			–
Transit country			.974 ($p = .922$)	1.04 ($p = .873$)			–
Destination country			.534* ($p = .056$)	1.41 ($p = .171$)			–
Internal trafficking			1.36 ($p = .311$)	.830 ($p = .375$)			–
U.S. aid/GDP	–	–	–	–	608.02** ($p = .011$)	81.73 ($p = .189$)	–
U.S. trade/ total trade	–	–	–	–	.487 ($p = .521$)	1.02 ($p = .879$)	–
EU trade/ total trade	–	–	–	–	1.39 ($p = .618$)	1.15 ($p = .779$)	–
No. of news stories	–	–	–	–	–	–	1.0002** ($p = .040$)
No. of countries	134	132	116	114	121	120	138
No. of criminalizations	76	107	63	90	63	90	78
No. of obs.	2126	1918	1882	1692	1715	1586	2137
Prob. > χ^2	0.000	0.000	0.000	0.0001	0.000	0.000	0.000

